off the
motorway

"The essential guide for the glove box"

Travel Publishing Ltd

2nd Edition

Published by: Travel Publishing Ltd, 7a Apollo House, Calleva Park, Aldermaston, Berkshire RG7 8TN

ISBN 1-902-00781-6
© Travel Publishing Ltd

First Published: 2000, second edition 2002

Printing by: Ashford Colour Press, Gosport
Maps: © Maps in Minutes ™ (2002)
Authors: Paul and Shirley Smith
Cover Design: Amanda Gooch and Lines and Words, Aldermaston
Cover Photograph: The M6 motorway and Lune Valley, Lancashire © Freefoto.com

This book is dedicated to our good friend Jack Perry Crisp

the**preface**

A system of high-speed roads to link all the main areas of population was first considered as long ago as the 1920s and some detailed planning was undertaken in the following decade. World War II curtailed any advances along these lines but, in the late 1940s, surveys of routes were undertaken and the section of motorway between Junctions 4 and 8 on the M5 was the first in the country to have its line established by an order under the Special Roads Act of 1949. The first section of motorway was not built for another nine years until the Preston By-Pass (between Junctions 29 and 32 on the M6) opened on December 5th, 1958.

Since those early days, motorway and trunk road construction has continued apace but, with the meteoric growth in personalized transport, large stretches of motorway are regularly utilized well beyond the designed capacity.

Nonetheless, despite the jams and hold-ups, many travellers still consider this form of transport to be the most cost-effective and motorway travel is more popular than ever.

With this in mind it was felt that a travel guide concentrating specifically on motorways would prove to be of significant benefit to the millions of travellers who use these routes every year and the first edition of **Off the Motorway** was published in June 2000. This is a comprehensive guide to the facilities to be found at each junction as well as between junctions, coupled with a detailed description of landmarks and places of interest along the route. The guide is designed to not only direct motorway drivers to the many different types of facilities along the way but also to provide interesting information on places close to the motorway, many of which can be visited without significant diversion should the traveller wish to relieve a tedious journey.

Coming off at a junction can sometimes prove to be something of a lottery, especially if running short of fuel, and the primary purpose of this guide is to inform travellers of all food, fuel and accommodation available within a radius of about one mile from each junction, with precise details of opening times and the facilities available at each site. From a practical viewpoint, junctions on urban motorway stretches have been omitted as there are many facilities freely available and within easy reach. At junctions within urban areas only the main roads have been included.

Each motorway has an introduction describing the route and detailing information on the major landmarks visible (listing them in sequence as if travelling from Junction 1). Obviously perspectives will vary depending upon which direction the vehicle is travelling in and, similarly, some views may be obstructed in the summer when the trees screening the carriageways have a full complement of leaves.

Minor injuries not necessitating a 999 call, can happen all too often and the nearest **Accident and Emergency Hospital** to each junction has been identified, along with the route. In our experience very few hospitals are signed from junctions and trying to locate one with an active A&E department can prove to be time-consuming and frustrating. We are indebted to Ambulance Control Centres up and down the country for their help in compiling this information. The **Places of Interest** sections - located with the information for each junction - describe some of the attractions within easy reach of the motorway and which could conveniently be used for journey breaks.

The first edition was very well received and, as well as updating all the information for the routes previously dealt with, we have now taken the opportunity to considerably expand the number of motorways with the inclusion of the M25, all the radial routes out of London, the M27 in Hampshire and the M18 and M180 around Doncaster. As well as this expansion, photographs have been included and this second edition has been redesigned in full colour.

We would like to thank staff at Tourist Information Centres, Motorway Maintenance Departments and Highways Agency offices across the country for their generous assistance in supplying us with information.

Note:

Marker Posts are found at 100m (328yds) intervals along motorways and major trunk routes. With the widespread use of mobile telephones, when calling for assistance at the side of the motorway it is essential that the operator is told which motorway you are on, the direction being travelled and the nearest marker post to the vehicle.

Bibliography:

A History of British Motorways by George Charlesworth, Thomas Telford Ltd (1984).
ISBN 0 7277 0159 2

the Contents

how to use

Off the Motorway has been specifically designed as an easy to use guide so there is no need for complicated instructions.

■ Locating a Motorway

Each of the motorways covered in the guide can be found in it's own self-contained section and the information is presented in exactly the same way for each motorway. Simply refer to the contents page for the relevant page number.

■ Locating a Motorway Junction

All junctions are listed in numerical order from Junction 1 upwards within each motorway section so locating a junction couldn't be simpler.

■ Locating Facilities, Places of Interest and Hospitals

All facilities, places of interest and A & E Hospitals are presented after the map of each junction and the facilities are pinpointed on the junction map. The location of the places of interest can be found on the motorway maps at the beginning of the sections covering each motorway.

■ Notes

Not all Public Houses within a mile of the junction are listed. Although our policy is to be as comprehensive as possible, only those establishments offering food or accommodation at the time of the survey are incorporated within this guide. Similarly, some of those premises undergoing refurbishment, and not open for business at the time of the survey may not be included as information may not be available.

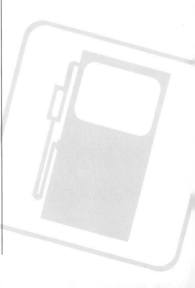

symbols

Short descriptions of the symbols used to describe the facilities at each junction may be found on the outside back cover. You may however find the following more detailed explanations of use when deciding where to stop.

⛄ Licensed premises serving alcoholic beverages

🍴 Food and non-alcoholic drinks available

⛽ Petrol and/or diesel fuel

24 HOUR Open 24 hours. (Some filling stations may close for a short period to effect staff changeovers)

£ Cash dispensing machine available on site, or adjacent (as at supermarkets)

WC Toilets available for customers use at filling stations. Please note that at some of those premises indicated as open for 24 hours toilets may not be available for the total duration if access is only gained through a shop area which is closed overnight for security reasons

♿ At filling station sites, this indicates that the toilets, although they may not have been specifically adapted, are considered suitable for the use of wheelchair customers. At pubs, restaurants and hotels, this either indicates that the buildings have been fully adapted for disabled access or that the buildings are considered suitable to accommodate wheelchair customers

🚶 Children are welcome in public houses for meals if accompanied by parents and entirely at the discretion of the management. Local licensing laws may apply regarding the hours during which children may be accommodated

B&B Guest house or Bed and Breakfast accommodation

H Medium to large sized hotel

smH Small hotel

M Motel or budget accommodation

🐕 Pets allowed at the discretion of the management

the M1

Although not the first stretch of motorway to be constructed in this country, it was undoubtedly the opening of the initial 72 mile long section of the M1 between Berrygrove and Crick by Mr Ernest Marples, the Transport Minister, on November 2nd, 1959 that heralded the long-awaited Motorway Age. As originally constructed the M1 ran from the North Circular Road (A406) in North London to Stourton on the outskirts of Leeds. In 1972 it was extended into the city centre but in 1999 the motorway was diverted around the east side of the city and lengthened to join up with the A1(M) at Garforth.

Commencing at Staples Corner, North London, with a connection to the A406 at Junction 1, the motorway heads north out of the capital, and passes the Gateway Service Area at **Scratchwood**. This site had previously been utilized for a spectacular rail crash scene for the 1962 MGM film *The Password is Courage*. After crossing the M25 at Junction 6A, the M10 joins the motorway at Junction 7 as the M1 continues northwards skirting past Watford and the hat-making town of Luton. On the west side of the motorway just before Junction 13 is **Woburn Park** which forms the grounds of **Woburn Abbey**, founded in 1145 and replaced by a mansion in 1747. **Milton Keynes**, a modern city established in the 1970s and comprising the small towns of Bletchley, Newport Pagnell, Woburn Sands, Wolverton, Olney and Stoney Stanton, is on the west side at Junction 14 and, between Junctions 15 and 16, Northampton is on the east side. **Northampton** has been renowned for its boot and shoe manufacture since the Middle Ages. The town has been of some importance as during the 11thC it was the residence of the King and in 1131 Henry I assembled Parliament here and the Barons swore fealty to his daughter the Empress Matilda.

Between Junctions 16 and 17 three modes of transport run parallel together; the M1, the **Grand Union Canal**, constructed between 1793 and 1805, and the former **London & Birmingham Railway** line which opened in 1838. The latter two were originally built to link Birmingham and London but rapidly became part of larger communication networks connecting the north and south of the country. Radio masts on the west side pinpoint the former **BBC Transmitting Station** which opened on July 25th, 1925 and was used for the first regular national radio broadcasts.

Clearly visible between Junctions 18 and 19, the radio masts at **Rugby** have been a feature of the skyline for many years but most of

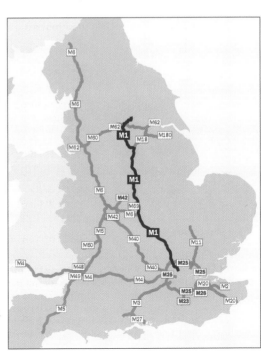

those on view are now redundant and may well be removed in the future. When the M1 was being constructed the former **Great Central Railway** main line between Sheffield and London was still operational and the two run side by side between Junctions 20 and 21. This railway was the last main line built to London from the north and opened in 1898 but, ironically was the first to close when it was truncated by BR to just a short section at the southern end on May 5th, 1969.

Town Hall Gardens, Leicester

The M69 joins the motorway from the west at Junction 21 whilst **Leicester** is on the east side between here and Junction 21A. The city, with its origins dating back over 2,000 years, is located on the banks of the River Soar and was and was fortified during the Roman occupation to protect the Fosse Way. Continuing north the motorway cuts through **Charnwood Forest**, now part of the National Forest, and passes Kegworth where aircraft can be seen flying over the carriageway as they land at **East Midlands Airport** to the west.

Between Junctions 24 and 25, the cooling towers of **Radcliffe on Soar Power Station** dominate the skyline to the east as the motorway crosses a series of lakes and weirs in the Trent Valley including the **Church Wine Water Treatment Plant**, with its 31ft deep and 614 million gallon capacity reservoir on the west side. As the motorway proceeds north to Junction 26 Nottingham is on the east side and two once-important canals are bridged; **The Erewash Canal** which opened in 1779 and formed part of the Grand Union route, linking the River Trent with the Cromford and Nottingham Canals at Langley Mill and **The Nottingham Canal**, which opened in 1796 and closed in 1937. **Nottingham** is of Saxon

River Trent, Nottingham

origin and, in Danish days was a town of importance standing high and commanding an extensive view of the Vale of Trent. In more recent times it was renowned as a centre of lacemaking.

Further north, beyond Junction 27 the motorway passes through what was an extensive coalfield and whilst redundant installations, including the former **Markham Colliery**, are in view at various points along the length, relics of England's older history can also be seen; **Hardwick Hall** overlooks the carriageways to the east just before Junction 29 and, further north, the remains of the 17thC **Bolsover Castle** are visible to the east. Hardwick Hall was built to the orders of Elizabeth Shrewsbury and completed in 1597 whilst a castle has stood at Bolsover since Norman times but the one visible today was begun in the reign of James I by Sir Charles Cavendish and dates from around 1615.

At Junction 32 the M1 takes a sharp turn to the west to pass between Rotherham and Sheffield as the M18 continues northwards to link up with the A1, Doncaster and Scunthorpe. **Sheffield** is England's fourth largest city and, despite the decline of traditional

Hardwick Hall

industries, is still a significant player in the world of steel, cutlery, engineering and toolmaking and now possesses a vibrant commercial, cultural and sporting reputation. Between Junctions 33 and 34 the site of **Tinsley Diesel Maintenance Depot** and marshalling yard is on the south west side of the motorway. Tinsley Diesel Depot opened in 1965 and was one of the largest in the country but by 1998 both the yard and the depot had become redundant and were abandoned. Junction 34 is where one of the major construction projects on the M1 was undertaken; to cross the River Don and the Sheffield to Rotherham railway line. **Tinsley Viaduct** opened in June 1968 and is a 0.75 mile long two-level steel box girder structure with a 20 span upper deck carrying the M1 and an 18 span lower deck accommodating the A631. This design was preferred on cost grounds by the Ministry of Transport to that of a reinforced concrete bridge but following the collapse of a steel box girder bridge at Milford Haven in 1970 the resultant enquiry, under the chairmanship of Dr Merrison, recommended additional strengthening measures. Traffic restrictions were placed on the viaduct and the additional work which commenced in 1973 took six years to complete and resulted in a final cost of twice that of a reinforced concrete structure! Here, **Meadowhall Shopping Centre**, typical of the redevelopments on disused steelworks sites that used to proliferate throughout this area, can be seen to the south. The cooling towers for **Blackburn Meadows Power Station**, with the wildlife conservation area beyond, are alongside the viaduct on the north west side.

Continuing north westwards, beyond Junction 36, **Wentworth Castle**, **Stainsborough Castle** and **Queen Anne's Obelisk** are all visible to the west. To the east can be seen **Worsbrough Mill Country Park**, with **Barnsley**, whose prosperity was once based on the local coal industry, visible beyond. Passing Woolley Edge Services an unusual feature is the proximity of an air shaft for **Woolley Tunnel** on the Barnsley to Wakefield line, adjacent to the northbound carriageway. Between Junctions 39 and 40 the ancient cathedral town of **Wakefield**, site of the Battle of Wakefield (1460), is passed on the east side and the River Calder (Calder & Hebble Navigation) is bridged. Interestingly, this bridge collapsed during construction! The

Sheffield Cathedral

M62 is crossed at Junction 42 and then the motorway splits at Junction 43 into the M621 (the reclassified portion of the M1 which used to terminate in Leeds), and the final section of the M1 which opened on February 4th, 1999 to form an eastern by-pass of Leeds and make an end-on connection with the A1 near Garforth at Junction 48.

Location of Places of Interest

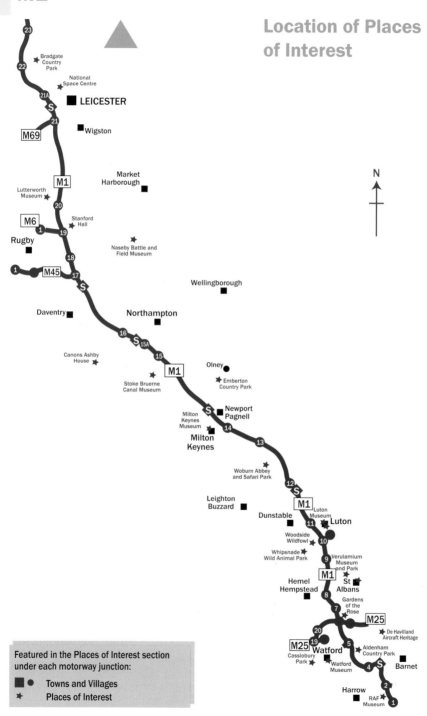

N

Featured in the Places of Interest section under each motorway junction:

■ ● Towns and Villages
★ Places of Interest

Location of Places of Interest

Harewood House

45

Lotherton Hall

LEEDS

Temple Newsam House

M1 47

46

7 44

M62

30

Castleford

31 3 M62

Dewsbury

41

40

Wakefield

Sandal Castle

Pontefract

National Coal Mining Museum

39

Hemsworth

Yorkshire Sculpture Park

38 S

M1

Cannon Hall Museum, Park & Gardens

37

Metrodome

Barnsley

Wigfield Farm

Worsbrough Mill Museum and Country Park

36

Elsecar Heritage Centre

Stocksbridge

Magna Science Adventure Centre

35

M18

Blackburn Meadows

Rotherham

1

Clifton Park Museum

Meadowhall

34

34 33

32

SHEFFIELD

Rother Valley Country Park

31

Tropical Butterfly House, Falconry & Wildlife Centre

Renishaw Gardens

S

Dronfield

Barrow Hill Roundhouse Railway Centre

30

Mr Straw's House

Chesterfield

M1

Bolsover Castle

St Mary and All Saints Church

29

Hardwick Hall

Clay Cross

S

Mansfield

Kirkby in Ashfield

28

Crich Tramway Village

Midland Railway Centre

Newstead Abbey

27

Ripley

D H Lawrence Museum

Hucknall

Eastwood

The American Adventure

26

NOTTINGHAM

Ilkeston

S

DERBY

25

Beeston

M1

Long Eaton

Donington Grand Prix Collection

24

Kegworth Museum

S

John Taylor Bellfoundry Museum

Swadlingcote

Loughborough

Great Central Railway

Charnwood Museum

Ashby-de-la-Zouch

23

Coalville

Snibston Discovery Park

Bradgate Country Park

22

N

Featured in the Places of Interest section under each motorway junction:

■ ● Towns and Villages

★ Places of Interest

M1 JUNCTION 2

THIS IS A RESTRICTED ACCESS JUNCTION
- Vehicles can only exit from the southbound lanes and travel south along the A1
- Vehicles can only enter the motorway along the northbound lanes from the A1 north carriageway

Nearest Northbound A&E Hospital

Watford General Hospital
Vicarage Road, Watford
WD1 8HB
Tel: (01923) 244366
Proceed to Junction 5 and take the A41 south and turn right along the A4008 towards Bushey. After about 1 mile turn right at the roundabout to Watford and continue along the A4145 to West Watford. The hospital is on the south side of Vicarage Road (A4145).
(Distance Approx 11.2 miles)

Nearest Southbound A&E Hospital

Barnet General Hospital
Wellhouse Lane, Barnet
EN5 3DJ
Tel: (020) 8216 4000
Take the A1 south and turn left along the B552 (Holders Hill Road). Follow the B552 to its end and turn right along the A411. After about 1.5 miles turn right into Wellhouse Lane and the hospital is on the left.
(Distance Approx 5.4 miles)

M1 JUNCTION 3

THERE IS NO JUNCTION 3

M1 BETWEEN JUNCS 2 & 4

LONDON GATEWAY SERVICES (WELCOME BREAK)
Tel: (020) 8906 0611
The Granary Restaurant, Burger King, La Brioche Doree, Days Inn & Shell Fuel.

M1 JUNCTION 4

THIS IS A RESTRICTED ACCESS JUNCTION
- Vehicles can only exit from the southbound lanes and travel south along the A41
- Vehicles can only enter the motorway along the northbound lanes from the A41 north carriageway

Nearest Northbound A&E Hospital

Watford General Hospital
Vicarage Road, Watford
WD1 8HB
Tel: (01923) 244366
Proceed to Junction 5 and take the A41 south and turn right along the A4008 towards Bushey. After about 1 mile turn right at the roundabout to Watford and continue along the

A4145 to West Watford. The hospital is on the south side of Vicarage Road (A4145).
(Distance Approx 7.2 miles)

Nearest Southbound A&E Hospital

Barnet General Hospital
Wellhouse Lane, Barnet
EN5 3DJ
Tel: (020) 8216 4000
Follow the A41 south and turn left at the second roundabout north along the A1. Turn right at the first roundabout along the A411 and after about 1.8 miles turn right into Wellhouse Lane and the hospital is on the left. (Distance Approx 4.6 miles)

FACILITIES

1   Canons Corner Service Station (Esso)

🅿 WC 24HOUR

Tel: (020) 8958 8166
1 mile south along the A410, on the left.
Access, Visa, Overdrive, All Star, Switch, Dial Card, Mastercard, Amex, Diners Club, Delta, AA Paytrak, UK Fuelcard, Shell Gold, BP Supercharge, Esso Cards.

2   McDonald's

🍴 ♿

Tel: (020) 8958 3482
1 mile south along the A410, on the left.
Open; 07.00-23.00hrs daily. "Drive-Thru" closes at 0.00hrs daily.

PLACES OF INTEREST

RAF Museum

Grahame Park Way, London
NW9 5LL Tel: (020) 8205 2266
website; www.rafmuseum.com

Follow the A41 south and the route is signposted. (4 miles)

Occupying 10 acres of what was once the historic Hendon Aerodrome over 70 aircraft are contained within 260,000 ft² of exhibition halls. Specially constructed walkways and platforms enable close inspection of the planes and other attractions include a Red Arrows Flight Simulator, "Touch and Try" Jet Provost cockpit, interactive gallery and a walk-through Sunderland Flying Boat.

The Battle of Britain Hall exhibit enables visitors to experience the sights and sounds of Britain's finest hour. Shop. Licensed Restaurant. Disabled access. Large grounds with indoor and outdoor picnic area

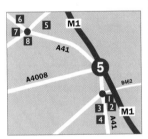

JUNCTION 5

Nearest A&E Hospital

Watford General Hospital
Vicarage Road, Watford
WD1 8HB
Tel: (01923) 244366
Take the A41 south and turn right along the A4008 towards Bushey. After about 1 mile turn right at the roundabout to Watford and continue along the A4145 to West Watford. The hospital is on the south side of Vicarage Road (A4145).
(Distance Approx 2.7 miles)

FACILITIES

1   Toby Carvery

Tel: (01923) 225826
0.5 miles south along the A41, on the left.
(Six Continents) Open all day. Carvery Open; Mon-Fri; 12.00-14.00hrs & 17.00-22.00hrs, Sat & Sun; 12.00-22.00hrs. Bar meals served Sun-Fri; 12.00-22.00hrs daily

2   Hilton National Watford Hotel

Tel: (01923) 235881
0.6 miles south along the A41, on the left.
The Patio Restaurant Open; Breakfast; Mon-Fri; 07.00-10.00hrs, Sat & Sun; 07.30-10.30hrs, Lunch; Sun-Fri; 12.30-14.00hrs, Sat; Closed, Dinner; 19.00-22.00hrs daily.

3   Elton Way Service Station (Total)

Tel: (01923) 699560
0.7 miles south along the A41, on the right.
Access, Visa, Overdrive, All Star, Switch, Dial Card, Master-card, Amex, Diners Club, Delta, Keyfuels, Total/Fina/Elf Cards.

4   Quinceys Bar & Restaurant

Tel: (01923) 229137
0.7 miles south along the A41, on the right.
(Scottish & Newcastle) Open all day; Meals served; Mon-Sat; 12.00-23.00hrs, Sun; 12.00-22.30hrs

5   Sainsbury's Filling Station

Tel: (01923) 681984

1 mile north along the A41, on the right.
Access, Visa, Overdrive, All Star, Switch, Dial Card, Mastercard, Amex, Delta, UK Fuelcard, JS Fuelcard. Disabled Toilets and Cash Machine in adjacent store.

6   BP Dome Filling Station
Tel: (01923) 672129
1 mile north along the A41, on the right.
Access, Visa, Overdrive, All Star, Switch, Dial Card, Mastercard, Amex, Diners Club, Delta, Routex, AA Paytrak, Shell Agency, BP Cards.

7   Shell Sceptre Service Station
Tel: (01923) 800920
1 mile north along the A41, on the left.
LPG. Access, Visa, Overdrive, All Star, Switch, Dial Card, Mastercard, Amex, Diners Club, Delta, UK Fuelcard, Shell Cards, Smartcard, BP Supercharge

8   Asda Filling Station

Tel: (01923) 250380
1 mile north along the A41, on the left.
Access, Visa, Overdrive, All Star, Switch, Dial Card, Mastercard, Amex, Diners Club, Delta, BP Supercharge, Asda Business Card. Open; Mon-Sat; 06.00-17.00hrs, Sun; 09.00-17.00hrs. Disabled Toilets and Cash Machines in adjacent store

PLACES OF INTEREST

Watford Museum
194 High Street, Watford
WD1 2HG

Tel: (01923) 232297
website: www.watford.gov.uk

Follow the A4008 into Watford (Signposted 2.2 Miles)

Displaying the town's history, the exhibits include a superb art collection, displays relating to printing and brewing and a tribute to the local football club. Disabled Access.

Cassiobury Park

Cassiobury Avenue, Watford
WD1 7SL
Tel: (01923) 235946

Follow the A41 north and A412 southwest through Watford (4.8 Miles)

With over 190 acres of open space and woodland it provides an area of natural beauty and historic interest. Visitors have access to the canal and lock, children's paddling pools, miniature railway and tennis courts. Café. Some disabled access.

Aldenham Country Park

Elstree WD6 3AT
Tel: (020) 8953 9602
website: www.hertfordshire.co.uk

Follow the A41 south and turn left along the A411 towards Elstree. (4.1 Miles)

Consisting of a large reservoir surrounded by 175 acres of woodland and parkland with an extensive network of footpaths. There is a rare breeds farm, Winnie-the-Pooh's 100 Acre Wood, children's adventure play area and picnic site. Fishing available. Refreshments. Disabled access.

JUNCTION 6

Nearest Northbound A&E Hospital

Hemel Hempstead General Hospital

Hillfield Road HP2 4AD
Tel: (01442) 213141

Proceed to Junction 8 and follow the A4147 to the second roundabout and the hospital is signposted to the right along the A4147 continuation. (Distance Approx 7.2 miles)

Nearest Southbound A&E Hospital

Watford General Hospital

Vicarage Road, Watford
WD1 8HB
Tel: (01923) 244366

Take the A412 south into Watford town centre and follow the A4145 south to West Watford. The hospital is on the south side of Vicarage Road (A4145). (Distance Approx 4.2 miles)

FACILITIES

1   Little Chef

Tel: (01923) 661842
0.1 miles north along the A405, on the right.
Open; 07.00-22.00hrs daily.

2   Classic Service Station (Total)

Tel: (01923) 680024
0.7 miles north along the A405, on the right.
Access, Visa, Overdrive, All Star, Switch, Dial Card, Mastercard, Amex, AA Paytrak, Diners Club, Delta, Total/Fina/Elf Card.

3   The Harvester at Garston

Tel: (01923) 672061
0.8 miles south along the A405, in Garston, on the right.
(Six Continents) Open all day. Meals served; Sun-Thurs; 12.00-21.00hrs, Fri & Sat; 12.00-22.00hrs

4   McDonald's

Tel: (01923) 671550
0.9 miles south along the A412, in Garston, on the right.
Open; 07.00-23.00hrs daily.

5   TGI Friday's

Tel: (01923) 672310
1 mile south along the A412, in Garston, on the right.
(Greene King) Open all day. Meals served; Sun-Fri; 12.00-23.00hrs daily, Sat; 11.00-23.00hrs

6   Travel Inn Metro

Tel: (0870) 242 8000
1 mile south along the A412, in Garston, on the right

PLACES OF INTEREST

The Gardens of the Rose

The Royal National Rose Society, Chiswell Green,

St Albans AL2 3NR
Tel: (01727) 850461
website; www.roses.co.uk
Follow the A405 north (2.2 Miles)
Over 30,000 roses create a stunning spectacle from early Spring to late Summer. These are complemented by a rich variety of companion plants including Spring bulbs, herbaceous borders, Lavenders and over 100 varieties of Clematis. Disabled access.

JUNCTS 6A & 7

JUNCTIONS 6A AND 7 ARE MOTORWAY INTERCHANGES ONLY AND THERE IS NO ACCESS TO ANY FACILITIES

JUNCTION 8

Nearest A&E Hospital
Hemel Hempstead General Hospital
Hillfield Road HP2 4AD
Tel: (01442) 213141
Follow the A4147 to the second roundabout and the hospital is signposted to the right along the A4147 continuation.
(Distance Approx 3.3 miles)

FACILITIES

1   Breakspear Way Service Station (BP)

Tel: (01442) 269003
0.4 miles west along the A414, on the left.
LPG. Access, Visa, Overdrive, All Star, Switch, Dial Card, Mastercard, Amex, Diners Club, Delta, Routex, AA Paytrak, Shell Agency, BP Cards. Wild Bean Café.

2   Holiday Inn Hemel Hempstead

Tel: 0870 400 9041
0.4 miles west along the A414, on the left.
The Junction Bar & Restaurant; Open all day. Breakfast 06.30-10.00hrs, Lunch 12.30-14.30hrs, Evening Meals 18.30-22.30hrs daily.

3   Shell Hemel Hempstead

Tel: (01442) 275010
0.5 miles west along the A414, on the right.
Visa, Delta, Mastercard, Switch, Diners Club, Amex, Overdrive, All Star, Dial Card, BP Agency, Shell Cards.

JUNCTION 9

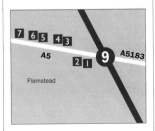

Nearest Northbound A&E Hospital
Luton & Dunstable Hospital
Lewsey Road, Luton LU4 0D
Tel: (01582) 491122
Proceed north to Junction 11 and take the A505 west. The hospital is on the north side of this road, adjacent to the motorway junction. (Distance Approx 6.1 miles)

Nearest Southbound A&E Hospital
Hemel Hempstead General Hospital
Hillfield Road HP2 4AD
Tel: (01442) 213141
Proceed to Junction 8, follow the A4147 to the second roundabout and the hospital is signposted to the right along the A4147 continuation. (Distance Approx 7.7 miles)

FACILITIES

1   The Harvester Flamstead

Tel: (01582) 842800
0.1 miles west along the A5, on the left.
(Six Continents) Open all day. Meals served; 12.00-22.00hrs daily

2   Express by Holiday Inn, Luton-Hemel

Tel: (01582) 841332
0.2 miles west along the A5, on the left.
Breakfast served; Mon-Fri; 06.30-09.30hrs, Sat & Sun; 06.30-11.30hrs.

3   Watling Street Filling Station (Shell Diesel)

Tel: (01582) 840215
0.4 miles west along the A5, on the right.

Access, Visa, Overdrive, Switch, Mastercard, Amex, Diners Club, UK Fuelcard, Shell Cards, Texaco Fastfuel, Securicor Fuelserv, IDS, Keyfuels, AS24. Open; 05.45-22.00hrs daily (24hr Credit/Fuel Card operated pumps available when closed)

4 Watling Street Café

Tel: (01582) 840270
0.4 miles west along the A5, on the right.
Open; Mon-Fri; 06.00-22.00hrs, Sat; 07.00-13.00hrs, Sun; 09.00-14.00hrs

5 Flamstead Filling Station (Shell)

Tel: (01582) 842098
0.5 miles west along the A5, on the right.
Mastercard, Visa, Switch, Amex, Diners Club, Dial Card, Overdrive, All Star, Shell Cards.

6 Waggon & Horses

Tel: (01582) 841932
0.7 miles west along the A5, on the right.
(Pub Partnership) Open all day.

7 Hertfordshire Moat House

Tel: (01582) 449988
1 mile west along the A5, on the right.
Borders Restaurant & Bar; Breakfast; Mon-Fri; 07.00-10.00hrs, Sat & Sun; 07.30-10.30hrs, Lunch; 12.30-14.00hrs daily, Dinner; Mon-Sat; 17.30-21.45hrs, Sun; 17.30-21.30hrs

PLACES OF INTEREST

Whipsnade Wild Animal Park

Whipsnade, Nr Dunstable, Bedfordshire LU6 2LF
Tel : (01582) 872171. Information Hotline Tel; 0990 200 123
website: www.whipsnade.co.uk

Follow the A5 north (Signposted 6 Miles)

One of Europe's largest Conservation Parks with 2,500 animals on view within a 600 acre parkland. Visitors may drive around or take one of the free Safari Tour Buses. Miniature Steam Railway. Children's Play Area. Café. Disabled Access

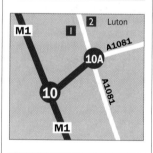

JUNCTS 10 & 10A

Nearest A&E Hospital
Luton & Dunstable Hospital
Lewsey Road, Luton LU4 0D
Tel: (01582) 491122
Proceed north to Junction 11 and take the A505 west. The hospital is on the north side of this road, adjacent to the motorway junction. (Distance Approx 3.7 miles)

FACILITIES

1 Stockwood Hotel

Tel: (01582) 721000
0.9 miles north along the A6 (Castle Street), in Luton, on the left.

2 Shell Motorway Station

Tel: (01582) 747430
1 mile north along the A6 (Castle Street), in Luton, on the right.
Access, Visa, Overdrive, All Star, Switch, Dial Card, Mastercard, Amex, Diners Club, Delta, UK Fuelcard, Shell Cards, Smartcard.

PLACES OF INTEREST

Stockwood Craft Museum & Gardens

Farley Hill, Luton LU1 4BH
Tel: (01582) 738714
website: www.luton.gov.uk

Follow the A6 north towards Luton (Signposted 1.8 Miles)
A craft museum featuring rural trades, and set within beautifully restored Period Gardens. The gardens represent over 1,000 years of English gardening and feature Knot, Mediaeval, Victorian and Italian styles. Other attractions include the Mossman Collection of Horse Drawn Vehicles and a Bee Gallery. Childrens Play Area. Gift Shop. Disabled Access.

Woodside Wildfowl Park

Woodside Road, Slip End Village, Luton LU1 4DG
Tel: (01582) 841044
website: www.woodsidefarm.co.uk

Follow the A1081 south, turn first right east towards Slip End and then left along the B4540. (Signposted 2.9 Miles)

One of England's largest poultry centres incorporating very rare breeds. Visitors can stroke, handle and feed the animals and poultry. Children's Farm. Leisure Complex. Farm and Gift Shops. Coffee Shop. Disabled Access.

Luton Museum & Art Gallery

Warndown Park, Luton LU2 7HA

Tel: (01582) 546721 or
Tel: (01582) 546739
website: www.luton.gov.uk

Follow the A6 north through Luton (Signposted 3.3 Miles).

The history of Luton and the surrounding district is featured in this Victorian mansion set in Wardown Park. Saxon jewellery, mediaeval guild books for Luton and Dunstable and the development of the hat industry are just some of the exhibits on display. Gift Shop. Tea Room. Disabled facilities.

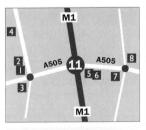

JUNCTION 11

Nearest A&E Hospital
Luton & Dunstable Hospital
Lewsey Road, Luton LU4 0D
Tel: (01582) 491122
Take the A505 west and the hospital is on the north side of

this road, adjacent to the motorway junction. (Distance Approx 0.4 miles)

FACILITIES

1 The Halfway House

Tel: (01582) 609938
0.5 miles west along the A505, on the right.
(Beefeater) Open all day. Breakfast; Mon-Fri; 07.00-09.00hrs, Sat & Sun; 08.00-10.00hrs. Meals served; Sun-Thurs; 12.00-22.30hrs, Fri & Sat; 12.00-23.00hrs.

2 Travel Inn

Tel: (01582) 609938
0.5 miles west along the A505, on the right.

3 Tesco Filling Station

Tel: (01582) 687500
0.5 miles west along the A505, on the left.
Access, Visa, Overdrive, All Star, Switch, Dial Card, Mastercard, Amex, Delta, AA Paytrak, Tesco Fuelcard. Disabled Toilets and Cash Machine in adjacent store.

4 Shell Wilbury Service Station

Tel: (01582) 479950
1 mile along Poynters Road, on the left.
Access, Visa, Overdrive, All Star, Switch, Dial Card, Mastercard, Amex, Diners Club, Delta, Shell Cards, BP Supercharge.

5 Travelodge Luton

Tel: (01582) 575955
0.1 miles east along the A505, on the right.

Bar Café Open; Breakfast; Mon-Fri; 07.00-10.00hrs, Sat & Sun; 08.00-11.00hrs, Lunch; 12.00-14.00hrs daily, Dinner; 18.00-22.00hrs daily.

6 Dunstable Road Filling Station (Jet)

Tel: (01582) 574366
0.1 miles east along the A505, on the right.
Access, Visa, Overdrive, All Star, Switch, Dial Card, Mastercard, Amex, Diners Club, Delta, Routex, BP Supercharge, Jet Cards. Open; Mon-Fri; 06.30-22.00hrs, Sat & Sun; 07.00-22.00hrs.

7 The Leicester Arms Harvester

Tel: (01582) 572718
0.5 miles east along the A505, on the right.
(Six Continents) Open all day Sat & Sun. Meals served; Mon-Fri; 12.00-14.30hrs & 17.00-21.30hrs, Sat & Sun; 12.00-22.00hrs

8 Empire Petrol Station (Esso)

Tel: (01582) 593886
0.8 miles east along the A505, on the left.
Visa, Access, Diners Club, Overdrive, Switch, All Star, Dial Card, Amex, Esso Cards.

PLACES OF INTEREST

Luton Museum & Art Gallery

Warndown Park, Luton LU2 7HA

Follow the A505 east and turn left along the A5228 north. (Signposted 2.5 Miles)

For details please see Junction 10 information

M1 BETWEEN JUNCS 11 & 12

TODDINGTON SERVICES (NORTHBOUND) (MOTO)
Tel: (01525) 878400
Fresh Express Self Service Restaurant, Burger King, Little Chef, Upper Crust, Harry Ramsden's & BP Fuel

TODDINGTON SERVICES (SOUTHBOUND) (MOTO)
Tel: (01525) 878424
Fresh Express Self Service Restaurant, Burger King, Little Chef, Upper Crust, Harry Ramsden's, Travelodge & BP Fuel

FOOTBRIDGE CONNECTION BETWEEN SITES

M1 JUNCTION 12

Nearest Northbound A&E Hospital

Bedford General Hospital
South Wing, Kempston Road MK42 9DJ
Tel: (01234) 355122
Proceed north to Junction 13 and take the A421 east to Bedford. Continue along the A6 and then the A5141 and the hospital is along this road. (Distance Approx 16.3 miles)

Nearest Southbound A&E Hospital

Luton & Dunstable Hospital
Lewsey Road, Luton LU4 0D
Tel: (01582) 491122
Proceed south to Junction 11 and take the A505 west. The hospital is on the north side of this road, adjacent to the motorway junction. (Distance Approx 5.5 miles)

FACILITIES

1   The Griffin Hotel

Tel: (01525) 872030
0.9 miles south along the A5120, on the left.
(Greene King) Open all day. Lunch; 12.00-14.00hrs daily, Evening meals; Mon-Sat; 19.00-21.00hrs

2   The Bell at Toddington

Tel: (01525) 872564
0.9 miles south along the A5120, on the right.
(Free House) Open all day. Meals served; Lunch; 12.00-15.00hrs daily, Evening meals Mon-Thurs; 18.00-21.00hrs.

3   Oddfellows Arms

Tel: (01525) 872021
1 mile south along the A5120, in Market Place, Toddington.
(Free House) Lunch; Fri, Sat & Sun; 12.00-14.00hrs, Evening Meals; Mon; 18.00-20.00hrs, Tues-Sat; 18.00-21.00hrs.

4   The Bombay Tandoori Restaurant

Tel: (01525) 872928
1 mile south along the A5120, in Market Place, Toddington.
Open; 18.30-23.30hrs daily.

5   The Red Lion

Tel: (01525) 872524
1 mile south along the A5120, in Market Place, Toddington.
(Free House) Open all day on Sat & Sun. Closed until 19.00hrs on Mon. Meals served; Tues-Sun; 12.00-14.30hrs & 19.00-21.30hrs.

PLACES OF INTEREST

Whipsnade Wild Animal Park

Whipsnade, Nr Dunstable, Bedfordshire LU6 2LF

Follow the A5120 south (Signposted 9 Miles)
For details please see Junction 9 Information

M1 JUNCTION 13

Nearest A&E Hospital

Bedford General Hospital
South Wing, Kempston Road MK42 9DJ
Tel: (01234) 355122
Take the A421 east to Bedford. Continue along the A6 and then the A5141 and the hospital is along this road. (Distance Approx 9.5 miles)

Or Alternatively

Milton Keynes General

Standing Way, Eaglestone
MK6 5LD
Tel: (01908) 660033
Take the A421 west to Milton
Keynes and continue into the
A4146. The hospital is along
this road. (Distance Approx 5.8
miles)

FACILITIES

1   Crawley Crossing (Keyfuels)

Tel: (01908) 281084
**0.3 miles east along the
A507, on the left.**
Diesel Direct, IDS, Keyfuels,
Securicor Fuelserv.

2   Truck Stop

Tel: (01908) 281086
**0.3 miles east along the
A507, on the left.**
Open; Mon-Fri; 06.00-
22.00hrs, Sat; 07.00-12.00hrs.

PLACES OF INTEREST

Woburn Safari Park

Woburn, Bedfordshire MK17 9QN
Tel: (01525) 290407
website: www.woburnsafari.co.uk

**Follow the A507 south.
(Signposted 2 Miles)**

Featuring a drive-through
Safari Park, with extensive
reserves, and a Worldwide
Leisure area with adventure
playgrounds, and animal
encounters and demonstration
features. Boating. Miniature
Railway. Gift Shop. Restaurant.
Disabled access.

Woburn Abbey

Woburn, Bedfordshire MK43 0TP
Tel: (01525) 290666
website:www.woburnabbey.co.uk

**Adjacent to Woburn Safari
Park.**

The home of the Marquess and
Marchioness of Tavistock, the
house contains one of the
most important private
collections of works of art in
the country. Surrounded by a
3,000 acre park containing
nine species of deer, there are
two gift shops, an antiques
centre, pottery and the Flying
Duchess Pavilion serves light
lunches and teas. Some
disabled access.

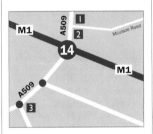

JUNCTION 14

Nearest A&E Hospital

Milton Keynes General

Standing Way, Eaglestone
MK6 5LD
Tel: (01908) 660033
Take the A509 towards Milton
Keynes and at the crossroads
bear right along the A4146. At
the roundabout junction with
the A421 turn right along the
A421 and this leads to the
hospital. (Distance Approx 4.1
miles)

FACILITIES

1   Courtyard by Marriott Hotel

Tel: (01908) 613688
**0.3 miles north along the
A509, on the right.**

The Courtyard Brasserie; Open;
Breakfast; Mon-Fri; 07.00-
09.30hrs, Sat & Sun; 07.00-
11.00hrs, Lunch; 12.00-
14.00hrs daily, Dinner; 19.00-
22.00hrs daily. Bar Meals
served all day.

2   The Old Stables Executive B&B at Hermitage Farm

Tel: (01908) 217766
**0.1 miles east along Moulsoe
Road, on the right.**

3   Total Filling Station

Tel: (01908) 354240
**0.7 miles south along the
A509, on the left.**
Visa, Access, Amex, Diners
Club, All Star, Overdrive, Dial
Card, Switch, Total Eurotraffic,
Total/Fina/Elf Cards

PLACES OF INTEREST

Milton Keynes Museum

Southern Way, Wolverton
MK12 5EJ Tel: (01908) 316222
website; www.mkmuseum.org.uk

**Follow the A505 east through
Central Milton Keynes, turn
right along the A5 and right
along the A422 (6.4 Miles)**

Housed in a beautiful Victorian
farmstead and grounds and
sited in Wolverton, England's
first railway town, there is a
Hall of Transport and exhibits
and displays reflecting the
agricultural and industrial
heritage of the area. Shop. Tea
Rooms. Disabled access.

Emberton Country Park

Nr Olney, Buckinghamshire
MK46 5DB

Tel: (01234) 711575
Take the A509 north towards

Olney (8 Miles)

Originally a gravel works, in 1965 it was transformed into an attractive parkland setting covering 205 acres. It caters for a wide variety of uses and interests including caravanning and camping, fishing, sailing, walking and picnic areas. Shop. Tea Rooms. Disabled access.

Olney

Olney Chamber of Trade Tel: (01234) 241161.
website;www.olney.org.uk

Follow the A509 north (Signposted 7.1 Miles)

A beautiful market town, with an attractive wide high street and market, it is home to a fascinating collection of architecturally varied buildings dating back many centuries. Although the earliest documentary evidence as to the existence of Olney is contained in a Saxon Charter of 979, a number of archaeological finds indicate that the area was occupied as early as 1600BC.

The Church of St Peter & St Paul dates from the 14thC and the bridge from the 19thC. The Cowper & Newton Museum (Tel: 01234-711516. website: www.cowperandnewtonmuseum.org.uk) in the Market Place was once the home of William Cowper from 1768 to 1786 and is dedicated to preserving the memory and artifacts of Cowper and his friend the Rev.John Newton, reformed slave trader and curate of Olney between 1764 and 1780. They collaborated in writing the Olney Hymns, of which "Amazing Grace" is the most well known.

M1 BETWEEN JUNCS 14 & 15

NEWPORT PAGNELL SERVICES (NORTHBOUND) (WELCOME BREAK)
Tel: (01908) 217722
Food Connection, La Brioche Doree, KFC, Burger King, Welcome Lodge & Shell Fuel

NEWPORT PAGNELL SERVICES (SOUTHBOUND) (WELCOME BREAK)
Tel: (01908) 217722
The Granary Restaurant & Shell Fuel

FOOTBRIDGE CONNECTION BETWEEN SITES

M1 JUNCTION 15

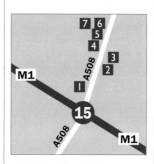

Nearest A&E Hospital

Northampton General Hospital
Cottarville, Off Billing Road NN1 5BD
Tel: (01604) 634700
Take the A508 north into Northampton and turn right along the A5123. The hospital is along this route. (Distance Approx 3.8 miles)

FACILITIES

1   The Hilton in Northampton

Tel: (01604) 700666
0.2 miles north along the A508, on the left.
Restaurant Open; Breakfast; Mon-Sat; 07.00-10.00hrs, Sun; 08.00-10.30hrs, Lunch; Mon-Fri; 12.30-14.00hrs, Sun; 13.00-14.30hrs, Dinner;19.00-22.00hrs daily. Bar snacks available throughout the day.

2   Grange Farm Service Station (Save)

Tel: (01604) 700498
0.5 miles north along the A508, on the right.
Keyfuels, Access, Visa, Overdrive, All Star, Switch, Dial Card, Mastercard, AA Paytrak, Delta, BP Supercharge, Save Card

3   Little Chef

Tel: (01604) 705722
0.5 miles north along the A508, on the right.
Open; 07.00-22.00hrs daily.

4   Midway Hotel

Tel: (01604) 769676
0.9 miles north along the A508, on the left.
(Toby Restaurant) Open all day. Restaurant Open; Mon-Sat; 12.00-14.00hrs & 17.30-22.00hrs, Sun; 12.00-22.00hrs. Bar meals served all day.

5   Burger King

Tel: (01604) 701078
0.9 miles north along the A508, on the left.
Open; 10.00-22.00hrs daily.

6 Little Chef

Tel: (01604) 701078
0.9 miles north along the A508, on the left.
Open; 07.00-22.00hrs daily.

7 Shell Northampton

Tel: (01604) 664940
0.9 miles north along the A508, on the left.
LPG. Access, Visa, Overdrive, All Star, Switch, Dial Card, Mastercard, Amex, Diners Club, Delta, AA Paytrak, BP Agency, Shell Cards.

PLACES OF INTEREST

Northampton

Follow the A508 north (Signposted 4.3 Miles)
For details please see Junction 16 information.

Within the town can be found ...

Central Museum and Art Gallery

Guildhall Road, Northampton
NN1 1DP

For details please see Junction 16 information.

The Canal Museum

Bridge Road, Stoke Bruerne, Towcester NN12 7SE
Tel: (01604) 862229
website: www.britishwaterways.co.uk

Follow the A508 south (3.8 Miles)
The Canal Museum portrays over 200 years of colourful waterways history, whilst the picturesque village of Stoke Bruerne contains canalside pubs. Waterside walks, boat trips to Blisworth Tunnel, restaurants and tearooms. Some disabled access.

JUNCTION 15A

APART FROM ROTHERSTHORPE SERVICES THERE ARE NO OTHER FACILITIES WITHIN ONE MILE OF THIS JUNCTION

ROTHERSTHORPE SERVICES (NORTHBOUND) (ROADCHEF)
Tel: (01604) 831888
En Route Restaurant, Wimpy Bar, Costa Coffee & BP Fuel

ROTHERSTHORPE SERVICES (SOUTHBOUND) (ROADCHEF)
Tel: (01604) 831888
En Route Restaurant, Wimpy Bar, Costa Coffee & BP Fuel

FOOTBRIDGE CONNECTION BETWEEN SITES

Nearest A&E Hospital

Northampton General Hospital
Cottarville, Off Billing Road
NN1 5BD
Tel: (01604) 634700
Take the A43 north and continue north along the A45. Turn right along the A5123 and the hospital is signposted along this route. (Distance Approx 4.5 miles)

PLACES OF INTEREST

Northampton

Follow the A43 north (Signposted 4.2 Miles)
For details please see Junction 16 information.

Within the town can be found ...

Central Museum and Art Gallery

Guildhall Road, Northampton
NN1 1DP

For details please see Junction 16 information.

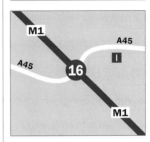

JUNCTION 16

Nearest A&E Hospital

Northampton General Hospital
Cottarville, Off Billing Road
NN1 5BD
Tel: (01604) 634700
Proceed to Junction 15A, take the A43 north and continue north along the A45. Turn right along the A5123 and the hospital is signposted along this route. (Distance Approx 8 miles)

FACILITIES

1 The Red Lion Pub & Café

Tel: (01604) 831914
0.5 miles east along the A45, on the right.
(Freehouse) Pub Open; Mon-Fri; Evenings only. Cafe Open; Mon-Fri; 06.00-21.30hrs

PLACES OF INTEREST

Northampton

Northampton Tourist Information Office, St Giles Square,

Northampton NN1 1DA
Tel: (01604) 622677
website: www.northampton.gov.uk/tourism

Follow the A45 east (Signposted 5 Miles)

Synonymous with the manufacture of footwear, the history of Northampton goes back to pre-Roman times with Iron Age settlements having been found in and around the town. Ever since King John bought a pair of shoes here for nine pence in the early 13thC the boot and shoe trade has flourished greatly and a world wide reputation established. Cromwell's Parliamentarians, with whom the town sided during the Civil War, were sent 1,500 pairs and many other armies, over the years, have been supplied with footwear made here.

Lace-making, the other industry here, was probably established during the 17thC in the wake of the influx of Protestant refugees from the Continent. The town was all but destroyed by the Great Fire of 1675 but was rebuilt in such a spacious and well-planned way that Daniel Defoe called it "the handsomest and best built town in all this part of England".

Today there is a fascinating mix of historic buildings; Norman churches, Victorian architecture, museums and an art gallery, and modern amenities. Reflecting on the major trade in the town, there are numerous factory shoe shops including Barker Shoes in Station Road, Earls Barton (Tel: 01604-810387) and Barratts in Barrack Road (Tel: 01604-718632).

Within the town can be found ...

Central Museum and Art Gallery

Guildhall Road, Northampton
NN1 1DP
Tel: (01604) 238548

website: www.northampton.gov.uk/museums

With two new galleries opening in 2002, visitors are able to view more examples from the largest collection of boots and shoes in the world, as well as displays of shoe fashions across the centuries and the machines that made them. There are exhibits showing the history of Northampton from the Stone Age to the present day and the Art Gallery has a fine collection of Italian 15thC to 18thC paintings and British art. Disabled access.

Canons Ashby House (NT)

Canons Ashby, Nr Daventry
NN11 3SD
Tel: (01327) 860044
website: www.nationaltrust.org.uk

Follow the A45 west, turn left through Nether Heyford and left along the A5. Canons Ashby is signposted along this route. (10.4 Miles)

One of the oldest and most romantic of Northamptonshire's great houses and home of the Dryden family since the 1550's. The house contains fascinating Elizabethan wall paintings and sumptuous Jacobean plasterwork, formal gardens with terraces, mediaeval church and parkland. Shop. Tea Room. Some disabled access.

M1

BETWEEN JUNCS 16 & 17

WATFORD GAP SERVICES (NORTHBOUND) (ROADCHEF)
Tel: (01327) 879001
Restaurant, Wimpy Bar, Costa Coffee & BP Fuel.

WATFORD GAP SERVICES (SOUTHBOUND) (ROADCHEF)
Tel: (01327) 879001
Restaurant, Wimpy Bar, Costa Coffee, Travel Inn & BP Fuel.

FOOTBRIDGE CONNECTION BETWEEN SITES

M1

JUNCTION 17

JUNCTION 17 IS A MOTORWAY INTERCHANGE ONLY WITH THE M45 AND THERE IS NO ACCESS TO ANY FACILITIES

M1

JUNCTION 18

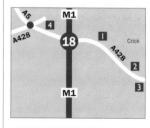

Nearest A&E Hospital

Hospital of St Cross

Barby Road, Rugby CV22 5PX
Tel: (01788) 572831

Take the A5 west and the A428 into Rugby. Turn left into Barby Road and the hospital is on the left. (Distance Approx 5.4 miles)

FACILITIES

1 Holiday Inn Rugby/Northampton

Tel: 0870 400 9059

0.3 miles east along the A428, on the left.

Junction Restaurant; Open; Breakfast; Mon-Fri; 06.30-10.00hrs, Sat & Sun; 07.30-11.00hrs, Lunch; Mon-Fri; 12.30-14.00hrs, Dinner; Mon-Sat; 18.30-21.30hrs, Sun; 19.00-21.30hrs.

2   The Wheatsheaf

Tel: (01788) 822284

1 mile east along the A428, in Crick, on the left.

(McManus Taverns) Open all day. Meals served; Mon-Sat; 12.00-14.30hrs & 18.00-22.00hrs, Sun; 12.00-14.30hrs & 18.00-21.30hrs

3   The Red Lion

Tel: (01788) 822342

1 mile east along the A428, in Crick, on the right.

(Free House) Meals served; Lunch; 12.00-14.00hrs daily, Evening Meals; Mon-Fri; 19.00-21.00hrs, Sat; 19.00-21.30hrs.

4   Ibis Hotel, Rugby East

Tel: (01788) 824331

0.3 miles west along the A5, on the right.

Bar Meals served 24 hours.

PLACES OF INTEREST

James Gilbert Rugby Football Museum

5 St Matthews Street, Rugby CV21 3BY Tel: (01788) 333889 website: www.james-gilbert.com

Follow the A428 into Rugby (5.2 Miles)

The museum is on the site where Gilbert footballs have been made since 1842. The birthplace of rugby union,

visitors can find out how Rugby gave its name to what became an international game. It contains many artefacts and there are practical demonstrations of the art of manufacturing the oval shaped ball. There is also "The Total Rugby Experience", an audio visual show, and a Factory Outlet shop.

Rugby School Museum

10 Little Church Street, Rugby CV21 3AW Tel: (01788) 556109 website: www.rugbyschool.net

Famously, the scene for "Tom Brown's Schooldays" and the birthplace of Rugby football, the museum tells the story of Rugby School, its pupils and the ethos that led it to the forefront of Public Schools and its outstanding influence on the development of the sport. Music and sound bring to life the displays which feature memorabilia of the game and of the many famous people who were pupils here. Tours of the school itself are arranged regularly.

Stanford Hall

Lutterworth, Leicestershire LE17 6DH

Follow the A428 east (Signposted 5.2 Miles)

For details please see Junction 19 information.

THIS IS A MOTORWAY INTERCHANGE WITH THE M6 AND A RESTRICTED ACCESS JUNCTION

■ **Vehicles can only exit from the southbound lanes.**
■ **Vehicles can only enter the motorway along the northbound lanes**

Nearest A&E Hospital

Hospital of St Cross

Barby Road, Rugby CV22 5PX Tel: (01788) 572831

Take the B5414 into Rugby and turn right along the A428. Turn left into Barby Road and the hospital is on the left. (Distance Approx 5.7 miles)

FACILITIES

1   The Chequers

Tel: (01788) 860318

0.5 miles east along the B5414, in Swinford, on the right.

(Pubmaster) Meals served; Tues-Sat; 12.00-14.00hrs & 18.00-21.00hrs, Sun; 12.00-14.00hrs

PLACES OF INTEREST

Stanford Hall

Lutterworth, Leicestershire LE17 6DH Tel: (01788) 860250 website: www.stanfordhall.co.uk

Signposted from the junction. (2.7 Miles)

Built by the Smiths of Warwick in the 1690's and still occupied by the Cave family, it contains antique furniture, fine pictures and family costumes. The grounds include a walled rose garden and nature trail and there is also a Motorcycle

Museum. Gift Shop. Tea Room. Limited disabled access.

Naseby Battle & Farm Museum.

Janet Hillyer Tel: (01604) 740662

Follow the A14 east, at the first junction turn right along the A50 and then first left to Naseby. (Signposted off the A14, 9.7 Miles).

(NB.Open 14.00-17.00hrs on Sun and Mon at Bank Holidays between Easter and September and By Appointment only).

The decisive battle of the Civil War, Naseby has played a significant part in English history. It was here on June 14th, 1645 that Cromwell defeated Charles I's Royalist army and brought about his surrender some 11 months later in Newark. Today, Naseby is one of the least spoilt of English battlefields and the adjacent museum contains a miniature layout of the battlefield with commentary as well as relics from the battle.

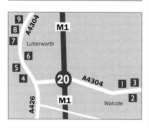

JUNCTION 20

Nearest Northbound A&E Hospital

Leicester Royal Infirmary

Infirmary Square, Leicester LE1 5WW
Tel: (0116) 254 1414

Proceed to Junction 21 and take the exit to Leicester. Follow the A5460 into the city and turn right along Upperton Road. Turn left at the end and the hospital is on the left.
(Distance Approx 15 miles)

Nearest Southbound A&E Hospital

Hospital of St Cross

Barby Road, Rugby CV22 5PX
Tel: (01788) 572831

Take the A426 into Rugby and turn left along the A428. Turn right into Barby Road and the hospital is on the left.
(Distance Approx 7.6 miles)

FACILITIES

> **LUTTERWORTH TOWN CENTRE IS WITHIN ONE MILE OF THIS JUNCTION**

1 The Tavern Inn

Tel: (01455) 553338

0.9 miles east along the A4304, in Walcote, on the left.

(Free House) Open all day. Meals served; 08.00-11.30 hrs (Breakfast only) and 11.30-21.30hrs daily

2 Walcote Service Station (Texaco)

Tel: (01455) 553911

1 mile east along the A4304, in Walcote, on the right.

Access, Visa, Overdrive, All Star, Switch, Dial Card, Mastercard, Amex, Diners Club, Delta, Texaco Cards. Open; 07.00-22.00hrs daily.

3 The Black Horse

Tel: (01455) 552684

1 mile east along the A4304, in Walcote, on the left.

(Free House) Meals served; Lunch; Fri; 12.00-14.00hrs & Sun; 12.00-14.30hrs, Evening Meals; 19.00-21.30hrs daily

4 The Fox Inn

Tel: (01455) 552677

0.5 miles west along the A4304, in Lutterworth, on the left.

(Laurel Pub Partnership) Meals served; Lunch; 12.00-14.30hrs daily, Evening Meals; Tues-Sat; 18.00-21.00hrs,

5 The Denbigh Arms

Tel: (01455) 553537

0.7 miles west along the A4304, in Lutterworth, on the left.

(Free House) Open all day. The Players Bar; Bar Snacks served 12.00-14.00hrs & 19.00-21.00hrs daily. Lambert's Restaurant; Breakfast; Mon-Fri; 07.00-09.30hrs, Sat & Sun; 08.00-10.00hrs, Lunch; Sun-Fri; 12.00-14.00hrs, Dinner; 19.00-21.00hrs daily.

6 The Shambles

Tel: (01455) 552620

0.8 miles west along the A4304, in Lutterworth, on the right.

(Banks's) Open all day. Meals served; Mon-Thurs; 11.00-14.00hrs & 17.00-19.00hrs, Fri; 11.00-14.00hrs, Sat; 12.00-14.30hrs, Sun; 12.00-15.30hrs. NB. Accommodation is bed only.

7 The Greyhound Hotel

Tel: (01455) 553307

0.9 miles west along the A4304, in Lutterworth, on the left.

(Free House) Open all day. Bar Snacks available; Mon-Sat; 12.00-14.00hrs & Sun-Thurs; 19.00-21.30hrs. Restaurant Open; Lunch; Mon-Sat; 12.00-14.00hrs, Evening Meals; 19.00-21.30hrs daily. The Vaults Bistro; Open; Thurs-Sat; 19.00-21.30hrs.

8   The Cavalier Inn

Tel: (01455) 552402
1 mile west along the A4304, in Lutterworth, on the left.
(Free House) Open all day. Meals served; Mon-Sat; 12.00-21.30hrs, Sun; 12.00-21.00hrs

9   Star St Mary's Filling Station (Texaco)

Tel: (01455) 200560
1 mile west along the A4304, in Lutterworth, on the left.
Access, Visa, Overdrive, All Star, Switch, Dial Card, Mastercard, Amex, Diners Club, Delta, Electron, Texaco Cards.

PLACES OF INTEREST

Lutterworth Museum

Churchgate, Lutterworth
LE17 4AN Tel: (01455) 284733

Follow the A426 west into Lutterworth (1 Mile)
Devoted to local history, this museum has a wealth of exhibits from Roman times to World War II.

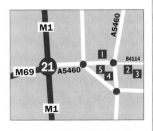

JUNCTION 21

Nearest A&E Hospital
Leicester Royal Infirmary
Infirmary Square, Leicester

LE1 5WW
Tel: (0116) 254 1414
Take the exit to Leicester, follow the A5460 into the city and turn right along Upperton Road. Turn left at the end and the hospital is on the left.
(Distance Approx 3.8 miles)

FACILITIES

1   Hilton Leicester

Tel: (0116) 263 0066
0.4 miles east along the A5460, on the left.
The Britisserie Restaurant; Open; Breakfast; 07.00-10.00hrs, Lunch; 12.00-14.00hrs, Dinner; 19.00-22.00hrs daily.

2   Asda Filling Station

Tel: (0116) 289 8174
0.9 miles east along the B4114 (Fosse Park Road), on the right.
Access, Visa, Overdrive, All Star, Switch, Dial Card, Mastercard, Amex, Diners Club, Delta, AA Paytrak, Asda Fuelcard. Disabled Toilets and Cash Machine available in adjacent store. Open; 06.00-00.00hrs daily. 24hr Credit Card operated pump available Mon-Fri.

3   McDonald's

Tel: (0116) 263 0563
1 mile east along the B4114 (Fosse Park Road), on the right.
Open; Mon-Thurs; 07.00-23.30hrs, Fri & Sat; 07.00-0.00hrs, Sun; 07.00-22.30hrs (Drive-Thru open until 23.30hrs)

4   Sainsbury's Filling Station

Tel: (0116) 263 1153
0.4 miles south along the B4114, at the Grove Park Triangle, on the right.
Access, Visa, Overdrive, All Star, Switch, Dial Card, Mastercard, Amex, Delta, AA Paytrak, Sainsburys Petrol Card. Disabled Toilets and Cash Machine available in adjacent store.

5   Pizza Hut

Tel: (0116) 289 2990
0.4 miles south along the B4114, at the Grove Park Triangle, on the right.
Open; 11.30-23.00hrs daily.

PLACES OF INTEREST

Leicester

Leicester Tourist Information Centre, 7/9 Every Street, Town Hall Square, Leicester LE1 6AG
Tel: (0116) 299 8888 website: www.discoverleicester.com

Follow the A5460 north (Signposted 4.2 Miles)
Standing on the River Soar, the origin of Leicester dates back over 2,000 years. The Romans built Fosse Way through it and walled the city, naming it Leirceastre, and there are still some remains of their occupation, Peacock Pavement; Roman pavements and Jewry Wall; A 70ft long portion of the city wall, being some of the more notable. Amongst the many fine buildings still to be seen are the 15thC Guild Hall (Tel: 0116-253 2569), 17thC Town Library and the Museum and Art Gallery.

Within the city can be found ....

Jewry Wall Museum

St.Nicholas Circle, Leicester

LE1 4JJ

Tel: (0116) 247 3021 website: www.leicestermuseums.ac.uk

Featuring early archaeology from pre-historic times to the Middle Ages the museum is adjacent to the Jewry Wall.

Belgrave Hall & Gardens

Church Road, Leicester LE4 5PE Tel: (0116) 266 6590. website: www.leicestermuseums.ac.uk

A delightful Queen Anne House dating from 1709 and displaying Edwardian elegance and Victorian cosiness. Set in beautiful gardens.

Castle Park

Tel: (0116) 299 8888

The historic core of Leicester where the Romans, Saxons and Normans settled. Full of fascinating buildings and delightful walks around the area in which the mediaeval town flourished and the industrial city was born. Museums and Specialist Shops.

M1
BETWEEN
JUNCS 21 & 21A

LEICESTER FOREST EAST SERVICES (WELCOME BREAK)

Tel: (0116) 238 6801
Days Inn & BP Fuel (Northbound)
BP Fuel (Southbound)
Food Connection Restaurant, Red Hen Restaurant, Burger King & KFC on Footbridge connecting sites

M1
JUNCTION 21A

THIS IS A RESTRICTED ACCESS JUNCTION

- Vehicles can only exit from the northbound lanes.
- Vehicles can only enter the motorway along the southbound lanes

THERE ARE NO FACILITIES WITHIN ONE MILE OF THIS JUNCTION

Nearest Northbound A&E Hospital

Leicester Royal Infirmary

Infirmary Square, Leicester LE1 5WW Tel: (0116) 254 1414

Take the A46 north and turn right along the A50 to Leicester. Bear right along the A594 and the hospital is on the right hand side of Infirmary Road in the city centre. (Distance Approx 6.1 miles)

Nearest Southbound A&E Hospital

Leicester Royal Infirmary

Infirmary Square, Leicester LE1 5WW Tel: (0116) 254 1414

Proceed to Junction 21 and take the exit to Leicester. Follow the A5460 into the city and turn right along Upperton Road. Turn left at the end and the hospital is on the left. (Distance Approx 6.5 miles)

PLACES OF INTEREST

National Space Centre

Exploration Drive, Leicester LE4 5NS Tel: (0116) 261 0261.

website: www.spacecentre.co.uk

Follow the A46 north (Signposted 5.3 Miles)

Opened in 2001, The National Space Centre is the UK's largest visitor attraction dedicated to space science and our understanding of space with five differently themed galleries showing the history and technology of space exploration and containing examples of rockets, satellites and capsules. Satellite Bar, Boosters Restaurant, Gift Shop. Disabled access.

M1
JUNCTION 22

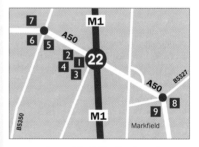

Nearest A&E Hospital

Leicester Royal Infirmary

Infirmary Square, Leicester LE1 5WW Tel: (0116) 254 1414

Take the exit to Leicester, follow the A50 through the city centre and the hospital is on the right. (Distance Approx 8.6 miles)

FACILITIES

1   Leicester North Services (Moto) (BP)

Tel: (01530) 244777

On the west side of the roundabout.
LPG. Access, Visa, Overdrive, All Star, Switch, Dial Card, Mastercard, Amex, Diners Club, Delta, Routex, AA Paytrak, Shell Agency, BP Cards

2 Little Chef

Tel: (01530) 244777
On the west side of the roundabout.
Open; 07.00-22.00hrs daily

3 Burger King

Tel: (01530) 244777
On the west side of the roundabout.
Open; 11.00-21.00hrs daily

4 Travelodge Leicester North

Tel: (01530) 244777
On the west side of the roundabout.

5 Flying Horse

Tel: (01530) 245610
0.5 miles west along the A511, on the left.
(Free House) Cantonese Restaurant Open; 12.00-14.00hrs & 17.30-23.00hrs daily

6 Flying Horse Garage (BP)

Tel: (01530) 242222
0.6 miles west along the A511, on the left.
Access, Visa, Overdrive, All Star, Switch, Dial Card, Mastercard, Amex, Diners Club, Delta, Shell Agency, BP Cards.
Open; 05.30-22.00hrs daily.

7 Browns Blue Filling Station (BP)

Tel: (01530) 249849

0.7 miles west along the A511, on the right.
Access, Visa, Overdrive, All Star, Switch, Dial Card, Mastercard, Amex, AA Paytrak, Diners Club, Delta, Routex, Shell Agency, BP Cards.

8 The Field Head Hotel

Tel: (01530) 245454
1 mile east along the A511, in Markfield, on the left.
(Free House) Meals served; Breakfast; Mon-Fri; 07.00-09.30hrs, Sat & Sun; 08.00-10.00hrs, Lunch; Mon-Sat; 12.00-14.00hrs, Dinner; Mon-Sat; 18.30-21.30hrs, Meals served all day Sun; 12.00-21.00hrs.

9 The Coach & Horses

Tel: (01530) 242312
1 mile east along the A511, in Markfield, on the right.
(Everards) Open all day Friday, Saturday & Sunday. Meals served; Mon-Thurs; 12.00-14.00hrs & 18.00-21.00hrs, Fri & Sat; 12.00-21.00hrs, Sun; 12.00-19.00hrs

PLACES OF INTEREST

Snibston Discovery Park

Ashby Road, Coalville
LE67 3LN
Tel: (01530) 278444
website:
www.leics.gov.uk/museums

Follow the A50 west to Coalville (4.2 Miles)

Based at the former Snibston Colliery the Discovery Park is full of hands-on displays and experiments. There are galleries devoted to Transport,

Engineering and Textile & Fashion plus graphic illustrations of 19thC life in a coal mine. There is a surface colliery tour and plenty of activities for children. Gift Shop. Café. Disabled facilities.

Bradgate Country Park Visitor Centre

Newtown Linford, Leicestershire LE6 0FA Tel: (0116) 236 2713

Follow the A50 east and bear left to Newtown Linford (Signposted off A50, 3.2 Miles)

In the centre of Bradgate Park, the Visitor Centre contains displays on Lady Jane Grey and the history of Bradgate Park and Swithland Wood. Within the grounds can be found the ruins of Bradgate House and the Old John Tower. Refreshments. Gift Shop. Some disabled access.

National Space Centre

Exploration Drive, Leicester
LE4 5NS

Follow the A50 south (Signposted 8.3 Miles)

For details please see Junction 21A information.

M1
JUNCTION 23

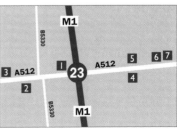

Nearest Northbound A&E Hospital
Derbyshire Royal Infirmary
London Road, Derby DE1 2XX

Tel: (01332) 347141

Proceed to Junction 24 and take the A6 west to Derby. The hospital is in the city centre, on the left hand side of the road. (Distance Approx 16 miles)

Nearest Southbound A&E Hospital

Leicester Royal Infirmary

Infirmary Square, Leicester LE1 5WW

Tel: (0116) 254 1414

Proceed to Junction 22 and take the exit to Leicester. Follow the A50 through the city centre and the hospital is on the right. (Distance Approx 13.2 miles)

FACILITIES

1   Junction 23 Lorry Park (Keyfuels)

Tel: (01509) 507480

0.3 miles west along the A512, on the right.

Diesel Fuel only. Access, Visa, Overdrive, All Star, Mastercard, AA Paytrak, UK Fuelcard, Securicor Fuelserv, IDS, Butler Fuels, Keyfuels. Café Open; Mon-Fri; 06.00-21.00hrs, Sat; 06.00-11.00hrs. Lounge Bar Restaurant Open; Mon-Fri; 12.00-21.00hrs.

2   The Delisle Arms

Tel: (01509) 650170

0.6 miles west along the A512, on the left.

(Inn Partnership) Open all day. Lunch; Mon-Sat; 12.00-14.30hrs, Sun (Carvery); 12.00-15.00hrs, Evening Meals; Mon-Sat; 18.00-21.00hrs.

3   Total Service Station

Tel: (01509) 650214

0.8 miles west along the A512, on the right.

Access, Visa, Overdrive, All Star, Switch, Dial Card, Mastercard, Amex, Diners Club, Delta, AA Paytrak, Total/Fina/Elf Cards. Open; 06.00-22.45hrs daily.

4   Charnwood BP Connect

Tel: (01509) 238530

0.6 miles east along the A512, on the right.

LPG. Access, Visa, Overdrive, All Star, Switch, Dial Card, Mastercard, Amex, Diners Club, Delta, Routex, AA Paytrak, Shell Agency, BP Cards. Wild Bean Café.

5   Temple Filling Station (Texaco)

Tel: (01509) 643770

0.6 miles east along the A512, on the left.

Access, Visa, Overdrive, All Star, Switch, Dial Card, Mastercard, Amex, Diners Club, Delta, BP Supercharge, Keyfuels, Texaco Cards. Open; Mon-Sat; 06.00-23.00hrs, Sun; 08.00-23.00hrs.

6   Quality Hotel

Tel: (01509) 211800

0.9 miles east along the A512, on the left.

Choices Restaurant; Breakfast; Mon-Sat; 07.00-09.30hrs, Sun; 07.30-10.00hrs, Lunch; Sun; 12.30-14.00hrs, Dinner; Mon-Sat; 19.00-21.30hrs, Sun; 19.00-21.00hrs.

7   The Harvester at Loughborough

Tel: (01509) 214165

1 mile east along the A512, on the left.

(Harvester) Open all day. Meals served; Sun-Fri; 12.00-21.00hrs, Sat; 12.00-22.00hrs.

PLACES OF INTEREST

John Taylor Bellfoundry Museum

Freehold Street, Nottingham Road, Loughborough LE11 1AR
Tel: (01509) 233414
website: www.taylorbells.co.uk

Follow the A512 east into Loughborough and continue along the A60 (3.8 Miles)

A unique museum, part of the world's largest working bellfoundry, relating to all aspects of bellfounding from early times and demonstrating the craft techniques of moulding, casting, tuning and the fitting up of bells. Museum Shop. Foundry tours. Some disabled access.

Great Central Railway

Loughborough Central Station, Great Central Road, Loughborough LE11 1RW
Tel: (01509) 230726
website: www.gcrailway.co.uk

Follow the A512 east into Loughborough and turn south along the A6 (Signposted along A6, 3.4 Miles)

The only preserved steam railway on a former main line, the Great Central Railway runs between Loughborough and Leicester North. Museum, working signal box and historic loco collection at Loughborough Station. Café. Gift Shop. Some disabled access.

Charnwood Museum

Queens Hall, Granby Street, Loughborough LE11 3DZ
Tel: (01509) 233754
website: www.charnwoodbc.gov.uk

Follow the A512 east into Loughborough (3 Miles)

The museum for the Borough of Charnwood, the displays include natural history, local history and exhibitions of industry and farming. Café. Gift Shop. Disabled access.

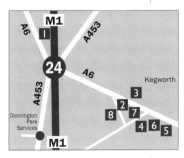

JUNCTION 23A

THIS IS A RESTRICTED ACCESS JUNCTION
- There is no exit to the A453 from the northbound carriageway
- There is no access from the A453 to the southbound carriageway

DONINGTON PARK SERVICES (MOTO)
Tel: (01509) 672220
Little Chef, Burger King, Fresh Express Self-Serve Restaurant, Harry Ramsden's, Travelodge & BP Fuel

Nearest A&E Hospital
Derbyshire Royal Infirmary
London Road, Derby DE1 2XX
Tel: (01332) 347141
Proceed to Junction 24 and take the A6 exit west to Derby. The hospital is in the city centre, on the left hand side. (Distance Approx 11.9 miles)

JUNCTION 24

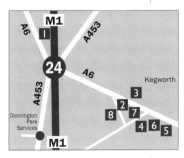

Nearest A&E Hospital
Derbyshire Royal Infirmary
London Road, Derby DE1 2XX
Tel: (01332) 347141
Take the A50 exit west to Derby. The hospital is in the city centre, on the left hand side. (Distance Approx 9.8 miles)

FACILITIES

DONINGTON PARK SERVICES (MOTO)
Tel: (01509) 672220
Little Chef, Burger King, Fresh Express Self-Serve Restaurant, Harry Ramsden's, Travelodge & BP Fuel

1   Hilton East Midlands Airport Hotel

Tel: (01509) 674000
0.1 miles west along the A6, on the right.
Restaurant Open; Breakfast; Mon-Fri; 07.00-09.30hrs, Sat & Sun; 07.30-10.00hrs, Lunch; Sun-Fri; 12.30-14.00hrs, Dinner; Mon-Sat; 19.00-22.00hrs, Sun; 19.00-21.30hrs

2   Kegworth Whitehouse Hotel

Tel: (01509) 672427
0.5 miles east along the A6, on the right.
The Garden Restaurant Open; Breakfast; Mon-Fri; 07.00-09.00hrs, Sat & Sun; 08.00-10.00hrs, Lunch; 12.00-14.00hrs daily, Dinner; 19.00-21.30hrs daily. Bar Meals served; 08.00-23.00hrs daily

3 Kegworth Service Station (Spot)

Tel: (01509) 673435
0.7 miles east along the A6, on the left.

Access, Visa, Overdrive, All Star, Switch, Dial Card, Mastercard, Amex, Delta. Open; Mon-Sat; 07.30-20.30hrs, Sun; 08.00-20.00hrs.

4   Ye Olde Flying Horse

Tel: (01509) 672253
0.9 miles east along the A6, in Kegworth, on the right. (Punch Taverns) Open all day. Meals served; Mon-Fri; 11.30-14.30hrs & 18.30-21.00hrs, Sat; 11.30-14.00hrs, Sun; 12.00-15.00hrs.

5   The Kegworth Lantern Hotel

Tel: (01509) 673989
0.9 miles east along the A6, in Kegworth, on the right. (Free House) Open all day. Meals served; Breakfast; 06.00-09.00hrs, Lunch; 12.00-14.00hrs, Evening Meals; 18.00-21.00hrs daily

6   Public Toilets

0.9 miles east along the A6, in Kegworth, on the right

7   Cottage Restaurant

Tel: (01509) 672449
1 mile along the High Street, in Kegworth, on the right. Open; Lunch; Tues-Fri; 12.00-14.00hrs, Sun; 12.00-14.30hrs, Dinner; Tues-Fri; 19.00-22.00hrs, Sat; 19.00-22.30hrs, Sun; 19.00-21.30hrs. Closed all day on Monday.

8   Yew Lodge Hotel

Tel: (01509) 672518
0.8 miles east, on Packington Hill, on the right. (Best Western) The Orchard Restaurant Open; Breakfast; Mon-Sat; 07.00-09.30hrs, Sun; 07.30-10.30hrs, Lunch; 12.00-

14.00hrs daily, Dinner; Mon-Sat; 18.30-21.30hrs, Sun; 19.00-21.00hrs

PLACES OF INTEREST

Donington Grand Prix Collection

Donington Park, Castle Donington, Derby DE74 2RP
Tel: (01332) 811027
website:
www.doningtoncollection.com

Follow the A6 west (Signposted 3.7 Miles)

The world's largest collection of Grand Prix racing cars with over 120 exhibits in 5 halls depicting the history of the sport from 1901 to the present day. Restaurant, Souvenir Shop. Disabled access

Kegworth Museum

52 High Street, Kegworth DE74 2DA Tel: (01509) 672886

Follow the A6 east into Kegworth (0.7 Miles)

The permanent displays include a Victorian parlour, saddlery, the local school, the knitting industry and British Legion memorabilia and history. Sections dealing with the Romans in Kegworth and the Victorian Garden will be opened during 2002/3. Some disabled access.

JUNCTION 24A

THIS IS A RESTRICTED ACCESS JUNCTION
- There is no access to the southbound carriageway
- There is no exit from the northbound carriageway

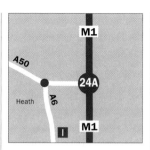

Nearest A&E Hospital
Derbyshire Royal Infirmary
London Road, Derby DE1 2XX
Tel: (01332) 347141
Take the A50 exit west to Derby. The hospital is in the city centre, on the left hand side. (Distance Approx 8.2 miles)

FACILITIES

1   Hilton East Midlands Airport Hotel

Tel: (01509) 674000
0.5 miles south along the A6, on the left.
Restaurant Open; Breakfast; Mon-Fri; 07.00-09.30hrs, Sat & Sun; 07.30-10.00hrs, Lunch; Sun-Fri; 12.30-14.00hrs, Dinner; Mon-Sat; 19.00-22.00hrs, Sun; 19.00-21.30hrs.

JUNCTION 25

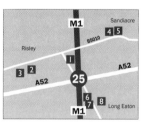

Nearest A&E Hospital
Queens Medical Centre
University Hospital, Derby Road, Nottingham NG7 2UH
Tel: (0115) 924 9924
Take the A52 east exit to Nottingham and the hospital is signposted along the route. (Distance Approx 5.6 miles)

FACILITIES

1   Holiday Inn Derby/ Nottingham

Tel: 0870 400 9062
0.4 miles north along the Risley Road, on the right.
Traders Restaurant & Bar; Open all day. Breakfast; Mon-Fri; 06.30-10.00hrs, Sat & Sun; 07.30-11.00hrs. Meals served all day; Mon-Sat; 12.00-22.30hrs, Sun; 12.00-22.00

2   Risley Hall Country House Hotel

Tel: (0115) 939 9000
0.8 miles west along the B5010, on the left.
The Garden Room Restaurant; Open; Breakfast; Mon-Fri; 07.00-09.30hrs, Sat & Sun; 08.00-09.30hrs, Lunch; Mon-Sat; 12.00-14.00hrs, Sun; 12.00-15.00hrs, Dinner; Mon-Sat; 19.30-21.30hrs, Sun; 18.30-21.30hrs.

3   The Risley Park

Tel: (0115) 939 2313
1 mile west along the B5010, on the left.
(Punch Taverns) Open all day. Meals served; Mon-Thurs; 11.30-21.30hrs, Fri & Sat; 11.30-22.00hrs, Sun; 12.00-21.00hrs

4   Sandiacre Service Station (Texaco)

Tel: (0115) 949 1398

1 mile east along the B5010, in Sandiacre, on the left.

Access, Visa, Overdrive, All Star, Switch, Dial Card, Mastercard, Amex, Diners Club, Delta, AA Paytrak, BP Supercharge, Texaco Cards. Open; Mon-Sat; 07.00-21.00hrs, Sun; 09.00-21.00hrs.

5   White Lion

Tel: (0115) 939 7123

1 mile east along the B5010, in Sandiacre, on the left.

(Enterprise Inns) Open all day. Meals served; Mon-Sat; 12.00-19.30hrs, Sun; 12.00-15.00hrs.

6   Novotel Hotel Nottingham/Derby

Tel: (0115) 946 5111

0.4 miles south along the Long Eaton Road, on the left.

The Garden Brasserie; Meals served daily throughout day from 06.00hrs to 0.00hrs.

7   Branaghans Restaurant & Bar

Tel: (0115) 946 2000

0.4 miles south along the Long Eaton Road, on the right.

Open; Mon-Thurs; 11.30-14.30hrs & 17.00-22.00hrs, Fri & Sat; 11.30-23.00hrs, Sun; 12.00-21.30hrs.

8   The Ramada Jarvis Nottingham/Derby Hotel

Tel: (0115) 946 0000

0.4 miles south along the Long Eaton Road, on the right

PLACES OF INTEREST

Derby

Derby Tourist Information, Assembly Rooms, Market Place, Derby DE1 3AH
Tel: (01332) 255802
website: www.visitderby.co.uk

Follow the A52 west (Signposted 7.2 Miles)

A Roman station named Derventio and established on the opposite bank of the River Derwent to today's town centre led to the rise of Derby. The Danes made it an important centre and it was here in 1717 that the first successful silk weaving in England was established. Amongst the many buildings that reflect the town's long history are the Bridge Chapel of 1330, the All Saints Cathedral which originated in 1509 and Derby School, founded in 1160 and re-instituted by Queen Mary in 1554.

Derby was an important railway junction as long ago as 1839 and the Midland Railway established extensive workshop premises here with the production of both locomotives and carriages undertaken on the site. Sadly, today they have all but disappeared but the city is still particularly renowned for two of its manufacturers; Rolls-Royce and Royal Crown Derby.

Within the city can be found ...

Derby Industrial Museum

Silk Mill Lane, Off Full Street, Derby DE1 3AR
Tel: (01332) 255308 website: www.derby.gov.uk/museums

Housed in a rebuilt version of Britain's first factory, the Silk Mill of 1717-1721, the museum contains galleries featuring Derbyshire industries, railway engineering, stationary power sources and the world's largest collection of Rolls Royce aero-engines. Gift Shop. Disabled access.

Royal Crown Derby Visitor Centre

194 Osmaston Road, Derby DE23 8JZ Tel: (01332) 712800 website: www.royal-crown-derby.co.uk

Follow the A52 west into Derby and take the A514 south towards Melbourne. (8 Miles)

A factory tour and demonstration area are utilized to show visitors how the world famous table and giftware is manufactured from the raw materials of bone ash, clay, stone and water. The traditional skills of hand gilding and flower making, handed down through the generations, are demonstrated by experienced craftsmen and there is a museum which traces the development of the company from 1748 to the present day. Restaurant. Factory Shop. Limited disabled access.

Nottingham

Follow the A52 east (Signposted 8.3 Miles)

For details please see Junction 26 information

Within the city can be found ...

The Caves of Nottingham

Drury Walk, Broad Marsh Shopping Centre, Nottingham NG1 7LS

For details please see Junction 26 information

Galleries of Justice

Shire Hall, High Pavement, Lace Market, Nottingham NG1 1HN

For details please see Junction 26 information

The Tales of Robin Hood

30-38 Maid Marian Way,
Nottingham NG1 6GF

For details please see Junction
26 information

M1
BETWEEN
JUNCS 25 & 26

**TROWELL SERVICES
(NORTHBOUND) (MOTO)**
Tel: (0115) 932 0291
Fresh Express Self Service
Restaurant, Little Chef,
Travelodge & Esso Fuel

**TROWELL SERVICES
(SOUTHBOUND) (MOTO)**
Tel: (0115) 932 0291
Fresh Express Self Service
Restaurant, Burger King, Harry
Ramsden's & Esso Fuel

**FOOTBRIDGE CONNECTION
BETWEEN SITES**

M1
JUNCTION 26

**Nearest Northbound A&E
Hospital**
Kings Mill Hospital
Mansfield Road, Sutton in
Ashfield NG17 4JL
Tel: (01623) 622515
Proceed north to Junction 28
and take the A38 east towards

Mansfield. At the junction with
the B6023 bear left and the
hospital is along this route.
(Distance Approx 13.5 miles)

**Nearest Southbound A&E
Hospital**
Queens Medical Centre
University Hospital, Derby
Road, Nottingham NG7 2UH
Tel: (0115) 924 9924
Take the A610 towards
Nottingham, turn right along
the A6514 (A52) and the
hospital is along this route.
(Distance Approx 4.6 miles)

FACILITIES

1   The Three Ponds

Tel: (0115) 938 3170
**1 mile north along the B600,
in Nuthall, on the left.**
(Kimberley Ales) Open all day.
Meals served; Mon-Sat; 11.00-
21.00hrs, Sun; 12.00-20.00hrs

2   Broxtowe Inn

Tel: (0115) 927 8210
**0.9 miles east along the
A610, on the right.**
(Scottish & Newcastle) Open all
day. Meals served; Mon-Sat;
12.00-21.30hrs, Sun; 12.00-
20.30hrs.

3   The Millers Barn

Tel: (0115) 951 9971
**1 mile east along the A610,
on the left.**
(Whitbread) Open all day.
Meals served; 12.00-22.30hrs
daily.

4   Travel Inn

Tel: (0115) 951 9971
**1 mile east along the A610,
on the left.**

5   St Mary's BP Connect

Tel: (0115) 927 2707
**1 mile east along the A610,
on the right.**
LPG. Access, Visa, Overdrive,
All Star, Switch, Dial Card,
Mastercard, Amex, Diners Club,
Delta, Routex, Shell Agency, BP
Cards. Wild Bean Café

6   Old Moor Lodge

Tel: (0115) 976 2200
**0.9 miles south along the
A6002, on the left.**
(Whitbread) Open all day.
Meals served; Mon-Sat; 11.30-
22.00hrs, Sun; 12.00-
22.00hrs

7   Star Woodhouse
(Texaco)

Tel: (0115) 975 8890
**1 mile south along the
A6002, on the left.**
Access, Visa, Delta,
Mastercard, Switch, Diners
Club, Amex, Electron, Solo,
Overdrive, All Star, Dial Card,
Texaco Cards

PLACES OF
INTEREST

Nottingham

Nottingham Tourist Information
Centre, 1-4 Smithy Row,
Nottingham NG1 2BY
Tel: (0115) 915 5330 website:
www.nottinghamcity.gov.uk

**Follow the A610 south
(Signposted 4.2 Miles)**
The city of Nottingham was
founded by Snot, the chief of a
6thC Anglo-Saxon tribe who
carved out dwellings in the
local sandstone and
established the settlement of
Snottingaham, "home of the
followers of Snot". A castle was

sited on top of the rock formation by the Normans and this was dismantled by Oliver Cromwell. The edifice seen today is just a 17thC mansion that was destroyed during a riot in 1831 and taken over and converted into a museum by the Corporation in 1875.

Beneath the castle is a honeycomb of caves, some utilized as dungeons, and passages the most famous of which is Mortimer's Hole used, it is said, by Edward III to enter the castle in 1330 and arrest Queen Isabella, his mother. At the base of Castle Rock, and set into the sandstone is "The Trip to Jerusalem" dating from 1189 and reputed to be the oldest pub in England. Nottingham, as it became known, is, of course, not only associated with the legend of Robin Hood but also renowned for the manufacture of lace.

Within the city can be found ...

The Caves of Nottingham

Drury Walk, Broad Marsh Shopping Centre, Nottingham NG1 7LS Tel: (0115) 924 1424 website: www.nottinghamshire tourism.co.uk

A unique audio tour through the 700 year old man made caves. On view are a mediaeval tannery, an air raid shelter, the pub cellars and the remains of Drury Hill, Nottingham's most historic street. Gift Shop. No disabled access.

Galleries of Justice

Shire Hall, High Pavement, Lace Market, Nottingham NG1 1HN Tel: (0115) 952 0555 website: www.galleriesofjustice.org.uk

A fascinating journey and interactive tour through time revealing the history of justice in England. Set in a Victorian courtroom, county gaol and early 20thC Police Station, visitors can witness how crime and punishment methods have

changed over the years, from public hangings to present day forensic science detection methods. Gift Shop. Café. Disabled Access.

The Tales of Robin Hood

30-38 Maid Marian Way, Nottingham NG1 6GF Tel: (0115) 948 3284 website: www.robinhooduk.com

An indoor family entertainment centre that relates the story of Robin Hood through an exciting 3-dimensional ride. There are exhibitions of mediaeval life and Robin Hood plus opportunities for visitors to try brass rubbings or archery. There is a children's play area, Gift Shop and Café. Full disabled access.

Midland Railway Centre

Butterley Station, Ripley, Derbyshire DE5 3QZ

Follow the A610 west (Signposted 9.8 Miles)

For details please see Junction 28 information.

DH Lawrence Birthplace Museum

8a Victoria Street, Eastwood, Nottingham NG16 3AW Tel: (01773) 717353

Follow the A510 west into Eastwood and turn right along the A608 (5 Miles)

This tiny terraced house is now a museum devoted to the writer's life and reflections on his time spent in Nottinghamshire. The countryside around Eastwood provided inspiration for novels such as "Sons & Lovers", "Women in Love" and "The Rainbow", as well as the controversial "Lady Chatterley's Lover". (NB The Durban House Heritage Centre, nearby in Mansfield Road has further information on DH Lawrence as well as exhibits on local history). Shop. No disabled access.

The American Adventure

Ilkeston, Derbyshire DE7 5SX Tel: (01773) 531521 website: www.americanadventure.co.uk

Follow the A610 west (Signposted 6.7 Miles)

Set in 390 acres of Derbyshire parkland it is the home to Europe's tallest SkyCoaster, a 200ft freefall ride. Amongst over 100 themed rides, Nightmare Niagara is the world's highest and wettest triple drop log flume. Restaurant. Gift Shop. Disabled Access.

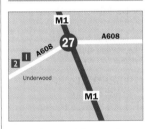

JUNCTION 27

Nearest Northbound A&E Hospital

Kings Mill Hospital

Mansfield Road, Sutton in Ashfield NG17 4JL Tel: (01623) 622515

Proceed north to Junction 28 and take the A38 east towards Mansfield. At the junction with the B6023 bear left and the hospital is along this route. (Distance Approx 8 miles)

Nearest Southbound A&E Hospital

Queens Medical Centre

University Hospital, Derby Road, Nottingham NG7 2UH Tel: (0115) 924 9924

Proceed to Junction 26, take the A610 towards Nottingham and turn right along the A6514

(A52). The hospital is along this route. (Distance Approx 10.1 miles)

FACILITIES

1   Sand Hills Tavern

Tel: (01773) 780330
0.9 miles west along the A608, on the right.
(Scottish Courage) Open all day. Bar Snacks available daily. Sunday Carvery; 12.00-14.30hrs.

2   Underwood Garage

Tel: (01773) 712554
1 mile west along the A608, on the right.
Access, Visa, Overdrive, All Star, Switch, Dial Card, Mastercard, Amex, Diners Club, Delta. Open; Mon-Sat; 08.00-18.30hrs, Sun; Closed.

PLACES OF INTEREST

Newstead Abbey & Park

Ravenshead, Nottinghamshire NG15 8GE Tel: (01623) 455900 website: www.newsteadabbey .org.uk

Follow the A608 east, signposted "Sherwood Forest" and then signposted to "Newstead Abbey" (6.6 Miles) The original priory was founded in c1170 and converted into a house, known as Newstead Abbey, by Sir John Byron in the 1540's. It was sold by Lord Byron in 1816 when he moved abroad and the building was refurbished in Gothic style to designs by John Shaw. The building contains many Byron relics and there are 30 beautifully preserved period

rooms. It is surrounded by superb grounds including the Japanese Gardens and two lakes. Gift Shop. Café. Limited disabled access.

JUNCTION 28

Nearest Northbound A&E Hospital
King's Mill Hospital
Mansfield Road, Sutton in Ashfield NG17 4JL
Tel: (01623) 622515
Take the A38 east towards Mansfield and at the junction with the B6023 bear left. The hospital is along this route. (Distance Approx 4.5 miles)

Nearest Southbound A&E Hospital
Queens Medical Centre
University Hospital, Derby Road, Nottingham NG7 2UH
Tel: (0115) 924 9924
Proceed to Junction 26, take the A610 towards Nottingham and turn right along the A6514 (A52). The hospital is along this route. (Distance Approx 13.5 miles)

FACILITIES

1   Meteor Service Station (BP)

Tel: (01773) 811268
0.8 miles west along the B6019, in South Normanton, on the right.

Access, Visa, Overdrive, All Star, Switch, Dial Card, Mastercard, Amex, Diners Club, Delta, Routex, AA Paytrak, Shell Agency, BP Cards. Open; Mon-Sat; 06.00-22.00hrs, Sun; 08.00-22.00hrs.

2   The Hawthorns

Tel: (01773) 811328
0.9 miles west along the B6019, in South Normanton, on the right.
(Free House) Open all day. Meals served; Mon & Tues; 12.00-14.30hrs & 17.30-21.00hrs, Wed-Sat; 12.00-21.00hrs, Sun; 12.00-15.00hrs.

3   Carnfield Service Station (BP)

Tel: (01773) 811251
1 mile west along the B6019, in South Normanton, on the left.
Access, Visa, Overdrive, All Star, Switch, Dial Card, Mastercard, Amex, Diners Club, Delta, Routex, AA Paytrak, Shell Agency, BP Cards

4   Renaissance Derby/ Nottingham Hotel

Tel: (01773) 812000
0.1 miles east along the A38, on the left.
Chatterley's; Open; Breakfast; 07.00-10.00hrs, Lunch; 12.30-14.00hrs, Dinner; 19.00-22.00hrs daily

5   The Castlewood

Tel: (01773) 862899
0.2 miles east along the A38, on the left.
(Brewsters) Open all day. Meals served all day Mon-Sat; 11.30-22.00hrs, Sun; 12.00-22.00hrs.

6   Travel Inn

Tel: (01773) 862899
0.2 miles east along the A38, on the left.

7   McArthur Glen Designer Outlet Mansfield

Tel: (01773) 545000
0.7 miles east along the A38, on the right.

There are numerous cafés and restaurants, including Madisons, Bitz N'Pizza, Burger King, Arkwright's Fish & Chips, Bradwell's Kiosk and Spud-U-Like within the Food Court. Open; Mon-Wed & Fri; 10.00-18.00hrs, Thurs; 10.00-20.00hrs, Sat; 09.00-18.00hrs, Sun; 11.00-17.00hrs.

PLACES OF INTEREST

Midland Railway Centre

Butterley Station, Ripley, Derbyshire DE5 3QZ
Tel: (01773) 747674 website: www.heritagerailways.co.uk

Follow the A38 west and turn south along the B6179 (Signposted 5.2 Miles)
More than 50 steam, diesel and electric locomotives, and more than 100 items of historic rolling stock are on display. There is a steam hauled passenger service and other attractions include narrow gauge, miniature and model railways, museum, country park and farm park and a demonstration signal box. Gift Shop. Some disabled access.

Crich Tramway Village

Crich, Matlock, Derbyshire DE4 5DP Tel: (01773) 852565 website: www.tramway.co.uk

Follow the A38 west (Signposted 7.7 Miles)
A collection of more than 70 restored horse, steam and electric trams from all over the world. Working trams take visitors along a mile of scenic track and exhibits include depots, power stations, workshops and a period street. Gift Shop. Café. Playgrounds. Picnic Areas. Disabled access.

M1 BETWEEN JUNCS 28 & 29

TIBSHELF SERVICES (NORTHBOUND) (ROADCHEF)
Tel: (01773) 876600
Food Fayre Self-Service Restaurant, Costa Coffee, Wimpy Bar, Dr Beaks Chicken, Travel Inn & Texaco Fuel

TIBSHELF SERVICES (SOUTHBOUND) (ROADCHEF)
Tel: (01773) 876600
Food Fayre Self-Service Restaurant, Costa Coffee, Wimpy Bar, Dr Beaks Chicken & Texaco Fuel.

FOOTBRIDGE CONNECTION BETWEEN SITES.

M1 JUNCTION 29

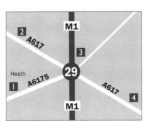

Nearest Northbound A&E Hospital

Chesterfield & North Derbyshire Royal
Calow, Chesterfield S44 5BL
Tel: (01246) 277271
Take the A617 west to Chesterfield and after 4.8 miles bear right at the roundabout along the A61(T). At the junction with the A619 and A632 turn right along the A632 and the hospital is along this road on the left hand side. (Distance Approx 6.1 miles)

Nearest Southbound A&E Hospital

Kings Mill Hospital
Mansfield Road, Sutton in Ashfield NG17 4JL
Tel: (01623) 622515
Take the A617 towards Mansfield and after 5.7 miles turn right along the A6075. The hospital is on the left hand side of this road. (Distance Approx 8.2 miles)

FACILITIES

1   Red House Service Station (Shell)

Tel: (01246) 850329
0.9 miles south along the A6010, on the right.
Access, Visa, Overdrive, All Star, Switch, Dial Card, Mastercard, Amex, Diners Club, Delta, AA Paytrak, Shell Cards, BP Agency, Smartcard. Open; Mon-Fri; 07.00-21.30hrs, Sat & Sun; 08.00-20.00hrs.

2   Heath Service Station (Esso)

Tel: (01246) 850525
0.6 miles west along the A617, on the right (Actual distance 2.2 miles).
Access, Visa, Overdrive, All Star, Switch, Dial Card,

Mastercard, Amex, Diners Club, Delta, AA Paytrak, Shell Gold, Shell Europe, Shell Agency, BP Supercharge, Esso Cards. Esso Bakery Shop Open; 06.00-18.00hrs daily.

3 Twin Oaks Motel

Tel: (01246) 855455
0.2 miles north along the Palterton Road, on the left.
Restaurant Open; Mon-Sat; 12.00-14.00hrs & 19.00-21.00hrs, Sun; 12.00-14.00. Bar Snacks available on Sun;18.00-21.00hrs

4 Ma Hubbard's

Tel: (01246) 857236
1 mile east along the A617, in Glapwell, on the left.
(Tetley's) Meals served; 12.00-15.00hrs & 17.00-21.00hrs daily.

PLACES OF INTEREST

St Mary and All Saints Church

Church Way, Chesterfield S40 1SF Tel: (01246) 206506

Follow the A617 west (Signposted 5.3 Miles)
The symbol of Chesterfield, the famous crooked spire, sits on top of the tower of this church, the largest in Derbyshire. There is much folklore devoted to how this curious shape came about but the answer would appear to be closely connected to the year when it was being constructed - 1349.

Precisely at this time, the Black Death was raging through the country and it is not inconceivable that many of the skilled craftsmen engaged in the construction work may have died, leaving less knowledgeable

workers to carry on. Certainly no cross braces, utterly essential for the 32 tons of tiles that it was to carry, were installed and green timber could easily have been utilized. These two elements, allied to the decaying of the timbers at the base of the 228ft spire would easily account for the deformation that is visible today. The church is open throughout the year and guided trips up the tower are available from time to time. Coffee Shop. Gift Shop. Disabled access to church.

Hardwick Hall (NT)

Doe Lane, Chesterfield, Derbyshire S44 5QJ
Tel: (01246) 850430 website: www.nationaltrust.org.uk

Signposted from Motorway (2.7 Miles)
A fine Elizabethan house designed for Bess of Hardwick, the Countess of Shrewsbury. Contains outstanding 16thC furniture, tapestries and needlework, many items known to have been in the house prior to 1601. Walled courtyards enclose superb gardens, orchards and a herb garden and a 300 acre country park contains many rare breeds of sheep and cattle. Some disabled access.

Bolsover Castle

Castle Street, Bolsover S44 6PR
Tel: (01246) 823349 and Tel: (01246) 822844 website: www.english-heritage.org.uk

Take the unclassified road east to Palterton and turn left to Bolsover. (3.7 Miles)
A castle has stood on this site since Norman times but nothing of the original edifice remains. The building on view today, more of a mansion than a castle, was constructed by Sir Charles Cavendish, during the reign of James I, and added to by his son the 1st Duke of Newcastle in c1660. It contains

elaborate fireplaces, panelling, wall paintings and an early indoor riding school. There is an audio tour and a Visitor Centre. Refreshments. Gift Shop. Limited disabled access.

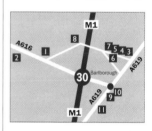

Nearest Northbound A&E Hospital

Rotherham District General Hospital
Moorgate Road, Rotherham S60 2UD
Tel: (01709) 820000
Proceed north to Junction 33, follow the A630 north, turn right along the A631, left along the A618 (Moorgate Road) and the hospital is on the left. (Distance Approx 12.1 miles)

Nearest Southbound A&E Hospital

Chesterfield & North Derbyshire Royal
Calow, Chesterfield S44 5BL
Tel: (01246) 277271
Take the A6135 east and at the first roundabout turn right along the A619 to Chesterfield. After about 6.5 miles turn left at the roundabout along the A61(T) and, at the junction with the A619 and A632, turn left along the A632. The hospital is along this road on the left hand side. (Distance Approx 9 miles)

FACILITIES

1   Bridgehouse Service Station (Total)

Tel: (01246) 810600
0.6 miles west along the A616, on the right.
Access, Visa, Delta, Mastercard, Switch, Diners Club, Amex, Overdrive, All Star, Dial Card, Total/Fina/Elf Cards.
Open; Mon-Fri; 07.00-21.00hrs, Sat & Sun; 07.30-20.00hrs

2   The Prince of Wales

Tel: (01246) 432108
1 mile west along the A616, on the left.
(Free House) Meals served; Lunch; 12.00-14.30hrs daily, Evening Meals; Mon-Sat; 18.00-20.30hrs.

3   De Rodes Arms

Tel: (01246) 810345
0.6 miles east along the A619, on the left.
(Whitbread) Open all day. Meals served; Mon-Sat; 11.30-22.00hrs, Sun; 12.00-22.00hrs.

4   Stonecroft

Tel: (01246) 810974
0.7 miles west off the A619, in Barlborough, on the right

5   The Rose & Crown

Tel: (01246) 810364
0.8 miles west off the A619, in Barlborough, on the right.
(Kimberley Ales) Meals served; Tues; 12.00-14.00hrs, Wed-Sat; 12.00-14.00hrs & 18.30-21.00hrs, Sun; 12.00-14.30hrs

6   The Apollo

Tel: (01246) 810346

0.9 miles west off the A619, in Barlborough, on the left.
(Pubmaster) Open all day. Meals served; Mon-Sat; 12.00-14.30hrs & 17.00-20.00hrs, Sun; 12.00-14.30hrs.

7   The Royal Oak

Tel: (01246) 573020
0.9 miles west off the A619, in Barlborough, on the right.
(Voyager) Open all day Sat & Sun. Meals served; Wed-Fri; 12.00-14.30hrs & 18.00-21.00hrs, Sat; 12.00-14.00hrs & 18.30-21.30hrs, Sun; 12.00-17.00hrs

8   Dusty Miller

Tel: (01246) 810507
1 mile west off the A619, in Barlborough, on the right.
(Freehouse) Open all day Sat. Meals served; Tues-Sat; 12.00-14.00hrs & 17.30-20.00hrs, Sun; 12.00-14.30hrs

9   Treble Bob

Tel: (01246) 813005
0.4 miles south along the A619, on the left.
(Tom Cobleigh) Open all day. Meals served; Mon-Sat; 12.00-22.00hrs, Sun; 12.00-21.30hrs.

10   Ibis Hotel, Barlborough

Tel: (01246) 813222
0.4 miles south along the A619, on the left

11   McDonald's

Tel: (01246) 819520
0.5 miles south along the A619, on the left.
Open; 07.30-23.00hrs daily

PLACES OF INTEREST

Mr Straw's House (NT)

7 Blyth Grove, Worksop S81 0JG
Tel: (01909) 482380 website: www.nationaltrust.org.uk

(NB. No access without pre-booked timed admission ticket)

Follow the A619 east into Worksop and northeast along the B6045 (8.9 Miles)

A semi-detached house built in c1901 which belonged to William Straw and his brother, Walter, has been internally preserved since the death of their mother in the 1930's. Contains 1920's wallpaper, furnishings and locally made furniture. There are also museum rooms and a period suburban garden.

Renishaw Hall, Gardens and Museum

Renishaw, Derbyshire S21 3WB
Tel: (01246) 432310
website: www.sitwell.co.uk

Follow the A616 west (2.9 Miles)

The beautiful formal Italian gardens and wooded park of Renishaw Hall are open to visitors, along with a nature trail, a Sitwell family museum, and art gallery and a display of Fiori De Henriques sculptures located in the Georgian stables. Café. Disabled Access.

Barrow Hill Roundhouse Railway Centre

Campbell Drive, Barrow Hill, Staveley, Chesterfield S43 2PN
Tel: (01246) 472450
website: www.barrowhill.org.uk

Take the A619 west, continue through Staveley and at Hollingwood turn right and follow the signposts to Barrow Hill. (5 miles)

A unique building housing steam, diesel and electric locomotives, and demonstrating the operations of an engine shed. Casual visitors are welcome to this industrial museum, with the regular special open weekends, featuring a large range of visiting locomotives and train rides well worthy of a visit. The site is generally flat and disabled visitors can be accommodated.

M1 BETWEEN JUNCS 30 & 31

WOODALL SERVICES (NORTHBOUND) (WELCOME BREAK)

Tel: (01142) 486434
The Granary Restaurant, KFC, McDonald's, & Shell Fuel

WOODALL SERVICES (SOUTHBOUND) (WELCOME BREAK)

Tel: (01142) 486434
Red Hen, The Granary Restaurant, KFC, Burger King, La Brioche Doree, Days Inn & Shell Fuel

FOOTBRIDGE CONNECTION BETWEEN SITES

M1 JUNCTION 31

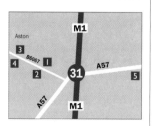

Nearest Northbound A&E Hospital

Rotherham District General Hospital
Moorgate Road, Rotherham S60 2UD
Tel: (01709) 820000
Proceed north to Junction 33, follow the A630 north, turn right along the A631, left along the A618 (Moorgate Road) and the hospital is on the left. (Distance Approx 6.7 miles)

Nearest Southbound A&E Hospital

Chesterfield & North Derbyshire Royal
Calow, Chesterfield S44 5BL
Tel: (01246) 277271
Proceed south to Junction 30 and take the A6135 east. At the first roundabout turn right along the A619 to Chesterfield. After about 6.5 miles turn left at the roundabout along the A61(T) and at the junction with the A619 and A632 turn left along the A632. The hospital is along this road on the left hand side. (Distance Approx 14.4 miles)

FACILITIES

1   Yellow Lion

Tel: (0114) 287 2283
0.4 miles west along the B6067, on the right.
(Enterprise Inns) Open all day. Meals served; Mon-Fri; 12.00-15.00hrs & 17.30-21.00hrs, Sat; 12.00-20.30hrs, Sun; 12.00-17.30hrs

2   Aston Hall Hotel

Tel: (0114) 287 2309
0.5 miles west along the B6067, on the left.
Restaurant Open; Mon-Sat; Breakfast; 07.00-09.45hrs, Lunch; 12.00-14.15hrs, Dinner;

19.00-21.30hrs, Sun; Breakfast; 07.00-09.45hrs, Lunch; 12.00-14.15hrs, Dinner; 19.00-21.15hrs

3   The Blue Bell

Tel: (0114) 287 1031
0.7 miles west along the B6067, on the right.
(Free House) Open all day. Meals served; Mon-Fri; 12.00-14.00hrs & 18.00-20.00hrs, Sat & Sun; 12.00-14.00hrs.

4   Aston Service Station (Jet)

Tel: (0114) 287 4167
0.9 miles west along the B6067, on the left.
Access, Visa, Overdrive, All Star, Switch, Dial Card, Mastercard, Amex, Diners Club, Delta, AA Paytrak, Jet Cards

5   The Red Lion Hotel

Tel: (01909) 771654
1 mile east along the A57, on the right.
(Laurel Pub Company) Open all day. Meals served; Mon-Sat; 12.00-22.00hrs, Sun; 12.00-21.30hrs.

PLACES OF INTEREST

Tropical Butterfly House, Falconry & Wildlife Centre

Woodsetts Road, North Anston S25 4EQ
Tel: (01909) 569416 website: www.butterflyhouse.co.uk

Follow the A57 east (Signposted along A57, 3.6 Miles)

A Wildlife Centre consisting of a butterfly house containing thousands of free flying butterflies, an Animal Nursery,

Bird of Prey Centre, Farm Corner and Nature Trail. Plenty of "hands-on" opportunities. Gift Shop. Café. Picnic Area. Disabled access.

Rother Valley Country Park

Mansfield Road, Wales Bar S26 5PQ Tel: (0114) 247 1452 (General Enquiries) website: www.bigwig.net/rothervalley

Follow the A57 west and turn left along the A618 (Signposted 3 Miles)

A landscaped leisure park with excellent facilities for water sports including sailing, windsurfing and canoeing and a 6,600 yards golf course with a driving range. There is a Visitor Centre, Craft Centre and Ranger Service. Equipment and cycles may be hired. Gift Shop. Café.

JUNCTION 32

JUNCTION 32 IS A MOTORWAY INTERCHANGE WITH THE M18 ONLY AND THERE IS NO ACCESS TO ANY FACILITIES

JUNCTION 33

Nearest A&E Hospital

Rotherham District General Hospital

Moorgate Road, Rotherham S60 2UD Tel: (01709) 820000 Follow the A630 north, turn right along the A631, left along the A618 (Moorgate Road) and the hospital is on the left. (Distance Approx 1.7 miles)

FACILITIES

1   Courtyard by Marriott Hotel

Tel: (01709) 830630 **0.7 miles west along the A631, on the right.** Restaurant Open; Breakfast; Mon-Fri; 07.00-09.30hrs, Sat & Sun; 07.30-10.00hrs, Lunch; Sun-Fri; 12.00-14.00hrs, Dinner; 18.30-21.30hrs daily.

2   Canklow Bridge (Total)

Tel: (01709) 726900 **1 mile west along the A631, on the left.** LPG. Access, Visa, Overdrive, All Star, Switch, Dial Card, Mastercard, Amex, Diners Club, Delta, UK Fuelcard, BP Supercharge, Total/Fina/Elf Cards.

3   Canklow Service Station

Tel: (01709) 382875 **1 mile west along the A631, on the right.** Access, Visa, Overdrive, All Star, Switch, Dial Card, Mastercard, Delta. Open; Mon-Fri; 07.00-20.00hrs, Sat; 08.00-17.00hrs.

PLACES OF INTEREST

Sheffield

Sheffield Visitor Information Centre, 1 Tudor Square, Sheffield S1 2LA. Tel: (0114) 201 1101 website: www.sheffieldcity.co.uk

Follow the A630 southwest (Signposted 6 Miles)

From Saxon times, Sheffield was the capital of Hallamshire and by the days of Henry II a castle had been constructed. It was within this fortress, demolished during the Civil War, that Mary, Queen of Scots was imprisoned for fourteen years from 1570. Standing on the River Don with its confluence with the River Sheaf, from which it gained its name, the city found world wide fame from its expertise in the manufacture of steel. Cutlery was made as early as the 14thC and the Company of Cutlers gained their charter in 1624. The present Cutlers Hall (Tel: 0114-272 8456) in Church Street, is in Grecian style and dates from 1832, the third such building to be erected on the site.

The Cathedral Church of St Peter and St Paul (Tel: 0114-275 3434), also in Church Street, was built in c1430 with parts added or altered until 1805. There are many fine Victorian structures including the Town Hall in Pinstone Street. Following the contraction of the steel industry in the 1970's some of the steel works sites have been revitalized with new projects including the Don Valley Stadium and the Meadowhall Shopping Centre.

Within the city can be found ...

Kelham Island Museum

Alma Street (Off Corporation Street), Sheffield S3 8RY

Tel: (0114) 272 2106
website: www.simt.co.uk

This living museum tells the story of Sheffield, its industry and life. The exhibits include the River Don Engine, the most powerful working steam engine in Europe, the Melting Shop, an interactive steelmaking display (only open on Sundays and School holidays) and workshops demonstrating cutlery manufacture.

Graves Art Gallery

Surrey Street, Sheffield S1 1XZ.
Tel: (0114) 278 2600 website:
www.sheffieldgalleries.org.uk

A wide-ranging collection of British art from the 16thC to the present, European paintings, a fine collection of watercolours, drawings and prints and the Grice Collection of Chinese Ivories forms the centrepiece to the collection of non-European artefacts.

Magna Science Adventure Centre

Sheffield Road, Templeborough, Rotherham S60 1DX
Tel: (01709) 720002 website:
www.magnatrust.org.uk

Follow the A630 North (Signposted 2.25 Miles)
The UK's first Science Adventure Centre and the biggest multi-storey, multi-media exhibition, Magna is an exciting high-tech hands-on experience demonstrating the power of earth, air, fire and water. O_2 Restaurant, Gift Shop. Full Disabled Access.

Rotherham

Rotherham Tourist Information Centre, Central Library, Walker Place, Rotherham S65 1JH
Tel: (01709) 835904
website: www.rotherham.gov.uk

Follow the A630 North (Signposted 3.2 Miles)
Where the rivers Rother and Don meet, the Romans worked iron here and built a fort on the south bank of the River Don at Templeborough and finds from excavations of the area can be seen at Clifton Park Museum.

In 1161 the monks of Rufford Abbey were given the right to prospect for, and to smelt, iron and plant an orchard, leading to the tradition in Rotherham of industry and agriculture existing side by side. Heavy industry put the town on the map when, in the early days of the Industrial Revolution, the Walker family established themselves here in 1746. The Walker Company manufactured cannons, some of which featured in such famous conflicts as the American War of Independence and the Battle of Trafalgar, and bridges, with those at Southwark and Sunderland being better known examples. The town's connection with bridges does not end there either, as Sir Donald Coleman Bailey, designer and inventor of the Bailey Bridge was born here in 1901. In total contrast to heavy engineering, Rockingham Pottery was produced here in the late 18thC and early 19thC.

Within the town can be found …

The Chapel of our Lady

Rotherham Bridge, Rotherham S60 1QJ Tel: (01709) 364737

One of only a few surviving complete bridge chapels, construction commenced in 1483 following a legacy of 3/4d (17p) from John Bokyng, master of the grammar school, and was probably completed, and paid for, by Thomas Rotherham. It was sumptuously furnished but only lasted until the reign of King Edward VI (1547-1553) when it closed and then saw a variety of commercial uses until reconsecrated in 1924 by the Bishop of Sheffield.

Clifton Park Museum

Clifton Lane, Rotherham S60 2AA
Tel: (01709) 382121
website: www.rotherham.gov.uk

Built in 1783 for the Rotherham ironmaster, Joshua Walker, the interior has little changed and now houses a fine collection of Rockingham Pottery including the Rhinoceros Vase which stands almost 4ft high. In addition there is also a collection of Yorkshire pottery, English glass, silver and British oil paintings and water colours. Café. Gift Shop. Limited disabled access.

JUNCTION 34

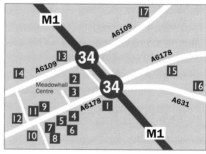

Nearest Northbound A&E Hospital

Northern General Hospital
Herries Road Sheffield
S5 7AU
Tel: (0114) 243 4343
Take the A6178 south and at the junction with the A6102 turn right. The hospital is on the right along this road.
(Distance Approx 2.6 miles)

Nearest Southbound A&E Hospital

Northern General Hospital

Herries Road Sheffield
S5 7AU
Tel: (0114) 243 4343
Take the A6109 south and at the junction with the A6102 turn right. The hospital is on the right along this road.
(Distance Approx 2.7 miles)

FACILITIES

1   Tinsley Transport Café

Tel: (0114) 244 2046
Adjacent to the south side of the roundabout.
Open; Mon-Fri; 06.00-14.30hrs, Sat & Sun; 06.00-09.30hrs

2   Meadowhall Shopping Centre

Tel: 08457 573 618
Adjacent to the west side of the junction.
There are numerous cafés and restaurants within the shopping centre. Open; Mon-Fri; 10.00-21.00hrs, Sat; 09.00 -19.00hrs, Sun; 11.00-17.00hrs

3   Sainsbury's Filling Station South

Tel: (0114) 235 4200
0.2 miles west along the A6178, on the right.
Access, Visa, Overdrive, All Star, Switch, Dial Card, Mastercard, Amex, Delta, AA Paytrak, UK Fuelcard, Sainsbury's Fuelcard. Open; Mon-Fri; 07.00-22.30hrs, Sat; 07.00-21.00hrs, Sun; 10.00-18.00hrs. Disabled Toilets and Cash Machines available in adjacent store.

4   Tinsley Filling Station (Jet)

Tel: (0114) 256 2343
0.3 miles west along the A6178, on the left.
LPG. Visa, Jet Card, Diners Club, Overdrive, All Star, Mastercard, Amex, Switch, Dial Card.

5   Pizza Hut

Tel: (0114) 256 2211
0.6 miles west along the A6178, on the left.
Open; Sun; 12.00-22.00hrs, Mon-Thurs; 11.30-22.00hrs, Fri & Sat; 11.30-23.00hrs.

6   McDonald's

Tel: (0114) 261 9269
0.6 miles west along the A6178, on the left.
'Drive-Thru' & Restaurant. Open; 07.00-0.00hrs daily.

7   KFC

Tel: (0114) 249 5210
0.8 miles west along the A6178, on the left in Broughton Lane.
Open; Sun & Mon; 11.00-23.30hrs, Tues-Thurs; 11.00-0.00hrs, Fri/Sat & Sat/Sun; 11.00-02.00hrs

8   Burger King

Tel: (0114) 242 6197
0.8 miles west along the A6178, on the left in Broughton Lane.
Open; Sun-Thurs; 10.00-0.00hrs, Fri/Sat & Sat/Sun; 10.00-03.30hrs

9   Carbrook Hall

Tel: (0114) 244 0117
0.8 miles west along the A6178, on the right.
(Punch Taverns) Open all day Mon-Fri. Meals served; 12.00-14.00hrs & 17.00-19.00hrs daily

10 The Stumble Inn

Tel: (0114) 244 1530
0.9 miles west along the A6178, on the left.
(Pubmaster) Open all day on Friday. Lunch; Mon-Fri; 12.00-14.00hrs; Sun; 12.00-15.00hrs

11 Arena Square

Tel: (0114) 243 2320
1 mile west along the A6178, on the right.
(Brewsters) Open all day. Meals served; Mon-Sat; 11.30-22.00hrs, Sun; 12.00-22.00hrs

12 Sheffield Travel Inn

Tel: (0114) 242 2802
1 mile west along the A6178, on the right.
The Potter's Bar & Restaurant; Breakfast; Mon-Fri; 07.00-09.00hrs, Sat & Sun; 08.00-10.00hrs, Dinner; 17.30-22.30hrs daily

13 Sainsbury's Filling Station North

Tel: (0114) 235 4200
0.2 miles west along the A6178, on the right.
Access, Visa, Overdrive, All Star, Switch, Dial Card, Mastercard, Amex, Delta, AA Paytrak, UK Fuelcard, Sainsbury's Fuelcard. Open; Mon-Fri; 07.00-22.30hrs, Sat; 07.00-21.00hrs, Sun; 10.00-18.00hrs. Disabled Toilets and Cash Machines available in adjacent store.

14 The Crown Pub and B&B

Tel: (0114) 243 1319
0.9 miles west along the A6109, on the right.
(Free House)

15 The Fox & Duck

Tel: (0114) 244 1938
0.4 miles east along the A6178, on the right.
(Avebury Taverns Ltd)

16 The Fairways

Tel: (01709) 838111
1 mile south along the A631, on the left.
(Millhouse Inns) Open all day
Mon-Sat. Meals served; Mon-Sat; 12.00-14.00hrs & 17.30-20.00hrs, Sun; 12.00-15.00hrs (Bookings only on Sundays)

17 Meadowbank Filling Station (Jet)

Tel: (01709) 740440
1 mile east along the A6109, on the left.
Access, Visa, Overdrive, All Star, Switch, Dial Card, Mastercard, Amex, Diners Club, Delta, BP Supercharge, Jet Card.

PLACES OF INTEREST

Sheffield

Follow the A631 west. (Signposted 4.2 Miles)
For details please see Junction 33 information

Within the city can be found ...

Kelham Island Museum

Alma Street (Off Corporation Street), Sheffield S3 8RY

For details please see Junction 33 information

Graves Art Gallery

Surrey Street, Sheffield S1 1XZ.

For details please see Junction 33 information

Meadowhall

Adjacent to the west side of Junction 34

Tel: 08457 573 618
website: www.meadowhall.co.uk

A large shopping centre with more than 270 shops and an 11 screen Warner Village cinema. Other features include the Oasis, a Mediterranean-style food court with a giant video wall, and The Lanes, an avenue of specialist and craft shops. Disabled Access

Magna Science Adventure Centre

Sheffield Road, Templeborough, Rotherham S60 1DX

Follow the A6178 east (Signposted 1 Mile)
For details please see Junction 33 information.

Rotherham

Follow the A6178 east (Signposted 2.9 Miles)
For details please see Junction 33 information.

Within the town can be found ...

The Chapel of our Lady

Rotherham Bridge, Rotherham S60 1QJ

For details please see Junction 33 information.

Clifton Park Museum

Clifton Lane, Rotherham S60 2AA

For details please see Junction 33 information.

Blackburn Meadows

Steel Street, Holmes, Rotherham S61 1DF

Tel: 07899 832660

Follow the A6109 east and turn right down Psalters Lane. (1.4 Miles)

An unusual haven for wildlife within an urban area, this conservation site has an extraordinary history. Part of the floodplain of the River Don, Holmes Farm was established here and then the land was taken over by the Tinsley Sewage Farm. Surprisingly, wildlife and especially migrating birds were attracted to the huge, liquid sewage lagoons but modern changes in waste management led them to start drying up and the local birdwatchers, aided by the local councils and Yorkshire Water, stepped in to save the site. The green heart of a projected large scale development of the Lower Don Valley it is planned to improve the facilities and build a Visitor Centre.

JUNCTION 35

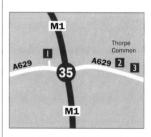

Nearest Northbound A&E Hospital

Barnsley & District General Hospital

Gawber Road, Barnsley S75 2PW
Tel: (01226) 730000
Proceed north to Junction 37, take the A628 east towards Barnsley, and after about 0.5 miles turn left at the traffic lights along Pogmoor Road. Turn left at the end of this road into Gawber Road and the hospital is immediately on the left. (Distance Approx 8.4 miles)

Nearest Southbound A&E Hospital

Northern General Hospital

Herries Road Sheffield
S5 7AU
Tel: (0114) 243 4343

Take the A629 west and after about 0.5 miles turn left along Nether Lane. At the end of this lane turn left along the A6135 and the hospital is on the right hand side of this road.
(Distance Approx 4 miles)

FACILITIES

1   The Travellers

Tel: (0114) 246 7870
0.2 miles west along the A629, on the right in Smithy Wood Road.

(Free House) Meals served; Mon-Sat; 12.00-14.30hrs & 18.00-20.30hrs, Sun; 12.00-15.00 & 18.00-20.30hrs.

2   Star Scholes (Texaco)

Tel: (0114) 257 4400
0.8 miles east along the A629, on the left.

Access, Visa, Delta, Mastercard, Switch, Diners Club, Amex, Electron, Solo, Overdrive, All Star, Dial Card, Texaco Cards.

3   The Sportsman's

Tel: (0114) 240 1824
1 mile east along the A629, on the left.

(Unique Pub Company) Open all day. Meals served; Mon-Sat; 12.00-21.30hrs, Sun 12.00-20.00hrs

---

THIS IS A RESTRICTED ACCESS JUNCTION
- Vehicles can only exit from the northbound lanes
- Vehicles can only enter the motorway along the southbound lanes

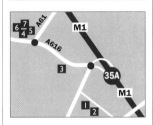

Nearest Northbound A&E Hospital

Barnsley & District General Hospital

Gawber Road, Barnsley
S75 2PW
Tel: (01226) 730000

Proceed north to Junction 37, take the A628 east towards Barnsley, and after about 0.5 miles turn left at the traffic lights along Pogmoor Road. Turn left at the end of this road into Gawber Road and the hospital is immediately on the left. (Distance Approx 6.9 miles)

Nearest Southbound A&E Hospital

Northern General Hospital

Herries Road Sheffield
S5 7AU
Tel: (0114) 243 4343

Proceed south to Junction 35 and take the A629 west. After about 0.5 miles turn left along Nether Lane and at the end of this lane turn left along the A6135. The hospital is on the right hand side of this road.
(Distance Approx 5.5 miles)

FACILITIES

1   Thorncliffe Arms

Tel: (0114) 245 8942
0.3 miles south along Warren Lane, on the right.

(Enterprise Inns) Open all day Fri & Sat, Lunch; Mon-Sat; 12.00-14.00hrs, Sun; 12.00-15.00hrs, Evening Meals; Mon-Fri; 18.00-21.00hrs, Sat; 18.00-21.30hrs, Sun; Closed.

2   The Miners Arms

Tel: (0114) 257 0092
0.3 miles south along Warren Lane, on the right.

(The Nice Pub Co.) Open all day. Meals served; Mon-Sat; 12.00-14.30hrs & 17.00-20.30hrs. Sun; 12.00-20.30hrs.

3   Truckers Café. (Transport)

0.4 miles north along the A616, on the left

4   McDonald's

Tel: (01226) 740025
1 mile north along the A616, on the right.
Open; 07.00-0.00hrs daily.

5   Wentworth Park Service Station (Save)

Tel: (01226) 350479
1 mile north along the A616, on the right.

Access, Visa, Overdrive, All Star, Switch, Dial Card, Mastercard, Delta, Routex, Keyfuels, AA Paytrak, UK Fuelcard.

6   Travel Inn

Tel: (01226) 350035

1 mile north along the A616, on the right

7   The Wentworth

Tel: (01226) 350035

1 mile north along the A616, on the right.

(Brewsters) Open all day. Meals served; Mon-Sat; 11.30-22.00hrs, Sun; 12.00-22.00hrs.

M1
JUNCTION 36

Nearest Northbound A&E Hospital

Barnsley & District General Hospital

Gawber Road, Barnsley
S75 2PW
Tel: (01226) 730000
Proceed north to Junction 37, take the A628 east towards Barnsley, and after about 0.5 miles turn left at the traffic lights along Pogmoor Road. Turn left at the end of this road into Gawber Road and the hospital is immediately on the left. (Distance Approx 5.3 miles)

Nearest Southbound A&E Hospital

Northern General Hospital

Herries Road Sheffield
S5 7AU
Tel: (0114) 243 4343
Proceed south to Junction 35 and take the A629 west. After about 0.5 miles turn left along Nether Lane and at the end of

this lane turn left along the A6135. The hospital is on the right hand side of this road. (Distance Approx 7.1 miles)

FACILITIES

1   Marston Hotel, Tankersley Manor

Tel: (01226) 744700

0.7 miles west along the A61, on the left.

Bar open all day. Meals served; 12.00-21.30hrs daily. Restaurant Open; Breakfast; Mon-Fri; 07.00-09.30hrs, Sat & Sun; 08.00-10.00hrs, Lunch; Mon-Fri; 12.00-14.00hrs, Sat; Closed; Sun; 12.00-14.30hrs, Dinner; 19.00-21.30hrs daily

2   McDonald's

Tel: (01226) 740025

1 mile west along the A61, on the right.

Open; 07.00-0.00hrs daily.

3   Wentworth Park Service Station (Save)

Tel: (01226) 350479

1 mile west along the A61, on the right.

Access, Visa, Overdrive, All Star, Switch, Dial Card, Mastercard, Delta, Routex, Keyfuels, AA Paytrak, UK Fuelcard.

4   Travel Inn

Tel: (01226) 350035

1 mile west along the A61, on the right

5   The Wentworth

Tel: (01226) 350035

1 mile west along the A61, on the right.

(Brewsters) Open all day. Meals

served; Mon-Sat; 11.30-22.00hrs, Sun; 12.00-22.00hrs.

6   Hilltop Service Station (Shell)

Tel: (01226) 284412

1 mile north along the A61, on the right.

Access, Visa, Overdrive, All Star, Switch, Dial Card, Mastercard, Amex, Diners Club, Delta, Routex, Keyfuels, AA Paytrak, Shell Cards, BP Agency. Open; Mon-Sat; 07.00-21.00hrs, Sun; 08.00-20.30hrs.

7   The Cross Keys

Tel: (01226) 742277

0.4 miles south along the A6135, on the left.

(Whitbread) Open all day on Sunday. Lunch; Mon-Sat; 12.00-14.00hrs, Evening Meals, Mon-Sat; 17.30-21.00hrs, Meals served all day Sundays; 12.00-21.00hrs.

8   Cross Keys Garage (Jet)

Tel: (01226) 743331

0.4 miles south along the A6135, on the left.

Access, Visa, Overdrive, All Star, Switch, Dial Card, Mastercard, Delta, UK Fuelcard, Jet Card. Open; Mon-Sat; 07.00-22.00hrs, Sun; 08.00-22.00hrs.

9   Hare & Hounds

Tel: (01226) 742283

0.5 miles south along the A6135, on the left.

(John Smith's) Open all day. Bar meals served; Mon-Fri; 12.00-14.00hrs & 17.30-21.30hrs, Sat; 12.00-14.00hrs & 19.00-21.30hrs. Restaurant Open; Mon-Sat; 19.00-21.30hrs, Sun 12.00-14.30hrs.

10 Hoyland Common Save Petrol Station

Tel: (01226) 746475
0.7 miles south along the A6135, on the right.
Access, Visa, Overdrive, All Star, Switch, Dial Card, Mastercard, Delta, AA Paytrak, Save Business Card. Open; 06.00-23.00hrs daily.

PLACES OF INTEREST

Worsbrough Mill Museum & Country Park

Off Park Road, Worsbrough Bridge, Barnsley S70 5LJ
Tel: (01226) 774527 website: www.barnsley.gov.uk

Follow the A61 north (Signposted 2.1 Miles)
A water powered corn mill dating from c1625 and a 19thC steam mill have been restored to full working order and form the centrepiece of this industrial museum which is surrounded by a 200 acre park.

Elsecar Heritage Centre

Wath Road, Elsecar, Barnsley S74 8HJ Tel: (01226) 740203 e-mail: stephen.duckworth @barnsley.gov.uk

Follow the A61 northeast (Signposted 2.9 Miles)
Situated in the South Yorkshire countryside, this science and history centre features "hands-on" science in the Power House and trips on the Elsecar Steam Railway. Displays include the interactive "Living History Exhibition" and interactive multi-media in the Newcomen Beam Engine Centre. Gift Shop. Tea Room. Disabled access.

Wigfield Farm

Haverlands Lane, Worsbrough Bridge, Barnsley S70 5NQ
Tel: (01226) 733702 e-mail: wigfieldfarm@barnsley.ac.uk

Follow the A61 northeast (Signposted along A61. 2.4 Miles)
An opportunity to view rare and traditional breeds of farm animals with milking demonstrations being held daily. There is also an Exotic Animal House featuring reptiles and snakes. Gift Shop. Café. Picnic and play areas. Disabled access.

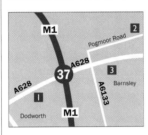

JUNCTION 37

Nearest A&E Hospital
Barnsley & District General Hospital
Gawber Road, Barnsley S75 2PW
Tel: (01226) 730000
Take the A628 east and after about 0.5 miles turn left at the traffic lights along Pogmoor Road. Turn left at the end of this road into Gawber Road and the hospital is immediately on the left. (Signposted. Distance Approx 1.3 miles)

FACILITIES

1 Brooklands Hotel & Restaurant

Tel: (01226) 299571
0.5 miles west along the A628, on the left.
Restaurant Open; Sun- Fri; 12.00-14.30hrs & 19.00-22.00hrs, Sat; 19.00-22.00hrs.

2 Intake 1 Jet Service Station

Tel: (01226) 286424
1 mile north along Pogmoor Road, on the left.
LPG. Access, Visa, Overdrive, All Star, Switch, Dial Card, Mastercard, Amex, Diners Club, Delta, Jet Card.

3 Shell Barnsley

Tel: (01226) 737100
0.6 miles east along the A628, on the right.
Access, Visa, Overdrive, All Star, Switch, Dial Card, Mastercard, Amex, Diners Club, Shell Cards, BP Agency.

PLACES OF INTEREST

Metrodome Leisure Complex

Queen's Ground, Queen's Road, Barnsley S71 1AN
Tel: (01226) 730060. website: www.themetrodome.co.uk

Follow the A628 into Barnsley, continue along Peel Street and Kendray Street (Signposted 1.8 Miles)
Britain's most exciting and imaginative indoor water based theme attraction, featuring the Terrorship 3000, Black Hole, Red River Cruiser and Lunar Run, the ultimate in aqua excitement challenge and daring! Dry facilities include squash, badminton and bowls. Café. Disabled access.

Cannon Hall Museum, Park & Gardens

Cawthorne, Barnsley S75 4AT
Tel: (01226) 790270

website: www.barnsley.gov.uk

Follow the A628 west and turn right towards Barugh Green. Turn left along the A635 to Cawthorne and it is signposted locally. (4.3 Miles)

The country house, remodelled by John Carr of York in the 18thC, houses a collection of pottery, furniture, paintings and glassware from the 18th to 20thC and is the Regimental Museum of the 13th/18th Royal Hussars. It is surrounded by 70 acres of parkland landscaped by Richard Woods in the 1760's, with lawns, a walled garden full of historic pear trees and lakes. Shop. Victorian Kitchen Café.

JUNCTION 38

Nearest Northbound A&E Hospital

Pinderfield Hospital

Aberford Road, Wakefield
WF1 4DG
Tel: (01924) 201688

Proceed north to Junction 39. Take the A636 east exit and after 2.5 miles turn right along the A638. At the junction of the A642 and A61 turn right along the A642 and the hospital is along this road on the left. (Distance Approx 7.7 miles)

Nearest Southbound A&E Hospital

Barnsley & District General Hospital

Gawber Road, Barnsley
S75 2PW
Tel: (01226) 730000

Take the A637 south towards Barnsley and at the roundabout carry straight on along the A635. Almost immediately turn first right into Redbrook Road and continue into Gawber Road. The hospital is on the right hand side. (Distance Approx 4.4 miles)

FACILITIES

1   The Old Post Office

🍴 🍽 ♿ 🚶

Tel: (01226) 387619
0.1 miles south along the A637, on the left.
(Free House) Open all day on Saturday. Lunch; Mon-Sat; 12.00-14.00hrs, Sun; 12.00-14.30hrs, Evening Meals; Mon, Wed & Thurs; 17.30-19.30hrs, Fri & Sat; 17.30-21.00hrs.

PLACES OF INTEREST

National Coal Mining Museum for England

Caphouse Colliery, New Road, Overton, Wakefield WF4 4RH
Tel: (01924) 848806
website: www.ncm.org.uk

Follow the A637 north (Signposted 5.4 Miles)

Displays and audio-visual presentations show mining conditions from the early days to the present whilst there is a one hour underground tour (warm clothes and sensible shoes recommended) of a real coal mine with an experienced local miner as a guide. Café. Gift Shop. Disabled access

Yorkshire Sculpture Park

Bretton Hall, West Bretton, Wakefield WF4 4LG
Tel: (01924) 830302
website: www.ysp.co.uk

Follow the A637 north (Signposted 1 mile)

One of Europe's leading open air galleries, set in 100 acres of 18thC parkland, with a programme of international exhibitions of contemporary sculpture. There are indoor galleries, a craft shop, café and sculpture bookshop. Electric scooters (pre-booked by telephone) are available and there are audio guides and braille information. The neighbouring Bretton Country Park contains a number of works by Henry Moore

M1
BETWEEN JUNCS 38 & 39

WOOLLEY EDGE SERVICES (NORTHBOUND) (MOTO)
Tel: (01924) 830371
Self Service Restaurant, Burger King, Travelodge & Esso Fuel

WOOLLEY EDGE SERVICES (SOUTHBOUND) (MOTO)
Tel: (01924) 830371
Self Service Restaurant, Burger King, Travelodge & Esso Fuel

ADJACENT ROADBRIDGE CONNECTION BETWEEN SITES

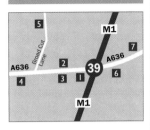

JUNCTION 39

Nearest Northbound A&E Hospital

Pinderfield Hospital

Aberford Road, Wakefield
WF1 4DG
Tel: (01924) 201688
Take the A636 east exit and after 2.5 miles turn right along the A638. At the junction of the A642 and A61 turn right along the A642 and the hospital is along this road on the left. (Distance Approx 4.3 miles)

Nearest Southbound A&E Hospital

Barnsley & District General Hospital

Gawber Road, Barnsley
S75 2PW
Tel: (01226) 730000
Proceed south to Junction 38. Take the A637 south towards Barnsley and at the roundabout carry straight on along the A635. Almost immediately turn first right into Redbrook Road and continue into Gawber Road. The hospital is on the right hand side. (Distance Approx 7.9 miles)

FACILITIES

1   Cedar Court Hotel, Wakefield

Tel: (01924) 276310

On the west side of the roundabout.
Capellos Restaurant Open; Breakfast; Mon-Fri; 07.00-10.00hrs, Sat; 07.30-10.30hrs, Sun; 08.00-10.30hrs, Lunch; Mon-Fri; 12.00-14.00hrs [Sat; Closed], Sun; 12.00-15.00hrs, Dinner; 19.00-22.00hrs daily.

2   Knight of Wakefield Total Filling Station

Tel: (01924) 274756
0.2 miles west along the A636, on the right.
Access, Visa, Overdrive, All Star, Switch, Dial Card, Mastercard, Delta, BP Supercharge, Total/Fina/Elf Card. Open; Mon-Fri; 07.00-20.00hrs, Sat; 08.00-19.00hrs, Sun; 09.00-19.00hrs.

3   King Fishers Fish & Chip Restaurant

Tel: (01924) 274994
0.2 miles west along the A636, on the left.
Open; Sun & Mon; 11.30-22.00hrs, Tues-Sat; 11.30-23.00hrs.

4   The British Oak

Tel: (01924) 275286
0.8 miles west along the A636, on the left.
(Tetley) Open all day. Meals served; 12.00-21.30hrs daily.

5   The Navigation Inn

Tel: (01924) 274361
0.5 miles along Broad Cut Lane, on the left.
(Free House) Open all day. Lunch; Mon-Sat; 12.00-14.00hrs, Sun; 12.00-15.00hrs, Evening Meals; Mon-Sat; 17.30-20.00hrs.

6   The New Inn

Tel: (01924) 255897

0.2 miles east along the A636, on the right.
(Punch Taverns) Open all day. Meals served; Mon-Sat; 12.00-20.00hrs, Sun; 12.00-15.00hrs.

7   Grange Service Station (Esso)

Tel: (01924) 371209
0.7 miles east along the A636, on the left.
Access, Visa, Overdrive, All Star, Switch, Dial Card, Mastercard, Amex, Diners Club, Delta, AA Paytrak. Shell Gold, BP Supercharge. Open; 07.00-22.00hrs daily.

PLACES OF INTEREST

Wakefield

Follow the A 636 north (Signposted 3.1 Miles)
For details please see Junction 40 information

Within the city can be found ...

The Cathedral Church of All Saints

Northgate, Wakefield WF1 1HG
For details please see Junction 40 information

The Chantry Chapel of St Mary on Wakefield Bridge
For details please see Junction 40 information

Sandal Castle

Off Manygates Lane, Sandal, Wakefield.

Follow the A636 east towards Wakefield, turn south along the A6186 and continue north along the A61. (Signposted along A61, 2.7 Miles)
For details please see Junction 40 information

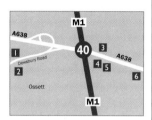

JUNCTION 40

Nearest A&E Hospital

Pinderfield Hospital
Aberford Road, Wakefield
WF1 4DG
Tel: (01924) 201688
Take the A638 east exit and at
the junction of the A642 and
A61 turn right along the A642.
The hospital is along this road
on the left. (Distance Approx
4.2 miles)

FACILITIES

**1   Mercury Service
Station (UK Fuels)**

Tel: (01924) 275680
**1 mile west along the
Dewsbury Road, in Ossett, on
the right.**
Red Diesel. Access, Visa,
Overdrive, All Star, Switch, Dial
Card, Mastercard, Amex, Diners
Club, Delta, Keyfuels, AA
Paytrak, BP Supercharge.
Open; Mon-Sat; 07.30-
20.00hrs, Sun; 10.00-
20.00hrs.

2   The Red Lion

Tel: (01924) 273487
**1 mile west along the
Dewsbury Road, in Ossett, on
the left.**
(Free House) Open all day.
Meals served; Mon; 12.00-
14.00hrs, Tues-Sat; 12.00-

14.00hrs & 19.00-22.00hrs,
Sun; 12.00-22.00hrs

3   Shell Ossett

Tel: (01924) 282570
**0.3 miles east along the
A638, on the left.**
Access, Visa, Overdrive, All
Star, Switch, Dial Card,
Mastercard, Amex, Diners Club,
Delta, UK Fuelcard, Shell
Cards, BP Agency.

4   Posthouse Wakefield

Tel: 0870 400 9082
**0.3 miles east along the
A638, on the right.**
Traders Restaurant Open; Mon-
Fri; 06.30-22.30hrs, Sat & Sun;
06.30-22.00hrs

**5   Ossett Service Station
(BP)**

Tel: (01924) 265947
**0.3 miles east along the
A638, on the right.**
Access, Visa, Overdrive, All
Star, Switch, Dial Card,
Mastercard, Amex, Diners Club,
Delta, Solo, Electron, BP Cards.
Open; Mon-Fri; 06.00-
22.30hrs, Sat & Sun; 07.00-
22.30hrs.

6   The Old Malt Shovel

Tel: (01924) 201561
**0.6 miles east along the
A638, on the right.**
(Free House) Open all day.
Meals served; Mon-Sat; 12.00-
14.00hrs, Sun; 12.00-15.00hrs

PLACES OF
INTEREST

Wakefield

Wakefield Tourist Information
Centre, Town Hall, Wood Street,
Wakefield WF1 2HQ

Tel: (01924) 305000/1
website: www.wakefield.gov.uk

**Follow the A638 east
(Signposted 2.4 Miles)**
This ancient Cathedral City
dates back to at least Roman
times and was once an inland
grain and cloth port. The
famous Battle of Wakefield
took place on Wakefield Green
in 1460 with defeat for the
Royalists. Amongst the fine
buildings are the parish
church, dating from the 14thC
and with the tallest spire in
Yorkshire, which became a
cathedral in 1888 and St
Mary's Chapel.

**Within the city can be
found ...**

**The Cathedral Church of
All Saints**
Northgate, Wakefield WF1 1HG
Tel: (01924) 373923 website:
www.wakefield-cathedral.org.uk

The Cathedral offers a quiet
and tranquil respite from the
lively and bustling pedestrian
precinct that surrounds it.
There are magnificent wood
carvings throughout the
building, notably the choir and
screen, and the stained glass
windows form a
comprehensive collection of
glass by Kempe who
contributed work to the
cathedral throughout his life.
Book Shop. Disabled access.

**The Chantry Chapel of St
Mary on Wakefield Bridge**
Curator; Kate Taylor
Tel: (01924) 372748
website: www.rcti.org.uk

Standing on Wakefield's
Mediaeval bridge, this chapel
is a very rare survival of the
once common practice in the
Middle Ages of siting places of
worship on bridges where
priests could minister to
travellers and say masses. The
stone bridge upon which it

stands was built in the 1340's and the tolls charged to use it were of considerable economic importance to the townspeople. The chapel was extensively restored in 1847.

Sandal Castle

Off Manygates Lane, Sandal, Wakefield

Follow the A631 into Wakefield and turn south along the A61 (Signposted along A61, 4 Miles)

This motte and bailey castle dates from the 12thC and the later stone castle, owned by Richard, Duke of York, overlooks the site of the Battle of Wakefield (1460). The structure was demolished upon the orders of Parliament after the siege of 1645 and the ruins are now part of a park.

NB. Artefacts and further information about Sandal Castle can be seen at Wakefield Museum, Wood Street, Wakefield WF1 2HQ. Tel: (01924) 305351. website: www.wakefield.gov.uk.

Nearest Northbound A&E Hospital

Leeds General Infirmary

Great George Street, Leeds LS1 3EX
Tel: (0113) 243 2799
Proceed north to Junction 7 (M621) and take the A61 north into Leeds city centre. The

hospital is signposted in the city. (Distance Approx 8 miles)

Nearest Southbound A&E Hospital

Pinderfield Hospital

Aberford Road, Wakefield WF1 4DG
Tel: (01924) 201688
Take the A650 exit east and continue along the A61. At the junction of the A642 and A61 turn left along the A642 and the hospital is along this road on the left. (Distance Approx 3.4 miles)

FACILITIES

1   The Bay Horse

Tel: (01924) 825926
0.3 miles west along the A650, on the right.
(Punch Retail) Open all day. Meals served; 12.00-20.00hrs daily.

2   Manor Service Station (BP)

Tel: (01924) 822260
0.3 miles west along the A650, on the left.
Access, Visa, Overdrive, All Star, Switch, Dial Card, Mastercard, Amex, Diners Club, Delta, Routex, UK Fuelcard, Shell Cards, BP Cards. Open; Mon-Fri; 06.00-22.00hrs, Sat & Sun; 07.00-22.00hrs.

3   Ardsley Esso Service Station

Tel: (01924) 823192
0.6 miles west along the A650, on the right.
Access, Visa, Overdrive, All Star, Switch, Dial Card, Mastercard, Amex, Diners Club, Delta, Shell Gold, Esso Cards. Open; 05.00-0.00hrs daily

4   The Malt Shovel

Tel: (01924) 875520
0.4 miles east along the A650, on the left.
(Enterprise Inns) Open all day. Meals served; Lunch; Mon-Sat; 12.00-14.00hrs, Sun; 12.00-14.30hrs. Evening Meals; Thurs & Fri; 17.30-19.30hrs.

5   The Poplars

Tel: (01924) 375682
0.8 miles east along the road to Wrenthorpe, on the left.

PLACES OF INTEREST

Wakefield

Follow the A 650 south (Signposted 3.1 Miles)
For details please see Junction 40 information

Within the city can be found ...

The Cathedral Church of All Saints
Northgate, Wakefield WF1 1HG
For details please see Junction 40 information

The Chantry Chapel of St Mary on Wakefield Bridge
For details please see Junction 40 information

Sandal Castle
Off Manygates Lane, Sandal, Wakefield.

Follow the A650 south into Wakefield and continue south along the A61.(Signposted along A61, 4.8 Miles)
For details please see Junction 40 information

M1
JUNCTION 42

THIS JUNCTION IS A
MOTORWAY INTERCHANGE
WITH THE M62 ONLY AND
THERE IS NO ACCESS TO ANY
FACILITIES

Nearest Northbound A&E Hospital

Leeds General Infirmary
Great George Street, Leeds
LS1 3EX
Tel: (0113) 243 2799
Proceed north to Junction 7
(M621) and take the A61 north
into Leeds city centre. The
hospital is signposted in the
city. (Distance Approx 6.8
miles)

Nearest Southbound A&E Hospital

Pinderfield Hospital
Aberford Road, Wakefield
WF1 4DG
Tel: (01924) 201688
Proceed south to Junction 41,
take the A650 exit east and
continue along the A61. At the
junction of the A642 and A61
turn left along the A642 and
the hospital is along this road.
(Distance Approx 4.6 miles)

M1
JUNCTION 43

THIS JUNCTION IS A
MOTORWAY INTERCHANGE
ONLY WITH THE M621 AND
THERE IS NO ACCESS TO ANY
FACILITIES

Nearest Northbound A&E Hospital

Leeds General Infirmary
Great George Street, Leeds
LS1 3EX
Tel: (0113) 243 2799
Proceed north to Junction 7
(M621) and take the A61 north
into Leeds city centre. The
hospital is signposted in the
city. (Distance Approx 4.2
miles)

Nearest Southbound A&E Hospital

Pinderfield Hospital
Aberford Road, Wakefield
WF1 4DG
Tel: (01924) 201688
Proceed south to Junction 41,
take the A650 exit east and
continue along the A61. At the
junction of the A642 and A61
turn left along the A642 and
the hospital is along this road.
(Distance Approx 6.4 miles)

M1
JUNCTION 44

Nearest Northbound A&E Hospital

Leeds General Infirmary
Great George Street, Leeds
LS1 3EX
Tel: (0113) 243 2799
Follow the B6481 north and
continue along the A61 into
Leeds city centre. The hospital
is signposted within the city.
(Distance Approx 4.1 miles)

Nearest Southbound A&E Hospital

Pinderfield Hospital
Aberford Road, Wakefield
WF1 4DG
Tel: (01924) 201688
Proceed south to Junction 41,
take the A650 exit east and
continue along the A61. At the
junction of the A642 and A61
turn left along the A642 and
the hospital is along this road.
(Distance Approx 7.6 miles)

FACILITIES

1   John O'Gaunts

Tel: (0113) 282 2243
**0.6 miles south along the
A639, on the left.**
(Whitbread) Closed on Mon.
Open all day Sun. Meals
served; Lunch; Tues-Fri; 11.30-
14.30hrs, Evening Meals; Tues-
Sat; 17.30-21.00hrs. Meals
served all day on Sundays;
12.00-21.00hrs.

**2   Rothwell Petrol
Station (BP)**

Tel: (0113) 282 1489
**1 mile south along the A639,
on the left.**
Access, Visa, Overdrive, All
Star, Switch, Dial Card,
Mastercard, Amex, Diners Club,
Delta, BP Cards, Shell Agency.

PLACES OF INTEREST

Leeds

**Follow the B6481 north and
continue along the A61.
(Signposted 4 Miles)**
For details please see Junction
27 (M62) information

Within the city centre ...

Royal Armouries

Armouries Drive, Leeds LS10 1LT

For details please see Junction 27 (M62) information

Thackray's Medical Museum

Beckett Street, Leeds LS9 7LN

Follow the B6481 north, continue along the A61 and then the A58 (3.8 Miles)

For details please see Junction 27 (M62) information

JUNCTION 45

THIS JUNCTION IS NOT CURRENTLY IN SERVICE AND HAS BEEN BUILT TO FACILITATE ACCESS TO THE EAST LEEDS RADIAL ROUTE. CONSTRUCTION IS PROJECTED TO START IN 2002

Nearest Northbound A&E Hospital

Leeds General Infirmary

Great George Street, Leeds LS1 3EX
Tel: (0113) 243 2799

Proceed north to Junction 46, take the A63 exit north and continue along the A64 and M64 into the city centre. The hospital is signposted within the city. (Distance Approx 8.6 miles)

Nearest Southbound A&E Hospital

Pinderfield Hospital

Aberford Road, Wakefield WF1 4DG
Tel: (01924) 201688

Proceed south to Junction 41, take the A650 exit east and

continue along the A61. At the junction of the A642 and A61 turn left along the A642 and the hospital is along this road. (Distance Approx 8.9 miles)

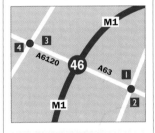

JUNCTION 46

Nearest A&E Hospital

Leeds General Infirmary

Great George Street, Leeds LS1 3EX
Tel: (0113) 243 2799

Take the A6120 exit north and continue along the A64 and M64 into the city centre. The hospital is signposted within the city. (Distance Approx 6 miles)

FACILITIES

1   The Old George

Tel: (0113) 286 2100
1 mile south along the A63, on the left.
(Beefeater) Open all day. Meals served 12.00-22.30hrs daily.

2   Hilton Leeds Garforth

Tel: (0113) 286 6556
1 mile south along the A63, on the right.
Duke's Restaurant Open; Breakfast; Mon-Fri; 07.00-09.30hrs, Sat & Sun; 08.00-10.00hrs, Lunch; Sun-Fri; 12.30-14.00hrs, Dinner;

19.00-21.300hrs daily. Bar meals are available 11.00-23.00hrs daily.

3   Austhorpe Filling Station (Texaco)

Tel: (0113) 284 0100
0.2 miles north along the A6120, on the right.
LPG. Access, Visa, Overdrive, All Star, Switch, Dial Card, Mastercard, Amex, Diners Club, Delta, BP Chargecard, Fast Fuel, Texaco Cards.

4   Sainsbury's Filling Station

Tel: (0113) 232 8154
0.3 miles north along the A6120, on the left.
Access, Visa, Overdrive, All Star, Switch, Dial Card, Mastercard, Amex, Delta, AA Paytrak. Toilets & Cash Machines available in adjacent store during store opening hours.

PLACES OF INTEREST

Harewood House

Harewood, Leeds LS17 9LQ
Tel: (0113) 288 6331
website: www.harewood.org

Follow the A63 north, continue along the A6120 and turn north along the A61 (Signposted 10 miles)

Designed by John Carr of York in the neo-classical style and completed in 1772, Harewood House is one of the great treasure houses of England with interiors and plaster work ceilings by Robert Adam and State Rooms furnished by Thomas Chippendale. Outstanding art collections include works by JMW Turner, Girtin, Reynolds, Gainsborough and Picasso, whilst The Gallery and the China Room display, amongst other things, examples of fine porcelain. The magnificent gardens were designed in the 1840's by Sir Charles Barry and the Terrace contains an Italian-style garden with ornate fountains. There are extensive walks around the grounds, boat trips around the lake, a Bird Garden and a children's adventure play ground. Café. Gift Shops. Disabled access.

Temple Newsam House

Leeds LS15 0AE
Tel: (0113) 264 7321 or (0113) 264 1358
website: www.leeds.gov.uk

Follow the A63 north (Signposted 2.1 miles)
Dubbed the "Hampton Court of the North", Temple Newsam is a magnificent Tudor-Jacobean country house set in 1,200 acres of parkland with 30 rooms recently restored to their original splendour and representing many of the different styles employed during its existence. The Home Farm has the largest collection of rare breeds in the country. Café. NB. House closed until Spring 2003 for refurbishment

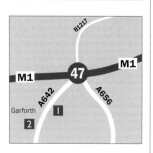

JUNCTION 47

Nearest A&E Hospital

Leeds General Infirmary
Great George Street, Leeds LS1 3EX
Tel: (0113) 243 2799

Proceed south to Junction 46, take the A6120 exit north and continue along the A64 and M64 into the city centre. The hospital is signposted within the city. (Distance Approx 8.9 miles)

FACILITIES

1   Aagrar Restaurant

Tel: (0113) 287 6606
0.6 miles south along the A642, on the left.
Open; Sun-Thurs; 18.00-23.30hrs, Sat; 17.30-23.30hrs

2   Toll Bar Garage (UK Fuel)

Tel: (0113) 286 2926
1 mile south along the A642, in Garforth, on the right.
Access, Visa, Mastercard, Amex, Delta. Open; Mon-Fri; 08.00-18.00hrs, Sat; 08.00-13.00hrs, Sun; Closed.

PLACES OF INTEREST

Lotherton Hall

Aberford, Yorkshire LS25 3EB
Tel: (0113) 281 3259
website: www.leeds.gov.uk

Signposted from junction. (2.6 miles)

A small Edwardian country house with period gardens, housing the Gascoigne Collection and displays of fashions up to recent times. The Gardens, created by Mrs

Gwendolen Gascoigne, retain their Edwardian character, whilst the Bird Garden is home to many rare and endangered species. Café.

JUNCTION 48

THIS IS A RESTRICTED ACCESS JUNCTION
- Vehicles can only exit from the northbound lanes and travel north along the A1
- Vehicles can only enter the motorway along the southbound lanes from the A1(M) south carriageway

Nearest A&E Hospital

Leeds General Infirmary
Great George Street, Leeds LS1 3EX
Tel: (0113) 243 2799

Proceed south to Junction 46, take the A6120 exit north and continue along the A64 and M64 into the city centre. The hospital is signposted within the city. (Distance Approx 10.2 miles)

MOTORWAY ENDS
(Total Length of Motorway 191.1 miles)

the M2

This motorway forms the strategic route from London and the West to the North Kent coast. Commencing at Junction 1, an end-on connection with the A2 just west of Rochester, the motorway heads south east before reaching the largest engineering project

River Medway, Rochester

along the route, the bridge over the River Medway between Junctions 2 and 3. Another motorway bridge, to double the capacity, is currently under construction here and alongside this is the 120ft high **Medway Viaduct** carrying the new 186 mph **Channel Tunnel Rail Link** (CTRL). Within this section, the CTRL runs parallel to the carriageways on the west side before entering the 2 miles long North Downs Tunnel under Junction 3 and Blue Bell Hill as it diverts south to run alongside of the M20. The Channel Tunnel Rail Link began in October 1998 and the first section,

between the Channel Tunnel and Fawkham Junction, is due to open in 2003 whilst the projected opening date for the complete line between London St Pancras and the Tunnel is 2007.

When construction of a rail Channel Tunnel was first discussed it was claimed that as well as giving a boost to the economy of the south east region of England, it would also be of national importance as through trains would be run from a number of major cities across the country as well as from London. It was undoubtedly this factor which gained the support of MPs across the country and assisted in the passage of the Channel Tunnel Bill through Parliament. The Channel Tunnel Act was passed in 1987 and although one of the clauses authorized the construction of enough trains to accommodate the number of anticipated services, another one released the Government from any legal requirement to provide them!

Within a few months of the commencement of the London-Paris service the rail operators announced that they felt that it

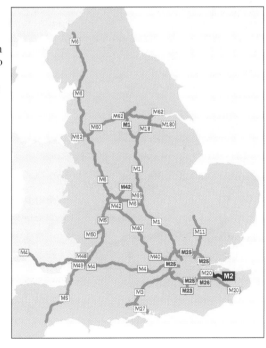

would be uneconomic to introduce any more routes at that time and that the situation would be reviewed periodically. As it stands today (2002), trains still only run from London to the Continent and £500,000 worth of brand new unused rolling stock continues to sit in sidings!

Between Junctions 2 and 5, the motorway by-passes the three historic towns of Rochester, Chatham and Gillingham. **Rochester** can trace its origins to some 2,000 years ago, having first been settled by the Celts, and it was an important crossing point over the River Medway during the Roman occupation. The first fleet of ships was built here by King Alfred to establish the Royal Navy, William the Conqueror built a castle and the town features heavily in the writings of Charles Dickens. **Chatham** was established as a major naval

World Naval Base, Chatham

dockyard by Henry VIII and for some 400 years was responsible for building many famous fighting ships including "HMS Victory". **Gillingham** is the home base for the Royal Engineers who, although formed primarily to provide logistic support for the army, have featured in a number of major historical landmarks and earned 50 Victoria Crosses in battles such as the defence of *Rorkes Drift* in the *Zulu War*.

Continuing west, Sittingbourne and Faversham are passed on the north side before the motorway ends at Junction 7 and diverges into the A299 to Whitstable and the A2 to Canterbury. **Faversham**, a limb of the Cinque Port of Dover, has been established for well over 2,000 years and was an important staging point on Watling Street during the Roman occupation.

Location of Places of Interest

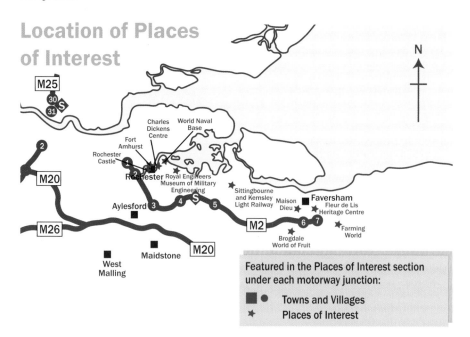

JUNCTION 1

THIS IS A RESTRICTED ACCESS JUNCTION.
- Vehicles cannot access the motorway from the A2 westbound
- Vehicles cannot exit along the A2 eastbound

Nearest Westbound A&E Hospital
Darent Valley Hospital
Darenth Wood Road, Dartford DA2 8DA
Tel: (01322) 428100
Follow the A2 west and take the B255 exit to Dartford. Take the second exit at the second roundabout and, at a third roundabout, follow the signs to Dartford along Watling Street. (Distance Approx 9.0 miles)

Nearest Eastbound A&E Hospital
Medway Maritime Hospital
Windmill Road, Gillingham ME7 5NY
Tel: (01634) 830000
Follow the A2 east into Gillingham and the hospital is signposted (Distance Approx 5.4 miles)

PLACES OF INTEREST

(ONLY ACCESSIBLE TO EASTBOUND TRAFFIC)

Rochester
Medway Visitor Information Centre, 95 High Street, Rochester ME1 1LX
Tel: (01634) 843666
Follow the A2 west (Signposted 2.6 Miles)
For details please see Junction 2 information

World Naval Base
The Historic Dockyard, Chatham ME4 4TW
Tel: (01634) 823800:
Follow the A2 west into Chatham (Signposted 4.5 Miles)
For details please see Junction 3 information

Fort Amherst
Dock Road, Chatham ME4 4UB
Tel: (01634) 847747
Follow the A2 west into Chatham and it is signposted north along the A231 Dock Road (4.1 Miles)
For details please see Junction 3 information

Royal Engineers Museum of Military Engineering
Prince Arthur Road, Gillingham ME4 4UG Tel: (01634) 406397
Follow the A2 west into Chatham and it is signposted north along the A231 Dock Road (4.5 Miles)
For details please see Junction 3 information

JUNCTION 2

Nearest Westbound A&E Hospital
Darent Valley Hospital
Darenth Wood Road, Dartford DA2 8DA
Tel: (01322) 428100
Proceed to Junction 1, follow the A2 west and take the B255 exit to Dartford. Take the second exit at the second roundabout and, at a third roundabout, follow the signs to Dartford along Watling Street. (Distance Approx 10.3 miles)

Nearest Eastbound A&E Hospital
Medway Maritime Hospital
Windmill Road, Gillingham ME7 5NY
Tel: (01634) 830000
Follow the A228 north, turn right along the A2 east into Gillingham and the hospital is signposted (Distance Approx 4.9 miles)

FACILITIES

1 Cuxton Auto Services (Independent)

Tel: (01634) 717987
0.9 miles south along the A228 on the right
Access, Visa, Overdrive, All Star, Switch, Dial Card, Mastercard. Open; Mon-Sat; 06.00-20.00hrs, Sun; 09.00-16.00hrs.

2   The White Hart

Tel: (01634) 711857
1 mile south along the A228 on the left.
(Shepherd Neame) Open all day. Meals served; Tues-Sat; 12.00-14.30hrs & 19.00-21.30hrs, Sun & Mon; 12.00-14.30hrs.

3 McDonald's

Tel: (01634) 719122

0.5 miles north along the A228 north, on the right in Medway Valley Leisure Park.
Open; Sun, Mon, Wed & Thurs; 10.00-0.00hrs, Fri & Sat; 10.00-01.00hrs

4 Chiquito's

Tel: (01634) 713816

0.5 miles north along the A228, on the right in Medway Valley Leisure Park.
Meals served; 12.00-21.30hrs daily

5 Exchange Bar & Grill

Tel: (01634) 719306

0.5 miles north along the A228, on the right in Medway Valley Leisure Park.
Meals served; 12.00-22.00hrs daily

6 Frankie & Benny's

Tel: (01634) 712209

0.5 miles north along the A228, on the right in Medway Valley Leisure Park.
Meals served; Sun-Thurs; 12.00-22.00hrs, Fri & Sat; 12.00-23.00hrs

7 Temple Farm Service Station (Esso)

Tel: (01634) 719286

0.6 miles north along the A228, on the right.
Access, Visa, Mastercard, Switch, Diners Club, Amex, Overdrive, All Star, Dial Card, UK Fuelcard, Keyfuels, Esso Cards, Shell Cards.

PLACES OF INTEREST

Rochester

Medway Visitor Information Centre, 95 High Street, Rochester ME1 1LX
Tel: (01634) 843666
website: www.medway.gov.uk

Follow the A228 north (Signposted 2.3 Miles)

The site was first settled some 2,000 years ago, by the Celts of the Belgic tribe and the ancient British name for Rochester was "Dourbryt", meaning "swift stream", a reference to the Medway, at the mouth of which it stands. Watling Street crossed the river here and in 43AD the Romans established the walled city of "Durobrivae" (The stronghold by the bridge), encompassing almost 23 acres.

Later the Saxons called it "Hrofesceaster" and King Alfred, determined to thwart Viking sea power, built a fleet of ships in Rochester to create England's first navy. William the Conqueror, aware of the strategic importance of the town, decreed that a castle be maintained here permanently and he also commissioned the building of Rochester Cathedral (Tel: 01634-843366) on the site of a Saxon church which had been founded by St Augustine in 604.

The town abounds in old and interesting buildings; Restoration House, where Charles II stayed on May 28th, 1660 on his way to London to take possession of the throne; 47 High Street, from where James II made an ignominious escape to France, and The Poor Travellers' House which dates from 1579 are fine examples of Rochester's historic past.

Within the town centre ...

Rochester Castle

The Keep, Rochester ME1 1SX
Tel: (01634) 402276

Built in 1088 by William's chief architect, Bishop Gundulph, on the site of a previous fortification of 480, Rochester Castle has featured heavily in the history of England. Henry I ordered the massive keep to be raised in 1125, King John held it in siege, the Dauphin captured it, Simon de Montfort successfully resisted the Barons and all assaults till the reign of Edward IV were so successfully repelled that it became known as the "Englishman's Castle".

Partially dismantled in 1610, it is still massive in construction, 113ft high, 70ft square and with walls of a breadth of 11ft to 13ft. Extensive views of the river and surrounding area can be taken from the battlements and there are models showing the development and construction of the castle.

The Charles Dickens Centre

Eastgate House, High Street, Rochester ME1 1EW
Tel: (01634) 844176

Set in an Elizabethan building, the museum is dedicated to the works and times of one of England's best known and loved authors. Dickens incorporated many of the local buildings within his stories, usually with a change of name; Eastgate House itself turning up in "The Mystery of Edwin Drood" as The Nun's House and in "The Pickwick Papers" as the Westgate House Seminary for Young Ladies.

The Charles Dickens Centre recreates scenes from some of his best known books and the latest laser disc technology is utilized to bring to life characters and scenes from his novels and the grim reality of Victorian England. Within the grounds of the house is the Charles Dickens Chalet. It was in this, whilst sited at his home Gads Hill Place, that Charles Dickens wrote his last words in June 1870, leaving "The Mystery of Edwin Drood" as unfinished

World Naval Base

The Historic Dockyard, Chatham ME4 4TW
Tel: (01634) 823800

Follow the A228 north (Signposted 4.2 Miles)
For details please see Junction 3 information

Fort Amherst

Dock Road, Chatham ME4 4UB
Tel: (01634) 847747

Follow the A228 north, turn right along the A2 into Chatham and it is signposted north along the A231 Dock Road (3.8 Miles)
For details please see Junction 3 information

Royal Engineers Museum of Military Engineering

Prince Arthur Road, Gillingham ME4 4UG
Tel: (01634) 406397

Follow the A228 north, turn right along the A2 into Chatham and it is signposted north along the A231 Dock Road (4.2 Miles)
For details please see Junction 3 information

JUNCTION 3

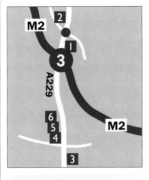

Nearest A&E Hospital
Medway Maritime Hospital
Windmill Road, Gillingham ME7 5NY
Tel: (01634) 830000
Follow the A229 north, bear right along the A230, turn right along the A2 and the hospital is signposted (Distance Approx 4 miles)

FACILITIES

1   Bridgewood Service Station (Esso)

Tel: (01634) 682089
0.5 miles north along the A229, on the right
Visa, Mastercard, Switch, Diners Club, Amex, Overdrive, All Star, Delta, Esso Cards.
Open; 06.00-22.00hrs daily.

2   Forte Posthouse Rochester

Tel: 0870 400 9069
1 mile north along the A229, on the left
Restaurant Open; Breakfast;

Mon-Fri; 06.30-09.30hrs, Sat & Sun; 07.00-10.30hrs, Lunch; Mon-Fri; 12.00-14.00hrs, Sun; 12.00-14.30hrs, Dinner; 18.00-22.00hrs daily.

3   Shell Cossington

Tel: (01634) 661900
1.4 miles south along the A229, on the left
Access, Visa, Mastercard, Switch, Diners Club, Amex, Overdrive, All Star, Dial Card, Delta, BP Supercharge, BP Agency, Esso Chargecard, Shell Cards.

4   Kit's Coty House Brasserie

Tel: (01634) 684445
0.8 miles south along the A229, on the right (via Aylesford turn off)
Open; Mon-Fri; 11.00-15.00hrs & 18.00-23.00hrs, Sat; 18.00-23.00hrs, Sun; 12.00-15.00hrs. NB. Children allowed in with parents on Sunday only.

5   Shell Bluebell Hill

Tel: (01634) 661000
0.8 miles south along the A229, on the right (Actual distance 2.8 miles)
Access, Visa, Overdrive, All Star, Switch, Dial Card, Mastercard, Amex, Diners Club, Delta, BP Cards, Shell Cards, Esso Card.

6   Little Chef

Tel: (01634) 862216
0.8 miles south along the A229, on the right (Actual distance 2.8 miles)
Open; 07.00-22.00hrs daily

PLACES OF INTEREST

World Naval Base

The Historic Dockyard, Chatham ME4 4TW
Tel: (01634) 823800 website: www.worldnavalbase.org.uk

Follow the A229 north (Signposted 4.6 Miles)

Established by Henry VIII and expanded by Elizabeth I, Chatham Dockyard has played a pivotal role in the history and survival of England. Over four centuries many famous fighting ships were built, including Nelson's "HMS Victory", launched in 1765 and today it is the site of an 80 acre historical and educational theme park with three ships moored for inspection; The ex-WWII Destroyer "HMS Cavalier", Spy submarine "HM Submarine Ocelot" and the last Victorian sail & steam sloop "HMS Gannet".

As well as the ships there are numerous displays and exhibits; Wooden Walls, featuring the manufacture of ships in days gone by, there is a working Ropery and the Royal National Lifeboat Institution has its National Exhibition Hall located here with some 15 lifeboats on view.

There are also numerous independent exhibitions within the site; The Conservation Unit (Tel: 01634-823800), RNXS Story (Tel: 01634-823800), Flagship Brewery (Tel: 01634-832828), Kent Police Museum (Tel: 01634-403260) and the Amtec Co-op (Tel: 01634-832627) with an exhibition of early metalworking. During the summer, visitors can take boat trips on the coal-fired paddle steamer "Kingswear Castle" (Tel: 01634-827648) with cruises from both Chatham and Rochester. Shop. Wheelwrights Restaurant. Some disabled access.

Fort Amherst

Dock Road, Chatham ME4 4UB
Tel: (01634) 847747

Follow the A229 north, bear right along the A230 into Chatham and it is signposted north along the A231 Dock Road (3.9 Miles)

Built in 1756 to protect the dockyard, Fort Amherst is one of Britain's finest Napoleonic fortresses. Displays, both static and live, exhibits and regular events reveal the lives of the soldiers and their families from those days right through to WWII. Beneath the fort are over 2,300ft of caverns and tunnels which have been excavated to provide stores, magazines, guardrooms and barracks whilst seven acres of the extensive fortifications and battlements have been restored as a park with picnic areas and nature trails. Visitor Centre. Café. Gift Shop. Some disabled access.

Royal Engineers Museum of Military Engineering

Prince Arthur Road, Gillingham ME4 4UG Tel: (01634) 406397

Follow the A229 north, bear right along the A230 into Chatham and it is signposted north along the A231 Dock Road (4.3 Miles)

Located in the Ravelin Building and featuring displays of real equipment, working models, a superb and dignified medal gallery, and a collection of costumes and curios, this one of the most fascinating and finest museums of its type in the world.

Whilst the Royal Engineers have a proud history in providing the army with logistic support they have also featured in landmarks in history; with 50 Victoria Crosses and 18 George Crosses being awarded. Major Charles Gordon, Gordon of Khartoum, was an RE and the Regiment conducted the heroic defence of Rorkes Drift (as featured in the film "Zulu"). The Courtyard Display shows the work undertaken since the end of WWII and how the Corps led in the military application of steam power, flight, diving and telecommunications as well as numerous other innovations.

The museum is complemented by the Corps Library, an extensive archive begun in 1813, with a collection of books, manuals, manuscripts, maps, plans and photographs. The Royal Engineers were famous pioneers in the early days of Association Football and it was near here, at "Great Lines", that they played and established their fine reputation in the FA Cup in the 1870s. Picnic Area. Refreshments. Museum Shop. Disabled access.

Maidstone

Tourist Information Office, The Gatehouse, Palace Gardens, Maidstone ME15 6YE
Tel: (01622) 602169 website: www.maidstone.gov.uk

Follow the A229 south (Signposted 5.0 Miles)

For details please see Junction 6 (M20) Information

Within the town centre can be found ...

Maidstone Museum and Art Gallery

Chillington Manor House, St Faith's Street, Maidstone ME14 1LH Tel: (01622) 754497

For details please see Junction 6 (M20) Information

The Tyrwhitt-Drake Museum

Archbishops Stables, Mill Street, Maidstone ME15 6YE Tel: (01622) 754497

For details please see Junction 6 (M20) Information

Museum of Kent Life

Lock Lane, Sandling ME14 3AU
Tel: (01622) 763936

Follow the A229 south and it is signposted along the route (3.6 Miles)

For details please see Junction 6 (M20) Information

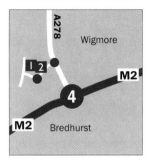

JUNCTION 4

Wigmore

Bredhurst

Nearest A&E Hospital

Medway Maritime Hospital

Windmill Road, Gillingham
ME7 5NY
Tel: (01634) 830000
Follow the A278 north, turn left along the A2 into Gillingham and the hospital is signposted (Distance Approx 4.1 miles)

FACILITIES

1   Sainsbury's Sava Centre Filling Station

Tel: (01634) 382400
1 mile west along Sharsted Way, on the right in Hempstead Valley Shopping Centre
Access, Visa, Mastercard, Switch, Diners Club, Amex, Overdrive, All Star, Dial Card, Delta, Sainsbury's Card. Toilets in adjacent store. Open; 06.30-22.00hrs daily

2   McDonald's

Tel: (01634) 268814
1 mile west along Sharsted Way, on the right in Hempstead Valley Shopping Centre
Open; 08.00-22.00hrs daily

PLACES OF INTEREST

Royal Engineers Museum of Military Engineering
Prince Arthur Road, Gillingham
ME4 4UG Tel: (01634) 406397

Follow the A278 north, turn left along the A2 and it is signposted north along the A231 Dock Road (5.6 Miles)
For details please see Junction 3 information

BETWEEN JUNCS 4 & 5

MEDWAY SERVICES (EASTBOUND) (MOTO)
Tel: (01634) 236900
Fresh Express Self Service Restaurant, Harry Ramsden's & BP Fuel

MEDWAY SERVICES (WESTBOUND) (MOTO)
Tel: (01634) 236900 Travelodge & BP Fuel
Burger King restaurant on Footbridge connecting both sites.

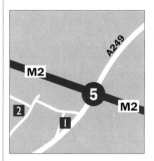

JUNCTION 5

Nearest A&E Hospital

Medway Maritime Hospital
Windmill Road, Gillingham
ME7 5NY
Tel: (01634) 830000
Proceed west to Junction 4, follow the A278 north, turn left along the A2 into Gillingham and the hospital is signposted (Distance Approx 7.6 miles)

FACILITIES

1   The Three Squirrels

Tel: (01795) 842449
0.9 miles south along the A249, on the right
(Free House) Open all day.
Meals served; Breakfast; 06.00-09.30hrs, Lunch; 12.00-15.00hrs, Dinner; 19.00-21.00hrs daily.

2   The Harrow

Tel: (01795) 842546
1 mile south in Stockbury
(Free House) Meals served; Mon-Sat; 12.00-14.00hrs & 18.30-21.00hrs, Sun; 12.00-14.00hrs.

PLACES OF INTEREST

Sittingbourne & Kemsley Light Railway

The Wall, Milton Regis, Sittingbourne
Tel: (01795) 424899

Follow the A249 north, turn right along the A2 and left along the B2005 (3.7 Miles)

The 2ft 6in gauge line was originally built in 1906 for the transportation of raw materials and finished goods between Lloyd's Sittingbourne Paper Mill and the wharves at Milton Creek. With the creek silting up, Ridham Dock was constructed after World War I and the line extended north to connect the new docks and the mill. In 1924 a new mill was opened at Kemsley, roughly between Sittingbourne and Ridham, and the little railway found itself in such demand that by 1940 it had no less than 9 steam locomotives and 2 fireless engines, for shunting at Kemsley Mill, and not only moved freight traffic but ran a passenger service for employees.

With the advent of the 1960s it became clear that road transport would inevitably take over, but the management (by now part of the Bowater Group) rather than sell it all for scrap made representations to the railway preservation fraternity to see if any group would wish to take it over. This generous and far-sighted gesture, sadly rare in these days of accountant-driven organizations, enabled the Locomotive Club of Great Britain to lease it and establish the Sittingbourne & Kemsley Light Railway as it is today with a line running between Sittingbourne and Kemsley Down and an interesting collection of steam locomotives and rolling stock. Refreshment Room. Gift Shop. Disabled access by prior arrangement.

JUNCTION 6

FAVERSHAM TOWN CENTRE IS WITHIN ONE MILE OF THE JUNCTION

Nearest Westbound A&E Hospital

Medway Maritime Hospital
Windmill Road, Gillingham
ME7 5NY
Tel: (01634) 830000
Proceed west to Junction 4, follow the A278 north, turn left along the A2 into Gillingham and the hospital is signposted (Distance Approx 18.3 miles)

Nearest Eastbound A&E Hospital

Kent & Canterbury Hospital
Ethelbert Road, Canterbury
CT1 3NG
Tel: (01227) 766877
Proceed east to Junction 7, follow the A2 into Canterbury and the hospital is signposted in the city. (Distance Approx 9.9 miles)

FACILITIES

1   The Ship Inn

Tel: (01795) 532408
1 mile west along the A2 on the right, in Ospringe.
(Enterprise Inns) Open all day Fri, Sat & Sun. Meals served; Mon-Wed; 11.30-14.30hrs & 19.30-21.00hrs, Thurs; 11.30-14.30hrs, Fri-Sun; 11.30-21.00hrs,

2   The Elephant

Tel: (01795) 590157
0.6 miles north along The Mall, on the right
Meals served; Sun 12.00-16.00hrs only

3   The Railway Hotel

Tel: (01795) 533173
1 mile north along Station Road, on the left
(Shepherd Neame) Open all day. Meals Served; Mon & Tues 12.00-14.30hrs (Evenings bookings only), Wed-Sat; 12.00-14.30hrs & 18.30-21.30hrs, Sun; 12.00-14.30hrs

4   The Windmill

Tel: (01795) 536505
0.8 miles east along the A2, on the left
(Shepherd Neame) Open all day Sat & Sun. Meals served; Mon-Fri; 12.00-14.30hrs & 18.00-20.30hrs, Sat & Sun; 12.00-20.30hrs.

5   Read's Restaurant with Rooms

Tel: (01795) 535344
0.9 miles east along the A2, on the right
Restaurant Open; Tues-Sat; 12.00-14.00hrs & 19.00-

21.00. Accommodation available Tues-Sat.

6 Macknade Shell

Tel: (01795) 542910

1 mile east along the A2, on the left

Access, Visa, Mastercard, Switch, Diners Club, Amex, Overdrive, All Star, Dial Card, AA Paytrak, BP Supercharge, BP Agency, Esso Europe, Shell Cards. Open; Mon-Sat; 06.00-22.00hrs, Sun; 07.00-22.00hrs.

PLACES OF INTEREST

Faversham

website: www.faversham.org.

Follow the A251 north (Signposted 1 Mile)

A settlement was established here at least 2,000 years ago, the Romans constructed the first road, Watling Street, through the area and, following their withdrawal, the Jutes and Saxons took over. In 811AD King Kenulf granted it a charter and by mediaeval times it had become a thriving town and port. Well favoured by monarchs through the ages and known as the "King's Port" during the reign of Edward I, warships were constructed at the Creek and mediaeval warehouses still stand in the dock area.

Faversham was, and still is, a Limb of the Cinque Port of Dover, retaining the right to elect a Baron to the assembly of these ancient towns, and the prosperity of the area is intrinsically linked to the trading through the port. At various times in its history Faversham has dealt in everything from oysters to gunpowder and has not been averse to indulging in the odd smuggling activity either. The town is packed with over 400 listed buildings, including the 16thC Guildhall, Abbey Street, a complete and well preserved 16thC street, the 18thC Chart Gunpowder Mills (Tel: 01795-534542) as well as more modern examples such as the former London Chatham & Dover Railway engine sheds at the east end of Faversham Station.

Within the town centre ...

Fleur de Lis Heritage Centre & Tourist Information Office

13 Preston Street, Faversham ME13 8NS Tel: (01795) 534542 website: www.faversham.org

Located within a 15thC former inn, audio-visual, colourful displays and bygones are used to illustrate how the town has evolved. In this building the plot to murder Thomas Arden, the town's Mayor, in 1551, was hatched and upstairs is a doorway once used by James II. Run by the "Faversham Society", local walking tours can be arranged from here.

Brogdale World of Fruit

Brogdale Road, Faversham ME13 8XZ Tel: (01795) 535286

website: www.brogdale.org.uk

Follow the A251 north, turn left along the A2 and it is signposted along the route. (1.6 miles)

Home to The National Fruit Collection, the largest in the world, over 2,300 different varieties of apple, 550 of pear, 350 of plum, 220 of cherry and 320 varieties of bush fruits as well as smaller collections of nuts and vines are grown here in 150 acres of orchards. Not only spectacular in blossom time, they are also at their best in late summer and autumn when the ripe fruit is ready for picking. The Plant Centre is open throughout the year for the sale of trees, bushes and fruit. Miniature Railway. Gift Shop. Orchard Tea Rooms. Disabled access.

Maison Dieu

Ospringe St., Ospringe, Nr Faversham ME13 8TL Tel: (01795) 534542

Follow the A251 north and turn left along the A2 (1.2 Miles)

A half-timbered mediaeval building, dating from the 13thC, it was once part of a complex which served as a Royal Lodge, pilgrims hostel, hospital and almshouse for retired royal retainers. The interior houses a museum tracing the history of the area from Roman times, through the Saxon and mediaeval periods and includes some fascinating information about the house itself.

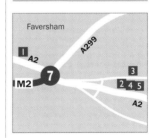

Nearest Westbound A&E Hospital

Medway Maritime Hospital

Windmill Road, Gillingham ME7 5NY Tel: (01634) 830000

Proceed west to Junction 4, follow the A278 north, turn left along the A2 into Gillingham and the hospital is signposted. (Distance Approx 20.0 miles)

Nearest Eastbound A&E Hospital

Kent & Canterbury Hospital
Ethelbert Road, Canterbury
CT1 3NG
Tel: (01227) 766877
Follow the A2 east into Canterbury and the hospital is signposted in the city.
(Distance Approx 8.2 miles)

FACILITIES

1   Macknade Shell

Tel: (01795) 542910
1 mile west along the A2, on the right
Access, Visa, Mastercard, Switch, Diners Club, Amex, Overdrive, All Star, Dial Card, AA Paytrak, BP Supercharge, BP Agency, Esso Europe, Shell Cards. Open; Mon-Sat; 06.00-22.00hrs, Sun; 07.00-22.00hrs.

2   Tenterden House B&B

Tel: (01227) 751593
0.7 miles east on the right in Boughton Street

3   The White Horse Restaurant & Hotel

Tel: (01227) 751343
0.9 miles east on the left in Boughton Street
(Shepherd Neame) Open all day. Meals served; 12.00-14.30hrs & 19.00-21.30hrs daily

4   The Garden Hotel & Vines Restaurant

Tel: (01227) 751411
0.9 miles east on the right in Boughton Street
Vines Restaurant Open; Mon-Sat; 12.00-15.00hrs & 19.00-21.00hrs, Sun; 12.00-15.00hrs

5   The Queen's Head

Tel: (01227) 751369
1 mile east on the right in Boughton Street
(Shepherd Neame) Open all day Fri, Sat & Sun. Meals served; 12.00-14.30hrs & 18.00-21.30hrs daily.

PLACES OF INTEREST

Farming World
Nash Court, Boughton Nr Faversham ME13 9SN
Tel: (01227) 751144

Follow the A2 east and it is signposted along the route (2.0 Miles)
Farming World, as well as Shire horses and rare breeds of domestic and farm animals on view, has a nature trail through delightful orchards and the opportunity to "pick your own" fruit and vegetables. There is also a Birds of Prey Centre, a farm-fresh produce and gifts stall, a Museum of Agricultural Memorabilia, and an exciting adventure playground and mini toddlers area. Picnic area. Refreshments. Disabled access.

MOTORWAY ENDS
(Total Length of Motorway
24.7 Miles)

---

the M3

This motorway forms the major road transport link between London and the south coast ports of Southampton and Portsmouth. Commencing at Junction 1, an end-on connection with the A316 in Sunbury, the carriageways run eastwards passing the **Queen Mary Reservoir**, the most southerly of a number of reservoirs stretching some 7 miles north to Datchet, on the north side and **Shepperton**, associated with the making of films since the 1930s, on the south. The motorway continues east, negotiating its way through numerous smaller lakes and reservoirs and crosses the River Thames before passing under the M25 at Junction 2. Between here and Junction 3, the route is screened with light woods as it crosses over **Chobham Common** and Sandhurst, the home of the famous **Sandhurst Military Academy** since 1807, is passed on the north side as the motorway reaches Junction 4. To the south of the short section between here and Junction 4A are the towns of **Farnborough**, where the first powered flight was made in this country in 1908 and is now the site of the Royal Aircraft Establishment and **Aldershot**, which has been an important army base since 1854. Between Junctions 4A and 5 the town of **Fleet** is passed on the south side.

Just east of Junction 5, on the south side, Butter Wood can be seen on the slopes of **Greywell Hill**. The Basingstoke Canal passes through this hill by means of the 1,230 yard long **Greywell Tunnel**. It was last used by a commercial boat in 1914 and although now closed and no longer navigable, as the result of subsequent roof falls, natural springs within the tunnel feed water to the restored section of the canal and the tunnel still finds use as a conservation site for the winter hibernation and breeding of several species of bats. **The Basingstoke Canal** opened in 1794 and ran for 37 miles between Basingstoke and the River Wey at Byfleet. Continuing south eastwards the motorway passes **Basingstoke** to the north before turning south at Junction 8 and running parallel to the A33 through heavily wooded areas, including **Mitcheldever Wood**. Approaching Junction 9 the carriageways crosses the River Itchen before **Winchester** and its magnificent Cathedral come into view on the west side between Junctions 9 and 10. Winchester, which can trace its history to at least 450BC, became the capital of England in 871AD. William the Conqueror commenced construction of the Cathedral in 1079 and commissioned the Domesday Book here in 1086.

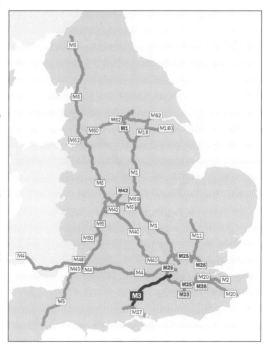

Westgate Museum, Winchester

The area immediately south east of Winchester is a nature reserve containing interesting archaeology and featuring wild flowers and rare butterflies, but despite protests from conservationists, the section between Junctions 9 and 10 was eventually built to pass through **St Catherine's Hill**, where Celtic tribes settled in 450BC, and **Twyford Down** both of which form an integral part of this conservation area. At Junction 11 the motorway crosses the River Itchen again and an interesting **abandoned railway viaduct** is on view on the west side. This viaduct carried the Didcot, Newbury & Southampton Railway line into Winchester from 1858 until 1966 and most of the trackbed within the city has been converted into public roads.

The section between Junctions 11 and 12 follows the route of the former A33 and involved rebuilding and expansion of the carriageways to motorway standard. The motorway continues south, slipping between **Chandlers Ford**, to the west and **Eastleigh**, to the east and utilizing the former A33 Chandlers Ford By-pass which opened in 1967 and was upgraded to motorway standard in 1993. Eastleigh expanded beyond all recognition (in a similar fashion to Crewe, Swindon and Doncaster) when it was selected as an ideal site for a major railway installation in the late 19thC. The London & South Western Railway moved its Carriage Works here in 1891, the Locomotive Works in 1910 and opened large engine sheds in 1903. The motorway ends at Junction 14 where it joins the M27 (Junction 4), the A27 and the A33 into the historic port of **Southampton**.

Location of Places of Interest

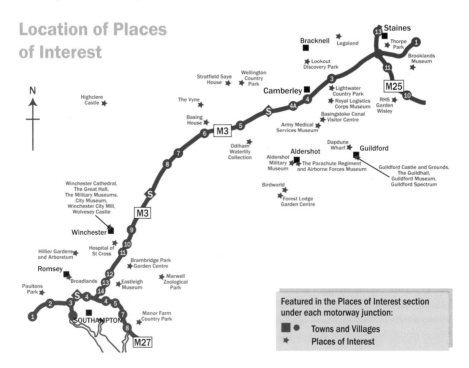

Featured in the Places of Interest section under each motorway junction:

■ ●   Towns and Villages

✳   Places of Interest

M3 JUNCTION 2

THIS JUNCTION IS A MOTORWAY INTERCHANGE WITH THE M25 ONLY AND THERE IS NO ACCESS TO ANY FACILITIES.

Nearest A&E Hospital

St Peter's Hospital

Guildford Road, Ottershaw, Chertsey KT16 0PZ
Tel: (01932) 872000
Proceed south [anti-clockwise] along the M25 to Junction 11 and follow the A317 south. The hospital is signposted from the junction (Distance Approx 3.9 miles)

M3 JUNCTION 3

THE TOWN OF BAGSHOT IS WITHIN ONE MILE OF THIS JUNCTION

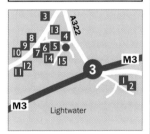

Lightwater

Nearest Westbound A&E Hospital

Frimley Green Hospital

Portsmouth Road, Frimley, Camberley GU16 5UJ
Tel: (01276) 604604
Proceed west to Junction 4 and the hospital is signposted from the junction (Distance Approx 5.3 miles)

Nearest Eastbound A&E Hospital

St Peter's Hospital

Guildford Road, Ottershaw, Chertsey KT16 0PZ
Tel: (01932) 872000
Proceed east to Junction 2 and follow the M25 south [anti-clockwise] to Junction 11. Follow the A317 south and the hospital is signposted from the junction (Distance Approx 10.8 miles)

FACILITIES

1 Red Lion

Tel: (01276) 472236
0.6 miles south in Lightwater, on the left
(Hampshire Pub Group) Meals served; Tues-Sat; 12.00-14.00hrs & 18.00-21.00hrs, Sun & Mon; 12.00-14.00hrs

2 BP Lightwater

Tel: (01276) 473114
0.8 miles south in Lightwater, on the left
Access, Visa, Overdrive, All Star, Switch, Dial Card, Mastercard, Amex, AA Paytrak, Diners Club, Delta, Routex, Shell Agency, BP Cards. Open; 06.30-22.00hrs daily

3 The Cricketers Inn

Tel: (01276) 473196
1 mile north along the A322, on the left (on the A30)
(Travel Inn) Open all day. Meals served; Mon-Fri; 12.00-15.00hrs & 18.00-22.00hrs, Sat & Sun; 12.00-22.00hrs

4 The White Hart

Tel: (01276) 473640
0.6 miles west along the road to Bagshot, on the right
(Unique Pub Company) Open all day. Meals served; Mon-Sat; 12.00-15.00hrs & 18.00-22.00hrs, Sun; 12.00-15.00hrs

5 The Three Mariners

Tel: (01276) 473768
0.7 miles west along the through road past Bagshot, on the left
(Perfect Pub Company) Open all day. Meals served; Mon-Sat; 12.00-15.00hrs, Sun; 12.00-17.00hrs

6 Safeway Filling Station Bagshot (BP)

Tel: (01276) 476469
0.8 miles west along the A30, on the left
LPG. Access, Visa, Delta, Mastercard, Switch, Diners Club, Amex, Electron, Solo, Overdrive, All Star, Dial Card, Shell Agency. BP Cards

7 Jack's of Bagshot

Tel: (01276) 473193
0.8 miles west along the A30, on the left
Open; 07.00-23.00hrs daily

8 Redflash Service Station (Total)

Tel: (01276) 473881
0.9 miles west along the A30, on the right
Access, Visa, Overdrive, All Star, Switch, Dial Card, Mastercard, Amex, Diners Club, Delta, Total/Fina/Elf Cards. Open; Mon-Sat; 07.00-22.00hrs, Sun; 08.00-22.00hrs

9 Mogul Indian Restaurant

Tel: (01276) 475114
0.9 miles west along the A30, on the right
Open; 12.00-14.30hrs & 18.00-23.30hrs daily

10 Windle Brook

Tel: (01276) 479942
1 mile west along the A30, on the right
(Brewers Fayre) Open all day. Meals served; Mon-Sat; 11.30-22.00hrs, Sun; 12.00-22.00hrs

11 The Fighting Cocks

Tel: (01276) 473160
1 mile west along the A30, on the left
(Carlsberg Tetley) Open all day

12 Belvedere Italian Restaurant

Tel: (01276) 475583
1 mile west along the A30, on the left
Open; Mon-Fri; 12.00-14.30hrs & 19.00-22.30hrs, Sat; 19.00-23.00hrs

13 The Old Barn Restaurant

Tel: (01276) 476673
1 mile north along the A30, on the right
Open; Sun-Tues; 11.00-23.00hrs, Wed-Sat; 11.00-0.00hrs

14 Hardy's Tex Mex Bar & Restaurant

Tel: (01276) 477477
0.8 miles west in Bagshot, on the right
Open; Sun-Thurs; 18.00-22.00hrs, Fri & Sat; 18.00-22.30hrs

15 Kings Arms

Tel: (01276) 473812
0.8 miles west in Bagshot, on the left
(Hungry Horse) Open all day. Meals served; 12.00-21.45hrs daily

PLACES OF INTEREST

Lightwater Country Park

The Avenue, Lightwater
GU18 5RG
Tel: (01276) 479582

Follow the A322 south (Signposted 0.4 Miles)
Lightwater Park, situated on the edge of Lightwater Village and extending for some 145 acres, was once part of the vast Bagshot Heath, which originally stretched as far as Bracknell and Windsor. The area occupied by the park has a recorded history dating back to Saxon times with the heathland being commonly used for sheep grazing and the 423ft high Curley Hill utilized as a source of gravel until 1910.

Today the heathland is a Site of Special Scientific Interest and a huge diversity of wildlife can be seen within the park which, apart from the heathland, also embraces habitats such as ponds, meadows, scrub and lowland bog.. There is a Heathland Trail, Nature Trail, and Bridleway and the facilities include a Children's Playground, Picnic areas, a Fitness Circuit, the Lightwater Leisure Centre (Tel: 01276-472662) and a Visitor Centre. Some disabled access.

The Royal Logistics Corps Museum

The Princess Royal Barracks, Deepcut, Camberley
GU16 6RW
Tel: (01252) 340871

Follow the A322 north, turn left along the A30 and then left along the B3015 to Deepcut (5.8 miles)
Incorporating the Royal Corps of Transport, Royal Army Ordnance Corps, Royal Pioneer Corps, Army Catering Corps and the Postal & Courier Service, this museum was built in 1995 to house the large collections amassed by the Trustees of the constituent Corps. Transport, clothing, accommodation, food, ammunition and communications are the solid foundations of any army and the displays and tableaux show how well it has been supported over some 500 years with all these essential elements to ensure that it serves as an efficient fighting force. Gift Shop. Disabled access.

The Lookout Discovery Park

Nine Mile Road, Bracknell
RG12 7QW

Follow the A322 north and it is signposted along the route (4.4 Miles)
For details please see Junction 10 (M4) Information.

M3 JUNCTION 4

Nearest A&E Hospital

Frimley Green Hospital

Portsmouth Road, Frimley,
Camberley GU16 5UJ
Tel: (01276) 604604

Follow the A331 south
(Signposted from the junction.
Distance Approx 1 mile)

FACILITIES

1 Sainsbury's Filling Station

Tel: (01276) 676829

0.5 miles north along the
A331, on the right

Access, Visa, Delta,
Mastercard, Switch, Amex,
Electron, Solo, Overdrive, All
Star, Dial Card, BP
Supercharge, Sainsbury's Fuel
Card. Disabled Toilets and
Cash Machines available in
adjacent store.

2 Ye Olde White Hart

0.8 miles east in Frimley town
centre, on the left

Meals served daily

3 Gallant Chinese Restaurant

Tel: (01276) 681321

0.8 miles east in Frimley town
centre, on the left

Open; Mon-Sat; 12.00-
14.00hrs & 18.00-23.00hrs

PLACES OF INTEREST

The Basingstoke Canal Visitor Centre

Mytchett Place Road, Mytchett,
Camberley GU16 6DD
Tel: (01252) 370073 website:
www.basingstoke-canal.co.uk

Follow the A331 south, turn
left towards Mytchett and it
is signposted along the route.
(2.7 Miles)

Considered to be one of
Britain's most beautiful
waterways, this restored canal
is not only a recreational
amenity but also a noted
wildlife habitat. The special
quality of the water has led to
the establishment of one of the
largest collections of aquatic
plants and invertebrates in the
country and this resulted in
most of the canal being
designated as a Site of Special
Scientific Interest in 1995.
There are plenty of
opportunities for pleasant
walks, fishing and boating trips
along its 32 miles through
unspoilt countryside and there
is a play area and picnic area
with camping and caravanning
facilities also available. Visitor
Centre. Tea Room.

Army Medical Services Museum

Keogh Barracks, Ash Vale,
Aldershot GU12 5RQ
Tel: (01252) 340212 e-mail:
museum@keogh72.freeserve.co.uk

Take the A331 south, turn left
towards Mytchett, follow the
signboards for "Basingstoke
Canal Visitor Centre" and it is
signposted along the route.
(2.9 Miles)

Having taken part in every
campaign and battle fought by
the British Army since 1660,
this museum relates the story
of the dedication and gallantry
of the Royal Army Medical
Corps and its forefathers, the
Army Nursing Services, the
Royal Army Dental Corps and
the Royal Veterinary Corps.
Exhibits include a display of
over 20 Victoria Crosses
awarded to the services,
Florence Nightingale's carriage
and some of her other
artefacts, dental instruments

used on Napoleon as well as a
fine collection of uniforms. Gift
Shop. Disabled access.

Aldershot

Tourist Information Centre,
Aldershot Military Museum,
Queens Avenue, Aldershot
GU11 2LG Tel: (01252) 320968

**Follow the A321 south and
continue along the A325
(Signposted 5.8 Miles)**

Originally just a small village of
some 800 inhabitants, the
decision by the Army in 1854
to establish a major camp here
has led it to become a town
with a population of 55,000. As
a result of this concentration,
there are two important
military museums within
Aldershot

The Parachute Regiment & Airborne Forces Museum

Browning Barracks, Aldershot
GU11 2BU Tel: (01252) 349619

(Signposted within the town)

It was the army at Aldershot
who pioneered flying in Britain,
building their aircraft sheds at
nearby Farnborough where the
Royal Aircraft Establishment is
sited today. This museum
traces the history of military
aviation from those pioneering
days, through the two world
wars and the establishment of
the British Airborne Forces in
1940 to the present day.
Amongst the many interesting
exhibits are displays of
equipment and dioramas. Gift
Shop. Disabled access.

Aldershot Military Museum

Queens Avenue, Aldershot
GU11 2LG Tel: (01252) 314598

(Signposted within the town)

The history of the expansion of
Aldershot is related in this
museum, devoted to the
communities of the Aldershot

Military Town and the adjoining civil towns of Aldershot and Farnborough. Located in the middle of the Army Camp and housed within the last two surviving Victorian barrack blocks, the exhibits include a Victorian Barrack Room and an Edwardian kitchen as well as displays of military hardware and a feature on Samuel Franklin Cody who made the first powered flight in this country, at Farnborough in 1908. Light refreshments. Picnic Area. Gift Shop. Disabled access.

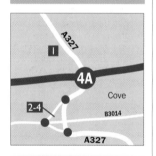

JUNCTION 4A

Nearest A&E Hospital

Frimley Green Hospital
Portsmouth Road, Frimley, Camberley GU16 5UJ
Tel: (01276) 604604

Proceed east to Junction 4 and the hospital is signposted from the junction (Distance Approx 3.1 miles)

FACILITIES

1 Crown & Cushion

Tel: (01252) 545253
0.4 miles north along the A327, on the left
(Punch Retail) Open all day. Meals served; Mon-Sat; 12.00-

15.00hrs & 17.00-21.00hrs, Sun; 12.00-18.00hrs

2 TCS Fleet Service Station (Total)

Tel: (01252) 772630
1 mile south along the road to Cove, on the left
Access, Visa, Overdrive, All Star, Switch, Dial Card, Mastercard, Amex, AA Paytrak, Diners Club, Delta, Total/Fina/ Elf Cards. Open; Mon-Sat; 06.00-23.00hrs, Sun; 07.00-23.00hrs

3 Harvester at Fleet

Tel: (01252) 816655
1 mile south along the road to Cove, on the left
(Six Continents) Open all day on Sun. Meals served; Mon-Sat; 12.00-14.30hrs & 17.00-21.00hrs, Sun; 12.00-21.00hrs

4 Wayfarer's Lodge

Tel: (01252) 774600
1 mile south along the road to Cove, on the left

BETWEEN JUNCS 4A & 5

FLEET SERVICES (WESTBOUND) (WELCOME BREAK)
Tel: (01252) 621656
Burger King, KFC, The Granary Restaurant, La Brioche Doree French Café, Red Hen Restaurant, Kenco Coffee Bar, Days Inn and Shell Fuel

FLEET SERVICES (EASTBOUND) (WELCOME BREAK)
Tel: (01252) 621656 McDonald's,

The Granary Restaurant & Shell Fuel

FOOTBRIDGE CONNECTION BETWEEN SITES

JUNCTION 5

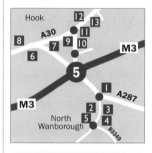

Nearest Westbound A&E Hospital

North Hampshire Hospital
Aldermaston Road, Basingstoke RG24 9NA
Tel: (01256) 473202

Proceed west to Junction 6, follow the A339 north and the hospital is signposted along the route. (Distance Approx 7.5 miles)

Nearest Eastbound A&E Hospital

Frimley Green Hospital
Portsmouth Road, Frimley, Camberley GU16 5UJ
Tel: (01276) 604604

Proceed east to Junction 4 and the hospital is signposted from the junction (Distance Approx 10.6 miles)

FACILITIES

1 The Lord Derby

Tel: (01256) 702283
0.6 miles south along the A287, on the north side of the roundabout

(Free House) Meals served; 12.00-14.00hrs & 19.00-21.30hrs daily

2   Bluebeckers Mill House

Tel: (01256) 702953

0.7 miles south along the B3349, on the right in North Warnborough

(Bluebeckers & Edwins) Meals served; Mon-Fri; 12.00-14.30hrs & 17.30-22.00hrs, Sat & Sun; 12.00-15.00hrs & 17.30-22.30hrs

3   The Jolly Miller

Tel: (01256) 702085

0.7 miles south along the B3349, on the left in North Warnborough

(Free House) Open all day. Bar snacks served all day. Meals served; Mon-Thurs; 11.30-14.30hrs & 18.30-22.00hrs, Fri & Sat; 11.30-22.00hrs, Sun; 12.00-22.00hrs

4   Q8 North Warnborough

Tel: (01256) 701620

0.9 miles south along the B3349, on the left in North Warnborough

Access, Visa, Overdrive, All Star, Switch, Dial Card, Mastercard, Amex, Diners Club, Delta, Q8 Cards

5   The Swan

Tel: (01256) 702727

0.9 miles south along the B3349, on the right in North Warnborough

(Free House) Meals served; Mon & Wed-Sat; 12.00-14.30hrs & 18.30-20.30hrs, Sun; 12.00-14.30hrs

6   Gate of India Restaurant

Tel: (01256) 761216

0.8 miles west along the A287, on the left

Open; Mon-Sat; 18.00-23.30hrs, Sun; 12.00-15.00hrs & 18.00-22.00hrs

7   Dorchester Arms

Tel: (01256) 762690

0.8 miles west along the A287, on the right

(Eldridge Pope) Open all day, every day, during summer and on Saturdays in winter. Meals served; Mon-Fri; 12.00-14.00hrs & 19.00-21.00hrs, Sat; 12.00-14.30hrs & 19.00-21.00hrs, Sun; 12.00-15.00hrs.

8   Hanover International Hotel

Tel: (01256) 764161

1 mile west along the A30, on the right

Restaurant Open; Mon-Sat; 07.00-10.00hrs, 12.30-14.30hrs & 19.00-21.45hrs, Sun; 08.00-10.30hrs, 12.30-14.30hrs & 19.00-21.45hrs.

9   Hook Tandoori Restaurant

Tel: (01256) 764844

0.7 miles north along Station Road on the left, in Hook

Open; Mon-Sat; 18.00-23.30hrs, Sun; 18.00-22.30hrs

10 The Raven Hotel

Tel: (01256) 762541

0.7 miles north along Station Road on the right, in Hook

(Greene King) Open all day. Restaurant Open; Mon-Sat;

12.00-14.30hrs & 18.30-22.00hrs, Sun; 12.00-14.30hrs. Bar Snacks available; 12.00-14.30hrs & 18.30-22.00hrs daily.

11 White Hart Hotel

Tel: (01256) 762462

0.8 miles east along the A30 on the right, in Hook

(Punch Retail) Open all day. Bar snacks served all day. Meals served; Mon-Sat; 12.00-14.30hrs & 18.30-21.30hrs, Sun; 12.00-21.00hrs.

12 Albany Service Station (Total)

Tel: (01256) 763612

0.9 miles east along the A30 on the left, in Hook

Access, Visa, Mastercard, Switch, Diners Club, Amex, Overdrive, All Star, Dial Card, Delta, Total/Fina/Elf Cards. Open; 07.00-22.00hrs daily

13 Star Hook (Texaco)

Tel: (01256) 740660

0.9 miles east along the A30 on the right, in Hook

LPG. Access, Visa, Mastercard, Switch, Electron, Solo, Diners Club, Amex, Overdrive, All Star, Dial Card, Delta, UK Fuelcard, Texaco Cards. Open; 06.30-22.30hrs daily.

PLACES OF INTEREST

Birdworld

Holt Pound, Farnham GU10 4LD Tel: (01420) 22140 website: www.birdworld.co.uk

Take the A287 south and follow the brown and white cockatoo sign boards. (12.3 Miles)

Located within extensive gardens, this impressive bird sanctuary is the largest Bird Park in the country. Featuring a full range of exotic and domestic varieties, the attractions include the Penguin Island, a Parrots in Flight Aviary and Underwater World, full of colourful aquatic fish and reptiles, as well as the Jenny Wren Farm where children can meet all the farm animals. Visitors can enjoy a ride on The Safari Train and there are numerous play and picnic areas within the site. Gift Shop. Restaurant. Disabled access.

Adjoined by ...

Forest Lodge Garden Centre

Holt Pound, Farnham GU10 4LD Tel: (01420) 23275

A previous winner of the Garden Centre of the Year Award, as well as four Awards of Merit from the Garden Centre Association for excellence, Forest Lodge is set in 6.5 glorious acres. More in the style of a large garden than an ordinary garden centre, each area flows naturally into the next and there is a full selection of indoor and outdoor plants including a fine collection of specimen varieties. The Squirrel's Pantry Restaurant. Gift Shop. Disabled access.

Odiham Waterlily Collection

Wychwood, Farnham Road, Odiham, Hook RG29 1HS Tel: (01256) 702800 e-mail: cnhenley@aol.com

Follow the A287 east. (2.8 Miles)

Started in 1961, the Odiham Waterlily Collection is based on 8 raised ponds, each containing some 33 waterlilies and all within easy visiblity, particularly for visitors in wheelchairs. Over the years it

has grown to become the largest collection of Hardy Waterlilies in the world and since 1989 has been registered with the National Council for the Conservation of Plants and Gardens. Plants, including waterlilies and marginals can be purchased at the adjacent Wychwood Waterlily Farm. Disabled access

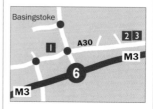

JUNCTION 6

Nearest A&E Hospital

North Hampshire Hospital
Aldermaston Road, Basingstoke RG24 9NA Tel: (01256) 473202
Follow the A339 north and the hospital is signposted along the route. (Distance Approx 2.9 miles)

FACILITIES

1   Basingstoke Hilton

Tel: (01256) 460460
1 mile west along the A30, on the right
Restaurant Open; Mon-Fri; 07.00-10.00hrs, 12.00-14.00hrs & 19.00-22.00hrs, Sun; 08.00-10.30hrs, 12.00-14.00hrs & 19.00-22.00hrs

2   Alan Gibson (Esso)

Tel: (01256) 355221
1 mile east along the A30, on the left

Access, Visa, Mastercard, Switch, Diners Club, Amex, Overdrive, All Star, Dial Card, Delta, AA Paytrak, Shell Gold, Esso Cards. Open; 07.00-22.00hrs daily.

3   Oliver's Restaurant

Tel: (01256) 321018
1 mile east along the A30, on the left
Open; 12.00-22.00hrs daily

PLACES OF INTEREST

Basing House

Redbridge Lane, Basing, Basingstoke RG24 7HB Tel: (01256) 467294 e-mail: musmat@hants.gov.uk

Follow the A30 east (Signposted 1.1 Miles)

The magnificent Tudor fortified mansion of Basing House was built in 1530 by the first Marquis of Winchester on the site of two previous castles, one Saxon and the other Norman. Queen Elizabeth I stayed here twice, the second occasion lasted for 13 days and proved to be so ruinously expensive that the host had to demolish part of the house to pay for it. It was beseiged for three years by Cromwell's troops during the Civil War before being captured in 1645 and razed to the ground.

Excavations at the site have revealed many items dating back to the Iron Age and these are housed in the New Museum, whilst the Old Museum, built on the site of the original powder magazine, contains examples of Tudor and Elizabethan crafts and artefacts. Other attractions include a restored garden, towers, earthworks, a tunnel and the great barn that survived the Civil War siege. Picnic Area. Gift Shop. Disabled access.

The Vyne [NT]

Sherborne St John,
Nr Basingstoke RG24 9HL
Tel: (01256) 883858 website:
www.nationaltrust.org.uk/
regions/southern

**Take the A339 north, follow
the signboards to
"Basingstoke District
Hospital", and it is
signposted along this route
(5.9 Miles)**

The name probably originates
from a Roman vine-growing
estate on the site and the
present Tudor mansion of brick
and stone was built between
1500 and 1520 for Lord
Sandys, a Chancellor to Henry
VIII. The chapel, with
Renaissance glass, and
panelled long gallery date from
this period and it was the first
building to acquire a classical
portico when Chaloner Chute,
Speaker in the House of
Commons, altered the house in
1654 to the designs of John
Webb. Further alterations were
carried out in the 1760s with
the installation of a Palladian
staircase and decoration of
some rooms in the rococo
style.

The house is set in 17 acres of
classic English parkland with
extensive lawns, lakes,
herbaceous borders, a
Summerhouse garden, wild
garden and woodland walks.
Restaurant. Shop. Full Disabled
access to gardens and partial
access to house.

JUNCTION 7

Nearest Westbound A&E Hospital

Royal Hampshire County Hospital

Romsey Road, Winchester
SO22 5DG

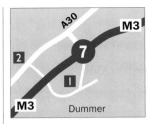
Dummer

Tel: (01962) 863535
Proceed west to Junction 9 and
follow the signs to Winchester.
Turn right along the B3330 and
proceed along the B3331 and
B3040 and the hospital is
signposted along the route.
(Distance Approx 14.6 miles)

Nearest Eastbound A&E Hospital

North Hampshire Hospital

Aldermaston Road,
Basingstoke RG24 9NA
Tel: (01256) 473202
Follow the A30 north, turn left
along the A340 and the
hospital is signposted along
the route. (Distance Approx 5.8
miles)

FACILITIES

1 The Queen Inn

Tel: (01256) 397367
**0.5 miles south in Dummer,
on the right**
(Unique Pub Company) Meals
served; Mon-Sat; 11.30-
14.30hrs & 18.30-21.30hrs,
Sun; 12.00-15.00hrs & 10.00-
21.30hrs.

2 The Sun Inn

Tel: (01256) 397234
**1 mile south along the A30,
on the right**
(CCC Leisure [Courage]) Open
all day Fri, Sat & Sun. Meals
served; Mon-Thurs; 12.00-
14.30hrs & 17.30-21.30hrs, Fri
& Sat; 12.00-21.30hrs, Sun;
12.00-20.00hrs.

JUNCTION 8

**THIS IS A RESTRICTED
ACCESS JUNCTION**
- Vehicles can only exit along the
westbound lanes and travel west
along the A303
- Vehicles can only enter along
the eastbound lanes from the
A303 east carriageway

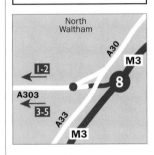

Nearest Westbound A&E Hospital

Royal Hampshire County Hospital

Romsey Road, Winchester
SO22 5DG
Tel: (01962) 863535
Proceed west to Junction 9 and
follow the signs to Winchester.
Turn right along the B3330 and
proceed along the B3331 and
B3040 and the hospital is
signposted along the route.
(Distance Approx 12.4 miles)

Nearest Eastbound A&E Hospital

North Hampshire Hospital

Aldermaston Road,
Basingstoke RG24 9NA
Tel: (01256) 473202
Proceed east to Junction 7,
follow the A30 north, turn left
along the A340 and the hospital
is signposted along the route.
(Distance Approx 8.7 miles)

FACILITIES

1 Little Chef

Tel: (01256) 397761
0.8 miles west along the A303, on the right (Actual distance 2.8 miles).
Open; 07.00-22.00hrs daily.

2 Mitcheldean Service Station (Esso)

Tel: (01256) 397448
0.8 miles west along the A303, on the right (Actual distance 2.8 miles)
LPG. Access, Visa, Mastercard, Switch, Diners Club, Amex, Overdrive, All Star, Dial Card, Delta, Shell Gold, BP Supercharge, Esso Cards.

3 Little Chef

Tel: (01256) 398490
0.9 miles west along the A303, on the left.
Open; 07.00-22.00hrs daily

4 Burger King
Tel: (01256) 398490
0.9 miles west along the A303, on the left.
Open; 10.00-21.00hrs daily

5 BP Popham

Tel: (01256) 397160
0.9 miles west along the A303, on the left
Access, Visa, Overdrive, All Star, Switch, Dial Card, Mastercard, Amex, AA Paytrak, Diners Club, Delta, Routex, Shell Agency, BP Cards.

M3 BETWEEN JUNCS 8 & 9

WINCHESTER SERVICES (WESTBOUND) (ROAD CHEF)
Tel: (01962) 791135.
Costa Coffee, Wimpy, Dr Beaks Chicken, En Route Self Service Restaurant, Travel Inn & Texaco Fuel

WINCHESTER SERVICES (EASTBOUND) (ROAD CHEF)
Tel: (01962) 791135.
Costa Coffee, Wimpy, Dr Beaks Chicken, En Route Self Service Restaurant & Texaco Fuel

M3 JUNCTION 9

WINCHESTER CITY CENTRE IS WITHIN ONE MILE OF THIS JUNCTION

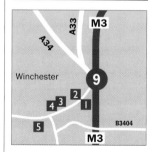

Nearest A&E Hospital
Royal Hampshire County Hospital
Romsey Road, Winchester
SO22 5DG
Tel: (01962) 863535
Follow the signs to Winchester, turn right along the B3330 and proceed along the B3331 and B3040 (Signposted along route. Distance Approx 2.5 miles)

FACILITIES

1 Tesco Filling Station

Tel: (01962) 749400
0.1 miles west along Easton Lane, on the left
Access, Visa, Mastercard, Switch, Amex, Overdrive, All Star, Dial Card, Delta, AA Paytrak, UK Fuelcard, BP Supercharge, Tesco Fuelcard. Cash Machines available in adjacent store (Open 24hrs)

2 Shell Winnall

Tel: (01962) 876810
0.1 miles west along Easton Lane, on the right.
Access, Visa, Overdrive, All Star, Switch, Dial Card, Mastercard, Amex, AA Paytrak, Diners Club, Delta, BP UK Agency, Shell Cards.

3 First In, Last Out

Tel: (01962) 865963
0.7 miles west along Easton Lane, on the right.
(Punch Taverns) Open all day. Meals served; 12.00-14.30hrs & 18.00-21.00hrs daily

4 The Ship

Tel: (01962) 852892
0.8 miles west along Wales Street, on the right.
(Elders Pope) Open all day. Meals served; Mon-Sat: 12.00-14.00hrs.

5 Willow Tree

Tel: (01962) 877255
0.9 miles west along Wales Street, on the left
(Greene King) Open all day Fri, Sat & Sun. Meals served; Mon-Sat 12.00-14.30hrs & 18.00-22.00hrs, Sun 12.00-15.00hrs.

PLACES OF INTEREST

Winchester

Winchester Tourist Information Office, Guildhall, The Broadway, Winchester SO23 9LJ
Tel: (01962) 840500 website: www.winchester.gov.uk

Follow the signs to Winchester (2 miles)

Sited on the River Itchen, Winchester was an important city even in pre-Roman times. Celtic tribes settled on St Catherine's Hill in 450BC and Iberians, Britons and Belgae became occupiers of the town of Caer Gwent (White City) that was subsequently established. In 70AD the Romans commenced the fortification of the city with the construction of a wall and renamed it Venta Belgarum but, following their withdrawal in 400AD the city, as did most of England, descended into the chaos of the Dark Ages.

It was the arrival of the Saxons in the 7thC that firmly fixed Winchester into the fabric of English history when Christianity was established here by King Cynegils in 635AD and King Alfred made the city his capital in 871AD. In 1066, the city fell to William the Conqueror who built a palace and a castle, commissioned the construction of the present Cathedral in 1079 and compiled the great survey of England, the Domesday Book, in 1086.

For the next 700 years or so, Winchester prospered through its Royal patronage and many of the fine buildings constructed in this period can be seen throughout the town. The 14thC Pilgrim Hall, part of the original Pilgrim School which provided lodgings for pilgrims to the shrine of St Swithun is in The Close and the 12thC Hospital of St Cross is at St Cross just south of the city centre.

The oldest school in England, Winchester College in College Street (Tel: 01962-621209) was founded in 1382 by William of Wykeham, Lord Chancellor and Bishop of Winchester, whilst the Peninsula Barracks, home of the Military Museums, were built on the site of the King's House, the only part of a grand palace commissioned by Charles II that saw completion.

Within the city can be found ...

Winchester Cathedral

1 The Close, Winchester SO23 9LS
Tel: (01962) 857224 website: www.winchester-cathedral.org.uk

The first cathedral, of Saxon origin, was built in the 7thC and replaced in 1079 by William the Conqueror with the largest Cathedral in England, being some 556ft long and 88ft wide at the choir. Additions and alterations were made in 1189, 1346, 1367 and 1404 with other modifications being subsequently carried out from time to time and major repair work took place in the early 1900s when rotting timbers were replaced by masonry at the east end; a hazardous operation that took 6 years and had to be undertaken by a diver, William Walker.

Within the cathedral, there are many fine carvings, superbly crafted masonry and rich decorations such as those employed in the Bishop Waynflete's Chantry of 1486. Relics housed here include bones of early kings such as Canute and Rufus whilst the library contains the illuminated Winchester Bible, a 10thC copy of Bede's history and the first American Bible. Mary Tudor married Philip of Spain here on July 25th, 1554 and amongst those buried at the cathedral are Jane Austen (1775-1817), who resided at No.8 College Street for the last six weeks of her life, and Izaak Walton (1593-1683). The Visitor Centre, which details its history, also has a gift shop and restaurants. Disabled access.

The Great Hall

Castle Avenue, Winchester SO23 8PJ Tel: (01962) 846476

This is the only surviving part of Winchester Castle that was constructed by William the Conqueror following the fall of the city in 1066 and laid seige to and destroyed by the Parliamentarians in 1651. Henry III was born in the castle in 1207 and the Great Hall, built in 1235, was the scene of many Parliaments and great trials; Sir Walter Raleigh was tried here in 1603 and Judge Jeffreys held a "Bloody Assize" in 1685. The building now houses the Round Table which, although purporting to be connected to the legend of King Arthur, is of mediaeval origin rather than from the 8thC, the period during which he is believed to have existed. Shop. Disabled access.

The Military Museums

Peninsula Barracks, Romsey Road, Winchester SO23 8TS

Within this site are four major military museums;

The King's Royal Hussars Museum in Winchester (Tel: 01962-828541) which details the history of three famous Cavalry Regiments and includes a display on The Charge of the Light Brigade during the Crimean War.

The Light Infantry Museum (Tel: 01962-828550) which shows the story of a modern Regiment and includes features on recent conflicts such as the Gulf War.

The Gurkha Museum (Tel: 01962-828536) showing their historic and heroic service to the British Crown and details of Nepal, their homeland.

The Royal Green Jackets Museum (Tel: 01962-828549) with displays of campaigns conducted over five continents and a magnificent diorama of Waterloo.

And, at Serle's House, Southgate Street, Winchester SO23 9EG ...

The Royal Hampshire Regiment Museum (Tel: 01962-863658) which details the history of the Regiment from its formation in 1702.

All museums have a gift shop and disabled access.

City Museum

The Square, Winchester SO23 9ES Tel: (01962) 848269 website: www.winchester.gov.uk/heritage/home.htm

Re-opened in 2000 after extensive refurbishment, the museum displays local archaeology and the history of the city through to modern times. Exhibits include parts of Roman mosaic floors, 1stC grave finds, coins minted in the city, mediaeval pottery and reconstructed Victorian shops as well as original drawings by Sir Christopher Wren for Charles II's Winchester Palace, which was only partially completed, and some personal belongings of Jane Austen. Disabled access.

Winchester City Mill [NT]

Bridge Street, Winchester SO23 8EJ Tel: (01962) 870057 website: www.winchestercitymill.co.uk

Constructed in 1744, the mill spans the River Itchen and has a small island garden and exceptional mill races. Milling demonstrations are conducted from time to time. Gift Shop.

Wolvesey Castle (Old Bishop's Palace)

College Street, Winchester SO23 9NB Tel: (01962) 854766

The residence of the Bishops of Winchester since 963AD the remains date back to the 14thC when it was considered to be one of the grandest buildings in mediaeval England. Alongside it is the present palace, of which one wing remains (not open to the public), and was constructed by Wren for Bishop Morley in 1684. Gift Kiosk. Light Refreshments. Limited disabled access.

Hospital of St Cross

St Cross Road, Winchester SO23 9SD Tel: (01962) 851375

Follow the signposts into Winchester, take the B3335 south and it is signposted along the route (2.9 Miles)
Founded in 1136 by Bishop Henry of Blois, half brother to King Stephen, this fine complex of mediaeval almshouses was originally built to accommodate 13 poor men and in 1445 a second foundation, for men of "noble poverty" was added by Cardinal Beaufort.

The 25 inmates of the Hospital wear traditional and distinctive dress; Those of the Blois foundation, nowadays aged men, have a black gown, mediaeval cap and display a silver cross of St John on the left breast whilst the men of "noble poverty" wear a mulberry coloured gown, cardinal's hat and tassels. Both are regular sights in Winchester today. The Church, Brethren's Hall and Kitchen and the Master's Garden are open to visitors who may also request the Wayfarer's Dole, a sliver of bread and a small portion of beer served in a horn mug with a glass bottom. Café. Gift Shop. Disabled access.

M3
JUNCTION 10

THIS IS A RESTRICTED ACCESS JUNCTION
- Vehicles can only enter along the westbound lanes
- Vehicles can only exit along the eastbound lanes

WINCHESTER CITY CENTRE IS WITHIN ONE MILE OF THIS JUNCTION

Nearest Westbound A&E Hospital
Royal Hampshire County Hospital
Romsey Road, Winchester SO22 5DG
Tel: (01962) 863535
Proceed west to Junction 11, follow the A3090 north and turn right along the B3040 (Signposted along route. Distance Approx 4.0 Miles)

Nearest Eastbound A&E Hospital
Royal Hampshire County Hospital
Romsey Road, Winchester SO22 5DG
Tel: (01962) 863535
Follow the B3330 north, turn left along the B3331 and continue along the B3040 (Signposted along route. Distance Approx 2.2 miles)

FACILITIES

1 BP St Cross

 £

Tel; (01962) 855032
1 mile west along St Cross Road (B3335) on the right
LPG. Access, Visa, Mastercard, Switch, Diners Club, Amex, Overdrive, All Star, Dial Card, Shell UK, BP Cards. Open; 07.00-22.00hrs daily

2 Mrs RA Blockley B&B

Tel: (01962) 852073
1 mile west along St Cross Road (B3335), on the left

3 Queen Inn

Tel: (01962) 853898
1 mile west along Kingsgate Road, on the left
(Greene King) Meals served; Mon-Sat; 11.00-14.15hrs & 18.00-21.00hrs, Sun; 12.00-14.00hrs & 18.00-21.00hrs.

4 Murco Filling Station

Tel: (01962) 865760
0.3 miles north along Bar End Road (B3330), on the left
Access, Visa, Delta, Mastercard, Switch, Diners Club, Amex, Overdrive, All Star, Dial Card, Murco Cards.

PLACES OF INTEREST

Winchester

Follow the B3330 north (Signposted 1 mile)

Within the city can be found ...

Winchester Cathedral

1 The Close, Winchester
For details please see Junction 9 information

The Great Hall

Castle Avenue, Winchester
For details please see Junction 9 information

The Military Museums

Peninsula Barracks, Romsey Road, Winchester SO23 8TS
For details please see Junction 9 information

City Museum

The Square, Winchester
For details please see Junction 9 information

Winchester City Mill [NT]

Bridge Street, Winchester
For details please see Junction 9 information

Wolvesey Castle (Old Bishop's Palace)

College Street, Winchester
For details please see Junction 9 information

Hospital of St Cross

St Cross Road, Winchester SO23 9SD

Take the Garnier Road exit west, turn left at the end along the B3335 (St Cross Rd) and it is signposted along the route (1.4 Miles)
For details please see Junction 9 information

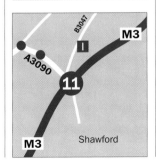

Nearest A&E Hospital

Royal Hampshire County Hospital
Romsey Road, Winchester SO22 5DG
Tel: (01962) 863535
Follow the A3090 north and turn right along the B3040 (Signposted along route. Distance Approx 2.9 Miles)

FACILITIES

1 The Bell Inn

Tel: (01962) 865284
1 mile north along the B3335, on the right
(Greene King) Open all day Fri & Sat. Meals served; Mon-Tues & Thurs-Sat; 12.00-14.00hrs & 18.00-20.00hrs, Wed & Sun; 12.00-14.00hrs

PLACES OF INTEREST

Winchester

Follow the A3090 west and turn right along the B3335 (Signposted 2.8 miles)
For details please see Junction 9 information

Within the city can be found ...

Winchester Cathedral

1 The Close, Winchester SO23 9LS
For details please see Junction 9 information

The Great Hall

Castle Avenue, Winchester SO23 8PJ
For details please see Junction 9 information

The Military Museums

Peninsula Barracks, Romsey Road, Winchester SO23 8TS

For details please see Junction 9 information

City Museum

The Square, Winchester

For details please see Junction 9 information

Winchester City Mill [NT]

Bridge Street, Winchester

For details please see Junction 9 information

Wolvesey Castle (Old Bishop's Palace)

College Street, Winchester

For details please see Junction 9 information

Hospital of St Cross

St Cross Road, Winchester

Follow the A3090 west, turn right along the B3335 and it is signposted along the route (1.1 miles)

For details please see Junction 9 information

Marwell Zoological Park

Colden Common,
Nr Winchester SO21 1JH
Tel: (01962) 777407
website: www.marwell.org.uk

Follow the B3335 south (Signposted 5.7 Miles)

Fine specimens of birds, reptiles, mammals, insects, fish and plants from around the world are on view here, with many of the animals rare, endangered or extinct in the wild. There are children's amusements, an adventure playground, a free road train and play and picnic areas. Gift Shop. Restaurant. Disabled access.

JUNCTION 12

Nearest Northbound A&E Hospital

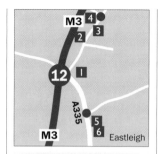

Eastleigh

Royal Hampshire County Hospital

Romsey Road, Winchester
SO22 5DG
Tel: (01962) 863535

Proceed to Junction 11, follow the A3090 north and turn right along the B3040 (Signposted along route. Distance Approx 6.3 Miles)

Nearest Southbound A&E Hospital

Southampton General Hospital

Tremona Road, Shirley
SO16 6YD
Tel: (023) 8077 7222

Proceed to Junction 14, follow the A33 south, bear right along the A35 and it is signposted along the route (Distance Approx 6.1 Miles)

FACILITIES

1   The Otter

Tel: (023) 8025 2685
0.2 miles north along the Otterbourne Road, in Boyatt Lane on the right
(Whitbread) Open all day. Meals served; Mon-Sat; 11.00-14.30hrs & 18.00-21.30hrs, Sun; 12.00-14.30hrs & 18.00-22.30hrs

2   The White Horse

Tel: (01962) 712830
0.7 miles north along the Otterbourne Road, on the left,
in Otterbourne
(Interbrew) Open all day. Meals served; Mon-Sat; 12.00-14.30hrs & 18.00-21.00hrs, Sun; 12.00-18.00hrs.

3   The Old Forge

Tel: (01962) 717191
0.9 miles north along the Otterbourne Road, on the right, in Otterbourne
(Six Continents Retail) Open all day. Meals served; Mon-Sat; 12.00-22.00hrs, Sun; 12.00-21.00hrs

4   Williams Convenience Store, Garage & Post Office (Esso)

Tel (01962) 713150
1 mile north along the Otterbourne Road, on the left, in Otterbourne
Access, Visa, Mastercard, Switch, Diners Club, Amex, Overdrive, All Star, Dial Card, Delta, UK Fuelcard, BP Super-charge, Shell Gold, Esso Cards. Open; 07.00-22.00hrs daily

5   The Ham Farm

Tel: (023) 8061 9181
1 mile south along the A335, on the left
(Harvester) Open all day Sat & Sun. Meals served; Mon-Fri; 12.00-14.30hrs & 17.00-21.15hrs, Sat; 12.00-22.00hrs, Sun; 12.00-21.00hrs

6   Travelodge

Tel: (023) 8061 6813
1 mile south along the A335, on the left

PLACES OF INTEREST

Brambridge Park Garden Centre

Kiln Lane, Brambridge, Eastleigh
SO50 6HT
Tel: (01962) 713707

Follow the A335 south, turn left along the B3335 and turn left at the second crossroads (2.5 Miles)

Originally part of the estate of the 18thC Brambridge House, the old walled garden is now occupied by the Brambridge Park Garden Centre. Apart from those on sale, there are displays of exotic plants and "World Gardens" a series of plots laid out in the various styles adopted in other countries. The surrounding woods and meadows are also part of the garden centre and this conservation area has a nature trail to help visitors explore the wildlife at close quarters. "Country House" Coffee Shop. Gift Shop. Disabled access

M3

JUNCTION 13

VEHICLES ENTERING THE M3 SOUTHBOUND CANNOT ACCESS THE M27 EASTBOUND

EASTLEIGH TOWN CENTRE IS WITHIN ONE MILE OF THIS JUNCTION

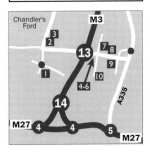

Nearest Northbound A&E Hospital

Royal Hampshire County Hospital

Romsey Road, Winchester
SO22 5DG
Tel: (01962) 863535

Proceed to Junction 11, follow the A3090 north and turn right along the B3040 (Signposted along route. Distance Approx 8.8 Miles)

Nearest Southbound A&E Hospital

Southampton General Hospital

Tremona Road, Shirley
SO16 6YD
Tel: (023) 8077 7222

Proceed to Junction 14, follow the A33 south, bear right along the A35 and it is signposted along the route (Distance Approx 4.2 Miles)

FACILITIES

1   Asda Filling Station

Tel: (023) 8026 8341
1 mile south along Bournemouth Road (B3043), on the left
Access, Visa, Delta, Mastercard, Switch, Diners Club, Amex, Electron, Solo, Overdrive, All Star, Dial Card, Asda Card. Toilets and Cash Machines available in adjacent store. Open; 06.00-0.00hrs daily. (24hr Credit Card operated pumps available when kiosk is closed)

2   Rowles Garage (Esso)

Tel: (023) 8025 5432
0.6 miles north along Bournemouth Road (B3043), on the right
Access, Visa, Mastercard, Switch, Diners Club, Amex, Overdrive, All Star, Dial Card, Delta, UK Fuelcard, BP Supercharge, Esso Cards.

Open; Mon-Fri; 06.30-22.30hrs, Sat & Sun; 08.00-21.00hrs.

3   The Hut

Tel: (023) 8026 6626
0.6 miles north along Bournemouth Road (B3043), on the right
(Beefeater) Open all day. Meals served; 12.00-21.00hrs daily

4   The Gateway

Tel: (023) 8065 0541
Adjacent to the motorway junction, on the A335
(Brewers Fayre) Open all day. Meals served; Mon-Sat; 11.30-22.00hrs, Sun; 12.00-22.00hrs

5   Travel Inn

Tel: (023) 8065 0541
Adjacent to the motorway junction, on the A335

6   Holiday Inn Eastleigh

Tel: 0870 400 9075
0.2 miles east along Leigh Road (A335), on the right

7   The Leigh

Tel: (023) 8061 2174
0.2 miles east along Leigh Road (A335), on the left
(Enterprise Inns) Open all day. Meals served; Sun-Thurs; 12.00-16.00hrs & 18.00-21.00hrs, Fri; 12.00-18.00hrs, Sat; 12.00-15.00hrs.

8   The Guest House

Tel: (023) 8039 8401
0.3 miles east along Leigh Road (A335), on the left.

9   The Good Companions

Tel: (023) 8062 9001
0.6 miles east along Leigh

Road (A335), on the right
(Courage) Open all day. Meals
served; Sun-Fri; 12.00-
14.30hrs

**10   Monks Brook Service
Station (Total)**

Tel: (023) 8064 1722
**0.5 miles south along
Passfield Avenue, on the left**
Access, Visa, Mastercard,
Switch, Diners Club, Amex,
Overdrive, All Star, Dial Card,
Delta, UK Fuelcard, Total/Fina/
Elf Cards. Open; Mon-Fri; 06.30-
23.00hrs, Sat; 07.00-23.00hrs,
Sun; 07.00-22.00hrs.

PLACES OF INTEREST

Eastleigh Museum

25 High Street, Eastleigh
SO50 5LF Tel: (023) 8064 3026
e-mail: musmst@hants.gov.uk

**Follow the A335 east (1.4
Miles)**

Eastleigh was established as a
railway town when the London &
South Western Railway moved
its workshops here from Nine
Elms in London. The Carriage
Works opened in 1891, the
Locomotive Works in 1910 and
with large engine sheds opening
in 1903 it became one of the
most important railway centres
in the country. This integral part
in the life of the town is reflected
in the museum's themes of a
typical Victorian terraced house,
home to Mr Brown, an engine
driver, and his wife Mrs Brown as
it would have looked in the
1930s, a display on the Erecting
Shops at the works and a mock-
up of the footplate of the former
Southern Railway's No.828, a
Class S15 4-6-0 locomotive built
at Eastleigh prior to WWII. Light
Refreshments. Gift Shop.
Disabled access.

JUNCTION 14

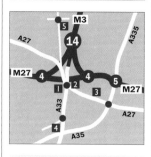

Nearest A&E Hospital
**Southampton General
Hospital**
Tremona Road, Shirley
SO16 6YD
Tel: (023) 8077 7222
Proceed to Junction 14, follow
the A33 south, bear right along
the A35 and it is signposted
along the route (Distance
Approx 4.2 Miles)

FACILITIES

**1   Clock Service Station
(Total)**

Tel: (023) 8076 3100
**0.1 miles north along the
A27, on the left**
Access, Visa, Overdrive, All
Star, Switch, Dial Card,
Mastercard, Amex, AA Paytrak,
Diners Club, Delta, Total/Fina/
Elf Cards.

2   Hilton Southampton

Tel: (023) 8070 2700
**0.2 miles north along the
A27, on the right**
The Britisserie Restaurant
Open; Breakfast; Mon-Fri;
07.00-10.00hrs, Sat & Sun;
07.00-10.30hrs, Lunch; Sun-
Fri; 12.00-14.00hrs, Dinner;
19.00-21.30hrs daily

3   Stoneham Arms

Tel: (023) 8058 6732
**0.8 miles east along the A27,
on the left**
(Enterprise Inns) Open all day.
Meals served; 12.00-15.00hrs
daily

4   Basset House

Tel: (023) 8076 6972
**1 mile south along the A33,
on the right**

5   Asda Filling Station

Tel: (023) 8026 8341
**1 mile north along
Bournemouth Road, on the
right**
Access, Visa, Delta,
Mastercard, Switch, Diners
Club, Amex, Electron, Solo,
Overdrive, All Star, Dial Card,
Asda Card. Toilets and Cash
Machines available in adjacent
store. Open; 06.00-0.00hrs
daily. (24hr Credit Card
operated pumps available
when kiosk is closed)

PLACES OF INTEREST

Southampton

**Follow the A33 south
(Signposted 2 Miles)**
For details please see Junction
5 (M27) information

> **MOTORWAY ENDS AND ALSO
> MERGES WITH THE M27**
> (Total Length of Motorway 57.1
> Miles)

the M4

Linking London, Bristol and South West Wales, the M4 is the principal east-west route in the southern half of England. The motorway commences at Junction 1 with an end-on connection to the A4 at Chiswick via a flyover which opened in 1959, and heads due west along a 1.5 miles long viaduct. To the south, planes can be seen circling whilst waiting to land at **Heathrow Airport** and, after crossing the M25 at Junction 4B, the carriageways pass between the **Queen Mother Reservoir** (the most northerly of a number of reservoirs stretching some 7 miles south to Sunbury) on the south side and **Ditton Park** to the north. Ditton Park was the manorial seat of the Montague family and some of the very first experiments in the development of radar were conducted in the grounds by Robert Watson-Watt prior to World War II.

Further west, at Junction 6, **Windsor Castle**, one of a ring of defences established around London by William the Conqueror, dominates the skyline to the south as it overlooks Windsor and Eton. **Eton College** is one of the oldest schools in England, having been founded in the 15thC. Between Junctions 6 and 7 **Slough**, famous for its massive trading estate, is on the north side and the River Thames is bridged just before Junction 8/9. **Maidenhead**, one of the original stops on the London to Bath coaching route, is passed to the north. Between Junctions 10 and 12, **Reading**, the County Town of Berkshire, is on the north side and at the west end of Junction 11 the modern lines of the Madejski Stadium, the home ground of Reading FC (and currently London Irish RUFC) which

opened in August 1998, can be seen to the north. Reading was the scene of a fierce battle between the Danes and Saxons in King Alfred's day and, in the 12ᵗʰC, Parliament was assembled here on several occasions. One of Reading Jail's most famous residents was Oscar Wilde who survived the harsh treatment and managed to write *De Profundus* and *The Ballad of Reading Jail* during his two years of occupancy. Just before Junction 12 the motorway passes through a series of small lakes adjoining the River Kennett and the Kennett & Avon Canal after it bridges the former Great Western Railway main line.

The motorway continues westwards across the North Wessex Downs through Wiltshire to **Swindon** which it by-passes on the south side of the town between Junctions 15 and 16. Swindon has a history going back to the days of Sweyn, father of Canute, but it was the arrival of the Great Western

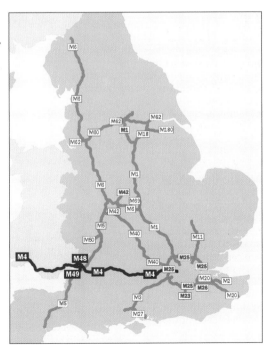

River Thames, Sonning

Railway that transformed it into a bustling town with the construction of a large railway works and extensive engine sheds which opened on January 1st, 1843. A few miles before Junction 17, on the south side, is RAF Lyneham (from which military aircraft can frequently be seen taking off and landing) hidden behind the hill. Continuing west the motorway skirts past the north side of Bristol before turning north west at Junction 19, where it connects with the M32, and crosses the M5 at Junction 20, the Almondsbury Interchange. **Bristol** has been a major crossing point since Saxon times but it was during the Middle Ages that the city became established as a major seaport and trading centre.

At Junction 21 the motorway splits into two with the M48 (the original M4) veering to the north west and the M4 continuing on a slightly more direct route south westwards before they both cross the River Severn by means of two spectacular bridges. Designated on its current site as the first crossing as long ago as 1947, the M48 opened on September 8th, 1966 and is effected by two main structures; the **Severn Suspension Bridge** and the **Wye Bridge & Viaduct**. The suspension bridge is sited between Aust Cliff and Beachley Peninsula, where the River Severn is almost exactly one mile wide at high water, and the main span is 3,240ft. Over 126,000 yards^3 of concrete and 18,500 tons of steel were utilized in the construction which commenced in 1961. The Wye Bridge, a cable-stayed structure with a main span of 770ft, crosses the River Wye and the South Wales to Gloucester railway line between Beachley and Chepstow.

On the M4, the easternmost end of the bridge crosses over the path of the **Severn Tunnel**, the longest rail tunnel in Britain at 4 miles 628 yards and built by Isambard Kingdom Brunel for the Great Western Railway. The crossing here is effected by the **Second Severn Crossing**, a Cable Stayed Bridge, the construction of which commenced in early 1992. The overall length of the structure is 3 miles 127 yds with the main span having a length of 1,496ft (just 20ft longer than the Queen Elizabeth II Bridge on the A282/M25) and 418,000 yards^3 of concrete and 30,000 tons of steel were utilized. The bridge was formally opened on June 5th, 1996.

The two motorways link up on the west side of the river at Junction 23 where it continues westwards as the M4. At Junction 25A the River Usk is bridged and **Newport** is on view on the south side before the carriageways pass under Brynglas through the 330 yard long Crindau Tunnel, the first motorway tunnel in Britain. Newport was originally a Bronze Age settlement and developed into a significant town through Roman and Norman times. The town possesses a transporter bridge, one of only five examples of this design still in existence in the world. **The Monmouthshire & Brecon Canal**, which opened in 1796, is bridged and the River Ebbw is crossed

Clifton Suspension Bridge, Bristol

Castell Coch

before **Cardiff** is passed on the south side between Junctions 30 and 32. Cardiff became the richest coal-exporting city in the world during the 19thC and is now the capital of the Principality of Wales, thanks to the entrepreneurial skill of the Marquess of Bute, home to the Welsh Assembly and a thriving centre for sport and culture.

Just west of Junction 30 **Ruperra Castle** is in view to the north on the side of the 580ft high Coed Criag Ruperra This four storey tall make-believe castle, was completed in 1626 by Sir Thomas Morgan and rebuilt in 1785 following a fire. It was restored in 1909, abandoned in 1935 and taken over for army billeting in 1941. On December 6th of that year the interior was totally destroyed by a fire and all that remains today are the walls. **Tongwynlais** can be seen on the north side of Junction 32 with the fairy tale **Castell Coch**, built for the 3rd Marquess of Bute, nestling in the trees on the hillside above the town.

As the motorway proceeds westwards panoramic views south across to **St Fagans**, famous for its castle and Museum of Welsh Life, can be seen before it passes **Bridgend** on the south side and turns north at Junction 37 to follow the coastline to Port Talbot. Bridgend, known in Welsh as *Pen-y-Bontar Ogwr* (the crossing of the River Ogmore) was once regarded as so vital a route that no less than two castles were constructed here, one on each side of the river. Between Junctions 38 and 40, the **Corus Steel Plant** is visible on the west side and the bizarre edifice of **Margam Castle** can be seen amongst the trees in Margam Country Park to the east. The castle was constructed as a Tudor & Gothic style folly in 1840 for Christopher Rice Mansel Talbot and was badly destroyed by a fire in 1977.

Between Junctions 40 and 41 **Port Talbot** is on the west side with the floodlights of the Talbot Athletic Ground, home of Aberavon RUFC, clearly in view. Port Talbot was named after the Talbot family who developed the docks in the 19thC and in the 1960s British Steel and the British Transport Docks Board constructed a new deep water harbour here. A viaduct then bridges the River Avan, with **Aberavon** on the west side and the 850ft high **Mynydd Dinas** on the east. Aberavon, now part of Port Talbot, was the site of an 11thC castle erected by Caradoc, son of Jeslyn ab Cwrgan, a Welsh prince.

Beyond Junction 41 the motorway climbs out of Port Talbot and a long viaduct carries it over the River Neath and Outer Basin with views west to **Baglan** and **Swansea Bay** and east to **Briton Ferry**. The River Tawe is bridged at Junction 45 as it veers west and **Swansea**, once an important port with significant ship-building and copper smelting industries and the birth place of Dylan Thomas, is passed along its north side between Junctions 45 and 47 before the motorway turns north to terminate at **Pont Abraham** at Junction 49 and forms an end-on connection with the A48 to Carmarthen and the A483 to Ammanford.

Swansea Marina

Location of Places
of Interest

LONDON

M25

Stanley Spencer Gallery

Uxbridge

Maidenhead

Eton College

Slough

Wireless Museum

Basildon Park

Beale Park

7

6

5

4

3

2

1

The Living Rainforest

Dorney Court

Windsor

M4

13

Reading

A329(M)

M4

14

Windsor Castle

12

10

13

Newbury

11

Bracknell

Legoland

M25

Museum of English Rural Life

Lookout Discovery Park

Stratfield Saye House

Wellington Country Park

Highclere Castle

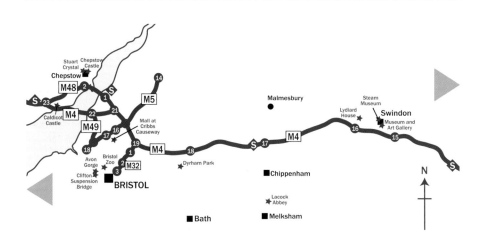

Stuart Crystal

Chepstow Castle

Chepstow

14

M48

2

S

M5

Malmesbury

Steam Museum

S

23

1

Lydiard House

Swindon

Caldicot Castle

M4

22

21

Museum and Art Gallery

M49

16

Mall at Cribbs Causeway

M4

16

15

17

18

19

M4

18

17

M4

Avon Gorge

Bristol Zoo

2

M32

Dyrham Park

N

Clifton Suspension Bridge

3

BRISTOL

Chippenham

Lacock Abbey

Bath

Melksham

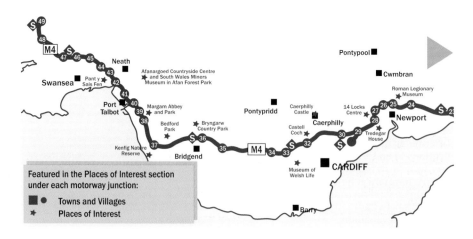

S

49

48

M4

47

46

45

Neath

Pontypool

Cwmbran

44

43

Afanargoed Countryside Centre and South Wales Miners Museum in Afan Forest Park

Roman Legionary Museum

Swansea

Pant y Sais Fen

42

Port Talbot

41

40

39

Margam Abbey and Park

Pontypridd

Caerphilly Castle

14 Locks Centre

27

26

25

24

S

38

Bedford Park

Bryngarw Country Park

Caerphilly

28

Newport

Kenfig Nature Reserve

37

36

35

M4

34

Castell Coch

33

32

30

29

Tredegar House

Bridgend

Museum of Welsh Life

31

S

CARDIFF

Barry

**Featured in the Places of Interest section
under each motorway junction:**

■ ● Towns and Villages

✳ Places of Interest

M4 JUNCTION 2

THIS IS AN URBAN MOTORWAY AND A VARIETY OF FACILITIES ARE WITHIN EASY REACH OF THIS JUNCTION

Nearest A&E Hospital
The Ealing Hospital
Uxbridge Road, Southall
UB1 3HW
Tel: (020) 8967 5000
Follow the A4 west, turn right along the A3002 and continue along the A4020. The hospital is on the left. (Distance Approx 3.6 miles)

M4 BETWEEN JUNCS 2 & 3

HESTON SERVICES (WESTBOUND) (MOTO)
Tel: (020) 8580 2000
Fresh Express Self Service Restaurant, Burger King, Harry Ramsden's, Travelodge & BP Fuel

HESTON SERVICES (EASTBOUND) (MOTO)
Tel: (020) 8580 2000
Little Chef, Burger King, Travelodge & BP Fuel

M4 JUNCTION 3

THIS IS AN URBAN MOTORWAY AND A VARIETY OF FACILITIES ARE WITHIN EASY REACH OF THIS JUNCTION

Nearest A&E Hospital
The Ealing Hospital
Uxbridge Road, Southall
UB1 3HW
Tel: (020) 8967 5000
Follow the A312 north and turn right along the A4020. The hospital is on the right.
(Distance Approx 4.1 miles)

M4 JUNCTION 4

THIS IS AN URBAN MOTORWAY AND A VARIETY OF FACILITIES ARE WITHIN EASY REACH OF THIS JUNCTION

Nearest A&E Hospital
Hillingdon Hospital
Pield Heath Road, Hillingdon
UB8 3NN
Tel: (01895) 238282
Follow the A408 north, turn right along the B465 and left along the A437. (Distance Approx 2.7 Miles)

M4 JUNCTION 4B

THIS JUNCTION IS A MOTORWAY INTERCHANGE WITH THE M25 ONLY AND THERE IS NO ACCESS TO ANY FACILITIES

Nearest A&E Hospital
Wexham Park Hospital
Wexham Road, Slough
SL2 4HL
Tel: (01753) 633000
Proceed west to Junction 5 and take the A4 exit north. Turn right along the A412 and the hospital is signposted.
(Distance Approx 6.4 Miles)

M4 JUNCTION 5

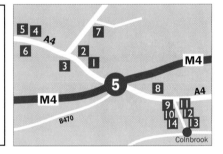

Nearest A&E Hospital
Wexham Park Hospital
Wexham Road, Slough
SL2 4HL
Tel: (01753) 633000
Take the A4 exit north, turn right along the A412 and the hospital is signposted.
(Distance Approx 4.3 Miles)

FACILITIES

1 Toby Carvery, Langley
Tel: (01753) 591212
0.2 miles north along the A4, on the right.
(Six Continents) Open all day. Bar Meals served; Mon-Sat; 12.00-22.00hrs. Carvery; Open; Mon-Fri; 12.00-14.00hrs

& 17.00-22.00hrs, Sat & Sun; 12.00-23.30hrs.

2 Inn Keeper's Lodge, Langley

Tel: (01753) 5912120.
0.2 miles north along the A4, on the right.
(Six Continents)

3 The Montagu Arms

Tel: (01753) 543009
0.3 miles north along the A4, on the left.
(Harvester) Open all day. Meals served; Sun-Thurs; 12.00-22.00hrs, Fri & Sat; 12.00-23.00hrs

4 St Francis House

Tel: (01753) 578888
1 mile north along the A4, on the right

5 Slough East Service Station (Total Fina)

Tel: (01753) 574041
1 mile north along the A4, on the right.
Keyfuels, Access, Visa, Overdrive, All Star, Switch, Dial Card, Mastercard, Amex, AA Paytrak, Diners Club, Delta, BP Supercharge, Total/Fina/Elf Cards. Open; 06.00-23.00hrs daily. Hot Snacks available.

6 Tesco Express Filling Station (Esso)

Tel: (01753) 671679
1 mile north along the A4, on the left.
Access, Visa, Delta, Mastercard, Switch, Diners Club, Amex, Electron, Solo, Overdrive, All Star, Dial Card, Esso Cards. Open; 06.00-0.00hrs daily

7 BP Langley Connect

Tel: (01753) 583058
0.7 miles east along Parlaunt Road, on the right.
Access, Visa, Overdrive, All Star, Switch, Dial Card, Mastercard, Amex, AA Paytrak, Diners Club, Delta, Routex, BP Cards, Shell Agency. Wild Bean Café. Open; 07.00-23.00hrs daily.

8 BP Brands Hill Connect

Tel: (01753) 545531
0.3 miles south along the A4, on the left.
LPG. Access, Visa, Overdrive, All Star, Switch, Dial Card, Mastercard, Amex, AA Paytrak, Diners Club, Delta, Routex, BP Cards, Shell Agency. Wild Bean Café.

9 Quality Hotel Heathrow

Tel: (01753) 684001
0.4 miles south along the A4, on the right.
The Season Brasserie Open; Mon-Fri; 06.30-22.00hrs, Sat & Sun; 07.30-22.00hrs. Bar Meals served 10.30-23.00hrs daily

10 Brands Hill Lodge

Tel: (01753) 680377
0.6 miles south along the Colnbrook Road, on the right

11 Regent House

Tel: (01753) 683093
0.6 miles south along the Colnbrook Road, on the left

12 Gibtel Café

Tel: (01753) 683093
0.6 miles south along the Colnbrook Road, on the left.
Open; Mon; 07.00-15.00hrs, Tues-Thurs; 07.00-20.00hrs, Fri; 07.00-15.00hrs, Sat; 07.00-

12.00hrs.

13 The Crown

Tel: (01753) 682026
0.8 miles south along the Colnbrook Road, on the left.
(Punch Taverns) Meals served; Mon-Sat; 12.00-15.00hrs & 19.00-21.00hrs

14 Golden Cross Service Station (BP)

Tel: (01753) 686321
1 mile south along the Colnbrook Road, on the right.
Access, Visa, Overdrive, All Star, Switch, Dial Card, Mastercard, Amex, AA Paytrak, Diners Club, Delta, Routex, BP Cards, Shell Agency. Open; Mon-Sat; 06.00-21.00hrs, Sun; 08.00-21.00hrs.

PLACES OF INTEREST

Museum of Ancient Wireless & Historic Gramophone Apparatus

Tel: (01753) 542242

Follow the B470 west (2 Miles) Open by Appointment Only.

Located in Datchet, this small private museum features a unique and fascinating collection of vintage wireless, gramophone, phonograph, telephone, wire and tape-recording apparatus. The enthusiastic innovator Capt. Maurice Seddon, also renowned as the inventor of medical heated clothing, is on hand to share his considerable expertise and opinions (in any one of five languages) with visitors. The extensive collection includes a large stock of redundant, but serviceable, spare parts many of which are available for sale.

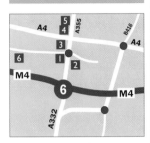

M4 JUNCTION 6

Nearest A&E Hospital

Wexham Park Hospital

Wexham Road, Slough
SL2 4HL
Tel: (01753) 633000
Follow the A355 north, turn right along the A4 and left along the B416. The hospital is signposted. (Distance Approx 3.8 Miles)

FACILITIES

1 Copthorne Hotel Slough/Windsor

Tel: (01753) 516222
0.3 miles north along the A355, on the left.
The Verandah Restaurant; Breakfast; Mon-Fri; 06.30-10.00hrs, Sat & Sun; 07.30-11.00hrs, Lunch; Mon-Fri; 12.00-14.00hrs, Dinner; 18.30-22.00hrs daily. Bar Meals served 10.00-22.00hrs daily.

2 Courtyard Slough/ Windsor Marriott Hotel

Tel: (01753) 551551
0.3 miles north along the A355, on the right.
The Brasserie; Breakfast; Mon-Fri; 06.30-09.30hrs, Sat & Sun; 07.30-11.00hrs, Lunch; Mon-Fri; 12.30-14.00hrs, Dinner; 18.30-22.30hrs daily. Bar Meals

served 10.00-22.00hrs daily.

3 Gino's Grill Café & Restaurant

Tel: (01753) 531868
0.7 miles north along the A355, on the left.
Open; Mon-Fri; 07.00-15.30hrs, Sat; 07.00-14.00hrs.

4 The Three Tuns

Tel: (01753) 521911
0.7 miles north along the A355, on the left.
(Scottish & Newcastle) Open all day. Meals served; Mon-Fri; 12.00-15.00hrs & 18.00-21.00hrs, Sat; 12.00-15.00hrs, Sun; 12.00-16.00hrs. Bar Snacks available all day.

5 Farnham Road Service Station (Total)

Tel: (01753) 534848
0.9 miles north along the A355, on the left.
Access, Visa, Overdrive, All Star, Switch, Dial Card, Mastercard, Amex, Diners Club, Delta, Total/Fina/Elf Cards.

6 The Earl of Cornwall

Tel: (01753) 578333
1 mile west along Cippenham Lane, on the left.
(Laurel Pub Company) Open all day. Meals served; 12.00-14.00hrs daily.

PLACES OF INTEREST

Eton College & Museum of Eton Life

High Street, Eton SL4 6DW
Tel: (01753) 671177
website: www.etoncollege.com

Follow the A332 south. (Signposted 1.4 Miles)
Founded in 1440 by Henry VI,

Eton College is one of the oldest schools in the country. Although the architecture is mainly of the 16thC with additions in 1889, earlier buildings such as the Lower School and Long Chamber of 1500 and the chapel, constructed between 1476 and 1482, are on view. The library, which stands on the site of the south cloisters and was erected in 1730, contains many rare manuscripts, including the original of Gray's Elegy. Still a bastion of privilege and a foundation stone of the British Establishment many political and commercial leaders can be counted amongst its former pupils.

Windsor Castle

Windsor SL4 1NJ Visitor Office
Tel: (01753) 868286
website: www.royal.gov.uk.

Follow the A332 south (Signposted 2 Miles)
Following the Norman Conquest of England in 1066 a strategic ring of defences was established around London, each of one days march apart and one days march from the Tower of London, at the centre. A stronghold of earth and timber was constructed on a steep chalk hill overlooking the River Thames at Windsor and it was quickly rebuilt in stone to a plan much as it is seen today. Improved and enlarged over the ages it was following the restoration of the monarchy and under Charles II that the role of the castle changed from that of a fortification to a royal palace.

The state apartments contain some of the finest works of art, armour, pictures and interiors in the world and it was part of this section that was destroyed by a fire in November 1992. Ironically, it was this fire that signalled a shift in the relationship between the Royal family and the public. The Government's immediate response to underwrite all the costs of repairs was met with a nationwide disbelief as to why taxpayers should have to bail out one of the world's richest women, and this feeling was endorsed when a national appeal raised very little. Today, partially as a result of the proceeds raised from the opening of Buckingham Palace to visitors, the £37m restoration has been completed.

Legoland Windsor

Winkfield Road, Windsor SL4 4AY
Tel: 08705 040404
website: www.legoland.co.uk.

Follow the A332 south (Signposted 3.3 Miles)
An 150 acre major children's adventure park packed with exciting rides, hands-on features, displays and exhibitions all with the Lego theme and designed to enhance creativity, fun, development, play and learning. Restaurants. Gift Shops. Disabled access.

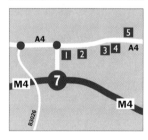

JUNCTION 7

Nearest A&E Hospital

Wexham Park Hospital,
Wexham Road, Slough SL2 4HL Tel: (01753) 633000
Proceed east to Junction 6, follow the A355 north, turn right along the A4 and left along the B416. The hospital is signposted. (Distance Approx 5.5 Miles)

FACILITIES

1   The Huntercombe

Tel: (01628) 663177
Adjacent to south east side of roundabout.
(Unique Pub Co) Open all day. Meals served; Sun; 12.00-16.00hrs. Bar snacks served all day daily.

2   Kai Leung Chinese Restaurant

Tel: (01628) 666411
0.3 miles east along the A4, on the right.
Open: Mon-Fri; 12.00-14.00hrs & 18.00-23.00hrs, Sat & Sun; 18.00-23.00hrs.

3   KFC

Tel: (01628) 603020
0.4 miles east along the A4, on the right.
Open: Sun-Thurs; 11.30-0.00hrs, Fri/Sat & Sat/Sun; 11.30-01.00hrs

4   Slough West Service Station (Esso)

Tel: (01628) 666877
0.5 miles east along the A4, on the right.
Access, Visa, Overdrive, All Star, Switch, Dial Card, Mastercard, Amex, AA Paytrak, Diners Club, Delta, BP Supercharge, Shell Gold, Esso Cards.

5   McDonald's

Tel: (01753) 531816
0.8 miles east along the A4, on the left.
Open; 07.00-23.00hrs daily

PLACES OF INTEREST

Dorney Court

Dorney, Nr Windsor SL4 6QP
Tel: (01628) 604638
website: www.dorneycourt.co.uk

Follow the A4 west and turn left along the B3026 (1.4 Miles)
Built in c1440, Dorney Court is one of the finest Tudor Manor Houses in England. The rooms contain 15th & 16thC oak, beautiful 17thC lacquer furniture and 400 years of history of the family who still live here. The very first pineapple to be raised in England was grown here and presented to Charles II in 1661. Visitors can enjoy lunch or afternoon tea in the walled garden at the Plant Centre and, during June to September, there is the opportunity to pick-your-own fruit and vegetables. Gift Shop. Limited disabled access.

JUNCTION 8/9

Nearest Eastbound A&E Hospital

Wexham Park Hospital
Wexham Road, Slough SL2 4HL
Tel: (01753) 633000
Proceed to Junction 6, follow the A355 north, turn right along the A4 and left along the

B416. The hospital is signposted. (Distance Approx 8.7 Miles)

Nearest Westbound A&E Hospital

Royal Berkshire Hospital

London Road, Reading
RG1 5AN
Tel: (0118) 987 5111

Proceed to Junction 10, follow the A329(M) north and turn left along London Road (Signposted from end of A329[M]. Distance Approx 12.5 Miles)

FACILITIES

1   Brayswick Service Station (Esso)

Tel: (01628) 623315
0.8 miles north along the A308, on the right.
Access, Visa, Overdrive, All Star, Switch, Dial Card, Mastercard, Amex, Diners Club, Delta, Shell Gold, Esso Cards.

2   Empire Of India Restaurant

Tel: (01628) 624100
0.8 miles north along the A308, on the right.
Open; 12.00-14.00 & 18.00-0.00hrs daily

3   The Old Coach House

Tel: (01628) 671244
0.8 miles north along the A308, on the right

PLACES OF INTEREST

Stanley Spencer Gallery

King's Hall, High Street, Cookham on Thames, Berkshire SL6 9SJ
Tel: (01628) 471885

website: www.cookham.com

Follow the A308(M) and A308 north, turn right along the A4 and left along the B4442 to Cookham. (Signposted in Cookham area, 5 Miles)

The gallery is exclusively devoted to the works of Sir Stanley Spencer, who died in 1959, and is unique in Britain inasmuch as it is in the village of his birthplace. Located in the former Victorian Methodist Chapel that he used to attend as a child, there are also displays, memorabilia and artefacts devoted to his life. The gallery contains a permanent collection of his work and over a thousand pictures have been shown since it opened in 1962. Sales Desk. Disabled access.

JUNCTION 10

> **THIS JUNCTION IS A MOTORWAY INTERCHANGE WITH THE A329(M) ONLY AND THERE IS NO ACCESS TO ANY FACILITIES**

Nearest A&E Hospital

Royal Berkshire Hospital

London Road, Reading
RG1 5AN
Tel: (0118) 987 5111

Follow the A329(M) north and turn left along London Road (Signposted from end of A329[M]. Distance Approx 5.2 Miles)

PLACES OF INTEREST

Look Out Discovery Park

Nine Mile Ride, Bracknell
RG12 7QW Tel: (01344) 354400

website: www.bracknell-forest.gov.uk/lookout

Follow the A329(M) south (Signposted from motorway 5.9 Miles)

A hands-on science and nature exhibition featuring over 70 exhibits, including a hot air balloon. Set within 2,600 acres of woodland there are nature walks and mountain bike trails, with bikes available for hire. There is also a children's adventure playground, Coffee Shop and Gift Shop.

JUNCTION 11

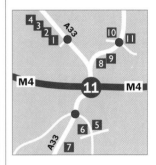

Nearest A&E Hospital

Royal Berkshire Hospital

London Road, Reading RG1 5AN   Tel: (0118) 987 5111

Take the A33 north and turn right along the A4. (Distance Approx 2.9 Miles)

FACILITIES

1   Millennium Madejski Hotel

Tel: (0118) 945 1100
0.7 miles north along the A33, on the left.
Le Café Brasserie Open; Breakfast; 06.30-10.30hrs, Lunch; 12.00-14.30hrs,

Dinner; 18.30-22.00hrs daily.
The Cilantro Restaurant; Open;
Mon-Sat; 19.00-22.00hrs

2 Pizza Hut

Tel: (0118) 945 1100
**0.8 miles north along the
A33, on the left in Reading
Gate Retail Park.**
Open; 12.00-23.00hrs daily

3 McDonald's

Tel: (0118) 975 2343
**0.8 miles north along the
A33, on the left in Reading
Gate Retail Park.**
Open; 08.00-23.00hrs daily

4 KFC

Tel: (0118) 957 3541
**0.8 miles north along the
A33, on the left in Reading
Gate Retail Park.**
Open; Sun-Thurs; 11.30-
0.00hrs, Fri/Sat & Sat/Sun;
11.30-01.00hrs

5 The Swan

Tel: (0118) 988 3674
**0.5 miles south along the
Basingstoke Road, on the left
in Three Mile Cross.**
(Free House) Open all day Mon-
Sat. Meals served; Mon-Sat;
12.00-15.00hrs & 18.00-
22.00hrs, Sun; 12.00-
15.00hrs & 19.00-22.30hrs.

6 Roman Road Service Station (BP)

Tel: (0118) 988 2334
**0.5 miles south along the
Basingstoke Road, on the
right in Three Mile Cross.**
LPG. Access, Visa, Overdrive,
All Star, Switch, Dial Card,
Mastercard, Amex, AA Paytrak,
Diners Club, Delta, Routex, BP
Cards, Shell Agency. Open;
07.00-22.00hrs daily

7 Swallowfields Service Station (Repsol)

Tel: (0118) 988 6065
**1 mile south along the A33,
on the left.**
Keyfuels, Access, Visa,
Overdrive, All Star, Switch, Dial
Card, Mastercard, Amex, AA
Paytrak, Diners Club, Delta, BP
Supercharge, Repsol Card.
Toilets available between
07.00-20.00hrs only.

8 Little Chef

Tel: (0118) 931 3465
**0.4 miles north along the
B3031, on the right.**
Open; 07.00-22.00hrs daily

9 Shell Fairfield

Tel: (0118) 922 4500
**0.5 miles north along the
B3031, on the right.**
LPG. Access, Visa, Overdrive,
All Star, Switch, Dial Card,
Mastercard, Amex, Diners Club,
Delta, BP Agency, Shell Cards.

10 Holiday Inn Reading South

Tel: 0870 400 9067
**0.8 miles north along the
B3031, on the left.**
Restaurant Open; Breakfast;
Mon-Fri; 06.30-10.00hrs, Sat &
Sun; 07.30-11.00hrs, Lunch;
Sun-Fri; 12.30-14.30hrs,
Dinner; Mon-Sat; 18.30-
22.30hrs, Sun; 18.300-
21.30hrs.

11 Whitley Wood Garage (BP)

Tel: (0118) 931 0785
**0.9 miles north along the
B3031, on the right.**
Access, Visa, Delta,
Mastercard, Switch, Diners
Club, Amex, Overdrive, All Star,
Dial Card, Shell Agency, BP

Cards. Open; Mon-Sat; 06.00-
22.00hrs, Sun; 07.00-22.00hrs

PLACES OF INTEREST

Museum of English Rural Life

University of Reading,
Whiteknights, Reading RG6 6AG
Tel: (0118) 931 8663
website: www.ruralhistory.org

**Follow the B3350 east and
turn left along the A327 (2.6
Miles)**
Established in 1951 by
Reading University as a centre
of information and research on
all aspects of country living,
the museum contains farm
implements, tools and
domestic equipment. There is
also a records resource
including manuscripts,
photographs, prints and
drawings. Book Shop, Limited
disabled access.

Wellington Country Park

Riseley, Nr Reading RG7 1SP
Tel: (0118) 932 6444
website: www.wellington-country-
park.co.uk

**Follow the A33 south
(Signposted 4.7 Miles)**
A 350 acre park surrounding a
35 acre lake and containing
many activities both for adults
and children. There are several
nature trails, a deer park, an
animal farm, an adventure
playground, a miniature railway
and a crazy golf course.
Activities at the lake include
coarse fishing, from the banks,
and boating and there are
picnic areas and barbecue
sites. Gift shop. Café. Some
disabled access.

Stratfield Saye House

Stratfield Saye, Reading RG7 2BZ
Tel: (01256) 882882 website:
www.stratfieldsayehouse.co.uk

Follow the A33 south (Signposted 7.7 Miles)

Presented to the Duke of Wellington in 1817, this elegant and stylish house has been the family home ever since. Within the beautiful grounds, which include many rare trees, is the grave of Copenhagen, the Iron Duke's famous charger. The Wellington Exhibition graphically illustrates his life and the exhibits include his magnificent funeral carriage. Gift Shop. Tea Room.

(NB. Closed for extensive refurbishment until Spring 2003)

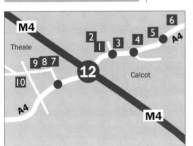

M4 BETWEEN JUNCS 11 & 12

READING SERVICES (WESTBOUND) (MOTO)
Tel: (0118) 956 6966
Fresh Express Self Service Restaurant, Burger King, Little Chef, Travelodge & BP Fuel

READING SERVICES (EASTBOUND) (MOTO)
Tel: (0118) 956 6966
Fresh Express Self Service Restaurant, Burger King, Upper Crust, Travelodge & BP Fuel

M4 JUNCTION 12

Nearest A&E Hospital
Royal Berkshire Hospital
London Road, Reading
RG1 5AN
Tel: (0118) 987 5111
Follow the A4 east into Reading (Distance Approx 4.7 Miles)

FACILITIES

1   Pincents Manor Hotel
Tel: (0118) 932 3511
0.2 miles east along the A4, on the left.
The Oak Restaurant Open; Breakfast; 07.00-10.00hrs, Lunch; 12.00-14.00hrs, Dinner; 19.00-21.30hrs daily. Bar Meals available; 10.00-22.00hrs daily.

2   McDonald's
Tel: (0118) 941 5744
0.2 miles east along the A4, on the left.
Open; 07.00-23.00hrs daily

3   Sainsbury's Filling Station
Tel: (0118) 938 2200
0.2 miles east along the A4, on the left.
Access, Visa, Overdrive, All Star, Switch, Dial Card, Mastercard, Amex, Delta, AA Paytrak, UK Fuelcard, Sainsburys Fuel Card

4   BP Express Calcot
Tel: (0118) 942 7912
0.8 miles east along the A4, on the left.
Access, Visa, Overdrive, All Star, Switch, Dial Card, Mastercard, Amex, AA Paytrak, Diners Club, Delta, Routex, BP Cards, Shell Agency. Open; 06.00-

22.00hrs daily.

5   Calcot Hotel
Tel: (0118) 941 6423
0.9 miles east along the A4, on the left.
The Wybourn Room Restaurant Open; Breakfast; Mon-Fri; 07.00-09.00hrs, Sat & Sun; 08.00-10.00hrs, Lunch; Sun-Fri; 12.00-14.00hrs, Dinner; 19.00-22.00hrs daily.

6   Murdochs Restaurant
Tel: (0118) 945 1344
1 mile east along the A4, on the left.
Open; Lunch; Wed & Fri; 12.00-14.00hrs, Dinner; 18.00-21.30hrs daily.

7   The Bull

Tel: (0118) 930 3478
0.7 miles on the right, in Theale village.
(Wadworth) Open all day. Meals served; Mon-Sat; 12.00-14.00hrs

8   The Falcon
Tel: (0118) 930 2523
0.7 miles on the right, in Theale village.
(Unique Pub Company) Open all day. Meals served; Mon-Fri; 12.00-14.00hrs & 18.00-20.00hrs.

9   The Village Café & Pizza
Tel: (0118) 932 3433
0.8 miles on the right, in Theale village.
Open; Mon-Sat; 07.30-15.00hrs & 18.00-22.00hrs, Sun; 10.00-14.00hrs & 18.00-22.00hrs

10   The Red Lion

Tel: (0118) 930 2394
1 mile on the left, in Theale village.
(Pubmaster) Open all day Tues-Sun. Meals served; Mon-Sat; 12.00-14.00hrs & 19.00-21.00hrs, Sun; 12.00-14.30hrs

PLACES OF INTEREST

Basildon Park (NT)

Lower Basildon, Reading
RG8 9NR Tel: (0118) 984 3040
website: www.nationaltrust.org.uk

Follow the A4 south, turn right along the A340 and continue along the A340 (Signposted "Beale Park" 7.8 Miles)
A classical Georgian 18thC house set in a beautiful garden and 400 acres of parkland, Basildon Park was built on a fortune made in the East Indies. The mansion later held the art collection of a wealthy industrialist but by the conclusion of World War II, it had been reduced to a near ruin after being a billet for British and American troops as well as a prisoner of war camp.

In the 1950's it was rescued by Lord & Lady Iliffe who lovingly restored it before handing it over to the National Trust in 1978. It contains an unusual octagonal drawing room, fine plasterwork, Graham Sutherland's studies for Coventry Cathedral and a decorative shell room and there are woodland walks. Licensed Restaurant. NT Shop. Limited disabled access.

Beale Park

Lower Basildon, Reading
RG8 9NH Tel: (0118) 984 5172
website: www.bealepark.co.uk

Just north of Basildon Park (see above)
The park contains a diverse range of activities centred around an amazing collection of rare birds and animals. The attractions include a variety of activity and play areas for children, a deer park, children's fun fair, a model boat exhibition, picnic areas and gardens and walks. Shop. Café. Disabled access.

JUNCTION 13

Nearest Eastbound A&E Hospital
Royal Berkshire Hospital
London Road, Reading
RG1 5AN
Tel: (0118) 987 5111
Proceed to Junction 12 and take the A4 east to Reading (Distance Approx 16.2 Miles)

Nearest Westbound A&E Hospital
Princess Margaret Hospital
Okus Road, Swindon
SN1 4JU
Tel: (01793) 536231
Proceed to Junction 15 and follow the A419 north. (Signposted within the town. Distance Approx 24.3 Miles)

FACILITIES

CHIEVELEY SERVICES (MOTO)
Tel: (01635) 248024
Fresh Express Self Service Restaurant, Harry Ramsden's, Little Chef, Upper Crust, Burger King, Travelodge & BP Fuel

1   The Hilton Newbury North Hotel

Tel: (01635) 247010
0.1 miles south along the A34, on the right (2.3 miles detour required to gain access).
Quotes Restaurant; Breakfast; Mon-Fri; 07.00-9.30hrs, Sat & Sun; 07.30-10.00hrs, Lunch; Sun-Fri; 12.30-14.00hrs, Dinner; Sun-Thurs; 19.00-22.00hrs, Fri & Sat; 18.30-21.30hrs.

2   Ye Olde Red Lion

Tel: (01635) 248379
0.9 miles north along the Chieveley Road, on the left, in Chieveley.
(JC Taverns) Meals served; Mon-Sat; 11.15-14.30hrs & 18.00-21.30hrs, Sun; 12.00-15.00hrs.

PLACES OF INTEREST

Highclere Castle

Near Newbury, Berkshire
RG20 9RN Tel: (01635) 253210
website: www.highclerecastle.co.uk

Follow the A34 south (10.2 Miles)
Designed by Sir Charles Berry, Highclere Castle is considered to be the finest Victorian house still in existence. The castle is the family home of Lord & Lady Carnarvon and the ornate architecture is supplemented by fine period furniture and an art collection including works by Gainsborough, Reynolds and Van Dyck. Exhibitions include displays on the Tomb of Tutankhamun, discovered by the 5th Earl of Carnarvon and Howard Carter, and horse racing, the present Earl being engaged as the Racing Manager to the monarch. The magnificent parkland

surrounding the castle is dominated by the Cedars of Lebanon and the sweeping vistas, inset with follies, present breathtaking views and relaxing walks. Gift Shop. Restaurant & Tea Rooms. Limited disabled access.

The Living Rainforest

Hampstead Norreys, Thatcham. Berkshire RG18 0TN
Tel: (01635) 202444
website: www.livingrainforest.org

Follow the A34 north, take the first exit and turn right towards Hermitage and, at the end, turn left along the B4009 towards Hampstead Norris. (5.5 miles)

Experience the sheer beauty of this unique rainforest conservation project created under 20,000 ft^2 of glass and containing a stunning collection of dramatic and endangered rare plant species and rainforest creatures, including the tamarin monkeys, that thrive in tropical temperatures. The Living Rainforest is the World Land Trust's UK Conservation and Education Centre and qualified staff are on hand to give guided tours. Picnic Area. Café. Gift Shop. Disabled access.

JUNCTION 14

Nearest Eastbound A&E Hospital

Royal Berkshire Hospital

London Road, Reading
RG1 5AN
Tel: (0118) 987 5111
Proceed to Junction 12 and take the A4 east to Reading
(Distance Approx 23.9 Miles)

Nearest Westbound A&E Hospital
Princess Margaret Hospital

Okus Road, Swindon
SN1 4JU
Tel: (01793) 536231
Proceed to Junction 15 and follow the A419 north. (Signposted within the town. Distance Approx 16.6 Miles)

FACILITIES

1   The Pheasant Inn

Tel: (01488) 648284
0.4 miles north along the B4000, on the right.
(Free House) Open all day. Meals served; Mon-Sat; 12.30-14.30hrs & 19.30-21.30hrs, Sun; 12.30-15.00hrs. "Comfort" Food available all day.

2   Tally Ho!

Tel: (01488) 682312
0.9 miles south along the A338, on the left.
(Wadworth) Open all day Sat & Sun. Meals served; 12.00-14.30hrs & 18.00-21.30hrs daily.

BETWEEN JUNCS 14 & 15

MEMBURY SERVICES (WESTBOUND) (WELCOME BREAK)
Tel: (01488) 72336

La Brioche Doree French Café, Food Connection Restaurant, Burger King, KFC, Red Hen Restaurant, Days Inn & BP Fuel

MEMBURY SERVICES (EASTBOUND) (WELCOME BREAK)
Tel: (01488) 72336
Food Connection Restaurant, Burger King & BP Fuel

FOOTBRIDGE CONNECTION BETWEEN SITES.

JUNCTION 15

Nearest A&E Hospital
Princess Margaret Hospital

Okus Road, Swindon
SN1 4JU
Tel: (01793) 536231
Follow the A419 north. (Signposted within the town. Distance Approx 4.6 Miles)

FACILITIES

1   Kingsbridge House

Tel: (01793) 522861
1 mile north along the A4259, on the left

2   The Plough Inn

Tel: (01793) 740342
0.4 miles south along the A346, on the right.

(Arkells) Open all day Mon-Fri. Meals served; 12.00-14.00hrs & 19.00-22.30hrs daily. Bar Snacks available; 16.00-19.00hrs daily

3 Chiseldon Camp Service Station (Esso)

Tel: (01793) 740251
1 mile south along the A346, on the right.
Access, Visa, Overdrive, All Star, Switch, Dial Card, Mastercard, Amex, AA Paytrak, Diners Club, Delta, BP Supercharge, Shell Gold, Esso Cards.

PLACES OF INTEREST

Swindon Museum & Art Gallery

Bath Road, Swindon SN1 4BA
Tel: (01793) 466556
website: www.swindon.gov.uk

Follow the A419 north into Swindon (1.5 Miles)
The museum contains artefacts dating from Roman times and, amongst other exhibits, a comprehensive local studies section illustrating life in Swindon. The art gallery houses one of the most important collections of British 20thC Art. Established in 1944 the collection ranges from Sir George Clausen of 1896 to 1986 and Gillian Ayres, and embraces works by such major exponents as Lowry, Nicolson, Sutherland and Moore. Gift Shop. Limited disabled access.

JUNCTION 16

Freshbrook

Nearest A&E Hospital
Princess Margaret Hospital
Okus Road, Swindon
SN1 4JU
Tel: (01793) 536231
Follow the A3102 east.
(Signposted within the town. Distance Approx 2.8 Miles)

FACILITIES

1 Hilton Swindon

Tel: (01793) 881777
0.1 miles north along the A3102, on the left.
Minsky's Restaurant; Breakfast; Mon-Fri; 06.30-10.00hrs, Sat & Sun; 07.00-10.00hrs, Lunch; Sun-Fri; 12.30-14.00hrs, Dinner; 19.00-21.45hrs daily

2 The Lydiard

Tel: (01793) 881490
0.1 miles north along the A3102, on the left.
(Beefeater) Open all day. Restaurant Open; Mon-Thurs; 07.00-09.00hrs & 12.00-22.00hrs, Fri; 07.00-09.00hrs & 12.00-23.00hrs, Sat; 08.00-10.00hrs & 12.00-23.00hrs, Sun; 08.00-10.00hrs & 12.00-21.00hrs. Bar Meals available 12.00-22.00hrs daily.

3 Travel Inn

Tel: (01793) 881490
0.1 miles north along the A3102, on the left

4 Save Petrol Station

Tel: (01793) 881654
0.5 miles north along the A3102, on the left.
Keyfuels, Access, Visa, Overdrive, All Star, Switch, Dial Card, Mastercard, Delta, Save Card. Open; 06.00-23.00hrs daily.

5 Sally Pusseys Inn

Tel: (01793) 852430
0.9 miles west along the A3102, on the right.
(Arkells) Open all day. Meals served; Mon-Fri; 08.00-21.00hrs, Sat; 11.00-22.00hrs, Sun; 12.00-21.00hrs

PLACES OF INTEREST

Lydiard House & Park

Hook Street, Lydiard Tregoze, Swindon SN5 9PA
Tel: (01793) 770401
website: www.swindon.gov.uk

Follow the A3102 east and turn left along the B4534 (Signposted 1.7 Miles)
Lydiard Park is the delightful, yet little known, home of the Viscounts Bolingbroke which was rescued from ruin by Swindon Corporation in 1943 and restored to its former glory. The elegant ground floor apartments contain ornate plasterwork and original family furnishings are preserved alongside portraits of the St John family who lived here from Elizabethan times. Other attractions include the Blue Dressing Room, devoted to the

talented 18thC society artist Lady Diana Spencer, and a 17thC painted window by Abraham Van Linge. The Visitor Centre houses countryside displays and a café and there are extensive paths and trails through the parkland as well as adventure playgrounds for children. Gift Shop. Limited disabled access.

Steam-Museum of the Great Western Railway

Kemble Drive, Swindon SN2 2TA Tel (01793) 466646 website: www.steam-museum.org.uk

Follow the A3102 east (Signposted "Outlet Centre" 3.2 Miles)

The No.20 Shop in the former GWR Railway Works has been beautifully restored and converted into a new museum facility to show the story of the works and the Great Western Railway and their place in railway history. Featuring static and interactive displays as well as famous locomotives, carriages and wagons, there is also the Railway Village Museum nearby which demonstrates the domestic lives of those who were employed by the GWR in the early 1900s. Café. Gift Shop. Disabled access.

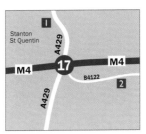

Nearest Eastbound A&E Hospital

Princess Margaret Hospital

Okus Road, Swindon SN1 4JU Tel: (01793) 536231 Proceed to Junction 16 and follow the A3102 east. (Signposted within the town. Distance Approx 15.2 Miles)

Nearest Westbound A&E Hospital

Frenchay Hospital

Frenchay Park Road, Frenchay, Bristol BS16 1L Tel: (0117) 970 1212 Proceed to Junction 19 and then follow the M32 to Junction 1. Take the A4174 east exit and the hospital is signposted. (Distance Approx 19.1 miles)

FACILITIES

1   Murco Filling Station

Tel: (01666) 837161 **0.7 miles north along the A429, on the left.** Access, Visa, Overdrive, All Star, Switch, Dial Card, Mastercard, Amex, AA Paytrak, Delta, BP Supercharge, Murco Cards. Country Choice Hot Snacks available; 06.00-22.00hrs daily.

2   Silvey Truckstop Chippenham (UK Fuels)

Tel: (01249) 750645 **0.8 miles east along the B4122, on the right.** Diesel Fuel Only (24hr card operated pumps). Access, Mastercard, Visa, Switch, Securicor Fuelserv, IDS, Keyfuels, AS24, Q8 Card, Silvey Card. Café Open; Mon 06.30hrs-Sat 11.00hrs.

PLACES OF INTEREST

Malmesbury

Malmesbury Tourist Information Centre, Town Hall, Market Lane, Malmesbury SN16 9BZ Tel: (01666) 823748 website: www.malmesbury-towncouncil.com

Follow the A429 north (Signposted 5.5 Miles)

England's oldest borough, the hill-top town is dominated by the impressive remains of the Norman Abbey. St Aldhelm, the first abbot, created a place of pilgrimage in the 7thC and Athelstan, the first King of England, chose Malmesbury as his capital and was buried here. In 1010 Elmer, a monk, attempted to fly, making himself a set of wings and launching himself 620ft from the top of the Abbey roof. He survived and, despite breaking both legs, enjoyed a long life. There are delightful walks around the town and beside the River Avon.

Lacock Abbey & The Fox Talbot Museum of Photography (NT)

Chippenham, Wiltshire SN15 2LG Tel: (01249) 730227 website: www.nationaltrust.org.uk

Follow the A429 south past Chippenham and continue along the A350 towards Melksham. Lacock is signposted on the left. (7.7 Miles)

A 13thC abbey, it was acquired by Sir William Sharington, one time treasurer at the Bristol Mint, in 1540 and adapted as a Tudor mansion by adding an octagonal tower and twisted chimneys whilst retaining the 13th & 15thC cloisters, chapter house and nuns parlour. The house was altered in neo-

Gothic style in 1753 with further modifications being made in 1828. It was here in 1839-41 that William Fox Talbot perfected his talbotype technique which laid the foundations of modern photography and the adjacent museum is devoted to this achievement. Gift Shop. Limited disabled access.

M4
BETWEEN JUNCS 17 & 18

LEIGH DELAMERE SERVICES (EASTBOUND) (MOTO)
Tel: (01666) 837691
Self Service Restaurant, Fresh Express, Harry Ramsden's, Burger King, Little Chef, Upper Crust, Travelodge & Esso Fuel

LEIGH DELAMERE SERVICES (WESTBOUND) (MOTO)
Tel: (01666) 837691
Self Service Restaurant, Fresh Express, Harry Ramsden's, Burger King, Little Chef, Upper Crust, Travelodge & Esso Fuel

ROADBRIDGE AND FOOTBRIDGE CONNECTIONS BETWEEN SITES.

M4
JUNCTION 18

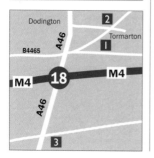

Nearest A&E Hospital
Frenchay Hospital
Frenchay Park Road, Frenchay, Bristol BS16 1LE
Tel: (0117) 970 1212
Proceed west to Junction 19 and then follow the M32 to Junction 1. Take the A4174 east exit and the hospital is signposted. (Distance Approx 8.7 miles)

FACILITIES

1　The Compass Inn

Tel: (01454) 218242
0.4 miles north along the Tormarton Road, on the right.
(Best Western) Bittles Restaurant; Open; 07.00-22.30hrs daily.

2　Chestnut Farm B&B

Tel: (01454) 218563
0.8 miles north along the Tormarton Road, on the left

3　The Crown Inn at Tolldown

Tel: (01225) 891231
1 mile south along the A46, on the left.
(Wadworth) Meals served; Sun-Thurs; 12.00-14.15hrs & 19.00-21.30hrs, Fri & Sat; 12.00-14.15hrs & 19.00-22.00hrs

PLACES OF INTEREST

Dyrham Park (NT)

Dyrham, Nr Chippenham, Wiltshire SN14 8E

Tel: (01179) 372501 website: www.nationaltrust.org.uk

Follow the A46 south (Signposted 2.6 Miles)

A country mansion built in c1698 to designs by William Talman for William Blathwayt, politician and Secretary of State to William III in Flanders. The house contains portraits and tapestries, furniture used by Pepys and Evelyn, the diarists, and rooms panelled in oak, walnut and cedar. There is a park, garden and orangery and a number of picnic sites. Licensed Restaurant. Gift Shop. Limited disabled access.

M4
JUNCTION 19

THIS JUNCTION IS A MOTORWAY INTERCHANGE WITH THE M32 ONLY AND THERE IS NO ACCESS TO ANY FACILITIES

Nearest A&E Hospital
Frenchay Hospital
Frenchay Park Road, Frenchay, Bristol BS16 1LE
Tel: (0117) 970 1212
Follow the M32 to Junction 1 and take the A4174 east exit and the hospital is signposted. (Distance Approx 1.5 miles)

PLACES OF INTEREST

Bristol

Follow the M32 south (Signposted 5.6 Miles)
For details please see M5 Junction 16 & 17 information

M4 JUNCTION 20

THIS JUNCTION IS A MOTORWAY INTERCHANGE WITH THE M5 ONLY AND THERE IS NO ACCESS TO ANY FACILITIES

Nearest A&E Hospital

Frenchay Hospital
Frenchay Park Road,
Frenchay, Bristol BS16 1LE
Tel: (0117) 970 1212
Proceed east to Junction 19 and then follow the M32 to Junction 1. Take the A4174 east exit and the hospital is signposted. (Distance Approx 4.9 miles)

M4 JUNCTION 21

THIS JUNCTION IS A MOTORWAY INTERCHANGE WITH THE M48 ONLY AND THERE IS NO ACCESS TO ANY FACILITIES

M4 JUNCTION 22

THIS JUNCTION IS A MOTORWAY INTERCHANGE WITH THE M49 ONLY AND THERE IS NO ACCESS TO ANY FACILITIES

Nearest Westbound A&E Hospital

The Royal Gwent Hospital
Cardiff Road, Newport
NP20 2UB
Tel: (01633) 234234

Proceed to Junction 24 and follow the A48 west (Signposted along route. Distance Approx 15.9 miles)

Nearest Eastbound A&E Hospital

Frenchay Hospital
Frenchay Park Road,
Frenchay, Bristol BS16 1LE
Tel: (0117) 970 1212
Proceed to Junction 19 and then follow the M32 to Junction 1. Take the A4174 east exit and the hospital is signposted. (Distance Approx 10 miles)

M48 LOOP JUNCTION 1

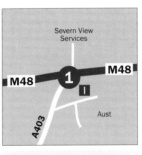

Nearest Westbound A&E Hospital

The Royal Gwent Hospital
Cardiff Road, Newport
NP20 2UB
Tel: (01633) 234234
Proceed to Junction 24 and follow the A48 west (Signposted along route. Distance Approx 18.4 miles)

Nearest Eastbound A&E Hospital

Frenchay Hospital
Frenchay Park Road,
Frenchay, Bristol BS16 1LE
Tel: (0117) 970 1212
Proceed to Junction 19 and then follow the M32 to Junction 1. Take the A4174

east exit and the hospital is signposted. (Distance Approx 9 miles)

FACILITIES

SEVERN VIEW SERVICES (MOTO)
Tel: (01454) 633199
Little Chef, Burger King, Travelodge & BP Fuel

1   Boars Head

Tel: (01454) 632278
0.4 miles south in Aust Village.
(Eldridge Pope) Meals served; Tues-Sat; 12.00-14.30hrs & 18.00-21.30hrs, Sun & Mon; 12.00-14.30hrs

M48 LOOP JUNCTION 2

THERE ARE NO FACILITIES WITHIN ONE MILE OF THIS JUNCTION

Nearest Westbound A&E Hospital

The Royal Gwent Hospital
Cardiff Road, Newport
NP20 2UB
Tel: (01633) 234234
Proceed to Junction 24 and follow the A48 west (Signposted along route. Distance Approx 15.3 miles)

Nearest Eastbound A&E Hospital

Frenchay Hospital
Frenchay Park Road,
Frenchay, Bristol BS16 1LE
Tel: (0117) 970 1212
Proceed to Junction 19 and then follow the M32 to Junction 1. Take the A4174 east exit and the hospital is

signposted. (Distance Approx 12 miles)

PLACES OF INTEREST

Chepstow Castle

Chepstow, Monmouthshire NP6 5EZ Tel: (01291) 624065 website: www.cadw.wales.gov.uk

Follow the A466 north (Signposted 2.1 Miles)
Standing guard over a strategic crossing point into Wales, Chepstow Castle was amongst the first of the Norman stone-built strongholds. It was constructed by William fitz Osbern to secure his territories along the Welsh borders and was improved and added to over the centuries until it ceased to have a military use in 1690. It is one of the few castles in Britain in which the evolution of mediaeval military architecture can be traced from start to finish. A major exhibition entitled "A Castle at War" reflects the changing role of Chepstow through the Middle Ages and there are displays of life sized models of the mediaeval lords and a dramatic Civil War battle scene. Gift Shop. Limited disabled access.

Sited opposite to the castle ...

Stuart Crystal

Bridge Street, Chepstow, Monmouthshire NP6 5EZ Tel: (01291) 620135

A Visitor Centre and Factory Shop featuring an exhibition of old glass, a glass engraving display and an audio visual presentation on glass making. There is a glass repair and personalized glassware service, and also a picnic area. Coffee Shop.

M4 JUNCTION 23

THIS JUNCTION IS A MOTORWAY INTERCHANGE WITH THE M48 ONLY AND THERE IS NO ACCESS TO ANY FACILITIES

M4 JUNCTION 23A

Nearest Westbound A&E Hospital
The Royal Gwent Hospital
Cardiff Road, Newport NP20 2UB Tel: (01633) 234234
Proceed to Junction 24 and follow the A48 west (Signposted along route. Distance Approx 7.5 miles)

Nearest Eastbound A&E Hospital
Frenchay Hospital
Frenchay Park Road, Frenchay, Bristol BS16 1LE Tel: (0117) 970 1212
Proceed to Junction 19 and then follow the M32 to Junction 1. Take the A4174 east exit and the hospital is signposted. (Distance Approx 18.4 miles [via M4])

FACILITIES

MAGOR SERVICES (FIRST)
Tel: (01633) 881515
Burger King, Self Service Restaurant, Comfort Inns Lodge & Esso Fuel

1　Reliance Garage (Esso)

Tel: (01633) 880229
1 mile along the B4245 east, on the right.
Access, Visa, Overdrive, All Star, Switch, Dial Card, Mastercard, Amex, AA Paytrak, Diners Club, Delta, BP Supercharge, Shell Gold, Esso Cards. Open; Mon-Sat; 07.30-19.30hrs, Sun; 10.00-14.00hrs.

2　Wheatsheaf Inn

Tel: (01633) 880608
1 mile along the B4245 east, in Magor.
(Laurel Pub Partnership) Open all day. Meals served; Mon-Sat; 12.00-21.30hrs, Sun; 12.00-15.00hrs

PLACES OF INTEREST

Caldicot Castle & Country Park

Caldicot, Monmouthshire NP6 4HU Tel: (01291) 420241 website: www.caldicotcastle.co.uk

Follow the B4245 east (Signposted 4.7 Miles)
Caldicot Castle's well preserved fortifications were founded by the Normans and fully developed by the late 14thC. Restored as a family home by a wealthy Victorian, the castle offers the chance to explore mediaeval walls and

towers in a setting of tranquil gardens and wooded country park. There are personal stereo sound tours, play areas and picnic and barbecue sites within the park. Castle Shop, Tea Room. Limited disabled access

M4
JUNCTION 24

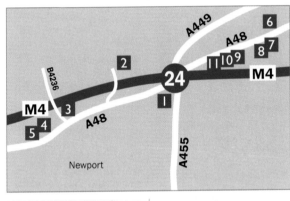

Nearest A&E Hospital
The Royal Gwent Hospital
Cardiff Road, Newport
NP20 2UB Tel: (01633) 234234.
Follow the A48 west (Signposted along route. Distance Approx 3.6 miles)

FACILITIES

1 Holiday Inn Newport

Tel: (01633) 412777
0.1 miles west along the A48, on the left.
Harpers Bar & Restaurant; Restaurant Open; Breakfast; Mon-Fri; 06.30-09.30hrs, Sat & Sun; 07.00-11.00hrs, Lunch; Sun; 12.00-14.00hrs Dinner; 19.00-22.00hrs daily. Bar Meals served 09.00-22.30hrs daily.

2 Celtic Manor Hotel

Tel: (01633) 413000
0.2 miles west along the A48, on the right.
The Olive Tree Restaurant; Breakfast; 07.00-10.30hrs daily, Lunch; 12.30-14.30hrs daily, Dinner; 19.00-22.30hrs daily. Owen's Restaurant; Open; Tues-Sat; 19.00-23.00hrs. The Patio Brasserie; Open; 19.00-22.30hrs daily.

3 The Toby Carvery, Coldra

Tel: (01633) 282155
0.6 miles west along the A48, on the right.
(Six Continents) Open all day. Meals served; 12.00-22.00hrs daily

4 Treberth Service Station (Esso)

Tel: (01633) 281241
0.8 miles west along the A48, on the right.
Access, Visa, Overdrive, All Star, Switch, Dial Card, Mastercard, Amex, Diners Club, Delta, Esso Cards.

5 Man of Gwent

Tel: (01633) 281263
1 mile west along the A48, on

the right.
(Scottish & Newcastle) Open all day. Meals served; Mon-Sat; 11.00-21.30hrs, Sun; 12.00-21.00hrs

6 Hilton Newport

Tel: (01633) 413733
0.2 miles east along the A48, on the left.
Seasons Restaurant; Breakfast; Mon-Sat; 07.00-10.00hrs, Sun; 08.00-10.00hrs, Lunch; Sun; 12.30-15.00hrs, Dinner; Mon-Sat; 19.00-22.00hrs, Sun; 19.00-21.30hrs. Café Chino; Open; Mon-Fri; 09.00-17.00hrs.

7 Taylor's Garage (Independent)

Tel: (01633) 412354
0.2 miles east along the A48, on the right.
Access, Visa, Mastercard, Switch, Diners Club, Amex, Overdrive, All Star, Dial Card, Delta, Keyfuels, BP Supercharge. Open; Mon-Fri; 07.00-20.00hrs, Sat & Sun; 07.00-19.00hrs.

8 Lynwood Café

Tel: (01633) 412354
0.2 miles east along the A48, on the right.
Open; Mon-Fri; 07.00-15.00hrs, Sat; 08.00-12.00hrs

9 McDonald's

Tel: (01633) 412087
0.1 miles east along the A48, on the right.
Open; 07.00-23.00hrs daily. "Drive Thru" Open until 0.00hrs on Fri & Sat.

10 Travel Inn
Tel: (01633) 411390
0.1 miles east along the A48, on the right

11　The Coldra

Tel: (01633) 411390

0.1 miles east along the A48, on the right.

(Beefeater) Open all day. Meals served; Mon-Fri; 12.00-14.30hrs & 17.30-22.45hrs, Fri; 12.00-14.30hrs & 17.00-23.00hrs, Sat; 12.00-23.00hrs, Sun; 12.00-21.00hrs

PLACES OF INTEREST

Roman Legionary Museum

High Street, Caerleon, Newport NP6 1AE Tel: (01633) 423134 website: www.nmgw.co.uk

Follow the A48 south and turn right along the B4236 (Signposted 1.9 Miles)
The legionary fortress of "Isca" was one of the principal military bases in Roman Britain. The museum illustrates the history of Roman Caerleon and the daily life of its garrison with a display of many fascinating discoveries, including a remarkable collection of engraved gemstones from the Fortress Baths, an intriguing labyrinth mosaic, tombstones and arms and equipment of the Roman soldiers. An amphitheatre, Barracks, Baths and Roman remains are to be seen nearby. The Capricorn Centre, sited next door, is an educational facility for schools and families. Gift Shop. Limited disabled access.

M4 JUNCS 25 & 25A

THESE TWO JUNCTIONS ARE ADJACENT. ALTHOUGH EACH

ONE HAS A RESTRICTED ACCESS, THE COMBINATION IS SUCH THAT VEHICLES ARE ABLE TO ENTER AND EXIT IN BOTH DIRECTIONS

THERE ARE NO FACILITIES WITHIN ONE MILE FOR VEHICLES EXITING FROM JUNCTION 25A

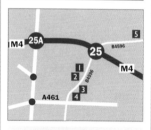

Nearest A&E Hospital
The Royal Gwent Hospital
Cardiff Road, Newport NP20 2UB
Tel: (01633) 234234
Follow the A4042 south and continue along the A48 (Signposted along route. Distance Approx 2.1 miles)

FACILITIES

FROM JUNCTION 25

1　The Victoria Inn

Tel: (01633) 258252

0.4 miles south along the B4596, on the right.

(Punch Taverns) Open all day. Meals served; 12.00-15.00hrs & 18.00-21.00hrs daily

2　Polash Tandoori Restaurant

Tel: (01633) 252891

0.5 miles south along the B4596, on the right.

Open; Mon-Thurs; 18.00-0.00 hrs, Fri/Sat & Sat/Sun; 18.00-01.30hrs, Sun; 18.00-0.00hrs.

3　Ashburton House

Tel: (01633) 211140

0.6 miles south along the B4596, on the left

4　Caerleon Service Station (Esso)

Tel: (01633) 266581

0.7 miles south along the B4596, on the left.

Access, Visa, Overdrive, All Star, Switch, Dial Card, Mastercard, Amex, Diners Club, Shell Gold, Esso Cards. Open; 07.00-23.00hrs daily

5　St Julian Inn

Tel: (01633) 243548

1 mile north along the B4596, on the left.

(Courage) Open all day. Meals served; Mon-Sat; 11.30-14.45hrs & 18.00-20.45hrs

PLACES OF INTEREST

Newport

Newport Tourist Information Centre, John Frost Square, Newport NP9 1H2 Tel: (01633) 842962 website: www.newport.gov.uk/tourism

Follow the A4042 south (Signposted 1.6 Miles)
Bronze Age fishermen settled around the estuary of the River Usk and, later the Celtic Silures built hill forts overlooking it. On the western edge of their empire, the Romans built a fortress at Caerleon to defend the river crossing and later the Normans arrived to build a castle on Stow Hill.

In the 14thC a new castle was constructed next to a river crossing and around this a new town grew to become Newport. The most famous landmark in the town is the recently renovated Transporter Bridge, which opened in 1906 and was erected to provide a crossing between the east and west banks of the Usk. This is one of only two working in Britain, Middlesbrough has the other, and there are now believed to be only five such examples in the world of this unusual form of transport which allows traffic to cross the river without obstructing shipping.

JUNCTION 26

NEWPORT TOWN CENTRE IS WITHIN ONE MILE OF THIS JUNCTION

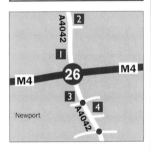

Nearest A&E Hospital
The Royal Gwent Hospital
Cardiff Road, Newport
NP20 2UB
Tel: (01633) 234234
Follow the A4042 south and continue along the A48 (Signposted along route. Distance Approx 2.1 miles)

FACILITIES

1   The Borderer

Tel: (01633) 858667
0.4 miles north along the A4051, on the left.
(Harvester) Open all day. Meals

served; Sun-Thurs; 12.00-21.00hrs, Fri & Sat; 12.00-22.00hrs

2   Malpas BP Service Station

Tel: (01633) 858057
1 mile north along the A4051, on the right.
Access, Visa, Overdrive, All Star, Switch, Dial Card, Mastercard, Amex, AA Paytrak, Diners Club, Delta, Routex, BP Cards.

3   Shell Newport

Tel: (01633) 820000
0.7 miles south along the A4051, on the right.
LPG. Access, Visa, Overdrive, All Star, Switch, Dial Card, Mastercard, Amex, AA Paytrak, Delta, Routex, Shell Cards.

4   The Old Rising Sun

Tel: (01633) 223452
0.9 miles south along the A4051, on the left.
(Freehouse) Open all day. Meals served; Mon-Wed; 11.00-15.00hrs, Thurs & Fri; 11.00-15.00hrs & 18.00-20.00hrs, Sat; 11.00-15.00hrs, Sun; 12.00-15.00hrs. Meals can be served at other times by prior notification.

PLACES OF INTEREST

Newport

Follow the A4042 south (Signposted 1.6 Miles)
For details please see Junction 25 information.

JUNCTION 27

Nearest A&E Hospital
The Royal Gwent Hospital
Cardiff Road, Newport
NP20 2UB
Tel: (01633) 234234
Follow the B4591 east, bear right along the B4240 and turn left along the A48. (Signposted along route. Distance Approx 1.8 miles)

FACILITIES

1   Star High Cross (Texaco)

Tel: (01633) 898400
0.2 miles north along the B4591, on the left.
Access, Visa, Mastercard, Switch, Electron, Solo, Diners Club, Amex, Overdrive, All Star, Dial Card, Delta, Texaco Cards.
Open; 06.00-23.00hrs daily

2   Cefn Smithy Service Station (Total)

Tel: (01633) 894021
0.5 miles north along the B4591, on the right.
Access, Visa, All Star, Switch, Dial Card, Mastercard, Amex, Diners Club, Total/Fina/Elf Cards.

3 The Rising Sun Hotel & Restaurant

Tel: (01633) 895126

0.8 miles north along the B4591, on the left.

(Scottish Courage) Open all day Fri & Sat. Meals served; Mon-Sat; 12.00-14.15hrs & 18.00-21.30hrs, Sun; 12.00-14.15hrs

4 The Olde Oak

Tel: (01633) 892883

0.9 miles north along the B4591, on the right in Ruskin Avenue.

(Inspired Inns) Open all day Sat & Sun. Meals served; Mon-Sat; 12.00-14.30hrs & 18.30-21.30hrs, Sun; 12.00-15.00hrs.

PLACES OF INTEREST

Newport

Follow the B4591 east (Signposted 2.2 Miles)

For details please see Junction 25 information.

Fourteen Locks Canal Centre

Cwm Lane, Rogerstone NP10 9GN Tel: (01633) 894802 website: www.newport.gov.uk/tourism

Follow the B4591 north towards Risca (Signposted along this route 1 Mile)

On the Monmouthshire Canal which opened in 1796, Fourteen Locks is a complicated system of locks, ponds, channels, tunnels and weirs designed to enable barges to be lowered or raised 168ft in 0.5 miles with the minimum wastage of water. At the Visitor Centre, an exhibition traces the growth and decline of the canal in Gwent and a

display explains how the locks and water storage system worked. There are numerous walks and picnic sites around the canal centre.

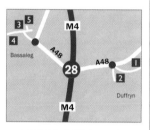

Nearest A&E Hospital

The Royal Gwent Hospital

Cardiff Road, Newport NP20 2UB Tel: (01633) 234234.

Follow the A48 east. (Signposted along route. Distance Approx 2 miles)

FACILITIES

1 Newport Filling Station (BP)

Tel: (01633) 815921

0.9 miles east along the A48, on the right.

Access, Visa, Overdrive, All Star, Switch, Dial Card, Mastercard, Amex, AA Paytrak, Diners Club, Delta, Routex, BP Cards, Shell Agency

2 The Stonehouse

Tel: (01633) 810541

0.9 miles east along the B4239, on the left.

(Whitbread) Open all day. Meals served; Mon-Sat; 11.30-22.00hrs, Sun; 12.00-22.00hrs.

3 The Tredegar Arms

Tel: (01633) 893247

0.9 miles north along the A468, on the right.

(Laurel Pub Company) Open all day. Meals served; 12.00-14.30hrs & 18.00-21.30hrs daily.

4 Bassaleg BP Service Station

Tel: (01633) 893321

1 mile north along the A468, on the left.

Access, Visa, Overdrive, All Star, Switch, Dial Card, Mastercard, Amex, Diners Club, Delta, Routex, BP Cards, Shell Agency. Open; Mon-Fri; 07.30-20.30hrs, Sat; 07.30-20.00hrs, Sun; 09.00-20.00hrs.

5 Junction 28 Restaurant

Tel: (01633) 891891

1 mile north along Forge Lane, on the left, in Station Approach.

Open; Mon-Sat; 12.00-14.00hrs & 17.30-21.30hrs, Sun; 12.00-16.00hrs.

PLACES OF INTEREST

Tredegar House & Park

Newport NP1 9YW Tel: (01633) 815880 website: www.members.fortunecity.com/tredegarhouse

Follow the A48 south. (Signposted 0.8 Miles)

Set in a beautiful 90 acre park, Tredegar House is one of the best examples of a 17thC, Charles II mansion in Britain with some parts of the building dating back to the early 1500's. All the rooms have been restored and reflect the rise and fall of the home's former owners, the Morgan family of whom the most notorious member was Sir Henry Morgan, the pirate. The second Lord Tredegar, Godfrey Morgan, survived the Charge of the Light Brigade and his horse is buried in the grounds.

The stunning state rooms are adorned with fine paintings, carvings and elaborate ceilings; illustrating the opulence of William Morgan, the builder of the house. There is a children's adventure playground and nature lakeside walks, as well as walled gardens and a beautiful Orangery. Craft Workshops. Gift Shop. Tea Room. Disabled access.

M4
JUNCTION 29

THIS IS A RESTRICTED ACCESS MOTORWAY INTERCHANGE WITH THE A48(M) ONLY

- Vehicles can only exit along the A48(M) from the southbound lanes.
- Vehicles can only enter the motorway from the A48(M) along the northbound lanes.

THERE ARE NO FACILITIES WITHIN ONE MILE OF THIS JUNCTION

Nearest Westbound A&E Hospital
University Hospital of Wales
Heath Park, Cardiff CF4 4XW
Tel: (029) 2074 7747
Follow the A48(M) and A48 (Signposted. Distance Approx 7.1 Miles)

Nearest Eastbound A&E Hospital
The Royal Gwent Hospital
Cardiff Road, Newport

NP20 2UB
Tel: (01633) 234234
Proceed to Junction 28 and follow the A48 east. (Signposted along route. Distance Approx 4.3 miles)

PLACES OF INTEREST

Cardiff
Cardiff Tourist Information Centre, 16 Wood Street, Cardiff CF10 1ES
Tel: (029) 2022 7281 website: www.cardiffmarketing.co.uk

Follow the A48(M) west (Signposted 6 Miles)
Once a walled town with five gates, a Benedictine priory, a Dominican house, a Franciscan and two churches, Cardiff, in 150 years rose grew to become the capital of the Principality of Wales, a major seaport, and a university city. The prosperity of the city was founded upon the establishment of the first Dock, opened in 1839 and upon which the Marquess of Bute risked the whole of his fortune. It became the richest coal exporting city in the world with an extensive port of 5 docks, 12 graving docks, 5 miles of quays and great timber basins and the legacy of this wealth is reflected in the Victorian and Edwardian architecture to be found in the city.

Today the docks have all but disappeared and they are now the centre of a 2,700 acre redevelopment to revitalize the area.

Within the city centre...

Cardiff Castle
Castle Street, Cardiff CF1 2RB
Tel: (029) 2087 8100 website: www.cardiff-info.com/castle

A motte with wooden buildings was raised in c1093 on the site of a Roman fortification; the present stone keep was erected to replace wooden buildings in the late 12thC and additions were made in the 15th and each subsequent century following. In 1861 the 3rd Marquess of Bute and William Burges designed additions in the Gothic, Arab and Classical Greek idioms. There are also two military museums, splendid gardens, gift shop and a tea room. Some disabled access

National Museum & Gallery
Cathays Park, Cardiff CF1 3NP
Tel: (029) 2039 7951
website: www.nmgw.ac.uk

No other British museum offers a similar range of art, natural history and science under one roof. There is a spectacular exhibition on the creation of Wales, complete with animated Ice Age creatures and simulated Big Bang, there are natural history galleries with woodland and wildlife displays and the art section includes works from Canaletto to Cezanne. Gift Shop. Restaurant. Disabled access.

Cardiff Bay: Millennium Waterfront
Cardiff Bay Visitor Centre
Tel: (029) 2046 3833 website: www.cardiff.gov.uk

(Signposted from Motorway)
Europe's largest regeneration project, a Covent Garden on the waterfront with entertainment, arts, places to eat and a range of leisure attractions including; Techniquest (Tel: 029-2047 5475) and the Atlantic Wharf Leisure Village (Tel: 029-2025 6261) with a 12-screen multiplex cinema, 26 lane Hollywood Bowl, micro brewery, family entertainment complex, nightclubs, cafes and bars.

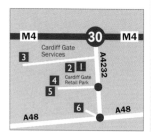

JUNCTION 30

Nearest A&E Hospital
University Hospital of Wales
Heath Park, Cardiff CF4 4XW
Tel: (029) 2074 7747
Follow the A48 south
(Signposted. Distance Approx
5.3 Miles)

FACILITIES

1   Cardiff Gate Services
(Total)

Tel: (029) 2073 5618
Adjacent to the south west
side of roundabout.
Access, Visa, Overdrive, All
Star, Switch, Dial Card,
Mastercard, Amex, Diners Club,
Delta, Securicor Fuelserv,
Keyfuels, UK Fuelcard, Maxol,
Self Diesel, Total/Fina/Elf
Cards.

2   Ibis Hotel Cardiff Gate

Tel: (029) 2073 3222
Adjacent to the south west
side of roundabout.
Restaurant Open; 06.30-
22.30hrs daily.

3   Toby Carvery, Cardiff
Gate

Tel: (029) 2054 1132

Adjacent to the south west
side of roundabout.
(Six Continents) Open all day.
Carvery Open; Mon-Fri; 12.00-
14.00hrs & 17.00-22.00hrs,
Sat; 12.00-22.00hrs, Sun;
12.00-21.30hrs. Bar Meals
served; 12.00-22.00hrs daily

4   McDonald's

Tel: (029) 2073 3228
0.5 miles south along the
A4232, on the right, in Cardiff
Gate Retail Park.
Open; Sun-Thurs; 07.30-
23.00hrs, Fri & Sat; 07.30-
0.00hrs.

5   Asda Filling Station

Tel: (029) 2034 0276
0.5 miles south along the
A4232, on the right, in Cardiff
Gate Retail Park.
Access, Visa, Overdrive, All
Star, Switch, Dial Card,
Mastercard, Amex, Diners Club,
Delta, BP Supercharge, Asda
Business Card. Open; Mon-Sat;
07.00-22.30hrs, Sun; 09.00-
17.30hrs. (24hr card operated
pumps available). Toilets and
Cash Machine available in
adjacent store.

6   Campanile Hotel
Cardiff

Tel: (029) 2054 9044
1 mile south along the
A4232, on the right.
The Bistro Restaurant; Open;
12.00-14.00hrs & 19.00-
22.00hrs daily

PLACES OF INTEREST

Cardiff

Follow the A48 south
(Signposted 5 Miles)
For details please see Junction
29 information

Within the city centre...

Cardiff Castle

Castle Street, Cardiff CF1 2RB

For details please see Junction
29 information

National Museum &
Gallery

Cathays Park, Cardiff CF1 3NP

For details please see Junction
29 information

Cardiff Bay: Millennium
Waterfront

For details please see Junction
29 information

JUNCTION 31

THERE IS NO JUNCTION 31

JUNCTION 32

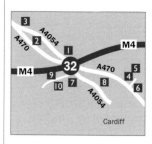

Nearest A&E Hospital
University Hospital of Wales
Heath Park, Cardiff CF4 4XW
Tel: (029) 2074 7747
Follow the A470 south
(Distance Approx 2.4 Miles)

FACILITIES

1   Quality Hotel Cardiff

Tel: (029) 2052 9988

0.1 miles north along the A4054, on the right.

The Hillside Restaurant; Breakfast; Mon-Fri; 07.00-09.45hrs, Sat & Sun; 07.30-10.00hrs, Dinner; Mon-Sat; 19.00-21.45hrs, Sun; 19.00-21.30hrs. Bar Snacks available; 12.00-22.00hrs daily

2   Old Tom Inn

Tel: (029) 2081 1865

0.6 miles north along the A4054, on the left, in Tongwynlais.

(Whitbread) Open all day. Meals served; Mon-Sat; 11.00-21.00hrs, Sun; 12.00-21.00hrs

3   The Lewis Arms

Tel: (029) 2081 0330

0.6 miles north along the A4054, on the right, in Tongwynlais.

(Brain's) Open all day. Meals served; Mon-Sat; 12.00-14.45hrs & 18.00-20.45hrs, Sun; 12.00-14.45hrs

4   Toby Carvery, Whitchurch

Tel: (029) 2069 2554

1 mile south along the A470, on the left.

(Six Continents) Open all day. Restaurant Open; Mon-Sat; 12.00-14.00hrs & 17.00-22.00hrs, Sun; 12.00-22.00hrs. Bar meals served; 12.00-22.00hrs daily.

5   Inn Keeper's Lodge, Whitchurch

Tel: (029) 2069 2554

1 mile south along the A470, on the left.

(Six Continents)

6   BP Safeway Filling Station

Tel: (029) 2061 6141

1 mile south along the A470, on the left.

Access, Visa, Overdrive, All Star, Switch, Dial Card, Mastercard, Amex, Diners Club, BP Cards, Shell Agency. Open; 06.00-23.00hrs daily

7   Village Hotel & Leisure Club

Tel: (029) 2052 4300

0.1 miles south along the A4054, on the right.

Salingers Bar & Restaurant; Open; Mon-Sat; 12.00-14.00hrs & 18.00-22.30hrs, Sun; 12.30-22.00hrs. The Village Pub; Meals served; Mon-Sat; 12.00-21.30hrs, Sun; 12.00-21.00hrs. Café Copra; Open; 08.00-23.00hrs daily

8   The Holly Bush

Tel: (029) 2062 5037

0.4 miles south along the A4054, on the left.

(Six Continents) Open all day. Meals served; 12.00-14.00hrs & 17.30-22.00hrs daily.

9   Coryton Services (Esso)

Tel: (029) 2061 6044

Adjacent to the south west side of roundabout.

Access, Visa, Overdrive, All Star, Switch, Dial Card, Mastercard, Amex, AA Paytrak, Diners Club, Delta, BP Supercharge, Shell Gold, Esso Cards.

10   McDonald's

Tel: (029) 2069 1700

Adjacent to the south west side of roundabout.

Open; Sun-Thurs; 07.30-23.00hrs. Fri & Sat; 07.30-0.00hrs

PLACES OF INTEREST

Cardiff

Follow the A470 south (Signposted 4.2 Miles)

For details please see Junction 29 information

Within the city centre...

Cardiff Castle

Castle Street, Cardiff CF1 2RB

For details please see Junction 29 information

National Museum & Gallery

Cathays Park, Cardiff CF1 3NP

For details please see Junction 29 information

Cardiff Bay: Millennium Waterfront

For details please see Junction 29 information

Caerphilly Castle

Caerphilly CF83 1JD
Tel: (029) 2088 3143 website: www.cadw.wales.gov.uk

Follow the A480 north (Signposted 5.5 Miles)

Built by the Anglo-Norman lord, Gilbert de Clare, in the late 13thC to consolidate his control on the lands he had captured, it sprawls over 30 acres and is one of the largest castles in Britain. The ingenuity of the "walls within walls" fortifications and the scale of its water defences ensured that it was out of the range of military catapults and never taken in battle. Due to immense reconstructions carried out by the former owner, the 4th Marquess of Bute, and since 1947 by Government agencies, Caerphilly Castle can be viewed today as a splendid example of early military architecture. Gift Shop. Limited disabled access.

Castell Coch

Tongwynlais, Nr Cardiff CF15 7J
Tel: (029) 2081 0101 website:
www.cadw.wales.gov.uk

**Follow the A470 north
(Signposted 0.7 Miles)**

Built on the site of a mediaeval castle, Castell Coch was commissioned by the 3rd Marquess of Bute in 1865. The architect, William Burges, was given free reign to create a Victorian dream of the Middle Ages as a companion piece to the patron's home at Cardiff Castle and the result was the ultimate fairytale castle.

The conical towers and needle sharp turrets peek out from a wooded slope and present a vision more in tune with the Bavarian countryside, the pages of Sleeping Beauty, or even a Walt Disney creation than a Welsh hillside. The interior is extravagantly decorated in the "anything goes" spirit of the Victorian age and there are fantastic furnishings and fireplaces. Gift Shop. Tea Room. Disabled access (free) to ground floor only.

M4
JUNCTION 33

APART FROM CARDIFF WEST SERVICES THERE ARE NO OTHER FACILITIES WITHIN ONE MILE OF THIS JUNCTION

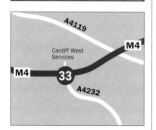

Nearest Westbound A&E Hospital

The Royal Glamorgan Hospital

Llantrisant CF72 8XR
Tel: (01443) 443443

Proceed to Junction 34 and it is signposted from the Junction. (Distance Approx 5 Miles)

Nearest Eastbound A&E Hospital

University Hospital of Wales

Heath Park, Cardiff CF4 4XW
Tel: (029) 2074 7747

Proceed to Junction 32 and follow the A470 south (Distance Approx 5.9 Miles)

FACILITIES

CARDIFF WEST SERVICES (MOTO)

Tel: (029) 2089 1141
Fresh Express Self Service Restaurant, Burger King, Travelodge & Esso Fuel

PLACES OF INTEREST

Cardiff

**Follow the A4232 south
(Signposted 7 Miles)**

For details please see Junction 29 information

Within the city centre...

Cardiff Castle

Castle Street, Cardiff CF1 2RB

For details please see Junction 29 information

National Museum & Gallery

Cathays Park, Cardiff CF1 3NP

For details please see Junction 29 information

Cardiff Bay: Millennium Waterfront

For details please see Junction 29 information

Museum of Welsh Life

St Fagans, Cardiff CF5 6XB
Tel: (029) 2057 3500
website: www.nmgw.ac.uk

**Follow the A4232 south
(Signposted 1.8 Miles)**

Over forty buildings have been taken down and rebuilt here to recreate Welsh daily life throughout history. Set in 100 acres of beautiful countryside, the open air museum follows the evolution of national life from a Celtic village of 2,000 years ago to a miner's cottage of the 1980's. Recent additions include a pre-fab and a house of the future. Gift Shop. Restaurant. Disabled access.

M4
JUNCTION 34

Nearest A&E Hospital

The Royal Glamorgan Hospital

Llantrisant CF72 8XR
Tel: (01443) 443443

Signposted from Junction. (Distance Approx 2.7 Miles)

FACILITIES

1   Miskin Manor Country Hotel

Tel: (01443) 224204

0.6 miles north along the A4119, on the left.

The Miskin Restaurant Open; Lunch; Sun-Fri; 12.00-14.00hrs, Dinner; 19.00-21.45hrs daily. (Pre-booking advisable).

2 Castell Mynach

Tel: (01443) 220940

0.7 miles north along the A4119, on the right.

(Vintage Inns) Open all day. Meals served; Mon-Sat; 12.00-22.00hrs, Sun; 12.00-21.30hrs.

3 Corner Park Garage (Texaco)

Tel: (01443) 224115

1 mile north along the A4119, on the left.

Access, Visa, Overdrive, All Star, Switch, Dial Card, Mastercard, Amex, Diners Club, Delta, BP Supercharge, Fast Fuel, Texaco Cards.

4 Llanerch Vineyard

Tel: (01443) 220940

1 mile west along the Hensol Road, in Hensol (Signposted). Café Open; 10.00-17.00hrs daily.

Nearest A&E Hospital

The Princess of Wales Hospital

Coity Road, Bridgend
CF31 1RQ
Tel: (01656) 752752

Proceed west to Junction 36 (Signposted from Junction. Distance Approx 4.9 Miles)

FACILITIES

1 Old Kings Head

Tel: (01656) 860203

1 mile north, on the right, in Pencoed.

(Punch Taverns) Open all day. Kurtie's Kebabs; Meals served; 12.00-23.30hrs daily

2 Pencoed Service Station (Murco)

Tel: (01656) 863855

1 mile north, on the right, in Pencoed.

Access, Visa, Delta, Mastercard, Switch, Diners Club, Amex, Electron, Solo, Overdrive, All Star, Dial Card, Murco Cards.

3 Riverside Filling Station (BP)

Tel: (01656) 860783

1 mile north along the A473, on the left.

Access, Visa, Overdrive, All Star, Switch, Dial Card, Mastercard, Amex, AA Paytrak, Diners Club, Delta, Routex, BP Cards, Shell Agency. Open; 06.00-21.00hrs daily

4 Cross Roads Service Station (Texaco)

Tel: (01656) 863686

Adjacent to north east side of roundabout.

LPG. Keyfuels, Access, Visa, Overdrive, All Star, Switch, Dial Card, Mastercard, Amex, Diners Club, Delta, BP Supercharge, Fast Fuel, Texaco Cards.

5 McDonald's

Tel: (01656) 865484

Adjacent to north east side of roundabout.

Open; 07.30-23.00hrs daily

6 Pantruthyn Farm

Tel: (01656) 860133

Adjacent to north east side of roundabout.

(Brewsters) Open all day. Meals served; Mon-Sat; 11.30-22.00hrs, Sun; 12.00-22.00hrs

7 Travel Inn

Tel: (01656) 860133

Adjacent to north east side of roundabout

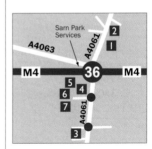

Nearest A&E Hospital

The Princess of Wales Hospital

Coity Road, Bridgend
CF31 1RQ
Tel: (01656) 752752

Signposted from Junction along A4061 south (Distance Approx 1.2 Miles)

FACILITIES

> **SARN PARK SERVICES (WELCOME BREAK)**
> Tel: (01656) 655332
> Red Hen Restaurant, Granary Restaurant, Welcome Lodge & Shell Fuel

1 The Royal Oak

Tel: (01656) 720083
0.7 miles north along the A4061, on the right.
(Inspired Inns) Open all day. Meals served; Mon-Sat; 10.15-23.00hrs, Sun; 12.00-15.00hrs. Bar Meals available; Mon-Sat; 19.00-21.00hrs.

2 The Masons Arms Hotel & Restaurant

Tel: (01656) 720253
1 mile north along the A4061, on the right.
Meals served; Mon-Sat; 12.00-14.30hrs & 18.00-22.00hrs, Sun; 12.00-15.00hrs

3 The Red Dragon
Tel: (01656) 654753
0.7 miles south along the Litchard Road, in Litchard.
(Scottish & Newcastle) Open all day. Meals served; 11.00-21.00hrs daily

4 Sainsbury's Filling Station

Tel: (01656) 648951
Adjacent to the south west side of the roundabout in The Derwen.
Access, Visa, Overdrive, All Star, Switch, Dial Card, Mastercard, Amex, Diners Club, Delta, Style Card, Sainsbury's Fuel Card. Toilets and Cash Machine are available in adjacent store.

5 McArthur Glen Designer Outlet

Tel: (01656) 665700
Adjacent to the south west side of the roundabout in The Derwen.
There are numerous cafés and restaurants, including Sidoli's, Harry Ramsden's, McDonald's, Madisons, Singapore Sam Chinese Restaurant, Fat Jackets and Costa Coffee, within the Food Court. (Open; Mon-Sat; 09.00-21.00hrs, Sun; 10.00-21.00hrs) and there is also a Pizza Hut (Open; 12.00-23.00hrs daily)

6 Express by Holiday Inn, Bridgend

Tel: (01656) 646200
Adjacent to the south west side of the roundabout in The Derwen.

7 The Farm Harvester Restaurant

Tel: (01656) 768668
Adjacent to the south west side of the roundabout in The Derwen.
(Harvester). Open all day. Meals served; 12.00-22.00hrs daily

PLACES OF INTEREST

Bryngarw Country Park
Brynmenyn, Nr Bridgend
CF32 8UU
Park Tel: (01656) 725155,
House Tel: (01656) 729009
website: www.bridgend.gov.uk

Follow the A4061 north (Signposted 1 Mile)
Bryngarw House, built in 1834, is set above a delightful ornamental garden, part of which is the exotic Japanese Garden of 1910. It is surrounded by a secluded 113 acre park with meadows, lake and woodland. The facilities include barbecue and picnic areas, a Visitor Centre and a children's play area. The Harlequin Restaurant serves cream teas, light refreshments and candle-lit dinners. Disabled facilities

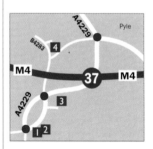

Nearest Eastbound A&E Hospital
The Princess of Wales Hospital
Coity Road, Bridgend
CF31 1RQ
Tel: (01656) 752752
Proceed to Junction 36 (Signposted from Junction. Distance Approx 6.8 Miles)

Nearest Westbound A&E Hospital
Neath General Hospital
Penrhiwtyn, Neath SA11 2LQ
Tel: (01639) 641161
Proceed to Junction 41, follow the A48 north and turn right along the A474. (Distance Approx 10.8 Miles)

FACILITIES

1   South Cornelly Service Station (Esso)

Tel: (01656) 746658
1 mile south along the A4229, on the left.
Access, Visa, Overdrive, All Star, Switch, Dial Card, Mastercard, Amex, AA Paytrak, Diners Club, Delta, BP Supercharge, Shell Gold, Esso Cards.

2   Leraj Indian Restaurant

Tel: (01656) 741174
1 mile south along the A4229, on the left.
Open; Mon -Fri; 18.00-0.00hrs, Sat & Sun; 12.00-14.30hrs & 18.00-0.00hrs.

3   The Three Horseshoes

Tel: (01656) 740037
0.7 miles south, on the left, in South Cornelly.
(Unique Pub Company) Meals served; Mon-Sat; 12.00-14.15hrs & 18.30-21.30hrs, Sun; 12.00-14.30hrs & 19.00-20.30hrs

4   The New House Inn

Tel: (01656) 747911
1 mile west, on the right in North Cornelly.
(Voyager) Open all day. Mon-Sat; 12.00-14.00hrs & 17.30-21.30hrs, Sun; 12.00-14.00hrs

PLACES OF INTEREST

Bedford Park

Cefn Cribwr, Nr Kenfig Hill, Bridgend Tel: (01656) 725155

Follow the A4228 north, continue along the A48 to Pyle and turn right along the B4281. (4.5 Miles)
Centred on a Scheduled Ancient Monument, the former Cefn Cribwr Ironworks established by John Bedford in the 1780's, Bedford Park is an interesting mix of industrial archaeology, rare plants, flowers and country walks and nature trails, all sited within 40 acres of parkland. There are children's play areas and classroom facilities.

Kenfig National Nature Reserve

Ton Kenfig, Bridgend CF33 4PT
Tel: (01656) 743386

Take the A4229 and follow signposts to Ton Kenfig (2.5 Miles)
This mecca for naturalists, birdwatchers and ramblers consists of 1,300 acres of fascinating dunescapes honeycombed with pathways and trails and containing more than 550 species of flowering plants, including 14 varieties of orchids. The 70 acre freshwater lake provides a haven for birds and the Kenfig Reserve Centre has an exhibition, mini nature reserve, shop and information on places to visit. Gift Shop. Limited disabled access.

M4
JUNCS 38 & 39

THESE ARE RESTRICTED ACCESS JUNCTIONS

JUNCTION 38:
■ Vehicles can only exit from the westbound lanes
■ Vehicles can only enter along the eastbound lanes

JUNCTION 39:
■ Vehicles can only enter along the westbound lanes.
■ Vehicles cannot exit at this junction in either direction

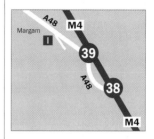

Nearest Eastbound A&E Hospital
The Princess of Wales Hospital
Coity Road, Bridgend CF31 1RQ
Tel: (01656) 752752
Proceed to Junction 36 (Signposted from Junction. Distance Approx 10.8 Miles)

Nearest Westbound A&E Hospital
Neath General Hospital
Penrhiwtyn, Neath SA11 2LQ
Tel: (01639) 641161
Proceed to Junction 41, follow the A48 north and turn right along the A474. (Distance Approx 6.8 Miles)

FACILITIES

1   The Twelve Knights

Tel: (01639) 882381
0.9 miles north along the A48, on the left.
(Noble House Company) Open all day. Meals served; Mon-Fri; 12.00-14.00hrs & 18.00-21.00hrs, Sat; 18.00-21.00hrs, Sun; 12.00-15.00hrs

PLACES OF INTEREST

Margam Abbey & Stones Museum

Margam, Port Talbot SA13 2TA
Margam Abbey
Tel: (01639) 871184
Stones Museum
Tel: (029) 2050 0200
website: www.cadw.wales.gov.uk

Follow the A48 east, adjacent to motorway junction (0.2 Miles)

Margam Abbey Church, founded in 1147, is the only Cistercian Foundation in Wales, whose nave is still intact and used for Christian worship. The Stones Museum, housed in an old school house, contains a collection of Christian memorials from the sub-Roman era right through to the hugely impressive "cart-wheel" crosses of the 10th & 11thC's, the finest example of which is the Cross of Conbelin. Restaurant. Gift Shop. Disabled access.

Margam Country Park

Margam, Port Talbot SA13 2TJ
Tel: (01639) 881635 website: www.neath-porttalbot.gov.uk

Follow the A48 east, adjacent to motorway junction (Signposted 0.5 Miles)

Set in 850 acres of glorious parklands, Margam Country Park offers something for all the family. The park, centred on Margam Castle, a Tudor/Gothic folly built in 1840, and the magnificent Orangery, constructed in 1789, contains a variety of attractions including splendid walks, Fairytale Land, a children's play area, Miniature Railway, Farm Trail, Pets Corner, boating and fishing. Gift Shop. Charlotte's Pantry. Disabled access.

M4 JUNCTION 40

Nearest Eastbound A&E Hospital
The Princess of Wales Hospital
Coity Road, Bridgend
CF31 1RQ
Tel: (01656) 752752
Proceed to Junction 36 (Signposted from Junction. Distance Approx 13.3 Miles)

Nearest Westbound A&E Hospital
Neath General Hospital
Penrhiwtyn, Neath SA11 2LQ
Tel: (01639) 641161
Proceed to Junction 41, follow the A48 north and turn right along the A474. (Distance Approx 4.3 Miles)

FACILITIES

PORT TALBOT TOWN CENTRE IS WITHIN ONE MILE OF THE JUNCTION.

THERE ARE NO FACILITIES ADJACENT TO THIS JUNCTION

PLACES OF INTEREST

Afanargoed Countryside Centre & South Wales Miners Museum in Afan Forest Park

Cynonville, Port Talbot SA13 3HG
Tel: (01639) 850564
website: www.forestry.gov.uk

Follow the A4107 east (Signposted 5.2 Miles)

This gateway to 9,000 acres of forest park, is ideal for quiet countryside recreation. Facilities are available for walking, cycling, for which cycles are available for hire, orienteering, camping and caravanning. The Visitor Centre contains a Gift Shop and Cafe and the adjacent South Wales Miners Museum, depicts the story of the miner and his family in the South Wales valleys. The range of outdoor exhibits also includes a blacksmith's shop and winding wheel. Disabled access.

M4 JUNCTION 41

PORT TALBOT TOWN CENTRE IS WITHIN ONE MILE OF THE SOUTH EXIT.

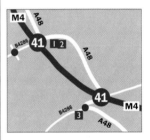

Nearest A&E Hospital
Neath General Hospital
Penrhiwtyn, Neath SA11 2LQ
Tel: (01639) 641161
Follow the A48 north and turn right along the A474. (Distance Approx 3.1 Miles)

FACILITIES

1   The Bagle Brook

Tel: (01639) 813017
0.2 miles south along the A48 from the north exit, on the right.
(Beefeater) Open all day. Meals served; Mon-Thurs 12.00-14.00hrs & 17.30-22.00hrs,

Fri; 12.00-14.00hrs & 17.30-22.30hrs, Sat; 12.00-22.30hrs, Sun; 12.00-21.00hrs

2   Travel Inn

Tel: (01639) 813017
0.2 miles south along the A48 from the north exit, on the right

3   Blanco's Café Bar

Tel: (01639) 896378
0.4 miles along the A48 from the south exit, on the right.
Meals served; 12.00-14.30hrs daily.

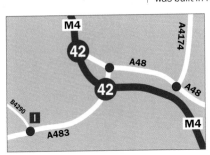

Nearest A&E Hospital
Neath General Hospital
Penrhiwtyn, Neath SA11 2LQ
Tel: (01639) 641161
Follow the A48 south and turn left along the A474. (Distance Approx 1.9 Miles)

FACILITIES

1   Shell Swansea Bay

Tel: (01792) 326900
1 mile west along the A483, on the right (From eastbound exit), 0.5 miles west along

the A483, on the right (From westbound exit)
Access, Visa, Overdrive, All Star, Switch, Dial Card, Mastercard, Amex, AA Paytrak, Diners Club, Delta, BP Supercharge, Shell Cards.

PLACES OF INTEREST

Swansea

Swansea Tourist Information Centre, Singleton Street, Swansea SA1 3QG. Tel: (01792) 468321
website: www.want2getaway.net

Follow the A483 west (Signposted 5 Miles)
The town was granted its charter in 1210 and the original motte and bailey castle was built in Norman times, only to be replaced by a stone structure in the late 13thC. In its heyday as a port the docks had over six miles of quays, but today these are all but gone and the Maritime Quarter, a modern leisure centre with a 600 berth marina, now occupies the area. A former warehouse on this waterfront has been converted into a Maritime & Industrial Museum (Tel: 01792-650351) tracing the development of Swansea as a seaport and detailing some of the traditional industries.

To the south of the town and sweeping west to the unspoilt Victorian village of Mumbles is the impressive Swansea Bay, part of the Gower Peninsula. One of Swansea's most famous sons, Dylan Thomas, is commemorated at the Dylan Thomas Centre (Tel: 01792-463980) on the banks of the River Tawe, whilst his

birthplace at 5 Cwmdonkin Drive still exists, although in private ownership as a dwelling.

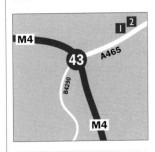

Nearest A&E Hospital
Neath General Hospital
Penrhiwtyn, Neath SA11 2LQ
Tel: (01639) 641161
Follow the A465 north and turn right along the A474 (Distance Approx 3.7 miles)

FACILITIES

1   Sgiwen Service Station (Total)

Tel: (01792) 326930
0.4 miles north along the A465, on the left.
Access, Visa, Delta, Mastercard, Switch, Diners Club, Amex Overdrive, Dial Card, Mastercard, Amex, Overdrive, All Star, Dial Card, Total/Fina/Elf Cards. Open; 06.00-23.00hrs daily

2   McDonald's

Tel: (01792) 817010
0.4 miles north along the A465, on the left.
Open; Sun; 07.30-0.00hrs, Mon-Wed; 07.30-23.00hrs, Thurs; 07.30-0.00hrs, Fri/Sat & Sat/Sun; 07.30-03.00hrs

PLACES OF INTEREST

Pant-y-Sais Fen

New Road, Jersey Marine
SA10 6JR Tel: (01639) 763207

Follow the A483 west (1.9 Miles)

A nature reserve and site of Special Scientific Interest, Pant-y-Sais Fen is one of the few wetlands remaining in the region and is a must for those who appreciate the flora and fauna only to be found in these areas. The site is adjacent to the Tennant Canal for onward towpath strolls and boardwalks provide environmental-friendly paths through the fen area. Disabled access.

JUNCTION 44

Birchgrove

Nearest Westbound A&E Hospital

Morriston Hospital

Morriston, Swansea
SA6 6NL
Tel: (01792) 702222
Proceed to Junction 45 (Signposted from the junction. Distance Approx 3 miles)

Nearest Eastbound A&E Hospital

Neath General Hospital

Penrhiwtyn, Neath SA11 2LQ

Tel: (01639) 641161

Proceed to Junction 43, follow the A465 north and turn right along the A474 (Distance Approx 3.7 miles)

FACILITIES

1   The Bowen Arms

Tel: (01792) 812321

0.5 miles south along the A4230, on the left.

(Entrepreneurs) Open all day. Meals served; Mon-Sat; 12.00-14.30hrs & 18.00-21.00hrs, Sun; 12.00-15.00hrs

2   DF & AM Bevan (Texaco)

Tel: (01792) 817505

0.6 miles south along the A4230, on the right.

LPG. Access, Visa, Mastercard, Switch, Electron, Solo, Diners Club, Amex, Overdrive All Star, Dial Card, Delta, BP Supercharge, Texaco Cards.

3   Llansamlet Service Station (Total)

Tel: (01792) 701330

0.7 miles west along the A48, on the right.

Access, Visa, Overdrive, All Star, Switch, Dial Card, Mastercard, Amex, AA Paytrak, Diners Club, Delta, Keyfuels, Diesel Direct, Total/Fina/Elf

---

Cards. Open; Mon-Fri; 07.00-22.00hrs, Sat & Sun; 08.00-20.00hrs.

PLACES OF INTEREST

Swansea

Follow the A48 west (Signposted 4.5 Miles)

For details please see Junction 42 information

JUNCTION 45

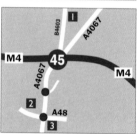

Nearest A&E Hospital

Morriston Hospital

Morriston, Swansea
SA6 6NL
Tel: (01792) 702222
Signposted from the junction (Distance Approx 1 mile)

FACILITIES

1   Millers Arms

Tel: (01792) 842614

0.7 miles north along the B4603, on the right, in Ynystawe.

(Laurel Pub Partnership) Open all day on Sat. Meals served; Mon; 11.30-14.00hrs, Tues-Sat; 11.30-14.00hrs & 18.00-21.30hrs, Sun; 12.00-14.30hrs.

2 McDonald's

Tel: (01792) 774295

1 mile south along the A4067, on the right.

Open; Sun-Thurs; 07.30-23.00hrs, Fri & Sat; 11.30-0.00hrs

3 Wychtree Service Station (Texaco)

Tel: (01792) 700071

1 mile south along the A4067, on the left.

Access, Visa, Overdrive, All Star, Switch, Dial Card, Mastercard, Amex, Diners Club, Delta, Texaco Cards.

PLACES OF INTEREST

Swansea

Follow the A4067 south (Signposted 3.7 Miles)

For details please see Junction 42 information

JUNCTION 46

THIS IS A RESTRICTED ACCESS JUNCTION

- Vehicles can only exit from the westbound lanes
- Vehicles can only enter the motorway along the eastbound lanes

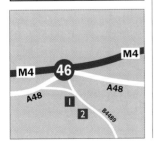

Nearest A&E Hospital
Morriston Hospital

Morriston, Swansea
SA6 6NL
Tel: (01792) 702222

Signposted from the junction
(Distance Approx 1.5 miles)

FACILITIES

1 Plough & Harrow

Tel: (01792) 771816

0.2 miles south along the B4489, on the right.

(Free House) Open all day. Meals served; Mon-Sat; 12.00-14.00hrs & 17.00-20.30hrs, Sun; 12.00-14.00hrs.

2 The Willow Guest House

Tel: (01792) 775948

0.4 miles south along the B4489, on the right

PLACES OF INTEREST

Swansea

Follow the B4489 south (Signposted 3.3 Miles)

For details please see Junction 42 information

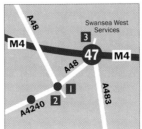

JUNCTION 47

Nearest A&E Hospital
Morriston Hospital

Morriston, Swansea
SA6 6NL
Tel: (01792) 702222

Proceed east to Junction 45
(Signposted from the junction.
Distance Approx 4.5 miles)

FACILITIES

SWANSEA WEST SERVICES (MOTO)

Tel: (01792) 896222

Burger King, Little Chef, Café Nescafé, Travelodge & BP Fuel

1 Cross Service Station (Total)

Tel: (01792) 222932

0.3 miles west along the A48, on the left, in Penllergaer.

Access, Visa, Delta, Mastercard, Switch, Diners Club, Amex, Overdrive, All Star, Dial Card, Total/Fina/Elf Cards. Open; Mon-Sat; 07.00-23.00hrs, Sun; 08.00-22.00hrs.

2 The Old Inn

Tel: (01792) 894097

0.3 miles west along the A48, on the left, in Penllergaer.

(Brain's) Open all day Sat. Restaurant Open; Mon-Fri; 12.00-14.15hrs & 18.00-21.30hrs, Sat; 12.00-14.15hrs & 18.00-22.00hrs, Sun; 12.00-14.30hrs & 19.00-21.15hrs. Bar Meals served; 12.00-14.30hrs & 18.00-21.30hrs daily.

3 McDonald's

Tel: (01792) 898655

Adjacent to north side of roundabout.

Open; 07.30-23.00hrs daily.

PLACES OF INTEREST

Swansea

Follow the A483 south (Signposted 5 Miles)

For details please see Junction 42 information

Nearest A&E Hospital
Morriston Hospital

Morriston, Swansea
SA6 6NL
Tel: (01792) 702222

Proceed east to Junction 45 (Signposted from the junction. Distance Approx 8.5 miles)

FACILITIES

1   The Black Horse Inn

Tel: (01792) 882239
0.8 miles west along the A4138, on the left.
(Brain's) Open all day. Meals served; Mon-Thurs; 12.00-15.00hrs & 17.00-21.00hrs, Fri & Sat; 12.00-21.00hrs, Sun; 12.00-16.00hrs.

2   The Gwyn Hotel

Tel: (01792) 882187

0.9 miles west along the A48, on the right, in Pontardulais.
Open all day. Meals served; Mon-Sat; 12.00-14.30hrs & 19.00-21.30hrs, Sun; 12.00-15.30hrs

3   Shell Central

Tel: (01792) 885741
1 mile west along the A48, on the right, in Pontardulais.
Access, Visa, Overdrive, All Star, Switch, Dial Card, Mastercard, Amex, Diners Club, Delta, BP Supercharge, Shell Cards. Open; Mon-Sat; 06.00-22.00hrs, Sun; 07.00-21.00hrs.

4   Smiths Arms

Tel: (01554) 820305
1 mile east along the B4297, on the left, in Llangennech.
(Crown Buckley Taverns) Open all day. Meals served; Mon-Sat; 12.00-14.00hrs & 18.00-21.00hrs, Sun; 12.00-18.00hrs

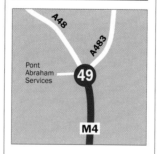

APART FROM PONT ABRAHAM SERVICES THERE ARE NO OTHER FACILITIES AT THIS JUNCTION

Nearest A&E Hospital
Morriston Hospital

Morriston, Swansea SA6 6NL
Tel: (01792) 702222

Proceed east to Junction 45 (Signposted from the junction. Distance Approx 11.2 miles)

FACILITIES

PONT ABRAHAM SERVICES (ROADCHEF)
Tel: (01792) 884663
Food Fayre Self-Service Restaurant & BP Fuel

MOTORWAY ENDS
(Total length of Motorway 189.0 miles or 190.7 miles via M48)

the **M5**

The primary road route into the South West of England, parts of which were surveyed in the 1940s, it extends from the Ray Hall Interchange with the M6 at Junction 8 to the west side of Exeter, linking up with the A30 and A38 onwards into Devon and Cornwall.

From its junction with the M6, the motorway heads south and between Junctions 1 and 3 passes through the West Midlands conurbation with the western edge of Birmingham on the east side and the area known as the "**Black Country**" to the west. Originally centred around Dudley this area now embraces Wolverhampton, West Bromwich and other small towns within the vicinity. The name is purported to have derived from the large seam of coal upon which it stood and became a 19thC base for the iron and steel industry. Continuing south past the western outskirts of **Birmingham**, a city rich in industrial history and now a thriving cultural, sporting and shopping centre, the motorway crosses the **Frankley Tunnel**, carrying water from the Elan Valley in Wales to Birmingham, and just after Frankley Services the Lickey Hills are visible on the east side, with the **MG Rover Plant** at Longbridge in view at the foot of the hill. Herbert Austin established the factory at Longbridge in November 1905 and its world famous products include the pre-war Austin 7 and the Mini.

The section of motorway between Junction 4 and the connection with the M50 at Junction 8 was the first in the country to have its line established by an order under the Special Roads Act [1949] and was the first part of the M5 to be built, opening as a 2-lane motorway on July 20th, 1962. The motorway continues south westwards from Junction 4A, where it links up with the M42,
and passes **Bromsgrove** on the east side. The bridge (marker post 31.6) just after this junction was involved in a bizarre accident in 1993 when a large crane, which was being transported northwards on the back of a low-loader, became unstable and its jib collided with the bridge, leaving a massive dent in the support girder. It was six years before the bridge was repaired taking 11 weeks, including total closure of the section on the night of September 25/26th, 1999, and at a cost of £245,000! Radio masts at the **BBC Droitwich Transmitting Station**, which opened on October 7th, 1934 to supplement the transmitter at Daventry (to be seen from the M1 motorway), dominate the skyline on the eastern side as the carriageways reach Junction 5.

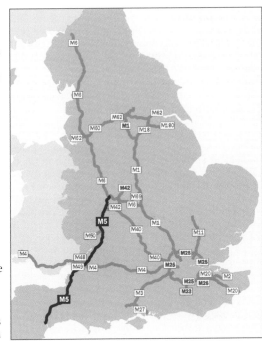

The section between here and Junction 6 passes the east side of **Droitwich**, a great town in the days of King John which was famous as a spa resort with its 100 foot deep well drawing up some of the most salienated water in Europe, some ten times stronger than sea water. Just south of Junction 5, the towers of the **Chateau Impney**, built in 1875 in the classic French chateau style of architecture, can be glimpsed through the trees. On the west side of the motorway, adjacent to Junction 6, is **Sixways** the home ground of Worcester RUFC and, on the top of the hill, the **transmittter mast** and headquarters of West Mercia Police. Continuing south west through Worcestershire the motorway passes the famous cathedral city of **Worcester** on the west side. This city dates from Saxon days and its industries include glove making and art pottery. The cathedral, which is in view just south of Junction 7, was rebuilt in Norman days and houses the tomb of King John. Between Junctions 7 and 8 an unusual structure known as "The Panorama" can be observed on the west side, sited on Knights Hill. This was part of the landscaping of Croome Court commissioned by the 6th Earl of Coventry in 1801, designed by James Wyatt and completed in about 1810.

Worcester Cathedral

The motorway connects with the M50 at Junction 8 before crossing the alluvial flood plain and River Severn with **Bredon Hill**, site of an Iron Age fort, in view to the east with the delightful village of **Bredon** nestling on the south bank of the river. Just south of the river, parts of **Tewkesbury** can be seen on the west side of the motorway near Junction 9. This town dates back to the 6thC, having taken its name from Theoc (becoming Theocsbury) an early missionary, and contains a well preserved Abbey dating back to 1123 as well as some Tudor buildings. As the motorway continues south through Gloucestershire the **Cotswold Hills** are in the distance to the east and the **Forest of Dean** to the west before it passes between **Gloucester**, on the west side, and **Cheltenham** to the east and reaches Junction 12. Gloucester, an important historic city, originated in Roman times, was rebuilt in 50AD and contains many mediaeval buildings. Henry III was crowned here in 1216 and the tomb of Edward II is in the cathedral, the 225ft high tower of which is visible from the motorway. Cheltenham is a spa town with mineral springs dating back to 1715 and possesses some fine Georgian buildings.

Just south of Junction 12 the motorway crosses over part of the disused former **RAF Moreton Valence** airfield. This was utilized as a training unit and aircraft factory until it closed when the last flight, a single Javelin, took off on July 25th, 1962. The redundant buildings have since been converted into an industrial park and part of the site was earmarked for a proposed service area as the short slip roads, built at the same time as the carriageways, will testify. Continuing south westwards, the 111ft high **Tyndale Monument**, comes into view between Junctions 13 and 14 on the east side at Nibley Knoll. This was erected between 1863 and 1866 as a memorial to William Tyndale who was born in North Nibley. He is reputed to have been the first scholar to translate the New Testament into English and this work formed the basis for the authorized version of the Bible. By referring to the original Greek and Hebrew sources, rather than the "approved" Latin translations, he was accused of heresy and in 1536 arrested and taken to Vilvorde, near Brussels. He was convicted and burned at the stake on October 6th, 1536. North Nibley also has a unique place in English history as the site of the last "private" battle which took place in 1471 between the rival barons William Lord Berkeley and the Viscount De Lisle.

As the motorway approaches Junction 15, where it passes under the M4, there are panoramic views eastwards across to the **Marlborough and Lambourn Downs**. Junction 15 is known as the "Almondbury Interchange". This four-level structure was opened in

September 1966, occupies 80 acres of land and includes some 7 miles of road.

Between Junction 15 and Junctions 18 and 18A, where the M4 connects with the M49, the historic port city of **Bristol** is passed to the south east with the Bristol Channel, straddled by the two Severn Bridges, and the Welsh Mountains beyond, in view to the north west. Continuing south west to Junction 19, the **Avonmouth Bridge**, with views of the Avon Gorge to the east, spectacularly carries the motorway over the River Avon. Opened in May 1974, the bridge is 4,550ft long with a 100ft clearance over high water and has a 570ft long main river span with two side spans of 370ft. On the north bank, **Avonmouth Docks and Works** are on the west side and **Shirehampton** is on the east. Just south west of Junction 19 the motorway splits into two levels as it clings to the side of Tickenham Hill with **Cudbury Camp**, an ancient fortification, towering over the carriageways. Here, there are splendid views to the west of the plateau stretching away to the coastal town of **Portishead** below Portishead Down with the Bristol Channel and Monmouthshire beyond.

Berkeley Castle

The genteel seaside town of **Clevedon** is on the west side of Junction 20. Clevedon has famous literary connections and Tennyson described the town as "the haven under the hill" in his work *In Memoriam*. Just beyond the junction the Blind Yeo River is bridged, **The Hand Stadium** (home ground of Clevedon Town FC) is on the east side and the **BBC Clevedon Transmitting Station**, opened in June 1939 and currently in use for the Radio 5 Live service, is on the west side. At Junction 21 the holiday town of **Weston super Mare** can be seen at the foot of Worlesbury Hill as the motorway turns due south and passes between the Bleadon and Mendip Hills. Beyond this point, **Brent Knoll** is clearly visible to the west before it reaches Junction 22. Brent Knoll, which can be seen from as far away as South Wales, was almost certainly an island before the Somerset Levels were drained. It rises to 450ft and is topped by the remains of an Iron Age fort. Several centuries later, its southern slope is reputed to have been the site of a battle against the Danes which was fought and won by King Alfred.

Between Junctions 22 and 23 the motorway passes **Highbridge**, once a busy coastal port, on the west side before traversing the Somerset Levels and crossing the River Brue and the Huntspill River. Just north of Junction 23, the adjacent towns of **Glastonbury**, a mecca for those encompassing such diverse beliefs as paganism, Christianity, Arthurian legend and the existence of UFO's, and **Street** an ancient settlement which became a thriving trading centre due largely to one entrepreneurial Quaker family (the Clarks), are visible in the distance, to the east, at the foot of Polden Hill. Continuing

Hestercombe Gardens

southwards, **Bridgwater**, with the tall chimney of the British Cellophane Works in view, is on the west side. Just before Junction 24 **Weston Zoyland**, pinpointed by the spire of the Church of St Mary, can be seen to the east. It was on the north side of this village that the Battle of Sedgemoor was fought in 1685 and the defeated rebels from the Duke of Monmouth's army were temporarily confined in the church. A little further south the River Parrett, the ex-Great Western Railway Bristol to Plymouth line and the Bridgwater and Taunton Canal are bridged by a 4,000ft long. 17 span viaduct. **The Bridgwater and Taunton Canal** originally opened in 1827 and although never officially closed was abandoned in the early part of the 20thC. It was restored and re-opened in 1994.

The town of **Taunton** is on the west side of Junction 25 and **Taunton Racecourse** is visible to the east. Taunton stands on the River Tone and has a castle dating from 702AD. The Duke of Monmouth was proclaimed as King here in 1685 and Judge Jeffries tried 509 rebels at the infamous Bloody Assizes in the Great Hall of the castle following the Battle of Sedgemoor. Taunton has the youngest racecourse in Britain, the 10 furlong oval track not being opened until 1927. The land was donated by Viscount Portman and the back straight passes over the site of Orchard House, a huge mansion that was razed to the ground in 1843 as a desperate measure to contain an outbreak of typhoid that decimated the family and staff. As the motorway turns westwards, between junctions 25 and 26 it passes **Poundisford Lodge**, a small H-shaped Tudor mansion, on the east side. The Lodge, renowned for its fine plasterwork and ceilings, stands in **Poundisford Park** a wooded deer park which once belonged to the Bishops of Winchester.

Between Junctions 26 and 27 the **Wellington Monument**, a landmark visible for miles around, can be seen on the south side. Sited on top of Monument Hill, it was erected in 1817-18 in honour of the 1st Duke of Wellington following his victory in the Battle of Waterloo in 1815. Just after Junction 26 the **Brendon Hills** are visible in the distance to the north and the **Blackdown Hills** to the south. Just east of Junction 27, the **Grand Western Canal and Country Park** is on the west side. The canal was conceived as a scheme to link the Bristol and English Channels. Only partially built, it was closed in 1962, but in the 1980s sections were restored and re-opened.

The motorway turns south at Junction 27 to follow the Culm Valley and a range of hills, including the 863ft high ancient settlement on **Huntsman Hill**, and the town of **Tiverton**, home of Blundell's School which was founded in 1604 and attended by Jan Ridd, the hero of RD Blackmore's *Lorna Doone*, are visible to the west. The town of **Cullompton**, a royal demesne in Saxon days, with a market that dates back to 1278, is adjacent to the west side of Junction 28. The carriageways south from Willand and by-passing Cullompton had originally been constructed in 1969 as part of the A38, but with the intention that they would eventually form part of the M5. They were upgraded and incorporated into the motorway in 1975. The route continues southwards along the valley before reaching Junction 30 and then swinging around the south side of **Exeter**, and crossing the River Exe and Exeter Canal by means of the 2,250ft long concrete Exe Viaduct between Junctions 30 and 31. Exeter was founded by the Celts in about 150BC, as Isca, and contains many

historical structures, including the oldest municipal building in England, The Guildhall and the 12thC Cathedral, the towers of which are visible from the motorway. The Exeter Canal, which runs parallel to the River Exe, was built in 1563 by John Trew to provide a navigable waterway into Exeter after Isabel, Countess of Devon built a weir across the river in the reign of Henry III.

The motorway ends at Junction 31 where the road diverges into the A38 to Plymouth and A30 to Okehampton.

Cathedral Close, Exeter

Location of Places of Interest

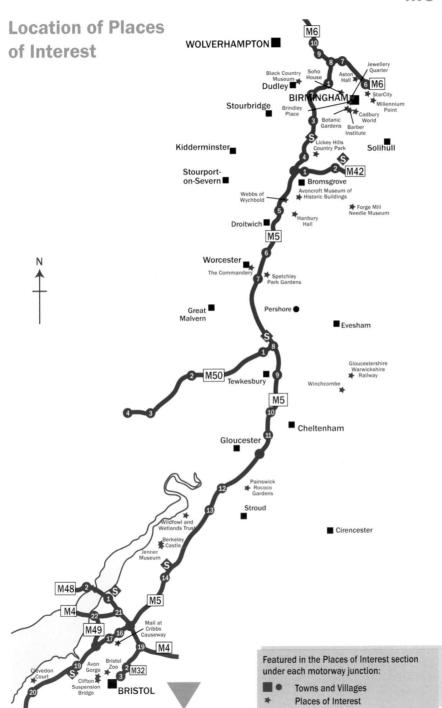

N

Featured in the Places of Interest section under each motorway junction:

■ ● Towns and Villages

★ Places of Interest

Location of Places of Interest

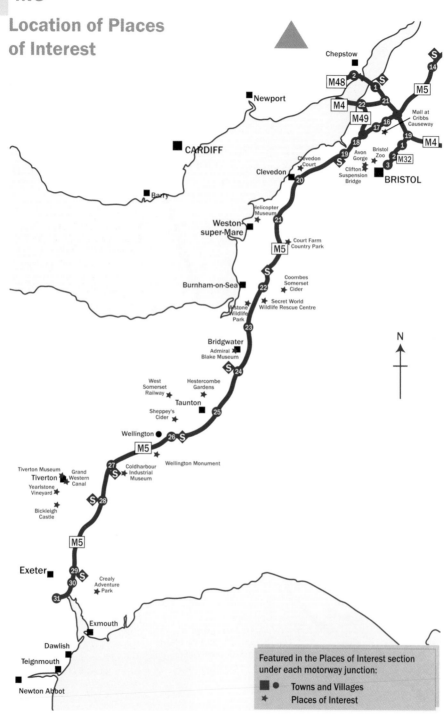

Featured in the Places of Interest section under each motorway junction:

■ ● Towns and Villages
★ Places of Interest

JUNCTION 1

> WEST BROMWICH TOWN
> CENTRE IS WITHIN ONE MILE
> OF THIS JUNCTION

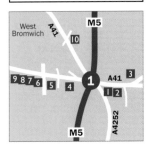

Nearest A&E Hospital

Sandwell District General Hospital

Hallam Street, West Bromwich B71 4HJ
Tel: (0121) 553 1831

Take the A41 west towards West Bromwich. Turn right at the roundabout along the A4031 and the hospital is on the right. (Distance Approx 1.8 miles)

FACILITIES

1   Hawthornes Petrol Station (BP)

Tel: (0121) 553 7666
0.2 miles east along the A41, on the right.
BP Cards, Routex, All Star, Overdrive, Diners Club, Switch, Visa, Mastercard.

2   The Hawthorns

Tel: (0121) 553 0915
0.4 miles east along the A41, on the right.
(Voyager) Meals served; Mon-Fri; 12.00-14.00hrs

3   Albion Filling Station (BP)

Tel: (0121) 551 1767
0.7 miles east along the A41, on the left.
BP Cards, Switch, Mastercard, Visa, Dial Card, All Star, Routex, Amex, Diners Club.

4   MI Bhattay & Sons, Esso Service Station

Tel: (0121) 525 4100
0.3 miles west along the Birmingham Road, on the left.
Esso Cards, Diners Club, Overdrive, Dial Card, All Star, Amex, Switch, Visa, Mastercard. Open; Mon-Sat; 07.30-22.00hrs, Sun; 09.00-21.00hrs.

5   Howard Johnson Hotel

Tel: (0121) 525 8333
0.7 miles west along the Birmingham Road, on the left.
Restaurant Open; Mon-Fri; 12.00-14.30hrs & 18.00-21.45hrs, Sat; 18.00-21.45hrs

6   Pizza Hut

Tel: (0121) 500 5232
1 mile west along the Birmingham Road, in the Farley Centre, West Bromwich.
Open; 11.30-23.00hrs daily.

7   McDonald's

Tel: (0121) 553 0436
1 mile west along the Birmingham Road, in the High Street, West Bromwich.
Open; 07.30-23.00hrs daily

8   KFC

Tel: (0121) 553 2119
1 mile west along the Birmingham Road, in the High Street, West Bromwich.
Open; Sun-Wed; 12.00-23.00hrs, Thurs; 12.00-0.00hrs, Fri/Sat; 12.00-03.00hrs, Sat/Sun; 11.00-02.00hrs

9   Shalimar Indian Cuisine

Tel: (0121) 553 1319
1 mile west along the Birmingham Road, in the High Street, West Bromwich.
Open 18.00-00.30hrs daily.

10 The Birmingham/ West Bromwich Moat House Hotel

Tel: (0121) 609 9988
0.3 miles north along Europa Avenue, on the right
Raferty's Restaurant Open; Breakfast; 07.00-09.30hrs daily, Lunch; Sun; 12.30-14.30hrs, Mon-Fri; 12.00-14.00hrs, Dinner; Mon-Sat; 18.30-22.00hrs, Sun; 19.00-21.30hrs.

PLACES OF INTEREST

Birmingham

Birmingham Convention & Visitor Bureau, 130 Colmore Row, Birmingham B3 3AP
Tel: (0121) 693 6300 website: www.birmingham.org.uk

Follow the A41 east (Signposted 4 miles)
Birmingham, Britain's second city, traditionally of industrial origins and the home base of a legion of world renowned brand names, has re-invented

itself in the last decade to become a major tourist destination and plays host to millions of conference and exhibition delegates from around the world.

Little more than a village at the time of the Domesday Book, its location alongside of the River Rea and adjacent to coal fields made it an ideal launch pad for the Industrial Revolution, and the attraction of entrepreneurs and engineering pioneers led to its rapid growth to become a fine Victorian city. Many of the buildings constructed during this period still remain and some of the earlier structures pre-dating this can still be found. The city centre, a very popular destination for shoppers and day trippers from all over the country, is undertaking a major rebuilding programme with reconstruction of the famous Bull Ring Centre the first phase of a £1billion plus investment in the expansion and modernization of the city.

Soho House

Soho Avenue, Off Soho Road, Handsworth, Birmingham B18 5LB Tel: (0121) 554 9122 website: www.bmag.org.uk

Follow A41 eastwards towards Birmingham and turn right into Soho Avenue (2.3 miles)

The former home of the industrialist pioneer Matthew Boulton who developed the steam engine in partnership with James Watt. Here, he met with some of the most important scientists, engineers and thinkers of his time - the Lunar Society. Refreshments. Gift Shop. Disabled access.

Museum of the Jewellery Quarter

75-79 Vyse Street, Hockley, Birmingham B18 6HA Tel: (0121) 554 3598 website: www.bmag.org.uk

Follow A41 east into the city centre and the route is signposted (3.3 miles)

The preserved "time-capsule" workshop of the family run firm of Smith & Pepper forms the centre-piece of this highly interesting and fascinating exhibition. Sited in the heart of the Jewellery Quarter, which for over 200 years has helped the city to become known as the "Workshop of the World", it demonstrates the skills and techniques utilized in manufacturing jewellery of the highest standard. Café. Gift Shop. Disabled access.

Brindley Place & Broad Street, Birmingham

Follow the A41 east into the city centre and the route is signposted "National Indoor Arena & Convention Centre" (4.5 miles)

The revitalized and dynamic west end of the city, centred around the International Convention Centre and National Indoor Arena. Enjoy the atmosphere of the waterside bars, night clubs, cafés and restaurants. Canal tours start from Gas Street Basin (Parties Afloat Tel: 0121-236 7057) and the National Sea Life Centre in The Waters Edge (Tel: 0121-633 4700) has spectacular walk-through aquaria. The Ikon Gallery (Tel: 0121-248 0708) holds exhibitions of contemporary art and the Museum & Art Gallery (Tel: 0121-303 2834), nearby, houses one of the world's finest collections of pre-Raphaelite Art. Symphony Hall, within the ICC complex and home of the CBSO, is rated as one of the greatest concert halls in the world.

Millennium Point

Curzon Street, Birmingham B4 7XG Tel: 0800 48 2000 website: www.millenniumpoint.org.uk

Follow the A41 east into the city centre and the route is signposted (6 miles)

The first part of a £6bn project to regenerate the east side of the city centre and one of Britain's latest, and largest, millennium projects to open, Millennium Point houses Think Tank (the country's most exciting new science centre; the Birmingham Museum of Science and Discovery with a hands-on journey through the past, present and future), an IMAX theatre, a Technology and Innovation Centre and the University of the First Age. The Hub, Millennium Point's social centrepiece, has a variety of shops and cafés and there is a children's play area in the gardens. Disabled Access.

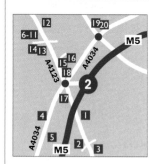

M5 JUNCTION 2

Nearest A&E Hospital
Sandwell District General Hospital

Hallam Street, West Bromwich B71 4HJ Tel: (0121) 553 1831

Proceed to Junction 1 and take the A41 west towards West Bromwich. Turn right at the roundabout along the A4031 and the hospital is on the right. (Distance Approx 4.2 miles)

FACILITIES

1 The New Navigation

Tel: (0121) 552 2525
0.4 miles south along the A4123, on the left in Titford Road.
(Punch Taverns) Open all day. Meals served; Mon-Fri; 12.00-14.00hrs, Sun; 12.00-14.30hrs

2 Cin Cin Italian Restaurant

Tel: (0121) 552 1752
0.5 miles south along the A4123, on the right.
Open; Mon-Fri; 12.00-14.00hrs, 19.00-22.30hrs, Sat; 18.30-22.30hrs, Sun 12.00-14.00hrs.

3 Wing Wah Chinese Restaurant

Tel: (0121) 552 0041
0.7 miles south along the A4123, on the left.
Open; 12.00-0.00hrs daily

4 Whiteheath Service Station (Esso)

Tel: (0121) 559 8369
0.6 miles west along the A4034, on the right.
Access, Visa, Mastercard, Switch, Diners Club, Amex, Delta, Overdrive, All Star, Dial Star, AA Paytrak, BP Supercharge, Shell Gold, Esso Cards. Open; Mon-Sat; 07.00-23.00hrs, Sun; 07.00-22.30hrs.

5 Broomfield Garage (Texaco)

Tel: (0121) 559 1217
0.8 miles west along the A4034, on the left.
Access, Visa, Mastercard, Switch, Electron, Solo, Diners Club, Amex, Delta, Overdrive, All Star, Dial Card, AA Paytrak, UK Fuelcard, Securicor Fuelserv, IDS, Keyfuels, Texaco Cards Open; 06.30-23.00hrs daily. (NB. 4* Leaded Petrol available here for classic cars and vehicles)

6 Little Chef

Tel: (0121) 552 2494
0.5 miles north along the A4123, on the left.
Open; 07.00-22.00hrs daily.

7 Travel Lodge, Oldbury

Tel: (0121) 552 2967
0.5 miles north along the A4123, on the left.

8 Osprey Filling Station (BP)

Tel: (0121) 552 3807
0.5 miles north along the A4123, on the left.
LPG. Access, Visa, Mastercard, Switch, Diners Club, Amex, Overdrive, All Star, Dial Card, Delta, UK Fuelcard. Open; 06.00-23.00hrs daily

9 Lakeside Brewsters

Tel: (0121) 552 3031
0.6 miles north along the A4123, on the left.
(Brewsters) Open all day. Meals served; Mon-Sat; 11.00-22.00hrs, Sun; 12.00-22.00hrs

10 Lakeside Travel Inn

Tel: (0121) 552 3031
0.6 miles north along the A4123, on the left.

11 KFC

Tel: (0121) 544 1819
0.6 miles north along the A4123, on the left.
Open; 11.30-00.00hrs daily

12 Bury Hill Petrol Station (BP)

Tel: (0121) 544 9074
0.9 miles north along the A4123, on the right.
Access, Visa, Mastercard, Switch, Diners Club, Amex, Overdrive, All Star, Dial Card, Delta, BP Cards.

13 Newbury Travel Filling Station (Ind)

Tel: (0121) 552 3262
0.6 miles along Newbury Lane, on the left.
Diesel & Red Diesel Fuel only. Access, Visa, Mastercard, Switch, Electron, Amex, Delta, Keyfuels. Open; Mon-Fri; 07.30-17.00hrs, Sat; 09.00-12.00hrs

14 Valentino Italian Restaurant

Tel: (0121) 552 4073
0.7 miles along Newbury Lane, on the left.
Open; Sun; 12.00-14.30hrs, Tues-Fri; 12.00-14.00hrs & 19.00-22.00hrs, Sat; 18.30-22.00hrs.

15 The One and Two Halves

Tel: (0121) 544 9621
0.1 miles north along the A4123, on the right.
(Tom Cobleighs) Open all day. Meals served; Mon-Sat; 12.00-22.00hrs, Sun; 12.00-21.30hrs.

16 Express by Holiday Inn, Birmingham/Oldbury

Tel: (0121) 511 0000
0.1 miles north along the A4123, on the right.

17 McDonald's

Tel: (0121) 541 2055
**0.1 miles, on the west side of
the Roundabout.**
Open; Sun-Thurs; 07.00-
23.00hrs, Fri-Sat; 07.00-
23.30hrs

18 TCS Birchley Park Filling Station (Total)

Tel: (0121) 552 6957
**0.1 miles, on the east side of
the Roundabout.**
Access, Visa, Mastercard,
Switch, Diners Club, Amex,
Overdrive, All Star, Dial Card,
Delta, UK Fuelcard, Total/Fina/
Elf Cards.

19 McDonald's

Tel: (0121) 552 9002
**0.6 miles north along the
A4034 in Halesowen Street,
Oldbury.**
Open; 07.00-23.00hrs daily.

20 Savacentre Filling Station

Tel: (0121) 665 2900
**0.7 miles north along the
A4034 in Halesowen Street,
Oldbury.**
Access, Visa, Mastercard,
Switch, Diners Club, Amex, All
Star, Dial Card, Overdrive,
Sainsbury's Fuel Card. Open;
Mon-Sat; 06.00-22.30hrs, Sun;
09.00-17.00hrs. Toilets and
Cash Machines in adjacent
store.

PLACES OF INTEREST

Birmingham

**Follow the A4123 south
(Signposted 6.5 miles)**
For details please see Junction
1 information.

The Black Country Living Museum

Tipton Road, Dudley DY1 4SQ
Tel: (0121) 557 9643
website: www.bclm.co.uk

**Follow A4123 north west
towards Dudley and the site
is signposted (3 miles)**
An open air museum where an
old fashioned village has been
created by the canal as a living
tribute to the skills and
enterprise of the people of the
Black Country, once the
industrial heart of Britain. A full
day is required to enjoy all the
attractions and tours. Disabled
Access to most of site.

Cadbury World

Bournville, Birmingham B30 2LD

**Follow Brown & White tourist
boards along the A4123 &
A4040. (7 miles).**
For details please see Junction
4 information.

Brindley Place & Broad Street, Birmingham

**Follow A4123 & A456 east
into the city centre and the
route is signposted "National
Indoor Arena & Convention
Centre" (6.5 miles)**
For details please see Junction
1 information.

Millennium Point

**Follow the A41 east into the
city centre and the route is
signposted (8 miles)**
For details please see Junction
1 information.

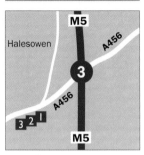

M5 JUNCTION 3

**Nearest A&E Hospital
City Hospital**
Dudley Road, Birmingham
B18 7QH
Tel: (0121) 554 3801
Follow the A456 east into
Birmingham and after about 3
miles turn left at Bearwood
along the A4040. Turn right at
the end of City Road along the
A457 (Dudley Road) and the
hospital is on the left.
(Distance Approx 5.3 miles)

FACILITIES

1 Little Chef

Tel: (0121) 585 5412
**0.8 miles west along the
A456, on the left.**
Open; 07.00-22.00hrs daily

2 BP Greenfields

Tel: (0121) 585 5105
**0.8 miles west along the
A456, on the left.**
LPG. Access, Visa, Mastercard,
Switch, Diners Club, Amex,
Overdrive, All Star, Dial card,
Delta, AA Paytrak, Shell Agency,
BP Cards. Open; Mon-Fri;
06.00-23.00hrs, Sat; 07.00-
23.00hrs, Sun; 07.00-
22.00hrs.

3 The Black Horse

Tel: (0121) 550 1465

0.8 miles west along the A456, on the left.

(Punch Taverns) Open all day. Meals served; 11.00-21.30hrs daily (Bar Snacks available between 11.00 and 18.00hrs)

PLACES OF INTEREST

Birmingham

Follow the A456 east (Signposted 6 miles)

For details please see Junction 1 information.

The Birmingham Botanical Gardens & Glasshouses

Westbourne Road, Edgbaston,

Birmingham B15 3TR Tel: (0121) 454 1860 website: www.birminghambotanical gardens.org.uk

Follow the A456 towards the city centre and turn right onto the B4129 (Norfolk Road). It is signposted Botanical Gardens (5 miles)

Enjoy fifteen acres of magnificent Ornamental gardens including Glasshouses housing exotic plants and birds. Dine in the Pavilion Restaurant where the Prime Minister, the Rt Hon Tony Blair MP and his wife hosted a dinner party on May 16th, 1998 for the G8 leaders and their wives during the Birmingham Summit. Childrens Discovery Garden and playground. Tea Room. Gift Shop. Disabled Access.

Brindley Place & Broad Street, Birmingham

Follow A456 east into the city centre and the route is signposted "National Indoor

Arena & Convention Centre" (6 miles)

For details please see Junction 1 information.

Millennium Point

Follow the A41 east into the city centre and the route is signposted (7.5 miles)

For details please see Junction 1 information.

M5 BETWEEN JUNCS 3 & 4

FRANKLEY SERVICES (SOUTHBOUND) (MOTO)

Tel: (0121) 550 3131
Fresh Express Self Service Restaurant, Little Chef, Burger King, Travelodge and Esso Fuel.

FRANKLEY SERVICES (NORTHBOUND) (MOTO)

Tel: (0121) 550 3131
Fresh Express Self Service Restaurant, Burger King, and Esso Fuel.

FOOTBRIDGE CONNECTION BETWEEN SITES

M5 JUNCTION 4

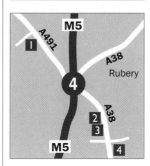

Nearest A&E Hospital

Selly Oak Hospital

Raddlebarn Road, Selly Oak, Birmingham B29 6JD Tel: (0121) 627 1627

Take the A38 north to Birmingham and into Selly Oak. The hospital is signposted within the city. (Distance Approx 7.4 miles)

Nearest Minor Injury Unit

The Princess of Wales Community Hospital

Stourbridge Road, Bromsgrove B61 0BB Tel: (01527) 488000

Follow the A38 into Bromsgrove. Signposted within the town. Opening Hours; 09.00-17.00, Monday to Friday. (Distance Approx 2.6 miles)

FACILITIES

1 Home Farm B&B

Tel: (01527) 874964

0.2 miles west along the A491, on the left.

2 Hilton Bromsgrove

Tel: (0121) 447 7888

0.8 miles south along the A38, on the right.

The Britisserie Restaurant Open; Mon-Fri; 07.00-10.00hrs, 12.00-14.00hrs, 19.00-21.30hrs, Sat; 07.00-10.00hrs, 19.00-21.30hrs, Sun; 07.30-10.00hrs, 12.00-14.00hrs, 19.00-21.30hrs.

3 Marlbrook Service Station (Total)

Tel: (01527) 570178

0.9 miles south along the A38, on the right.

Access, Visa, Mastercard, Switch, Diners Club, Amex, Overdrive, All Star, Dial Card, Delta, AA Paytrak, BP

Supercharge, Total/Fina/Elf Cards. Open; Mon-Fri; 07.00-22.00hrs, Sat; 08.00-22.00hrs, Sun; 08.00-13.00hrs.

4 Toby Carvery, Marlbrook

Tel: (01527) 878060

1 mile south along the A38, on the left.

(Toby Carvery) Open all day. Bar meals served; Mon-Sat; 11.00-23.00hrs. Carvery Open; Mon-Fri; 12.00-14.00hrs & 17.00-22.00hrs, Sat & Sun; 12.00-22.00hrs.

PLACES OF INTEREST

Birmingham

Follow the A38 north (Signposted 10.4 miles)

For details please see Junction 1 information.

Millennium Point

Follow the A41 east into the city centre and the route is signposted (11 miles)

For details please see Junction 1 information.

Cadbury World

Bournville, Birmingham B30 2LD
Booking: (0121) 451 4159 24hr
Information: (0121) 451 4180
website: www.cadburyworld.co.uk

Follow Brown & White tourist boards north east along the A38 and A4040 (7 miles)

For anyone who loves chocolate, a visit to Cadbury World is a trip to paradise. A fabulous family experience all about chocolate - sights, sounds, smells and, of course, tastes. Gift Shop. Restaurant. Disabled Access.

The Barber Institute of Fine Arts

University of Birmingham, Edgbaston, Birmingham B15 2TS
Enquiries: (0121) 414 7333 24hr
Information: (0121) 472 0962
website: www.barber.org.uk

Follow A38 north east towards city centre. Immediately after University site turn left along Edgbaston Park Road and first left into University Road East (7.6 miles).

One of the finest small picture galleries in the world with an art reference library of more than 35,000 volumes. The Institute, housed in a Grade 2 listed building was opened in 1939 and has acquired a collection of works of international significance. To those with any sort of interest in art, this is an unmissable visual delight. Disabled Access.

Lickey Hills Country Park

Warren Lane, Rednal, Birmingham B45 8ER
Tel: (0121) 447 7106 website: www.birmingham.gov.uk

Follow the A38 east towards Birmingham and after 3 miles turn right along the B4120 towards Rednal. At Rednal turn right along the B4096. (4.7 miles)

Over 500 acres of woodland, marshes and heaths with a variety of wildlife. Within the City of Birmingham the council is responsible for the maintenance of over a million trees and many of these can be seen in the panoramic views across the city from the viewing point on the top of the hills. The park has a visitor centre, café, children's play area and a trail suitable for disabled visitors.

M5 JUNCTION 4A

THIS JUNCTION IS A MOTORWAY INTERCHANGE WITH THE M42 ONLY AND THERE IS NO ACCESS TO ANY FACILITIES

M5 JUNCTION 5

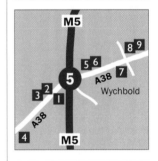

Nearest A&E Hospital
Worcester Royal Hospital
Charles Hastings Way, Worcester WR5 1DD
Tel: (01905) 763333
Proceed to Junction 6 and take the westbound exit along the A4440. The route is signposted A&E Hospital. (Distance Approx 8.6 miles)

Nearest Minor Injury Unit
The Princess of Wales Community Hospital
Stourbridge Road, Bromsgrove B61 0BB
Tel: (01527) 488000
Follow the A38 into Bromsgrove. Signposted within the town. Opening Hours; 09.00-17.00, Monday to Friday. (Distance Approx 5 miles)

FACILITIES

1 Robin Hood Inn

Tel: (01527) 861931
0.2 miles west along the A38, on the left.
(Six Continents) Open all day. Meals served; 12.00-21.00hrs daily.

2 Little Chef

Tel: (01527) 861594
0.3 miles west along the A38, on the right.
Open; 07.00 - 22.00hrs daily.

3 Travelodge

Tel: (01527) 861545
0.3 miles west along the A38, on the right.

4 Chateau Impney

Tel: (01905) 774411
1 mile west along the A38, on the left.
Jason's Carving Room; Open; Mon-Sat; 12.30-13.30hrs & 19.00-21.00hrs, Sun; 12.30-13.45hrs & 18.30-20.00hrs.
Angelique's Restaurant; Open; Mon-Fri; 12.30-13.30hrs & 19.00-21.00hrs, Sat; 19.00-21.00hrs.

5 McDonald's

Tel:
0.05 miles east along the A38, on the left.
(NB. There are currently no details available but this restaurant is due to open in the Autumn of 2002)

6 Express by Holiday Inn

0.05 miles east along the A38, on the left.
(NB. There are currently no details available but this hotel is due to open in the Autumn of 2002)

7 Wychbold Garage (Independent)

Tel: (01527) 861861
0.2 miles east along the A38, on the right.
Access. Visa, Delta, Mastercard, Switch, Electron. Attended Service. Open; Mon-Fri; 09.00-18.00hrs, Sat; 09.00-13.00hrs.

8 Poachers Pocket

Tel: (01527) 861413
0.3 miles east along the A38, on the left.
(Banks's) Open all day. Meals served Mon-Sat; 12.00-22.00hrs, Sun; 12.00-21.30hrs.

9 Murco Service Station

Tel: (01527) 861406
0.4 miles east along the A38, on the left.
Access, Visa, Mastercard, Switch, Electron, Solo, Dial Card, Overdrive, All Star, Delta, AA Paytrak, Amex, Murco Cards.

PLACES OF INTEREST

Webbs of Wychbold

Wychbold, Droitwich Spa, Worcestershire WR9 0DG
Tel: (01527) 861777 website: www.webbsofwychbold.co.uk

Follow the A38 east. Signposted from Junction 5 (1.2 miles)
One of the leading horticultural centres in the country extending over 55 acres and with excellent disabled access. The extensive facilities include a restaurant and large shop.

Avoncroft Museum of Historic Buildings

Stoke Heath, Worcestershire B60 4JR Tel: (01527) 831886
website: www.avoncroft.org.uk

Follow the A38 east and continue along the B4091 Signposted from Junction 5 (2.4 miles)
A fascinating collection of threatened buildings which have been carefully re-erected and restored. This open air museum also includes the national Collection of Telephone Kiosks. Picnic Area. Tea Room. Disabled Access.

Hanbury Hall [NT]

Droitwich, Worcestershire WR9 7EA Tel: (01527) 821214
website: www.nationaltrust.org.uk

Signposted from Junction 5 (4.5 miles)
An outstanding William and Mary red-brick house famed for its beautiful painted ceilings and staircase. Set in 400 acres of parkland and gardens. Accommodation available in the Lodge. Snack Bar and Shop. Limited disabled access.

M5 JUNCTION 6

Nearest A&E Hospital
Worcester Royal Hospital
Charles Hastings Way,

Worcester WR5 1DD
Tel: (01905) 763333
Take the westbound exit along the A4440 and the route is signposted A&E Hospital. (Distance Approx 2.6 miles)

FACILITIES

1 Travel Inn

Tel: (01905) 451240
0.1 miles west along the A4440, on the right.

2 The Three Pears

Tel: (01905) 451240
0.1 miles west along the A4440, on the right.
(Beefeater) Open all day. Meals served Sun-Thurs; 12.00-22.30hrs, Fri & Sat; 12.00-23.00hrs.

3 Poachers Pocket

Tel: (01905) 458615
0.8 miles west along the Warndon Road, on the right.
(Banks's) Open all day. Meals served Mon-Sat; 12.00-22.00hrs, Sun; 12.00-23.00hrs

4 BP Harmony Blackpole Road

Tel: (01905) 456574
1.8 miles west along the A449, in Blackpole, on the left.
Access, Visa, Overdrive, All Star, Switch, Dial Card, Mastercard, Amex, Diners Club, Delta, Routex, BP Cards, Shell Agency.

PLACES OF INTEREST

Worcester

Worcester Tourist Information Centre, The Guildhall, High Street, Worcester WR1 2EY
Tel: (01905) 726311 website: www.cityofworcester.gov.uk

Follow the A449 westwards (Signposted 4 miles)

The birthplace of Sir Edward Elgar, Worcester has an architectural heritage embracing the splendid Guildhall and magnificent Cathedral. The home of Worcester Porcelain, it is a major crossing point of the River Severn and river trips can be taken from the South Quay (Tel: 01905-422499). The pedestrianized High Street allows for leisurely shopping and for the sports orientated visitors the County Cricket Ground and Racecourse are adjacent to the city centre. The Museum & Art Gallery in Foregate Street (Tel: 01905-25371) features regular programmes of arts and craft exhibitions.

Within the city centre can be found ...

Worcester Cathedral

College Green, Worcester WR1 2LH Tel: (01905) 28854 or Tel: (01905) 21004 website: www.cofe-worcester.org.uk

A cathedral city since Saxon days, the magnificent edifice, with its 200ft tower, seen today dates back to Norman times. The crypt, now containing an exhibition of the history and archaeology of the early cathedral, was constructed in 1084 and the Chapter House and Cloisters, reminders of its monastic past, were built in the 12thC. King John (d1116) and Prince Arthur (d1502) are both buried here. Cloisters Tea Room. Gift Shop. Part disabled access.

Royal Worcester Visitor Centre

Severn Street, Worcester WR1 2NE (adjacent to Cathedral)
Tel: (01905) 21247 or Tel: (01905) 23221 website: www.royal-worcester.co.uk

The Museum of Worcester Porcelain contains rare porcelain displayed in period settings whilst visitors are able to view modern production techniques through the factory tours and take a behind the scenes look at the Design Department. Morning Coffee, Lunch and Afternoon Teas are available in the Warmstry Restaurant and a Factory Shop retails Bargain Seconds and Bestware. Disabled facilities.

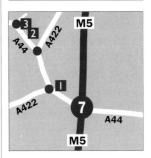

M5 JUNCTION 7

Nearest A&E Hospital
Worcester Royal Hospital
Charles Hastings Way, Worcester WR5 1DD
Tel: (01905) 763333
Take the westbound exit along the A44 and the route is signposted A&E Hospital. (Distance Approx 3 miles)

FACILITIES

1 The Swan

Tel: (01905) 351361
0.3 miles west along the A44, on the right.
(Banks's) Open all day. Meals

served; Mon-Sat; 12.00-
21.30hrs, Sun; 12.00-
21.00hrs.

2   Whittington Road BP Filling Station

Tel: (01905) 351245
1 mile west along the A44, on the right.
Access, Visa, Overdrive, All Star, Switch, Dial Card, Mastercard, Amex, Diners Club, Delta, BP Cards, Shell Agency.
Open; Mon-Fri; 07.00-22.00hrs, Sat; 07.00-21.00hrs, Sun; 08.00-21.00hrs

3   The Oak Apple

Tel: (01905) 355121
1 mile west along the A44, on the right.
(Banks's) Open all day. Meals served 12.00-21.00hrs daily.

PLACES OF INTEREST

Pershore

Pershore Tourist Information Centre, Wanderers World,
19 High Street, Pershore
WR10 1AA
Tel: (01386) 554262 website:
www.pershore-tourism.co.uk

Follow the A44 east (Signposted 7 miles)
A genuine old English market town with beautifully preserved Georgian architecture, fine old coaching inns and a magnificent Abbey considered by John Betjeman to be one of the best in Britain. Surrounded by the Vale of Evesham, Pershore nestles on the banks of the beautiful River Severn.

Within the town can be found ...

Pershore Heritage Centre

5 Bridge Street, Pershore
WR10 1AJ

Tel: (01386) 552827 website:
www.pershore-tourism.co.uk
An old beamed cottage containing many local displays.

Pershore Abbey

Pershore WR10 1DT
Tel: (01386) 561520 website:
www.pershoreabbey@fsnet.co.uk

Founded by King Oswald in 689AD and although only the choir now remains standing it is an impressive building and treasury of mostly 13thC architecture with a tall pinnacled tower.

Worcester

Follow the A44 north (Signposted 4 miles)
For details please see Junction 6 information.

Within the city centre can be found ...

Worcester Cathedral

College Green, Worcester
WR1 2LH

For details please see Junction 6 information.

Royal Worcester Visitor Centre

Severn Street, Worcester
WR1 2NE

(adjacent to Cathedral)
For details please see Junction 6 information.

Spetchley Park Gardens

Spetchley Park, Worcester
WR5 1RS Tel: (01905) 345213 or
Tel: (01905) 345224 website:
www.spetchleygardens.co.uk

Follow the A44 north, take the A4440 north east and turn east along the A422. (3 miles)
This lovely 30 acre private garden is a Plantsman's Paradise, containing a large collection of trees, shrubs and plants, many of which are rare or unusual. Tea Room. Limited disabled access.

The Commandery

Sidbury, Worcester WR1 2HU
Tel: (01905) 361821 website:
www.worcestercitymuseums.org.uk

Follow the A44 north. (2.4 miles)
A magnificent timber-framed building and Charles II's headquarters during the Battle of Worcester in 1651. Contains period rooms and Civil War displays. Gift Shop. Limited disabled access.

M5 BETWEEN JUNCS 7 & 8

STRENSHAM SERVICES (NORTHBOUND) (ROADCHEF)
Tel: (01684) 293004
Food Fayre Self-Service Restaurant, Wimpy Bar, Travel Inn & Texaco Fuel

STRENSHAM SERVICES (SOUTHBOUND) (ROADCHEF)
Tel: (01684) 293004
Food Fayre Self-Service Restaurant, Wimpy Bar & BP Fuel

M5 JUNCTION 8

JUNCTION 8 IS A MOTORWAY INTERCHANGE WITH THE M50 ONLY AND THERE IS NO ACCESS TO ANY FACILITIES

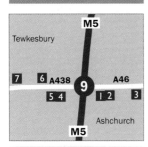

JUNCTION 9

Nearest A&E Hospital

Cheltenham General Hospital

Sandford Road, Cheltenham
GL53 7AN
Tel: (01242) 222222
Proceed to Junction 10 and
follow the A4019 into
Cheltenham. The hospital is
signposted from within the
town. (Distance Approx 9.1
miles)

Nearest Minor Injury Unit

Tewkesbury Hospital
Barton Road, Tewkesbury
GL20 5QN
Tel: (01684) 293303.
Follow the A438 into
Tewkesbury. Signposted from
within the town. Open 24
hours. (Distance Approx 1.5
miles)

FACILITIES

**1   BP Connect
Ashchurch**

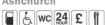

Tel: (01684) 293785
0.2 miles east along the A46,
on the right.
LPG. Access, Visa, Overdrive,
All Star, Switch, Dial Card,
Mastercard, Amex, Diners Club,
Delta, Routex, Shell Agency, BP
Cards. Wild Bean Café Open;
05.30-20.00hrs daily

2   Little Chef

Tel: (01684) 292037
0.2 miles east along the A46,
on the right
NB. Temporarily closed during
2002 for rebuilding.

3   Newton Farm B&B

Tel: (01684) 295903
0.5 miles east along the A46,
on the right.

4   Spa Villa B&B

Tel: (01684) 292487
0.6 miles west along the
A438, on the left.

**5   PJ Nicholls Filling
Station (Q8)**

Tel: (01684) 2975555
0.6 miles west along the
A438, on the left.
Access, Visa, Mastercard,
Switch, Electron, Solo, Diners
Club, Amex, Delta, Overdrive,
All Star, Dial Card, Q8 Cards.
Open; Mon-Sat; 07.00-
21.00hrs, Sun; 08.00-20.00hrs

6   The Canterbury

Tel: (01684) 297744
0.7 miles west along the
A438, on the right.
(Laurel Pub Company) Open all
day. Meals served; 12.00-
21.00hrs daily.

**7   Safeway Filling
Station**

Tel: (01684) 273268
1 mile west along the A438,
on the right.
Access, Visa, Overdrive, All
Star, Switch, Dial Card,
Mastercard, Electron, Solo,
Amex, Delta. Open; Mon-Fri;
07.00-22.00hrs, Sat; 07.00-
21.00hrs, Sun; 08.00-20.00hrs

PLACES OF INTEREST

Tewkesbury

Tewkesbury Tourist Information
Centre, 64 Barton St, Tewkesbury
GL20 5PX
Tel: (01684) 295027 website:
www.visitcotswoldsandsevernvale.gov.uk

**Follow the A438 west.
(Signposted 1.5 miles)**
Sited at the confluence of the
Severn and Avon Rivers, it was
unable to expand outwards
and, as a result, the narrow
streets became densely
packed with unusually tall
buildings; many of those built
in the 15th and 16th centuries
still remain today. The most
notable structure is the Abbey
which stands at the centre of a
"Y" formed by High Street,
Church Street and Barton
Street with the area between
being filled with narrow
alleyways and courtyards
containing some wonderful old
pubs and mediaeval cottages.
   The strategic position of the
town ensured that it had a
turbulent military history, with the
Battle of Tewkesbury, which took
place on May 4th, 1471 and saw
the Lancastrian army defeated in
the penultimate and most
decisive battle in the Wars of the
Roses, taking place to the south
of the town. A Battle Trail which
encompasses this area starts near
the Abbey. The town also changed
hands several times during the
Civil War.

**Tewkesbury Abbey &
Museum**

Church Street, Tewkesbury
GL20 5RZ Tel: (01684) 850959
website:
www.tewkesburyabbey.org.uk

**Follow the A438 west and
then A38 south (Signposted
1.9 miles)**
A parish church of cathedral-

like proportions it was founded in the 8thC and completely rebuilt at the end of the 11th. It was once the church of the Benedictine Abbey of Tewkesbury and was one of the last monasteries to be dissolved by Henry VIII. In 1540 the abbey was saved from destruction by the town burghers who purchased it from the Crown for £453. The main tower, 132ft high and 46ft square, is thought to be the largest Norman Church tower still in existence. There is a shop and the Refectory serves Tea & Coffee, Lunches and Afternoon Teas. Disabled access.

Winchcombe

Follow the A46 east, continue along the B4077 and the route is signposted (9 miles)

The attractive small town of Winchcombe was once a regional capital of Saxon Mercia and one of the town's more enduring legends concerns Kenelm, a popular child king who is said to have been martyred here by his jealous sister, Quendrida, in the 8thC. As a means of calming a mob of people who had gathered to voice their anger at this murderous act, legend has it that she recited Psalm 109 backwards, a deed which resulted in her being struck blind in an act of divine retribution. A shrine to St Kenelm, as he became known, during Mediaeval times was second only to Thomas a Beckett's as one of the foremost places of pilgrimage and Winchcombe prospered to become a walled town with an abbot.

However in 1539, the abbey was destroyed by Thomas Seymour of Sudeley following Henry VIII's Dissolution of the Monasteries and all that remains today is a section of a gallery which forms part of The George Inn. In the wake of this event the townspeople were forced to find an alternative source of income, and this they found in the form of a crop which had just been introduced from the New World; Tobacco. Although difficult to grow, the town proceeded to earn a good living from this until an Act of Parliament in 1670, forbidding home grown tobacco in favour of imports from the struggling colony of Virginia, brought it to an abrupt end. With that the town slipped into decline as any sort of commercial centre but many of the buildings erected during its period of prosperity can still be seen today and Winchcombe is well worthy of a visit.

Within the town can be found ...

Winchcombe Folk and Police Museum

Town Hall, High Street, Winchcombe GL54 5LJ Tel: (01242) 602925

The history of Winchcombe from Neolithic times to the present day is shown in a series of exhibits and there is an international display of police uniforms, caps, badges and equipment through the ages. Shop.

Winchcombe Railway Museum & Garden

23 Gloucester Street, Winchcombe GL54 5LX Tel: (01242) 602257

One of the largest collections of railway memorabilia and equipment has been assembled here, including a working signal box and a booking office. Many of the artefacts adorn the beautiful half-acre garden which is full of old and rare plants. Shop. Disabled access to most of the site.

Sudeley Castle

Winchcombe GL54 5JD Tel: (01242) 602308 website: www.stratford.co.uk/sudeley

Once the home of Queen Katherine Parr, this castle was the garrison headquarters of Prince Rupert during the Civil War and was twice besieged, in 1643 and 1644. The ravages of this conflict left it derelict and it was not until it was purchased in 1837 by John and William Dent that the huge restoration task began. The building now houses an impressive collection of furniture and paintings and the nine beautiful gardens that surround it cover 14 acres. St Mary's Church contains the marble tomb of Queen Katherine Parr, Henry VIII's sixth wife. Gift Shop and Plant Centre. Restaurant. Limited disabled access.

Gloucestershire Warwickshire Railway

Toddington Station, Toddington GL54 5DT Tel: (01242) 621405 website: www.gwsr.plc.uk

Follow the A46 east and continue along the B4077 to Toddington (8.8 miles)

Running the 6.5 miles from Toddington to Gotherington, the GWR has splendid views across the Vale of Evesham to the Malvern Hills and beyond to the Welsh Mountains. A variety of motive power is available with vintage steam and diesel locomotives and a diesel railcar utilized throughout the timetable. Originally part of the main line from Birmingham Snow Hill to Cheltenham, the preservation group are currently preparing the line onward to Cheltenham Racecourse Station and this section is due to re-open in 2003. Gift Shop. Café. Disabled access.

JUNCTION 10

THIS IS A RESTRICTED ACCESS JUNCTION

- Vehicles can only exit from the southbound lanes and travel east along the A4019
- Vehicles can only enter the motorway along the northbound lanes from the A4019 west carriageway

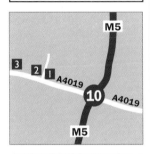

Nearest A&E Hospital

Cheltenham General Hospital

Sandford Road, Cheltenham GL53 7AN
Tel: (01242) 222222

Southbound; Take the A4019 into Cheltenham and turn right along the A46. The hospital is on this road. (Distance Approx 4.4 miles)

Northbound; Proceed north to Junction 9 and return to Junction 10. Take the A4019 into Cheltenham and turn right along the A46. The hospital is on this road. (Distance Approx 14 miles)

Nearest Minor Injury Unit

Tewkesbury Hospital

Barton Road, Tewkesbury GL20 5QN
Tel: (01684) 293303

Proceed to Junction 9 and follow the A438 into Tewkesbury. Signposted from within the town. Open 24 hours. (Distance Approx 6.4 miles)

FACILITIES

1 Stanborough Cottage

Tel: (01242) 680327
0.6 miles west along the A4019, on the right.

2 The Gloucester Old Spot

Tel: (01242) 680321
0.6 miles west along the A4019, on the right.
(Laurel Pub Company) Open all day. Meals served; Mon-Sat; 12.00-15.00hrs & 18.00-21.00hrs, Sun; 12.00-21.00hrs.

3 Silver Birches B&B

Tel: (01242) 680842
0.9 miles west along the A4019, on the right

PLACES OF INTEREST

Cheltenham

Cheltenham Tourist Information Centre, 77 Promenade, Cheltenham GL50 1PP
Tel: (01242) 522878 website: www.visitcheltenham.gov.uk

Follow the A4019 east. (Signposted 4.5 miles)

The chance discovery of a saline spring in 1715 by a local farmer subsequently transformed the character of Cheltenham, a small market town, forever. Some twenty years later Captain Henry Skillicorne saw the potential of this discovery and built an enclosure around the spring along with various buildings and a network of walks and rides which now form the tree-lined Promenade.

The town rapidly became a highly fashionable resort and by the 1820s huge amounts of money had been invested in constructing houses and buildings in the Neoclassical Regency style, most of which can be seen today. On a more modern note, Cheltenham is home to the Government tracking station, GCHQ.

Within the town centre can be found ...

Cheltenham Art Gallery & Museum

Clarence Street, Cheltenham GL50 3JT Tel: (01242) 237431
website: www.cheltenhammuseums.org.uk

Occupying three floors, the Art Gallery section holds a world-famous collection relating to the Arts and Crafts Movement, including fine furniture and exquisite metalwork, made by Cotswold craftsmen and inspired by William Morris, rare Chinese and English pottery and 300 years of painting by Dutch and English artists. The museum details the story of Edward Wilson, Cheltenham's Arctic explorer and shows the history of Britain's most complete Regency town as well as exhibiting archaeological treasures from the Cotswolds. Gift Shop. Cafe. Disabled access.

Holst Birthplace Museum

4 Clarence Road, Cheltenham GL52 2AY Tel: (01242) 524846
website: www.holstmuseum.org.uk

The birthplace of Gustav Holst, composer of The Planets, contains displays detailing the life of the famous musician. This Regency terraced house also shows the "upstairs-downstairs" way of life of Victorian and Edwardian times, including a working Victorian kitchen. Gift Shop.

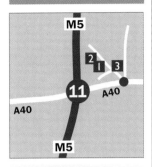

JUNCTION 11

Nearest A&E Hospital

Cheltenham General Hospital

Sandford Road, Cheltenham GL53 7AN
Tel: (01242) 222222
Follow the A40 into Cheltenham. The hospital is signposted from within the town. (Distance Approx 3.5 miles)

Or alternatively

Gloucestershire Royal Hospital

Great Western Road, Gloucester GL1 3PQ
Tel: (01452) 528555
Follow the A40 into Gloucester. The hospital is signposted within the town. (Distance Approx 3.7 miles)

FACILITIES

1   Briarfields Motel

Tel: (01242) 235324
0.9 miles east, in Churchdown Road, on the left.

2   White House Hotel

Tel: (01452) 713226
1 mile east, in Churchdown Road, on the left.

The Terrace Restaurant Open; Breakfast; Mon-Fri; 07.00-09.30hrs, Sat; 07.30-09.30hrs, Sun; 08.00-10.00hrs, Lunch; Sun-Fri; 12.00-14.00hrs, Dinner; Mon-Fri; 19.00-21.30hrs, Sat; 19.00-22.00hrs, Sun; 19.00-21.00hrs.

3   Thistle Cheltenham Hotel

Tel: (01242) 232691
0.9 miles east along the A40, on the left.
The Burford Restaurant Open; Breakfast; Mon-Fri; 07.00-10.00hrs, Sat & Sun; 07.30-11.00hrs, Lunch; 12.30-13.45hrs daily, Dinner; 19.00-21.45hrs daily.

PLACES OF INTEREST

Cheltenham

Follow the A40 east. (Signposted 3.8 miles)
For details please see Junction 10 information.

Within the city centre can be found ...

Cheltenham Art Gallery & Museum

Clarence Street, Cheltenham GL50 3JT

For details please see Junction 10 information.

Holst Birthplace Museum

4 Clarence Road, Cheltenham GL52 2AY

For details please see Junction 10 information.

Gloucester

Gloucester Tourist Information Centre, 28 Southgate Street, Gloucester GL1 2DP
Tel: (01452) 421188 website: www.visit-glos.org.uk

Follow the A40 west (Signposted 4.4 miles)

Originally a Roman settlement dating from the 1stC and known as Glevum, a Saxon monastery was established here in the 7thC. After the Norman invasion Gloucester Cathedral was established and the building was modified and rebuilt over the years. At 72ft x 38ft the great east window, constructed to celebrate victory at the Battle of Crecy in 1346, is the largest surviving mediaeval window in England. There are still many old buildings surviving within the city and the inland docks which by the end of the 1970s were totally derelict have been thoroughly refurbished and are now a thriving tourist attraction.

Within the city centre can be found ...

Beatrix Potter's House of the Tailor of Gloucester

9 College Court, Gloucester GL1 2NJ Tel: (01452) 422856

This recently refurbished attraction is housed in the building that Beatrix Potter sketched in 1897 and contains a large range of memorabilia and manuscripts. Shop. Limited Disabled access.

The National Waterways Museum

Llanthony Warehouse, Gloucester Docks, Gloucester GL1 2EH
Tel: (01452) 318054
website: www.nwm.demon.co.uk

Follow the A40 west (Signposted "Historic Docks" 4.7 miles)

Set in the Gloucester Docks, there is much to see and do at this museum, with informative displays bringing the fascinating history of the waterways to life in a traditional Victorian warehouse setting. Visitors can explore historic boats along the quayside, take part in an Interactive Canal Shares Game and see blacksmiths at work in the forge. Touch-screen computers can be used to design a canal boat or canal landscape and there is the opportunity to take part in a sack-hauling challenge.

The Interactive Gallery & Family Activity Room has been designed with children in mind, with plenty of hands-on displays, water toys, traditional costume, pulleys and puzzles. Visitors can enjoy lunch and refreshments in the friendly cafe, visit the well stocked museum shop and take a boat trip on the Queen Boadicea II or the King Arthur along the adjacent Gloucester & Sharpness Canal. Some disabled access.

JUNCTION 11A

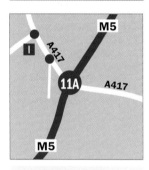

Nearest A&E Hospital

Gloucestershire Royal Hospital

Great Western Road, Gloucester GL1 3PQ
Tel: (01452) 528555
Follow the A417 into Gloucester. The hospital is signposted within the town.
(Distance Approx 2.8 miles)

FACILITIES

1   Holiday Inn Gloucester

Tel: 0870 400 9034

---

1 mile north along the A417, on the left.

Traders Bar & Restaurant. Open; Breakfast; Mon-Fri; 06.30-09.30hrs, Sat & Sun; 07.00-11.00hrs, Lunch; Sun-Fri; 12.00-14.00hrs, Dinner; Sun; 18.00-22.00hrs, Mon-Sat; 18.00-22.30hrs.

PLACES OF INTEREST

Gloucester

Follow the A417 west (Signposted 3.4 miles)
For details please see Junction 11 information.

Within the city centre can be found ...

The National Waterways Museum

Llanthony Warehouse, Gloucester Docks, Gloucester GL1 2EH

Follow the A417 west (Signposted "Historic Docks" 4.3 miles)
For details please see Junction 11 information.

Painswick Rococo Gardens

Painswick House, Painswick, Gloucestershire GL6 6TH
Tel: (01452) 813204
website: www.rocogarden.co.uk

Follow the A417 east and take the A46 south. (Signposted along A46 7 miles)

Commissioned by Benjamin Hyett in the 1740's, the gardens survived in that form until they were changed in the early 1800's to a more practical layout to grow fruit and vegetables. Over the years they gradually proved to be too expensive to maintain and were eventually abandoned in the 1950's.

Thanks to a painting of the

---

original garden by Thomas Robins in 1748 a reference was available and restoration, with private funding, began in 1984 when its historic importance became apparent as it was found to be the sole, complete, survivor from the brief Rococo period of English garden design (1720-1760). In 1988 control of the garden was handed over to the Painswick Rococo Garden Trust and they continued with the restoration of the 6 acre site. Coffee, Lunches and Teas available in the licensed Coach House Restaurant. Gift Shop. Partial Disabled access.

JUNCTION 12

THIS IS A RESTRICTED ACCESS JUNCTION
- Vehicles can only exit from the northbound lanes and travel west along the B4008
- Vehicles can only enter the motorway along the southbound lanes from the B4008 east carriageway

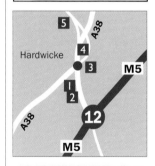

Nearest A&E Hospital

Gloucestershire Royal Hospital

Great Western Road, Gloucester GL1 3PQ
Tel: (01452) 528555
Northbound: Follow the A38 into Gloucester. The hospital is signposted within the town.
(Distance Approx 6.3 miles)

Southbound: Proceed south to Junction 13 and return to Junction 12. Follow the A38 into Gloucester. The hospital is signposted within the town. (Distance Approx 12.2 miles)

Nearest Minor Injury Unit
Stroud General Hospital
Trinity Road, Stroud
GL5 2HY
Tel: (01453) 562200
Proceed to Junction 13 and follow the A419 to Stroud. Signposted from within the town. Open 24 hours (Doctors in attendance between 09.00-12.30hrs and 14.00-16.30hrs only) (Distance Approx 8.6 miles)

FACILITIES

1   Cross Keys Filling Station (BP)

Tel: (01452) 721470
0.4 miles north along the B4008, on the left.
No LRP. Access, Visa, Overdrive, All Star, Switch, Dial Card, Mastercard, Amex, Diners Club, Delta, Routex, Shell Agency, BP Card. Open; Mon-Sat; 06.00-22.00hrs, Sun; 07.00-22.00hrs

2   Little Chef

Tel: (01452) 720132
0.4 miles north along the B4008, on the left.
Open; 07.00-22.00hrs daily

3   Hardwicke Garage (UK Petrol)

Tel: (01452) 720239
0.5 miles north along the A38, on the right.
Access, Visa, Mastercard, Switch, Electron, Solo. Open; Mon-Fri; 08.00-17.00hrs, Sat; 08.00-13.00hrs, Sun; Closed.

4   The Cross Keys

Tel: (01452) 720113
0.5 miles north along the A38, on the right.
(Laurel Pub Company) Meals served; Sun-Fri; 12.00-14.00hrs, & 19.00-21.00hrs, Sat; 11.00-14.00hrs & 19.00-21.30hrs

5   The Morning Star

Tel: (01452) 720028
1 mile north along the B4008, in Quedgeley, on the left.
(Whitbread) Open all day. Meals served; Mon-Sat; 12.00-14.45hrs & 18.00-20.45hrs. Sun; 12.00-18.00hrs

PLACES OF INTEREST

LOCAL PLACES OF INTEREST ARE BEST ACCESSED FROM JUNCTIONS 11A OR 13

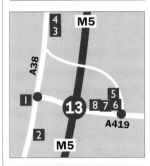

Nearest A&E Hospital
Gloucestershire Royal Hospital
Great Western Road, Gloucester GL1 3PQ
Tel: (01452) 528555

Proceed to Junction 12 and follow the A38 into Gloucester. The hospital is signposted within the town. (Distance Approx 9.2 miles)

Nearest Minor Injury Unit
Stroud General Hospital
Trinity Road, Stroud
GL5 2HY
Tel: (01453) 562200
Follow the A419 to Stroud. Signposted from within the town. Open 24 hours. (Doctors in attendance between 09.00-12.30hrs and 14.00-16.30hrs only) (Distance Approx 5.4 miles)

FACILITIES

1   Fromebridge Mill

Tel: (01452) 741796
0.2 miles west along the A419, adjacent to the roundabout.
(Greene King) Open all day. Bar Meals served; 12.00-20.00hrs daily. Restaurant Open; Mon-Sat; 12.00-15.00hrs & 18.00-21.30hrs, Sun; 12.00-15.00hrs & 18.00-21.00hrs

2   Fromebridge Self Serve (Total)

Tel: (01452) 740753
0.9 miles south along the A38, on the left.
Access, Visa, Overdrive, All Star, Switch, Dial Card, Mastercard, Amex, Diners Club, Delta, Total/Fina/Elf Cards. Open; Mon-Sat; 07.00-21.30hrs, Sun; 09.00-21.30hrs.

3   The Old Forge

Tel: (01452) 741306
1 mile north along the A38, on the right.
(Free House) Open all day Sat. Meals served; Tues-Sat; 12.00-

14.00hrs & 18.00-21.00hrs.
Sun; 12.00-14.00hrs

4　The Whitminster

Tel: (01452) 740234
**1 mile north along the A38,
on the right.**
(Free House) Meals served;
Sun; 12.00-15.00hrs & 17.00-
21.30hrs, Mon-Sat; 17.00-
21.30hrs

5　Little Chef

Tel: (01453) 828847
**0.5 miles east along the
A419, on the left.**
Open; 07.00-22.00hrs daily

6　Oldbury Service Station (Shell)

Tel: (01453) 828688
**0.5 miles east along the
A419, on the left.**
LPG. Access, Visa, Mastercard,
Switch, Diners Club, Amex,
Delta, Overdrive, All Star, Dial
Card, AA Paytrak, Securicor
Fuelserve. Shell Cards.

7　Burger King

Tel: (01453) 828847
**0.5 miles east along the
A419, on the left.**
Open; 10.00-22.00hrs daily.

8　Travelodge Stonehouse

Tel: (01453) 828590
**0.5 miles east along the
A419, on the left**

PLACES OF INTEREST

The Wildfowl & Wetlands Trust

Slimbridge, Gloucestershire
GL2 7BT Tel: (01453) 890333
website: www.wwt.org.uk

**Follow the A38 south.
(Signposted 5.5 miles)**
The Trust was founded by Sir
Peter Scott in 1946 and
Slimbridge now has the world's
largest collection of exotic
wildfowl. It is the only place in
Europe where all six types of
flamingoes can be seen and in
winter up to 8,000 wild birds fly
in to this 800 acre reserve on
the River Severn. Other
attractions include a Tropical
House and an indoor Wonder of
Wetlands exhibit and there is a
licensed restaurant as well as
picnic areas. Disabled facilities.
No dogs, other than guide dogs,
are allowed into the grounds.

Berkeley Castle

Berkeley, Gloucestershire
GL13 9BQ

**Follow the A38 south and
Berkeley is signposted. (9
miles)**
For details please see Junction
14 information

Jenner Museum

The Chantry, Church Lane,
Berkeley GL13 9BN (Adjacent to
castle)

**Follow the A38 south and
Berkeley is signposted. (9
miles)**
For details please see Junction
14 information

Painswick Rococo Garden

Painswick House, Painswick,
Gloucestershire GL6 6TH

**Follow the A419 east into
Stroud and take the A46
north. (Signposted along A46
8.8 miles)**
For details please see Junction
11A information

**MICHAEL WOOD SERVICES
(SOUTHBOUND) (WELCOME
BREAK)**
Tel: (01454) 260631
Granary Restaurant, Burger King
& BP Fuel

**MICHAEL WOOD SERVICES
(NORTHBOUND) (WELCOME
BREAK)**
Tel: (01454) 260631
Granary Restaurant, Burger King,
Days Inn & BP Fuel

**FOOTBRIDGE CONNECTION
BETWEEN SITES.**

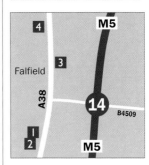

Nearest A&E Hospital
Frenchay Hospital
Frenchay Park Road,
Frenchay, Bristol BS16 1LE
Tel: (0117) 970 1212
Proceed south to Junction 15,
take the M4 east to Junction
19 and then follow the M32 to
Junction 1 Take the A4174 east
exit and the hospital is
signposted. (Distance Approx
12.3 miles)

FACILITIES

1 The Huntsman House Inn

Tel: (01454) 260239
0.5 miles south along the A38, in Falfield, on the right.
(Whitbread) Open all day.
Meals served; 12.00-14.30hrs & 18.00-21.00hrs daily.

2 Mill Lane Filling Station (Total)

Tel: (01454) 260286
0.6 miles south along the A38, in Falfield, on the right.
Access, Visa, Overdrive, All Star, Switch, Dial Card, Mastercard, Amex, Diners Club, Delta, AA Paytrak, Total/Fina/ Elf Cards. Toilets available for occasional customer use at staff discretion. Open; Mon-Sat; 07.00-23.00hrs, Sun 08.00-22.00hrs.

3 The Gables Hotel

Tel: (01454) 260502
0.5 miles north along the A38, in Falfield, on the right.
Bar open all day; Bar Meals served; 12.30-14.00hrs & 18.30-22.00hrs daily.
Restaurant Open; Mon-Sat; 18.30-22.00hrs, Sun Carvery; 12.00-14.00hrs.

4 Stone Garage (UK Fuels)

Tel: (01454) 260551
1 mile north along the A38, in Stone, on the left.
Access, Visa, Overdrive, All Star, Switch, Dial Card, Mastercard, Amex, Delta, Electron, Solo, AA Paytrak. Open; Mon-Fri; 08.00-18.00hrs, Sat; 09.00-14.00hrs, Sun; Closed.

PLACES OF INTEREST

The Wildfowl & Wetlands Trust

Slimbridge, Gloucestershire
GL2 7BT

Follow the A38 north and the site is signposted. (10 miles)
For details please see Junction 13 information

Berkeley Castle

Berkeley, Gloucestershire
GL13 9BQ Tel: (01453) 810332
website: www.berkeley-castle.com

Follow the A38 north and Berkeley is signposted. (5.4 miles)

Built between 1117 and 1153 on the site of a Saxon fort, Berkeley Castle is the oldest castle in England still to be inhabited. It was here in 1215 that the barons of the West met before setting out to witness the sealing of the Magna Carta by King John at Runnymede, but the incident which gave the castle its greatest notoriety and place in English history was the brutal murder of King Edward II in 1327. The dungeon where this took place can today be viewed along with the 14thC Great Hall, circular keep, state apartments and mediaeval kitchens within the castle as well the Elizabethan terraced garden which surrounds it. These grounds also include a free-flight butterfly house, tea room, gift shop and a large well-stocked deer park.

Jenner Museum

The Chantry, Church Lane, Berkeley GL13 9BN (Adjacent to castle) Tel: (01453) 810631
website:www.jennermuseum.com

Follow the A38 north and Berkeley is signposted. (5.4 miles)

The home of Dr Edward Jenner, discoverer of vaccination against Smallpox. The son of a local parson, he was apprenticed to a surgeon in Chipping Sodbury, later moving on to St George's Hospital in London to become a student under John Hunter, and then returning to Berkeley to practice as a country doctor. It was whilst he was still an apprentice that he noticed that those who had, at some stage, been infected with cowpox did not contract smallpox and he was now able to continue his studies into this phenomenon. His work, over several decades, led to the first vaccination against smallpox and virtually eradicated a disease that in the 1600's is estimated to have killed 60 million people worldwide.

The beautiful Georgian house and gardens, including the Temple of Vaccinia, where he vaccinated the poor, remain much as they were in the Doctor's day and a modern display of computer games and CD ROMs show the importance of the science of immunology, which he founded, in modern medicine. Gift Shop.

M5 JUNCTION 15

> THIS JUNCTION IS A MOTORWAY INTERCHANGE WITH THE M4 ONLY AND THERE IS NO ACCESS TO ANY FACILITIES

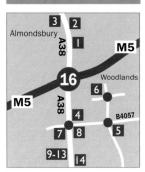

JUNCTION 16

Nearest A&E Hospital
Southmead Hospital,
Southmead Road, Westbury
on Trym, Bristol BS10 5NB
Tel: (0117) 950 5050
Take the A38 south to Filton
and the hospital is signposted.
(Distance Approx 3.8 miles)

FACILITIES

**1   Almondsbury
Interchange Hotel &
Restaurant**

Tel: (01454) 613206
0.3 miles north along the
A38, on the right.
Oliver's Restaurant Open;
Breakfast; 07.00-09.00hrs
daily, Lunch; Mon-Fri; 12.00-
13.30hrs, Dinner; Mon-Sat;
19.00-21.30hrs.

2   The Swan Hotel

Tel: (01454) 625671
0.4 miles north along the
A38, on the right.
(Wizard Inns) Open all day.
Meals served; Mon-Sat; 11.00-
21.30hrs, Sun; 12.00-21.00hrs

3   Rocklands Restaurant

Tel: (01454) 612208

0.6 miles north along the
A38, on the left.
Open at weekends. Prior
booking only.

4   Hilton Bristol

Tel: (01454) 201144
0.2 miles south along the
A38, on the left.
Chandler's Restaurant Open;
Breakfast; Mon-Fri; 07.00-
09.30hrs, Sat; 07.30-10.00hrs,
Sun; 08.30-10.30hrs, Lunch;
Mon-Fri; 12.30-14.00hrs, Sun;
13.00-14.45hrs, Dinner;
19.00-21.45hrs daily.

5   The Bradley Stoke

Tel: (01454) 202193
0.6 miles east along the
B4057, on the right.
(Punch Retail) Open all day.
Meals served; Mon-Sat; 11.00-
21.30hrs, Sun; 12.00-21.30hrs

6   The Orchard

Tel: (01454) 201202
1 mile along Woodlands Lane,
on the left.
(Six Continents) Open all day.
Meals served; Mon-Thurs;
12.00-14.00hrs & 17.30-
21.00hrs, Fri & Sat; 12.00-
14.00hrs & 17.30-22.00hrs,
Sundays; 12.00-21.00hrs.

7   Aztec Hotel

Tel: (01454) 201090
0.3 miles south along the
A38, on the right.
Restaurant Open; Breakfast;
Mon-Fri; 07.00-09.30hrs, Sat &
Sun; 08.30-10.00hrs, Lunch;
Mon-Fri; 12.30-14.00hrs,
Dinner; Mon-Sat; 19.15-
21.45hrs, Sun; 19.15-
21.15hrs.

8   Travellers Rest

Tel: (01454) 612238
0.4 miles south along the

A38, on the left.
(The Hungry Horse) Open all
day. Meals served; Mon-Sat;
12.00-22.00hrs, Sun; 12.00-
21.30hrs

9   Radnor B&B

Tel: (01454) 618390
0.5 miles south along the
A38, on the right.

10 Dove Court B&B

Tel: (01454) 612271
0.6 miles south along the
A38, on the right.

11 The Jays Guest House

Tel: (01454) 612771
0.6 miles south along the
A38, on the right.

**12 The Willow Hotel &
Licensed Restaurant**

Tel: (01454) 612276
0.6 miles south along the
A38, on the right.
Open for meals; 19.00-
21.30hrs daily

**13 Star Patchway
(Texaco)**

Tel: (01454) 453000
0.7 miles south along the
A38, on the right.
Access, Visa, Mastercard,
Switch, Electron, Solo, Diners
Club, Amex, Delta, Overdrive,
All Star, Dial card, AA Paytrak,
Fast Fuel, Texaco Cards.

**14 Stokebrook Service
Station (Esso)**

Tel: (0117) 969 2115
1 mile south along the A38,
on the left.
Access, Visa, Mastercard,
Switch, Diners Club, Amex,
Delta, Overdrive, All Star, Dial
card, AA Paytrak, BP
Supercharge, Shell Gold, Esso

Cards. Open; 05.00-23.00hrs daily

PLACES OF INTEREST

Bristol

Bristol Tourist Information Centre, Wildscreen Walk, Harbourside, Bristol BS1 5DB
Tel: (0117) 926 0767 website: www.visitbristol.co.uk

Follow the A38 south (Signposted 7 miles)
Founded during Saxon times, this strategically-important bridging point at the head of the Avon gorge soon became a major port and market centre and, by the early 11thC Bristol had its own mint and was trading with other ports throughout western England, Wales and Ireland. In 1067 the Normans built a massive stone keep, at a site still known as Castle Park, and this structure was all but destroyed at the end of the Civil War. During the middle ages the town expanded enormously to accommodate the huge increases in the export trade in wool and importation of wines from Spain and France. Many of the fine buildings constructed during this period, and subsequently, can be seen today within the city centre.

Within the city centre can be found ...

Bristol City Museum & Art Gallery

Queen's Road, Clifton, Bristol BS8 1RL Tel: (0117) 922 3571
website: www.bristol-city.gov.uk/museums

A treasure house of wonderful exhibits, including an exceptional collection of Chinese glass. Gift Shop. Café.

SS Great Britain & The Matthew

Great Western Dock, Gas Ferry Road, Bristol BS1 6TY
Tel: (0117) 926 0680 website: www.ss-great-britain.com

Isambard Kingdom Brunel's SS Great Britain, built in the city in 1843, was the world's first iron-hulled, propeller-driven, ocean-going vessel. After a working life of 43 years it languished in the Falkland Islands, utilized as a storage hulk, until 1970 when it was saved, brought back to its home dock and ultimately restored to its former glory. The Matthew is a replica of John Cabot's 15thC ship which sailed from Bristol on the voyage that discovered Newfoundland in 1497. This replica re-enacted the journey in 1997.

Bristol Cathedral

College Green, Bristol BS1 5TJ
Tel: (0117) 926 4879
website: www.bristol-cathedral.co.uk

Founded in the 12thC as the great church of an Augustine abbey, several original Norman features remain, including the south east transept walls, chapter house, gatehouse and east side of the abbey cloisters. Following the Dissolution of the Monasteries in 1539, Henry VIII elevated the church status to that of cathedral but the structure was not fully completed until the 19thC when a new nave was built in sympathetic style to the existing choir. The building contains some exceptional monuments and tombs. Gift Shop. Refectory. Limited disabled access.

John Wesley's Chapel

36 The Horsefair, Bristol BS1 3JE
Tel: (0117) 926 4740

website: www.methodist.org.uk/new.room

Built in 1739 it is the oldest Methodist building in the world. The Chapel, constructed to cope with the huge response to John Wesley's open air preaching to the poor in Bristol, remains wonderfully unspoilt. Visitors are able to see the living rooms, above the Chapel, where John stayed with his brother and some of the first pioneering Methodist preachers.

Harvey's Wine Cellars

12 Denmark Street, Bristol BS1 5DQ
Tel: (0117) 927 5036

Learn the history of wine in the 13thC cellars and take in the wonderful collection of antique displays. Guided tours and tutored tastings are available. Restaurant. Gift Shop.

Bristol Industrial Museum

Princes Wharf, Wapping Road, Bristol BS1 4RN
Tel: (0117) 925 1470
website: www.bristol-city.gov.uk/museums

Houses a fascinating record of the achievements of the city's industrial pioneers, including those with such household names as Harvey, Fry, Wills and McAdam. Visitors can find out about Bristol's history as a port, view the aircraft and aero engines made in the city since 1910, and inspect some of the many famous motor vehicles which have borne the Bristol name since Victorian times. During the summer, working demonstrations of some of the larger exhibits can be seen. These include a giant crane, steam railway, printing workshop and a variety of motor vessels. Gift Shop. Disabled access.

JUNCTION 17

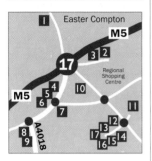

Nearest A&E Hospital

Southmead Hospital

Southmead Road, Westbury on Trym, Bristol BS10 5NB Tel: (01179) 505050 Take the A4018 to Bristol (West) and the hospital is signposted. (Distance Approx 3.1 miles)

FACILITIES

1 The Fox

Tel: (01454) 632220
1 mile north along the B4055, in Easter Compton, on the left.
(Unique Pub Co) Meals served; Mon-Sat; 12.00-14.00hrs & 18.30-21.30 hrs, Sun; 12.00-14.00hrs

2 Asda Filling Station

Tel: (0117) 969 3973
In the Regional Shopping Centre, on the south side of the roundabout, on the left.
LPG. Access, Visa, Mastercard, Switch, Diners Club, Amex, Delta, Overdrive, All Star, Dial Card, AA Paytrak, Asda Fuelcard. Open; Mon-Sat; 07.00-22.30hrs, Sun; 09.00-16.30hrs. (24hr Credit Card

operated pumps available when shop is closed)

3 McDonald's

Tel: (0117) 950 3977
In the Regional Shopping Centre, on the south side of the roundabout, on the left.
Open; 07.30-23.00hrs daily

4 Travelodge

Tel: (0117) 950 1530
0.2 miles south along the A4018, on the right.

5 The Lamb & Flag

Tel: (0117) 950 1490
0.2 miles south along the A4018, on the right.
(Harvester) Open all day. Meals served; Mon-Fri; 12.00-14.30hrs & 17.00-21.30hrs, Sat; 12.00-21.30hrs, Sun; 12.00-21.00hrs.

6 Cribbs Lodge Hotel

Tel: (0117) 950 0066
0.3 miles south along the A4018, on the right.

7 Harry Ramsden's

Tel: (0117) 959 4100
0.3 miles south along the A4018, on the left.
Open; Mon-Thur; 12.00-21.30hrs, Fri & Sat; 12.00-22.00hrs, Sun; 12.00-20.00hrs.

8 Cribbs Causeway Shell Station

Tel: (0117) 941 9400
0.6 miles south along the A4018, on the right
LPG. Access, Visa, Overdrive, All Star, Switch, Dial Card, Mastercard, Amex, Diners Club, Delta, Shell Cards, BP Agency Card.

9 BP Severnway Filling Station

Tel: (0117) 950 0414
1 mile south along the A4018, on the right.
LPG. Access, Visa, Overdrive, All Star, Switch, Dial Card, Mastercard, Amex, Diners Club, Delta, Routex, AA Paytrak, UK Fuelcard, Shell Agency, BP Cards. Open; Thur-Sat; 24hrs, Sun-Wed; 06.00-22.00hrs.

10 McDonald's

Tel: (0117) 950 1523
0.6 miles south along the A4018 on the right.
Restaurant Open; 07.30-23.00hrs daily.

11 The Mall

Tel: (0117) 903 0303
1 mile south along Highway Road, on the left.
(Signposted).
There are 16 cafés and restaurants within the shopping centre. Open; Mon-Fri; 10.00-21.00hrs, Sat; 09.00-19.00hrs, Sun; 11.00-17.00hrs.

12 KFC

Tel: (0117) 959 1492
1 mile south along Highway Road, in The Venue Leisure Complex on the right.
Open; 11.00-0.00hrs daily

13 Burger King

Tel: (0117) 959 0712
1 mile south along Highway Road, in The Venue Leisure Complex on the right.
Open; 10.00-0.00hrs daily

14 Chiquito's

Tel: (0117) 959 1459
1 mile south along Highway

Road, in The Venue Leisure Complex on the right.
Open; Mon-Sat; 12.00-23.00hrs, Sun; 12.00-22.30hrs

15 Frankie & Benny's

Tel: (0117) 959 1180
1 mile south along Highway Road, in The Venue Leisure Complex on the right.
Open; Mon-Sat; 12.00-23.00hrs, Sun; 12.00-22.30hrs

16 Bella Pasta

Tel: (0117) 959 0982
1 mile south along Highway Road, in The Venue Leisure Complex on the right.
Open; Sun-Thurs; 12.00-22.00hrs, Fri & Sat; 12.00-23.00hrs.

17 TGI Fridays

Tel: (0117) 959 1987
1 mile south along Highway Road, in The Venue Leisure Complex on the right.
Open; Sun-Thurs; 12.00-22.30hrs, Fri & Sat; 12.00-23.30hrs

PLACES OF INTEREST

The Mall at Cribbs Causeway

Bristol BS34 5DG
Tel: (0117) 915 5326
Information Line:
Tel: (0117) 903 0303
website: www.mallcribbs.com

Adjacent to junction and signposted

A new shopping centre with 130 top names, 15 cafés and restaurants and a wealth of excellent facilities and attractions all under one roof. Creche. Play Area. Accessibility Unit

Bristol

Follow the A4018 south (Signposted 5.5 miles)
For details please see Junction 16 information.

Within the city centre can be found ...

Bristol City Museum & Art Gallery

Queen's Road, Clifton, Bristol BS8 1RL

For details please see Junction 16 information.

SS Great Britain & The Matthew

Great Western Dock, Gas Ferry Road, Bristol BS1 6TY

For details please see Junction 16 information.

Bristol Cathedral

College Green, Bristol BS1 5TJ

For details please see Junction 16 information.

John Wesley's Chapel

36 The Horsefair, Bristol BS1 3JE

For details please see Junction 16 information.

Harvey's Wine Cellars

12 Denmark Street, Bristol BS1 5DQ

For details please see Junction 16 information.

Bristol Industrial Museum

Princes Wharf, Wapping Road, Bristol BS1 4RN

For details please see Junction 16 information.

Bristol Zoo Gardens

Clifton, Bristol BS8 3HA
Tel: (0117) 970 6176

Information Line
Tel: (0117) 973 8951
website: www.bristolzoo.org.uk

Follow the A4018 south and A4176 west (Signposted 5.1 miles)

A great place to enjoy a real life experience and see over 300 species of wildlife in beautiful gardens. Gorilla Island, Twilight World, Bug World, The Rainforest Species Exhibit and the Seal and Penguin Coasts, with underwater viewing, provide a fascinating insight into our natural world. Café and Restaurant. Garden. Disabled facilities.

Clifton Suspension Bridge & Visitor Centre

Bridge House, Sion Place, Bristol BS8 4AP
Tel: (0117) 974 4664 website: www.clifton-suspension-bridge.org.uk

Follow the A4018 south and A4176 west (Signposted 6 miles)

Sited 1.5 miles west of the city centre, the bridge, which is suspended more than 245ft above the Avon Gorge was designed by the great Victorian engineer, Isambard Kingdom Brunel. This graceful structure was completed in 1864 and offers drivers and pedestrians a magnificent view over the city and surrounding landscape. Before you cross it call in to the Visitor Centre* and learn the fascinating story behind the bridge and inspect the superb scale model. Gift Shop. Disabled access.

(*NB. The Visitor Centre is currently being relocated and is due to open in 2003 on a new site adjacent to the bridge)

THERE ARE TWO ACCESS POINTS TO THIS JUNCTION
■ The distances quoted below have been taken from the southernmost access point

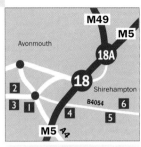

Nearest A&E Hospital

Southmead Hospital,

Southmead Road, Westbury on Trym, Bristol BS10 5NB
Tel: (01179) 505050

Take the A4 into Bristol and the hospital is signposted within the city (Distance Approx 6.8 miles)

FACILITIES

1   Bradford Hotel

Tel: (0117) 982 3211
0.1 miles, at the corner of Portway and Avonmouth Road.

2   Avonmouth Filling Station (Q8)

Tel: (0117) 982 5921
0.2 miles west along the Avonmouth Road, in Avonmouth, on the right.
Access, Visa, Overdrive, All Star, Switch, Dial Card, Mastercard, Amex, Diners Club, Delta, Key Fuels, BP Super-charge, Securicor Fuelserv, UK Fuels, Q8 Cards. Open; Mon-Fri; 06.00-20.00hrs, Sat; 07.00-15.00hrs, Sun; Closed.

3   Miles Arms Hotel

Tel: (0117) 982 2317
0.2 miles west along the Avonmouth Road, in Avonmouth, on the left.
(Six Continents) Open all day. Meals served; Mon-Fri; 12.00-14.30hrs & 18.00-21.00hrs,

Sat; 19.00-21.00hrs, Sun; 12.00-14.00hrs & 19.00-21.00hrs

4   Hope & Anchor

Tel: (0117) 982 2691
0.2 miles south along the B4054, on the right.
(Enterprise Inns) Open all day. Meals served; Mon-Sat; 11.00-21.30hrs, Sun; 12.00-18.00hrs

5   Shirehampton Texaco

Tel: (0117) 937 9040
1 mile south along the B4054, on the right in Shirehampton.
Access, Visa. Overdrive, All Star, switch, Dial Card, Mastercard, Amex, Diners Club, Delta, Texaco Cards.

6   Shirehampton Lodge Hotel

Tel: (0117) 907 3480
1 mile south along the B4054, on the left, in Shirehampton

PLACES OF INTEREST

Bristol

Follow the A4 south (Signposted 6 miles)
For details please see Junction 16 information.

Within the city centre can be found ...

Bristol City Museum & Art Gallery

Queen's Road, Clifton, Bristol BS8 1RL

For details please see Junction 16 information.

SS Great Britain & The Matthew

Great Western Dock, Gas Ferry Road, Bristol BS1 6TY

For details please see Junction 16 information.

Bristol Cathedral

College Green, Bristol BS1 5TJ

For details please see Junction 16 information.

John Wesley's Chapel

36 The Horsefair, Bristol BS1 3JE

For details please see Junction 16 information.

Harvey's Wine Cellars

12 Denmark Street, Bristol BS1 5DQ

For details please see Junction 16 information.

Bristol Zoo Gardens

Clifton, Bristol BS8 3HA

Follow the A4 south (Signposted 5.6 miles)
For details please see Junction 17 information.

Bristol Industrial Museum

Princes Wharf, Wapping Road, Bristol BS1 4RN

For details please see Junction 16 information.

Clifton Suspension Bridge & Visitor Centre

Follow the A4 south (Signposted 5.7 miles)
For details please see Junction 17 information.

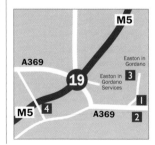

Nearest A&E Hospital

Southmead Hospital

Southmead Road, Westbury on Trym, Bristol BS10 5NB
Tel: (0117) 950 5050
Proceed to Junction 18 and take the A4 to Bristol. The hospital is signposted within Bristol. (Distance Approx 9.1 miles)

FACILITIES

> **GORDANO SERVICES (WELCOME BREAK)**
> Tel: (01275) 373624
> Burger King, KFC, Red Hen Restaurant, Granary Restaurant, Days Inn & Shell Fuel.
> NB. During some periods on Friday evenings and Saturdays during the summer months this service area is extremely busy and access may be closed by the police.

1   The Rudleigh Inn

Tel: (01275) 372363
0.6 miles south along the A369, on the left.
(Free House) Open all day. Food served Mon-Sat;11.00-22.00hrs, Sun; 12.00-21.30hrs.

2   Tynings

Tel: (01275) 372608
0.6 miles south along the A369, on the right.

3   The Kings Arms

Tel: (01275) 372208
0.5 miles east, in Easton in Gordano, on the left.
(Unique Pub Co) Meals served; Mon-Sat; 12.00-14.00hrs & 17.30-21.30hrs, Sun; 12.00-14.00hrs.

4   The Priory

Tel: (01275) 378411
0.8 miles south along the Portbury Road, on the right.
(Vintage Inns) Open all day. Meals served; Mon-Sat; 12.00-22.00hrs, Sun; 12.00-21.30hrs

PLACES OF INTEREST

Avon Gorge Nature Reserve

Follow the A369 south to Bristol (3.5 miles)

Sited on the western side of the river it offers some delightful walking through Leigh Woods to the summit of an iron age hill fort.

Clifton Suspension Bridge & Visitor Centre

Follow the A369 south to Bristol (4.7 miles)

For details please see Junction 17 information.

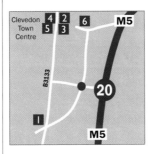

M5
JUNCTION 20

Nearest A&E Hospital

Weston General Hospital

Grange Road, Uphill, Weston super Mare BS23 4TQ
Tel: (01934) 636363
Proceed to Junction 21 and take the A370 to Weston super Mare. The hospital is signposted from the junction. (Distance Approx 11.4 miles)

Nearest Minor Injury Unit

Clevedon Hospital

Old Street,Clevedon BS21 6BS
Tel: (01275) 872212
Follow the route into Clevedon town centre. (Distance approx 1 mile) Open; 08.00-21.00hrs daily. [NB. No doctor on site].

FACILITIES

> **CLEVEDON TOWN CENTRE IS WITHIN ONE MILE OF THIS JUNCTION**

1   Tesco Filling Station

Tel: (01275) 517400
0.8 miles south along the B3133, on the right.
Access, Visa, Overdrive, All Star, Switch, Dial Card, Mastercard, Amex, Delta, AA Paytrak, Open; 07.00-0.00hrs daily. Toilets and Cash Machines available in adjacent store (Open 24 hours)

2   Grapevine Café & Bistro

0.8 miles north in the Town Square, in Clevedon town centre.

3   Public Toilets

0.8 miles north in the Town Square, in Clevedon town centre.

4   Old Street Garage (Esso)

Tel: (01275) 872596
0.8 miles north in Old Street, in Clevedon town centre.
Access, Visa, Overdrive, All Star, Switch, Dial Card, Mastercard, Amex, Diners Club, Delta, Esso Cards. Attended service for disabled drivers. Open; 06.30-22.00hrs daily.

5 Ye Olde Bristol Inn

Tel: (01275) 872073

1 mile north in Chapel Hill, in Clevedon town centre.

(Scottish & Newcastle) Open all day. Food served; Mon-Thurs; 11.00-21.30hrs, Fri & Sat; 11.00-19.00hrs, Sun; 12.00-19.00hrs.

6 Clevedon Garages (Shell)

Tel: (01275) 873701

0.9 miles along Tickenham Road, in Clevedon, on the right.

Access, Visa, Overdrive, All Star, Switch, Dial Card, Mastercard, Amex, Diners Club, Delta, Shell Cards, BP Agency Cards.

PLACES OF INTEREST

Clevedon

Follow the B3133 west (Signposted 0.7 miles)

A genteel seaside town, with a population of 20,000 it has been a stylish holiday resort and residential centre since the latter half of the 18thC. Devoid of most of the popular attractions associated with holiday resorts, it does boast of a recently-restored slim and elegant pier which, amongst other things, is utilized as a landing stage by large pleasure steamers such as the Balmoral and the Waverley, the only surviving seagoing paddle steamers in the world. Clevedon's appeal is in the romantic, Coleridge and Thackeray both lived and worked here, rather than the dramatic and it has managed to retain an atmosphere of tranquil refinement which still has a certain charm.

Clevedon Court [NT]

Tickenham Road, Clevedon, Somerset BS21 6QU

Tel: (01275) 872257 website: www.nationaltrust.org.uk

Follow the B3133 west (Signposted 1.5 miles)

An outstanding and virtually unaltered, 14thC manor house incorporating a massive 12thC tower and 13thC great hall, it contains many striking Eltonware pots and vases and a fine collection of Nailsea glass. The house looks out over a beautiful 18thC terraced garden. Tea Room. Limited disabled access.

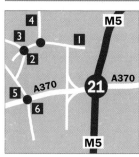

JUNCTION 21

Nearest A&E Hospital

Weston General Hospital

Grange Road, Uphill, Weston super Mare
BS23 4TQ

Tel: (01934) 636363

Take the A370 to Weston super Mare. The hospital is signposted from the junction. (Distance Approx 5.3 miles)

FACILITIES

1 Woolpack Inn

Tel: (01934) 521670

0.5 miles west along the

B3440, on the right.

(Free House) Meals served; Mon-Fri; 12.00-14.00hrs & 18.00-22.00hrs, Sat; 12.00-14.30hrs & 18.00-22.00hrs, Sun; 12.00-14.30hrs & 19.00-21.00hrs.

2 The Summer House

Tel: (01934) 520011

0.9 miles west along the B3440, on the left.

(Banks's) Open all day. Restaurant open; Mon-Thurs; 12.00-14.30hrs & 17.30-22.00hrs, Fri & Sat; 12.00-22.00hrs, Sun; 12.00-21.00hrs. Bar meals served; 12.00-17.30hrs daily.

3 Weston Motoring Centre (BP)

Tel: (01934) 511414

0.9 miles west along the B3440, on the right.

Access, Visa, Overdrive, All Star, Switch, Dial Card, Mastercard, Amex, Diners Club, Delta, BP Cards, Shell Agency, AA Paytrak.

4 Sainsbury's Filling Station

Tel: (01934) 516088

1 mile west along Queen's Way, on the left.

Visa, Access, Mastercard, Switch, Eurocard, Delta, All Star, Overdrive, Amex, Dialcard, AA Paytrak. Toilets and Cash Machines in adjacent Store. Open; Mon-Fri; 06.30-00.30hrs, Sat; 06.30-22.30hrs, Sun; 08.00-18.00hrs.

5 Safeway Filling Station

Tel: (01934) 515067

0.9 miles west along the A370, on the right.

Access, Visa, Overdrive, All Star, Switch, Dial Card,

Mastercard, Amex, Delta, BP Supercharge. Open; Mon-Fri; 06.00-22.30hrs, Sat; 06.00-21.30hrs, Sun; 08.00-20.00hrs.

6   The Bucket & Spade

Tel: (01934) 521235
0.9 miles along the A370, on the left.
(Punch Retail) Meals served; Mon-Thurs; 11.00-21.00hrs, Fri & Sat; 11.00-22.00hrs, Sun; 12.00-21.30hrs.

PLACES OF INTEREST

Weston super Mare

Weston super Mare Tourist Information Centre, Beach Lawns, Weston super Mare BS23 1AT Tel: (01934) 888800 website: www.somersetcoast.com

Follow the A370 west (Signposted 3.5 miles)
From existing as a small fishing hamlet in 1811, within 100 years it had grown to become Somerset's second largest town with a population of well over 50,000. The Grand Pier, the focal point of a seafront packed with assorted attractions, as well as the splendid Winter Gardens and Pavilion overlooking the long safe and sandy beach combine to make this a very popular holiday resort.

Court Farm Country Park

Wolvershill Road, Banwell, Weston super Mare BS24 6DL Tel: (01934) 822383

Follow the A370 west and turn south west towards Barnwell (Signposted 1.9 miles)
A super day out for all the family on this working farm with over 20,000 ft^2 of

undercover entertainment, great in all weathers. Enjoy the hands on experience of bottle feeding of the young animals and there are free tractor rides, an "Amazing Maze" and an Indoor Adventure Playground. Café. Gift Shop. Disabled access.

The Helicopter Museum

The Airport, Locking Moor Road, Weston super Mare BS22 8PL Tel: (01934) 635227 website: www.helicoptermuseum.co.uk

Follow the A370 towards Weston super Mare (Signposted with "propeller" 3 miles)
The home of the world's largest collection of helicopters and autogyros and the only museum in Britain dedicated to the rotary wing aircraft. Now totally under cover, over 60 exhibits are on view and there are also displays on their history and development, a Heli-Adventure Play Area and a conservation hangar where the machines are restored. Gift Shop. Café. Disabled access.

SEDGEMOOR SERVICES (SOUTHBOUND) (ROADCHEF)
Tel: (01934) 750888 Food Fayre Self-Service Restaurant, Wimpy Bar & Esso Fuel

SEDGEMOOR SERVICES (NORTHBOUND) (WELCOME BREAK)
Tel: (01934) 750730 Granary Self-Serve Restaurant, Burger King, Welcome Lodge & Shell Fuel

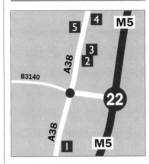

Nearest A&E Hospital
Weston General Hospital
Grange Road, Uphill, Weston super Mare
BS23 4TQ
Tel: (01934) 636363
Take the A38 north to Weston super Mare. The hospital is signposted within the town.
(Distance Approx 7.2 miles)

Nearest Minor Injury Unit
Bridgwater Hospital
Salmon Parade, Bridgwater
TA6 5AH
Tel: (01278) 451501
Proceed to Junction 23 and take the A38 south to Bridgwater and the hospital is signposted within the town.
(Distance Approx 8.2 miles)
Open: 09.00-20.00hrs daily
[Doctor not in attendance 17.00-20.00hrs]

FACILITIES

1   The Bristol Bridge Inn

Tel: (01278) 787269
1 mile south along the A38, on the left.
(Free House) Open all day Tues-Sun. Bar Snacks served; Tues-Sat; 11.00-23.00hrs, Sun; 12.00-22.30hrs.

2 The Fox & Goose

Tel: (01278) 760223

0.4 miles north along the A38, on the right.

(Free House) Open all day. Meals served; Mon-Sat; 10.30-22.30hrs, Sun; 12.00-19.00hrs

3 BWOC Garages (Keyfuels)

Tel: (01278) 760542

0.4 miles north along the A38, on the right.

Access, Visa, Mastercard, Delta, Switch, Electron, Solo, Overdrive, All Star, Dial Card, AA Paytrak, BP Supercharge, Keyfuels Open; Mon-Fri; 06.30-20.00hrs, Sat; 07.00-20.00hrs, Sun; 08.00-20.00hrs

4 The Goat House Café & Restaurant

Tel: (01278) 760995

0.8 miles north along the A38, on the right.

Open; Mon-Thurs; 09.00-16.00hrs, Fri & Sat; 09.00-16.00hrs & 19.00-23.00hrs, Sun; 09.00-17.00hrs.

5 Battleborough Grange Hotel

Tel: (01278) 760208

0.8 miles north along the A38, on the left.

Restaurant Open; 12.00-14.00hrs & 19.00-21.30hrs daily

PLACES OF INTEREST

Alstone Wildlife Park

Alstone Road, Highbridge TA9 3DT Tel: (01278) 782405

Follow the A38 south through Highbridge (Signposted on A38 2.8 miles)

A small non-commercial family run park with a huge variety of interesting and amusing fur and feathered friends including a herd of Red Deer, Llamas, Emus, Ponies, Pigs, Owls, Waterfowl and Theodore the friendly camel. Picnic Area. Light refreshments available.

Coombes Somerset Cider

Japonica Farm, Mark TA9 4QD Tel: (01278) 641265

Follow the A38 north towards Cheddar and after 200 yards turn right to Mark (Signposted "Mark, Cider Farm & Tea Rooms" 2.7 miles)

Founded in 1919, this family-owned firm still makes cider in the traditional way, using local cider apple varieties and maturing the cider in oak vats. Visitors can see this process from start to finish and sample the products. There is also an interesting video of the cider maker's year and a museum. Disabled access.

JUNCTION 23

Nearest Northbound A&E Hospital

Weston General Hospital

Grange Road, Uphill, Weston super Mare BS23 4TQ Tel: (01934) 636363

Proceed to Junction 22 and take the A38 north to Weston super Mare. The hospital is signposted within the town. (Distance Approx 13 miles)

Nearest Southbound A&E Hospital

Musgrove Park Hospital

Taunton TA1 5DA Tel: (01823) 333444

Proceed to Junction 25 and take the A358 west to Taunton. The hospital is signposted within the town. (Distance Approx 14.7 miles)

Nearest Minor Injury Unit

Bridgwater Hospital

Salmon Parade, Bridgwater TA6 5AH Tel: (01278) 451501

Take the A38 south to Bridgwater and the hospital is signposted within the town. (Distance Approx 3.1 miles) Open: 09.00-20.00hrs daily [Doctor not in attendance 17.00-20.00hrs]

FACILITIES

1 The Puriton Inn

Tel: (01278) 683464

0.2 miles along the Puriton Road, on the left.

(Whitbread) Meals served; Mon-Sat; 11.30-14.00hrs & 18.00-21.00hrs, Sun; 12.00-14.00hrs & 19.00-21.00hrs.

2 Rockfield House

Tel: (01278) 683561

0.2 miles east along the A39, on the right.

3 The Admiral's Table

Tel: (01278) 685671

0.6 miles south along the A38, on the left.

(Eldridge, Pope & Co) Open all day, meals served 07.00-22.00hrs daily.

PLACES OF INTEREST

Admiral Blake Museum

Blake Street, Bridgwater
TA6 3NB

Follow the A38 south to Bridgwater and it is signposted within the town. (3.4 miles)

For details please see Junction 24 information

Secret World Wildlife Rescue Centre

East Huntspill, Somerset
TA9 3PZ Tel: (01278) 783250
website: www.secretworld.co.uk

Follow the A39 east towards Street and turn north along the B3134 to East Huntspill (5.3 miles)

Featured regularly on TV in programmes such as HTV's "Cross Country", the BBC's "Animal People" and "The Really Wild Show" as well as C4's "Pet Rescue", this centre is now established as a wild animal hospital and rehabilitation centre. Although originally opened as a tourist attraction, it is still open to visitors on five weekends of the year. Disabled access

Alstone Wildlife Park

Alstone Road, Highbridge
TA9 3DT

Follow the A38 north towards Highbridge (Signposted on A38 4.4 miles)

For details please see Junction 22 information.

JUNCTION 24

Nearest A&E Hospital

Musgrove Park Hospital
Taunton TA1 5DA

Tel: (01823) 333444

Proceed to Junction 25 and take the A358 west to Taunton. The hospital is signposted within the town. (Distance Approx 9.9 miles)

Nearest Minor Injury Unit

Bridgwater Hospital

Salmon Parade, Bridgwater
TA6 5AH
Tel: (01278) 451501

Take the A38 north to Bridgwater and the hospital is signposted within the town. (Distance Approx 2.2 miles) Open: 09.00-20.00hrs daily [Doctor not in attendance 17.00-20.00hrs]

FACILITIES

BRIDGWATER SERVICES (FIRST)
Tel: (01278) 456800
Burger King, Lodge, Restaurant & BP Fuel

1   The Boat & Anchor Inn

Tel: (01278) 662473
1 mile along the Huntworth Road, on the right.
(Free House) Meals served; 12.00-15.00hrs & 18.00-21.00hrs daily. (Sun Carvery; 12.00-15.00hrs)

2   Compass Tavern

Tel: (01278) 662283

0.3 miles south along the A38, on the left.
(Enterprise Inns) Open all day. Bar meals served; 12.00-21.00hrs daily. Meals served; 12.00-21.30hrs daily (June-September), 12.00-15.00hrs & 18.00-21.30hrs daily (October-May)

3   Quantock View Guest House

Tel: (01278) 663309
0.3 miles south along the A38, on the left.

4   Grahams Transport Stop Café

Tel: (01278) 663052
0.5 miles south along the A38, on the left.
Open; Mon; 07.00-20.30hrs, Tues-Thurs; 06.30-20.30hrs, Fri; 06.30-17.00hrs, Sat; 07.00-11.00hrs.

5   Woods Filling Station (UK Petrol)

Tel: (01278) 663076
0.5 miles south along the A38, on the left.
Access, Visa, Mastercard, Switch, Electron, Solo, Delta, Overdrive, All Star, Dial Card, AA Paytrak, UK Fuelcard, Securicor Fuelserv, IDS, Keyfuels. Open; Mon-Sat; 07.00- 21.00, Sun; 09.00-18.00hrs.

6   Taunton Road Service Station (BP)

Tel: (01278) 427486
0.7 miles north along the A38, on the right.
Access, Visa, Mastercard, Switch, Diners Club, Amex, Overdrive, All Star, Dial Card, Shell Agency, BP Cards.

PLACES OF INTEREST

Admiral Blake Museum

Blake Street, Bridgwater
TA6 3NB Tel: (01278) 456127
website: www.sedgemoor.gov.uk

Follow the A38 north to Bridgwater and it is signposted within the town. (2.1 miles)

The birthplace of Admiral Blake is now utilized as the Town Museum and, as well as featuring events in his life, houses a variety of exhibits related to the local history. Blake was an important officer in Cromwell's army and twice defended Taunton against overwhelming Royalist odds. In his fifties he was given command of the British navy and went on to win important battles against the Dutch and Spanish and re-established Britain's naval supremacy in Europe. One of the exhibits is a three-dimensional model of one of his most famous victories, the Battle of Santa Cruz. There is also a similar diorama of the Battle of Sedgemoor and exhibitions of artefacts dating from the Neolithic period to the Second World War and a section dealing with shipping. Gift Shop. Limited disabled access.

JUNCTION 25

Nearest A&E Hospital

Musgrove Park Hospital
Taunton TA1 5DA
Tel: (01823) 333444
Take the A358 west to Taunton and the hospital is signposted within the town. (Distance Approx 3.4 miles)

FACILITIES

1   The Black Brook Tavern

Tel: (01823) 443121
0.1 miles east along the A358, on the left.
(Scottish & Newcastle) Open all day. Meals served in Tavern; Mon-Sat; 12.00-22.00hrs, Sun; 12.00-21.30hrs. Carvery Restaurant; Open Mon-Thurs; 12.00-14.00hrs & 18.00-21.30hrs, Fri; 12.00-14.00hrs & 18.00-22.00hrs, Sat; 12.00-22.00hrs, Sun; 12.00-21.30hrs.

2   Premier Lodge

Tel: (01823) 443121
0.1 miles east along the A358, on the left.

3   Countryways Accommodation

Tel: (01823) 442326
0.9 miles east along the A358, on the left.

4   Ruishton Inn

Tel: (01823) 442285
0.5 miles east, in Ruishton, on the left.
(Wadworths) Open all day Sat & Sun. Meals served; Mon-Sat; 12.00-13.45hrs & 19.00-21.45hrs, Sun; 12.00-13.45hrs

5   Holiday Inn, Taunton

Tel: 0870 400 9080
0.1 miles west along the A358, in Blackbrook Business Park, on the left.
Junction Restaurant Open; Breakfast; Mon-Fri; 06.30-10.00hrs, Sat & Sun; 07.30-11.00hrs, Lunch; Sun-Fri; 12.30-14.30hrs, Dinner; Mon-Sat; 18.30-22.00hrs, Sun; 19.00-22.00hrs

6   Taunton Deane Filling Station (Murco)

Tel: (01823) 332002
0.1 miles west along the A358, in Blackbrook Business Park, on the left.
Access, Visa, Delta, Mastercard, Switch, Amex, Overdrive, All Star, Dial Card, Murco Cards. Hot Food available; 07.00-16.00hrs daily

7   The Taunton Harvester

Tel: (01823) 442221
0.1 miles west along the A358, in Blackbrook Business Park, on the left.
(Six Continents) Open all day. Meals served; Sun-Fri; 12.00-21.00hrs, Sat; 12.00-22.00hrs.

8   Express by Holiday Inn, Taunton

Tel: (01823) 624000
0.1 miles west along the A358, in Blackbrook Business Park, on the left.

9   Sainsbury's Filling Station

Tel: (01823) 443163
0.3 miles west along the A358, in Hankridge Farm, on the right.
LPG. Visa, Access, Mastercard, Switch, Delta, Overdrive, All Star, Dial Card, Amex, JS Fuelcard. Cash Machines available in adjacent Store.

10 Pizza Hut

Tel: (01823) 444747
0.3 miles west along the
A358, in Hankridge Farm, on
the right.
Open; Sun-Thurs; 11.30-
23.00hrs, Fri & Sat; 11.30-
0.00hrs.

11 The Hankridge Arms

Tel: (01823) 444405
0.3 miles west along the
A358, in Hankridge Farm, on
the right.
(Hall & Woodhouse) Open all
day. Meals served in Bar &
Restaurant; Sun-Thurs; 12.00-
14.30hrs & 18.30-21.30hrs, Fri
& Sat; 12.00-14.30hrs &
18.30-22.00hrs.

12 Travelodge Taunton

Tel: (01823) 444702
0.3 miles west along the
A358, in Hankridge Farm, on
the right.

13 McDonald's

Tel: (01823) 443765
0.3 miles west along the
A358, in Riverside Park, on
the right.
Open; Sun-Thurs; 07.30-
23.30hrs, Fri & Sat; 07.30-
00.00hrs. ("Drive Thru" service
only after 23.00hrs daily)

14 Tramonte's Italian Restaurant

Tel: (01823) 323377
0.3 miles west along the
A358, in Riverside Park, on
the right.
Open; Tues & Wed; 17.30-
22.30hrs, Thurs-Sat; 12.00-
14.30hrs & 17.30-22.30hrs

15 Central Service Station (Esso)

Tel: (01823) 333587
0.8 miles north all along the
A38, on the right.
Access, Visa, Overdrive, All
Star, Switch, Dial Card,
Mastercard, Amex, Diners Club,
Delta, Shell Gold, Esso Cards.
Open; Mon-Sat; 07.00-
20.00hrs, Sun; 08.30-
18.00hrs

16 The Bathpool Inn

Tel: (01823) 272545
0.9 miles north along the
A38, on the right.
(Enterprise 9) Open all day.
Meals served; 12.00-15.00hrs
& 18.00-21.00hrs daily.

17 White Lodge Travel Inn

Tel: (01823) 321112
0.6 miles along Corfe Road,
on the right.

18 White Lodge

Tel: (01823) 321112
0.6 miles along Corfe Road,
on the right.
(Beefeater) Open all day. Meals
served; Mon-Thurs; 12.00-
14.30hrs & 17.00-21.45hrs,
Fri; 12.00-14.30hrs & 17.00-
22.15hrs, Sat; 12.00-22.45hrs,
Sun; 12.00-20.45hrs.

PLACES OF INTEREST

Taunton

Taunton Tourist Information
Centre, The Library, Paul Street,
Taunton TA1 3PF
Tel: (01823) 336344 website:
www.heartofsomerset.com

**Follow the A358 west.
(Signposted 1.9 miles)**

The county town of Somerset,
Taunton, was founded in the
8thC as a military camp by the
Saxon King Ine and, by Norman
times it had grown to have its
own Augustine monastery,
minster and castle. This castle
was the focus of two important
sieges during the Civil War and
in 1685 the Bloody Assizes
were held here in which the
infamous Judge Jeffreys
sentenced 150 followers of the
Duke of Monmouth to death.
The much-altered castle today
houses the Somerset County
Museum (Tel: 01823-320201)
and part of the old monastic
gatehouse in the Priory
grounds, nearby, has been
restored and is now in use as
The Somerset County Cricket
Museum (Tel: 01823-275893).
Taunton was a thriving wool
and textile centre and much of
the wealth generated was
expended on many of the fine
buildings still to be seen in the
town centre.

West Somerset Railway

Bishops Lydeard Station, Bishops
Lydeard TA4 3BX
Tel: (01643) 704996 website:
www.w-somerset-railway.co.uk

**Follow the A358 west and
follow the WSR signposts.
(7.1 miles)**

The West Somerset Railway
recreates the era of a Great
Western Railway country
branch line, connecting
Bishops Lydeard with the
holiday resort of Minehead.
Enjoy a steam hauled train ride
through some 20 miles of
glorious Somerset scenery as it
weaves its way past the
Quantock Hills and along the
Bristol Channel. There is a
visitor centre, giftshop and
refreshment room at the
Bishops Lydeard Station and a
large giftshop and refreshment
room at Minehead. Disabled
access to trains at all stations
except Doniford Halt and
disabled toilets are provided at
Minehead and Bishops
Lydeard.

Hestercombe Gardens

Hestercombe, Cheddon Fitzpaine, Taunton TA2 8LG
Tel: (01823) 413923 website: www.hestercombegardens.com

Follow the A358 west, A38 north and follow signposts to Cheddon Fitzpaine (3.3 miles)

Fifty acres of formal gardens and parkland, including the famous Edwardian Gardens designed by Sir Edwin Lutyens and Gertrude Jekyll, and the Georgian Landscape Garden with lakes, temples and delightful woodland walks. Tea Room. Gift Shop. Limited Disabled access.

BETWEEN JUNCS 25 & 26

TAUNTON DEANE SERVICES (SOUTHBOUND) (ROADCHEF)
Tel: (01823) 271111 RoadChef Restaurant, Wimpy Bar, Dr Beaks Chicken, Costa Coffee, Travel Inn & Shell Fuel

TAUNTON DEANE SERVICES (NORTHBOUND) (ROADCHEF)
Tel: (01823) 271111 RoadChef Restaurant, Wimpy Bar, & Shell Fuel

FOOTBRIDGE CONNECTION BETWEEN SITES.

JUNCTION 26

Nearest A&E Hospital

Musgrove Park Hospital
Taunton TA1 5DA
Tel: (01823) 333444
Follow the A38 route to Taunton. The hospital is

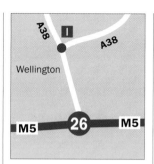

signposted within the town. (Distance Approx 4.7 miles)

FACILITIES

1 Piccadilly Filling Station (Independent)

 [WC]

Tel: (01823) 661469
1 mile north along the A38, on the left.
Access, Visa, Mastercard, Diners Club, Delta, Overdrive, All Star, Dial Card. Open; 07.00-21.00hrs daily

PLACES OF INTEREST

Wellington

Follow the A38 south (Signposted 2.2 miles)
An old market town with broad streets containing fine Georgian buildings including the neo-classical town hall. Once an important producer of woven cloth and serge, the prosperity of the town owed much to Quaker entrepreneurs and the Fox banking family. The much-altered perpendicular style church contains the ostentatious tomb of Sir John Popham, the judge who presided at the trial of Guy Fawkes. Present-day Wellington is a pleasant and prosperous shopping centre.

Wellington Monument

Follow the A38 south and it is signposted from Wellington. (4.4 miles)
An 170ft obelisk constructed in honour of the Duke of Wellington on the estate bought for him by the nation following his victory at the Battle of Waterloo. Although the foundation stone was laid in 1817, lack of funds led to a radical simplification of the design and the edifice was not finally completed until two years after his death, in 1854.

Visitors who would like to make the 235 step climb to the top should telephone Mr HR Pocock at Monument Farm on Tel: (01823) 680303 prior to arrival to arrange for provision of the key. It is strongly advised to take a torch as there are no windows in the monument!

Sheppy's Cider Family Centre

Three Bridges, Bradford on Tone, Taunton TA4 1ER
Tel: (01823) 461233 website: www.sheppyscider.com

Follow the A38 north to Bradford on Tone (2.8 miles)
A 370 acre farm with 47 acres of cider orchards producing a wide variety of apples. The attractions include nature walks, cider sampling and tours of the cellars and press room. There is a museum with cidermaking video, cider shop, licensed tea room (Seasonal) and picnic and childrens play areas. Disabled toilets and full disabled access.

West Somerset Railway

Bishops Lydeard Station, Bishops Lydeard TA4 3BX

Take the A38 north and follow the WSR signposts. (9.6 miles)
For details please see Junction 25 information

JUNCTION 27

Nearest Southbound A&E Hospital

Royal Devon & Exeter Hospital

Barrack Road, Wonford, Exeter EX2 5DW.
Tel: (01392) 411611
Proceed to Junction 30 and take the A379 west to Exeter. The hospital is signposted within the town. (Distance Approx 17 miles)

Nearest Northbound A&E Hospital

Musgrove Park Hospital

Taunton TA1 5DA
Tel: (01823) 333444
Proceed to Junction 26 and take the A38 route to Taunton. The hospital is signposted within the town. (Distance Approx 13.5 miles)

Nearest Minor Injury Unit

Tiverton District Hospital

William St. Tiverton
EX16 6DJ
Tel: (01884) 253251
Take the A36 west into Tiverton and the hospital is signposted within the town. Open 24 hours (Distance Approx 6 miles)

FACILITIES

TIVERTON SERVICES (MOTO)
Tel: (01884) 822010

Little Chef, Burger King, Travelodge & Shell Fuel

1   The Waterloo Cross

Tel: (01884) 840328
0.4 miles east along the A38, at Waterloo Cross, on the right.
(Eldridge, Pope & Co) Open all day on Sun. Meals served; Mon-Sat; 12.00-14.00hrs & 18.00-21.00hrs. Sun; 12.00-21.00hrs.

2   The Old Well Garden Centre & Coffee Shop

Tel: (01884) 840873
0.5 miles east along the A38, at Waterloo Cross, on the right.
Open; 09.30-17.00hrs daily.

3   Parkway House Hotel

Tel: (01884) 820255
0.9 miles south of the A373, in Sampford Peverell, on the right.
Cezanne's Restaurant & Bar; Meals served; 12.00-21.30hrs daily. (Disabled access to Restaurant.)

4   Kellands Garage (Texaco)

Tel: (01884) 820264
1 mile south of the A373, in Sampford Peverell, on the right.
Access, Visa, Mastercard, Switch, Electron, Solo, Diners Club, Amex, Delta, Overdrive, All Star, Dial Card, UK Fuelcard, Keyfuels, Texaco Cards. Open; Mon-Sat; 06.00-21.00hrs, Sun; 08.00-21.00hrs

5   Public Toilets

WC

1 mile south of the A373, in Sampford Peverell, on the right.

PLACES OF INTEREST

Tiverton

Tiverton Tourist Information Centre, Phoenix Lane, Tiverton
Tel: (01884) 255827 website: www.devonshireheartland.co.uk

Follow the A361 west (Signposted 6 miles)

A town of pre-Saxon origin, it stands high above the junction of the Rivers Exe and Lowman, leading to its original name of Twyford-ton (two ford town). Firmly established by the 16thC as a thriving centre for the woollen industry it was almost destroyed by fire on no less than three occasions 1598, 1612 and 1731. Tiverton Castle, originally constructed in the 12thC and taken by siege by the Roundheads in 1645 is just one of many interesting buildings to be found within the town centre.

Within the town centre can be found ...

Tiverton Museum

St.Andrew Street, Tiverton
EX16 6PH
Tel: (01884) 256295 website: www.tivertonmuseum.org.uk

Covering nearly half an acre and illustrating the history of the district from Roman times to the present day, it is one of the largest social history museums in the South West. Particularly noted for its collection of agricultural equipment, other galleries include civic displays, domestic artefacts, railway items and toys and dolls. Gift Shop. Disabled access.

Grand Western Canal

Canal Hill, Tiverton EX16 4HX

Follow the A361 to Tiverton and it is signposted within the town. (6.1 miles)

It was originally conceived as a

barge canal linking Taunton and Topsham and thereby making a navigable link between the Bristol and English Channels. In the end only a short section, opened in 1814, was built to this standard with a smaller "tub boat" canal being constructed between Lowdwells and Taunton and officially opening in 1838. This tub boat section closed in 1864 and the original barge canal, disused since 1924, was officially closed in 1962. It is this stretch, restored and re-opened in the 1980's, that forms the centrepiece of the Grand Western Canal and Country Park.

The Grand Western Horseboat Company (Tel: 01884-253345) runs horse drawn barge trips, to which there is disabled access (by prior arrangement), and hires out rowing boats and self-drive boats by the day. There is a Gift Shop, Restaurant Barge and picnic area as well as walks within the country park. Adjacent to the car park is Lime Kiln Cottage, a listed 16thC thatched building, where the Canal Tea Rooms and Gardens (Tel: 01884-252291), specializing in home-made cakes and traditional Devon cream teas, may be found.

Coldharbour Industrial Museum

Uffculme, Cullompton
EX15 3EE
Tel: (01884) 840960 website: www.coldharbourmill.org.uk

Follow the A38 east and follow the signs to Willand. Signposted along this route. (2 miles)
A working wool museum demonstrating how old Victorian spinning, carding, and machines produce knitting wool and the Devon tartan. The 1910 steam engine and the recently restored 1867 beam engine are currently on display as is the New World Tapestry

which tells the story of the colonization of the Americas in cartoon style. The Mill is surrounded by a water garden and delightful walks and there is a mill shop and restaurant. Disabled access is available by prior arrangement.

JUNCTION 28

CULLOMPTON TOWN CENTRE IS WITHIN ONE MILE OF THIS JUNCTION

Nearest A&E Hospital
Royal Devon & Exeter Hospital
Barrack Road, Wonford, Exeter EX2 5DW.
Tel: (01392) 411611
Proceed to Junction 30 and take the A379 west to Exeter. The hospital is signposted within the town, (Distance Approx 13.3 miles)

Nearest Minor Injury Unit
Tiverton District Hospital
William Street, Tiverton
EX16 6BJ
Tel: (01884) 253251
Take the road into Cullompton and follow the B3181 north to Willand. Take the B3391 west to Tiverton and the hospital is signposted within the town. Open 24 hours. (Distance Approx 8.6 miles)

FACILITIES

CULLOMPTON SERVICES (MARGRAM)
Tel: (01884) 38054
Little Chef and McDonald's & BP Fuel

1   Oakdale B&B

Tel: (01884) 33428
0.6 miles east along the A373, on the right.

2   Aller Barton Farm

Tel: (01884) 32275
0.7 miles east along the A373, on the right.

3   The Weary Traveller

Tel: (01884) 32317
0.1 miles west along the Cullompton Road, on the left. (Laurel Pub Partnership) Open all day Fri-Sun. Meals served; Mon-Thurs; 12.00-14.00hrs & 18.30-21.00hrs, Fri-Sat; 12.00-14.00hrs & 18.30-21.30hrs.

4   Public Toilets
WC
0.4 miles west along the Cullompton Road, in Cullompton, on the left.

5   Court House B&B

Tel: (01884) 32510
0.4 miles west along the Cullompton Road, on the right.

6   Tandoori Spice

Tel: (01884) 32060
0.4 miles north along the B3181, in Cullompton, on the left.
Open; 17,30-0.00hrs daily

7   The Market House Inn

Tel: (01884) 32339

0.5 miles south along the B3181, in Cullompton, on the left.

(Laurel Pub Partnership) Open all day. Meals served; 12.00-15.00hrs daily

8 The Manor House Hotel

Tel: (01884) 32281

0.5 miles south along the B3181, in Cullompton, on the right.

(Free House) Open all day. Meals served; 12.00-15.00 & 17.00-22.00hrs only

9 White Hart Inn

Tel: (01884) 33260

0.6 miles south along the B3181, in Cullompton, on the left.

(Courage) Meals served; Mon-Sat; 12.00-14.30hrs & 18.30-21.00hrs.

10 Exeter Road Garage (Esso)

Tel: (01884) 32726

0.8 miles south along the B3181, in Cullompton, on the right.

LPG. Access, Visa, Mastercard, Switch, Diners Club, Amex, Delta, Overdrive, All Star, Dial Card, BP Supercharge, Shell Gold, Esso Cards. Open; 07.00-21.00hrs daily

11 The Bell Inn

Tel: (01884) 35672

0.8 miles south along the B3181, in Cullompton, on the right.

(Heavitree) Open all day. Meals served; Mon-Sat; 11.00-14.30hrs & 18.30-20.30hrs, Sun; 12.00-14.30hrs & 18.30-20.30hrs.

12 The Inglenook Licensed Restaurant

Tel: (01884) 33685

1 mile south along the B3181, in Cullompton, on the right.

Meals served; Tues-Sat; 18.30-22.00hrs, Sun; 12.00-14.30hrs

PLACES OF INTEREST

Bickleigh Castle

Bickleigh, Tiverton, Devon
EX16 8RP
Tel: (01884) 855363

Take the west exit into Cullompton and follow the signs to Bickleigh (7.5 miles)

A Royalist stronghold for over 900 years the castle includes an 11thC Chapel, guard room, great hall and a "Tudor" bedroom. Bickleigh Castle stands in a picturesque moated garden and the displays include Cromwellian arms and armour. Restaurant. Limited disabled access.

Yearlstone Vineyard

Bickleigh, Tiverton, Devon
EX16 8RI
Tel: (01884) 855700 website: www.yearlstone.com

Take the west exit into Cullompton and follow the signs to Bickleigh (7.5 miles)

Free tasting sessions are available here at Devon's oldest vineyard, magnificently sited in the Exe Valley. Pick up a tour guide and stroll amongst the rows of vines, see how West Country wines are produced and then enjoy comparing vintages and varieties. Farm Shop. Limited disabled access.

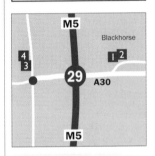

M5
JUNCTION 29

THIS IS A RESTRICTED ACCESS JUNCTION

- Vehicles can only enter the motorway (northbound) from the eastbound carriageway of the A30
- Vehicles can only enter the motorway (southbound) from the westbound carriageway of the A30
- Northbound and southbound vehicles can only exit along the eastbound carriageway of the A30

Nearest A&E Hospital

Royal Devon & Exeter Hospital

Barrack Road, Wonford, Exeter EX2 5DW.
Tel: (01392) 411611

Southbound: Proceed to Junction 30 and take the A379 west to Exeter. The hospital is signposted from the junction. (Distance Approx 3.4 miles)

Northbound: Take the A30 east, turn around at the end of the dual carriageway section and follow the A30 into Exeter. The hospital is signposted within the town. (Distance Approx 2.5 miles)

FACILITIES

1 The Black Horse Inn

Tel: (01392) 366649

0.8 miles east along London Road, on the left.
Meals served; 12.00-14.00hrs & 18.00-21.30hrs daily.

2 The Firs

Tel: (01392) 361821
0.9 miles east along London Road, on the left.

3 Express by Holiday Inn, Exeter

Tel: (01392) 261000
0.4 miles west along the A30, on the right.

4 The Barn Owl

Tel: (01392) 449011
0.4 miles west along the A30, on the right.
(Six Continents) Meals served; Mon-Sat; 12.00-22.00hrs, Sun; 12.00-21.30hrs.

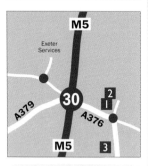

Nearest A&E Hospital
Royal Devon & Exeter Hospital
Barrack Road, Wonford, Exeter EX2 5DW
Tel: (01392) 411611
Take the A379 west to Exeter and the hospital is signposted from the junction. (Distance Approx 2.4 miles)

FACILITIES

EXETER SERVICES (MOTO)
Tel: (01392) 274044
Fresh Express Restaurant, Harry Ramsden's, Burger King, Travelodge & Esso Fuel

1 The Halfmoon Inn

Tel: (01392) 873515
0.5 miles south along the A376, in Clyst St Mary.
(Heavitree) Meals served; 12.00-14.00hrs & 19.00-21.30hrs daily

2 The Maltsters

Tel: (01392) 873445
0.5 miles south along the A376, in Clyst St Mary.
(Whitbread) Open all day Mon-Sat. Meals served; 12.00-14.00hrs daily.

3 Redlands BP Service Station

Tel: (01392) 873040
1 mile south along the A376, on the right.
Access, Visa, Overdrive, All Star, Switch, Dial Card, Mastercard, Amex, Diners Club, Delta, Routex, BP Cards, Shell Agency. Open; Mon-Sat; 07.00-19.00hrs (Oct-Apr), 07.00-20.00hrs (May-Sept), Sun; 09.00-19.00hrs. (24hr Credit Card operated pumps available when shop is closed)

PLACES OF INTEREST

Exeter

Exeter Tourist Information Centre, Civic Centre, Paris Street, Exeter EX1 1JJ
Tel: (01392) 265700
website: www.exeter.gov.uk

Follow the signboards (3.1 miles)
An historic city with a majestic Norman cathedral, many fine old buildings and a wealth of excellent museums. It was established by the Celtish tribe of Dumnonii some 200 years before the Romans arrived and established it as the city of Isca, a walled and fortified stronghold. In the dark ages the city became a major ecclesiastical centre with King Cenwealh founding an abbey in 670AD on the site of the present cathedral. The city was ransacked by the Vikings in the 9thC and they occupied it twice before they were defeated by King Alfred.

William the Conqueror took the city in 1086 and the Normans then constructed Rougemont Castle and commenced work on St Peter's Cathedral, a task that was not completed until 1206. A port of some importance, the town prospered for many years and this is reflected in the quality and variety of buildings within the city.

Crealy Adventure Park

Clyst St Mary, Exeter EX5 1DR
Tel: (01395) 233200
website: www.crealy.co.uk

Follow the A3052 east (Signposted along this route 2.6 miles)
A huge outdoor adventure ground featuring many attractions for children and adults, including roller coaster and carousel rides and the Farm Nursery and World of Pets allow for hands-on experience with small animals. Restaurant, Cafés, Kiosks, Gifts & Toy Shop.

the M6

Commencing at Junction 19 of the M1 near Rugby, this motorway forms the primary route north through north west England, linking Scotland to the Midlands and south of England.

The motorway heads due west and between Junctions 1 and 2 slip roads mark the site of a proposed Service Area at Harborough for which a bridge to connect the east and westbound sites was constructed at the same time as the motorway was built. This bridge survived, as a concrete beam supported upon two concrete pillars, in splendid isolation for some thirty years or so until it was demolished during the night of January 28th/29th, 2000 as part of a carriageway renewal scheme. Approaching Junction 2 the motorway crosses the West Coast Main Line from London Euston to Glasgow and the **Oxford Canal**. The northern section of the Oxford Canal, from Coventry to Banbury was originally opened in 1778 and followed a very circuitous route to avoid extensive earthworks. This was rectified by the Oxford Canal Company in 1830 who rebuilt the waterway and reduced the overall mileage by 14 miles.

Continuing west the motorway passes **Coventry** to the south between Junction 2 (where the motorway links up with the M69) and Junction 3. Coventry, once known as the "City of Three Spires" and inextricably linked with the famous ride of Lady Godiva, stands on the River Sherbourne and is one of the oldest cities in England, a convent having been established here in the 6thC. For those travelling west just after Corley Services the city of **Birmingham** comes into view, stretching right across the horizon with the Lickey Hills on

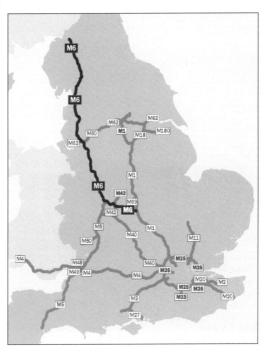

the extreme left, the BT Tower in the middle and Sutton Coldfield on the right before the carriageways meet with the M42 at Junction 4. The M6 was originally designed to carry 80,000 vehicles per day but even in 1973 it was over-capacity and, as any traveller who has struggled to make progress along the section from here to Junction 10A would testify, the situation has deteriorated with some 120,000 vehicles using it daily, making this the busiest stretch of motorway in Europe.

From this point to Junction 7, the motorway traverses the northern suburbs of Birmingham, passing through the **Castle Vale Estate** which, on the north side close to Junction 4, was built on the site of the former Spitfire Factory and airfield and, on the south side was built on the site of the Bromford Bridge Racecourse which closed on June 21st, 1965. The Spitfire factory was responsible for producing 13,000 fighters and was utilized in immediate post war days for the British Industries Fair. The **Fort Dunlop** building on the north side past Junction 5, and currently being refurbished as a "prestigious life-style complex", was the site of the world's largest poster between January and June 2001 when an advertisement commissioned by the Ford Motor Company, measuring 400ft x 70ft and weighing more than 2 tons, was installed on the side of the building.

Continuing westwards the **Aston Expressway** (A38[M]), a short council owned motorway can be seen on the south side of Junction 6. This opened on May 1st, 1972 and possesses two unique features; it has no central reservation, so that a tidal flow traffic management scheme can operate during rush hours, and is bridged by a vinegar main linking two parts of the HP Sauce factory. A couple of sporting venues can be seen on the south of the carriageways, **Villa Park**, home ground of Aston Villa since 1897, with the Jacobean **Aston Hall** beyond are just west of Junction 6 whilst the **Alexander Sports Stadium** is the home track of Birchfield Harriers and current venue for the AAA Championships and trials.

Between Junctions 7 and 8 the hard shoulders were dispensed with on February 9th, 1998 and re-classified as motorway lanes in a pilot scheme to ease congestion. Junction 8, a large triangular configuration known as the Ray Hall Interchange, links the M6 with the M5, and the south side of **Walsall**, traditionally the centre of the leather industry and renowned for the manufacture of saddles, is on the north side of the junction whilst the 8.5 mile long **Tame Valley Canal**, fully opened in 1844, runs along the south side. Between here and Junction 10, where it turns northwards, the motorway passes **Bescot Yard** on the south side. Bescot Marshalling Yard opened in 1892 and still has a major role today in forming freight trains for progress across the UK and onto the continent. In recent years part of the yard has been used for the storage of redundant diesel locomotives. Further west, **Bescot Diesel Depot** and former steam engine shed can be seen. The former steam engine shed closed on March 28th, 1966 and is one of the very few that still remains standing.

Continuing northwards Junction 10A links up with the M54 and Junction 11 is currently being reconstructed to provide a connection with the **M6 Toll** (formerly known

as the "Birmingham Northern Relief Road"), Britain's first toll motorway. Between Junctions 13 and 14 the County town of **Stafford** is by-passed along the west side with **Stafford Castle** visible on a hill at the northern end of the section. The castle was established in the 11thC and rebuilt in stone by Ralph, 1st Earl of Stafford in 1350. It saw action in the Civil War in 1643, after which the Parliamentarians ordered its demolition. Sir George Jerningham, claimant to the title, partially rebuilt the keep in Gothic style but the castle was finally abandoned in 1949. Just before Junction 14 the motorway crosses the River Sow, the West Coast Main Line and a wide peat bog by means of the 3,500ft long **Creswell**

Cannock Chase

Viaduct. The carriageways continue north through Staffordshire, passing **Stoke and the Potteries**, the manufacturing base for some of the world's finest tableware, on the east side between Junctions 15 and 16.

The motorway progresses through Cheshire and crosses the M56 at Junction 20 before reaching the largest bridge on the route, **The Thelwall Viaduct**. The 4,400ft long northbound viaduct is the original bridge, opened in July 1963 and measuring 90ft high with a 336ft centre span, it carried three lanes of traffic in both directions. The later, southbound, structure was completed in July 1995 but the completed Thelwall Viaduct, with two bridges each carrying four lanes, was not fully operational until refurbishments to the original one were finished in December 1996. This spans the **Manchester Ship**

Pottery Museum, Stoke on Trent

Canal which opened in 1894 and, from the bridge to the west, the cooling towers of **Fiddlers Ferry Power Station** and **Runcorn Bridge** can be seen in the distance beyond Warrington, an important industrial and commercial centre with many imposing Georgian and Victorian buildings. **Altrincham** and the western outskirts of **Manchester**, with the Pennines beyond, are visible on the east side. At the south end of the viaduct the **Bridgewater Canal**, opened in 1776 and now part of the Cheshire Ring Canal Walk, is bridged whilst, at the north end, the **River Mersey** and the Mersey Way Trail are crossed.

From the north bank of the River Mersey the motorway continues northwards and approaching Junction 23 the former **Liverpool & Manchester Railway** main line is bridged. This was opened on September 15th, 1830 by the Duke of Wellington and was the first full-scale inter city railway, exclusively powered by locomotives and providing a strictly timetabled service for both passengers and freight, the prototype on which all subsequent railways throughout the world were modelled. The M62 is crossed at Junction 21A and, after passing **Haydock Racecourse**, which opened in 1898, on the east side of Junction 24, the M6 links up with the M59 at Junction 26. Along this section **Wigan**, one of the oldest places in Lancashire, and **Bolton**, synonymous with the textile industry, as well as the **Pennine Mountains**, can be seen in a panoramic view on the east side and just before Junction 27 the 800ft long **Gathurst Viaduct** bridges the River Douglas, Leeds & Liverpool Canal (opened in 1780) and the ex-Lancashire & Yorkshire Railway Wigan to Southport line. The motorway then crosses the M65 at Junction 29.

The section between Junctions 29 and 32 was the first stretch of motorway to be built in this country. Known as the Preston By-Pass it originally comprised two lanes in each direction and was opened on December 5th, 1958. Reconstruction to a 3-lane motorway was completed in March 1966. The M61 joins the M6 from the south at Junction 30 as the motorway passes **Preston** on the west side. In Saxon days Preston was "Priest's Town" and later became the ancient capital of the Duchy of Lancaster. In 1715 the Old Pretender was proclaimed King in the Market Place and, 30 years later the Young Pretender was also proclaimed King on the same spot. Continuing northwards, Junction 32, which connects with the M55, has the distinction of being the first three-level interchange built in this country. As the motorway approaches Lancaster so the scenery starts to change dramatically to the east and approaching Forton Services the 1,300ft high **Forest of Bowland** is visible in the far distance with **Beacon Fell Country Park** (870ft high) and the 700ft high **Grizedale** with a cairn at 615ft in the near distance.

Between Junctions 33 and 34, **Lancaster University**, which was founded in 1964, and the town of **Lancaster**, a county town steeped in history, are passed on the west side whilst the dome of the Ashton Memorial can be seen in **Williamson Park**. This park was developed on the site of an old quarry in about 1896 and the dome is believed to be the first known example of a pre-stressed concrete structure. To the east, just before Junction 34, Cragg Wood is visible on the slopes of **Black Fell** (1,350ft high). As the motorway continues north across the fells the trackbed of the former Midland Railway Lancaster to Hellifield line and the River Lune are bridged approaching Junction 35 with Warton and **Warton Crag** (535ft high) beyond on the west side. **Crag Lot** (465ft high) and **Carnforth** is passed on the west side at Junction 35. The station at Carnforth was used in the classic

film *Brief Encounter* with Trevor Howard and Celia Johnson. Continuing north to Junction 36 the **Lancaster Canal** is bridged and the **River Keer** is crossed just after Burton in Kendal Services and Borwick and **Borwick Hall**, an Elizabethan manor house constructed in 1595, are passed on the east side. The Lancaster Canal and Tewitfield Locks - a flight of 8 locks rising some 76ft - run parallel to the eastern side of the motorway before passing under the carriageway. The Lancaster Canal and Tewitfield Locks, a flight of 8 rising 76ft, were opened on June 18th, 1819. A large section of the canal is impassable, having been blocked by the M6 and other roads. Just before Junction 36 **Dalton Crags** (515ft high) are visible to the east and **Farleton Fell** is on the same side as the Lancaster Canal is bridged once again.

Beyond Junction 36, close to Killington Lake Services, the town of **Kendal** can be glimpsed between the hills to the west and there is a panoramic view of the **Cumbrian Mountains** on the same side. Kendal was founded on the woollen industry in 1331 and remained an important industrial centre until the 19thC. This lively and bustling town is now the "tourist capital" of South Lakeland and has plenty to

Lancaster Castle

offer the inquisitive visitor. At the southern end of the 8.5 miles long section between Junctions 37 and 38, **Lambrigg Fell** (1,108ft high) is visible to the west, and **Firbank Fell** (1,040ft high) to the east. The West Coast Main Line is bridged and the stone viaduct that carried the former London & North Western Railway line from Tebay to Hellifield over the River Lune can be seen on the east side whilst, just after Junction 37, **Howgill** (1,184ft high) and **Fell Head** (2,040ft high) are to the east and **Dillicar Common** (1,145ft high) is to the west. To reduce excavation work the motorway was split into two levels along this stretch through the Lune Valley, dominated by the 1,240ft high **Jeffrey's Mount** on the west side and **Langdale Fells** (1,594ft high) on the other. The **Roman Fort** at Low Borrowbridge is on the west side as Borrow Beck is bridged approaching Junction 38. Here too, at the northern end of the valley, the village of **Tebay** can be seen on the east side, beyond the former engine shed and station sites, on the west side of the railway line. Tebay was a very important railway centre during steam days. Between 1846 and 1968 it provided banking locomotives for the long climb up to Shap Summit and was also a junction of the Hellifield, Lancaster, Carlisle and Barnard Castle lines. Today only the electrified West Coast Main Line to Glasgow is operational.

From Junction 38 as the motorway starts the long climb up to the 1,033ft high Shap Summit the West Coast Main Line can be seen alongside the west side of the carriageways with views across the valley to **Shap Fells** (1,710ft high) and the **Cumbrian Mountains** beyond. Approaching Junction 39 **The Shap Wells Hotel**, built in 1833 and used on innumerable occasions by Royal shooting parties, can be seen in the near distance to the west. **Crosby Ravensworth Fell** (1,315ft high) is on the east side before the summit is reached at the northern end of this section at Junction 39. Between Junctions 39 and 40 there is a panoramic view across to the east in which **Maulds Meaburn Moor** (960ft high), the **Lune Forest** (2,468ft high) and **Dufton Fell** (2,516ft high) can be seen with the Pennines beyond in the distance. The motorway carriageways diverge beyond Junction 39 and it is along here that the unusual spectacle of sheep grazing on the central reservation of a motorway, albeit wide enough to enclose a field, is on view. With land cost relatively low, the engineers were able to economize on earthworks by fitting the carriageways to the land contours. Just before Penrith is reached at Junction 40, a **tracking station**, used for civil aviation and looking like a white spherical structure, is visible on clear days on top of the 2,780ft high **Great Dun Fell** in the distance to the east.

Penrith Castle

The town of Penrith, an ancient Saxon capital, is adjacent to the east side of Junction 40 with the 940ft high **Beacon Hill Pike and Tower** beyond. The tower was built in 1719 and marks the place where, since 1296, beacons were lit to warn the townsfolk of an impending attack. The beacon was last lit during the Napoleonic wars in 1804. At the north end of the section, just before Junction 41, **Skirwith Fell** (2,930ft high) is on the east side and the River Petterill is bridged. As the motorway continues northwards, beyond Junction 41, **Lazonby Hill** (810ft high) is to the east side and **Langwathby**, **Great Salkend** and **Lazonby** can be seen in the valley on the same side. Just past Southwaite Services **Brackenburgh** is on the west side and **Voreda**, the site of a Roman Fort which was established by Agricola alongside a former Roman Road (now part of the A6), is passed on the east side. Travelling further north, a range of fells, including **Newbiggin** (1,940ft high), **Scarrowmanwick** (1,580ft high) and **Renwick Fells** (1,830ft high) are on view to east.

Carlisle is by-passed on the west side between Junctions 42 and 44 and, approaching Junction 43, Harraby is to the west and Scotby to the east as the Settle & Carlisle line is bridged. The **Settle and Carlisle Railway Line** was the last main line to reach Carlisle and was built by the Midland Railway in 1875. It has survived many closure threats over the years and is now famous for the steam specials that are run over its length. The ex-Newcastle & Carlisle Railway line, opened on July 19th, 1836 and the first one to reach Carlisle, is bridged close to Junction 43 where the River Eden, with **Carlisle** beyond is visible to the west. The historic City of Carlisle was established as a Roman Station and since then was fought for over many years, first by other European invaders and then between the English and the Scots. The course of **Hadrians Wall** is crossed just before Junction 44. Hadrians Wall was originally constructed by the Romans between 122-130AD and ran for about 75 miles from the Tyne to the Solway. Of little military or strategic use, it was rebuilt three times before it was finally abandoned in about 400AD. The M6 ends at Junction 44 and diverges into the A74 to Glasgow and the A7 to Edinburgh via the Borders.

Location of Places of Interest

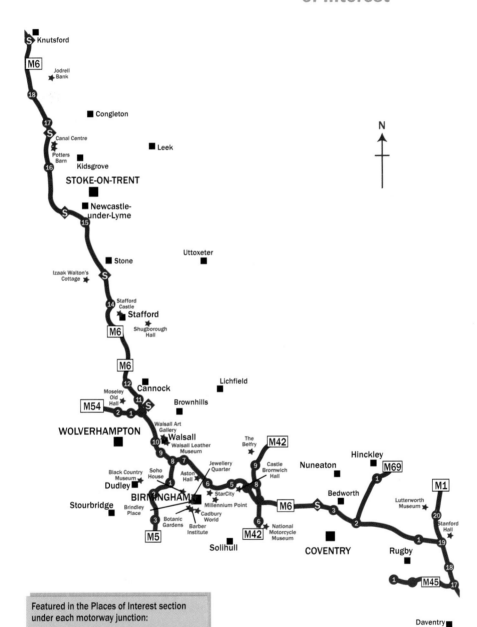

Featured in the Places of Interest section
under each motorway junction:

■ ● Towns and Villages
✦ Places of Interest

Location of Places of Interest

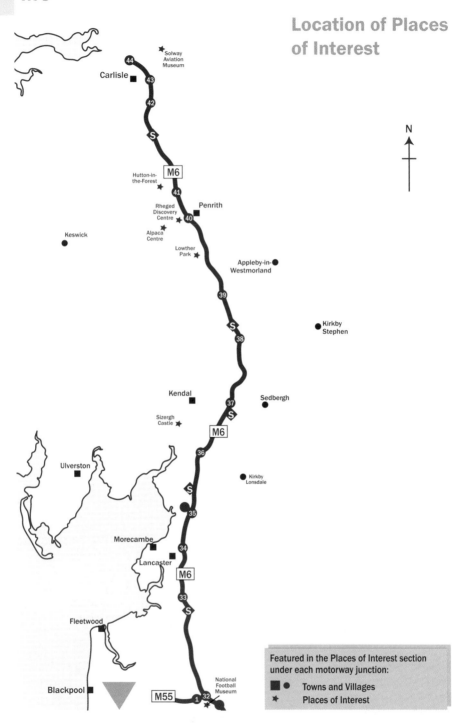

N

Solway Aviation Museum

Carlisle

44
43
42
S

M6

Hutton-in-the-Forest

41

Penrith

Rheged Discovery Centre
40

Keswick

Alpaca Centre

Lowther Park

Appleby-in-Westmorland

39

Kirkby Stephen

S
38

Kendal

Sedbergh

37
S

Sizergh Castle

M6

36

Ulverston

Kirkby Lonsdale

S

35

Morecambe

34

Lancaster

M6

33

S

Fleetwood

Blackpool

M55

National Football Museum

1 32

Featured in the Places of Interest section
under each motorway junction:

■ ● Towns and Villages
★ Places of Interest

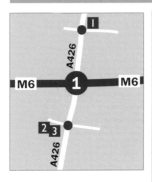

M6
JUNCTION 1

Nearest A&E Hospital
Hospital of St Cross
Barby Road, Rugby
CV22 5PX
Tel: (01788) 572831
Take the A426 into Rugby and turn left along the A428. Turn right into Barby Road and the hospital is on the left.
(Distance Approx 3.5 miles)

FACILITIES

THERE ARE NO FACILITIES WITHIN ONE MILE OF THIS JUNCTION

1 **Star Gibbets Cross (Texaco)**

Tel: (01788) 861500
1.3 miles north along the A426, on the right.
Access, Visa, Overdrive, All Star, Switch, Dial Card, Mastercard, Amex, AA Paytrak, Diners Club, Delta, BP Supercharge, Fast Fuel, Texaco Cards. Open; Mon-Fri; 06.30-22.30hrs, Sat & Sun; 07.00-22.00hrs

2 **Express by Holiday Inn, Rugby**

Tel: (01788) 550333

1.3 miles south along the A426, on the right

3 **The Bell & Barge**

Tel: (01788) 569466
1.3 miles south along the A426, on the right
(Harvester) Open all day. Meals served; Mon-Sat; 12.00-22.00hrs, Sun; 12.00-21.00hrs.

PLACES OF INTEREST

James Gilbert Rugby Football Museum

5 St Matthews Street, Rugby
CV21 3BY

Follow the A426 into Rugby and turn east along the A428 (Signposted 3.0 Miles)
For details please see M1 Junction 18 information.

Rugby School Museum

10 Little Church Street, Rugby
CV21 3AW

For details please see M1 Junction 18 information.

M6
JUNCTION 2

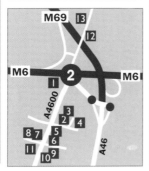

Nearest A&E Hospital
Coventry & Warwickshire Hospital
Stoney Stanton Road, Coventry CV1 4FH
Tel: (024) 7622 4055
Follow the A4600 south and turn right along the A4053 (Signposted in city) (Distance Approx 4.3 Miles)

FACILITIES

1 **Hilton Coventry**

Tel: (024) 7660 3000
Adjacent to south side of roundabout.
Voyagers Restaurant Open; Breakfast; Mon-Sat; 07.00-10.00hrs, Sun; 07.30-10.30hrs, Lunch; Mon-Fri; 12.00-14.00hrs, Dinner; 19.00-22.00hrs daily

2 **Big W Café**

Tel: (024) 7660 4519
0.3 miles south along the A4600, on the left in Cross Point Business Park.
Open; Mon-Sat; 08.00-22.00hrs, Sun; 10.30-17.00hrs

3 **Burger King**

Tel: (024) 7660 3661
0.3 miles south along the A4600, on the left in Cross Point Business Park.
Open; 10.00-22.00hrs daily.

4 **Pizza Hut**

Tel: (024) 7660 3040
0.3 miles south along the A4600, on the left in Cross Point Business Park.
Open; Sun-Fri; 12.00-23.00hrs, Sat; 11.30-23.30hrs

5 **Holiday Inn Coventry**

Tel: 0870 400 9021

0.4 miles south along the A4600, on the left.

Rotisserie Restaurant open; Breakfast; Mon-Fri; 06.30-09.30hrs, Sat & Sun; 07.00-11.00hrs, Lunch; Mon-Fri; 12.30-14.00hrs, Sun; 12.30-15.00hrs, Dinner; Mon-Sat; 18.30-22.30hrs, Sun; 19.00-22.00hrs.

6 Asda Filling Station

Tel: (024) 7661 3426

0.5 miles south along the A4600, on the left.

Access, Visa, Overdrive, All Star, Switch, Dial Card, Mastercard, Amex, Diners Club, Delta, AA Paytrak, Asda Cards. Open; Mon-Sat; 06.00-22.30hrs, Sun; 08.00-17.00hrs. Disabled Toilets & Cash Machine available in adjacent store during shop opening hours.

7 McDonald's

Tel: (024) 7661 2492

0.6 miles south along the A4600, on the right.

Open; 07.00-23.00hrs [Drive Thru open until 0.00hrs Sat & Sun]

8 Hotel Campanile

Tel: (024) 7662 2311

0.6 miles south along the A4600, on the right.

Bistro & Restaurant open; Lunch; 12.00-14.00hrs daily, Dinner Mon-Sat; 19.00-22.00hrs daily. (Light meals available on Sun between 19.00 & 22.00hrs)

9 Mount Pleasant

Tel: (024) 7661 2406

0.7 miles south along the A4600, on the left.

(Greene King) Open all day. Food served Mon-Sat; 12.00-

21.30hrs, Sun; 12.00-20.00hrs.

10 Woodway BP Petrol Station

Tel: (024) 7660 2928

0.7 miles south along the A4600, on the left.

Access, Visa, Overdrive, All Star, Switch, Dial Card, Mastercard, Amex, Diners Club, Delta, Routex, AA Paytrak, UK Fuelcard, Shell Agency, BP Cards, IDS, Keyfuels, AS24

11 Star Walsgrave (Texaco)

Tel: (024) 7684 1990

0.7 miles south along the A4600, on the right.

Access, Visa, Overdrive, All Star, Switch, Dial Card, Mastercard, Amex, Diners Club, Delta, BP Supercharge, Texaco Cards.

12 Rose & Castle

Tel: (024) 7661 2822

0.8 miles north along the B4065, in Ansty, on the right. (Freehouse) Open all day on Sun. Meals served; Mon-Sat; 12.00-15.00hrs & 18.00-23.00hrs, Sun; 12.00-22.30hrs

13 Ansty Hall Hotel

Tel: (024) 7661 2222

1 mile north along the B4065, on the left.

The Shilton Restaurant; Open; 12.00-14.30hrs & 19.00-21.00hrs daily.

PLACES OF INTEREST

Coventry

Coventry Tourist Information Centre, Bayley Lane, Coventry CV1 5RN Tel: (024) 7622 7264

website: www.coventry.org

Follow the A4600 south (Signposted 4.5 Miles)

Standing on the River Sherbourne, Coventry is one of the oldest cities in England with a history that begins with a 6thC convent, destroyed in 1016 and a monastery constructed by Earl Leofric and his wife Godgifu (Godiva) for the Benedictines in 1043. For over a thousand years Coventry has been a manufacturing centre, initially with wool and cloth, ribbons and watches and then bicycles, motor cycles and cars. Six hundred years ago it was rated fourth amongst England's cities in power and importance and, despite its large scale destruction during World War II, many of the early buildings still survive. The notable exception, of course, is Coventry Cathedral which was all but razed to the ground on November 14th, 1940 but gave rise to a dynamic new building which became the focal point for the post-war rebuilding of the city. The legend of Lady Godiva, and her naked ride in protest at the high taxes imposed by her husband, is inextricably linked with Coventry and there is a statue of her in Broadgate.

Within the city centre can be found ...

Coventry Cathedral & Visitors Centre

7 Priory Row, Coventry CV1 5ES

Tel: (024) 7622 7597 website; www.coventrycathedral.org

The impressive, post-war, St Michael's Cathedral, designed by Sir Basil Spence in 1954, stands alongside the ruins of the 14thC edifice destroyed in the blitz during 1940 and contains a superb tapestry by Graham Sutherland. The Visitors Centre features an historic exhibition with an audio visual display "The Spirit of Coventry" in the undercroft of the cathedral. The international department continues the work of reconciliation and the cathedral community prays daily for peace. Restaurant. Gift Shop. Disabled access.

Museum of British Road Transport

St Agnes Lane, Hales Street, Coventry CV1 1PN
Tel: (024) 7683 2425
website; www.mbrt.co.uk

The evolution of transport from the earliest of cycles through to the latest high-tech motor industry developments are shown in this display of British cars, cycles and motorcycles, the largest in the world. Other attractions include the record breaking Thrust 2 and Thrust SSC cars and the Blitz Experience, a re-enactment of the bombing raids on Coventry during 1940. Gift Shop. Disabled access.

Herbert Art Gallery & Museum

Jordan Well, Coventry CV1 5QP
Tel: (024) 7683 2381 website: www.coventrymuseum.org.uk

The "Godiva City" exhibition, a display of 1,000 years of Coventry's history, is the centrepiece of the Museum whilst Graham Sutherland's working drawings for the Cathedral tapestry, paintings by LS Lowry, John Collier and David Cox and sculpture by Henry Moore and Jacob Epstein are featured in the Art Gallery. Tea Room. Gift Shop. Disabled access.

St Mary's Guildhall

Bayley Lane, Coventry CV1 5RN
Tel: (024) 7683 3041

An important mediaeval building that has been pivotal in the history of the city since the 14thC. Superb

craftsmanship is evident in the stone, glass, timber and thread work and six royal portraits hang in the hall that at one time had played host to Elizabeth I, incarcerated Mary Queen of Scots and been used as an arsenal during the Civil War.

JUNCTION 3

Nearest A&E Hospital
Coventry & Warwickshire Hospital,
Stoney Stanton Road, Coventry CV1 4FH
Tel: (024) 7622 4055
Take the A444 south exit to Coventry and follow this route to the city centre. Turn left along the St Nicholas Ringway, take the first exit and follow the B4109 north into Stoney Stanton Road. The hospital is on the left. (Distance Approx 3.9 miles)

FACILITIES

1   Star Exhall (Texaco)

Tel: (024) 7649 4300
1 mile north along the B4113, on the left.
Access, Visa, Overdrive, All Star, Switch, Dial Card, Mastercard, Amex, Diners Club,

Delta, Texaco Cards. Open; 06.45-22.30hrs daily

2   The Lord Raglan

Tel: (024) 7636 0260
0.9 miles north along the B4113, on the right.
(Vanguard) Open all day. Meals served; Mon-Fri; 12.00-14.00hrs

3   The Longford Engine

Tel: (024) 7636 5556
0.9 miles south along the B4113, in Longford, on the left.
(Bass) Open all day. Breakfast/Lunch; 09.00-15.00hrs daily, Evening meals; 17.00-20.00hrs daily

4   Novotel Coventry

Tel: (024) 7636 5000
0.5 miles east along the B4113, on the right.
Garden Brasserie Restaurant Open; 06.00-0.00hrs daily. Bar Snacks served 11.00-0.00hrs daily.

PLACES OF INTEREST

Coventry

Follow the A444 south (Signposted 4.7 Miles)
For details please see Junction 2 information.

Within the city centre can be found ...

Coventry Cathedral & Visitors Centre

7 Priory Row, Coventry CV1 5ES

For details please see Junction 2 information.

Museum of British Road Transport

St Agnes Lane, Hales Street, Coventry CV1 1PN

For details please see Junction 2 information.

Herbert Art Gallery & Museum

Jordan Well, Coventry CV1 5QP

For details please see Junction 2 information.

St Mary's Guildhall

Bayley Lane, Coventry CV1 5RN

For details please see Junction 2 information.

M6
BETWEEN JUNCS 3 & 4

CORLEY SERVICES (WESTBOUND) (WELCOME BREAK)

Tel: (01676) 540111
KFC, La Brioche Doree, Red Hen Restaurant, Granary Restaurant, Burger King & Shell Fuel

CORLEY SERVICES (EASTBOUND) (WELCOME BREAK)

Tel: (01676) 540111
Granary Restaurant, Caffé Primo, Burger King & Shell Fuel

FOOTBRIDGE CONNECTION BETWEEN SITES

M6
JUNCTION 4

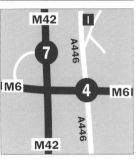

Nearest A&E Hospital
Heartlands Hospital

Bordesley Green East, Birmingham B9 5SS Tel: (0121) 424 3263

Take the A446 north exit and proceed to the first roundabout. Turn left along the B4114 and continue into the B4128. Follow this route for about 4 miles and the hospital is on the left hand side. (Distance Approx 6.6 miles)

FACILITIES

1   The George & Dragon

Tel: (01675) 466586
0.8 miles north along the B4117, in Coleshill, on the left.
(Punch Taverns) Meals served; Mon-Fri; 12.00-14.00hrs & 18.00-22.00hrs, Sat; 12.00-14.00hrs & 17.30-22.00hrs, Sun; 12.00-14.00hrs & 19.00-22.00hrs.

PLACES OF INTEREST

National Motorcycle Museum

Coventry Road, Bickenhill, Solihull B92 0EJ
Tel: (0121) 704 2784.
website:
www.nationalmotorcyclemuseum.co.uk
Follow the M42 south to Junction 6. Leave the motorway and the entrance is adjacent to the roundabout. (2.5 Miles)
A unique collection of over 700 beautifully restored British motorcycles dating from 1898 to the 1990's and outlining the history of a once world-dominating industry. Café. Gift Shop. Limited disabled access.

M6
JUNCTION 4A

> THIS JUNCTION IS A MOTORWAY INTERCHANGE WITH THE M42 ONLY AND THERE IS NO ACCESS TO ANY FACILITIES

M6
JUNCTION 5

> THIS IS A RESTRICTED ACCESS JUNCTION
> - Vehicles can only exit from the westbound lanes.
> - Vehicles can only enter the motorway along the eastbound lanes.

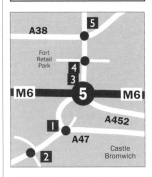

Nearest Eastbound A&E Hospital
Heartlands Hospital

Bordesley Green East, Birmingham B9 5SS
Tel: (0121) 424 3263

Continue to Junction 4, take the A446 north exit and proceed to the first roundabout. Turn left along the B4114 and continue into the B4128. Follow this route for about 4 miles and the hospital is on the left hand side. (Distance Approx 11.4 miles)

Nearest Westbound A&E Hospital

Heartlands Hospital

Bordesley Green East,
Birmingham B9 5SS
Tel: (0121) 424 3263

Take the A47 west towards
Birmingham and turn left along
the A4040. Follow this route for
about 1 mile and turn right
along Bordesley Green East
(B4128). The hospital is on the
left along this road. (Distance
Approx 3.6 miles)

FACILITIES

1   BP Clock Garage

Tel: (0121) 749 1833
0.6 miles south along the
A452, on the right.
Access, Visa, Overdrive, All
Star, Switch, Dial Card,
Mastercard, Amex, Diners Club,
Delta, Routex, AA Paytrak, Shell
Agency, BP Cards.

2   The Hunters Moon

Tel: (0121) 748 8951
1 mile west along the A47, on
the left.
(Six Continents) Meals served;
Mon-Fri; 12.00-15.00hrs.

3   The Fort Jester

Tel: (0121) 747 2908
0.1 miles north along the
A452, on the left.
(Punch Taverns) Open all day.
Meals served; Mon-Sat; 12.00-
22.00hrs, Sun; 12.00-21.30hrs

4   Express by Holiday Inn, Castle Bromwich

Tel: (0121) 747 6633
0.1 miles north along the
A452, on the left

5   The Tyburn House

Tel: (0121) 747 2128
1 mile north along the A452,
on the right.
(Bass) Open all day. Meals
served; 12.00-20.00hrs daily

PLACES OF INTEREST

Castle Bromwich Hall Gardens Trust

Chester Road, Castle
Bromwich, Birmingham
B36 9BT Tel: (0121) 749 4100
website:
www.cbhgt.swinternet.co.uk

**Follow the A47 east and bear
left along the B4118
(Birmingham Road).
(Signposted 1.2 Miles)**

An oasis of tranquility within
10 acre walled gardens lovingly
recreated and restored to their
18thC splendour. Features
include a maze, summer
house, greenhouse and Holly
Walk. Refreshments.

M6
JUNCTION 6

**GRAVELLY HILL
INTERCHANGE**

This interchange is better known
as Spaghetti Junction, a term
coined by a local journalist upon
seeing the first aerial view of the
proposed scheme, and is the
largest motorway interchange in
Europe. Such is its renown and
notoriety that the name features
as a term in "20th Century Words"
published by Oxford University
Press. At its highest point the
road is more than 80ft above
ground level.

Nearest A&E Hospital

City Hospital

Dudley Road, Birmingham
B18 7QH
Tel: (0121) 554 3801

Take the A38(M) into
Birmingham and at the second
exit turn right along the
Newtown Middleway (A4540).
Follow this route to its junction
with the A457 and turn right.
The hospital is on the right
hand side of this route (Dudley
Road). (Distance Approx 4
miles)

Alternative A&E Department for Children up to the age of 16

The Birmingham Children's
Hospital, Steelhouse Lane,
Birmingham B4 6NH
Tel: (0121) 333 9999

Take the A38(M) into
Birmingham and it is
signposted at the end of this
short motorway. (Distance
Approx 2.2 miles)

FACILITIES

1   The Rossmore Hotel

Tel: (0121) 377 7788
0.7 miles north along the
A5127, on the left

2   BP Sixways

Tel: (0121) 373 1973

1 mile north along the A5127, on the left.
Access, Visa, Overdrive, All Star, Switch, Dial Card, Mastercard, Amex, Diners Club, Delta, Routex, AA Paytrak, UK Fuelcard, Shell Agency, BP Cards, Securicor Fuelserv, IDS, Keyfuels.

3 BJ Banning (Total)

Tel: (0121) 327 2741
0.2 miles south along the A5127, on the left.
Access, Visa, Overdrive, All Star, Switch, Dial Card, Mastercard, Diners Club, Delta, AA Paytrak, Total/Fina/Elf Cards. Open; Mon-Fri; 07.30-18.00hrs, Sat; 07.30-13.30hrs.

4 Star Expressway Service Station (Texaco)

Tel: (0121) 328 1186
0.6 miles south along the A5127, on the left.
Access, Visa, Overdrive, All Star, Switch, Dial Card, Mastercard, Amex, Diners Club, Delta, AA Paytrak, Texaco Cards, UK Fuelcard.

5 Gravelly Park Service Station (Total)

Tel: (0121) 327 0026
0.5 miles east along the A38, on the right.
Access, Visa, Overdrive, All Star, Switch, Dial Card, Mastercard, Amex, Diners Club, Delta, Keyfuels, Solo, Electron, Total/Fina/Elf Cards. Open; Mon-Fri; 07.00-20.00hrs, Sat; 08.00-17.00hrs.

6 Midland Link Service Station (Esso)

Tel: (0121) 350 4493
0.7 miles east along the A38, on the left.
Access, Visa, Overdrive, All Star, Switch, Dial Card,

Mastercard, Amex, Diners Club, Delta, AA Paytrak, Shell Gold, Esso Cards.

7 StarCity

Tel: 0870 844 6600
0.8 miles south along the Heartlands Spine Road, on the left.
There are numerous cafés and restaurants within the leisure complex.

PLACES OF INTEREST

StarCity

Heartlands Spine Road, Birmingham B7 5TR
Tel: 0870 844 6600 website: www.starcitym6j6.com

Follow the A5127 south towards Birmingham and turn left along the Heartlands Spine Road. (Signposted 0.8 Miles)
The first of a new generation of state-of-the-art US-style urban entertainment centres, designed by the Jerde Partnership and containing the largest cinema in Europe, the Warner Village, a 30 screen megaplex seating 6,200 people. Vibrant leading edge facilities incorporating themed pubs, bars and restaurants, retail shops, casino, tenpin bowling, pool and snooker, electronic games and a leisure club can all be found on two levels and under one roof. The complex is laid out in a street and walkways format surrounding a central atrium and events plaza. Disabled Access

Aston Hall

Trinity Road, Aston, Birmingham B6 6JD
Tel: (0121) 327 0062
website: www.bmag.org.uk

Take the A6127 south towards Birmingham and follow the signboards to Aston Villa FC. (1.8 Miles)
The region's finest Jacobean country house, built between 1618 and 1635 by Sir Thomas Holte. Containing elaborate plasterwork ceilings and friezes, a magnificent carved oak staircase and a spectacular 136ft Long Gallery. The period rooms contain fine furniture, paintings, textiles and metalwork.

Birmingham

Follow the A38(M) south (Signposted 2.3 Miles)
For details please see Junction 1 (M5) information.

Brindley Place & Broad Street, Birmingham

Follow the A38(M) south into the city centre and the route is signposted "National Indoor Arena & Convention Centre" (3 Miles)
For details please see Junction 1 (M5) information.

Millennium Point

Curzon Street, Birmingham B4 7XG

Follow the A38(M) south into the city centre and the route is signposted. (3 Miles)
For details please see Junction 1 (M5) information.

Soho House

Soho Avenue, Off Soho Road, Handsworth, Birmingham B18 5LB.

Follow the A38(M) south towards Birmingham and turn west along the A4540. Turn north along the A41 and left into Soho Avenue. (3.7 Miles)
For details please see Junction 1 (M5) information.

Museum of the Jewellery Quarter

75-79 Vyse Street, Hockley,

Birmingham B18 6HA.

Follow the A38(M) south towards Birmingham and turn west along the A4540. Turn south along the A41 and the route is signposted. (3.6 Miles)

For details please see Junction 1 (M5) information.

Cadbury World

Bournville, Birmingham B30 2LD

Follow the A38(M) south and the brown & white tourist boards along the A38 & A4040. (7 miles).

For details please see Junction 4 (M5) information.

JUNCTION 7

Nearest Westbound A&E Hospital

Walsall Manor Hospital

Moat Road, Walsall WS2 9PS
Tel: (01922) 721172
Proceed to Junction 9 and take the A4148 north. The hospital is on the left hand side of Pleck Road on this route. (Distance Approx 4.6 miles)

Nearest Eastbound A&E Hospital

Sandwell District General Hospital

Hallam Street, West Bromwich B71 4HJ
Tel: (0121) 553 1831
Take the A34 towards Birmingham and after 0.5 miles turn right along the A4041 to West Bromwich. Turn left along All Saints Way (A4031), first left into Church Vale, continue into Hallam Street and the hospital is on the left. (Distance Approx 3.3 miles)

FACILITIES

1   Holiday Inn, Birmingham

Tel: 0870 400 9009
0.4 miles north along the A34, on the right.
Traders Bar & Restaurant; Meals served; Mon-Fri; 06.30-22.30hrs, Sat & Sun; 07.30-22.30hrs

2   The Beacon

Tel: (0121) 357 2567
0.6 miles north along the A34, on the left.
(Harvester) Open all day. Meals served 12.00-22.30hrs daily.

3   Express by Holiday Inn, Birmingham North

Tel: (0121) 358 4044
0.6 miles north along the A34, on the left

4   TCS Beacon Service Station (Total)

Tel: (0121) 358 8800
0.6 miles north along the A34, on the right.
Access, Visa, Delta, Mastercard, Switch, Amex, Diners Club, Total/Fina/Elf Cards.

5   The Bell Inn

Tel: (0121) 357 7461
1 mile north along the A34, on the left.
(Ember Inns) Open all day. Meals served; 12.00-20.00hrs daily

6   Shell Great Barr

Tel: (0121) 358 4622
0.2 miles south along the A34, on the right (Actual distance 1.8 miles)
LPG, Access, Visa, Overdrive, All Star, Switch, Dial Card, Mastercard, Amex, Diners Club, Delta, BP Supercharge, Shell Cards. Open; 07.00-22.40hrs daily.

7   Scott Arms

Tel: (0121) 357 8780
0.6 miles south along the A34, on the right
(Six Continents) Open all day. Meals served; Mon-Fri; 11.00-14.00hrs & 17.00-20.00hrs, Sat; 11.00-14.00hrs, Sun; 12.00-14.00hrs.

JUNCTION 8

RAY HALL INTERCHANGE.

THIS JUNCTION IS A MOTORWAY INTERCHANGE ONLY WITH THE M5 AND THERE IS NO ACCESS TO ANY FACILITIES

Nearest Westbound A&E Hospital

Walsall Manor Hospital

Moat Road, Walsall WS2 9PS
Tel: (01922) 721172
Proceed to Junction 9 and take the A4148 north. The hospital is on the left hand side of Pleck Road on this route. (Distance Approx 2.5 miles)

Nearest Eastbound A&E Hospital

Sandwell District General Hospital

Hallam Street,
West Bromwich B71 4HJ
Tel: (0121) 553 1831

Proceed to Junction 7, take the A34 towards Birmingham and after 0.5 miles turn right along the A4041 to West Bromwich. Turn left along All Saints Way (A4031), first left into Church Vale, continue into Hallam Street and the hospital is on the left. (Distance Approx 4.8 miles)

Nearest Southbound A&E Hospital (via M5)

Sandwell District General Hospital

Hallam Street,
West Bromwich B71 4HJ
Tel: (0121) 553 1831

Proceed to Junction 1 and take the A41 west towards West Bromwich. Turn right at the roundabout along the A4031 and the hospital is on the right. (Distance Approx 4.8 miles)

JUNCTION 9

Nearest A&E Hospital

Walsall Manor Hospital

Moat Road, Walsall
WS2 9PS
Tel: (01922) 721172

Take the A4148 north and the hospital is on the left hand side

of Pleck Road on this route. (Distance Approx 1.4 miles)

FACILITIES

1 Bescot House Hotel & Restaurant

Tel: (01922) 622447
0.1 miles north along the A461, on the right.
Restaurant Open; Mon-Sat; 19.00-21.30hrs.

2 Abberley Hotel

Tel: (01922) 627413
0.3 miles north along the A4148[N], on the right

3 The Forge & Fettle Tap House

Tel: (01922) 622499
1 mile north along the A4148[N], on the left.
(Banks's) Open all day. Meals served; 11.00-22.00hrs daily.

4 Morrissons Filling Station

Tel: (01922) 616177
0.5 miles east along the A4148[E], on the left.
Access, Visa, Overdrive, All Star, Switch, Dial Card, Mastercard, Delta, AA Paytrak, BP Supercharge, Morrissons Account Card. Toilets & Cash Machines in adjacent store. Open; Mon-Fri; 06.30-22.30hrs, Sat; 07.00-22.00hrs, Sun; 08.00-22.00hrs.

5 Grange Garage (Q8)

Tel: (01922) 626734
0.5 miles east along the A4148[E], on the right.
Access, Visa, Overdrive, All Star, Switch, Dial Card, Mastercard. Open; Mon-Sat;

07.30-20.00hrs, Sun; 09.00-20.00hrs.

6 McDonald's

Tel: (01922) 635747
0.7 miles east along the A4148 on the right, in Broadwalk Retail Park.
Open; 07.30-23.00hrs daily. [Fri-Sun; "Drive-Thru" remains open until 23.30hrs.]

7 Chinese Restaurant

Tel: (0121) 502 2218
0.4 miles south along the A461, on the left.
NB. A Chinese Restaurant is due to open here in mid-2002. No further details are available

8 The Horse & Jockey

Tel: (0121) 556 0464
0.5 miles south along the A461, on the right.
(Punch Taverns) Meals served; Mon-Fri; 12.00-14.30hrs & 17.00-21.00hrs, Sat; 11.00-14.30hrs & 17.00-21.00hrs, Sun; 12.00-17.00hrs

9 BP Safeway Wednesbury

Tel: (0121) 505 2205
0.9 miles south along the A461, on the right.
Access, Visa, Overdrive, All Star, Switch, Dial Card, Mastercard, Amex, Diners Club, Delta.

10 Burger King

Tel: (0121) 556 2100
0.4 miles south, on the right, in Junction 9 Retail Park (Access gained 0.1 miles south along the A461, on the left).
Open; Mon-Sat; 09.00-21.00hrs, Sun; 09.00-19.00hrs

PLACES OF INTEREST

Walsall Leather Museum

Littleton Street West, Walsall
WS2 8EQ Tel: (01922) 721153
website: www.walsall.gov.uk

Follow the A4148 north into Walsall (1.9 Miles)

From the earliest of days, leather has been a vital material in the daily life of Britain and this is reflected in the wide range of samples of the craft exhibited here. Jugs, bottles, bridles, saddles, luggage, clothing, musical instruments and forge bellows are just some of the examples on display. Walsall is renowned as the British leathergoods capital, over a hundred companies in the area are still involved in the manufacture of leather goods, and this museum captures the atmosphere of the original workshops. Gift Shop. Coffee Shop. Disabled access.

Also in the town centre can be found ...

The New Art Gallery Walsall

Gallery Square, Walsall
WS2 8LG Tel: (01922) 654400
website; www.artatwalsall.org.uk

Designed by Caruso St John Architects the landmark building was completed in 1999 and opened in 2000. The whole of the third floor is dedicated to the display of contemporary and historic art in beautiful naturally lit galleries of international specification. The first and second floors, a series of intimate, interconnected rooms house the Garman Ryan Collection and, at ground floor level, a Discovery Gallery with a 3-storey childrens house and art gallery create an active involvement in the creative

processes of art. Disabled access. Café. Gift Shop. Restaurant.

JUNCTION 10

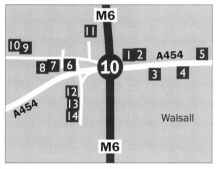

Nearest A&E Hospital

Walsall Manor Hospital

Moat Road, Walsall
WS2 9PS
Tel: (01922) 721172
Take the A454 east towards Walsall and turn right along Pleck Road (A4148) The hospital is on the right. (Distance Approx 0.8 miles)

FACILITIES

1   Hills Transport Café

Tel: (01922) 722593
0.2 miles east along the A454, on the left.
Open; Mon-Fri; 07.30-16.00hrs, Sat; 07.30-10.30hrs

2   The Parkbrook

Tel: (01922) 622970
0.3 miles east along the A454, on the left.
(Punch Taverns) Open all day Sat & Sun. Meals served; Mon-Sat; 12.00-14.00hrs & 18.00-20.00hrs, Sun; 12.00-14.30hrs.

3   Primley Service Station (Esso)

Tel: (01922) 634532
0.4 miles east along the A454, on the right.
Access, Visa, Overdrive, All Star, Switch, Dial Card, Mastercard, Amex, Diners Club, Delta, AA Paytrak, Shell Gold, BP Supercharge, Esso Cards. Open; Mon-Fri; 06.00-23.00hrs, Sat; 06.00-22.00hrs, Sun; 07.00-22.00hrs

4   Save Petrol Station

Tel: (01922) 638054
0.6 miles east along the A454, on the right.
Access, Visa, Mastercard, Switch, Electron, Solo, Amex, Overdrive, All Star, Dial Card, BP Supercharge, Savecard. Open; 06.00-23.00hrs daily

5   The Orange Tree Pub and B&B

Tel: (01922) 625119
0.9 miles east along the A454, on the left.
(Inn Partnership) Open all day Fri-Mon. Meals served; Fri-Mon; 12.00-20.30hrs, Tues-Thurs; 16.00-21.00hrs

6   Lane Arms

Tel: (01922) 623490
0.4 miles west along the B4464, in Bentley, on the left.
(Highgate Ales) Open all day Fri-Sun; Meals served; Mon-Sat; 12.00-14.30hrs & 18.00-20.00hrs

7 The Greedy Pig Café

Tel: (01922) 722998
0.5 miles west along the
B4464, in Bentley, on the left.
Open; Mon-Fri; 08.00-
14.00hrs, Sat; 08.00-12.00hrs

8 Euro Curries

Tel: (01922) 746786
0.5 miles west along the
B4464, in Bentley, on the left.
Due to open during 2002

**9 County Bridge Service
Station (Esso)**

 |wc|

Tel: (01902) 605734
1 mile west along the B4464,
on the right.
Access, Visa, Overdrive, All
Star, Switch, Dial Card,
Mastercard, Amex, Diners Club,
Delta, Shell Gold, Esso UK
Cards. Open; 06.00-23.00hrs
daily.

10 The Red Lion

Tel: (01902) 365921
1 mile west along the B4464,
on the right.
(Voyager) Open all day. Meals
served; Mon-Sat; 12.00-14.00
hrs & 18.00-20.00hrs, Sun;
12.00-15.00hrs

11 Quality Hotel & Suites

Tel: (01922) 724444
On the west side of the
roundabout (Signposted
"Hotel").
Restaurant Open; Breakfast;
Mon-Fri; 07.00-09.30hrs, Sat &
Sun; 08.00-10.00hrs, Lunch;
Sun-Fri; 12.00-15.00hrs,
Dinner; 19.00-22.00hrs daily.

12 Deep Pan Pizza

Tel: (0121) 568 8053
0.6 miles south along Bentley
Mill Way, on the right.

Open; Sun-Thurs; 12.00-
23.00hrs, Fri & Sat; 12.00-
0.00hrs.

**13 Cho Garden Chinese
Restaurant**

Tel: (0121) 526 7173
0.6 miles south along Bentley
Mill Way, on the right.
Open; Mon-Sat; 12.00-
14.00hrs & 17.30-22.30hrs,
Sun; 12.00-15.00hrs & 17.30-
22.30hrs

**14 Cinnamon Court
Restaurant**

Tel: (0121) 568 6664
0.6 miles south along Bentley
Mill Way, on the right.
Open; Sun-Thurs; 17.30-
23.30hrs, Fri & Sat; 17.30-
0.00hrs

PLACES OF INTEREST

Walsall Leather Museum

Littleton Street West, Walsall

**Follow the A454 east into
Walsall (1.3 Miles)**

For details please see Junction
10 information

**Also in the town centre
can be found ...**

**The New Art Gallery
Walsall**

Gallery Square, Walsall

For details please see Junction
10 information

JUNCTION 10A

THIS JUNCTION IS A
MOTORWAY INTERCHANGE
ONLY WITH THE M54 AND
THERE IS NO ACCESS TO ANY
FACILITIES

M6 BETWEEN JUNCS 10A & 11

**HILTON PARK SERVICES
(NORTHBOUND) (MOTO)**
Tel: (01922) 412237 Fresh
Express Self Service Restaurant,
Burger King, Harry Ramsden's,
Little Chef & BP Fuel.

**HILTON PARK SERVICES
(SOUTHBOUND) (MOTO)**
Tel: (01922) 412237 Fresh
Express Self Service Restaurant,
Harry Ramsden's, Burger King,
Travelodge & BP Fuel.

**FOOTBRIDGE CONNECTION
BETWEEN SITES.**

JUNCTION 11

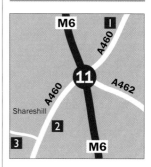

**Nearest Northbound A&E
Hospital**
**Staffordshire General
Hospital**
Weston Road, Stafford
ST16 3SA
Tel: (01785) 257731
Proceed to Junction 13. Take
the A449 exit north into
Stafford, continue along the
A49 and then the A34. At the
roundabout turn right along the
A518 east towards Weston and

the hospital is on the left. (Distance Approx 11.6 miles)

Nearest Southbound A&E Hospital

Walsall Manor Hospital

Moat Road, Walsall
WS2 9PS
Tel: (01922) 721172

Proceed to Junction 10, take the A454 east towards Walsall and turn right along Pleck Road (A4148). The hospital is on the right. (Distance Approx 6.5 miles)

FACILITIES

1   The Wheatsheaf

Tel: (01922) 412304
0.2 miles north along the A460, on the left.
(Banks's) Open all day. Meals served 12.00-21.00hrs daily.

2   M6 Diesel

Tel: (01922) 412995
0.7 miles west along the A460, on the left.
Securicor Fuelserv, Keyfuels, IDS, UK Fuels, All Star, Overdrive, AS24, Morgan Fuels, Access, Visa, Amex, Diners Club, Mastercard, Switch. Open; Continuously between 17.00hrs on Sunday to 22.00hrs Friday. Sat; 07.00-15.00hrs. (NB. 24hr Fuel Card operated pumps available when kiosk is closed)

3   The Elms

Tel: (01922) 412063
1 mile west, in Shareshill, on the left.
(Six Continents) Open all day Fri-Sun. Meals served; Mon-Sat; 12.00-14.00hrs & 18.30-21.00hrs, Sun; 12.00-14.30hrs.

PLACES OF INTEREST

Moseley Old Hall (NT)

Moseley Old Hall Lane, Fordhouses, Wolverhampton WV10 7HY Tel: (01902) 782808 website: www.nationaltrust.org.uk

Follow the A460 west, proceed past Junction 1 (M54) and turn right along Moseley Road. (2.9 Miles)

An Elizabethan house where the Whitgreave family sheltered King Charles II after the Battle of Worcester in 1651. The richly panelled walls cover ingenious hiding-holes that were originally designed to accommodate Catholic priests and it was in one of these that he was concealed from Cromwell's troops. An exhibition recounts this event and fine furniture, documents, portraits and other relics of the Whitgreaves are on display. The garden is recreated in 17thC style with a formal knot and planted with varieties of herbs and plants from three centuries ago. Shop. Tea Room. Disabled access.

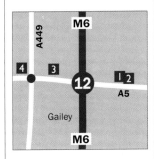

JUNCTION 12

Nearest Northbound A&E Hospital

Staffordshire General Hospital

Weston Road, Stafford
ST16 3SA
Tel: (01785) 257731

Proceed to Junction 13. Take the A449 exit north into Stafford, continue along the A49 and then the A34. At the roundabout turn right along the A518 east towards Weston and the hospital is on the left. (Distance Approx 8.9 miles)

Nearest Southbound A&E Hospital

Walsall Manor Hospital

Moat Road, Walsall
WS2 9PS
Tel: (01922) 721172

Proceed to Junction 10, take the A454 east towards Walsall and turn right along Pleck Road (A4148). The hospital is on the right. (Distance Approx 9.2 miles)

FACILITIES

1   The Hollies Transport Café and B&B

Tel: (01543) 503435
1 mile east along the A5, on the left.

2   Oak Farm Hotel & Restaurant

Tel: (01543) 462045
1 mile east along the A5, on the left.
Open for Evening Meals only; Mon-Sat; 19.00-21.15hrs.

3   Gailey Service Station (Texaco)

Tel: (01902) 791172
0.8 miles west along the A5, on the right.

Access, Visa, Overdrive, All Star, Switch, Dial Card, Mastercard, Amex, Diners Club, Delta, AA Paytrak, BP Supercharge, Texaco Cards. Open; Mon-Sat; 06.00-23.00hrs, Sun; 08.00-23.00hrs

4 The Spread Eagle

Tel: (01902) 790212

1 mile west along the A5, on the right.

(Tavern Table) Open all day. Meals served; Mon-Sat; 12.00-22.00hrs, Sun; 12.30-21.30hrs

PLACES OF INTEREST

Weston Park

Weston under Lizard, Near Shifnal, Shropshire TF11 8LE Tel: (01952) 850207
website: www.weston-park.com

Follow the A5 east (Signposted along route. 8.2 Miles)

Built in 1671 in the restoration style and the home of the Earls of Bradford, the house contains paintings by Holbein, Van Dyck, Bassano, Reynolds, Gainsborough and Lely, Tapestries by Gobelins and Aubusson and fine 17thC silver. The parkland that surrounds the house has matured over several hundred years into a masterpiece of unspoilt landscape and contains fallow deer and rare breeds of sheep. There are some wonderful architectural features within the park too, including the Roman Bridge and Temple of Diana, both designed and built by James Paine for Sir Henry Bridgeman in c1760. For the children, there is a Woodland Adventure Playground, Pets Corner and Deer Park as well as a 1.5

miles long miniature railway. Weston Park was chosen to host a meeting of the world leaders during the Birmingham G8 Summit of 1998. Old Stables Tea Room. Gift Shop.

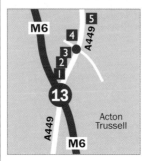

Acton Trussell

Nearest A&E Hospital

Staffordshire General Hospital

Weston Road, Stafford
ST16 3SA
Tel: (01785) 257731

Take the A449 exit north into Stafford, continue along the A49 and then the A34. At the roundabout turn right along the A518 east towards Weston and the hospital is on the left. (Distance Approx 3.7 miles)

FACILITIES

1 Express by Holiday Inn, Stafford

Tel: (01785) 212244

0.1 miles north along the A449, on the left

2 Fatty Arbuckles

Tel: (01785) 212221

0.1 miles north along the A449, on the left

Open; 12.00-22.00hrs daily.

3 Catch Corner

Tel: (01785) 245867

0.1 miles north along the A449, on the left.

(Tom Cobleigh) Open all day. Meals served; Mon-Fri; 12.00-22.00hrs, Sun; 12.00-21.30hrs daily.

4 Acton Gate Service Station (Total)

Tel: (01785) 782900

0.5 miles north along the A449, on the left.

Access, Visa, Delta, Mastercard, Switch, Diners Club, Amex, Overdrive, All Star, Dial Card, Total/Fina/Elf Cards. Open; Mon-Fri; 06.00-23.00hrs, Sat; 08.00-22.30hrs, Sun; 08.00-22.00hrs.

5 The Garth Hotel

Tel: (01785) 256124

1 mile north along the A449, on the right.

(Corus Regal) Bar meals served 12.00-21.00hrs daily. Restaurant Open; Lunch; Sun-Fri; 12.00-14.00hrs, Evening Meals; Mon-Sat; 19.00-21.45hrs, Sun; 19.00-21.30hrs.

PLACES OF INTEREST

Stafford

Stafford Tourist Information Centre, Market Street, Stafford ST16 2LQ Tel: (01785) 619619
website: www.staffordbc.gov.uk

Follow the A449 north (Signposted 3.6 Miles)

Sited on the banks of the River Sow, the county town of Staffordshire is of Saxon origin but very few traces of this period remain. There are, however, some excellent period buildings within the town centre including the Ancient High House, an Elizabethan building, William Salt Library, Chetwynd House, built in 1750 and now the town's Post Office, and The Noell Almshouses. A castle was erected here during Norman times.

Within the town centre can be found ...

Ancient High House

Greengate Street, Stafford
ST16 2JA Tel: (01785) 619130
website: www.staffordbc.gov.uk

The largest timber framed house in England, it was built in 1595 by the Dorrington family and is now a heritage and exhibition centre housing the Yeomanry Museum and Tourist Information Centre. Shop.

William Salt Library

Eastgate Street, Stafford
ST16 2LT Tel: (01785) 278372
website: www.staffordshire.gov.uk/archives/salt.htm

An 18thC town house now containing the county archive and history section.

Stafford Castle & Visitor Centre

Newport Road, Stafford
ST16 1DJ Tel: (01785) 257698
website: www.staffordbc.gov.uk

Follow the A449 into Stafford and take the A518 southwest towards Newport. (4.3 Miles)

Originally a motte and bailey castle of the Norman period, the stone keep was destroyed during the Civil War. The purpose built Visitor Centre displays artefacts from archaeological digs and contains a fascinating audio-visual presentation, scale models and hands-on equipment. Shop.

Shugborough Hall

Shugborough, Milford,
Nr Stafford ST17 0XB

Tel: (01889) 881388 website; www.staffordshire.gov.uk

Follow the A446 north (Signposted 6.3 Miles)

The 17thC seat of the Earls of Lichfield, the magnificent 900 acre estate includes Shrugborough Park Farm, a Georgian farmstead built in 1805 for Thomas, Viscount Anson, and now home to rare breeds and demonstrations of traditional farming methods. The mansion itself is a splendid piece of architecture, altered several times over its 300 years, but always retaining the distinct grandeur. The vast rooms, with their ornate plasterwork and cornicing, contain an impressive collection of paintings, ceramics, silverware and a wealth of elegant French furniture. The Staffordshire County Museum has been established in the former stable and kitchen wing of the house, whilst in the beautiful parkland surrounding the mansion, can be found an outstanding collection of neoclassical monuments and the Lady Walk leads along the banks of the River Sow to the delightful terraced lawns and rose garden. Restaurant. Gift Shop. Limited disabled access.

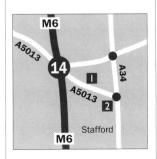

Nearest A&E Hospital
Staffordshire General Hospital
Weston Road, Stafford
ST16 3SA
Tel: (01785) 257731
Take the A5013 into Stafford, proceed along the A34 and follow the A518 east towards Weston. The hospital is on the left. (Distance Approx 2.7 miles)

FACILITIES

1   **Tillington Hall Hotel**

Tel: (01785) 253531
0.5 miles south along the A5013, on the left.
(Best Western) Restaurant Open; Mon-Fri; 12.30-13.45hrs & 19.00-21.45hrs, Sat; 19.00-21.45hrs, Sun; 19.00-21.00hrs.

2   **Brookhouse Service Station (Total)**

Tel: (01785) 229700
1 mile south along the A5013, in Stafford, on the right.
Access, Visa, Delta, Mastercard, Switch, Diners Club, Amex, Overdrive, All Star, Dial Card, Total/Fina/Elf Cards. Open; Mon-Sat; 07.00-23.00hrs, Sun; 08.00-22.00hrs.

PLACES OF INTEREST

Stafford

Follow the A5013 south (Signposted 2.4 Miles)
For details please see Junction 13 information

Within the town centre can be found ...

Ancient High House

Greengate Street, Stafford
ST16 2JA

For details please see Junction 13 information

William Salt Library

Eastgate Street, Stafford
ST16 2LT

For details please see Junction 13 information

Stafford Castle & Visitor Centre

Newport Road, Stafford
ST16 1DJ

Follow the A5013 south into Stafford and take the A518 southwest towards Newport. (3.6 Miles)

For details please see Junction 13 information

Shugborough Hall

Shugborough, Milford,
Nr Stafford ST17 0XB

Follow the A5013 south into Stafford and take the A51 east (Signposted 7.1 Miles)

For details please see Junction 13 information

Izaak Walton's Cottage

Worston Lane, Shallowford,
Nr Great Bridgeford,
Staffordshire ST15 0PA
Tel: (01785) 760278
website: www.staffordbc.gov.uk

Follow the A5013 west through Great Bridgeford and turn right (Signposted 3.1 Miles)

A pretty 17thC half timbered cottage, once owned by the famous biographer and author of "The Compleat Angler" and bequeathed to Staffordshire Borough Council by him. Today it is a registered museum on angling with period room displays and there is an authentic 17thC herb garden, picnic area and orchard. Souvenir Shop.

BETWEEN JUNCS 14 & 15

STAFFORD SERVICES (NORTHBOUND) (MOTO)
Tel: (01785) 811188 Self Service Restaurant, Burger King, Little Chef, Travelodge & BP Fuel

STAFFORD SERVICES (SOUTHBOUND) (ROADCHEF)
Tel: (01785) 826300 Food Fayre Self-Service Restaurant, Costa Coffee Shop, Wimpy Bar, Dr Beaks Chicken, Travel Inn & Esso Fuel

JUNCTION 15

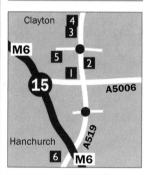

**Nearest A&E Hospital
North Staffordshire Royal Infirmary**
Princes Road, Hartshill, Stoke
ST4 7JN
Tel: (01782) 715444
Take the A5006 exit east and proceed along the A500 to Stoke. Follow the A52 signposts towards Newcastle-under-Lyme and continue into Hartshill Road. The hospital is in Princes Road on the left. (Distance Approx 4 miles)

FACILITIES

1   Holiday Inn, Stoke on Trent

Tel: 0870 400 9077
0.2 miles north along the A519, on the left.
Traders Bar & Restaurant; Bar open all day. Bar meals served 10.30-22.30hrs daily. Restaurant Open; Mon-Fri; 06.30-10.00hrs, 12.30-14.00hrs & 18.30-22.00hrs, Sat & Sun; 07.00-11.00hrs & 18.00-22.00hrs.

2   BP Swift Service Station

Tel: (01782) 713308
0.4 miles north along the A519, on the right.
Access, Visa, Overdrive, All Star, Switch, Dial Card, Mastercard, Amex, Diners Club, Delta, Routex, Shell Agency, BP Cards. Open; Mon-Sat; 07.00-22.00hrs, Sun; 09.00-21.00hrs

3   Clayton Lodge Hotel
Tel: (01782) 613093
1 mile north along the A519, on the left.
(Jarvis) Restaurant Open; Lunch; Mon-Thu; 12.00-13.45hrs, Sun; 12.00-14.45hrs, Evening Meals; Mon-Sat; 19.00-21.00hrs, Sun; 18.30-20.30hrs. Bar Snacks usually available on Fri & Sat.

4   Clayton Service Station (Esso)

Tel: (01782) 613189
1 mile north along the A519, on the left.
Access, Visa, Overdrive, All Star, Switch, Dial Card, Mastercard, Amex, Diners Club, Delta, Shell Gold, BP Supercharge, Esso Cards.

Open; Mon-Fri; 06.00-23.00hrs, Sat-Sun; 07.00-22.00hrs.

5   Westbury Tavern

Tel: (01782) 638766
0.8 miles north along the Westbury Road, on the left. (Punch Taverns) Open all day. Meals served; Mon-Sat; 12.00-14.00hrs & 17.00-20.00hrs, Sun; 12.00-14.30hrs.

6   Hanchurch Manor Hotel

Tel: (01782) 643030
0.8 miles south along the A519, on the right.

PLACES OF INTEREST

Stoke on Trent

Stoke on Trent Tourist Information Centre, Quadrant Road, Hanley, Stoke on Trent ST1 1RZ
Tel: (01782) 236000
website;
www.stoke.gov.uk/tourism

Follow the A500 east (Signposted 3.4 Miles)
It was the presence of the essential raw materials for the manufacture and decoration of ceramics, in particular marl clay, coal and water that led to the concentration of pottery manufacture in this area. Production started in the 17thC but it was the entrepreneurial skills of Josiah Wedgwood and Thomas Minton that created a form of flow line production, bringing individual potters together into large factories, and caused a massive rise in output in the 18thC. Alongside of these, hundreds of small establishments were thriving and producing a whole range of more utilitarian chinaware

creating, what was described in the late 19thC when production was at its height, the most unhealthy area in the country! The city of Stoke on Trent was only established as recently as 1910 when Fenton joined the five towns immortalized by Arnold Bennett; Tunstall, Burslem, Hanley, Longton and Stoke. For those interested in Victorian and Industrial architecture this is a wonderful place to visit. Factory shops, many selling high quality seconds, abound in this area and visitors are advised to obtain the leaflet "Visit the Potteries for a China Experience" either from within the area or by contacting the TIC, 'phone number above. There are also many museums and visitor centres devoted to pottery and ceramics and these are all signposted within the area;

The Potteries Museum and Art Gallery

Bethesda Street, Hanley
ST1 3DE
Tel: (01782) 232323
website;
www.stoke.gov.uk/museums

Gladstone Pottery Museum

Uttoxeter Road, Longton
ST3 1PQ
Tel: (01782) 319232
website; www.stoke.gov.uk/gladstone

Etruria Industrial Museum

Lower Bedford Street, Etruria
ST4 7AF
Tel: (01782) 233144
website; www.stoke.gov.uk/museums

The Wedgwood Story

Barlaston ST12 9ES
Tel: (01782) 204218
website; www.wedgwood.com

Royal Doulton Visitor Centre

Nile Street, Burslem
ST6 2AJ
Tel: (01782) 292434
website;
www.royal-doulton.com/rd/visitors

The World of Spode

Spode Works, Church Street,
Stoke on Trent
ST4 1BX
Tel: (01782) 744011
website; www.spode.co.uk

The Dudson Museum

Hope Street, Hanley ST1 5DD Tel: (01782) 285286

The Dudson Factory Cash & Carry

Nile Street, Burslem ST6 2BB Tel: (01782) 821075

M6

BETWEEN JUNCS 15 & 16

KEELE SERVICES (NORTHBOUND) (WELCOME BREAK)
Tel: (01782) 626221 Granary Restaurant & Shell Fuel

KEELE SERVICES (SOUTHBOUND) (WELCOME BREAK)
Tel: (01782) 626221 Granary Restaurant, La Brioche Doree & Shell Fuel

KFC AND BURGER KING RESTAURANTS ON FOOTBRIDGE CONNECTING BOTH SITES.

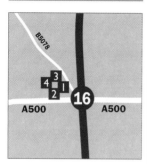

A500   **16**   A500

Nearest A&E Hospital
North Staffordshire Royal Infirmary
Princes Road, Hartshill, Stoke ST4 7JN
Tel: (01782) 715444
Follow the A500 east into Stoke and at the first roundabout turn right along the A34. After about 1.3 miles turn left at the roundabout along the A52, Proceed along Hartshill Road and the hospital is on the right in Princes Road. (Distance Approx 8.6 miles)

FACILITIES

1   Little Chef

Tel: (01270) 883115
0.1 miles north along the B5078, on the left.
Open; 07.00-22.00hrs daily.

2   Travelodge Crewe

Tel: (01270) 883157
0.1 miles north along the B5078, on the left

3   Burger King

Tel: (01270) 883115
0.1 miles north along the B5078, on the left
Open; 10.00-22.00hrs daily

4   Barthomley Service Station (Total)

Tel: (01270) 883212
0.1 miles north along the B5078, on the left
Access, Visa, Overdrive, All Star, Switch, Dial Card, Mastercard, Amex, Diners Club, Delta, Total Card. Open; 07.00-23.00hrs daily.

PLACES OF INTEREST

The Railway Age

Crewe Heritage Centre, Vernon Way, Crewe CW1 2DB Tel: (01270) 212130
website: www.therailwayage.co.uk

Follow the A500 west, and A5020 northwest to Crewe (Signposted Crewe Station 5.6 Miles)
Built on the site of the former huge Crewe North Engine Sheds, the exhibition shows the railway history of the town. There are three full sized signal boxes on view, including Crewe North Junction which overlooks the station and the locomotives on site include the former L&NWR "Cornwall" and the Gas Turbine Locomotive No.18000 which was built as a prototype in 1950. The Advanced Passenger Train, an abortive attempt to perfect the tilting train as the next generation of express passenger rolling stock for the 1980's, is also in the yard. There are a considerable number of models and hands-on displays. Café. Souvenir Shop. Limited Disabled access.

Hack Green Secret Nuclear Bunker

PO Box 127, Nantwich CW5 8AQ Information Line Tel: (01270) 629219
website: www.hackgreen.co.uk

Follow the A500 west into Nantwich and A530 south. (Signposted from Nantwich, 11.2 Miles)
One of the more unusual tourist destinations! RAF Hack Green was a WWII operational radar station and an extensive underground concrete command centre was built here in the 1950's, becoming a secret Regional Government Headquarters in the 1980's. Had nuclear war broken out, this is where 130 civil servants and military commanders would have ruled what was left of north west England. The maze of passages and rooms contains fascinating displays of all the paraphernalia required for communications and administration and an exhibition of authentic equipment shows the awesome power of nuclear weapons. NAAFI style canteen. Some disabled access.

Stapeley Water Gardens

London Road, Stapeley, Nantwich, Cheshire CW5 7LH
Tel: (01270) 623868 website: www.stapeleywatergardens.co.uk

Follow the A500 west (Signposted 7.9 Miles)
Set within 64 acres it is now the world's largest water garden centre. There is also an Angling Centre and the Palms Tropical Oasis incorporating the "World of Frogs" exhibition. Restaurant. Café. Gift Shop. Disabled access.

M6
BETWEEN JUNCS 16 & 17

SANDBACH SERVICES (NORTHBOUND) (ROADCHEF)
Tel: (01270) 767134 Food Fayre Self-Service Restaurant, Costa Coffee, Wimpy Bar & Esso Fuel

SANDBACH SERVICES (SOUTHBOUND) (ROADCHEF)
Tel: (01270) 767134 Food Fayre Self-Service Restaurant, Costa Coffee, Wimpy Bar & Esso Fuel

FOOTBRIDGE CONNECTION BETWEEN SITES.

JUNCTION 17

Nearest Northbound A&E Hospital

South Manchester University Hospital

Southmoor Road, Wythenshawe, Manchester M23 9LT
Tel: (0161) 998 7070
Proceed to Junction 19 and take the A556 north. Continue along the A56 into Altrincham and turn right along the A560. At the crossroads with the A5144 turn right and after about 0.1 miles turn left into Clay Lane. Turn left at the end and continue along Dobbinetts Lane. The hospital is along this road. (Distance Approx 21 miles)

Nearest Southbound A&E Hospital

Leighton Hospital

Middlewich Road, Leighton, Nr Crewe CW1 4QJ
Tel: (01270) 255141
Take the A5022 south towards Crewe and the hospital is signposted along this route. (Distance Approx 9 miles)

FACILITIES

> **SANDBACH TOWN CENTRE IS WITHIN ONE MILE OF THIS JUNCTION**

1   Saxon Cross Hotel

Tel: (01270) 763281
0.2 miles north along the A5022, on the left.
Restaurant Open; Mon-Sat; 12.00-14.00 hrs & 19.00-21.30hrs, Sun; 12.00-14.00hrs.

2   Chimney House Hotel & Restaurant

Tel: (01270) 764141
0.3 miles east along the A534, on the right.
Restaurant Open; Breakfast; 07.00-09.30hrs daily, Lunch; Sun-Fri; 12.00-14.00hrs, Dinner; 18.30-22.00hrs daily.

3   Star Saxon Cross Service Station (Texaco)

Tel: (01270) 758980
0.1 miles west along the A534, on the left.
Access, Visa, Overdrive, All Star, Switch, Dial Card, Mastercard, Amex, Diners Club, Electron, Solo, Delta, AA Paytrak, Texaco Cards. NB Not open on Christmas Day.

4   Café Symphony Restaurant & Wine Bar

Tel: (01270) 763664
0.7 miles west along Congleton Road, on the right.
Open; Tues-Fri; 12.00-14.00hrs & 17.30-22.00hrs, Sat; 17.30-22.00hrs, Sun; 12.00-14.30hrs & 17.30-22.00hrs

5   The Military Arms

Tel: (01270) 765442

0.9 miles west along the Sandbach Road, in Sandbach, on the right.
(Inn Partnership) Open all day. Meals served; 12.00-20.00hrs daily

6   Fortune Palace Cantonese Restaurant

Tel: (01270) 763255
0.9 miles west along Congleton Road, in Sandbach, on the right in Green Street.
Open; Tues-Sun; 17.00-0.00hrs.

7   Sallys Café

Tel: (01270) 761985
0.9 miles west along Congleton Road, in Sandbach, on the right in Green Street.
Open; Mon-Sat; 09.15-15.30hrs.

8   Sandbach Service Station (Ind)

Tel: (01270) 763395
1 mile west along Congleton Road, in Sandbach, in Bradwall Road.
Access, Visa, Switch, Mastercard, Amex, Diners Club, Delta, Electron, Solo. Open; Mon-Fri; 07.30-17.30hrs, Sat; 07.30-13.00hrs, Sun; Closed.

PLACES OF INTEREST

The Canal Centre

Hassall Green, Nr Sandbach CW11 4YB
Tel: (01270) 762266 website: www.brindleysrestaurant.co.uk

Follow the A534 west and turn left along the A533. (Signposted "Canal Centre & Potters Barn" along A533, 3.4 Miles)

An ideal place to take time out to relax, at this 200 years old canal centre on the Trent & Mersey Canal. Watch boats passing through the locks whilst enjoying lockside refreshments in the tea room, browse in the gift shop which includes handmade and painted canal and craft ware or dine in the licensed restaurant. Limited disabled access.

Connected by a short walk along the canal towpath to ...

The Potters Barn

Roughwood Lane, Hassall Green, Nr Sandbach CW11 4XX Tel: (01270) 884080 website: www.thepottersbarn.co.uk

A traditional pottery set amidst beautiful Cheshire countryside. There are workshops, a showroom gallery and a picnic area. Limited disabled access.

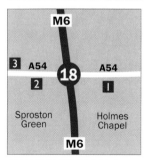

Nearest Northbound A&E Hospital

South Manchester University Hospital

Southmoor Road, Wythenshawe, Manchester M23 9LT
Tel: (0161) 998 7070

Proceed to Junction 19 and take the A556 north. Continue along the A56 into Altrincham and turn right along the A560. At the crossroads with the A5144 turn right and after about 0.1 miles turn left into Clay Lane. Turn left at the end and continue along Dobbinetts Lane. The hospital is along this road. (Distance Approx 17 miles)

Nearest Southbound A&E Hospital

Leighton Hospital

Middlewich Road, Leighton, Nr Crewe CW1 4QJ
Tel: (01270) 255141

Take the A54 exit west and after about 2.7 miles turn left along the A530. The hospital is along this road. (Distance Approx 8.6 miles)

FACILITIES

1 Star Croco Service Station (Texaco)

Tel: (01477) 536910
0.6 miles east along the A54, on the right.

Access, Visa, Overdrive, All Star, Switch, Dial Card, Mastercard, Amex, Electron, Solo, Diners Club, Delta, Fast Fuel, Texaco Cards. Open; Mon-Fri; 07.00-21.00hrs, Sat & Sun; 08.00-21.00hrs.

2 The Fox & Hounds

Tel: (01606) 832303
0.6 miles west along the A54, on the left.

(Inn Partnership) Home cooked food served daily; 12.00-14.20hrs and 18.30-21.20hrs.

3 Sproston Service Station (Save)

Tel: (01606) 832387
0.8 miles west along the A54, on the right.

Access, Visa, Overdrive, All Star, Switch, Dial Card, Mastercard, Delta, Save Card. Open; 06.00-23.00hrs daily.

PLACES OF INTEREST

Jodrell Bank Science Centre, Planetarium & Arboretum

Lower Withington, Nr Macclesfield SK11 9DL
Tel: (01477) 571339 website: www.jb.man.ac.uk/scicen

Follow the A54 east through Holmes Chapel and take the A535 north (Signposted 4.6 Miles)

The Science Centre, alongside of the Lovell Radio Telescope, contains many hands-on science exhibits relating to space, science and the environment and the Planetarium gives a vivid visual experience of the universe. A 35 acre Arboretum contains many beautiful trees and wildlife and there is an Environmental Discovery Centre. Picnic Area. Play Area. Shop. Café. Disabled access.

M6 BETWEEN JUNCS 18 & 19

KNUTSFORD SERVICES (NORTHBOUND) (MOTO)
Tel: (01565) 634167 Burger King & BP Fuel.

KNUTSFORD SERVICES (SOUTHBOUND) (MOTO)
Tel: (01565) 634167 Burger King & BP Fuel.

FRESH EXPRESS SELF-SERVICE RESTAURANT AND LITTLE CHEF ON FOOTBRIDGE CONNECTING BOTH SITES

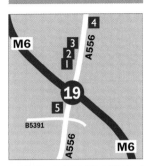

JUNCTION 19

Nearest Northbound A&E Hospital

South Manchester University Hospital

Southmoor Road, Wythenshawe, Manchester M23 9LT
Tel: (0161) 998 7070
Take the A556 exit north, continue along the A56 into Altrincham and turn right along the A560. At the crossroads with the A5144 turn right and after about 0.1 miles turn left into Clay Lane. Turn left at the end and continue along Dobbinetts Lane. The hospital is along this road. (Distance Approx 9.1 miles)

Nearest Southbound A&E Hospital

Leighton Hospital

Middlewich Road, Leighton, Nr Crewe CW1 4QJ
Tel: (01270) 255141
Proceed to Junction 18 and take the A54 west exit. Turn left along the A530 and the hospital is on this road. (Distance Approx 16.8 miles)

FACILITIES

1   Little Chef

Tel: (01565) 755049

0.1 miles north along the A556, on the left.
Open; 07.00-22.00hrs daily.

2   Travelodge Knutsford

Tel: (01565) 652187
0.1 miles north along the A556, on the left.

3   BP Tabley Mere

Tel: (01565) 755127
0.1 miles north along the A556, on the left.
Access, Visa, Overdrive, All Star, Switch, Dial Card, Mastercard, Amex, Diners Club, Delta, AA Paytrak, UK Fuelcard, Shell Agency, BP Cards. Open; 06.00-22.00hrs daily

4   The Old Vicarage Private Hotel

Tel: (01565) 652221
0.2 miles north along the A556, on the right

5   The Windmill

Tel: (01565) 632670
0.1 miles south along the A556, on the right.
(Robinson's) Meals served daily

PLACES OF INTEREST

Anderton Boat Lift

Anderton, Northwich CW9 6FA Visitor Centre
Tel: (01606) 77699 website: www.northwich.uk.com

Follow the A556 west into Northwich, take the A533 north and it is signposted along this route (7.6 miles)

At Anderton, the River Weaver and Trent & Mersey Canal, completed in 1777, are adjacent but there is a height difference of 50ft. A transfer centre was established here, but it required the costly and time consuming process of the unloading and trans-shipping of goods and it was obvious that some sort of physical link was required between the two, but the solution turned out to be unique in this country. Edward Leader Williams, the Weaver Navigations Trust Engineer, suggested the use of a "boat carrying lift" and in consultation with Edwin Clarke, a prominent civil engineer, he produced a design that was a magnificent example of the Victorian's mastery of cast iron and hydraulics. The first boat lift was completed in 1875 and replaced by the existing one in 1908. Commercial traffic ceased in the mid-1960s and it closed, life expired, in 1982. It is in the hands of the Waterways Trust and since the completion of its restoration and re-opening in 2002 has been operated by British Waterways.

Tatton Park

Knutsford, Cheshire WA16 6QN
Tel: (01625) 534400 website: www.tattonpark.org.uk

Follow the A556 north and turn right along the A50 (Signposted 2.8 Miles)

The home of the Egerton family since the late 16thC, the present Neo-classical mansion was begun in the late 18thC and built around an earlier house from Charles II's time. The 54 acres of ornamental and woodland gardens were laid out by Humphry Repton and featured the one mile long Tatton Mere, winding through them and the 400 yards long Broad Walk of tall trees leading to an 1811 replica of a Greek monument on the edge of the 1,000 acres of deerpark. There is a 1930's working farm, children's playground and speciality shops selling local produce. Gift Shop. Restaurant. Limited disabled access.

Arley Hall & Gardens

Great Budworth, Nr Northwich
CW9 6NA
Tel: (01565) 777353 website:
www.arleyestate.zuunet.co.uk

Follow the B5391 west (Signposted 6.9 Miles)
Famous for its 12 acres of award winning gardens, Arley Hall is a fine example of the early Victorian Jacobean style. Lunches and light refreshments are provided in the Tudor Barn. Gift Shop. Plant Nursery. Disabled access.

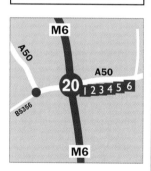

JUNCTION 20

THIS IS ALSO PART OF A MOTORWAY INTERCHANGE WITH THE M56 JUNCTION 9

Nearest A&E Hospital
Warrington Hospital
Lovely Lane, Warrington
WA5 1QG
Tel: (01925) 635911
Take the A50 north into Warrington and continue through the town centre along the A570 towards Prescot. At the roundabout junction of the A570, B5210 and Lovely Lane, turn right into Lovely Lane and

the hospital is on the right. (Distance Approx 5.4 miles)

FACILITIES

1　Poplar 2000 Services Restaurant

Tel: (01925) 757777
0.1 miles east along the A50, on the right.

2　McDonald's

Tel: (01925) 758759
0.1 miles east along the A50, on the right.
Open; 07.00-23.30hrs daily

3　Public Toilets & Showers

0.1 miles east along the A50, on the right.

4　Poplar 2000 Service Station (Total)

Tel: (01925) 754478
0.1 miles east along the A50, on the right.
LPG. Access, Visa, Overdrive, All Star, Switch, Dial Card, Mastercard, Amex, Diners Club, Delta, Total Cards. Cash machine available in adjacent amenities area.

5　Poplar 2000 Diesel Service Station

Tel: (01925) 757777
0.1 miles east along the A50, on the right.
Diesel Fuel Only. Access, Visa, Overdrive, All Star, Switch, Dial Card, Mastercard, Routex, AA Paytrak, UK Fuelcard, Securicor Fuelserv, IDS, Keyfuels, AS24, Allied Fuels, PCS Card, & BP Diesel Cards. Cash machine available in adjacent amenities area.

6　Travelodge Lymm

Tel: (01925) 757031
0.1 miles east along the A50, on the right.

PLACES OF INTEREST

Walton Hall & Gardens

Walton Lea Road, Higher Walton, Warrington WA4 6SN Tel: (01925) 601617 website:
www.warrington.gov.uk

Follow the M56 west to Junction 11 and take the A56 north (Signposted 9.1 Miles)
Set amidst beautiful Cheshire countryside, there is something for everyone at Walton Hall & Gardens. Apart from the formal gardens there is a Heritage Centre, a Children's Zoo, Pitch'n'Putt and Crazy Golf courses, a putting green and a bowling green all set amidst the extensive grounds. Gift Shop. Coffee Shop.

Catalyst, The Museum of the Chemical Industry

Mersey Road, Widnes, Cheshire WA8 0DF Tel: (0151) 420 1121 website: www.catalyst.org.uk

Follow the M56 west to Junction 12 (Signposted 11.1 Miles)
Catalyst is where science and technology really come alive through interactive and hands-on displays. Over 100 exhibits help the visitor explore the impact of chemicals on every day life, through scenes from the past, hands-on displays and multi-media programmes which summon up the sights, sounds and even the smells of yesterday. Apart from the exciting science exhibition, there is a roof top observatory with which to view Cheshire

and there is a nature trail through the adjacent Spike Island Water Park with its thriving wildlife. Café. Gift Shop. Disabled access.

Lymm Dam

Off Crouchley Lane, Lymm, Nr Warrington WA13 0AN
Tel: (01925) 758195 website: www.warrington.gov.uk

Follow the B5158 north and turn right along the A56 (2.5 Miles)

Lymm Dam was constructed in 1824 with the creation of a turnpike road from Warrington to Stockport and, with the remains of a slitting mill, forms a delightful country park. Sited within the Mersey Forest and adjacent to the Trans Pennine Trail, it is comprised of a variety of woodland and meadow settings and is the home for a wide range of wildlife. Picnic areas.

JUNCTION 21

Nearest A&E Hospital
Warrington Hospital

Lovely Lane, Warrington
WA5 1QG
Tel: (01925) 635911
Take the A57 west to Warrington and continue along the A49. At the roundabout junction of the A49, A570 and the A50 turn right along the

A570 and proceed through the town centre towards Prescot. At the junction with the B5210, the first major roundabout, turn right into Lovely Lane and the hospital is on the right. (Distance Approx 5.2 miles)

FACILITIES

1   The Rope & Anchor

Tel: (01925) 814996
0.9 miles west along the A57, in Woolston, on the right.
(Scottish & Newcastle) Open all day. Meals served; Mon; 12.00-14.30hrs, Tues-Fri; 12.00-14.30hrs & 17.00-19.30hrs, Sat; 12.00-18.00hrs, Sun; 12.00-17.30hrs

2   Holiday Inn, Warrington

Tel: (01925) 838779
0.1 miles north along the B5210, on the left.
The Junction Restaurant Open; Breakfast; Mon-Fri; 06.30-10.00hrs, Sat & Sun; 07.30-11.30hrs, Lunch; Sun-Fri; 12.00-14.00hrs, Dinner; 18.30-21.45hrs daily. Bar Snacks available throughout the day.

JUNCTION 21A

THIS JUNCTION IS A MOTORWAY INTERCHANGE ONLY WITH THE M62 AND THERE IS NO ACCESS TO ANY FACILITIES

JUNCTION 22

THERE ARE NO FACILITIES WITHIN ONE MILE OF THIS JUNCTION

Nearest A&E Hospital
Warrington Hospital

Lovely Lane, Warrington
WA5 1QG
Tel: (01925) 635911
Take the A49 south and continue along the A49 towards Warrington. At the first set of traffic lights, the junction with the A574, turn right into Kerfoot Street, continue along Folly Lane and the hospital is on the left just past the railway bridge. (Distance Approx 4.3 miles)

PLACES OF INTEREST

Gullivers World

Warrington, Cheshire WA5 5YZ
Information Line
Tel: (01925) 444888
website: www.gulliversfun.co.uk

Follow the A49 west and continue along the A574 (Signposted along route, 4.6 Miles)

Specifically designed for families with children between the age of two and thirteen years all 40 rides and attractions are aimed to cater for their specific needs. Set within a beautiful parkland there is a huge variety of attractions including themed displays and live shows. Catering for the younger market, great emphasis is placed on making the park as safe as possible. There are a number of cafés and restaurants. Disabled Access.

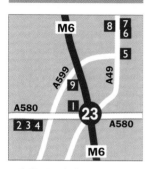

JUNCTION 23

Nearest Northbound A&E Hospital

Royal Albert Edward Infirmary

Wigan Lane, Wigan WN1 2NN
Tel: (01942) 244000
Proceed to Junction 25 and take the A49 north. At the first roundabout turn right along the B5238. Bear right at the junction with the A49 and turn left along the B5375. After about 0.5 miles bear right along the B5376 and the hospital is on the right along this road. (Distance Approx 6.9 miles)

Nearest Southbound A&E Hospital

Warrington Hospital

Lovely Lane, Warrington WA5 1QG
Tel: (01925) 635911
Proceed south to Junction 22 and take the A49 south and continue along the A49 towards Warrington. At the first set of traffic lights, the junction with the A574, turn right into Kerfoot Street, continue along Folly Lane and the hospital is on the left just past the railway bridge. (Distance Approx 7.3 miles)

FACILITIES

1　Haydock Island (Shell)

Tel: (01925) 293690
0.1 miles west along the A580, on the right.
LPG. Access, Visa, Overdrive, All Star, Switch, Dial Card, Mastercard, Amex, Diners Club, Delta, BP Supercharge, Shell Cards.

2　New Boston Service Station (Total)

Tel: (01942) 716227
1 mile west along the A580, on the left.
Access, Visa, Overdrive, All Star, Switch, Dial Card, Mastercard, Amex, Diners Club, Delta, UK Fuelcard, Securicor Fuelserv, Keyfuels, Total/Fina/Elf Cards.

3　Little Chef

Tel: (01942) 272048
1 mile west along the A580, on the left.
Open; 07.00-22.00hrs daily.

4　Travelodge Haydock

Tel: (01942) 272055
1 mile west along the A580, on the left

5　Holiday Inn, Haydock

Tel: 0870 400 9039
0.4 miles north along the A49, on the right.
The Junction Restaurant Open; Breakfast; Mon-Fri; 06.30-10.00hrs, Sat & Sun; 07.30-11.00hrs, Lunch; Sun-Fri; 12.30-14.30hrs, Dinner; 18.30-22.30hrs daily.

6　The Bay Horse

Tel: (01942) 725032
0.9 miles north along the A49, on the right.
(Scottish & Newcastle) Open all day. Meals served; Sun-Thurs; 12.00-21.30hrs, Fri & Sat; 12.00-22.00hrs.

7　Premier Lodge

Tel: (01942) 725032
0.9 miles north along the A49, on the right

8　The Angel

Tel: (01942) 728704
1 mile north along the A49, on the left.
(Burtonwood) Open all day on Sundays. Meals served; Mon-Sat; 11.30-14.30hrs & 17.30-21.30hrs, Sun; 12.00-21.30hrs.

9　Haydock Thistle Hotel

Tel: (01942) 272000
0.6 miles west along the A599, on the left.
The Beechers Restaurant Open; Breakfast; Mon-Fri; 07.00-10.00hrs, Sat; 07.00-11.00hrs, Sun; 08.00-11.00hrs, Lunch; Sun-Fri; 12.00-14.00hrs, Dinner; Mon-Sat; 19.00-21.45hrs, Sun; 19.00-20.30hrs.

JUNCTION 24

THIS IS A RESTRICTED ACCESS JUNCTION
- Vehicles can only exit from the southbound lanes.
- Vehicles can only enter the motorway along the northbound lanes.

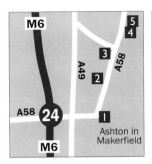

Nearest Northbound A&E Hospital

Royal Albert Edward Infirmary

Wigan Lane, Wigan
WN1 2NN
Tel: (01942) 244000

Proceed to Junction 25 and take the A49 north. At the first roundabout turn right along the B5238. Bear right at the junction with the A49 and turn left along the B5375. After about 0.5 miles bear right along the B5376 and the hospital is on the right along this road. (Distance Approx 5.6 miles)

Nearest Southbound A&E Hospital

Warrington Hospital

Lovely Lane, Warrington
WA5 1QG
Tel: (01925) 635911

Proceed south to Junction 22 and take the A49 south and continue along this road towards Warrington. At the first set of traffic lights, the junction with the A574, turn right into Kerfoot Street, continue along Folly Lane and the hospital is on the left just past the railway bridge. (Distance Approx 8.6 miles)

FACILITIES

ASHTON IN MAKERFIELD TOWN CENTRE IS WITHIN ONE MILE OF THIS JUNCTION.

---

1 KFC

Tel: (01942) 723146
0.6 miles east along the A58, in Ashton in Makerfield, on the right.
Open; 11.00-0.00hrs daily.

2 Sir Thomas Gerard

Tel: (01942) 713519
0.7 miles east along the A58, in Ashton in Makerfield, on the left
(Wetherspoon) Open all day. Meals served; Mon-Sat; 11.00-22.00hrs, Sun; 12.00-21.30hrs.

3 The Robin Hood

Tel: (01942) 721560
0.8 miles east along the A58, in Ashton in Makerfield, on the left.
(Scottish & Newcastle) Open all day. Meals served; 12.00-18.00hrs daily

4 The Rockleigh Hotel

Tel: (01942) 727156
1 mile east along the A58, in Ashton in Makerfield, on the right.
Grill Room Open; 19.00-21.00hrs daily

5 Caledonian Service Station (Esso)

Tel: (01942) 718352
1 mile east along the A58, in Ashton in Makerfield, on the right.
Access, Visa, Overdrive, All Star, Switch, Dial Card, Mastercard, Amex, Diners Club, Delta, Shell Euro, BP Supercharge, Esso Cards.
Open; 06.30-23.00hrs daily.

THIS IS A RESTRICTED ACCESS JUNCTION

- Vehicles can only exit from the northbound lanes.
- Vehicles can only enter the motorway along the southbound lanes.

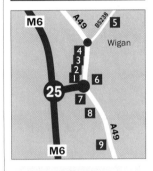

Nearest A&E Hospital

Royal Albert Edward Infirmary

Wigan Lane, Wigan WN1 2NN
Tel: (01942) 244000

Take the A49 north and at the first roundabout turn right along the B5238. Bear right at the junction with the A49 and turn left along the B5375. After about 0.5 miles bear right along the B5376 and the hospital is on the right along this road. (Distance Approx 3.5 miles)

FACILITIES

1 Travel Inn

Tel: (01942) 493469
0.2 miles north along the A49, on the left

2 Wheat Lea Park

Tel: (01942) 493469

0.2 miles north along the A49, on the left.
(Whitbread) Open all day. Meals served; 11.30-22.00hrs daily

3 McDonald's

Tel: (01942) 230139
0.5 miles north along the A49, on the left.
Open; 07.30-0.00hrs daily.

4 Marus Bridge Service Station (BP)

Tel: (01942) 242437
0.6 miles north along the A49, on the left.
Access, Visa, Overdrive, All Star, Switch, Dial Card, Mastercard, Amex, Diners Club, Delta, Routex, Shell Agency, BP Cards.

5 Wigan Service Station (Esso)

Tel: (01942) 707154
1 mile north along the B5288, on the right.
Access, Visa, Overdrive, All Star, Switch, Dial Card, Mastercard, Amex, Diners Club, Delta, Shell Gold, BP Supercharge, Esso Cards.

6 Goose Green (Shell)

Tel: (01942) 823900
0.2 miles north along the A49, on the right.
Access, Visa, Overdrive, All Star, Switch, Dial Card, Mastercard, Amex, Diners Club, Shell Cards.

7 The Red Lion Restaurant

Tel: (01942) 831089
0.1 miles south along the A49, on the right.
Open; 12.00-21.00hrs daily

8 The Cranberry Hotel

Tel: (01942) 243519
0.1 miles south along the A49, on the right.
Bar Snacks available 19.00-21.00hrs daily

9 The Park Hotel

Tel: (01942) 270562
0.3 miles south along the A49, on the right.
(Burtonwood) Open all day. Meals served; 12.00-21.00hrs daily.

PLACES OF INTEREST

Wigan Pier

Wallgate, Wigan WN3 4EU
Tel: (01942) 323666
website: www.wiganpier.net

Follow the A49 north (Signposted 3.1 Miles)

Set in an 8.5 acre site alongside the Leeds-Liverpool Canal, Wigan Pier offer hours of entertainment, education and interaction for all the family. For over a 100 years the pier, at the canal basin, was the hub of industrial Wigan with its sidings, warehouses, loading bays and barges all busy with the movement of coal and cotton. With the decline of both the waterways and these traditional industries the pier became derelict, but in the mid 1980's it was totally renovated and reopened as a heritage centre. Today the exhibitions include the "Way We Were", Opie's Museum of Memories, the Trencherfield Mill Engine and the Machinery Hall. There are waterbus trips, available throughout the year, and canal boat cruises in the summer. Gift Shops. Café. Disabled access.

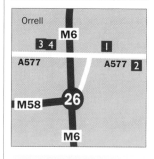

Nearest A&E Hospital

Royal Albert Edward Infirmary

Wigan Lane, Wigan WN1 2NN
Tel: (01942) 244000

Take the A577 east into Wigan and proceed north along the A49 towards Preston. Turn left along the B5375 and bear right along the B5376. The hospital is on the right hand side of this road. (Distance Approx 4.5 miles)

FACILITIES

1 KFC

Tel: (01942) 216849
0.6 miles east along the A577, on the left.
Open; 11.00-0.00hrs daily.

2 Pemberton Service Station (Esso)

Tel: (01942) 706307
1 mile east along the A577, on the right.
Access, Visa, Overdrive, All Star, Switch, Dial Card, Mastercard, Amex, Diners Club, Delta, Shell Gold, BP Supercharge, Esso Cards.

3   The Priory Wood

Tel: (01942) 211516
0.1 miles west along the
A577, on the right.
(Beefeater) Open all day. Meals
served; Mon-Thurs; 12.00-
14.30hrs & 17.30-22.00hrs,
Fri; 12.00-14.30hrs & 17.30-
22.30hrs, Sat; 12.00-23.00hrs,
Sun; 12.00-21.00hrs.

4   Travel Inn

Tel: (01942) 211516
0.1 miles west along the
A577, on the right

PLACES OF INTEREST

Wigan Pier

Wallgate, Wigan WN3 4EU

**Follow the A577 east
(Signposted 2.9 Miles)**

For details please see Junction
25 information.

Nearest Northbound A&E Hospital
Chorley & South Ribble District Hospital

Preston Road, Chorley
PR7 1PP
Tel: (01257) 261222
Take the A5209 east towards

Standish and continue along
the B5239. Turn left at the end
along the A5106 and after
about 3.5 miles continue into
the A6 through Chorley and the
hospital is on the left at
Hartwood. (Distance Approx 7
miles)

Nearest Southbound A&E Hospital
Royal Albert Edward Infirmary

Wigan Lane, Wigan WN1 2NN
Tel: (01942) 244000
Take the A5209 east towards
Standish and turn right along
the A49. Follow this route into
Wigan and the hospital is on
the right hand side. (Distance
Approx 3.8 miles)

FACILITIES

1   BP Connect Crow Orchard

Tel: (01257) 421390
0.1 miles west along the
A5209, on the right.
LPG. Access, Visa, Delta,
Mastercard, Switch, Diners
Club, Amex, Overdrive, All Star,
Dial Card, Routex, BP Cards.
Wild Bean Café Open; 06.00-
20.00hrs daily.

2   The Wrightington Hotel & Country Club

Tel: (01257) 425803
0.4 miles west along the
A5209, on the right.
(Best Western) Restaurant
Open; Mon-Sat; 19.00-
21.30hrs

3   The Tudor Inn

Tel: (01257) 425977
0.6 miles north along the
B5250, on the right.
(Greenalls) Open all day Sat &
Sun. Meals served; Wed-Fri;
12.00-14.00hrs & 18.00-

20.00hrs, Sat & Sun; 12.00-
20.00hrs.

4   Wigan Standish Moat House

Tel: (01257) 499988
0.6 miles east along the
A5209, on the left.
Restaurant Open; Breakfast;
07.00-10.00hrs Daily, Lunch,
Mon-Sat; 12.00-14.30hrs, Sun;
12.00-15.30hrs, Dinner; Mon-
Thurs; 19.00-21.30hrs, Fri &
Sat; 19.00-22.00hrs, Sun;
19.00-21.00hrs.

5   The Charnley Arms

Tel: (01257) 424619
0.6 miles east along the
A5209, on the right.
(Scottish & Newcastle) Open all
day. Meals served; Sun-Fri;
12.00-21.00hrs, Sat; 12.00-
21.30hrs.

6   Premier Lodge

Tel: (01257) 424619
0.6 miles east along the
A5209, on the right

7   Standish Service Station (Total)

Tel: (01257) 473660
0.7 miles east along the
A5209, on the right.
Access, Visa, Overdrive, All
Star, Switch, Dial Card,
Mastercard, Amex, Diners Club,
Delta, BP Supercharge, Total
Fina Cards.

PLACES OF INTEREST

Haigh Country Park

Haigh, Wigan WN2 1PE
Tel: (01942) 832895
website: www.haighhall.co.uk

**Follow the A5209 east
(Signposted 5.6 Miles)**

There are a number of walks and nature trails, marked out and of varying lengths and difficulty. Rangers are on hand to help and advise and at certain times also lead guided walks. For the visually impaired there are Audio Trails for which a tape player, Braille map and guide can be borrowed from the Information Centre whilst there is a route suitable for pushchairs and wheelchair users. Adventure activities, such as rock climbing, archery and an obstacle course can be pre-booked. Model Village, Gardens, Crazy Golf. Gift Shop. Café. Craft Studio. Some disabled access.

Martin Mere Wildlife & Wetland Centre

Fish Lane, Burscough, Lancashire L40 0TA
Tel: (01704) 895181
website: www.wwt.org.uk

Follow the A5209 west (Signposted 8.8 Miles)

A huge number and wide variety of species of tame swans, geese, ducks and flamingos are on view within the 40 acres of wildfowl gardens and 300 acres of wild refuge. There is a children's area where some of the birds can be hand fed, spacious hides for bird observation, picnic area and art and craft gallery. Gift Shop. Café.

Camelot Theme Park

Park Hall Road, Charnock Richard, Chorley PR7 5LP
Tel: (01257) 453044 website: www.camelotthemepark.co.uk

Follow the A5209 west and turn right along the B5250 to Heskin Green. (Signposted 3.6 Miles)

A theme park containing over 100 rides, shows and attractions, including live jousting and Merlin's Magic Show. Gift Shop. Café. Some disabled access.

M6 BETWEEN JUNCS 27 & 28

CHARNOCK RICHARD (NORTHBOUND) (WELCOME BREAK)

Tel: (01257) 791494 Granary Restaurant, La Brioche Doree French Café, Welcome Lodge & Shell Fuel

CHARNOCK RICHARD (SOUTHBOUND) (WELCOME BREAK)

Tel: (01257) 791494 Granary Restaurant & Shell Fuel.

KFC, BURGER KING & RED HEN RESTAURANT ON FOOTBRIDGE CONNECTING BOTH SITES.

M6 JUNCTION 28

Nearest Northbound A&E Hospital

Royal Preston Hospital

Sharoe Green Lane North, Fulwood, Preston PR2 9HT
Tel: (01772) 716565

Proceed north to Junction 29 and take the A6 west exit. Follow the road through Preston town centre and turn right along the B6241. The hospital is on this road. (Distance Approx 7.9 miles)

Nearest Southbound A&E Hospital

Chorley & South Ribble District Hospital

Preston Road, Chorley PR7 1PP
Tel: (01257) 261222

Take the B5256 east exit and turn right along the A49. After about 1.7 miles turn left along the B5248 and turn right at the end along the A6. The hospital is about 0.2 miles on at the junction of the A6 and B5252. (Distance Approx 4.3 miles)

FACILITIES

LEYLAND TOWN CENTRE IS WITHIN ONE MILE OF THIS JUNCTION.

1   Jarvis Leyland Hotel

Tel: (01772) 422922

0.1 miles west along the B5256, on the left.

Restaurant Open; Breakfast; Mon-Fri; 07.00-09.30hrs, Sat & Sun; 08.00-10.00hrs, Lunch; Sun-Fri; 12.00-14.00hrs, Dinner; 19.00-21.30hrs daily.

2   Canberra Total Service Station

Tel: (01772) 425900

0.4 miles west along the B5256, in Leyland, on the left.

Access, Visa, Overdrive, All Star, Switch, Dial Card, Mastercard, Amex, Diners Club, Delta, Total/Fina/Elf Cards. Open; Mon-Sat; 06.30-22.00hrs, Sun; 08.00-22.00hrs.

3   The Original Ship

Tel: (01772) 456674

1 mile along Westgate, in Leyland, on the right.
(Scottish & Newcastle) Open all day. Meals served; Tues-Sat; 12.00-15.00hrs, Sun; 12.00-17.00hrs.

4   Leyland Garage (Texaco)

Tel: (01772) 455414
1 mile along Westgate, in Leyland, on the right.
Access, Visa, Overdrive, All Star, Switch, Dial Card, Mastercard, Amex, Diners Club, Delta, Electron, Solo, UK Fuelcard, Securicor Fuelserv, Keyfuels, Texaco Cards. Open; Mon-Fri; 07.00-21.00hrs, Sat; 07.30-19.30hrs, Sun; 08.00-19.30hrs.

5   Shell Leyland

Tel: (01772) 450940
0.5 miles south along the A49, on the right.
Access, Visa, Overdrive, All Star, Switch, Dial Card, Mastercard, Amex, Diners Club, Delta, BP Agency, Esso Europe, Shell Cards.

6   Rydal Petroleum (Ind)

Tel: (01772) 455253
0.5 miles north along the A49, on the right.
Access, Visa, Solo, Overdrive, All Star, Switch, Dial Card, Mastercard, Delta, Open; 07.00-22.00hrs daily. (NB. Opening times may be slightly reduced during winter)

7   Top Wok Chinese Restaurant

Tel: (01772) 624888
0.5 miles north along the A49, on the left.
Open; 17.30-23.00hrs daily

8   The Hayrick

Tel: (01772) 434668
0.2 miles east along the B5256, on the right.
(Scottish & Newcastle) Open all day. Meals served; 12.00-20.00hrs daily.

PLACES OF INTEREST

British Commercial Vehicle Museum

King Street, Leyland,
Nr Preston PR5 1LE
Tel: (01772) 451011
Follow the B5356 west. (Signposted 0.7 Miles)
Sited on the former Leyland South Works, where for many years commercial vehicles were manufactured, this is a museum devoted to that genre with exhibits dating from the horse-drawn era to the present day, including the famous Popemobile. Imaginative displays utilize sound and lighting effects to bring the exhibits to life. Gift Shop. Café. Disabled access to ground floor only.

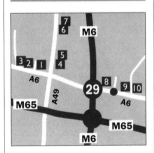

Nearest Northbound A&E Hospital
Royal Preston Hospital
Sharoe Green Lane North, Fulwood, Preston PR2 9HT
Tel: (01772) 716565
Take the A6 west exit and follow the road through Preston town centre. Turn right along the B6241 and the hospital is on this road. (Distance Approx 5.9 miles)

Nearest Southbound A&E Hospital
Chorley & South Ribble District Hospital
Preston Road, Chorley PR7 1PP
Tel: (01257) 261222
Take the A6 south exit and the hospital is at the junction with the B5252. (Distance Approx 4.2 miles)

FACILITIES

1   Sainsbury's Filling Station

Tel: (01772) 627762
0.6 miles west along the A6, on the right.
Access, Visa, Overdrive, All Star, Switch, Dial Card, Mastercard, Amex, Delta, Sainsbury's Fuel Card. Open; Mon-Fri; 06.00-0.00hrs, Sat; 06.00-22.00hrs, Sun; 07.00-22.00hrs. Disabled Toilets and Cash machines available in adjacent store.

2   The Millers

Tel: (01772) 324100
0.7 miles west along the A6, on the right.
(Scottish & Newcastle) Open all day. Meals served; Mon-Sat; 12.00-22.00hrs, Sun; 12.00-21.00hrs.

3   Lodge Inn

Tel: (01772) 324100
0.7 miles west along the A6, on the right

4   Ye Olde Hob Inn

Tel: (01772) 336863
0.5 miles north along the B6528, in Bamber Bridge, on the right.
(Free House) Open all day. Meals served; Mon; 12.00-14.00hrs, Tues-Sat; 12.00-14.00hrs & 18.00-21.00hrs, Sundays; 12.00-21.00hrs.

5   Bamber Bridge Service Station (Total)

Tel: (01772) 324410
0.6 miles north along the B6258, in Bamber Bridge, on the right.
Access, Visa, Overdrive, All Star, Switch, Dial Card, Mastercard, Amex, Diners Club, Delta, Total/Fina/Elf Cards.
Open; Mon-Sat; 07.00-22.00hrs, Sun; 08.00-21.00hrs.

6   The Black Bull

Tel: (01772) 335703
0.7 miles north along the B6258, in Bamber Bridge, on the right.
(Unique Pub Co) Open all day. Meals served; Tues-Sun; 12.00-14.00hrs & 17.00-20.30hrs.

7   The Mackenzie

Tel: (01772) 463902
0.8 miles north along the B6258, in Bamber Bridge, on the right.
(Whitbread) Open all day. Meals served; 12.00-15.00 hrs & 17.00-19.00hrs daily.

8   Novotel Preston

Tel: (01772) 313331
0.1 miles east along the A6, on the left.
The Garden Brasserie Restaurant Open; 06.00-0.00hrs daily

9   Clayton Brook Service Station (Esso)

Tel: (01772) 336064
0.7 miles east along the A6, on the left.
Access, Visa, Overdrive, All Star, Switch, Dial Card, Mastercard, Amex, Delta, Shell Gold, Esso Cards.

10 Brook House Hotel

Tel: (01772) 336403
1 mile east along the A6, on the left.
Restaurant Open; Mon-Thurs; 18.30-20.30hrs

PLACES OF INTEREST

Hoghton Tower

Hoghton, Preston, Lancashire PR5 0SH Tel: (01254) 852986 website: www.hoghtontower.co.uk

Follow the A6 south towards Chorley and turn left along the B5256. (5.3 Miles)
Ancestral home of the de Hoghton family since Norman times, the house was rebuilt in 1565 and restored during the late 19thC. Relics of James I's visit in 1617 are preserved here and it was in the magnificent Banqueting Hall that he famously knighted the beef "Sir Loin". William Shakespeare started his working life here and the house contains some fine 17thC panelling. Café. Gift Shop. No Disabled access.

M6
JUNCTION 30

TRIS JUNCTION IS A MOTORWAY INTERCHANGE ONLY WITH THE M61 AND THERE IS NO ACCESS TO ANY FACILITIES

M6
JUNCTION 31

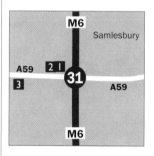

Nearest A&E Hospital
Royal Preston Hospital
Sharoe Green Lane North, Fulwood, Preston PR2 9HT
Tel: (01772) 716565
Take the A59(T) west exit and at the roundabout turn right along the A5085. At the crossroads with the A6063 and a minor road, turn right along the minor road and left at the end along the B6241. The hospital is along this road. (Distance Approx 3.2 miles)

FACILITIES

1   Tickled Trout Service Station (BP)

Tel: (01772) 877656
0.1 miles west along the A59, on the right.

Access, Visa, Overdrive, All Star, Switch, Dial Card, Mastercard, Amex, Diners Club, Delta, Routex, Shell Agency, BP Cards.

2 Tickled Trout Hotel

Tel: (01772) 877671

0.1 miles west along the A59, on the right.

(MacDonald) Restaurant Open; Lunch; Sun-Fri; 12.00-14.00hrs, Dinner; Mon-Sat; 19.00-21.30hrs, Sun; 19.00-21.00hrs

3 New Hall Lane Filling Station (BP)

Tel: (01772) 794212

0.8 miles west along the A59, on the left.

Access, Visa, Overdrive, All Star, Switch, Dial Card, Mastercard, Amex, Diners Club, Delta, Shell Agency, BP Cards.

PLACES OF INTEREST

Harris Museum & Art Gallery

Market Square, Preston PR1 2PP Tel: (01772) 258248 website: www.visitpreston.com

Follow the A59 west into Preston (Signposted 3.2 Miles)

Designed by James Hibbert in the Greek revival style, this magnificent listed building was opened in 1893. Funded by a local successful businessman and reminiscent of the British Museum, as well as the fine collection of paintings and watercolours by major 19thC British artists there is also an excellent exhibition of the story of Preston. Gift Shop. Café. Disabled access.

The National Football Museum

Sir Tom Finney Way, Deepdale, Preston PR1 6RU Tel: (01772) 908442 website: www.nationalfootballmuseum.com e-mail: enquiries@national footballmuseum.com

Follow the A59 west (Signposted 2 miles)

Developed in the 1860's as Association Football and organized into a Football League in 1888, Football (or Soccer, as it is known to distinguish it from other inferior forms of "football") rapidly became the world's most popular sport - both for playing and watching. The museum is packed with a fascinating collection of artefacts, mementos, photographs and film recording the development and history of this great game. Café. Gift Shop. Disabled Access.

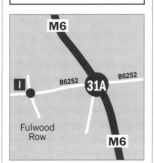

M6 JUNCTION 31A

THIS IS A RESTRICTED ACCESS JUNCTION

- Vehicles can only exit from the northbound lanes.
- Vehicles can only enter the motorway along the southbound lanes.

Nearest A&E Hospital

Royal Preston Hospital

Sharoe Green Lane North, Fulwood, Preston PR2 9HT Tel: (01772) 716565

Proceed north to Junction 32 and take the M55 west. At Junction 1 take the A6 south exit and at the crossroads turn left along the B6241. The hospital is along this road. (Distance Approx 5 miles)

FACILITIES

1 The Anderton Arms

Tel: (01772) 700104

0.6 miles west along the B6242, on the right.

(Six Continents) Open all day. Meals served; 12.00-20.00hrs daily.

M6 JUNCTION 32

THIS JUNCTION IS A MOTORWAY INTERCHANGE ONLY WITH THE M55 AND THERE IS NO ACCESS TO ANY FACILITIES

M6 BETWEEN JUNCS 32 & 33

FORTON SERVICES (NORTHBOUND) (COMPASS) Tel: (01524) 791775 Fresh Express Self-Service Restaurant, Burger King, Travelodge and Shell & BP Fuel

FORTON SERVICES (SOUTHBOUND) (COMPASS) Tel: (01524) 791775 Little Chef,

Burger King and Shell & BP Fuel

FOOTBRIDGE CONNECTION BETWEEN SITES.

M6
JUNCTION 33

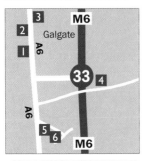

Nearest Northbound A&E Hospital

Royal Lancaster Infirmary

Ashton Road, Lancaster LA1 4RT Tel: (01524) 65944

Take the A6 north and after about 3 miles turn left at a crossroads along a minor road towards Scotforth. Turn right at the end along the A588 and the hospital is along this road. (Distance Approx 3.9 miles)

Nearest Southbound A&E Hospital

Royal Preston Hospital

Sharoe Green Lane North, Fulwood, Preston PR2 9HT Tel: (01772) 716565

Proceed south to Junction 32 and take the M55 west. At Junction 1 take the A6 south exit and at the crossroads turn left along the B6241. The hospital is along this road. (Distance Approx 16.3 miles)

FACILITIES

1   The Plough Inn

Tel: (01524) 751337

0.7 miles north along the A6, in Galgate, on the left. (Pubmistress) Open all day. Meals served; 12.00-20.30hrs daily

2   Green Dragon

Tel: (01524) 751062

0.9 miles north along the A6, in Galgate, on the left. (Thwaites) Open all day except Wednesday. Meals served; Thurs-Tues; 12.00-14.00hrs & 17.00-20.00hrs, Sat & Sun; 12.00-21.00hrs.

3   New Inn

Tel: (01524) 751643

0.9 miles north along the A6, in Galgate, on the right. (Mitchells) Meals served; 12.00-18.30hrs daily.

4   Hampson House Hotel

Tel: (01524) 751158

0.4 miles east along Hampson Lane, on the left. Restaurant Open; 12.00-14.00hrs & 18.30-21.30hrs daily.

5   Salt Oke South B&B

Tel: (01524) 752313

0.3 miles south along the A6, on the left.

6   Bay Horse Inn

Tel: (01524) 791204

0.9 miles south along the Abbeystead Road, on the right.

(Mitchells) Closed all day on Monday. Meals served; Tues-Sat; 12.00-14.00hrs & 19.00-21.30hrs, Sun; 12.00-16.00hrs.

PLACES OF INTEREST

Lancaster

Lancaster Tourist Information Office, 29 Tower Hill, Lancaster LA1 1YN. Tel: (01524) 32878 website: www.lancaster.gov.uk

Follow the A6 north (Signposted 5.4 Miles)

As early as the 10thC Athelstan had lands in the area, but it was the arrival of Roger of Pitou, cousin of William the Conqueror, who established Lancaster as his base to supervise the large areas of Lancashire given to him by the king. He built Lancaster Castle to keep out the marauding Scots and this was strengthened by John of Gaunt, Duke of Lancaster in the 15thC.

Unusually, it is still in use today, as a prison, so it can mostly only be viewed from the outside although visitors can enter the 18thC Shire Hall and Crown Court.

As with many ancient cities there are many fine period buildings still to be seen, including the Priory Church of St Mary, established in 1094 and rebuilt in the 14th & 15thC's, the Priory Tower, rebuilt in 1759 as a navigational landmark, and the Judge's Lodgings in Church Street, dating from the 1620's and now housing two museums; The Museum of Childhood and the Gillow & Town House Museum (Tel: 01524-32808) containing many examples of the fine workmanship of Gillows, the famous Lancaster cabinet makers.

The city's wealth during the 17th and 18thC's and until its decline in the nineteenth was undoubtedly based upon its maritime operations and this period is celebrated at St George's Quay which, with its great stone warehouses and superb Custom House form the Maritime Museum (Tel: 01524-64637)

Within the city can be found ....

Ashton Memorial & Williamson Park

Quernmore Road, Lancaster LA1 1UX Tel: (01524) 33318
website: www.lancaster.gov.uk

The great green copper dome of the memorial can be seen for miles around and is a magnificent viewpoint from which Morecambe Bay, the Lakeland Hills and the Forest of Bowland are all visible. It was built by John Belcher and completed in 1909 and is believed that the pre-stressed concrete dome is the first known example of such a construction. Today it houses exhibitions and multi-screen presentations about the life and Edwardian times of John Williamson, later Lord Ashton, who was the town's largest employer and the Liberal MP for many years. Williamson Park was his idea for providing employment for local people caused by the cotton famine crisis in the textile industry during the American Civil War of the 1860's. Constructed on old quarry workings, it opened in 1896, and there is now a Butterfly House in the restored Edwardian Palm House and the Conservation Garden and Wildlife Pool which opened in 1991. Gift Shop. Tea Room. Disabled Access.

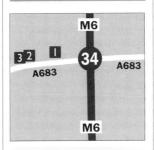

JUNCTION 34

Nearest A&E Hospital
Royal Lancaster Infirmary
Ashton Road, Lancaster
LA1 4RT Tel: (01524) 65944
Take the A683 exit west and continue along the A6 south. Turn right at the roundabout along the A588 and the hospital is along this road. (Distance Approx 3.1 miles)

FACILITIES

1   Holiday Inn, Lancaster

Tel: 0870 400 9047
0.2 miles west along the A683, on the right.
Traders Bar & Restaurant Open; Breakfast; Mon-Fri; 06.30-10.00hrs, Sat & Sun; 07.30-11.00hrs, Lunch; Sun-Fri; 12.00-14.00hrs, Dinner; 18.00-22.00hrs daily. Bar menu available all day.

2   Lancaster Town House

Tel: (01524) 65527
0.9 miles west along the A683, on the right

3   Shell Lancaster

Tel: (01524) 590900
1 mile west along the A683, on the right.
Access, Visa, Overdrive, All

Star, Switch, Dial Card, Mastercard, Amex, Diners Club, Delta, BP Agency, Shell Cards.

PLACES OF INTEREST

Lancaster

Lancaster Tourist Information Office, 29 Tower Hill, Lancaster LA1 1YN

Follow the A683 west. (Signposted 2 Miles)
For details please see Junction 33 information

Within the city can be found ....

Ashton Memorial & Williamson Park

Quernmore Road, Lancaster LA1 1UX

For details please see Junction 33 information

JUNCTION 35

Nearest Northbound A&E Hospital

Westmorland General Hospital
Burton Road, Kendal
LA9 7RG
Tel: (01539) 732288
Proceed north to Junction 36, take the A590 north exit and continue into the A591.

Continue along the A6 and at the Onal Park roundabout turn south east along the A65 and the hospital is along this road. (Distance Approx 14.9 miles)

Nearest Southbound A&E Hospital

Royal Lancaster Infirmary

Ashton Road, Lancaster LA1 4RT Tel: (01524) 65944

Proceed to Junction 34 and take the A683 exit west. Continue along the A6 south and turn right at the roundabout along the A588. The hospital is along this road. (Distance Approx 7.2 miles)

FACILITIES

1   Truckhaven (Esso)

Tel: (01524) 736699

0.2 miles west along the A601(M), on the left.

Access, Visa, Overdrive, All Star, Switch, Dial Card, Mastercard, Amex, Diners Club, Delta, AA Paytrak, Shell Gold, BP Supercharge, Esso Cards, Securicor Fuelserv, Keyfuels. Open; Mon-Thurs; 24hrs, Fri; 0.00-23.00hrs, Sat; 07.00-23.00hrs, Sun; 07.00-0.00hrs

2   Truckhaven Motel & Restaurant

Tel: (01524) 736699

0.2 miles west along the A601(M), on the left.

Restaurant Open; Mon-Thurs; 05.30-23.00hrs. Fri; 05.30-22.30hrs, Sat; 05.30-22.00hrs, Sun; 14.00-20.00hrs.

3   Norjac Garage (Shell)

Tel: (01524) 732208

1 mile south along the A6, on the right.

Access, Visa, Overdrive, All Star, Switch, Dial Card,

Mastercard, Amex, Diners Club, Delta, BP Agency, BP Supercharge, Shell Cards.

4   Morgano's French Restaurant

Tel: (01524) 730154

On north side of the roundabout adjacent to Junction 35A in the Pine Lake Resort.

Open; Breakfast; 09.00-10.30hrs daily, Lunch; 12.30-15.00hrs daily, Dinner; 18.00-21.30hrs daily

5   The Longlands Hotel

Tel: (01524) 781256

1 mile east along the A6070, on the right.

(Free House) Open all day. Meals served:12.00-14.30hrs & 17.30-21.00hrs.

6   The Eagles Head

Tel: (01524) 732457

1 mile east along the B6254, in Over Kellet, on the right.

(Free House) Open all day on Sat & Sun. Meals served; 12.00-14.00hrs & 18.30-21.00hrs daily

M6
BETWEEN JUNCS 35 & 36

BURTON IN KENDAL SERVICES (NORTHBOUND ONLY) (MOTO)
Tel: (01524) 781234 Burger King, Harry Ramsden's, Fresh Express Self-Service Restaurant, Travelodge & BP Fuel.

M6
JUNCTION 36

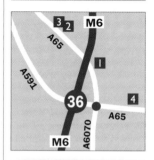

Nearest Northbound A&E Hospital

Westmorland General Hospital

Burton Road, Kendal LA9 7RG Tel: (01539) 732288

Take the A590 north exit and continue into the A591. Continue along the A6 and at the Onal Park roundabout turn south east along the A65 and the hospital is along this road. (Distance Approx 7.1 miles)

Nearest Southbound A&E Hospital

Royal Lancaster Infirmary

Ashton Road, Lancaster LA1 4RT Tel: (01524) 65944

Proceed to Junction 34 and take the A683 exit west. Continue along the A6 south and turn right at the roundabout along the A588. The hospital is along this road. (Distance Approx 14.8 miles)

FACILITIES

1   Canal Garage (Shell) & M6 Diesel Services (Independent)

Tel: (01539) 567280

0.6 miles north along the

A65, on the right.
LPG. Access, Visa, Overdrive,
All Star, Switch, Dial Card,
Mastercard, Amex, Diners Club,
Delta, Esso Europe, BP
Supercharge, BP Agency, IDS,
Securicor Fuelserv, UK
Fuelcard, Keyfuels, Shell Cards.

2   Crooklands Motor Company

Tel: (01539) 567414
0.9 miles north along the A65, on the right.
Mastercard, Delta, Visa, Switch,
Access. Open; Mon-Sat; 08.00-
18.00hrs. Attended Service.

3   Crooklands Hotel & Restaurant

Tel: (01539) 567432
1 mile north along the A65, on the right.
(Best Western) Boskins
Restaurant Open; 12.00-
14.00hrs daily, Fri & Sat;
18.30-21.00hrs (Light Snacks
available 14.00-18.00hrs
daily). Hayloft Restaurant
Open; 19.00-21.00hrs daily

4   Beckside B&B, 4 Nook Cottages

Tel: (01539) 567387
1 mile east along the A65, in Nook, on the left

PLACES OF INTEREST

Kendal

**Follow the A591 north
(Signposted 7.5 Miles)**
For details please see Junction
37 information.

Sizergh Castle (NT)

Sizergh Nr Kendal LA8 8AE
Tel: (01539) 560070

website:
www.nationaltrust.org.uk

Follow the A591 north. (4.6 Miles)
Home of the Strickland family
for over 750 years, the castle
reflects the turbulent history of
this part of the country. The
14thC pele tower contains
some exceptional Elizabethan
carved wooden chimney-pieces
and there is a good collection
of contemporary oak furniture
and portraits. The castle is
surrounded by handsome
gardens, including a beautiful
rock garden, and the estate
has flower-rich limestone
pastures and ancient
woodland. Gift Shop. Tea
Room. Limited disabled
access.

Kirkby Lonsdale

Kirkby Lonsdale Tourist
Information Office, 24 Main
Street, Kirkby Lonsdale
LA6 2AE Tel: (015242) 71437
website:
www.kirkbylonsdale.co.uk

**Follow the A65 east.
(Signposted 5.4 Miles)**
Now by-passed by the main
roads to the north it has
retained its character and
remains a very traditional and
handsome market town where
life still revolves around the
market place and the 600
years old cross. Thought to
have been settled by
marauding seafarers there is,
in the origin of its name, more
than a suggestion that Kirkby
Lonsdale has links with the
Danes. Visitors today will find
lovely Georgian buildings
crowding along the winding
main street with interesting
alleyways and courtyards to
discover, excellent shops to
browse in, and some wonderful
tea shops.

**KILLINGTON LAKE SERVICES
(SOUTHBOUND ONLY)
(ROADCHEF)**
Tel: (01539) 620739 Food Fayre
Self-Service Restaurant, Wimpy
Bar, Costa Coffee, Travel Inn & BP
Fuel

**THERE ARE NO FACILITIES
WITHIN ONE MILE OF THIS
JUNCTION**

**Nearest A&E Hospital
Westmorland General
Hospital**
Burton Road, Kendal
LA9 7RG
Tel: (01539) 732288
Take the A684 exit west and
after about 1 mile turn left
along an unclassified road.
Turn right at the end along the
B6254 and the hospital is
along this route. (Distance
Approx 6.1 miles)

PLACES OF INTEREST

Kendal

Kendal Tourist Information Office,
Town Hall, Highgate, Kendal
LA9 4DL. Tel: (01539) 725758
website: www.kendaltown.org.uk

**Follow the A684 west
(Signposted 6.3 Miles)**
Sited in the valley of the River
Kent, it was once one of the
most important woollen textile

centres of northern England. The Kendal woollen industry was founded in 1331 by John Kemp, a Flemish weaver, and it flourished until it was overtaken in the 19thC by the huge West Riding of Yorkshire mills. The town was also famous for its Kendal Bowmen, skilled archers who were instrumental in the defeat of the Scots at the Battle of Flodden Field in 1513. Once a bustling town, major traffic now by-passes it, the narrow streets of Highgate, Stramongate and Stricklandgate are still busy and the fine stagecoaching inns of the 17th & 18thC's, to which Prince Charles Edward is said to have retreated after his abortive 1745 rebellion, still line the streets. The numerous alleyways throughout the town are known as yards, a distinctive feature of Kendal inasmuch as they formed a series of defences for the townspeople against the threat of raids by the Scots. The ruins of Kendal Castle, high on a hill overlooking the town, stand on the site of one of the original Roman camps that guarded the route to the Scottish border, and Katherine Parr, the last of Henry VIII's six wives, lived at this castle in the 16thC before she was married. An exhibition at Kendal Museum of Natural History & Archaeology on Station Road (Tel: 01539-721374) tells the castle's story with computer interactives and reconstructions.

Sedbergh

Sedbergh Tourist Information Office, 72 Main Street, Sedbergh LA10 5AD Tel: (01539) 620125 website:
www.yorkshiredales.org.uk

Follow A684 west (Signposted 4.6 Miles)

This old market town, with its cobbled streets, was first granted a charter in 1251 to hold fairs and a market. The old norse name for the settlement here was "Setberg" meaning flat-topped hill which perfectly describes Sedbergh's location on top of the Howgill Fells. The old major routes, from Lancaster to Newcastle and Kendal to York, passed through the town and, during the 19thC, the town bustled with the constant stream of stage coaches. Today it is a focal point for the surrounding rural communities and much of the heart of the town, where many of the older buildings still survive, has been deemed a Conservation Area. Sedbergh lies within the boundaries of the Yorkshire Dales National Park and is a major National Park Centre.

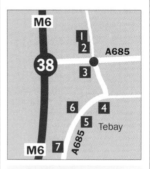

JUNCTION 38

Nearest Northbound A&E Hospital

Penrith New Hospital

Bridge Lane, Penrith
CA11 8HX
Tel: (01768) 245300
Proceed north to Junction 40 and take the A66 exit east. Turn left at the roundabout and the hospital is on the right. (Distance Approx 17 miles)

Nearest Southbound A&E Hospital

Westmorland General Hospital

Burton Road, Kendal
LA9 7RG
Tel: (01539) 732288
Proceed to Junction 37 and take the A684 exit west. After about 1 mile turn left along an unclassified road and then turn right at the end along the B6254. The hospital is in this road. (Distance Approx 14.5 miles)

FACILITIES

1   M6 Diesel Services (Independent)

Tel: (01539) 624336
0.1 miles north along the B6260, on the left.
LPG, Access, Visa, Overdrive, All Star, Switch, Dial Card, Mastercard, Diners Club, Delta, Routex, Securicor Fuelserv, Morgan Fuelcard, UK Fuelcard, IDS, Keyfuels, AS24.

2   Junction 38 Café

Tel: (01539) 624505
0.1 miles north along the B6260, on the left.
Open 24 hours daily (NB. Closed between Sat 17.30 & Sun 07.00hrs and Sun 22.30 & Mon 07.00hrs during winter season)

3   Primrose Cottage B&B

Tel: (01539) 624791
0.1 miles south along the A685, in Tebay, on the right

4   Public Toilets

WC

0.2 miles south along the A685, in Tebay, on the left

5 Carmel Guest House

Tel: (01539) 624651
0.3 miles south along the A685, in Tebay, on the left

6 Cross Keys Inn

Tel: (01539) 624240
0.4 miles south along the A685, in Tebay, on the right.
(Free House) Open all day Fri, Sat & Sun. Meals served; 12.00-14.30hrs & 18.00-21.00hrs daily.

7 Barnaby Rudge Tavern and B&B

Tel: (01539) 624328
0.9 miles south along the A685, in Tebay, on the right.
(Free House). Meals served; 12.00-14.00hrs & 19.00-21.00 hrs daily.

PLACES OF INTEREST

Kirkby Stephen

Kirkby Stephen Tourist Information Office, Market Street, Kirkby Stephen CA17 4QN
Tel: (017683) 71199
website: www.visiteden.org.uk

Follow the A685 east (Signposted 11.7 Miles)
Set amidst hills and heath-clad moors, intersected by upland valleys with small streams and on the pretty River Eden, it was the Norsemen who first established a village here. The Vikings named it "Kirke and bye", meaning churchtown and although it is essentially part of the Eden Valley, Kirkby Stephen has a strong Yorkshire Dales feel about it. The northern end of this delightful little town is dominated by the

13thC St Stephen's Church and between here and the market place stand the cloisters which served for a long time as a butter market. It gained some importance during the expansion of the railways in the 19thC, with the Settle and Carlisle line passing on the western side and the North Eastern Railway establishing an engine shed and large station within the town on its Darlington to Tebay line. Indeed much of today's A685 was built on the trackbed of the latter following its total closure in the 1970's.

M6 BETWEEN JUNCS 38 & 39

TEBAY SERVICES (NORTHBOUND) (WESTMORLAND LTD)
Tel: (01539) 624511 Restaurant, Coffee Shop, Westmorland Hotel, Coffee Bar & Texaco Fuel

TEBAY SERVICES (SOUTHBOUND) (WESTMORLAND LTD)
Tel: (01539) 624511 Restaurant & Texaco Fuel

A unique concept in motorway services with a philosophy based on home cooking and giving the traveller that something special. This independent company utilizes local produce, including some organic vegetables, and home ground spices to produce delicious English food as well as traditional Indian curries. The food is cooked to order outside of normal hours. Cakes and bread are freshly baked on the premises and barbecued steaks and burgers are a speciality.

M6 JUNCTION 39

THERE ARE NO FACILITIES WITHIN ONE MILE OF THIS JUNCTION

Nearest Northbound A&E Hospital
Penrith New Hospital
Bridge Lane, Penrith
CA11 8HX
Tel: (01768) 245300
Proceed north to Junction 40 and take the A66 exit east. Turn left at the roundabout and the hospital is on the right. (Distance Approx 12 miles)

Nearest Southbound A&E Hospital
Westmorland General Hospital
Burton Road, Kendal
LA9 7RG
Tel: (01539) 732288
Proceed to Junction 37 and take the A684 exit west. After about 1 mile turn left along an unclassified road and then turn right at the end along the B6254. The hospital is in this road. (Distance Approx 19.9 miles)

M6 JUNCTION 40

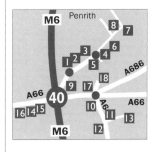

Nearest A&E Hospital

Penrith New Hospital

Bridge Lane, Penrith
CA11 8HX
Tel: (01768) 245300
Take the A66 exit east, turn left
at the roundabout along the A6
and the hospital is on the right.
(Distance Approx 0.7 miles)

FACILITIES

PENRITH TOWN CENTRE IS
WITHIN ONE MILE OF THIS
JUNCTION

**1 Mark Johns Motors
(Texaco)**

Tel: (01768) 892906
0.2 miles north along the
A592, on the left.
Access, Visa, Delta,
Mastercard, Switch, Diners
Club, Amex, Electron, Solo,
Overdrive, All Star, Dial Card,
Texaco Cards. Open; Mon-Fri;
07.00-21.00hrs, Sat; 07.00-
20.00hrs, Sun; 08.00-
20.00hrs.

**2 Red Rooster Road
Stop & Takeaway**

Tel: (01768) 895818
0.2 miles north along the
A592, on the left.
Open; Mon-Sat; 07.00-
18.00hrs, Sun; 08.00-
18.00hrs. (NB. Remains open
later during summer months)

**3 Davidsons Junction 40
(Esso)**

Tel: (01768) 867101
0.2 miles north along the
A592, on the left.
Bunkering of Diesel Fuel for
Commercial Vehicles Only. All
pumps are 24hr credit/fuel
card operated and most
bunkering cards are accepted.

4 Agricultural Hotel

Tel: (01768) 862622
0.6 miles north along the
A592, on the right.
(Jennings) Open all day. Meals
served; 12.00-14.00hrs &
18.00-20.30hrs daily

5 The Station Hotel

Tel: (01768) 866714
0.6 miles north along the
A592, on the right
(Free House)

**6 Safeway Filling
Station**

Tel: (01768) 867631
0.7 miles north along the
A592, on the right.
Access, Visa, Mastercard,
Switch, Amex, Electron, Solo,
Overdrive, All Star, Dial Card.
Open; Mon-Sat; 07.00-
22.00hrs, Sun; 08.00-
20.00hrs. Cash Machines
available in adjacent store

**7 Glen Cottage Hotel &
Restaurant**

Tel: (01768) 210826
1 mile north along the A592,
in Penrith, on the right.
Villa Bianca Restaurant
(Italian) Open (Summer);
12.00-14.00hrs & 18.00-
21.30hrs daily, (Winter); Mon-
Sat; 18.00-21.30hrs. Disabled
facilities in Restaurant.

8 The Royal Hotel

Tel: (01768) 862670
1 mile north along the A592,
in Penrith, on Wilson Row.
(Free House) Open all day.
Meals served; Mon-Fri; 12.00-
14.00hrs & 18.00-21.00 hrs.
Sat & Sun; 12.00-21.00hrs

**9 North Lakes Hotel &
Spa**

Tel: (01768) 868111
Adjacent to north side of the
roundabout at the junction.
Restaurant Open; Breakfast;
Mon-Fri; 07.30-09.30hrs, Sat &
Sun; 08.00-10.00hrs, Lunch;
Mon-Fri; 12.30-14.00hrs, Sat &
Sun; Closed, Dinner; Mon-Sat;
19.00-21.30hrs, Sun;19.00-
20.45hrs

10 Eamont House B&B

Tel: (01768) 863345
0.9 miles south along the A6,
in Eamont Bridge, on the right

11 The Beehive Inn

Tel: (01768) 862081
1 mile south along the A6, in
Eamont Bridge, on the left.
(Pubmaster) Open all day Sat &
Sun. Meals served; Mon-Sat;
Lunch; 12.00-15.00hrs,
Evening Meals; 18.00-
21.00hrs, Sun; 12.00-
21.00hrs.

12 The Crown

Tel: (01768) 892092
1 mile south along the A6, in
Eamont Bridge, on the right.
(Free House) Open all day Sat
& Sun. Meals served; Mon-Fri;
11.00-14.30hrs & 18.00-
21.00hrs, Sat; 11.00-21.00hrs,
Sun; 12.00-21.00hrs

13 Lowther Glen B&B

Tel: (01768) 864405
1 mile south along the A6, in
Eamont Bridge, in Lowther
Glen.

14 Little Chef

Tel: (01768) 868303
0.4 miles west along the A66,
on the left.
Open; 07.00-23.00hrs daily

15 Travelodge Penrith

Tel: (01768) 866958
0.4 miles west along the A66, on the left

16 Rheged Forecourt (Texaco)

Tel: (01768) 860023
0.6 miles west along the A66, on the left.

Access, Visa, Delta, Mastercard, Switch, Diners Club, Amex, Electron, Solo, Overdrive, All Star, Dial Card, Texaco Cards. Cash Machines in adjacent Rheged.

17 Bridge Lane Service Station (Esso)

Tel: (01768) 899303
0.8 miles north along the A6, on the left.

Access, Visa, Delta, Mastercard, Switch, Diners Club, Amex, Overdrive, All Star, Dial Card, Shell Gold, Esso Cards

18 Shell Penrith

Tel: (01768) 212900
1 mile north along the A6, on the right.

Access, Visa, Delta, Mastercard, Switch, Diners Club, Amex, Overdrive, All Star, Dial Card, BP Agency, BP Supercharge, Shell Cards.

PLACES OF INTEREST

Penrith

Penrith Tourist Information Office, Robinson's School, Middlegate, Penrith CA11 7PT
Tel: (01768) 867466
website: www.visiteden.co.uk

Follow the A592 east (Signposted 1 Mile)

The capital of the Kingdom of Cumbria in the 9th & 10thC's, it was ransacked by Scottish raiders in the 14thC and the evidence of its former vulnerability can still be seen in the charming mixture of narrow streets and wide open spaces, such as Great Dockray and Sandgate, into which cattle were herded during the raids. Penrith has a splendid Georgian church, St Andrew's, of Norman origin but extensively rebuilt between 1719 and 1772, surrounded by a number of interesting buildings.

The ruins of Penrith Castle bear witness to the town's importance in defending the surrounding countryside. It was built around 1399 and enlarged for the Duke of Gloucester, later Richard III, when he was Lord Warden of the Marches and responsible for keeping the peace along the borders. The castle has been in ruins since 1550 but still remains an impressive monument.

Within the town centre can be found...

Penrith Museum

Robinson's School, Middlegate, Penrith CA11 7PT
Tel: (01768) 212228
website: www.visiteden.co.uk

Set in a 300 year old school, the museum records the local history of Penrith and its surrounding area.

The Alpaca Centre

Snuff Mill Lane, Stainton, Penrith CA11 0HA
Tel: (01768) 891440 website: www.thealpacacentre.co.uk

Follow the A6 west, turn left along the A592 towards Ullswater and then second right (1.6 Miles)

This unique centre is located in rolling countryside near to Lake Ullswater and has been developed to expand the knowledge of the Alpaca, its products and viability as a farm animal for fibre production. The animals can be viewed from the edge of the paddock or from within the adjacent tea room. The "Spirit of Andes" shop has a wide variety of Alpaca goods and clothing for sale. Disabled Access.

Rheged

Redhills, Penrith CA11 0DQ
Tel: (01768) 868000
website; www.rheged.com

Follow the A66 west (Signposted 0.6 Miles)

Named after Cumbria's Celtic Kingdom, Rheged is Europe's largest grass covered building and international award-winning day out. Three giant movies are shown daily on a cinema screen as big as six double decker buses! Rheged – The Movie is a dramatic journey of myths, legends and spectacular views of Cumbria - The Lake District, while Everest – The Movie is a breathtaking journey to the top of the world and Shackleton's Antarctic Adventure is simply the greatest survival story of all time.

Everest – The Movie is also the perfect introduction to The Helly Hansen National Mountaineering Exhibition (permanent) also at Rheged. This celebration of Britain's illustrious mountaineering history includes original 1953 Everest footage and the Mallory and Irvine collection. There is free parking and entry to this breathtaking building, where you will also find the finest in local craft and gift shops, pottery demonstrations, Artists' Exhibitions, a Restaurant, an indoor children's play area and a 24 hour Texaco petrol forecourt and Shop.

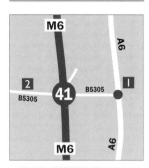

JUNCTION 41

Nearest A&E Hospital

Penrith New Hospital

Bridge Lane, Penrith
CA11 8HX
Tel: (01768) 245300
Proceed south to Junction 40
and take the A66 east. Turn
left at the roundabout and the
hospital is on the right.
(Distance Approx 3.9 miles)

FACILITIES

1   Stoneybeck Inn

Tel: (01768) 862369
**1 mile east along the B5305,
at the junction with the A6.**
(Free House) Open all day on
Sun. Lunch; 12.00-14.20hrs,
Evening Meals; 18.00-
21.00hrs daily.

**2   Woodlands Garage
(Texaco)**

Tel: (01768) 864019
**0.3 miles west along the
B5305, on the right.**
Access, Visa, Delta,
Mastercard, Switch, Diners
Club, Amex, Electron, Solo,
Overdrive, All Star, Dial Card.
Open; Mon-Fri; 08.30-
18.00hrs, Sat; 08.30-13.00hrs,

Sun; Closed. (NB. Attended
service available if required.)

PLACES OF INTEREST

Hutton-in-the-Forest

Penrith CA11 9TH
Tel: (017684) 84449
**Follow the B5305 towards
Wigton. (Signposted from
motorway, 2.1 Miles)**
The romantic and historic
home of Lord and Lady
Inglewood, dating from the
14thC when it was originally
built as a pele tower.
Alterations and additions over
the centuries, both inside and
out, show a varying range of
architectural styles with the
long gallery, unusual in a north
of England home, dating from
the 1630's whilst the hall of
c1680 is dominated by the
Cupid Staircase. Many of the
upstairs rooms date from the
mid-18th and 19thC's and the
house features fine collections
of furniture, tapestries,
portraits and ceramics. The
grounds, set in the mediaeval
Forest of Inglewood, include a
beautiful 18thC walled garden,
17thC topiary terraces and an
extensive Victorian woodland
walk. Tea Room. Gift Shop.
Limited disabled access.

BETWEEN JUNCS 41 & 42

**SOUTHWAITE SERVICES
(NORTHBOUND) (MOTO)**
Tel: (01697) 473476
Burger King, Harry Ramsden's,
Fresh Express Self-Service
Restaurant & Esso Fuel

**SOUTHWAITE SERVICES
(SOUTHBOUND) (MOTO)**
Tel: (01697) 473476
Little Chef, Burger King, Harry
Ramsden's, Fresh Express Self-
Service Restaurant, Travelodge &
Esso Fuel

**FOOTBRIDGE AND VEHICLE
BRIDGE CONNECTION
BETWEEN SITES.**

JUNCTION 42

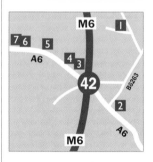

Nearest A&E Hospital

Cumberland Infirmary

Newtown Road, Carlisle
CA2 7HY
Tel: (01228) 523444
Take the A6 north into Carlisle,
bear right at the end following
the route to the A7 north and
at the roundabout turn left
along the A595 towards
Cockermouth. After about 0.6
miles bear right along the
B5307 and the hospital is on
the right hand side of this road.
(Distance Approx 5 miles)

FACILITIES

1   Lowther Arms

Tel: (01228) 560905
**1 mile north along the B6263,
in Cumwhinton, on the left in
Garlands Road.**

(Free House) Meals served; Tues-Sun; 12.00-14.00hrs & 18.00-21.00hrs

2 Exelby Services (BP) & Transport Café

Tel: (01228) 542766
0.1 miles south along the A6, on the left.
Red Diesel. Access, Visa, Delta, Mastercard, Switch, Diners Club, Amex, Overdrive, All Star, Dial Card, Routex, UK Fuelcard, Securicor Fuelserv, IDS, Keyfuels, Total/Fina/Elf Cards, BP Cards. Food is available in the Transport Café; Mon-Fri; 07.00-19.00hrs.

3 Border Gate

Tel: (01228) 532073
0.1 miles north along the A6, on the right.
(Brewer's Fayre) Open all day. Meals served; Mon-Fri; 07.00-09.00hrs & 12.00-22.00hrs, Sat & Sun; 08.00-10.00hrs & 12.00-22.00hrs

4 Travel Inn

Tel: (01228) 532073
0.1 miles north along the A6, on the right.

5 Carleton Filling Station (BP)

Tel: (01228) 592479
0.5 miles north along the A6, on the right.
Access, Visa, Delta, Mastercard, Switch, Diners Club, Amex, Overdrive, All Star, Dial Card, Routex, UK Fuelcard, Securicor Fuelserv, Shell Agency, BP Cards. Open; Mon-Sat; 07.00-22.00hrs, Sun; 08.00-22.00hrs.

6 The Green Bank

Tel: (01228) 528846

0.9 miles north along the A6, on the right.
(Scottish & Newcastle) Open all day. Meals served; Mon-Fri; 12.00-13.00hrs & 18.00-20.00hrs, Sat & Sun; 12.00-14.00hrs & 18.00-20.00hrs

7 Dhaka Tandoori Restaurant

Tel: (01228) 523855
0.9 miles north along the A6, on the right.
Open; Mon-Sat; 18.00-23.30hrs, Sun; 12.00-23.30hrs

PLACES OF INTEREST

Carlisle

Carlisle Tourist Information Centre, Old Town Hall, Greenmarket, Carlisle CA3 8JH Tel: (01228) 625600 website: www.historic-carlisle.org.uk

Follow the A6 north (Signposted 4.1 Miles)
A great Roman centre, and the military base for the Petriana Regiment, Luguvalium, as Carlisle was known during this period, also became a major civilian settlement with fountains, mosaics, statues and centrally heated homes. There is an extensive collection of Roman remains, from both the city and the Cumbrian section of Hadrians Wall in the Tullie House Museum & Art Gallery in Castle Street (Tel: 01228-534781).

There has been a castle at Carlisle since at least 1092 when William Rufus first built a palisaded fort but there was almost certainly a fortress prior to this, and Roman times, as the name of the city comes from the Celtic "Caer Lue", hill fort. Like many great mediaeval cities, Carlisle was surrounded by walls

and the best place to view these 11thC structures is in a street called West Walls, at the bottom of Sally Port Steps and near the Tithe Barn. Many fine buildings still remain, including the Guildhall of 1407, now a museum (Tel: 01228-534781), Carlisle Cathedral, founded in 1122 (Tel: 01228-548151) and the Old Town Hall of the 17thC and now in use as the Tourist Information Centre.

Within the city can be found ...

Carlisle Castle

Castle Way, Carlisle CA3 8UR Tel: (01228) 591922 website: www.historic-carlisle.org.uk

During the Scottish occupation in the 12thC, King David laid out a new castle with stone removed from Hadrian's Wall and the keep can still be seen, enclosed by massive inner and outer walls. The present castle is entered though a 14thC gatehouse, complete with portculis, and contains a maze of vaulted passages, chambers, staircases, towers and dungeons. It was beseiged for eight months during the Civil War by the Parliamentarians under General Leslie and after it was captured the castle was repaired and rebuilt utilizing stone from the adjacent Cathedral. Indeed some six out of the eight bays were used rendering Carlisle Cathedral to one of the smallest in England. Today the castle also contains the King's Own Royal Border Regiment Museum. Gift Shop. Limited disabled access.

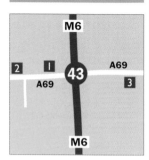

JUNCTION 43

Nearest A&E Hospital
Cumberland Infirmary
Newtown Road, Carlisle
CA2 7HY
Tel: (01228) 523444
Take the A69 west into Carlisle, turn right at the end and left at the roundabout along the A595 towards Cockermouth. After about 0.6 miles bear right along the B5307 and the hospital is on the right hand side of this road. (Distance Approx 3 miles)

FACILITIES

1   Tesco Filling Station

Tel: (01228) 600400
0.2 miles west along the A69, on the right.
Access, Visa, Overdrive, All Star, Switch, Dial Card, Mastercard, Amex, Delta. Disabled Toilets and Cash Machines available in adjacent store (Open 24 hours)

2   Brunton Park Service Station (Esso)

Tel: (01228) 528715
0.7 miles west along the A69, on the right.
Access, Visa, Delta, Mastercard, Switch, Diners Club, Amex, Overdrive, All Star,

Dial Card, Shell Gold, Shell Agency BP Supercharge, Esso Cards. Open; 06.00-0.00hrs daily

3   The Waterloo

Tel: (01228) 513347
0.6 miles east along the A69, on the right.
(Inn Partnership) Meals served; 12.00-14.30hrs & 19.00-20.45 daily.

PLACES OF INTEREST

Carlisle
Follow the A69 west (Signposted 2.3 Miles)
For details please see Junction 42 information

Within the city can be found ...

Carlisle Castle
Castle Way, Carlisle CA3 8UR
For details please see Junction 42 information

JUNCTION 44

Nearest A&E Hospital
Cumberland Infirmary
Newtown Road, Carlisle
CA2 7HY
Tel: (01228) 523444

Take the A7 south into Carlisle, cross the river and turn right along the A595. After about 0.6 miles bear right along the B5307 and the hospital is on the right hand side of this road. (Distance Approx 3 miles)

FACILITIES

1   Holiday Inn, Carlisle

Tel: 0870 400 9018
0.1 miles south along the A7, on the right. (NB. Entrance in Parkhouse Lane).
Traders Bar & Grill Open; Breakfast; Mon-Fri; 06.30-10.00hrs, Sat & Sun; 07.00-11.00hrs, Lunch; Sun-Fri; 12.00-14.30hrs, Dinner; Mon-Sat; 18.30-22.30hrs, Sun; 18.30-22.00hrs

2   BP Kingstown Filling Station (BP)

Tel; (01228) 523031
0.3 miles south along the A7, on the right.
LPG. Access, Visa, Delta, Mastercard, Switch, Diners Club, Amex, Electron, Solo, Overdrive, All Star, Dial Card, Shell Agency, UK Fuels, BP Cards. Food on the Move Café. Open; 06.00-22.00hrs daily.

3   The Kingstown Hotel & Steak House

Tel: (01228) 515292
0.5 miles south along the A7, on the left.
Steak House Restaurant Open; Sat & Sun; 19.00-22.00hrs (Pre-booking only)

4   The Coach & Horses

Tel: (01228) 525535
0.5 miles south along the A7, on the left.
(Scottish & Newcastle) Open all

day. Meals served; Mon-Sat; 12.00-14.00hrs & 18.30-21.00hrs, Sun; 12.00-14.30hrs & 18.30-21.00hrs.

5   Newfield Grange Motel & Restaurant

Tel: (01228) 819926
0.7 miles south along the A7, in Newfield Drive, on the left.
Restaurant Open; 18.00-22.00hrs daily

6   Gosling Bridge

Tel: (01228) 515294
0.9 miles south along the A7, on the left.
(Scottish & Newcastle) Open all day. Meals served all day; Sun-Thurs; 12.00-21.30hrs, Fri & Sat; 12.00-22.00hrs.

7   Premier Lodge

Tel: (01228) 515294
0.9 miles south along the A7, on the left

8   McDonald's

Tel: (01228) 512701
0.3 miles west along Parkhouse Road, on the left.
Open; Mon-Thurs; 07.30-21.00hrs, Fri & Sat; 07.30-23.00hrs, Sun; 08.00-21.00hrs

9   BP Truckstop Motel

Tel: (01228) 534192
0.4 miles west along Parkhouse Road, in Kingstown Industrial Estate, on the left

10   BP Truckstop

Tel (01228) 534192
0.4 miles west along Parkhouse Road, in Kingstown Industrial Estate, on the left.
Red Diesel & Diesel Fuel only.
Access, Visa, Delta,

Mastercard, Switch, Diners Club, Amex, Electron, Solo, Overdrive, All Star, Dial Card, Routex, UK Fuelcard, Securicor Fuelserv, Keyfuels, BP Cards

11   Asda Carlisle Filling Station

Tel: (01228) 526550
0.6 miles west along Parkhouse Road, on the left.
Access, Visa, Delta, Mastercard, Switch, Diners Club, Amex, Overdrive, All Star, Dial Card, Asda Cards. Disabled Toilets available in adjacent store during opening hours. Open; Mon-Sat; 07.00-22.00hrs, Sun; 09.00-16.30hrs.

12   Harker Service Station

Tel: (01228) 674274
0.6 miles north along the A7, on the left.
Access, Visa, Delta, Mastercard, Switch, Electron, Solo, Routex, UK Fuelcard, Securicor Fuelserv, AS24. Open; Mon-Fri; 07.30-20.00hrs, Sat; 08.00-18.00hrs, Sun; 09.00-18.00hrs. (NB Diesel Fuel available on 24 hour card operated pumps)

13   The Hill Cottage B&B

0.8 miles north along the A7, on the right

14   The Steadings B&B

Tel: (01228) 523019
0.9 miles east along the A689, on the right

PLACES OF INTEREST

Carlisle

Follow the A7 south (Signposted 2.1 Miles)

For details please see Junction 42 information

Within the city can be found ...

Carlisle Castle

Castle Way, Carlisle CA3 8UR

For details please see Junction 42 information

Solway Aviation Museum

Carlisle Airport, Carlisle CA6 4NW Tel: (01228) 573823 website: www.solway-aviation-museum.org.uk

Follow the A689 east (Signposted 6.4 Miles)
The recently expanded outdoor collection now includes examples of a Canberra bomber, a Vampire, a Sea Prince, a Phantom bomber, a Vulcan B2 bomber, a Meteor night fighter, an English Electric Lightning, a Westland helicopter and a Nimrod nose section. The indoor museum with displays of a wartime airfield and an air raid shelter amongst numerous exhibits now forms part of the Edward Houghey Aviation Heritage Centre. Gift Shop. Café and Restaurant. Picnic Area. Disabled Access.

MOTORWAY ENDS
(Total length of motorway 225.2 miles)

the **M11**

This motorway, which was completed in 1980, forms the major route from London to Cambridge and Newmarket. Commencing at Junction 4 where it connects with the North Circular Road (A406) in Woodford, the motorway heads north past the **Woodford Green AC Sports Ground** on the east side and passes under the Woodford to Newbury Park tube line before reaching Loughton and the magnificent ancient hornbeam coppice of **Epping Forest** on the west side of Junction 5.

Continuing north, the motorway passes under the M25 at Junction 6 and between Junctions 7 and 8 by-passes the "new town" of **Harlow**, a lively and vibrant town with some very good museums and several sites of historic interest and **Bishop's Stortford** on the west side. Of ancient origin, Bishop's Stortford was originally known as "Esterteferd" and when it was sold in 1060 to the Bishops of London it became "Bishop's Esterteferd", later corrupted to the present spelling. **Hatfield Forest**, a Royal deer park since Tudor times, is on the east side of the carriageway at the north end of this section. At Junction 8 a road connection, which is being significantly upgraded, is made with London's third airport, **Stansted**, to the east of the motorway. Along this section, the former **Great Eastern Railway London to Cambridge** line runs alongside the carriageways to the east and approaching Junction 9, **Saffron Walden** is passed on the same side. The ancient town of Saffron Walden was known as "Waledana" by Ancient Britons, and takes the rest of its name from the Saffron Crocus, utilized as a dye and condiment in mediaeval times.

As it continues to head north the motorway passes **Duxford Airfield**, formerly a World War II airbase and now an Imperial War Museum site, on the west side of Junction 10, and then, approaching Junction 11, crosses the Hitchin to Cambridge railway line and bridges the River Granta. It by-passes the city of **Cambridge** on the east side between Junctions 10 and 13, bridging the River Cam (originally known as the River Grant) just after Junction 11. Cambridge began as an early British primitive fort on a low hill north of the current town centre and it subsequently flourished as a market and river trading centre but it was not until after the arrival of students fleeing the Oxford riots of 1209 that Cambridge was established as a university town. The motorway ends at Junction 14 and forms an end-on connection with the A14 to Huntingdon and the A1 north.

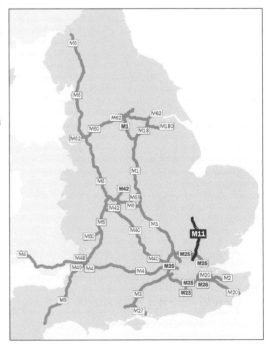

Location of Places of Interest

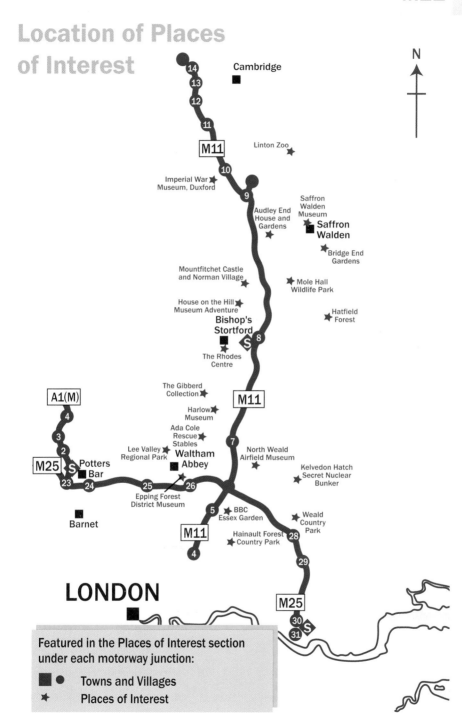

N

14
13
12
11

M11

Cambridge

Linton Zoo

10

Imperial War
Museum, Duxford

9

Audley End
House and
Gardens

Saffron
Walden
Museum

**Saffron
Walden**

Bridge End
Gardens

Mountfitchet Castle
and Norman Village

Mole Hall
Wildlife Park

House on the Hill
Museum Adventure

**Bishop's
Stortford**

Hatfield
Forest

8

S

The Rhodes
Centre

The Gibberd
Collection

M11

A1(M)

4

Harlow
Museum

Ada Cole
Rescue
Stables

3

2

Lee Valley
Regional Park

**Waltham
Abbey**

7

North Weald
Airfield Museum

M25

S

Potters
Bar

Kelvedon Hatch
Secret Nuclear
Bunker

23

24

25

26

Epping Forest
District Museum

5

BBC
Essex Garden

Weald
Country
Park

28

Barnet

M11

Hainault Forest
Country Park

4

29

LONDON

M25

30

31

S

Featured in the Places of Interest section
under each motorway junction:

■ ●   Towns and Villages

✶   Places of Interest

M11

JUNCTION 4

THIS IS A RESTRICTED ACCESS JUNCTION.

■ Vehicles can not access the northbound carriageways from the A1400

■ Vehicles can not exit to the A1400 from the southbound carriageways

Nearest A&E Hospital

King George's Hospital

Barley Lane, Goodmayes, Ilford IG3 8YB

Tel: (020) 8983 8000

Follow the A406 south and, at the first exit, turn left along the A12 (Signposted along A12. Distance Approx 2.3 miles)

JUNCTION 5

THIS IS A RESTRICTED ACCESS JUNCTION.

■ Vehicles can not access the northbound carriageways.

■ Vehicles can not exit from the southbound carriageways

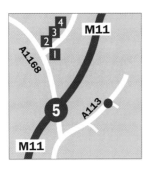

Nearest Northbound A&E Hospital

Princess Alexandra Hospital

Hamstel Road, Harlow CM20 1QX

Tel: (01279) 444455

Proceed north to Junction 7 and it is signposted along the A414 north. (Distance Approx 11.3 miles)

Nearest Southbound A&E Hospital

King George's Hospital

Barley Lane, Goodmayes, Ilford IG3 8YB

Tel: (020) 8983 8000

Proceed south to Junction 4, follow the A406 south and, at the first exit, turn left along the A12 (Signposted along A12. Distance Approx 6.2 miles)

FACILITIES

1   Chigwell Express (BP)

Tel: (020) 8502 0687

0.4 miles north along the A1168, on the right

Access, Visa, Mastercard, Switch, Diners Club, Amex, Overdrive, All Star, Dial Card, Delta, UK Fuelcard, BP Cards, Shell Agency.

2   Sir Winston Churchill

Tel: (020) 8508 7160

0.4 miles north along the A1168, on the right

(Scottish & Newcastle) Open all day. Meals served; 11.00-21.00hrs daily.

3   Taste of Raj

Tel: (020) 8508 6493

0.5 miles north along The Broadway, on the left

Open; 18.00-23.00hrs daily

4   El Kaz Taberna

Tel: (020) 8502 0440

0.5 miles north along The Broadway, on the left

Open; Sun-Thurs; 15.00-0.00hrs, Fri & Sat; 12.00-01.00hrs.

PLACES OF INTEREST

BBC Essex Garden

Crowther Nurseries, Ongar Road, Abridge RM4 1AA

Tel: (01708) 688581

Follow the A113 north into Abridge (3.3 Miles)

A working garden consisting of a vegetable plot, two small greenhouses, herbaceous and shrub border and over 400 varieties of clematis. There is an adjoining plant nursery and a number of farmyard animals are on the site. Shop. Café. Lego Corner. Partial disabled access.

Hainault Forest Country Park

Romford Road, Chigwell IG7 4QN

Tel: (020) 8500 7353

Follow the A113 north and turn right along the A112. (Signposted along route. 4 Miles)

Visit the rare breeds farm, enjoy a stroll or just relax alongside of the lake, all located within over 600 acres of ancient woodland. Various workshops and events throughout the year. Picnic Areas. Visitor & Interpretation Centre. Café. Varying disabled access.

JUNCTION 6

THIS JUNCTION IS A MOTORWAY INTERCHANGE WITH THE M25 ONLY AND THERE IS NO ACCESS TO ANY FACILITIES.

Nearest Northbound A&E Hospital

Princess Alexandra Hospital

Hamstel Road, Harlow
CM20 1QX
Tel: (01279) 444455

Proceed north to Junction 7 and it is signposted along the A414 north. (Distance Approx 8.0 miles)

Nearest Southbound A&E Hospital

King George's Hospital

Barley Lane, Goodmayes, Ilford IG3 8YB
Tel: (020) 8983 8000

Proceed south to Junction 4, follow the A406 south and, at the first exit, turn left along the A12 (Signposted along A12. Distance Approx 9.6 miles)

JUNCTION 7

Nearest A&E Hospital

Princess Alexandra Hospital

Hamstel Road, Harlow
CM20 1QX
Tel: (01279) 444455

Signposted from Junction along A414 north. (Distance Approx 3.3 miles)

FACILITIES

1 The Rainbow & Dove

Tel: (01279) 415419

0.4 miles north along Hastingwood Road on the left
(Inn Business) Meals served; 12.00-14.30 hrs & 19.00-21.00hrs daily

2 McDonald's

Tel: (01279) 454367

0.1 miles south along the B1393, on the left
Open; 07.00-23.00hrs daily

3 Cross Keys Café

1 mile south along the B1393, on the left
Open; Mon-Fri; 07.00-14.00hrs, Sat & Sun; 07.00-15.00hrs

4 Shell Harlow

Tel: (01279) 635980

0.4 miles north along the A414, on the left
LPG. Access, Visa, Mastercard, Switch, Diners Club, Amex, Overdrive, All Star, Dial Card, Shell Cards, BP Cards, Esso Cards.

5 Little Chef

Tel: (01279) 417057

0.4 miles north along the A414, on the left
Open; 07.00-22.00hrs daily

6 BP Connect Harlow Gate Service Station

Tel: (01279) 432391

0.4 miles north along the A414, on the right
Access, Visa, Overdrive, All Star, Switch, Dial Card, Mastercard, Amex, AA Paytrak, Diners Club, Delta, Routex. Shell Agency, BP Cards. Wild Bean Café.

7 The Gatekeeper

Tel: (01279) 424495

0.5 miles north along the A414, on the right.
(Beefeater) Open all day. Restaurant Open; Mon-Sat; 12.00-22.30hrs, Sun; 12.00-21.00hrs. Bar Meals served; 12.00-22.00hrs daily.

8 Moat House Hotel

Tel: (01279) 829988

1 mile north along the A414, on the left
Restaurant Open; Breakfast; 07.00-10.00hrs daily, Lunch; Sun-Fri; 12.30-13.45 daily, Dinner; 19.00-21.45hrs daily.

PLACES OF INTEREST

North Weald Airfield Museum

Ad Astra House, Hurricane Way, North Weald Bassett CM16 6AA
Tel: (01992) 523010

Follow the A414 south and turn right towards North Weald Bassett (2.7 Miles)

Devoted to the history of the airfield from 1916 to date, the museum contains photographs, records and artefacts, such as uniforms, as well as a video exhibit detailing a day to day account of life at North Weald. Guided tours of the site can be arranged for large groups and veteran aircraft fly from the airfield from time to time.

The Gibberd Collection

The Town Hall, The High, Harlow CM20 1HJ
Tel: (01279) 446763

Follow the A414 into Harlow (2.7 Miles)
Founded by Sir Frederick Gibberd, planner of Harlow New Town, the Gibberd Collection of British watercolours, as well as showing works by the founder also exhibits paintings by Blackadder, Sutherland, Nash and Frink. Disabled access.

Also within the town centre ...

Harlow Museum

Passmores House, Third Avenue, Harlow CM18 6YL
Tel: (01279) 454959

Occupying a Georgian house and set within picturesque gardens which include a lovely pond, the museum has extensive and important Roman, post-mediaeval and early 20thC collections as well as a full programme of temporary exhibitions. Gift Shop. Some disabled access.

Ada Cole Rescue Stables

Broadlands, Nazeing, Nr Waltham Abbey EN9 2DH
Tel: (01992) 892133 website: www.adacolestables.sagenet.co.uk

Follow the A414 towards Harlow, turn left along the A1169 and then left along the B1133 to Nazeing (Signposted in Nazeing 4.3 miles)
Founded in 1932 in memory of Ada Cole, a pioneer campaigner for equine justice,

Broadlands is a centre for the rescue, rehabilitation and, eventual, safe re-homing of ponies, horses, donkeys and mules. The facilities for visitors include a Pets Corner, Visitors Centre, shop and café and there is the opportunity to join a scheme to sponsor some of the animals that are unsuitable for re-homing

Nearest Northbound A&E Hospital

Addenbrookes Hospital
Hills Road, Cambridge CB2 2QQ
Tel: (01223) 245151
Proceed to Junction 11, follow the A1309 north, turn right along the A1134 and it is signposted along this route (Distance Approx 24.5 miles)

Nearest Southbound A&E Hospital

Princess Alexandra Hospital
Hamstel Road, Harlow CM20 1QX
Tel: (01279) 444455
Proceed south to Junction 7 and it is signposted along the A414 north. (Distance Approx 12.9 miles)

FACILITIES

BIRCHANGER GREEN SERVICES (WELCOME BREAK)
Tel: (01279) 653388
Granary Restaurant, Red Hen Restaurant, KFC, Burger King, Caffe Primo, Welcome Lodge and Shell Fuel.

1   Start Hill Service Station (Esso)

Tel: (01279) 503959
0.1 miles east along the A120, on the left
Access, Visa, Mastercard, Switch, Diners Club, Amex, Overdrive, All Star, Dial Card, Delta, BP Supercharge, Esso Cards, Shell Cards.

2   Great Hallingbury Manor B&B

Tel: (01279) 506475
0.4 miles south along the Great Hallingbury Road, on the left

3   Yew Tree Farm Guest House

Tel: (01279) 758875
0.4 miles south along the Great Hallingbury Road, on the right

4   The Hop Poles

Tel: (01279) 757042
1 mile south along the Great Hallingbury Road, on the left
(Free House) Meals served; 12.00-14.00hrs & 18.00-21.00hrs daily

5   The Three Willows Birchanger
Tel: (01279) 815913
1 mile north along the A414, on the right

6 Stansted Manor Hotel

Tel: (01279) 859800
0.2 miles west along the
A120, on the right
Restaurant Open; Breakfast;
07.00-09.30hrs, Lunch; 12.00-
14.30hrs, Dinner; 19.30-
22.00hrs daily

7 The Nag's Head

Tel: (01279) 654553
0.9 miles west along the
A1250, on the left
(Punch Retail) Open all day.
Meals served; Mon-Sat; 11.00-
22.00hrs, Sun; 12.00-
22.00hrs

8 Pearse House

Tel: (01279) 757400
0.6 miles west along
Parsonage Lane, on the left

PLACES OF INTEREST

Bishop's Stortford

Tourist Information Office, The Old
Monastery, Windhill, Bishop's
Stortford CM23 2ND Tel: (01799)
510444

**Follow the A1250 west
(Signposted 2.4 Miles)**
Of ancient origin it was
originally known as
"Esterteferd" and may have
been named after the family or
small clan who controlled the
crossing here. The town which
grew up at the ford became the
site of Waytemore Castle on an
artificial 42ft high mound and
one of the fortifications
reputedly constructed by
Edward the Elder (d924AD) to
protect the countryside from
the invading Danes. This was
improved by William the

Conqueror and survived for
over 500 years before being
demolished, the remains of
which can be seen in the
Castle Gardens.

The town itself was sold in
1060 to the Bishops of London
and became known as Bishop's
Esterteferd, later corrupted to the
present spelling of Bishop's
Stortford. The development of the
town's two traditional industries,
malting and brewing, was greatly
aided by the completion of the
Stort Navigation in 1769 and the
location of the town on the route
between Cambridge, Newmarket
and London ensured a healthy
economy with numerous
hostelries and inns catering for
stage-coach travel. Today there is
much to see in the town dating
from those times, several of the
old inns are still in business, as
well as a rich collection of 16thC
and 17thC buildings.

Within the town can be found ...

The Rhodes Centre

South Road, Bishop's Stortford
CM23 3JG Tel: (01279) 651746

Opened by the Cecil Rhodes
Birthplace Trust in 1938 to
commemorate the life and
times of Bishop's Stortford's
most famous son, it is situated
in two early Victorian houses
known as Netteswell and
Thorley Bourne. Born in 1853,
Cecil Rhodes was one of the
nine children of the Rev
William Francis and Louisa
and, within its seventeen
rooms, the museum details his
early life in the town as well as
his career in Africa culminating
in the establishment of
Rhodesia. Shop.

Mountfitchet Castle & Norman Village

Stansted Mountfitchet CM24 8SP
Tel: (01279) 813237 website:
www.gold.enta.net

**Follow the A120 west
(Signposted 3.3 Miles)**
The original castle was built
here in 1066 by William the
Conquerer and the motte and
bailey structure has been
reconstructed, along with the
Norman village, to
demonstrate how life was in
those times. There are siege
weapons on view, including two
giant catapults, and visitors are
able to climb to the top of the
siege tower as well as mingle
with the many domestic
animals that wander through
the site. Picnic area. Gift Shop.
Café. Disabled access.

Sited adjacent to the Castle ...

House on the Hill Museum Adventure

Stansted Mountfitchet CM24 8SP
Tel: (01279) 813237
website: www.gold.enta.net

As well as housing the world's
largest toy museum, with over
50,000 toys from Victorian
times to the 1970s on display,
there is also a hands-on
exhibition of Vintage
Amusement and Slot Machines
and a display of memorabilia
of stars from the music and
entertainment world. Gift
Shop. Collectors Shop (Tel:
01279-813567).

Mole Hall Wildlife Park

Widdington, Nr Newport, Saffron
Walden CB11 3SS
Tel: (01799) 540400 website:
http://www.molehall.co.uk

**Follow the A120 west and
turn right along the B1383
(Signposted 9.2 miles)**
Contained within nearly 20
acres and surrounding a
private fully moated 13thC
manor house, the park
features a fascinating range of
wild and domestic animals
from across the world. Of
especial interest are the

Formosa Sika Deer, which are extinct in the wild, llamas, flamigos, chimpanzees, muntjac, wallabies and otters as well as many other species. There is also a tropical Butterfly Pavilion which, apart from butterflies, also houses lovebirds, small monkeys, snakes, spiders and there are small pools accommodating goldfish, toads and terrapins. Deer Safari Rides. Picnic Area. Café. Gift Shop. Some disabled access.

Hatfield Forest [NT]

Takeley, Bishop's Stortford CM22 6NE
Tel: (01279) 870678 e-mail: ahdurs@smtp.ntrust.org.uk

Follow the A120 east and it is signposted in Takeley (2.5 Miles)

A rare surviving example of a mediaeval Royal Hunting forest, it comprises of nearly 1,000 acres of ancient coppice woodland, grassland with magnificent pollarded trees, two ornamental lakes, a stream and marsh reserve as well as the 18thC Shell House. Of great historical and ecological importance, it is designated as a Site of Special Scientific Interest and a National Nature Reserve, there are excellent walks through the estate and good fishing to be had at the lakes. Café. Disabled access (Electric buggy available if booked in advance)

Audley End House & Gardens

Audley End, Saffron Walden CB11 4JS Tel: (01799) 522399

Follow the A120 west and turn right along the B1383 (Signposted 10.0 Miles)

For details please see Junction 9 information

JUNCTION 9

THIS IS A RESTRICTED ACCESS JUNCTION.
- Vehicles can not access the northbound carriageways.
- Vehicles can not exit from the southbound carriageways

Nearest Northbound A&E Hospital
Addenbrookes Hospital
Hills Road, Cambridge CB2 2QQ
Tel: (01223) 245151
Proceed to Junction 11, follow the A1309 north, turn right along the A1134 and it is signposted along this route (Distance Approx 10.7 miles)

Nearest Southbound A&E Hospital
Princess Alexandra Hospital
Hamstel Road, Harlow CM20 1QX
Tel: (01279) 444455
Proceed south to Junction 7 and it is signposted along the A414 north. (Distance Approx 26.6 miles)

FACILITIES

1   The Crown House Hotel & Restaurant

Tel: (01799) 530515
0.8 miles south along the B1383, on the left in Great Chesterford
Restaurant Open; Breakfast; Mon-Fri; 07.00-09.00, Sat & Sun; 08.00-09.30hrs, Lunch; 12.00-14.00hrs daily, Dinner; 19.00-21.00hrs daily.

2   Crown & Thistle
Tel: (01799) 530278
1 mile south along South Street, on the right in Great Chesterford
(Pubmaster) Meals served; Mon-Sat; 12.00-14.30hrs & 19.00-21.30hrs, Sun; 12.30-15.00hrs

3   Plough
Tel: (01799) 530283
1 mile south along High Street in Great Chesterford
(Greene King) Open all day Sat & Sun. Meals served; Mon-Sat; 12.00-14.30hrs & 18.30-20.30hrs, Sun; 12.00-14.30hrs & 19.00-20.30hrs.

PLACES OF INTEREST

Saffron Walden

Tourist Information Office, 1 Market Place, Market Square, Saffron Walden CB10 1HR
Tel: (01799) 510444

Follow the B184 south (Signposted 4.5 Miles)

Known as "Waledana" by Ancient Britons, there are remnants of their extensive earthwork fortifications around the town; The "Paille" or "Battle Ditches", an ancient encampment of about 30 acres, yielded no less than 180 skeletons of Saxon origin during 19thC digs and, on the common, is the best surviving earth maze in England. These mazes were once numerous but only eight now survive, their origin and use are obscure and are thought to be pre-Christian and connected to early fertility rites.

The Normans constructed a castle here in the 12thC on the foundations of a Saxon fortress and the remains of the keep are on view adjacent to the museum on Castle Hill. The town takes the rest of its name from the Saffron Crocus, utilized as a dye and condiment and the growing of which was the most important industry from the time of Edward III through to the end of the 18thC. A large part of the town, and the street plan, dates from the Middle Ages and many fine timbered buildings with overhanging upper floors and pargetting, still survive from this period.

Within the town can be found ...

Saffron Walden Museum

Museum Street, Saffron Walden
CB10 1JL
Tel: (01799) 510333

Opened in 1835 "to gratify the inclination of all who value natural history", it traces the history of the area both from archaeological and from natural history perspectives. Exhibits include; The Earth Beneath Your Feet, looking at local fossils, rocks and minerals; The Discovery Centre, a woodland display of British wildlife; Worlds of Man, showing articles from the peoples of other continents and Ages of Man, a gallery tracing the history and archaeology of the area. Disabled access.

Bridge End Gardens

Bridge Street, Saffron Walden

A fine example of an early Victorian garden, Bridge End

Gardens are a tranquil and attractive oasis in the centre of the town. The Victorian Hedge Maze, which has been completely replanted and faithfully copies the original design, can be visited by appointment (Please contact the TIC).

Linton Zoo

Hadstock Road, Linton
CB1 6NT Tel: (01223) 891308

Follow the A11 north and it is signposted along the route (7.4 Miles)

Set in 16 acres of spectacular gardens, Linton Zoo is a major wildlife breeding centre and part of the inter-zoo breeding programme for endangered species. The collections include wild cats, birds, snakes and insects and for children there are quiz trails, pony rides, a bouncy castle and a play area. Picnic areas. Café. Disabled access

Audley End House & Gardens

Audley End, Saffron Walden CB11 4JS Tel: (01799) 522399

Follow the B1383 south (Signposted 6.4 Miles)

Originally the site of the Benedictine Abbey of Walden, following the Dissolution it was given to Lord Audley by Henry VIII and he built a house in the grounds. When Lord Howard of Walden, 1st Earl of Suffolk, inherited the estate in 1603 he commenced construction of a great Jacobean House which eventually consisted of two large courts built around the ruins of the monastery.

After the Restoration of the Monarchy, Charles II acquired the house but this was restored to the Howards in 1701 and in 1721 the 5th Earl commissioned the architect Sir John Vanbrugh to re-model it. On his advice the outer court was demolished and the

interior modified, but following these alterations the building slowly deteriorated until Lord Braybrooke restored it between 1762 and 1797 and this is the condition in which it is seen today. Considered to be one of the most magnificent houses in England with the Great Hall and Robert Adam's Painted Drawing Room just two of the architectural highlights, there are also fine paintings by Holbein, Lely and Canaletto to be seen.

There is a natural history collection of over 1,000 stuffed animals and birds and the superb gardens, created by "Capability" Brown, include a lake and "Temple of Concord" to George II in which visitors are able to stroll, picnic or just relax. Parterre Restaurant. Shop. Disabled access to grounds, facilities and ground floor of house.

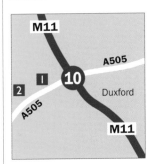

JUNCTION 10

Nearest Northbound A&E Hospital

Addenbrookes Hospital
Hills Road, Cambridge
CB2 2QQ
Tel: (01223) 245151

Proceed to Junction 10, follow the A1309 north, turn right along the A1134 and it is signposted along this route (Distance Approx 7.4 miles)

Nearest Southbound A&E Hospital

Princess Alexandra Hospital

Hamstel Road, Harlow
CM20 1QX
Tel: (01279) 444455

Proceed south to Junction 7 and it is signposted along the A414 north. (Distance Approx 29.9 miles)

FACILITIES

1 Aerodrome Service Station (Texaco)

 WC £

Tel: (01223) 499100

0.4 miles west along the A505, on the right

Access, Visa, Mastercard, Switch, Diners Club, Amex, Overdrive, All Star, Dial Card, Delta, UK Fuelcard, Securicor Fuelserv, Keyfuels, Fast Fuel, Texaco Cards. Open; Mon-Sat; 06.00-20.00hrs, Sun; 06.30-20.00hrs

2 Duxford Service Station (Total)

 WC

Tel: (01223) 832412

0.7 miles west along the A505, on the right

Visa, Mastercard, Switch, Diners Club, Amex, All Star, Dial Card, Delta, AA Paytrak, BP Cards, Total/Fina/Elf Cards, Open; Mon-Fri; 06.30-21.00hrs, Sat; 07.00-21.00hrs, Sun; 08.00-20.00hrs.

PLACES OF INTEREST

Imperial War Museum Duxford

Duxford Cambridge CB2 4QR Tel: (01223) 835000
website: www.iwm.org.uk

Follow the A505 west (0.3 Miles)

Europe's premier aviation museum with over 400,000 visitors annually, Duxford was an active airfield throughout WWII and the site perpetuates this period with preserved hangars, control tower and Operations Room forming the heart of the 85 acre complex. There are over 7 acres of indoor exhibition space and 180 historic aircraft are on show with special features that include the "Battle of Britain" Exhibition, The American Air Museum and The Land Warfare Hall. There are regular air shows and special events throughout the year and visitors are able to view historic aircraft restoration as it is undertaken. Picnic Site. Self-Service Restaurant. Shop. Disabled access.

Audley End House & Gardens

Audley End, Saffron Walden CB11 4JS Tel: (01799) 522399

Follow the A505 east (Signposted 10.5 Miles)

For details please see Junction 9 information

Saffron Walden

Tourist Information Office, 1 Market Place, Market Square, Saffron Walden CB10 1HR Tel: (01799) 510444

Follow the A505 east and turn right along the A1301 (Signposted 8.9 Miles)

For details please see Junction 9 information

Linton Zoo

Hadstock Road, Linton CB1 6NT Tel: (01223) 891308

Follow the A505 east (Signposted 8.0 Miles)

For details please see Junction 9 information

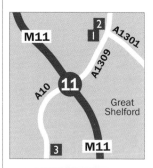

Nearest A&E Hospital

Addenbrookes Hospital

Hills Road, Cambridge
CB2 2QQ
Tel: (01223) 245151

Follow the A1309 north, turn right along the A1134 and it is signposted along this route (Distance Approx 2.8 miles)

FACILITIES

1 Waitrose Café

Tel: (01223) 845777

0.9 miles north along the A1309, on the left in Trumpington

Open; Mon-Thurs; 08.30-19.30hrs, Fri; 08.30-20.30hrs, Sat; 08.00-19.30hrs, Sun; 10.00-15.30hrs. Cash Machine in adjacent store.

2 Shell Trumpington

Tel: (01223) 846990

1 mile north along the A1309, on the left in Trumpington

Access, Visa, Mastercard, Switch, Diners Club, Amex, Overdrive, All Star, Dial Card, Delta, Shell Cards, Esso Cards. Open; 06.00-0.00hrs daily

3 Old English Gentleman

Tel: (01223) 870287

1 mile south along the A10, on the left in Harston

(Pubmaster) Meals Served; Mon-Sat; 12.00-14.00hrs, Sun; 12.00-15.00hrs. Thurs Steak Night; 18.30-22.00hrs.

PLACES OF INTEREST

Cambridge

Tourist Information Office, Wheeler Street, Cambridge CB2 3QB Tel: (01223) 322640

Follow the A1309 north (Signposted 3.8 Miles)

This historic university town began as a primitive fort on a low hill north of the current town centre and the early British name was "Caer Grant" (Fort by River Grant). The Saxons translated this as "Grantcaester", then it was changed to "Grante-bryege" and over a period of time this was eventually corrupted to Cambridge and from this the river became known as the Cam at some time around 1600.

Standing at the point where the forest met the fen, and at the lowest fording point of the river, it was settled by an Iron Age Belgic tribe, then the Romans, Saxons and subsequently the Normans who built a wooden motte and bailey castle. This was rebuilt in stone by Edward I but all that now remains is the 40ft high mound upon which it stood. The town flourished as a market and river trading centre but it was not until after the arrival of students fleeing the Oxford riots of 1209 that Cambridge was established as a University town.

The first college, Peterhouse, was founded by the Bishop of Ely in 1281 and by the end of the following century, Clare, Pembroke, Gonville & Caius, Trinity Hall and Corpus Christi Colleges had been formed and today there are now 31 with the most recent, Robinson College, the gift of self-made millionaire Mr David Robinson. The town abounds in historical buildings of wide architectural styles and periods and all the Colleges are well worth a visit with "unmissable" locations such as Kings College Chapel, The Great Court in Trinity College and Pepys Library in Magdalene College as well as a host of world-class museums.

JUNCTION 12

Nearest A&E Hospital

Addenbrookes Hospital

Hills Road, Cambridge CB2 2QQ Tel: (01223) 245151

Proceed south to Junction 11, follow the A1309 north, turn right along the A1134 and it is signposted along this route (Distance Approx 5.1 miles)

1 The Rupert Brooke

Tel: (01223) 840295

1 mile south along the Trumpington Road on the left, in Grantchester.

(Laurel Pub Company) Open all day Sat & Sun. Meals served; 12.00-14.30hrs & 18.30-21.30hrs daily

2 Burwash Manor Farm Tea Rooms

Tel: (01223) 264821

0.7 miles west along the Barton Road on the left.

Open; Mon-Fri; 10.00-16.30hrs, Sat; 10.00-17.00hrs, Sun; 11.00-17.00hrs.

3 White Horse

Tel: (01223) 262327

1 mile south along the A603, on the right.

(Greene King) Open all day. Meals served; 11.30-21.30hrs daily.

4 Wallis & Son (Q8)

Tel: (01223) 263911

1 mile south along the A603, on the left.

LPG. Access, Visa, Overdrive, All Star, Switch, Dial Card, Mastercard, Amex, Diners Club, Delta, Routex. Q8 Card. Open; 07.00-23.00hrs daily.

PLACES OF INTEREST

Cambridge

Follow A603 east (Signposted 3.2 Miles)

For details please see Junction 11 information.

M11
JUNCTION 13

THIS IS A RESTRICTED
ACCESS JUNCTION.
- Vehicles can not access the
northbound carriageways.
- Vehicles can not exit from the
southbound carriageways

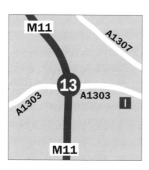

Nearest A&E Hospital

Addenbrookes Hospital

Hills Road, Cambridge
CB2 2QQ
Tel: (01223) 245151

Proceed south to Junction 11,
follow the A1309 north, turn
right along the A1134 and it is
signposted along this route
(Distance Approx 7.0 miles)

FACILITIES

1   McDonald's

Tel: (01223) 366753
1 mile east along the A1303,
on the right
Open; Mon-Sat; 08.00-
23.00hrs, Sun; 10.00-23.00hrs

PLACES OF INTEREST

Cambridge

Follow the A1303 east
(Signposted 2.2 Miles)
For details please see Junction
11 information.

M11
JUNCTION 14

THIS IS A RESTRICTED
ACCESS JUNCTION.
- Vehicles can not exit along the
A45 [W] or A1307 from the
northbound carriageways.
- Vehicles can not access the
southbound carriageways from
the A45 [E] or A1307

Nearest A&E Hospital

Addenbrookes Hospital

Hills Road, Cambridge
CB2 2QQ
Tel: (01223) 245151

Proceed south to Junction 11,
follow the A1309 north, turn
right along the A1134 and it is
signposted along this route
(Distance Approx 8.5 miles)

FACILITIES

THERE ARE NO FACILITIES
WITHIN ONE MILE OF THE
JUNCTION

MOTORWAY ENDS
(Total Length of Motorway 49.1
Miles)

the M18

When originally opened in November 1967, the M18 just provided the short, but important, link between the M1 at Junction 32 and the A1 (M) at Wadworth, south west of Doncaster. By the end of 1978 it had been extended north east to by-pass Doncaster along the west side, link up with the M180 to Scunthorpe and terminate with a connection to the M62 at Junction 7.Commencing with its connection with Junction 32 of the M1 at Thurcroft, to the east of Sheffield, the motorway heads north west, and by-passes **Rotherham**, a town with a long association with the engineering industry, to the west of Junction 1 before slipping between the 472ft high **Birchwood Hill** at Maltby (close to the dramatic ruins of **Roche Abbey**) to the east and the 467ft high **Conisbrough Park** and the 11thC **Conisborough Castle** which boasts the oldest circular keep in England, on the north side. The carriageways then turn north eastwards as

Museum of South Yorkshire Life, Doncaster

they veer through **Edlington** and **Wadworth Woods** before reaching Junction 2 where they cross the A1 (M) by means of the **Wadworth Viaduct**. This structure was the final part of the motorway to be completed when the viaduct opened in December 1978.

The motorway continues eastwards past Junction 3 before passing the **Rossington Main Colliery** to the south and bridging the **East Coast Main Line**. It then swings north around the south east corner of Doncaster, slips under the Doncaster to Gainsborough line and passes the remains of **Cantley Windmill**, in view on the east side before reaching Junction 4. **Doncaster** was known as "Danum" during the Roman occupation, the site having been chosen as it was the lowest crossing point over the River Don. In more recent times it was the location of the Railway Works of the Great Northern Railway which are still open and have the distinction of producing some of the finest steam engines ever built. This reputation culminated in the pre-World War II construction of the A4 Class of locomotives, a member of which No.4468 "Mallard" holds the world speed record for a steam locomotive of 126 mph. Doncaster Racecourse on Town Moor has hosted the St Leger classic horse race since 1776.

Continuing northwards the motorway connects with the M180 at Junction 5, and crosses the **Stainforth & Keadby Canal**, which opened in 1802 as part of the Sheffield & South Yorkshire Navigations, to join up with the River Trent at Keadby. It passes Thorne on the east side of junction 6 and then traverses **Dikes Marsh and Reedholme Common** before bridging the **Aire & Calder Navigation** at Junction 7. The Aire & Calder Navigation was constructed in the 1790s to connect the West Riding of Yorkshire to the River Ouse at Goole. It was modernized in the 1970s and is now capable of handling 700 tons vessels. Here the M18 ends with a connection to the M62.

Location of Places of Interest

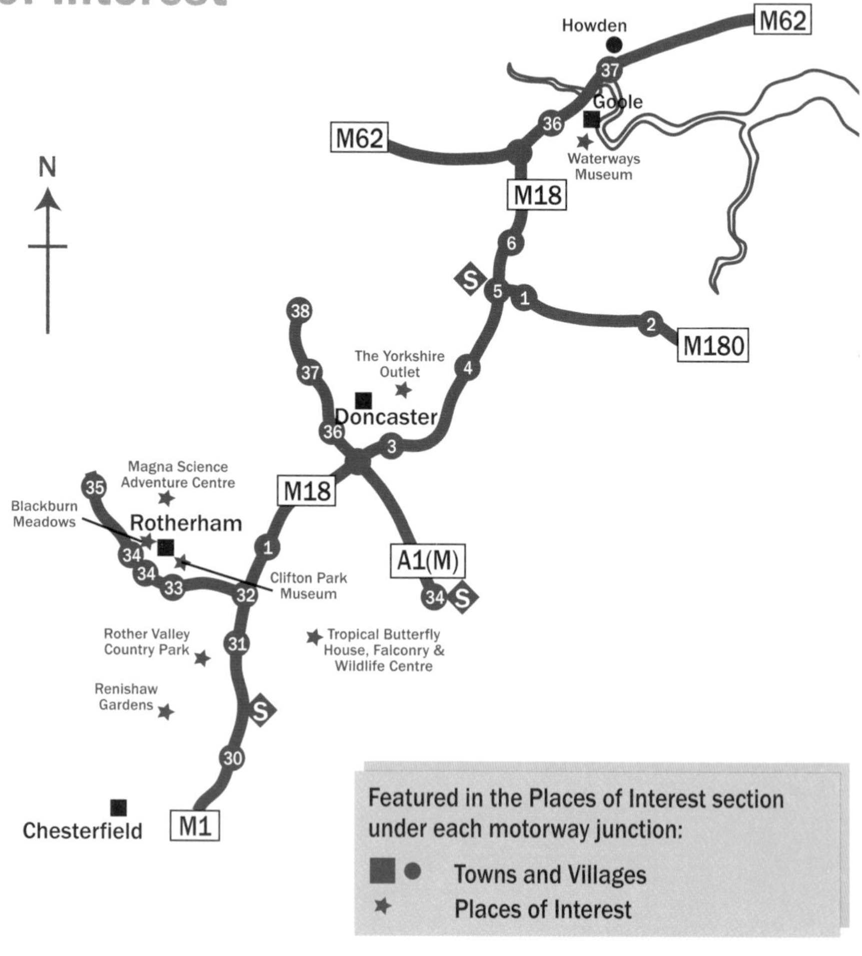

Featured in the Places of Interest section under each motorway junction:

■ ●   Towns and Villages

★   Places of Interest

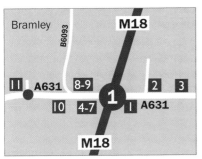

JUNCTION 1

Bramley
B6093
M18

A631 8-9
10 4-7 1 I A631

M18

Nearest A&E Hospital
Rotherham District General Hospital
Moorgate Road, Rotherham
S60 2UD
Tel: (01709) 820000
Follow the A631 west, turn right along Moorgate Road (A618) and the hospital is on the left. (Distance Approx 4 miles)

FACILITIES

1 Steering Wheel Service Station (Total)

Tel: (01709) 546494
0.1 miles east along the A631, on the right
LPG. Access, Visa, Overdrive, All Star, Switch, Dial Card, Mastercard, Amex, AA Paytrak, Diners Club, Delta, BP Supercharge, Electron, Solo, Total/Fina/Elf Cards.

2 Hellaby Hall Hotel

Tel: (01709) 702701
0.4 miles east along the A631, on the left
The Attic Restaurant Open; Breakfast; Mon-Fri; 07.00-09.00hrs, Sat & Sun; 08.00-10.00hrs, Lunch; Sun-Fri;

12.00-14.00hrs, Dinner; 19.00-22.00hrs daily. The Italian Restaurant Open; Lunch; Tues-Sat; 12.00-14.00hrs, Dinner; 18.00-22.00hrs daily

3 Save Retail Service Station

Tel: (01709) 813307
0.8 miles east along the A631, on the left
Access, Visa, Overdrive, All Star, Switch, Dial Card, Mastercard, Amex, Delta, Electron, Solo, Save Card. Open; 06.00-23.00hrs daily

4 Ibis Hotel

Tel: (01709) 730333
Adjacent to west side of roundabout
Bar Meals available 12.00-22.00hrs daily

5 Sir Jack

Tel: (01709) 530306
0.1 miles west along the A631, on the left
(Free House) Open all day. Meals served; Mon-Sat; 12.00-22.00hrs, Sun; 12.00-21.30hrs

6 McDonald's

Tel: (01709) 700344
0.1 miles west along the A631, on the left
Open; 07.00-0.00hrs daily

7 Morrison's Filling Station
Tel: (01709) 780150
0.2 miles west along the

A631, on the left
Access, Visa, Delta, Mastercard, Switch, Amex, Electron, Solo, Overdrive, Dial Card. Disabled Toilets and Cash Machines available in adjacent store. Open; Mon-Fri; 06.30-22.30hrs, Sat; 07.00-22.00hrs, Sun; 08.00-22.00hrs.

8 White Rose Filling Station (Total)

Tel: (01709) 702758
0.2 miles west along the A631, on the right
Access, Visa, Overdrive, All Star, Switch, Mastercard, Amex, Diners Club, Delta, Electron, Solo, Total/Fina/Elf Cards. Open; 05.00-23.00hrs daily

9 Little Chef

Tel: (01709) 545466
0.2 miles west along the A631, on the right
Open; 07.00-22.00hrs daily

10 The Travellers

Tel: (01709) 704341
0.4 miles west along the A631, on the left
(Voyager) Open all day. Meals served; Mon-Thurs; 12.00-14.00 & 17.30-20.30hrs, Fri & Sat; 12.00-14.00hrs & 17.00-20.00hrs, Sun; 12.00-15.00hrs

11 Masons Arms
Tel: (01709) 542223
1 mile west along the A631, on the right
(Laurel Pub Company) Open all day Mon-Sat. Meals served; Mon; 12.00-14.30hrs, Tues-Thurs; 12.00-14.30hrs & 18.00-19.45hrs, Fri & Sat; 12.00-14.30hrs & 18.00-20.45hrs

PLACES OF INTEREST

Rotherham

Follow the A631 west (Signposted 4.1 Miles)

For details please see Junction 33 [M1] information.

Within the town can be found ...

The Chapel of our Lady

Rotherham Bridge, Rotherham S60 1QJ

For details please see Junction 33 [M1] information.

Clifton Park Museum

Clifton Lane, Rotherham S60 2AA

For details please see Junction 33 [M1] information.

JUNCTION 2

THIS JUNCTION IS A MOTORWAY INTERCHANGE WITH THE A1 (M) ONLY AND THERE IS NO ACCESS TO ANY FACILITIES

Nearest Northbound A&E Hospital

Doncaster Royal Infirmary

Armthorpe Road, Doncaster DN2 5LT

Tel: (01302) 366666

Proceed north to Junction 3, follow the A6182 north, turn right along the A18 and at the second roundabout turn left along Armthorpe Road and the hospital is signposted. (Distance Approx 7 miles)

Nearest Southbound A&E Hospital

Rotherham District General Hospital

Moorgate Road, Rotherham S60 2UD

Tel: (01709) 820000

Proceed south to Junction 1, follow the A631 west, turn right along Moorgate Road (A618) and the hospital is on the left. (Distance Approx 10 miles)

Nearest A&E Hospital

Doncaster Royal Infirmary

Armthorpe Road, Doncaster DN2 5LT

Tel: (01302) 366666

Follow the A6182 north, turn right along the A18 and at the second roundabout turn left along Armthorpe Road and the hospital is signposted. (Distance Approx 5.7 miles)

FACILITIES

1   Pizza Hut

Tel: (01302) 366690

1 mile north in The Yorkshire Outlet

Open; 11.30-23.00hrs daily

2   McDonald's

Tel: (01302) 321593

1 mile north in The Yorkshire Outlet

Open; 07.00-22.00hrs daily

3   The Lakeside

Tel: (01302) 361134

1 mile north in The Yorkshire Outlet

(Beefeater) Open all day. Meals served; Mon-Sat; 12.00-22.00hrs, Sun; 12.00-21.00hrs

4   Travel Inn

Tel: (01302) 361134

1 mile north in The Yorkshire Outlet

PLACES OF INTEREST

The Yorkshire Outlet

White Rose Way, Doncaster Lakeside DN4 5JH

Tel: (01302) 366444 website; www.theyorkshireoutletcentre.co.uk

Follow the A6182 north (Signposted 1 mile)

A modern shopping centre with over 40 stores and shops including a coffee bar. Children's Play Area. Disabled access.

JUNCTION 3

THERE ARE NO FACILITIES WITHIN ONE MILE OF THIS JUNCTION

Nearest A&E Hospital

Doncaster Royal Infirmary

Armthorpe Road, Doncaster
DN2 5LT Tel: (01302)
366666

Follow the A630 west, continue
along the A18, turn right at the
second roundabout along
Armthorpe Road and the
hospital is signposted.
(Distance Approx 5 miles)

M18 JUNCTION 5

THIS JUNCTION IS A
MOTORWAY INTERCHANGE
WITH THE M180 ONLY AND,
APART FROM DONCASTER
SERVICES, THERE IS NO
ACCESS TO ANY FACILITIES

Nearest Eastbound A&E Hospital (Via M180)

Scunthorpe General Hospital

Cliff Gardens, Scunthorpe
DN15 7BH
Tel: (01724) 282282

Proceed east to Junction 3
(M180), follow the M181 north
and turn right along the A18
(Signposted. Distance Approx
15.6 miles)

Nearest Eastbound A&E Hospital (Via M62)

Goole & District Hospital

Woodland Avenue, Goole
DN14 6RX
Tel: (01724) 282282

Proceed to Junction 36 (M62)
and follow the A614 east
(Signposted. Distance Approx
11.2 miles)

Nearest Westbound A&E Hospital (Via M62)

Pontefract General Infirmary

Friarwood Lane, Pontefract
WF8 1PL

Tel: (01977) 600600

Proceed to Junction 33 (M62),
follow the A1 north and turn
left along the A628.
(Signposted in town. Distance
Approx 21.6 miles)

Nearest Southbound A&E Hospital

Doncaster Royal Infirmary

Armthorpe Road, Doncaster
DN2 5LT
Tel: (01302) 366666

Proceed south to Junction 4,
follow the A630 west, continue
along the A18, turn right at the
second roundabout along
Armthorpe Road and the
hospital is signposted.
(Distance Approx 9.1 miles)

FACILITIES

**DONCASTER (NORTH)
SERVICES (MOTO)**
Tel: (01302) 847700
**Fresh Express Self Serve
Restaurant, Burger King,
Travelodge & BP Fuel**

M18 JUNCTION 6

THORNE IS WITHIN ONE MILE
OF THIS JUNCTION

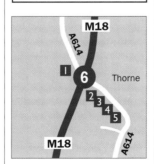

Nearest Eastbound A&E Hospital (Via M62)

Goole & District Hospital

Woodland Avenue, Goole
DN14 6RX
Tel: (01724) 282282

Proceed to Junction 36 (M62)
and follow the A614 east
(Signposted. Distance Approx
9.3 miles)

Nearest Westbound A&E Hospital (Via M62)

Pontefract General Infirmary

Friarwood Lane, Pontefract
WF8 1PL
Tel: (01977) 600600

Proceed to Junction 33 (M62),
follow the A1 north and turn
left along the A628.
(Signposted in town. Distance
Approx 19.7 miles)

Nearest Southbound A&E Hospital

Doncaster Royal Infirmary

Armthorpe Road, Doncaster
DN2 5LT
Tel: (01302) 366666

Proceed south to Junction 4,
follow the A630 west, continue
along the A18, turn right at the
second roundabout along
Armthorpe Road and the
hospital is signposted.
(Distance Approx 11 miles)

FACILITIES

1   The John Bull Inn

Tel: (01405) 814677
**Adjacent to the west side of
the roundabout**
(Free House) Open all day.
Meals served; Mon-Thurs;
12.00-14.00hrs & 18.00-
21.00hrs, Fri-Sun; 12.00-
14.30hrs & 18.00-21.00hrs

2   Smalleys Garage (Q8)

Tel: (01405) 812110
0.3 miles south along the A614, on the right
Access, Visa, Overdrive, All Star, Switch, Dial Card, Mastercard, Delta, Electron, Solo, BP Supercharge, Q8 Cards. Open; Mon-Fri; 08.00-20.00hrs, Sat; 08.00-19.00hrs, Sun; 09.00-16.00hrs

3   The Delves Café

Tel: (07929) 003436
0.4 miles south along the A614, on the right
Open; Mon-Fri; 08.00-17.30hrs, Sat & Sun; 07.00-17.30hrs

4   Adams Garage (Independent)

Tel: (01405) 812345
0.6 miles south along the A614, on the right in Thorne
Access, Visa, Overdrive, All Star, Switch, Dial Card, Mastercard, Amex, Delta, Electron, Solo. Open; Mon-Sat; 07.00-20.00hrs, Sun; 08.00-20.00hrs

5   The Gate Tea Rooms

Tel: (01405) 813634
0.8 miles south along the A614, on the right in Thorne
Open; Mon-Sat; 09.00-16.00hrs

M18
JUNCTION 7

THIS JUNCTION IS A MOTORWAY INTERCHANGE WITH THE M62 ONLY AND THERE IS NO ACCESS TO ANY FACILITIES

Nearest Eastbound A&E Hospital (Via M62)
Goole & District Hospital
Woodland Avenue, Goole
DN14 6RX
Tel: (01724) 282282
Proceed to Junction 36 (M62) and follow the A614 east (Signposted. Distance Approx 4.6 miles)

Nearest Westbound A&E Hospital (Via M62)
Pontefract General Infirmary
Friarwood Lane, Pontefract
WF8 1PL
Tel: (01977) 600600
Proceed to Junction 33 (M62), follow the A1 north and turn left along the A628. (Signposted in town. Distance Approx 15 miles)

Nearest Southbound A&E Hospital
Doncaster Royal Infirmary, Armthorpe Road, Doncaster
DN2 5LT
Tel: (01302) 366666
Proceed south to Junction 4, follow the A630 west, continue along the A18, turn right at the second roundabout along Armthorpe Road and the hospital is signposted. (Distance Approx 15.7 miles)

MOTORWAY MERGES WITH THE M62
(Total Length of Motorway 26.7 Miles)

the **M20** and **M26 spur**

Commenced in 1958 but not completed until 1991, the 50.1 miles long M20 was originally built to link the Channel Ferry ports of Dover and Folkestone with the M25. The 8 miles long M26 opened in 1980 to facilitate a more direct route for eastbound traffic off the M25.

Originating at Junction 1 (Junction 3 of the M25), the motorway heads south east with the north edge of the **Kent Downs** on the south side and passes along the north side of **Brands Hatch Race Track**. Brands Hatch opened in 1926 as a bicycle track and it was not until 1960 that it hosted a Grand Prix motor race. Jim Clark was the first driver to achieve a 100 mph average lap here on his way to winning the 1964 European GP. The

Leeds Castle

Grand Prix track is currently 2.6 miles long and the Indy Circuit is 1.2 miles. The M26 (running from Junction 5 of the M25) merges from the west at Junction 3 as the motorway veers eastwards and continues to Junction 5 where **Aylesford** is on the north side. Aylesford was the site of a great battle in 455AD between the Jutes, led by Hengist and Horsa, and the ancient Britons.

Between Junctions 6 and 7 the carriageways pass Maidstone on the south side and, on the north side, between here and Junction 13, the **Channel Tunnel Rail Link** (described in the M2 section) runs alongside the carriageways. **Maidstone** is the former capital of West Kent and straddles the River Medway. It grew up on the site of an important meeting place and has retained many Elizabethan and Georgian buildings. It is here that the distinction between "Kentish Man" and "Man of Kent" is made, with the former living to the west of the river and the latter to the east. The motorway between Junctions 4 and 7, the Maidstone By-pass, opened in September 1961 and was the first part of the M20 to be completed, but the 14 miles section from Junctions 7 to 9, following the southern edge of the Kent Downs, was shelved from the original project and not constructed for another thirty years.

Between Junctions 9 and 10 the town of **Ashford** is on the south side. Ashford was referred to in Shakespeare and the town is proud to be the home of the first volunteer Fire Service in the country formed in 1826. Continuing eastwards the motorway passes **Folkestone Racecourse** just before Junction 11 on the south side and the **Channel Tunnel Terminal** can be seen on

Folkestone Harbour

the north side just past Junction 11A. Folkestone Racecourse was established in 1898 and is located at Westenhanger, site of the former headquarters of Queen Elizabeth I's Kent army. The **Channel Tunnel Rail Link's Cheriton Depot**, which opened in 1992, is on the north side of Junction 12 and **Folkestone** is to the south as the motorway ends at Junction 13 and makes an end-on connection with the A20 to Dover. Folkestone, the site of an ancient fort, is principally an Edwardian town with the unusual feature of possessing a series of cliff top lawns and gardens rather than a traditional seafront.

Location of Places of Interest

N

M25
St John's Jerusalem
Eynsford and Lullingstone
M20
Trosley Country Park
1 Rochester
2
Faversham
4 Lullingstone Park Visitor Centre
Coldrum Long Barrow
Aylesford 3
4 S
5
2 3 4
Museum of Kent Life
M2
6 7
M26
5 6 7
M25 5
Maidstone Museum and Art Gallery
S
8
Manor Park Country Park
West Malling
Tyrwhitt-Drake Museum of Carriages
Maidstone
Sevenoaks
Knole
Leeds Castle
M20
9
Kent Battle of Britain Museum
10
Port Lympne Wild Animal Park and Garden
11 11A 12 13
Folkestone
Romney, Hythe and Dymchurch Railway
Hythe

Featured in the Places of Interest section under each motorway junction:

■ ● Towns and Villages
✱ Places of Interest

M26 SPUR — JUNCTION 2A

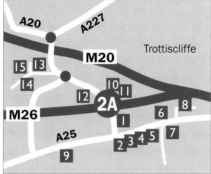

Nearest Eastbound A&E Hospital

Maidstone Hospital
Hermitage Lane, Maidstone
ME16 9QQ
Tel: (01622) 729000
Follow the A26 east and turn right along the B2246 (Signposted. Distance approx 8.2 Miles)

Nearest Westbound A&E Hospital (Via M25)

East Surrey Hospital
Canada Avenue, Redhill RH1 5RH
Tel: (01737) 768511
Proceed west to Junction 6 (M25) and follow the B2235 south. Turn right along the A25 into Redhill, turn left along the A23 and the hospital is signposted along this route. (Distance Approx 25.4 miles)

Nearest Minor Injury Unit

Sevenoaks Hospital
Hospital Road, Sevenoaks TN13 3PG
Tel: (01732) 455155
Follow the A25 west into Sevenoaks and the hospital is on the south side, at the end of Bradbourne Vale Rd. Opening Hours; 08.00-20.00hrs daily. (Distance Approx 7.4 miles)

FACILITIES

1   Forte Posthouse Maidstone/Sevenoaks
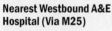
Tel: 0870 400 9054

0.1 miles south along the A20 on the left
Restaurant Open; Breakfast; Mon-Fri; 06.30-09.30hrs, Sat & Sun; 07.30-10.30hrs, Lunch; 12.30-14.30hrs daily, Dinner; 17.30-22.30hrs daily

2   Ming Chinese Restaurant

Tel: (01732) 883427
0.3 miles east along the A20 on the right
Open; Mon-Sat; 12.00-14.30hrs & 18.00-23.00hrs, Sun; 12.30-14.30hrs & 18.00-23.00hrs

3   Royal Oak

Tel: (01732) 884214
0.3 miles east along the A20 on the right
(Beefeater) Open all day. Restaurant Open; Mon-Fri; 12.00-14.00hrs & 18.00-22.00hrs, Sat; 12.00-22.00hrs, Sun; 12.00-21.00hrs. Bar meals served; 12.00-22.00hrs daily.

4   Travel Inn

Tel: (01732) 884214
0.3 miles east along the A20 on the right

5   Save Service Station (Save)

Tel: (01732) 987378
0.4 miles east along the A20 on the right
Securicor Fuelserv, Access, Visa, Overdrive, All Star, Switch, Dial Card, Mastercard, Amex, Diners Club, Delta.

6   The Vineyard Restaurant

Tel: (01732) 882330
0.5 miles east along the A20 on the left
Open; Tues-Sat; 12.00-14.30hrs & 19.00-22.00hrs, Sun; 12.00-14.30hrs

7   Shell Offham

Tel: (01732) 877900
0.7 miles east along the A20 on the right
Access, Visa, Mastercard, Switch, Diners Club, Amex, Overdrive, All Star, Dial Card, Delta, UK Fuelcard, Shell Cards. Open; 07.00-23.00hrs daily

8   Westfield Farm B&B

Tel: (01732) 843209
1 mile east along St Vincents Lane on the left

9   Brickmakers Arms

Tel: (01732) 883594
1 mile west along the A25, on the left.
(Shepherd Neame) Meals served; 12.00-14.00hrs & 18.30-21.30hrs daily

10 Petropolis Wrotham (Total)
Tel: (01732) 783810
0.2 miles north along the A20, on the right
Access, Visa, Mastercard,

Switch, Diners Club, Amex, Overdrive, All Star, Dial Card, Delta, Total Cards. Open ; 05.00-22.30hrs daily

11 Oakdene Café

Tel: (01732) 884152
0.2 miles north along the A20, on the right
Open; Mon, Tues, Thur & Fri; 06.00-18.30hrs, Wed; 06.00-22.00hrs, Sat & Sun; 06.00-17.00hrs.

12 The Moat

Tel: (01732) 882263
0.3 miles north along the A20, on the left
(Beefeater) Open all day Sat & Sun. Meals served; Mon-Fri; 12.00-14.00hrs & 17.30-21.00hrs, Sat; 12.00-22.00hrs, Sun; 12.00-21.00hrs

13 The Bull Inn

Tel: (01732) 789800
1 mile north in Wrotham
(Free House) Open all day Sun. Meals served; Mon-Sat; 12.00-14.30hrs & 18.00-22.00hrs, Sun; 12.00-21.30hrs.

14 Rose & Crown

Tel: (01732) 882409
1 mile north in Wrotham
(Shepherd Neame) Meals served; Sun-Thurs; 12.00-14.00hrs, Fri & Sat; 12.00-14.00hrs & 19.00-21.00hrs

15 George & Dragon

Tel: (01732) 884298
1 mile north in Wrotham
(Courage) Open all day Fri, Sat & Sun. Meals served; Mon-Sat 12.00-14.00hrs & 19.00-21.00hrs, Sun; 12.00-15.15hrs & 19.00-21.00hrs.

PLACES OF INTEREST

Trosley Country Park

Waterloo Road, Vigo DA13 0SG
Tel: (01732) 823570

Follow the A2 north, turn right along the A227 and it is signposted along the route (3.2 Miles)
Covering 160 acres of the North Downs this park was once part of Trosley Towers Estate and contains a Special Site of Scientific Interest. The chalk grassland slopes were created by early settlers who cleared the land to graze livestock but after the area was vacated was left to scrub over. Today, part of the conservation work within the park involves the removal of this scrub and re-introduction of grazing animals to help to preserve the Chalk Grasslands and thereby support many rare and important plants and animals such as the Chalkhill Blue Butterfly and the rare Musk Orchid. There are two walks of varying difficulty within the park and part of the 153 miles long North Downs Way from Farnham in Surrey to Dover in Kent passes through the site. There is an Orienteering Trail, Picnic area, Visitors Centre and a Café. Some disabled access.

Coldrum Long Barrow

Follow the A2 east and turn first left to Trottiscliffe (Utilize the NT Car Park, off Pinesfield Lane, Trottiscliffe. 3 Miles)
Sited on a plateau beyond Trottiscliffe and with a commanding view eastwards across the Medway Valley, this magnificent archaeological site contains the remains of a Neolithic Long Barrow. This 5,000 year old antiquity consisted of 24 huge stone

columns marking the perimeter of a circular long barrow of some 50ft in diameter. Although today only four of the 12ft x 10ft columns, which are not of local stone, are left and the burial mound has long since disappeared, it still remains both evocative and mysterious.

M20 JUNCTION 1

SWANLEY TOWN CENTRE IS WITHIN ONE MILE OF THIS JUNCTION

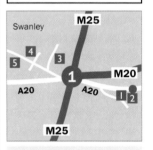

Nearest Westbound A&E Hospital
Queen Mary's Hospital
Frognal Avenue, Sidcup DA14 6LT
Tel: (020) 8302 2678
Follow the A20 west into Sidcup, turn right along the A222 and the hospital is on the right. (Signposted along route. Distance Approx 4.8 miles)

Nearest Northbound A&E Hospital (Via M25)
Darent Valley Hospital
Darenth Wood Road, Dartford DA2 8DA
Tel: (01322) 428100
Proceed north to Junction 2 (M25) and follow the A2 east towards Bluewater, take the first exit (and then the second exit at the roundabout) and, at a second roundabout, follow

the signs to Dartford along Watling Street (Signposted. Distance approx 5.7 miles)

Nearest Eastbound A&E Hospital

Maidstone Hospital

Hermitage Lane, Maidstone
ME16 9QQ
Tel: (01622) 729000
Proceed east to Junction 5, follow the A20 west and turn left along the B2246 (Signposted. Distance Approx 18.4 miles)

FACILITIES

1   The Farningham

Tel: (01322) 861500
0.9 miles east along the A20, on the right
(Courage) Open all day. Meals served; Mon-Fri; 12.00-14.30hrs & 19.00-21.00hrs, Sat; 12.00-22.00hrs, Sun; 12.00-20.00hrs

2   WJ King (Total/Fina)

Tel: (01322) 862366
1 mile east along the A20, on the right
LPG. Access, Visa, Mastercard, Switch, Overdrive, All Star, Dial Card, Delta, Total/Fina/Elf Card, WJ King Card

3   The Olympic

Tel: (01322) 615126
0.8 miles north along Beechenlea Lane
(Swanley Town Council) Meals served; Mon-Thurs; 12.00-14.30hrs, Fri & Sat; 12.00-14.30hrs & 18.00-21.30hrs, Sun; 12.00-15.00hrs

4   Jet Service Station (Jet)

Tel: (01322) 662955

0.9 miles west along the B2173 on the right, in Swanley
Access, Visa, Overdrive, All Star, Switch, Dial Card, Mastercard, Amex, Diners Club, Delta, Jet Card. NB Toilets only available between 06.00 & 22.00hrs daily.

5   Lullington Castle

Tel: (01322) 662027
1 mile west along the B2173 on the left, in Swanley
(Greene King) Open all day. Meals served; Mon-Thur; 12.00-15.00hrs & 18.00-21.00hrs, Fri; 12.00-19.00hrs, Sat; 12.00-16.00hrs, Sun; 12.00-16.00hrs.

PLACES OF INTEREST

St John's Jerusalem (NT)

Sutton-at-Hone, Dartford
DA4 9HQ Regional Office
Tel: (01892) 890651

Follow the A20 east to Farningham and turn left along the A225. (3.3 miles)
For details please see Junction 3 (M25) Information

Eynsford and Lullingstone

Follow the A20 east and turn right along the A225 (Signposted 3.3 miles)
For details please see Junction 3 (M25) Information

Also within the area ...

Lullingstone Park Visitor Centre

Kingfisher Bridge, Castle Road, Nr Eynsford DA4 0JF
Tel: (01322) 865995

For details please see Junction 3 (M25) Information

M20

JUNCTION 2

THIS IS A RESTRICTED ACCESS JUNCTION
- The only access is westbound at Junction 2 (south)
- The only exit is eastbound at Junction 2 (north)

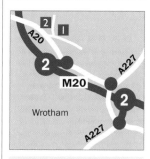

Nearest Eastbound A&E Hospital

Maidstone Hospital

Hermitage Lane, Maidstone
ME16 9QQ
Tel: (01622) 729000
Proceed east to Junction 5, follow the A20 west and turn left along the B2246 (Signposted. Distance Approx 11.0 miles)

Nearest Westbound A&E Hospital

Queen Mary's Hospital

Frognal Avenue, Sidcup
DA14 6LT
Tel: (020) 8302 2678
Proceed west to Junction 1, follow the A20 west into Sidcup, turn right along the A222 and the hospital is on the right. (Signposted along route. Distance Approx 13.6 miles)

Nearest Northbound A&E Hospital (Via M25)

Darent Valley Hospital

Darenth Wood Road, Dartford
DA2 8DA

Tel: (01322) 428100
Proceed west to Junction 1 and then north to Junction 2 (M25). Follow the A2 east towards Bluewater, take the first exit (and then the second exit at the roundabout) and, at a second roundabout, follow the signs to Dartford along Watling Street (Signposted. Distance approx 14.1 miles)

FACILITIES

1 The Hilltop Hotel

Tel: (01732) 822696
0.3 miles north along the A20, on the right in Labour in Vain Road
Restaurant Open; Mon-Sat; 18.00-21.00hrs, Sun; 13.00-17.00hrs

2 Horse & Groom

Tel: (01732) 822696
0.4 miles north along the A20, on the right
(Free House) Open all day. Meals served; Mon-Fri; 11.00-16.00hrs & 18.00-21.00hrs, Sat & Sun; 11.00-21.00hrs.

PLACES OF INTEREST

Trosley Country Park

Waterloo Road, Vigo DA13 0SG
Tel: (01732) 823570

Follow the A20 east, bear left along the A227 and it is signposted along the route (2.3 Miles)
For details please see the Junction 2A (M26) information

Coldrum Long Barrow

Follow the A20 east, turn left along the A227 and turn right to Trottiscliffe (Utilize the NT Car Park, off Pinesfield Lane,

Trottiscliffe. 3.6 Miles)
For details please see the Junction 2A (M26) information

THIS IS A RESTRICTED ACCESS MOTORWAY INTERCHANGE WITH THE M26 ONLY AND THERE IS NO ACCESS TO ANY FACILITIES.

- Vehicles can only exit along the M26 from the westbound lanes
- Vehicles can only enter the motorway from the M26 along the eastbound lanes.

Nearest Eastbound A&E Hospital

Maidstone Hospital

Hermitage Lane, Maidstone ME16 9QQ
Tel: (01622) 729000
Proceed east to Junction 5, follow the A20 west and turn left along the B2246 (Signposted. Distance Approx 8.1 miles)

Nearest Westbound A&E Hospital (Via M20)

Queen Mary's Hospital

Frognal Avenue, Sidcup DA14 6LT
Tel: (020) 8302 2678
Proceed west to Junction 1, follow the A20 west into Sidcup, turn right along the A222 and the hospital is on the right. (Signposted along route. Distance Approx 15.1 miles)

Nearest Westbound A&E Hospital (Via M26 & M25)

East Surrey Hospital

Canada Avenue, Redhill RH1 5RH
Tel: (01737) 768511
Proceed west to Junction 6 (M25) and follow the B2235 south. Turn right along the A25

into Redhill, turn left along the A23 and the hospital is signposted along this route. (Distance Approx 26.3 miles)

Nearest Northbound A&E Hospital (Via M20 & M25)

Darent Valley Hospital

Darenth Wood Road, Dartford DA2 8DA
Tel: (01322) 428100
Proceed west to Junction 1 and then north to Junction 2 (M25). Follow the A2 east towards Bluewater, take the first exit (and then the second exit at the roundabout) and, at a second roundabout, follow the signs to Dartford along Watling Street (Signposted. Distance approx 17.0 miles)

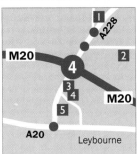

Nearest Eastbound A&E Hospital

Maidstone Hospital

Hermitage Lane, Maidstone ME16 9QQ
Tel: (01622) 729000
Proceed east to Junction 5, follow the A20 west and turn left along the B2246 (Signposted. Distance Approx 5.0 miles)

Nearest Westbound A&E Hospital (Via M20)

Queen Mary's Hospital

Frognal Avenue, Sidcup DA14 6LT

Tel: (020) 8302 2678

Proceed west to Junction 1, follow the A20 west into Sidcup, turn right along the A222 and the hospital is on the right. (Signposted along route. Distance Approx 18.2 miles)

Nearest Westbound A&E Hospital (Via M26 & M25)

East Surrey Hospital

Canada Avenue, Redhill RH1 5RH
Tel: (01737) 768511

Proceed west to Junction 6 (M25) and follow the B2235 south. Turn right along the A25 into Redhill, turn left along the A23 and the hospital is signposted along this route. (Distance Approx 29.4 miles)

Nearest Northbound A&E Hospital (Via M20 & M25)

Darent Valley Hospital

Darenth Wood Road, Dartford DA2 8DA
Tel: (01322) 428100

Proceed west to Junction 1 and then north to Junction 2 (M25). Follow the A2 east towards Bluewater, take the first exit (and then the second exit at the roundabout) and, at a second roundabout, follow the signs to Dartford along Watling Street (Signposted. Distance approx 19.7 miles)

FACILITIES

1   Ham Hill Service Station (Shell)

Tel: (01634) 247920

0.9 miles north along the A228, on the left.

LPG. Access, Visa, Mastercard, Switch, Diners Club, Amex, Overdrive, All Star, Dial Card, Esso Eurocard, BP Supercharge, Shell Cards

2   Tesco Filling Station

Tel: (01622) 701400

0.9 miles east along Lunsford Road, on the right in Lunsford Park

Access, Visa, Mastercard, Switch, Diners Club, Amex, Overdrive, All Star, Dial Card, Delta, AA Paytrak, Tesco Card. Open; 06.00-0.00hrs daily. Disabled Toilets and Cash Machine available in adjacent store.

3   Castle Lake

Tel: (01732) 521630

0.3 miles south along the A228, on the left.

(Brewsters) Open all day. Meals served; Mon-Sat; 11.00-21.30hrs, Sun; 12.00-21.30hrs

4   Travel Inn

Tel: (01732) 521630

0.3 miles south along the A228, on the left.

5   Chimneys

Tel: (01732) 844888

0.6 miles south along the A228, on the left.

(Henry's Table) Open all day. Meals served; 12.00-14.00hrs & 18.00-22.30hrs daily

PLACES OF INTEREST

West Malling

Follow the A228 south (Signposted 1.7 Miles)

West Malling, somewhat larger than the usual village, was once called Town Malling and there are 11thC remains of its former importance during Norman times when it was the site of a castle, an abbey and a monastery. The keep of the castle, St Leonard's Tower, stands by the entrance to Manor Park, Malling Abbey,

founded by Bishop Gundulph in 1090AD on Saxon foundations, has an imposing gate tower and the monastery stands in Water Street. Other relics from the past include the Anglican Abbey for nuns in Swan Street, a mediaeval tilting post with a revolving cross bar and a later period in history is well represented by fine Georgian houses in the High Street

Within the town can be found ....

Manor Park Country Park

Off St. Leonard Street, West Malling Tel: (01622) 817623

Fifty two acres of preserved mature parkland of Douces Manor, including a lake, are contained within Manor Park Country Park. There are four interesting circular walks from the park including one that passes St Leonard's Tower. Picnic and Play Areas.

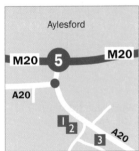

M20
JUNCTION 5

Nearest A&E Hospital

Maidstone Hospital

Hermitage Lane, Maidstone ME16 9QQ
Tel: (01622) 729000

Follow the A20 west and turn left along the B2246 (Signposted. Distance Approx 2.3 miles)

FACILITIES

1   The Sir Thomas Wyatt

Tel: (01622) 752515
0.7 miles south along the
A20, on the right
(Beefeater) Open all day. Bar
Meals served; Mon-Sat; 11.00-
22.00hrs, Sun; 12.00-
22.00hrs. Restaurant Open;
Mon-Fri; 11.00-14.30hrs &
17.00-22.00hrs, Sat & Sun;
11.00-22.00hrs

2   Travel Inn

Tel: (01622) 752515
0.7 miles south along the
A20, on the right

**3   Tudor Filling Station
(BP)**

Tel: (01622) 682416
1 mile south along the A20,
on the right
Access, Visa, Mastercard,
Switch, Electron, Diners Club,
Amex, Overdrive, All Star, Dial
Card, Delta, Shell Agency, BP
Cards.

PLACES OF INTEREST

Aylesford

**Follow the A20 west
(Signposted 1.1 Miles)**
Sitting on the banks of the
River Medway, Aylesford was
the site of a great battle in
455AD between the Jutes, led
by Hengist and Horsa, and the
ancient Britons. The victorious
Horsa died in the battle,
leaving Hengist and his son
Aesc to establish the kingdom
of the Cantware or "Men of
Kent" and this Esking dynasty
lasted for some 300 years.
Many of the timbered and
gabled buildings here reflect a

more recent history and its
importance as a crossing point
through the ages is
encapsulated in the five-
arched mediaeval bridge which
still spans the river. The Friary,
in the High Street, was built in
1240 and was the first
Carmelite order to be founded
in Europe. Following the
dissolution of the monasteries
it was rebuilt in 1675 and,
after the destruction of the
main part of the house by a fire
in the 1930s, the Carmelites
took over the house in 1949
and restored it to its former
glory.

Maidstone

Tourist Information Office, The
Gatehouse, Palace Gardens,
Maidstone ME15 6YE
Tel: (01622) 602169.

**Follow the A20 south
(Signposted 2.7 Miles)**
For details please see Junction
6 information

**Within the town centre
can be found ...**

**Maidstone Museum and
Art Gallery**

Chillington Manor House, St
Faith's Street, Maidstone
ME14 1LH Tel: (01622) 754497

For details please see Junction
6 information

**The Tyrwhitt-Drake
Museum of Carriages**

Archbishops Stables, Mill Street,
Maidstone ME15 6YE Tel:
(01622) 754497

For details please see Junction
6 information

JUNCTION 6

Nearest A&E Hospital
Maidstone Hospital
Hermitage Lane, Maidstone

ME16 9QQ
Tel: (01622) 729000
Proceed west to Junction 5,
follow the A20 west and turn
left along the B2246 (Signposted. Distance Approx 3.7 miles)

FACILITIES

1   Shell Cossington

Tel: (01634) 661900
0.8 miles north along the
A229, on the right
Access, Visa, Mastercard,
Switch, Diners Club, Amex,
Overdrive, All Star, Dial Card,
Delta, BP Supercharge,
BPAgency, Esso Chargecard,
Shell Cards.

**2   Kit's Coty House
Brasserie**

Tel: (01634) 684445
0.8 miles north along the
A229, on the left
Open; Mon-Fri; 11.00-15.00hrs
& 18.00-23.00hrs, Sat; 18.00-
23.00hrs, Sun; 12.00-
15.00hrs. NB. Children allowed
in with parents on Sunday only.

3   Bluebell Hill (Shell)

Tel: (01634) 661000
1 mile north along the A229,
on the left
Access, Visa, Overdrive, All
Star, Switch, Dial Card,
Mastercard, Amex, Diners Club,
Delta, BP Cards, Shell Cards,
Esso Card.

4 Little Chef

Tel: (01634) 862216
1 mile north along the A229,
on the left
Open; 07.00-22.00hrs daily

**5 Chatham Road
Service Station (BP)**

Tel: (01622) 683597
0.5 miles south along the
A229, on the right (Actual
distance 1.6 mile)
Access, Visa, Mastercard,
Switch, Diners Club, Amex,
Overdrive, All Star, Dial Card,
Delta, BP Cards

6 The Malta Inn

Tel: (01622) 717251
0.2 miles west along the
Aylesford Road, on the left
(Beefeater) Open all day. Meals
served; Mon-Sat; 12.00-
22.30hrs, Sun; 12.00-
22.00hrs

7 Travel Inn

Tel: (01622) 717251
0.2 miles west along the
Aylesford Road, on the left

**8 Aylesford Guest House
& Café**

Tel: (01622) 717208
0.8 miles west along Forstal
Road, on the right
Cafe Open; Mon-Fri; 07.00-
14.00hrs

**9 Aylesford Service
Station & Café**

Tel: (01622) 718119
1 mile west along Forstal
Road, on the left
LPG & Red Diesel. Keyfuels,
Access, Visa, Overdrive, All
Star, Switch, Dial Card,
Mastercard, Amex, Diners Club,
Fast Fuel, Securicor Fuelserv.

Open; Mon-Fri; 06.15-20.15,
Sat; 07.00-17.00hrs, Sun;
Closed.

10 The Running Horse

Tel: (01622) 752975
0.2 miles east along Sandling
Lane, on the left
(Harvester) Open all day. Meals
served; Mon-Fri; 12.00-
21.30hrs, Sat & Sun; 12.00-
22.00hrs

PLACES OF INTEREST

Maidstone

Tourist Information Office, The
Gatehouse, Palace Gardens,
Maidstone ME15 6YE
Tel: (01622) 602169. website:
www.maidstone.gov.uk

**Follow the A229 south
(Signposted 2.0 Miles)**

A former "station" for Roman
soldiers, Maidstone straddles
the River Medway, the ancient
boundary which separated
West and East Kent, and
developed on the site of an
important meeting place. The
name means "the people's
stone", it is likely that a stone
marked the site of the "moot",
and was the capital of West
Kent. It is here that the
distinction between "Kentish
Man" and "Man of Kent" is
made, with the former
occupying the west bank and
the latter the east.

As well as fruit and hop
production, the town's trade is
founded on weaving and dyeing
and the quarrying of local
sandstone and many of the fine
buildings reflect the years of
prosperity. The Archbishop's or
Old Palace, in Mill Street, was
constructed in 1348 and
belonged to the Archbishops of
Canterbury until the time of Henry
VIII. Its former stables, the old

tithe barn, are now occupied by
the Tyrwhitt-Drake Museum and
the beautiful Chillington Manor
House, in St Faith's Street and of
Tudor origin, houses the Museum
and Art Gallery. The fine, former
collegiate, Church of All Saints,
with 14th & 15thC additions was
built by Archbishop Courtenay in
1395 and, at the Old College, The
Master's House, with links to a
14thC ecclesiastical college which
was dissolved in 1547, has been
renovated and contains a 16thC
staircase and archways.

**Within the town centre
can be found ...**

**Maidstone Museum and
Art Gallery**

St Faith's Street, Maidstone
ME14 1LH
Tel: (01622) 754497 website:
www.mbcmus1.demon.co.uk

Located in Chillington Manor,
an Elizabethan manor house,
the museum houses a rich
variety of historical objects,
fine art and natural history. The
West Wing has recently been
refurbished and displays
include Japanese art,
European and British
paintings, ceramics, glass and
textiles from the 17thC to
20thC, an extensive
archaeological collection,
Natural History Galleries
incorporating an Ethnography
section, a Costume gallery and
Maidstone Connections, a
display of the social history of
the area. As well as these
exhibits, The Queen's Own
Royal West Kent Regimental
Museum is housed within the
complex. Gift Shop. Coffee
Shop.

**The Tyrwhitt-Drake
Museum of Carriages**

Archbishops' Stables, Mill Street,
Maidstone ME15 6YE Tel:
(01622) 754497

Established by Sir Garrard
Tyrwhitt-Drake, this display of
one of the finest collection of

carriages in the country first opened to visitors at this location in 1946. As well as being able to inspect the beautiful and historic building that houses it, the museum shows the huge variety of conveyances utilized prior to motorized transport, from Royal coaches to barrows and sedan chairs. Gift Shop. Disabled access.

Museum of Kent Life

Lock Lane, Sandling ME14 3AU
Tel: (01622) 763936

Follow the A229 south and it is signposted along the route (0.6 Miles)

An open air museum featuring 100 years of Kent history housed within ancient buildings including an Oast House, Hoppers Huts and a thatched barn. There are also herb, hop and market gardens and a Farmyard and Venture Playground provide a variety of activities and things to do indoors and out. Picnic Area. Tea Room. Gift Shop. Disabled access.

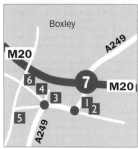

Nearest A&E Hospital

Maidstone Hospital

Hermitage Lane, Maidstone ME16 9QQ
Tel: (01622) 729000
Proceed west to Junction 5,

follow the A20 west and turn left along the B2246 (Signposted. Distance Approx 5.5 miles)

FACILITIES

1   The Newnham Court Inn

Tel: (01622) 734211
0.5 miles east along Bearsted Road, on the left in Newnham Court Shopping Village.
(Henrys Table) Open all day. Bar Meals served; 12.00-21.30hrs daily, Restaurant Open; Mon-Fri; 12.00-15.00hrs & 17.30-22.00hrs, Sat & Sun; 12.00-22.00hrs

2   Noble House Restaurant

Tel: (01622) 631268
0.5 miles east along Bearsted Road, on the left in Newnham Court Shopping Village.
Open; 12.00-14.00 & 17.00-23.00hrs daily

3   Maidstone Hilton Hotel

Tel: (01622) 734322
0.4 miles west along the A249, on the right
Season's Restaurant Open; Mon-Fri; 07.00-10.00hrs, 12.30-14.00hrs & 19.00-21.45hrs, Sat; 07.00-10.00hrs & 19.00-21.45hrs, Sun; 07.30-10.30hrs, 12.30-14.30hrs & 19.00-21.30hrs

4   Chiltern Hundreds Inn

Tel: (01622) 752335
0.5 miles west along the A249, on the right
(Chef & Brewer) Open all day. Meals served; Mon-Sat; 11.00-22.00hrs, Sun; 12.00-21.30hrs

5   The Russell Hotel

Tel: (01622) 692221
1 mile south along Boxley Road, on the left
(Best Western) Restaurant Open; Mon-Sat; 12.00-14.00hrs & 19.00-21.30hrs, Sun; 19.00-21.30hrs

6   The Bull Inn

Tel: (01622) 752888
0.9 miles north along Boxley Road, on the right
(Laurel Pub Partnership) Open all day. Meals served; Mon-Thur; 12.00-15.00hrs & 18.00-21.00hrs, Fri & Sat; 12.00-21.00hrs, Sun; 12.00-20.00hrs

PLACES OF INTEREST

Maidstone

Tourist Information Office, The Gatehouse, Palace Gardens, Maidstone ME15 6YE
Tel: (01622) 602169.

Follow the A249 south (Signposted 2.1 Miles)
For details please see Junction 6 information

Within the town centre can be found ...

Maidstone Museum and Art Gallery

Chillington Manor House, St Faith's Street, Maidstone ME14 1LH Tel: (01622) 754497

For details please see Junction 6 information

The Tyrwhitt-Drake Museum of Carriages

Archbishops Stables, Mill Street, Maidstone ME15 6YE Tel: (01622) 754497

For details please see Junction 6 information

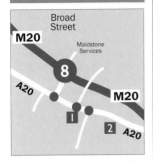

JUNCTION 8

Nearest Westbound A&E Hospital

Maidstone Hospital

Hermitage Lane, Maidstone
ME16 9QQ
Tel: (01622) 729000
Proceed west to Junction 5, follow the A20 west and turn left along the B2246 (Signposted. Distance Approx 8.6 miles)

Nearest Eastbound A&E Hospital

William Harvey Hospital

Kennington Road, Willesborough, Ashford
TN24 0LZ
Tel: (01233) 633331
Proceed east to Junction 10 and it is signposted from the motorway. (Distance Approx 16.9 miles)

FACILITIES

MAIDSTONE SERVICES (ROADCHEF)
Tel: (01622) 631100
Food Fayre Self Service Restaurant, Wimpy Bar, RoadChef Lodge & Esso Fuel

1   The Ramada Hotel & Resort

Tel: (01622) 631163

0.4 miles east along the A20, on the right
Rick's Bar & Grill (Tel: 01622-631111); Open all day. Breakfast; Mon-Fri; 07.00-09.30hrs, Sat & Sun; 08.00-10.30hrs, Lunch; Sun; 12.30-14.00hrs, Dinner; Sun-Thurs; 19.00-22.00hrs, Fri & Sat; 18.30-22.00hrs. Bar meals served Mon-Sat; 12.30-14.00hrs. Disabled access to the Restaurant.

2   The Park Gate Inn

Tel: (01622) 880985
1 mile east along the A20, on the right
(Six Continents) Open all day. Meals served; Mon-Sat; 12.00-22.00hrs, Sun; 12.00-21.30hrs

PLACES OF INTEREST

Leeds Castle
Broomfield, Maidstone
ME17 1PL
Tel: (01622) 765400
Information: 0870 600 8880
website: www.leeds-castle.co.uk

Follow the A20 east. (Signposted 2.0 Miles)
Standing on two islands in the middle of the River Lee, this strategic site was first utilized for a fortress in the 9thC with the present castle dating from the time of Edward I. It was Henry VIII who converted it into a royal stately country residence and it remained as such for 300 years with additions, such as the main building, designed to blend harmoniously with the rest of the structure. The 500 acres of parkland and extensive gardens, which include a Duckery, an avairy, a Maze & Grotto and a Vineyard, were laid out in the 18thC by Capability Brown. The castle itself contains superb furnishings and tapestries and

---

there is an exhibition of antique dog collars in the mediaeval Gate Tower. Gift Shops

JUNCTION 9

ASHFORD TOWN CENTRE IS WITHIN ONE MILE OF THIS JUNCTION

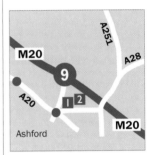

Nearest A&E Hospital

William Harvey Hospital

Kennington Road, Willesborough, Ashford
TN24 0LZ
Tel: (01233) 633331
Proceed east to Junction 10 and it is signposted from the motorway. (Distance Approx 3.2 miles)

FACILITIES

1   Ashford International Hotel

Tel: (01233) 219988
0.6 miles east along Simone Weil Avenue, on the left
Brasserie Open; Breakfast; 07.00-10.00hrs, Lunch; 12.30-14.30hrs & Dinner; 19.00-22.00hrs daily. The Alhambra Restaurant Open; Mon-Sat; 19.00-22.00hrs.

2 Sainsbury's Filling Station

Tel: (01233) 610841

0.8 miles east along Simone Weil Avenue, on the left in Warren Retail Park.

Access, Visa, Mastercard, Switch, Amex, Overdrive, All Star, Dial Card, Delta, Sainsbury's Cards. Disabled toilets available in adjacent store during store opening hours only.

JUNCTION 10

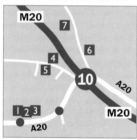

Nearest A&E Hospital

William Harvey Hospital
Kennington Road,
Willesborough, Ashford
TN24 0LZ
Tel: (01233) 633331
Signposted from the motorway. (Distance Approx 0.8 miles)

FACILITIES

1 The French Connection

Tel: (01233) 500755

1 mile south along the A2070 on the right, in Orbital Park (Brewer's Fare) Open all day. Meals served; Mon-Sat; 11.30-22.30hrs, Sun; 12.00-22.00hrs

2 Travel Inn

Tel: (01233) 500755
1 mile south along the A2070 on the right, in Orbital Park

3 McDonald's

Tel: (01233) 503587

1 mile south along the A2070 on the right, in Orbital Park
Open; 07.00-23.00hrs daily

4 Willesborough & Kennington Garages (Esso)

Tel: (01233) 623946/622808
0.5 miles west along the A292, on the right
Access, Visa, Overdrive, All Star, Switch, Dial Card, Mastercard, Amex, Diners Club, Delta, Esso Cards. NB Toilet facilities only available between 09.00 & 22.00hrs daily.

5 Windmill Café

Tel: (01233) 623969
0.6 miles west along the A292, on the left
Open; Mon-Fri; 08.00-14.00hrs, Sat; 08.00-13.00hrs, Sun; Closed

6 Warren Cottage Hotel

Tel: (01233) 621905
0.2 miles west along the A2070, on the right

7 The White Horse

Tel: (01233) 624257
0.6 miles west along the A2070, on the left
(Laurel Pub Partnership) Open all day. Meals served; Mon & Wed-Sat; 11.30-14.30hrs & 19.00-21.30hrs, Tues & Sun; 11.30-14.30hrs

JUNCTION 11

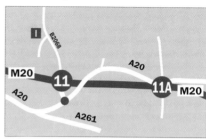

Nearest A&E Hospital

William Harvey Hospital
Kennington Road,
Willesborough, Ashford
TN24 0LZ
Tel: (01233) 633331
Proceed west to Junction 10 and it is signposted from the motorway. (Distance Approx 7.8 miles)

FACILITIES

1 The Drum Inn

Tel: (01303) 812125

0.9 miles north along the B2068 on the left, in Stanford North

(Greene King) Open all day Sat & Sun. Meals served; 12.00-14.30hrs & 18.00-21.30hrs daily

PLACES OF INTEREST

Port Lympne Wild Animal Park & Garden

Lympne, Nr Hythe CT21 4PD Tel: (01303) 264647
website: www.howletts.net

Follow the A20 west and turn left along the B2067. (Signposted 4.1 miles)
Created by John Aspinall and

dedicated to the preservation of rare and endangered animals, the 350 acre Wild Animal Wilderness contains Indian elephants, tigers, snow leopards, lions, monkeys, wolves, and many other rare and endangered animals as well as the largest captive group of black rhino in the world. Other attractions include a Gorilla House, an historic mansion, 15 acres of beautiful landscaped gardens, vineyards and stunning views of Romney Marsh. There is a free Safari Trailer Ride, suitable for disabled visitor use, and barbecues take place during the peak season. Conservatory Restaurant. Gift Shop. Disabled access.

Hythe

Tourist Information Office, En Route Building, Red Lion Square, Hythe CT21 5AU
Tel: (01303) 2677799

Follow the A20 south and turn left along the A261 (Signposted 3.0 miles)

Hythe goes back to at least 732AD when Ethelred, king of the Saxons, first granted it a charter. The name means "landing place", it was once one of the five Cinque ports, but the silting of the harbour rendered it redundant and it is now half a mile from the sea with no trace of the harbour remaining! Overlooked by the 11thC St Leonard's Church, the town is riddled with delightful ancient streets and passageways descending from Quarry Hill and contains innumerable period properties.

Within the town centre can be found ...

Romney Hythe & Dymchurch Railway

Headquarters: New Romney Station, New Romney TN28 8PL
Tel: (01797) 362353 website: www.rhdr.demon.co.uk

The world's smallest public railway, this 1ft 3in gauge (third full size) line runs for 14 miles from Hythe to Dungeness. Disabled access to trains available if pre-booked.

JUNCTION 11A

> **THIS JUNCTION IS AN EXIT POINT TO THE CHANNEL TUNNEL TERMINAL FOR WESTBOUND TRAFFIC ONLY AND THERE IS NO ACCESS TO ANY FACILITIES.**
>
> ■ There is no access to the eastbound carriageway
> ■ There is no exit from the westbound carriageway

JUNCTION 12

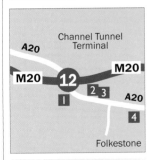

Nearest A&E Hospital
William Harvey Hospital
Kennington Road, Willesborough, Ashford TN24 0LZ
Tel: (01233) 633331
Proceed west to Junction 10 and it is signposted from the motorway. (Distance Approx 11.3 miles)

FACILITIES

1   Tesco Filling Station

Tel: (01303) 719400
0.1 miles east along the A20 on the right
LPG. Access, Visa, Mastercard, Switch, Electron, Amex, Overdrive, All Star, Dial Card, Delta, AA Paytrak, UK Fuelcard, BP Supercharge, Tesco Fuelcard. Cash Machine available in adjacent store.

2   Cheriton Filling Station (BP)
Tel: (01303) 276006
0.2 miles east along the A20 on the left
Access, Visa, Mastercard, Switch, Electron, Amex, Overdrive, All Star, Dial Card, Delta, Shell Cards, BP Cards.

3   The White Lion
Tel: (01303) 278276
0.4 miles east along the A20 on the left
(Free House) Open all day. Meals served; 07.00-15.00hrs daily

4   Royal Cheriton
Tel: (01303) 277007
0.9 miles east along the A20 on the right
(Free House) Open all day. Meals served; Mon-Sat; 12.00-14.30hrs

PLACES OF INTEREST

Folkestone

Tourist Information Office, Harbour Street, Folkestone CT20 1QN Tel: (01303) 258594

Follow the A20 east (Signposted 2.4 miles)
For details please see Junction 13 information

JUNCTION 13

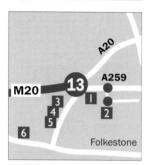

Folkestone

Nearest A&E Hospital

William Harvey Hospital
Kennington Road,
Willesborough, Ashford
TN24 0LZ
Tel: (01233) 633331
Proceed west to Junction 10
and it is signposted from the
motorway. (Distance Approx
12.5 miles)

FACILITIES

1 Sainsbury's Filling Station

Tel: (01303) 850810
0.7 miles east along the A259
on the right, in Park Farm
Industrial Estate
Access, Visa, Mastercard,
Switch, Amex, Overdrive, All
Star, Dial Card, Delta, AA
Paytrak, Sainsbury's Card.
Open; 06.00-0.00hrs daily.
Disabled toilets available in
adjacent store during store
opening hours only.

2 McDonald's

Tel: (01303) 249256
0.7 miles east along the A259
on the right, in Park Farm
Industrial Estate
Open; 08.00-23.00hrs daily

3 Burger King

Tel: (01303) 274275
0.2 miles south along the A20
on the right, in Cherry Garden
Lane
Open; 11.00-22.00hrs daily

4 Travel Inn

Tel: (01303) 273620
0.2 miles south along the A20
on the right, in Cherry Garden
Lane

5 The Brickfield

Tel: (01303) 273620
0.2 miles south along the A20
on the right, in Cherry Garden
Lane
(Brewster's) Open all day.
Meals served; Mon-Fri; 11.30-
22.00hrs, Sun; 12.00-
22.00hrs

6 The Morehall

Tel: (01303) 275347
0.9 miles west along the A20
on the right
(Punch Taverns) Open all day.
Meals served; Mon-Sat; 11.00-
23.00hrs, Sun; 12.00-
22.00hrs

PLACES OF INTEREST

Kent Battle of Britain Museum

Aerodrome Road, Hawkinge, Nr
Folkestone CT18 7AG
Tel: (01303) 893140

**Follow the A20 east and turn
left along the A260 to
Hawkinge. (2.0 miles)**
Exhibits including aircraft,
vehicles, weapons, flying
equipment, prints and relics
from over 600 crashed aircraft
are on show at this, the largest
and most important collection
of Battle of Britain artefacts in
the country. Café. Shop.
Disabled access

Folkestone

Tourist Information Office,
Harbour Street, Folkestone CT20
1QN Tel: (01303) 258594

**Follow the A20 south
(Signposted 1.9 miles)**
Although the second busiest
cross-Channel port on the
south coast, the unusual
feature of this seaside resort is
that it does not have a typical
seafront but a series of
delightful cliff top lawns and
flower gardens called "The
Leas". These run for the best
part of a mile and a half west
towards Sandgate and there is
a Victorian water-driven lift to
take residents from the cliff top
hotels down to the beach
below.

Much of the early history of this
Edwardian town is condensed
into an area known as "The
Lanterns" on Sandgate Road
where The Bayle, once the site of
an ancient fort, and the oldest
building in Folkestone, the 13thC
Church of St Mary and St
Eanswythe, may be found. Church
Street was home to traders in silk
and cloth and William Harvey,
discoverer of the circulation of
blood in the human body, was
born here in 1578. Amongst the
many visitor attractions within the
town are; the Rotunda Fun Park
(Tel: 01303-245245) and the
Russian Submarine (Tel: 01303-
240400) as well as historical sites
such as the Martello Tower No.3
(Tel: 01303-242113) and the
Museum & Art Gallery
(Tel: 01303-850213)

MOTORWAY ENDS
(Total Length of Motorway 50.1
Miles or 49.3 Miles utilizing M26)

the **M23**

This short 16.5 miles long motorway connects with the A23 just north of the M25 and, as well as forming a high speed route to Gatwick Airport, by-passes Redhill, Horley and Crawley before re-connecting with the A23 as it continues south to Brighton.

Originating at Junction 7 where it makes an end-on connection with the A23 to London, the motorway turns south, crosses the M25 at Junction 8 and continues south past **Redhill**, which rapidly developed following the arrival of the London

Wakehurst Place

& Brighton Railway in 1840, and then **South Nutfield** on the west side before reaching **Horley**, another town that expanded following the arrival of the railway, on the west side of Junction 9. In the area around this junction low flying aircraft pass over the carriageways from east to west as they approach **Gatwick Airport**. The site at Gatwick was bought by the Gatwick Racecourse Company in 1890 for use as a horse racing track and was also utilized by the Surrey Aero Club from 1930. In 1932 it was sold to the Redwing Co. and, in the following year, purchased by Airports Ltd who obtained a public licence from the Air Ministry in 1934 to allow commercial flying. Following the end of World War II, during which it had been requisitioned for military use, it was taken over by the Ministry of Civil Aviation and in 1952 was earmarked as the second London Airport. It closed in 1956

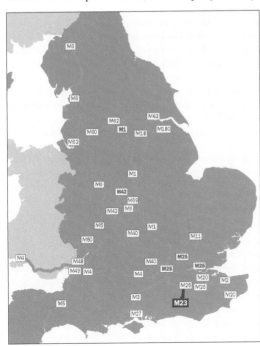

for rebuilding and is now the busiest single runway airport in the world and sixth busiest overall.

Continuing south from Junction 9 the carriageways sweep around the south east side of **Crawley** and pass through **Worth and Tilgate Forests** before re-joining the A23 at Junction 11. Crawley is probably of Saxon origin and was used as a stopping place in Regency days for Royal parties travelling to Brighton. Following the New Towns Act of 1946 it was amalgamated with Three Bridges and Ifield to create a modern town.

Nymans House

Location of Places of Interest

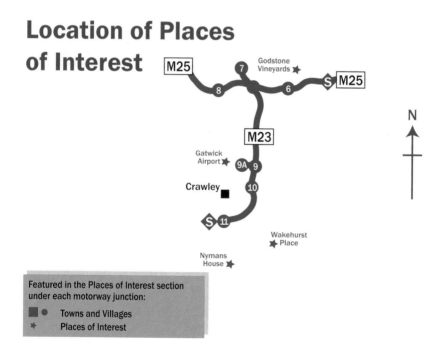

Featured in the Places of Interest section under each motorway junction:

■ ●   Towns and Villages

✷   Places of Interest

JUNCTION 7

THIS IS A RESTRICTED ACCESS JUNCTION
- Vehicles can only exit along the northbound lanes and travel north along the A23
- Vehicles can only enter along the southbound lanes from the A23 southbound carriageway

Nearest A&E Hospital

East Surrey Hospital

Canada Avenue, Redhill
RH1 5RH
Tel: (01737) 768511
Follow the A23 south into Redhill and the hospital is signposted along this route. (Distance Approx 5 miles)

FACILITIES

1   Little Chef

Tel: (01737) 557459
0.5 miles north along the A23 on the right.
Open; 07.00-22.00hrs daily

2   Burger King

Tel: (01737) 557459
0.5 miles north along the A23 on the right
Open; 11.00-21.00hrs daily

3   Hooley Service Station (Esso)

 WC 24 HOUR

Tel: (01737) 554390
0.8 miles north along the A23, on the right
LPG. Access, Visa, Overdrive, All Star, Switch, Dial Card, Mastercard, Amex, Diners Club, Delta, Esso Cards.

4   Star Lane BP Service Station

24 HOUR

Tel: (01737) 555217
0.9 miles north along the A23, on the left
Access, Visa, Overdrive, All Star, Switch, Dial Card, Mastercard, Amex, Diners Club, Delta, Routex, Shell Agency, UK Fuels, Keyfuels, IDS, BP Cards.

JUNCTION 8

THIS JUNCTION IS A MOTORWAY INTERCHANGE WITH THE M25 ONLY AND THERE IS NO ACCESS TO ANY FACILITIES.

Nearest A&E Hospital

East Surrey Hospital

Canada Avenue, Redhill
RH1 5RH
Tel: (01737) 768511
Proceed west to Junction 8 (M25), take the A217 south into Reigate, turn left along the A25 into Redhill, turn right along the A23 and the hospital is signposted along this route. (Distance Approx 8.4 miles)

JUNCS 9 & 9A

Nearest Northbound A&E Hospital

East Surrey Hospital

Canada Avenue, Redhill
RH1 5RH
Tel: (01737) 768511
Follow the A23 north to Redhill and the hospital is signposted along this route. (Distance Approx 5.1 miles)

Nearest Southbound A&E Hospital

Crawley Hospital

West Green Drive, Crawley
RH11 7DH
Tel: (01293) 600300
Proceed south to Junction 10, follow the A2011 west, continue along the A2004 into Crawley and it is signposted along the route (Distance Approx 4.9 miles)

FACILITIES

1   McDonald's

Tel: (01293) 569067
In entrance to Gatwick Airport South Terminal, adjacent to south side of roundabout at Junction 9A
Open; 07.00-23.00hrs daily ["Drive-Thru" remains open until 0.00hrs daily]

2 Star Gatwick Airport (Texaco)

Tel: (01293) 609100

In entrance to Gatwick Airport South Terminal, adjacent to south side of roundabout at Junction 9A

Access, Visa, Overdrive, All Star, Switch, Dial Card, Mastercard, Amex, Diners Club, Delta, Fast Fuel, Texaco Cards

3 Hilton London Gatwick Hotel

Tel: (01293) 518080

In entrance to Gatwick Airport South Terminal, adjacent to south side of roundabout at Junction 9A

The Garden Restaurant Open; Breakfast; 06.00-10.30hrs daily, Lunch; Sun-Fri; 12.00-14.30hrs, Dinner; 17.30-22.15hrs daily. Amy's Restaurant Open; 11.00-22.45hrs daily.

4 Star Market Gatwick North (Texaco)

Tel: (01293) 602500

0.9 miles west along the Junction 9A access road, adjacent to the roundabout

Access, Visa, Overdrive, All Star, Switch, Dial Card, Mastercard, Amex, Diners Club, Delta, Fast Fuel, Texaco Cards.

5 Gatwick Travel Inn Metro

Tel: 0870 238 3305

1 mile west along the Junction 9A access road, on the right

Potters Restaurant Open; 06.30-10.30hrs & 17.30-22.00hrs daily

6 Renaissance London Gatwick Hotel

Tel: (01293) 820169

1 mile west along the Junction 9A access road, on the right

The Pavilion Restaurant Open; Breakfast 06.00-11.00hrs, Lunch 11.00-14.00hrs & Dinner 18.30-21.30hrs daily. High Flyers Café Open; 11.00-23.00hrs daily

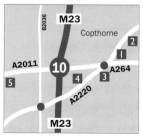

JUNCTION 10

Nearest A&E Hospital

Crawley Hospital

West Green Drive, Crawley RH11 7DH

Tel: (01293) 600300

Follow the A2011 west, continue along the A2004 into Crawley and it is signposted along the route (Distance Approx 3 miles)

FACILITIES

1 Kitsbridge House Hotel, Restaurant & Bar

Tel: (01342) 714422

0.7 miles east along the A264, adjacent to the left side of the roundabout

Restaurant Open; 19.00-22.00hrs daily

2 The Prince Albert

Tel: (01342) 712072

1 mile east along Brookhill Road in Copthorne, on the right

(Laurel Pub Partnership) Meals served; 12.30-14.30hrs daily. Outdoor barbecued meals available during Summer evenings.

3 Copthorne Gatwick Hotel

Tel: (01342) 714971

0.7 miles east along the A264, adjacent to the roundabout

The Lion D'Or Restaurant Open; Lunch; 12.00-14.30hrs daily, Dinner; 19.00-21.45hrs daily. The Brasserie Restaurant Open; Breakfast; 06.00-10.30hrs daily, Dinner; 18.00-22.30hrs daily

4 Crystal Motors Garage

Tel: (01293) 886691

1 mile south along the A2220, on the right

Access, Visa, Delta, Mastercard, Switch, Diners Club, Amex, Overdrive, All Star, Dial Card. Open; Mon-Fri; 07.00-19.45hrs, Sat & Sun; 08.00-18.30hrs

5 Ramada Plaza Gatwick Hotel

Tel: (01293) 561186

1 mile west along the A2011, on the left

The Arts Grill Open; Breakfast; 06.30-10.00hrs daily, Dinner; 18.30-22.00hrs daily. Bar Meals available 10.30-22,30hrs daily.

M23

JUNCTION 10A

THIS IS A RESTRICTED ACCESS JUNCTION

- Vehicles can only exit along the southbound lanes
- Vehicles can only enter along the northbound lanes

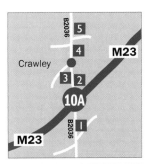

Nearest A&E Hospital
Crawley Hospital
West Green Drive, Crawley
RH11 7DH
Tel: (01293) 600300
Take the B2036 north and
follow the signs into the Town
Centre. The hospital is
signposted along the route
(Distance Approx 3.5 miles)

FACILITIES

1 The Cowdray Arms
Tel: (01444) 811280
1 mile south along the
B2036, on the left
(Greene King) Meals served;
Mon-Sat; 12.00-14.00hrs &
18.30-21.30hrs, Sun; 12.00-
15.00hrs & 19.00-21.00hrs

2 Europa Gatwick Hotel
Tel: (01293) 886666
0.1 miles north along the
B2036, on the right
The Mediterannee Restaurant
Open; Breakfast; Mon-Fri;
07.00-10.00hrs, Sat & Sun;
07.30-10.30hrs, Lunch; Sun;
12.30-15.30hrs, Dinner;
18.30-21.30hrs daily

**3 Barnwood Hotel &
Licensed Restaurant**
Tel: (01293) 425800
0.7 miles north along the
B2036, on the left

Restaurant Open; Breakfast;
07.00-09.30hrs daily, Dinner;
19.00-21.00hrs daily

**4 Star Market Pound
Hill (Texaco)**

Tel: (01293) 880540
0.8 miles north along the
B2036, on the right
Access, Visa, Delta,
Mastercard, Switch, Diners
Club, Amex, Electron, Solo,
Overdrive, All Star, Dial Card,
Fast Fuel, BP Supercharge,
Texaco Cards. Open; 07.00-
22.00hrs daily

5 The Hillside Inn

Tel: (01293) 880911
1 mile north along the B2036,
on the right
(Six Continents) Open all day.
Meals served; Mon-Sat; 12.00-
21.30hrs, Sun; 12.00-21.00hrs

JUNCTION 11

Nearest A&E Hospital
Crawley Hospital
West Green Drive, Crawley
RH11 7DH
Tel: (01293) 600300
Follow the A23 north into
Crawley and the hospital is
signposted along the route
(Distance Approx 2.2 miles)

FACILITIES

**PEASE POTTAGE SERVICES
(MOTO)**
Tel: (01293) 562852
Fresh Express Self Service
Restaurant, Burger King & Shell
Fuel

1 The Black Swan

Tel: (01293) 612261
0.6 miles west in Pease
Pottage, on the right
(Hall & Woodhouse) Open all
day. Meals served; 12.00-
22.00hrs daily

2 The Grapes

Tel: (01293) 526359
0.8 miles south along Old
Brighton Road South in Pease
Pottage, on the left
(King & Barnes) Open all day
Sat & Sun. Meals served; Mon-
Sat; 12.00-14.00hrs & 19.00-
21.00hrs, Sun; 12.00-
18.00hrs.

MOTORWAY ENDS
(Total Length of Motorway 16.5
Miles)

the M25

Conceived in 1905 and completed in October 1986, the 117 miles of the M25 make it the longest city by-pass in the world with the radius, struck from Charing Cross, varying between 13 and 22 miles. It is not quite a closed circle as the short 4.7 miles section embracing the Dartford River Crossing between Junctions 31 and 2 is all-purpose to accommodate non-motorway traffic. Somewhat despised and inspiring Chris Rea's hit single *Road to Hell*, it is an integral and essential piece of the motorway network allowing not only rapid movement between the outer suburbs of London but facilitating improved connections between the Channel ports and the Midlands and the North, traffic which would otherwise add to the congestion in the capital.

Knole House, Sevenoaks

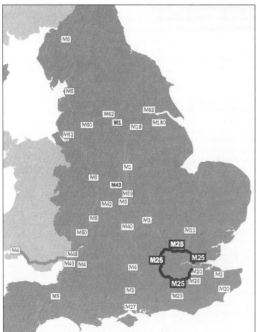

Commencing at Junction 2 the motorway heads south with panoramic views across **Darenth Valley** to the east before it reaches **Farningham Wood** on the east side just north of Junction 3. **Swanley** is adjacent to the west side of this junction and between here and Junction 5, where anti-clockwise traffic can connect with the M26, there is an extensive use of cuttings to hide the road as it passes through the Kent Downs. The motorway turns sharply to the west at Junction 5, where the town of **Sevenoaks**, once a Saxon market town and now a prosperous residential area on the commuter main line to London, is visible to the south, and it follows the southern edge of the North Downs to Junction 6. Between this point and Junction 7, and the connection with the M23, there are panoramic views to the south with the picturesque village of **Bletchingley** in view.

The short section between Junctions 7 & 8 by-passes **Reigate** to the south. Reigate was an important settlement in Norman times and a castle, long since demolished, was built here by the de Warenne family. The motorway continues north westwards across the North Downs to Junction 9, adjacent to the east side of **Leatherhead**, a pretty town set in the Mole Valley. Beyond Junction 9 there are extensive views across to the south and the River Mole meanders alongside of the motorway before the carriageways cross the London Waterloo to Guildford line. Extensive use of sound-proofing screens is made between Junctions 10, where the motorway links with the A3 to London and Portsmouth, and Junction 11 where the motorway spans the Woking to London Waterloo railway line and the junction of the River Wey Navigation and the 37 miles long **Basingstoke Canal** which opened in 1794.

RHS Wisley Gardens, nr Woking

The motorway continues northwards and the carriageways are crossed by the Lyne Bridge before crossing the M3 at Junction 12. **Lyne Bridge** is a cable-stayed concrete skew bridge and was the first example of this type of construction to be built for British Rail. It carries the Chertsey to Virginia Water line and following its formal opening on February 7th, 1979 by the British Rail Chairman Sir Peter Parker the first service train crossed it on February 12th. The River Thames, the Staines to Windsor & Eton branch line and numerous roads are all spanned at Junction 13, necessitating extensive bridge works and additional approach roadways. Between Junctions 13 and 14 the motorway slips between a series of reservoirs that stretch some seven miles north from the **Queen Mary Reservoir** near Sunbury to the **Queen Mother Reservoir** at Datchet and a high embankment containing the **Wraysbury Reservoir** can be seen on the west side.

Heathrow Airport is to the east of Junction 14 and between here and Junction 15, where the M4 is bridged, aircraft can be seen crossing the carriageways where the River Colne and the Colne Brook run alongside of the motorway. Continuing north the motorway crosses the Slough branch of the **Grand Union Canal** and passes **Woodlands Park Lake** on the east side before passing under the M40 at Junction 16. Beyond this junction the London Paddington to High Wycombe line crosses the carriageways,

Windsor Castle

unusually by means of the original brick built viaduct rather than a concrete replacement, and **Rickmansworth**, through which flow the River Colne and the Grand Union Canal, is passed on the east side between Junctions 17 and 18. The section between Junctions 17 and 19, where the motorway turns eastwards, was originally part of the A405 and was upgraded to motorway standard in the early 1980s.

Just east of Junction 19 a long viaduct carries the motorway over the Grand Union Canal, the River

Gade and the West Coast Main Line with **Kings Langley**, an historic village from which Edward I ruled for a short period, in view to the west. The 12.5 miles section between Junctions 19 and 23 was finished on October 29th, 1986 and completed the M25 route. The M1 passes under Junction 21 as the M25 continues eastwards past **Chiswell Green**, home to the Gardens of the Rose a two acre site that contains one of the most important rose collections in the world, to the north of Junction 21A. Just east of Junction 22, the **Mosquito Aircraft Museum** can be seen on the south side and between

St Albans Cathedral

Junctions 23 and 24, **Potters Bar**, a name which originated from the gates between the estates along the main road, is visible on the north side of the carriageway. This was the first section of the M25 motorway, first opened in September 1975 as part of the M16. At this time sections of the London Orbital were planned as separate relief roads and it was not until November of that year that the concept of drawing them all together as the M25 was arrived at. The motorway continues east over the **Enfield Chase** to Junction 25 where an aqueduct carries the New River over the carriageways. Aqueducts over motorways are very unusual and one of the very few other examples is the one that takes the Tame Valley Canal over the M5 north & southbound carriageways within the Ray Hall Interchange (Junction 8 of the M6) north west of Birmingham.

Immediately east of Junction 25, the London Liverpool Street to Cambridge line crosses the motorway before the carriageways enter the 711 yards long **Holmesdale Tunnel**. At the east end of this tunnel, the River Lee and Stort Canal are bridged and **Waltham Abbey**, built in the 12thC but whose origins go back to the 6thC, is passed on the north side before

Hunting Lodge, Epping Forest

reaching Junction 26. Continuing east the remnants of **Copped Hall** are on the north side before the motorway passes through the 514 yards long **Bell Common Tunnel**. This tunnel was extended eastwards to pass under Epping Foresters County Cricket ground at Mill Plain rather than through it. Epping Forest is passed on the south side before the M11 is crossed at Junction 27. **Epping Forest**, now just 5,600 acres, is all that remains of "the great forest of Essex", a Royal hunting ground that comprised 60,000 acres in 1640. The motorway continues to curve southwards and passes **Stapleford Airfield** on the south side before reaching Junction 28 with **Brentwood**, a town with quite a distinguished past despite its modern appearance, in view to the east and **Romford** to the west. The carriageways continue south, passing **Upminster** on the west side of Junction 29 to reach the end of the motorway at Junction 31, with **Purfleet**, whose esteemed Royal Hotel is said to have played host to Edward VII while still Prince of Wales, in view to the west and the huge **Lakeside Shopping Centre** to the east. At this point it makes an end-on connection with the A282 which links up with the M25 at Junction 2 on the south side of the River Thames.

The crossing is effected by a bridge and a tunnel. The **Queen Elizabeth II Bridge** carries the clockwise traffic and was formally opened on October 30th, 1991. Of the cable-stayed type it was the largest in Europe when built with an overall length of 9,422ft and a main span of 1,476ft. Over 18,750 tons of steel and 189,000 cubic yards of concrete were utilized in its construction and the whole thing was finished off with 48,800 gallons of paint. The anti-clockwise crossing is by means of the **Dartford Tunnels**. The first one (West Tunnel) was opened on November 18th, 1963 and is 4,701ft long with a carriage width of 21ft. Following the arrival of the M25 the second tunnel (East Tunnel) opened on May 16th, 1980 and was fractionally longer at 4,708ft with wider carriageways of 24ft. Both tunnels carry dual carriageways.

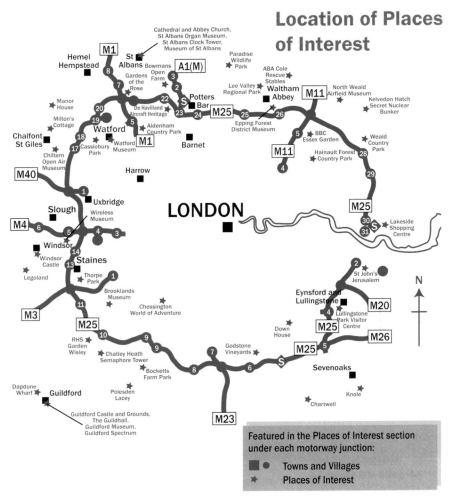

Location of Places of Interest

Featured in the Places of Interest section under each motorway junction:

■ ● Towns and Villages

★ Places of Interest

JUNCTION 2

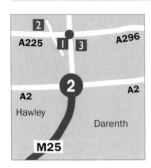

Nearest A&E Hospital

Darent Valley Hospital
Darenth Wood Road, Dartford
DA2 8DA
Tel: (01322) 428100
Follow the A2 east towards Bluewater, take the first exit (and then the second exit at the roundabout) and, at a second roundabout, follow the signs to Dartford along Watling Street (Signposted. Distance approx 2.4 miles)

FACILITIES

1 Dartford Service Station (Esso)

Tel: (01322) 220250
0.8 miles west along the A225, on the left
Access, Visa, Mastercard, Switch, Diners Club, Amex, Overdrive, All Star, Dial Card, UK Fuelcard, Shell Gold, Esso Cards

2 Elms Service Station (BP)

Tel: (01322) 290379
1 mile west along the A225, on the right
Access, Visa, Mastercard, Switch, Diners Club, Amex, Overdrive, All Star, Dial Card, Delta, Shell Agency, BP Cards

3 The Harvester Dartford Bridge

Tel: (01322) 287766
0.9 miles east along the A225, on the right
Open all day. Meals served; Sun-Fri; 12.00-21.30hrs, Sat; 12.00-22.00hrs

JUNCTION 3

SWANLEY TOWN CENTRE IS WITHIN ONE MILE OF THIS JUNCTION

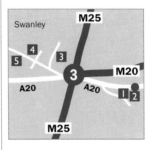

Nearest Clockwise A&E Hospital

Queen Mary's Hospital
Frognal Avenue, Sidcup
DA14 6LT
Tel: (020) 8302 2678
Follow the A20 west into Sidcup, turn right along the A222 and the hospital is on the right. (Signposted along route. Distance Approx 4.8 miles)

Nearest Anti-Clockwise A&E Hospital

Darent Valley Hospital
Darenth Wood Road, Dartford
DA2 8DA
Tel: (01322) 428100

Proceed north to Junction 2 and follow the A2 east towards Bluewater, take the first exit (and then the second exit at the roundabout) and, at a second roundabout, follow the signs to Dartford along Watling Street (Signposted. Distance Approx 5.7 miles)

FACILITIES

1 The Farningham

Tel: (01322) 861500
0.9 miles east along the A20, on the right
(Courage) Open all day. Meals served; Mon-Fri; 12.00-14.30hrs & 19.00-21.00hrs, Sat; 12.00-22.00hrs, Sun; 12.00-20.00hrs

2 WJ King (Total)

Tel: (01322) 862366
1 mile east along the A20, on the right
LPG. Access, Visa, Mastercard, Switch, Overdrive, All Star, Dial Card, Delta, Total/Fina/Elf Cards, WJ King Card

3 The Olympic

Tel: (01322) 615126
0.8 miles north along Beechenlea Lane
(Swanley Town Council) Meals served; Mon-Thurs; 12.00-14.30hrs, Fri & Sat; 12.00-14.30hrs & 18.00-21.30hrs, Sun; 12.00-15.00hrs

4 Jet Service Station (Jet)

Tel: (01322) 662955
0.9 miles west along the B2173 on the right, in Swanley
Access, Visa, Overdrive, All Star, Switch, Dial Card, Mastercard, Amex, Diners Club, Delta, Jet Card. NB Toilets only

available between 06.00 &
22.00hrs daily.

5   Lullington Castle

Tel: (01322) 662027
**1 mile west along the B2173
on the left, in Swanley**
(Greene King) Open all day.
Meals served; Mon-Thur;
12.00-15.00hrs & 18.00-
21.00hrs, Fri; 12.00-19.00hrs,
Sat; 12.00-16.00hrs, Sun;
12.00-16.00hrs.

PLACES OF INTEREST

St John's Jerusalem (NT)

Sutton-at-Hone, Dartford
DA4 9HQ Regional Office
Tel: (01892) 890651

**Follow the A20 east to
Farningham and turn left
along the A225. (3.3 Miles)**
A lovely manor house set on
the edge of the village of
Sutton at Hone, it was built in
the 13thC as a commandery of
the Knights Hospitallers and
parts of the original building
are still extant. The large
tranquil garden and chapel,
moated by the River Darent,
are open to the public.
Disabled access.

Eynsford and Lullingstone

**Follow the A20 east and turn
right along the A225
(Signposted 3.3 miles)**
Within this small area are three
sites of historic interest and a
Park and Visitor Centre.
Eynsford (Tel: 01959-565063)
is a picturesque village with a
number of timber framed
buildings, a ford crossing the
River Darent, and the remains,
a high curtain wall and stone
hall, of the 12thC Eynsford
Castle.
    The origins of nearby
Lullingstone Castle (Tel: 01322-

862114) date back to pre-
Norman times when a manor
house was located here. Added to
in the Tudor era it was largely
rebuilt in the 18thC but the Henry
VII gateway still remains. Both
Henry VIII and Queen Anne were
associated with Lullingstone and
the castle contains many Tudor
relics including panelling,
paintings and a collection of
armour, whilst in the grounds is
the Norman Church of St Botolph
which was restored during the
reign of Edward III. Shop. Café.
Disabled access
    Of even older antiquity is the
Lullingstone Roman Villa (Tel:
01322-863467) which, although
known about since the 19thC,
was only uncovered as recently as
1949 and is one of the best of
preserved sites. A glass and
timber pavilion covers the
excavated villa which comprises
of living rooms, deep room and
bath house and the fine mosaic
floor which was laid during the
4thC reconstruction of the villa
are on view. Although the deep
room contains relics of pagan
worship and a wall painting it is
the existence of this as a Christian
chapel which makes this private
Roman villa unique in Britain.
Shop. Disabled access.

Also within the area ...

Lullingstone Park Visitor Centre

Kingfisher Bridge, Castle Road, Nr
Eynsford DA4 0JF
Tel: (01322) 865995

Picnic areas, horse routes and
riverside walks are just some
of the leisurely activities
available within the 460 acres
of Lullingstone Park. This
mediaeval deer park includes
ancient pollarded trees, up to
33ft round, and chalk
grassland and there are guided
walks, special events and
children's holiday activity
programmes available at
various times throughout the
year. The facilities include a

Countryside Interpretation
Centre with an equipped
classroom, exhibitions, shop
and picnic and refreshment
areas.

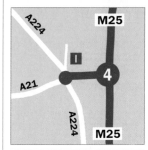

Nearest A&E Hospital
Queen Mary's Hospital

Frognal Avenue, Sidcup
DA14 6LT
Proceed north [anti-clockwise]
to Junction 3, follow the A20
west into Sidcup, turn right
along the A222 and the
hospital is on the right.
(Signposted along route.
Distance Approx 8.3 miles)

Nearest Minor Injury Unit
Sevenoaks Hospital

Hospital Road, Sevenoaks
TN13 3PG
Tel: (01732) 455155
Proceed south [clockwise] to
Junction 5, follow the A25 east
and the hospital is on the
south side, at the end of
Bradbourne Vale Rd. Opening
Hours; 08.00-20.00hrs daily.
(Distance Approx 6.9 miles)

FACILITIES

1   Bo Peep Restaurant

Tel: (01959) 534457
**0.5 miles north along the lane
to Well Hill, in Hewitts Road**

on the right
(Courage) Open all day Fri-Sun. Meals served; Mon-Sat; 12.00-14.00hrs & 19.00-21.45hrs, Sun; 12.00-14.00hrs

PLACES OF INTEREST

Down House

Luxted Road, Downe BR6 7JT

Tel: (01689) 859119. Booking Line Tel: 0870 603 0145

Follow the A21 west (Signposted along route 5.1 miles)

For more than forty years this was the family home of Charles Darwin whose work "On the Origin of the Species by means of Natural Selection" published in 1859, rightly or wrongly, changed many people's views about the beginning of mankind and life on our planet. Down House was the centre of his intellectual world and the study is full of notebooks and journals, and mementos from his voyage that took him to the Galapagos Islands. The house has been recently restored and visitors can wander along the "Sandwalk" in the gardens. Café. Gift Shop. Disabled access

M25
JUNCTION 5

THIS IS A MOTORWAY INTERCHANGE WITH THE M26 AND A RESTRICTED ACCESS JUNCTION.

■ Clockwise vehicles can only exit along the A21 and not access the M26
■ Vehicles can not access the M26 from the A21.

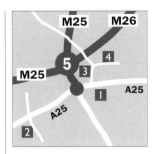

Nearest Clockwise A&E Hospital

East Surrey Hospital

Canada Avenue, Redhill RH1 5RH
Tel: (01737) 768511

Proceed westwards [clockwise] to Junction 6 and follow the B2235 south. Turn right along the A25 into Redhill, turn left along the A23 and the hospital is signposted along this route. (Distance Approx 16.7 miles)

Nearest Anti-Clockwise A&E Hospital

Queen Mary's Hospital

Frognal Avenue, Sidcup DA14 6LT
Tel: (020) 8302 2678

Proceed north [anti-clockwise] to Junction 3, follow the A20 west into Sidcup, turn right along the A222 and the hospital is on the right. (Signposted along route. Distance Approx 12.3 miles)

Nearest Minor Injury Unit

Sevenoaks Hospital

Hospital Road, Sevenoaks TN13 3PG
Tel: (01732) 455155

Follow the A25 east and the hospital is on the south side, at the end of Bradbourne Vale Rd. Opening Hours; 08.00-20.00hrs daily. (Distance Approx 2.4 miles)

FACILITIES

1 The Kings Head

Tel: (01732) 452081
0.5 miles east along the A25, on the right
(Free House) Meals served; Mon-Sat; 12.00-14.00hrs & 19.00-21.15hrs, Sun; 12.00-14.15hrs

2 White Horse Inn

Tel: (01959) 562837
0.9 miles west along the A25, on the left
(Scottish & Newcastle) Open all day. Meals served; 12.00-15.00hrs & 19.00-21.30hrs daily

3 The Bricklayers Arms

Tel: (01732) 743424
0.4 miles north along Chevening Road in Chipstead, on the left
(Harvey's) Meals served; Mon-Sat; 12.00-14.30hrs & 18.30-21.30hrs, Sun; 12.00-14.30hrs.

4 The George & Dragon

Tel: (01732) 460049
0.4 miles north along road to Chipstead, in Chipstead, on the left
(Free House) Meals served; Sun-Wed; 12.00-14.30hrs, Thurs-Fri; 12.00-14.30hrs & 18.00-21.00hrs

PLACES OF INTEREST

Sevenoaks

Sevenoaks Tourist Information Centre, Library Building, Buckhurst Lane, Sevenoaks TN13 1LQ Tel: (01732) 450305.

Follow the A25 east
(Signposted 2 miles)

Sited in a commanding position and at an important crossroads, although Sevenoaks origins can be traced back to at least Saxon times it was not officially mentioned until 1114AD when it appeared in a register of local churches as "Seovenaca". In 1955 a group of seven trees, taken from Knole Park, were planted on the common on the edge of the town. These were "replacements" for the original trees that legend had as giving the name to the area and had long since disappeared. Unfortunately these replacements suffered severe damage during the storm of October 1987. Despite its latter day role as a commuter town it has maintained its individuality, characterized by the warm tones of the building material, Kentish ragstone and the mellow tilehung houses built from locally made bricks. Picturesque cobbled back streets and specialist shops provide much for the visitor to enjoy.

Chartwell (NT)

Westerham, Kent TN16 1PS
Tel: (01732) 868381
Information Line:
Tel: (01732) 866368 (NB. No access without pre-booked timed admission ticket)
website:www.nationaltrust.org.uk

Follow the A25 west towards Westerham and, after 3.3 miles, turn left along the B2069 (Signposted 4.7 miles)

The home of Sir Winston Churchill since 1924, this unpretentious Victorian country house remains much as he left it with an impressive collection of mementos and historical artefacts of his life and career as a statesman. The house is set amidst beautiful terraced gardens overlooking the Weald and many of his paintings are on view in the Garden Studio. Restaurant. Gift Shop. Disabled access.

Knole (NT)

Sevenoaks TN15 0RP
Tel: (01732) 462100
Information Line
Tel: (01732) 450608
website:www.nationaltrust.org.uk

Follow the A21 south for 4 miles and turn left along the A225 towards Sevenoaks (5.8 miles)

Set in a 1,000 acre deer park, Knole was built by Thomas Bourchier when Archbishop of Canterbury (1454) and used as a retreat by bishops until Archbishop Cranmer relinquished it to Henry VIII. In 1566 Queen Elizabeth I granted it to her courtier Sir Thomas Sackville, 1st Earl of Dorset, who enlarged and embellished it in 1603-8. Still occupied today by the Sackville family, the house is virtually unaltered from this period and the thirteen state rooms on view contain magnificent collections: 17thC Royal Stuart furniture, silver furniture and the prototype of the Knole Settee, outstanding tapestries and textiles and important portraits by Van Dyck, Gainsborough and Reynolds. There are pleasant walks available in the deer park, in which over 200,000 trees have been planted in the wake of the storm of October 1987, and the private walled garden is open from time to time throughout the year. Tea Room. Shop. Limited disabled access.

Eynstone and Lullingstone

Follow the A25 east and turn north along the A225 (8.5 miles)

For details please see Junction 3 information.

For details please see Junction 3 information.

M25 BETWEEN JUNCS 5 & 6

CLACKET LANE SERVICES (CLOCKWISE) (ROADCHEF)
Tel: (01959) 565577 Restaurant, Coffee Bar, Wimpy Bar, Travel Inn & Total Fuel

CLACKET LANE SERVICES (ANTI-CLOCKWISE) (ROADCHEF)
Tel: (01959) 565577 Restaurant, Costa Coffee, Wimpy Bar & Total Fuel

FOOTBRIDGE CONNECTION BETWEEN SITES.

M25 JUNCTION 6

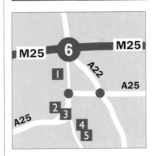

Nearest A&E Hospital

East Surrey Hospital
Canada Avenue, Redhill
RH1 5RH
Tel: (01737) 768511
Follow the B2235 south, turn right along the A25 into Redhill and turn left along the A23. The hospital is signposted along the A23. (Distance Approx 7.3 miles)

FACILITIES

1   Godstone Shell

Tel: (01883) 741700
0.4 miles south along the
B2235, on the right
Access, Visa, Delta,
Mastercard, Switch, Diners
Club, Amex, Overdrive, All Star,
Dial Card, BP Agency, Esso
Eurocard, Shell Cards.

2   The Hare & Hounds

Tel: (01883) 742296
0.7 miles south along the
B2235 in Godstone, on the
right
(Punch Taverns) Open all day.
Meals served; Mon-Thurs;
11.30-15.00hrs & 17.30-
21.30hrs, Fri-Sun; 11.30-
21.30hrs.

3   The Old Forge Café

Tel: (01883) 743230
0.8 miles south along the
B2235 in Godstone, on the
right
Open; Mon-Sat; 08.00-
16.00hrs

4   The White Hart

Tel: (01883) 742521
0.9 miles south along the
B2235 in Godstone, on the
left
(Beefeater) Open all day. Meals
served; Mon-Fri; 12.00-
14.30hrs & 17.00-22.30hrs,
Sat; 12.00-23.00hrs, Sun;
12.00-22.00hrs.

5   Coach House Restaurant & Godstone Hotel

Tel: (01883) 742461
0.9 miles south along the
B2235 in Godstone, on the
left

Restaurant Open; Breakfast;
07.30-10.00hrs, Lunch; 12.00-
14.00hrs, Dinner; 19.00-
22.00hrs daily

PLACES OF INTEREST

Godstone Vineyards

Quarry Road, Godstone
RH9 8ZA Tel: (01883) 744590

Follow the A22 north and turn
right along Quarry Road
(Signposted 1 Mile)

Established in 1985 and set in
50 acres of farmland, the
vineyards overlook the
beautiful Surrey countryside.
An initial 6.5 acres of gentle
south-facing terrain were
planted up and today visitors
are able to stroll through the
fields and even pick their own
grapes. The "Adopt-a-Vine"
Club is an opportunity to adopt
a personal vine, tend it and
eventually drink the wine that
it produces. Visitors are able to
taste the full range of wines
available in the Wine Shop and
morning coffee, lunches and
afternoon teas are served in
the Vineyard Garden Room.
Disabled access.

M25 JUNCTION 7

THIS JUNCTION IS A
MOTORWAY INTERCHANGE
WITH THE M23 ONLY AND
THERE IS NO ACCESS TO ANY
FACILITIES.

M25 JUNCTION 8

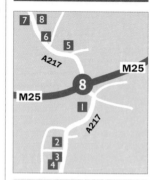

Nearest A&E Hospital

East Surrey Hospital
Canada Avenue, Redhill
RH1 5RH
Tel: (01737) 768511
Take the A217 south into
Reigate, turn left along the A25
into Redhill, turn right along
the A23 and the hospital is
signposted along this route.
(Distance Approx 5.3 miles)

FACILITIES

1   Bridge House Hotel & Lannis Restaurant

Tel: (01737) 244821
0.4 miles south along the
A217, on the right
Restaurant Open; Breakfast;
Mon-Sat; 07.30-09.30hrs, Sun;
08.00-09.30hrs, Lunch; Sun-
Fri; 12.30-14.30hrs, Dinner;
Mon-Thurs; 19.30-21.00hrs, Fri
& Sat; 19.30-21.30hrs

2   The Yew Tree

Tel: (01737) 244944
0.8 miles south along the
A217, on the right
(Unique Pub Company) Open
all day. Meals served; 12.00-
14.30hrs & 19.00-21.30hrs
daily

3 Reigate Manor Service Station (Esso)

Tel: (01737) 221150

0.8 miles south along the A217, on the right

Access, Visa, Overdrive, All Star, Switch, Dial Card, Mastercard, Amex, Diners Club, Delta, BP Supercharge, Shell Gold, Esso Cards.

4 Reigate Manor Hotel

Tel: (01737) 240125

0.9 miles south along the A217, on the right

(Best Western) Restaurant Open; Breakfast; 07.00-09.00hrs daily, Lunch; Sun-Fri; 12.00-14.00hrs, Dinner 19.30-21.45hrs daily

5 Oxford House Service Station (Total)

Tel: (01737) 831954

0.8 miles north along the A217, on the right

Access, Visa, Overdrive, All Star, Switch, Dial Card, Mastercard, Amex, Diners Club, Delta, Total/Fina/Elf Cards. Open; Mon-Sat; 06.00-22.00hrs, Sun; 07.00-22.00hrs

6 The Fox on the Hill

Tel: (01737) 832638

0.8 miles north along the A217, on the right

(Punch Pub Company) Open all day. Meals served; Mon-Sat 12.00-14.30hrs & 18.00-21.30hrs, Sun; 12.00-15.00hrs.

7 BP Connect Oak Tree Service Station

Tel: (01737) 832048

1 mile north along the A217, on the left

LPG. Access, Visa, Overdrive, All Star, Switch, Dial Card, Mastercard, Amex, AA Paytrak,

Diners Club, Delta, Routex. Shell Agency, BP Cards. Wild Bean Café.

8 Star Mogador (Texaco)

Tel: (01737) 831800

1 mile north along the A217, on the right

Access, Visa, Overdrive, All Star, Switch, Dial Card, Electron, Solo, Mastercard, Amex, Diners Club, Delta, Fast Fuel, Texaco Cards.

JUNCTION 9

LEATHERHEAD TOWN CENTRE IS WITHIN ONE MILE OF THE WESTBOUND/CLOCKWISE EXIT FROM THIS JUNCTION

Nearest A&E Hospital

Epsom General Hospital

Dorking Road, Epsom KT18 7EG

Tel: (01372) 735735

Follow the A243 south, turn left along the A24 towards Epsom and the hospital is signposted along this route. (Distance: From Westbound/Clockwise Exit: Approx 3.4 miles. From Eastbound/Anti-Clockwise Exit: Approx 4.5 miles)

FACILITIES

(From Eastbound/Anti-Clockwise Exit)

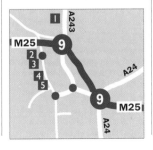

1 The Star

Tel: (01372) 843683

0.7 miles north along the A243, on the left

(Free House) Open all day Sun. Meals served; Mon-Thurs; 12.00-14.00 & 17.30-22.00hrs, Fri & Sat; 12.00-14.00 & 17.30-22.30hrs, Sun; 12.00-18.00hrs & 19.00-21.00hrs.

2 Manston Elms Guest House

Tel: (01372) 374514

0.5 miles south along Kingston Road on the right

3 Tesco Filling Station

Tel: (01372) 859400

0.5 miles south along Kingston Road on the right

Access, Visa, Overdrive, All Star, Switch, Dial Card, Mastercard, Electron, Amex, Diners Club, Delta. Tesco Fuelcard. Toilets and Cash Machines available in adjacent store. Open; 05.30-0.00hrs daily

4 The Royal Oak

Tel: (01372) 811988

0.8 miles south along Kingston Road on the right

(Greene King) Meals served; Mon-Fri; 12.00-14.30hrs

5 Lal Quila Indian Restaurant

Tel: (01372) 360884

0.9 miles south along Kingston Road on the right

Open; 12.00-14.30hrs & 18.00-0.00hrs daily

FACILITIES

(From Westbound/ Clockwise Exit)

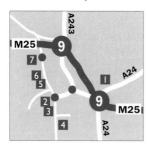

1 Silver Firs

Tel: (01372) 272122
0.7 miles north along the A24, on the left

2 The Plough

Tel: (01372) 377608
0.3 miles south along the A245, on the right
Open all day. Meals served; Mon-Sat; 11.00-23.00hrs, Sun; 12.00-22.30hrs

3 Kingscroft Service Station (Esso)

Tel: (01372) 361562
0.4 miles south along the A245, on the right
Access, Visa, Delta, Mastercard, Switch, Diners Club, Amex, Overdrive, All Star, Dial Card, Shell Gold, BP Supercharge, Esso Cards

4 Shell Leatherhead

Tel: (01372) 225110
0.6 miles south along the A245, on the left
Access, Visa, Overdrive, All Star, Switch, Dial Card, Mastercard, Amex, Diners Club, Delta, aa Paytrak, BP Supercharge, BP Agency, Esso Chargecard, Shell Cards. Open; 07.00-23.00hrs daily

5 Lal Quila Indian Restaurant

Tel: (01372) 360884
0.6 miles north along Kingston Road on the left
Open; 12.00-14.30hrs & 18.00-0.00hrs daily

6 The Royal Oak

Tel: (01372) 811988
0.7 miles north along Kingston Road on the left
(Greene King) Meals served; Mon-Fri; 12.00-14.30hrs

7 Tesco Filling Station

Tel: (01372) 859400
1 mile north along Kingston Road on the left
Access, Visa, Overdrive, All Star, Switch, Dial Card, Mastercard, Electron, Amex, Diners Club, Delta. Tesco Fuelcard. Toilets and Cash Machines available in adjacent store. Open; 05.30-0.00hrs daily

PLACES OF INTEREST

Polesden Lacey (NT)

Great Bookham, Nr Dorking RH5 6BD Tel: (01372) 452048
Information Line:
Tel: (01372) 458203
website: www.nationaltrust.org.uk

Follow the A243 south, continue along the A24 and A246 to Great Bookham and turn left towards Dorking (5.6 miles from Clockwise exit)
The writer Richard Brindley Sheridan, author of the plays "The School for Scandal" and "The Rivals", lived in a house on this site and his wife was responsible for laying out part of the gardens. The house was originally built in 1824 to designs by Thomas Cubitt but was extensively remodelled in 1906-9 and contains collections of fine paintings, furniture, porcelain and silver. King George VI and Queen Elizabeth the Queen Mother spent part of their honeymoon here and the extensive grounds contain a walled rose garden, lawns and landscape walks. Tea Room. Gift Shop. Disabled access.

Chessington World of Adventures

Leatherhead Road, Chessington KT9 2NE
Tel: 0870 444 7777
website: www.chessington.com

Follow the A243 north (Signposted along route. 2.9 miles from Anti-Clockwise exit)
Originally primarily a zoo, over 100 rides and amusements, including "Rattlesnake" and "Samurai" have become established favourites. Additions for 2002 are the New Vampire – the world's first bat-tastic coaster and Tomb Blaster an exciting inter-active ride to add to Chessington's well-established reputation amongst the leading amusement parks in the country. Amongst the attractions, "Rameses Revenge" is considered as one of the more spectacular, spinning riders through 360° whilst plummeting down towards a rock lined pit and water fountains, and for the less adventurous there is "Beanoland", with the New Dennis's Madhouse, a circus and gardens as well as the zoo with it's Trail of the Kings. Restaurant. Shop. Disabled access.

Bocketts Farm Park

Young Street, Fetcham KT22 9BS Tel: (01372) 363764
Follow the A243 south,

continue along the A24 and then the A246 to Fetcham (3.4 miles from Clockwise exit)

A great day out on a working farm with many play areas, inside and out, and loads of friendly farm animals. Look out for the pig racing which takes place at lunchtime on each mid-week day and then enjoy the delicious home made food in the tea room. Gift Shop. Disabled access.

JUNCTION 10

THERE ARE NO FACILITIES WITHIN ONE MILE OF THIS JUNCTION

Nearest Clockwise A&E Hospital
St Peter's Hospital

Guildford Road, Ottershaw, Chertsey KT16 0PZ
Tel: (01932) 872000

Proceed north [clockwise] to Junction 11 and follow the A317 south. The hospital is signposted from the junction (Distance Approx 6.4 miles)

Nearest Anti-Clockwise A&E Hospital
Royal Surrey County Hospital

Egerton Road, Guildford GU2 5XX
Tel: (01483) 571122

Follow the A3 south and the hospital is signposted along the route. (Distance Approx 9.7 miles)

Or alternatively
Epsom General Hospital

Dorking Road, Epsom KT18 7EG
Tel: (01372) 735735

Proceed east [anti-clockwise] to Junction 9 and follow the A243

south. Turn left along the A24 towards Epsom and the hospital is signposted along this route. (Distance Approx 10.8 miles)

PLACES OF INTEREST

Guildford

Guildford Tourist Information Centre, 14 Tunsgate, Guildford GU1 3QT Tel: (01483) 444333 website: www.guildfordborough.co.uk

Follow the A3 south (Signposted 8.2 miles)

Located on the attractive River Wey and with a wooded hill as its background, Guildford can trace its history back to at least Norman times when a castle was built here. Although it is now a bustling county town many early buildings still survive and the individual character, amongst its fine shops, has been retained. Apart from the castle and Guildhall there are a couple of inns, the "Lion" and the "Angel" both of some antiquity with the latter having a crypt that is reputed to have been constructed in the 13thC. The Grammar School was founded in 1550 and the "Hospital of the Holy Trinity" (Abbot's Hospital alms houses) was commenced in 1619 and is of special interest. Gifted to the town, it is built in red brick around a quadrangle with a gate house, turret, cupola and fine old chimney-stacks. Lewis Carroll has connections with the town, he stayed with his sisters at "The Chestnuts" on his visits here and his grave can be seen in the Mount Cemetery. Guildford Cathedral (Tel: 01483-565287), which was designed by Sir Edward Maufe and started in 1936 but not consecrated until 1961

overlooks the town from the top of Stag Hill, whilst in the valley, trips can be made from the Guildford Boat House (Tel: 01483-504494) along the National Trust's River Wey Navigation.

Within the town can be found ...

Guildford Castle & Grounds

Castle Street, Guildford GU1 3TU Tel: (01483) 444718 website: www.guildfordborough.co.uk

Guildford Castle was originally constructed by William the Conqueror as part of the strategic ring of defences around London, each of one days march apart and one days march from the Tower of London. Whilst Windsor Castle, part of this system, (See M4, Junction 6 information) was enlarged over the years and still remains, only the imposing stone keep built in the time of Henry II is left of Guildford Castle. Set amidst beautiful grounds it is a pleasant landmark right in the town centre.

The Guildhall

High Street, Guildford GU1 3AA Tel: (01483) 444035 website: www.guildfordborough.co.uk

Built in the 16th &17thC, the ground floor is of Tudor origin, the Guildhall was first utilized as a courtroom and Council Chamber and now houses a fine collection of Civic plate. The spectacular bracket clock which dominates the High Street was installed in 1683.

Guildford Museum

Castle Arch, Guildford GU1 3SX Tel: (01483) 444750 website: www.guildfordborough.co.uk

Located within a 17thC brick building adjoining the castle arch, the museum houses a collection of archaeological exhibits and artefacts tracing the history of the area from Prehistoric times through to the Middle Ages. These include items from the 6thC Saxon cemetery at Guildown, mediaeval tiles from Chertsey Abbey and examples of Wealden ironwork, needlework and needlework implements. A section is devoted to Lewis Carroll (Charles Dodgson) who died in Guildford in 1898 and displays letters and other memorabilia. The Muniment Room houses over 100,000 documents relating to Guildford and the district. Gift Shop.

Guildford Spectrum

The Leisure Complex, Parkway, Guildford GU1 1UP
Tel: (01483) 443322 website: www.guildfordspectrum.co.uk

Situated in landscaped parkland, the facilities include a ten-pin bowling centre, leisure pool with flumes, spas and wave machine, soft play area, American Pool deck and an Olympic sized ice rink. Other facilities include licensed bars and catering outlets. Disabled access.

Dapdune Wharf (NT)

River Wey Navigations, Wharf Road, Guildford GU1 4RR
Tel: (01483) 561389
website: www.nationaltrust. org.uk/southern

The Wey was one of the first British rivers to be made navigable, the 15.5 mile link between Guildford and Weybridge, on the River Thames, opened to barge traffic in 1653 with an extension down to Godalming opening in 1764. Dapdune Wharf was originally constructed as the barge-building site for the river and today the Visitor Centre gives a fascinating insight into the history of this 19.5 miles long waterway. Within the centre the restored Wey barge "Reliance" can be inspected and there are

interactive displays in the former Carbide Store, Stable and Smithy. The towpath is open throughout and there is a family trail and picnic area. Tea Room. Disabled access

RHS Garden Wisley

Woking GU23 6QB
Tel: (01483) 224234
website: www.rhs.org.uk.

Follow the A3 south (Signposted 1 mile)

Covering over 240 acres, Wisley is the magnificent flagship of the Royal Horticultural Society, in demonstrating the very best in gardening practices and acting as a working encyclopaedia for gardeners of all levels throughout the year. It is not necessary, however, to be a keen gardener to appreciate the beauty and enchantment of the superb gardens. Café. Gift Shop. Disabled access.

Chatley Heath Semaphore Tower

Ockham Common
Tel: (01732) 458822

Take the A3 exit and follow the signs to Effingham. (Utilize the Semaphore Car Parks in Old Lane, Ockham Common. 1 mile)

Situated on Chatley Heath and accessed via well marked trails through the 700 acres of heath and woodland, the Semaphore Tower was once part of the Royal Navy's signalling system for relaying messages between Portsmouth and the Admiralty in London. Although the semaphore system soon fell into disuse this unique building has remained in good order and is open for inspection at weekends and Bank Holidays. As well as offering outstanding views across the surrounding landscape it contains an interesting exhibition and a model collection. Tea Room. Gift Shop

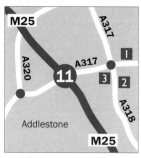

Nearest A&E Hospital

St Peter's Hospital
Guildford Road, Ottershaw, Chertsey KT16 0PZ
Tel: (01932) 872000

Follow the A317 south and the hospital is signposted from the junction (Distance Approx 1.7 miles)

FACILITIES

1   The Woburn Arms

Tel: (01932) 563314
0.9 miles east along the road to Addlestonemoor, on the left
(Unique Supply Line) Open all day. Meals served; Mon-Sat; 09.30-14.30hrs & 18.00-22.00hrs, Sun; 09.30-14.30hrs

2   TCS Addlestone Service Station (Total)

Tel: (01932) 839960
1 mile south along the A318, on the left
LPG. Access, Visa, Overdrive, All Star, Switch, Dial Card, Mastercard, Amex, Diners Club, Amex, AA Paytrak, Delta, Total/Fina/Elf Cards. Café Bonjour. Open; Mon-Fri; 06.30-23.00hrs, Sat & Sun; 07.00-23.00hrs.

3 The George

Tel: (01932) 820784

1 mile south along the A318, on the right

(Courage) Open all day. Meals served; Mon-Sat; 12.00-14.00hrs & 19.00-21.00hrs, Sun; 12.00-14.30hrs

PLACES OF INTEREST

Thorpe Park

Staines Road, Chertsey
KT16 8PN Tel: (01932) 569393
website: www.thorpepark.com

Follow the A320 (Signposted 3.7 miles)

Opened in 1979, within the 500 acre site is one of Britain's foremost amusement parks with such attractions as the Detonator, Vortex, Zodiac, Ribena Rumba Rapids, Tidal Wave and Pirates-4D. New for the 2002 season is the world's first ten looping coaster – Colossus. As well as the numerous rides there is a Model World and a man-made beach and pools with a traditional working farm and craft centre reached by a train or waterbus. Restaurant. Café. Shop. Disabled access.

Brooklands Museum

Brooklands Road, Weybridge
KT13 0QN Tel: (01932) 857381
website: www.motor-software.co.uk

Follow the A317 north into Weybridge and turn right along the B374 (Signposted in Weybridge 3.7 miles)

Recreating the 1920 and 1930s heyday of this famous old circuit, the first purpose built motor racing circuit and venue of the first 100 mile/hr motor ride, Brooklands Museum has plenty of racing

cars, motorbikes and bicycles on display in the restored clubhouse. Apart from land vehicles there are also aviation exhibits including "R for Robert" the Loch Ness Wellington Bomber and a comprehensive collection of vintage Vickers and Hawker planes. Tea Room. Shop. Disabled access.

JUNCTION 12

> THIS JUNCTION IS A MOTORWAY INTERCHANGE WITH THE M3 ONLY AND THERE IS NO ACCESS TO ANY FACILITIES.

Nearest A&E Hospital

St Peter's Hospital

Guildford Road, Ottershaw, Chertsey KT16 0PZ
Tel: (01932) 872000

Proceed south [anti-clockwise] to Junction 11 and follow the A317 south. The hospital is signposted from the junction (Distance Approx 3.9 miles)

JUNCTION 13

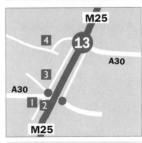

Nearest Clockwise A&E Hospital

Wexham Park Hospital

Wexham Road, Slough

SL2 4HL
Tel: (01753) 633000

Proceed north to Junction 15, turn west along the M4 to Junction 5 and take the A4 exit north. Turn right along the A412 and the hospital is signposted (Distance Approx 10.3 miles)

Nearest Anti-Clockwise A&E Hospital

St Peter's Hospital

Guildford Road, Ottershaw, Chertsey KT16 0PZ
Tel: (01932) 872000

Proceed south [anti-clockwise] to Junction 11 and follow the A317 south. The hospital is signposted from the junction (Distance Approx 7.0 miles)

Nearest Minor Injury Unit

Ashford Hospital

London Road, Ashford, Middlesex TW15 3AA
Tel: (01784) 884488

Take the A30 east and the hospital is on the left hand side adjacent to the junction with the B378. (Distance Approx 2.7 miles)

FACILITIES

1 The Iguana Bar & Oasis Restaurant

Tel: (01784) 432183

1.2 miles south along the A30, adjacent to the south side of the south roundabout

Bar open all day. Restaurant Open; Mon-Thurs; 12.00-15.00hrs & 17.30-21.30hrs, Fri/Sat; 12.00-01.00hrs, Sat/Sun; 18.00-01.00hrs, Sun; 12.00-15.00hrs

2 Runnymede Service Station (Total)

Tel: (01784) 430763

1.2 miles south along the A30, adjacent to the south

side of the south roundabout

Access, Visa, Overdrive, All Star, Switch, Dial Card, Mastercard, Amex, Diners Club, Amex, Delta, Electron, Solo, Total/Fina/Elf Cards. Open Mon-Sat; 07.00-23.00hrs, Sun; 08.00-22.00hrs

3 Runnymede Hotel & Spa

Tel: (01784) 436171

1.2 miles south along the A30, adjacent to the north side of the south roundabout

The Left Bank Restaurant Open; Breakfast; 07.00-09.30hrs daily, Lunch; Sun-Fri; 12.00-14.30hrs, Dinner; Mon-Sat; 19.00-22.30hrs

4 Tandoori & Balti Restaurant

Tel: (01784) 483578

0.4 miles west along the B376, on the right

Open; Tues-Sun; 12.00-14.30hrs & 18.00-23.00hrs

PLACES OF INTEREST

Thorpe Park

Staines Road, Chertsey KT16 8PN Tel: (01932) 569393

Follow the A30 south (Signposted 3.6 miles)

For details please see Junction 11 information

Windsor Castle

Windsor SL4 1NJ Visitor Office

Tel: (01753) 868286

Follow the A30 south and turn right along the A308 (Signposted 5.8 Miles)

For details please see M4 Junction 6 information.

Legoland

Winkfield Road, Windsor

SL4 4AY Tel: 0990 040404

Follow the A30 south, turn right and take the A308 into Windsor and turn left along the B3022. (Signposted 7 Miles)

For details please see M4 Junction 6 information.

Eton College & Museum of Eton Life

High Street, Eton SL4 6DW

Tel: (01753) 671177

Follow the B376 west (Signposted 6 Miles)

For details please see M4 Junction 6 information.

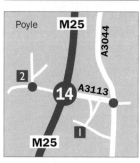

Nearest Clockwise A&E Hospital

Wexham Park Hospital

Wexham Road, Slough SL2 4HL

Tel: (01753) 633000

Proceed north to Junction 15, turn west along the M4 to Junction 5 and take the A4 exit north. Turn right along the A412 and the hospital is signposted (Distance Approx 8.4 miles)

Nearest Anti-Clockwise A&E Hospital

St Peter's Hospital

Guildford Road, Ottershaw, Chertsey KT16 0PZ

Tel: (01932) 872000

Proceed south [anti-clockwise] to Junction 11 and follow the A317 south. The hospital is signposted from the junction (Distance Approx 8.9 miles)

Nearest Minor Injury Unit

Ashford Hospital

London Road, Ashford, Middlesex TW15 3AA

Tel: (01784) 884488

Take the A3113 east, turn right along the A3044 and left along the B378. The hospital is at its junction with London Road (A30). (Distance Approx 2.8 miles)

FACILITIES

1 The Anchor

Tel: (01753) 682707

0.6 miles south along Horton Road on the right, in Stanwell Moor

(Greene King) Meals served; Mon-Fri; 12.00-14.00hrs & 17.00-19.00hrs, Sun; 13.00-16.00hrs

2 The Golden Cross

Tel: (01753) 682231

0.6 miles west along Poyle Road, on the left

(Greene King) Open all day. Meals served; Mon-Fri; 12.00-22.00hrs, Sat & Sun; 12.00-18.00hrs

THIS JUNCTION IS A MOTORWAY INTERCHANGE WITH THE M4 ONLY AND THERE IS NO ACCESS TO ANY FACILITIES.

Nearest A&E Hospital

Wexham Park Hospital

Wexham Road, Slough
SL2 4HL
Tel: (01753) 633000

Proceed west along the M4 to Junction 5 and take the A4 exit north. Turn right along the A412 and the hospital is signposted (Distance Approx 6.4 miles)

Nearest Minor Injuries Unit

Ashford Hospital

London Road, Ashford,
Middlesex TW15 3AA
Tel: (01784) 884488

Procced south [anti-clockwise] to Junction 14 and take the A3113 east. Turn right along the A3044, left along the B378 and the hospital is at its junction with London Road (A30). (Distance Approx 4.8 miles)

JUNCTION 16

> THIS JUNCTION IS A MOTORWAY INTERCHANGE WITH THE M40 ONLY AND THERE IS NO ACCESS TO ANY FACILITIES.

Nearest A&E Hospital

Wexham Park Hospital

Wexham Road, Slough
SL2 4HL
Tel: (01753) 633000

Proceed east along the M40 to Junction 1, take the A412 exit south and the hospital is signposted (Distance Approx 6.8 miles)

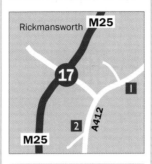

JUNCTION 17

Nearest Clockwise A&E Hospital

Watford General Hospital

Vicarage Road, Watford
WD1 8HB
Tel: (01923) 244366

Follow the A412 east into Watford and it is signposted in the town. (Distance Approx 5.7 miles)

Nearest Anti-Clockwise A&E Hospital

Wexham Park Hospital

Wexham Road, Slough
SL2 4HL
Tel: (01753) 633000

Proceed south to Junction 16 and then east along the M40 to Junction 1, take the A412 exit south to Slough and the hospital is signposted. (Distance Approx 12.0 miles)

FACILITIES

1 Whip & Collar

Tel: (01923) 774946
1 mile east along the A412, on the right in Mill End
(Free House) Meals served; 12.00-14.30hrs & 18.30-21.30hrs daily

2 The Cross

Tel: (01923) 773266
1 mile west along the A412, on the right in Maple Cross (Punch Retail) Open all day. Meals served; 12.00-14.30hrs daily

PLACES OF INTEREST

Chalfont St Giles

Follow the A412 south and turn first right. (Signposted 4.2 Miles)

This fine example of the archetypal English village dates from Roman times and one of the buildings, Stonewalls Farm, is mentioned in the Domesday Book. There are a number of interesting buildings here including an Elizabethan mansion, The Vache, that had started out as a farm in King John's day and by 1360 was a moated residence. Later it was the home to friends of Captain Cook and a monument to the great seafarer can be found in the grounds. Madame Tussaud started her first waxworks in the village and William Penn, founder of the state of Pennsylvania in the USA, lived here and he and his family are buried in the graveyard outside of the Quaker Meeting House at Jordans, nearby.

Within the village can be found ...

Milton's Cottage

Deanway, Chalfont St Giles
HP8 4JH Tel: (01494) 872313

A half-timbered Grade 1 listed building this is the only house used by John Milton to have survived. Dating from the 16thC he moved here in 1665 to escape the plague in London and, although he returned in

1666, wrote "Paradise Lost" and started "Paradise Regained". The cottage and garden have been preserved to encapsulate this period and the building is now home to a museum which includes many relics and an important collection of first editions of the blind poet's works. Shop. Disabled access.

Chiltern Open Air Museum

Newland Park, Gorelands Lane, Chalfont St Giles
HP8 4AB Tel: (01494) 872163

Follow the A412 south and turn first right. (Signposted 3.1 Miles)

This museum is of 45 acres and contains interesting and historial buildings from the Chiltern area that would otherwise have been demolished. Painstakingly dismantled and then rebuilt at the site, each building is utilized to house and display artefacts and implements appropriate to the building's use and history. Typical examples are as diverse as an Iron Age house, Victorian farmyard, Edwardian public convenience and a 1940s pre-fab. As well as the buildings there are fields farmed by mediaeval methods containing historic crops such as organic woad, from which indigo dye is extracted for use in dyeing demonstration, and a nature trail and adventure playground. Snacks. Shop. Some disabled access.

Nearest Clockwise A&E Hospital

Watford General Hospital
Vicarage Road, Watford

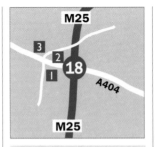

WD1 8HB
Tel: (01923) 244366
Follow the A404 south, turn left along the A412 into Watford and it is signposted in the town. (Distance Approx 5.0 miles)

Nearest Anti-Clockwise A&E Hospital

Wexham Park Hospital
Wexham Road, Slough
SL2 4HL
Tel: (01753) 633000
Proceed south to Junction 16 and then east along the M40 to Junction 1, take the A412 exit south to Slough and the hospital is signposted (Distance Approx 13.5 miles)

FACILITIES

1 The White Horse

Tel: (01923) 282227
0.3 miles west along the A404, on the left
(Greene King) Open all day Fri-Sun. Meals served; Mon-Sat; 12.00-14.15hrs & 18.00-21.15hrs, Sun; 12.00-15.00hrs

2 Chorleywood Shell

Tel: (01923) 285010
0.4 miles west along the A404, on the right
Access, Visa, Overdrive, All Star, Switch, Dial Card, Mastercard, Amex, Diners Club, Amex, Delta, BP Supercharge, Shell Cards.

3 Jenny Wren

Tel: (01923) 282053
0.5 miles west along the A404, on the right
(Six Continents) Open all day. Meals served; Mon-Sat; 12.00-22.00hrs, Sun; 12.00-21.30hrs

PLACES OF INTEREST

Manor House

Chenies, Rickmansworth
WD3 6ER Tel: (01494) 762888

Follow the A404 west and it is signposted along route (2.5 Miles)

Adjacent to the mediaeval village of Chenies, on the pretty River Chess, the origins of the Manor House date back to Henry VIII. The Tudor rooms contain tapestries and a doll collection and there is a 13thC crypt and a Priest's Hole. The neighbouring St Michael's Church has a Norman font and a north chapel constructed in 1556. As well as numerous monuments to the Russells, there are many fine brasses including remarkable specimens from 1484 and 1510. Home made teas. Shop.

THIS IS A RESTRICTED ACCESS JUNCTION.
- Vehicles can not access the clockwise carriageways
- Vehicles can not exit from the anti-clockwise carriageways.

Nearest Clockwise A&E Hospital

Watford General Hospital
Vicarage Road, Watford

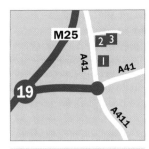

WD1 8HB
Tel: (01923) 244366
Follow the A411 south into Watford, take the A4145 south towards West Watford and the hospital is on the left side of Vicarage Road (Distance Approx 3.2 miles)

Nearest Anti-Clockwise A&E Hospital
Wexham Park Hospital
Wexham Road, Slough
SL2 4HL
Tel: (01753) 633000
Proceed south to Junction 16 and then east along the M40 to Junction 1, take the A412 exit south to Slough and the hospital is signposted (Distance Approx 16.4 miles)

FACILITIES

1 TCS Hunton Bridge Service Station (Total)

Tel: (01923) 267964
0.2 miles north along the A41, on the right
Access, Visa, Delta, Mastercard, Switch, Diners Club, Amex, Overdrive, All Star, Dial Card, Total/Fina/Elf Cards.

2 The Kings Head
Tel: (01923) 262307
0.7 miles north in Bridge Road, Hunton Bridge, on the right
(Punch Retail) Open all day.

Meals served; Mon-Sat; 12.00-15.00hrs & 19.00-21.00hrs, Sun; 12.00-15.00hrs

3 The Kings Lodge Hotel
Tel: (01923) 441141
0.7 miles north in Bridge Road, Hunton Bridge, on the right
(Mercury) Bar open all day. Meals served; Mon-Sat; 11.30-14.30hrs & 18.30-22.00hrs, Sun; 12.00-20.00hrs

PLACES OF INTEREST

Watford Museum
194 High Street, Watford
WD1 2HG

Follow the A411 south into Watford (Signposted 3.1 Miles)
For details please see Junction 5 (M1) information

Cassiobury Park
Cassiobury Avenue, Watford
WD1 7SL

Follow the A411 south towards Watford and turn right along the A412 (4.4 Miles)
For details please see Junction 5 (M1) information

JUNCTION 20

Nearest A&E Hospital
Watford General Hospital
Vicarage Road, Watford
WD1 8HB
Tel: (01923) 244366
Follow the A41 south and continue along the A411 into Watford, take the A4145 south towards West Watford and the hospital is on the left side of Vicarage Road (Distance Approx 4.4 miles)

Or alternatively
Hemel Hempstead General Hospital
Hillfield Road, Hemel Hempstead HP2 4AD
Tel: (01442) 213141
Follow the A41 north to Hemel Hempstead, turn right along the A414 and it is signposted along the route. (Distance Approx 4.6 miles)

FACILITIES

1 Rose & Crown

Tel: (01923) 290229
0.8 miles north along the A4251, on the left in Kings Langley
(Six Continents) Open all day. Meals served; 12.00-20.00hrs daily

2 The Saracens
Tel: (01923) 400144
0.9 miles north along the A4251, on the right in Kings Langley
(Free House) Meals served; Mon-Sat; 11.00-14.00hrs

3 Taste of India
Tel: (01923) 270668
0.9 miles north along the A4251, on the right in Kings Langley

Open; 12.00-14.30hrs &
18.00-23.30hrs daily

4 Oscars Pizza Bar & Restaurant

Tel: (01923) 263800
1 mile north along the A4251,
on the right in Kings Langley
Open; 12.00-22.30hrs daily

5 The Kings Head

Tel: (01923) 262307
0.8 miles south in Bridge
Road, Hunton Bridge, on the
right
(Punch Retail) Open all day.
Meals served; Mon-Sat; 12.00-
15.00hrs & 19.00-21.00hrs,
Sun; 12.00-15.00hrs

6 The Kings Lodge Hotel

Tel: (01923) 441141
0.8 miles south in Bridge
Road, Hunton Bridge, on the
right
(Mercury) Bar open all day.
Meals served; Mon-Sat; 11.30-
14.30hrs & 18.30-22.00hrs,
Sun; 12.00-20.00hrs

7 TCS Hunton Bridge Service Station (Total)

Tel: (01923) 267964
1 mile south along the A41,
on the left
Access, Visa, Delta,
Mastercard, Switch, Diners
Club, Amex, Overdrive, All Star,
Dial Card, Total/Fina/Elf Cards.

PLACES OF INTEREST

Watford Museum

194 High Street, Watford
WD1 2HG

Follow the A41 and then
A411 south into Watford
(Signposted 4.4 Miles)
For details please see Junction
5 (M1) information

Cassiobury Park

Cassiobury Avenue, Watford
WD1 7SL

Follow the A41 and then
A411 south towards Watford
and turn right along the A412
(5.7 Miles)
For details please see Junction
5 (M1) information

JUNCTION 21

THIS JUNCTION IS A
MOTORWAY INTERCHANGE
WITH THE M1 ONLY AND
THERE IS NO ACCESS TO ANY
FACILITIES.

JUNCTION 21A

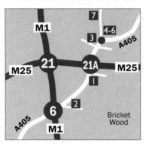

Nearest Clockwise A&E Hospital

Barnet Hospital

Wellhouse Lane, Barnet
EN5 3DJ
Tel: (020) 8216 4000
Proceed east to Junction 23,
follow the A1 south, at the
second roundabout turn left
along the A411 and the
hospital is signposted along
this route. (Distance Approx
12.2 miles)

Nearest Anti-Clockwise A&E Hospital

Watford General Hospital

Vicarage Road, Watford
WD1 8HB
Tel: (01923) 244366
Follow the A405 south and
continue along the A412 into
Watford. Take the A4145 south
towards West Watford and the
hospital is on the left side of
Vicarage Road (Distance
Approx 5.1 miles)

FACILITIES

1 Classic Service Station (Total)

Tel: (01923) 680024
0.1 miles south along the
A405, on the left
Access, Visa, Overdrive, All
Star, Switch, Dial Card,
Mastercard, Amex, AA Paytrak,
Diners Club, Delta, Total/Fina/
Elf Cards

2 Little Chef

Tel: (01923) 661842
0.6 miles south along the
A405, on the left
Open; 07.00-22.00hrs daily

3 Thistle St Albans Hotel

Tel: (01727) 854252
0.5 miles north along the
A405, on the left
The Noke Restaurant Open;
Breakfast; Mon-Fri; 07.30-
09.30hrs, Sat & Sun; 08.00-
10.00hrs, Lunch; 12.00-
14.00hrs daily, Dinner; 19.00-
21.30hrs daily. The Oak &
Avocado Restaurant Open;
Lunch; 12.00-14.00hrs daily,
Dinner; 19.00-22.00hrs daily.

4 Chiswell Shell

Tel: (01727) 819900

0.6 miles north along the A405, on the left

Access, Visa, Delta, Mastercard, Switch, Diners Club, Amex, Overdrive, All Star, Dial Card, Shell Cards

5   Little Chef

Tel: (01727) 839998
0.6 miles north along the A405, on the left
Open; 07.00-22.00hrs daily

6   Burger King

Tel: (01727) 839998
0.6 miles north along the A405, on the left
Open; 11.00-21.00hrs daily

7   The Three Hammers

Tel: (01727) 846218
1 mile north along the B4630, on the left
(Six Continents) Open all day. Meals served; Mon-Thurs; 12.00-20.00hrs, Fri & Sat; 12.00-21.00hrs, Sun; 12.00-16.00hrs

PLACES OF INTEREST

St Albans

Tourist Information Office, The Town Hall, Market Place, St Albans AL3 5DJ
Tel: (01727) 864511 website: www.stalbans.gov.uk

Follow the A405 north (Signposted 2.7 Miles)

An important settlement was sited here before the Romans established the town of Verulamium. The later town of St Albans was founded on the opposite side of the River Ver when Offa constructed a monastery in 793AD on the site of the first Christian martyrdom in England. The Saxon Abbey fell into disrepair,

but was solidly rebuilt, partially with bricks from the adjacent Roman sites, by the Normans. There is much in the town that survives from the various periods of its history; Nos 29 & 30 in the Market Place date from the 17thC, Hollywell Hill is mainly Georgian and St Peter's Street has some fine 18th & 19thC houses. St Albans today, with a variety of museums, restaurants and inns, proves to be an attractive and interesting destination for visitors.

Within the town centre ...

Cathedral & Abbey Church of St Alban.

Holywell Hill, St Albans
AL1 1BY

Tel: (01727) 860780 website: www.stalbanscathedral.org.uk

The Saxon Abbey Church and gate house are all that remained of the original edifice following the rebuilding of 1077. The core of the church, which dates from this period, is the second longest in England and the central tower was constructed in Roman brick pillaged from the remains of Verulamium. The original church was enlarged to the west in the 13thC and the Lady Chapel, later turned into a grammar school, added on the east side in the 14thC. The facilities include a Visitor Centre, audio-visual presentation, refectory and gift shop. Disabled access.

St Albans Organ Museum

320 Camp Road, St Albans
AL1 5PE Tel: (01727) 851557

Dance hall and theatre pipe organs, reproducing pianos and music boxes are just part of the magnificent collection of mechanical instruments housed here, all of which are in working order. Visitors can enjoy performances and the facilities include refreshments and a gift shop.

St Albans Clock Tower

Market Place, St Albans
AL4 0LB

Built between 1403 and 1412, this is one of the few belfries of the period to have survived. The original bell "Gabriel" is still housed in the tower that was constructed to symbolically assert the independence and wealth of the town from the dominance and power of the abbey. Fine views over the city and countryside may be obtained when the tower is open to the public at weekends and Bank Holidays.

Verulamium Museum & Park

St Michael's Street, St Albans
AL3 4SW

Tel: (01727) 751810 website: www.stalbans.gov.uk/museums

The museum charts the daily life and times of the major Roman city of Verulamium with the exhibits including magnificent mosaics and recreated rooms as well as a host of smaller artefacts. Other features include touch screen databases and hands-on discovery areas and the facilities include a Museum Shop and full disabled access.

The Park (Tel: 01727-846031) contains the remains of the Roman municipium of Verulamium, one of the three destroyed by Boadicea during the Icenian revolt. It was quickly rebuilt and the many fine buildings constructed then showed its importance. Much of this is now covered but remains of the walls, the Hypocaust and the site of the London Gate are still visible. The park, alongside of the River Ver, also contains fine trees and a lake and is an ideal spot for a picnic. The facilities include a childrens paddling pool, play area, crazy golf, tennis courts and a café.

Museum of St Albans

Hatfield Road, St Albans
AL1 3RR Tel: (01727) 819340
website: www.stalbans.gov.uk/
museum/

Taking over from where the Verulamium Museum leaves off, the Museum of St Albans traces the history and life of the town from the departure of the Romans through to today. It also features the "Tools of the Trade" exhibition of items from the Salaman Collection of trade tools and various special displays are held from time to time. The museum also has a wildlife garden and pond and there is a Museum Shop. Limited disabled access.

The Gardens of the Rose

The Royal National Rose Society, Chiswell Green, St Albans AL2 3NR.

Follow the A405 north and turn first left to Chiswell Green (1.3 miles)

For details please see M1 Junction 6 information.

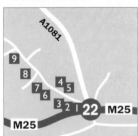

JUNCTION 22

Nearest Clockwise A&E Hospital

Barnet Hospital

Wellhouse Lane, Barnet
EN5 3DJ
Tel: (020) 8216 4000
Proceed east to Junction 23,

follow the A1 south, at the second roundabout turn left along the A411 and the hospital is signposted along this route. (Distance Approx 8.0 miles)

Nearest Anti-Clockwise A&E Hospital

Watford General Hospital

Vicarage Road, Watford
WD1 8HB
Tel: (01923) 244366
Proceed west to Junction 21A, follow the A405 south and continue along the A412 into Watford. Take the A4145 south towards West Watford and the hospital is on the left side of Vicarage Road (Distance Approx 9.3 miles)

FACILITIES

1 McDonald's

Tel: (01727) 827948
Adjacent to the north roundabout
Open; 07.00-23.00hrs daily ["Drive-Thru" open until 0.00hrs daily]

2 Sainsbury's Filling Station

Tel: (01727) 828151
0.1 miles west along road to London Colney, on the left
LPG. Access, Visa, Delta, Mastercard, Switch, Amex, Overdrive, All Star, Dial Card, JS Fuelcard

3 Starbuck's St Albans

Tel: (01727) 828112
0.2 miles west along road to London Colney, on the left in Hypermarket
Open; Mon-Fri; 08.00-21.00hrs, Sat; 09.00-21.00hrs, Sun; 11.00-17.00hrs

4 Colney Fox

Tel: (01727) 823698
0.5 miles west along road to London Colney, on the right
(Six Continents) Open all day. Meals served; Mon-Sat; 12.00-22.00hrs, Sun; 12.00-21.30hrs

5 Innkeeper's Lodge

Tel: (01727) 823698
0.5 miles west along road to London Colney, on the right

6 The Bull

Tel: (01727) 823160
0.6 miles west in London Colney, on the left
(Punch Pub Company) Open all day. Meals served; Mon-Sat; 12.00-14.00hrs

7 Green Dragon

Tel: (01727) 823214
0.7 miles west in London Colney, on the left
(Punch Taverns) Open all day Sat & Sun. Meals served; Mon-Sat; 12.00-14.30hrs & 18.00-21.00hrs, Sun; 12.30-14.30hrs

8 White Lion

Tel: (01727) 822123
0.8 miles west in London Colney, on the left
(Pubmaster) Open all day. Meals served; 12.00-15.00hrs daily

9 Lawrence Auto Services (Total)

Tel: (01727) 822825
1 mile west in London Colney, on the left
Access, Visa, Delta, Mastercard, Switch, Diners Club, Amex, Overdrive, All Star, Dial Card, Total Cards. Open; Mon-Fri; 07.30-20.00hrs, Sat;

09.00-19.00hrs, Sun; 09.00-14.00hrs

PLACES OF INTEREST

St Albans

Follow the A101 north (Signposted 3.7 Miles)
For details please see Junction 21A information.

Bowmans Open Farm

Coursers Road, London Colney, St Albans AL4 0PP
Tel: (01727) 822106 website: www.bowmansfarm.co.uk

From the roundabout on the north side of the exit, follow the route to Colney Heath (1.8 Miles)
Here at Hertfordshire's largest open farm visitors can enjoy an enjoyable and active day out with a variety of animals to meet, animal handling and falconry demonstrations amongst the activities. There are indoor and outdoor picnic and play areas and children's workshops to keep the younger family members amused. Restaurant. Gift Shop.

The de Havilland Aircraft Heritage

Mosquito Aircraft Museum, London Colney, St Albans AL2 1BU Tel: (01727) 822051 website: www.dehavilland museum.co.uk

Follow the B556 east (1.9 Miles)
The famous Mosquito Bomber was secretly developed at nearby Salisbury Hall from 1939 and many types of de Havilland aircraft are now on display in various forms of restoration. Visitors are allowed into some of the planes that, although they may not fly again, have many of the systems operational. There are

restoration workshops and a gift and book shop. Tea Room. Limited disabled access.

JUNCTION 23

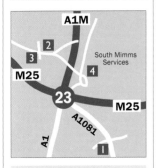

Nearest A&E Hospital

Barnet Hospital
Wellhouse Lane, Barnet EN5 3DJ
Tel: (020) 8216 4000
Follow the A1 south, at the second roundabout turn left along the A411 and the hospital is signposted along this route. (Distance Approx 5.1 miles)

FACILITIES

SOUTH MIMMS SERVICES (WELCOME BREAK)
Tel: (01707) 646333 Granary Express Self Service Restaurant, Granary Express Quick Service Restaurant. Red Hen, Burger King, Days Inn & BP Fuel

1   The Green Dragon

1 mile south along the A1081, on the right.
Meals served daily

2   Murco 124 Service Station

Tel: (01707) 654610

1 mile north along the road to South Mimms, on the right
Access, Visa, Overdrive, All Star, Switch, Dial Card, Mastercard, Amex, Delta, Murco Cards. Open; Mon-Sat; 06.00-23.00hrs, Sun; 08.00-22.00hrs

3   The White Hart

Tel: (01707) 642122
1 mile north along the road to South Mimms, on the left
(McMullens) Open all day. Meals served; Mon-Sat; 12.00-14.30hrs & 18.30-21.00hrs, Sun; 12.00-18.00hrs

4   Holiday Inn South Mimms

Tel: 0870 400 9072
0.2 miles north along the road to South Mimms, on the right
The Junction Restaurant Open; Breakfast; Mon-Fri; 06.30-10.30hrs, Sat & Sun; 07.30-10.30hrs, Lunch; Sun-Fri; 12.00-14.00hrs, Dinner; 18.30-22.30hrs daily. Bar snacks available throughout day.

JUNCTION 24

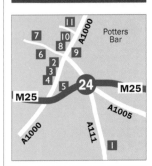

Nearest A&E Hospital

Barnet Hospital
Wellhouse Lane, Barnet EN5 3DJ

Tel: (020) 8216 4000

Follow the A111 north, turn left along the A1000 to Barnet, turn right along the A411 and the hospital is signposted along this route. (Distance Approx 4.4 miles)

FACILITIES

1 West Lodge Park Hotel & Restaurant

Tel: (020) 8440 8311

1 mile south along the A111, on the left

Restaurant Open; Breakfast; Mon-Fri; 07.00-09.45, Sat & Sun; 07.30-10.00hrs, Lunch; 12.30-14.00hrs, Sun; 12.30-14.30hrs, Dinner; Sun-Fri; 19.15-21.30hrs, Sat; 19.15-22.00hrs

2 Paparazzi Italian Restaurant

Tel: (01707) 662623

0.7 miles south along the A1000, on the right

Open; Mon-Sat; 12.00-14.30hrs & 18.00-23.00hrs

3 Potters Bar Café

Tel: (01707) 661181

0.7 miles south along the A1000, on the right

Open; Mon-Sat; 07.00-17.00hrs, Sun; 07.00-15.30hrs

4 Thai Rack Classic Restaurant

Tel: (01707) 663337

0.7 miles south along the A1000, on the right

Open; 12.00-14.30hrs & 18.00-23.00hrs daily

5 Murco Service Station

Tel: (01707) 642709

0.8 miles south along the

A1000, on the left

Access, Visa, Overdrive, All Star, Switch, Dial Card, Mastercard, Amex, Murco Cards. Open: Mon-Fri; 06.30-23.00hrs, Sat; 07.00-23.00hrs, Sun; 08.00-22.00hrs

6 Young's Chinese Restaurant

Tel: (01707) 652551

0.7 miles west along the A111, on the left

Open; Sun; 18.00-23.30hrs, Mon & Wed-Sat; 12.00-14.00hrs & 18.00-0.00hrs

7 Tesco Filling Station

Tel: (01707) 347500

0.8 miles west along the A111, on the right

Access, Visa, Delta, Mastercard, Switch, Amex, Electron, Overdrive, All Star, Dial Card, Tesco Fuelcard. Disabled Toilets and Cash Machine available in adjacent store.

8 Royal Elephant Thai Restaurant

Tel: (01707) 660668

0.7 miles north along the A1000, on the left

Open; Sun-Fri; 12.00-15.00hrs & 18.00-23.00hrs, Sat; 18.00-23.00hrs

9 The Meze Taverna Greek Restaurant

Tel: (01707) 664738

0.8 miles north along the A1000, on the right

Open; Tues-Fri; 12.00-13.30hrs & 18.00-22.00hrs, Sat & Sun; 18.00-23.00hrs

10 Dragon Garden Chinese Restaurant

Tel: (01707) 643040

0.8 miles north along the

A1000, on the left

Open; 12.00-14.30hrs & 18.00-22.30hrs daily

11 BP Potters Bar

Tel: (01707) 661375

0.9 miles north along the A1000, on the left

Access, Visa, Delta, Mastercard, Switch, Diners Club, Amex, Overdrive, All Star, Dial Card, Shell Agency, BP Cards.

PLACES OF INTEREST

Hatfield House, Park & Gardens

Hatfield AL9 5NQ
Tel: (01707) 262823

Follow the A111 north and turn right along the A1000 to Hatfield (6.4 Miles)

The original palace was completed in 1497 for Bishop Morton of Ely and after the Dissolution became a royal residence. Mary Tudor, the daughter of Henry VIII, lived here and, during her reign, her half-sister Princess Elizabeth was kept a virtual prisoner at Hatfield House. It was in 1558, in the park, that Elizabeth heard of her accession to the throne. James I swapped houses with Robert Cecil, 1st Earl of Salisbury, acquiring Theobalds in exchange, and the new owner set about building a great new Jacobean house here. Following the usual E-plan of Elizabethan houses it was completed in 1611 and measured nearly 300ft long and 150ft wide and today contains fine portraits, including a Zucherro of Elizabeth I, and many historical manuscripts and relics. Surrounded by a great park, there are magnificent organic gardens and nature trails and other attractions include a childrens play area and the National Collection of Model Soldiers. Gift and Garden Shops. Licensed Restaurant.

JUNCTION 25

Nearest Clockwise A&E Hospital

Princess Alexandra Hospital

Hamstel Road, Harlow
CM20 1QX
Tel: (01279) 444455

Follow the A10 north, turn right along the A414 into Harlow, turn right along the A1019 and it is signposted along the route (Distance Approx 13.4 miles)

Nearest Anti-Clockwise A&E Hospital

Barnet Hospital

Wellhouse Lane, Barnet
EN5 3DJ
Tel: (020) 8216 4000

Proceed west to Junction 24, follow the A111 north, turn left along the A1000 to Barnet, turn right along the A411 and the hospital is signposted along this route. (Distance Approx 10.0 miles)

FACILITIES

1   The Plough

Tel: (01992) 764888
0.7 miles south along the A10, on the left
(Laurel Pub Company) Open all day. Meals served; 12.00-21.00hrs daily

2   The Pied Bull

Tel: (01992) 710619
0.6 miles west along road to Bull's Cross, on the right
(Laurel Pub Company) Open all day. Meals served; Mon-Fri; 12.00-15.00hrs & 18.00-21.00hrs, Sat & Sun; 12.00-22.00hrs

3   McDonald's

Tel: (01992) 788261
0.3 miles east along the A105, on the right
Open; 07.00-23.00hrs daily

4   Burger King Drive Thru Express

Tel: (01992) 652666
0.3 miles east along the A105, on the right
Open; Sun-Thurs; 08.00-23.00hrs, Fri & Sat; 08.00-0.00hrs

5   Bullsmore Lane Service Station (BP)

Tel: (01992) 700778
0.3 miles east along the A105, on the right
Access, Visa, Overdrive, All Star, Switch, Dial Card, Mastercard, Amex, Diners Club, Delta, BP Cards.

6   TCS Bullsmoor Service Station (Total)

Tel: (01992) 659780
0.3 miles east along the A105, on the left
Access, Visa, Overdrive, All Star, Switch, Dial Card, Mastercard, Amex, Diners Club,

Delta, Electron, Solo, Total/ Fina/Elf Cards. Open; 06.00-23.00hrs daily

7   Tesco Express Filling Station (Esso)

Tel: (01992) 908300
0.9 miles east along the A105, on the left
Access, Visa, Delta, Mastercard, Switch, Diners Club, Amex, Electron, Solo, Overdrive, All Star, Dial Card, Shell Gold, Esso Cards, Open; 06.00-0.00hrs daily

8   Little Chef

Tel: (01992) 630788
0.4 miles north along the A10, on the right
Open; 07.00-22.00hrs daily

PLACES OF INTEREST

Paradise Wildlife Park

White Stubbs Lane, Broxbourne EN10 7QA Tel: (01992) 470490
website: www.pwpark.com

Follow the A10 north (Signposted 5.5 Miles)

Offering a fine selection of animals from monkeys to lions and zebras to tigers, additional attractions include the Dinosaur Wood with full scale models of dinosaurs, Cheetah Retreat, Squirrel Monkey Rainforest and the Parrot Olympics Show. There are also several themed adventure playgrounds, including an indoor play area for the under 5's, and an outdoor paddling pool. Full range of catering available. Picnic areas. Disabled access.

JUNCTION 26

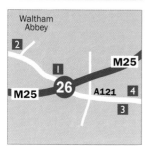

Nearest Clockwise A&E Hospital

Princess Alexandra Hospital
Hamstel Road, Harlow
CM20 1QX
Tel: (01279) 444455
Proceed east to Junction 27, follow the M11 north to Junction 7 and it is signposted along the A414 north. (Distance Approx 12.0 miles)

Or alternatively

King George's Hospital
Barley Lane, Goodmayes, Ilford IG3 8YB
Tel: (020) 8983 8000
Proceed east to Junction 27, turn south along the M11 to Junction 4, follow the A406 south and, at the first exit, turn left along the A12 (Signposted along A12. Distance Approx 13.6 miles)

Nearest Anti-Clockwise A&E Hospital

Barnet Hospital
Wellhouse Lane, Barnet
EN5 3DJ
Tel: (020) 8216 4000
Proceed west to Junction 24, follow the A111 north, turn left along the A1000 to Barnet, turn right along the A411 and the hospital is signposted along this route. (Distance Approx 14.2 miles)

FACILITIES

1 The Marriott Hotel in Waltham Abbey

Tel: (01992) 717170
Adjacent to north side of north roundabout
The Seasons Restaurant Open; Breakfast; Mon-Sat; 06.30-10.30hrs, Sun; 07.00-11.00hrs, Lunch; Mon-Sat; 12.30-13.45hrs, Sun; 13.00-14.30hrs, Dinner; Mon-Sat; 19.00-22.00hrs, Sun; 19.00-21.30hrs

2 The Green Man

Tel: (01992) 717486
1 mile west along the A121, on the right
(Six Continents) Open all day. Meals served; Mon-Fri; 12.00-15.00hrs & 18.00-21.00hrs, Sat & Sun; 12.00-21.00hrs

3 The Volunteer

Tel: (01992) 713705
0.3 miles east along the A121, on the right
(McMullens) Open all day. Meals served; Mon-Sat; 12.00-14.30hrs & 18.00-21.00hrs, Sun; 12.00-15.00hrs

4 The Woodbine

Tel: (01992) 713050
0.4 miles east along the A121, on the left
(Punch Lease) Open all day, Meals served; Mon-Sat; 12.00-15.00hrs & 18.30-21.30hrs, Sun; 12.00-15.00hrs

PLACES OF INTEREST

Waltham Abbey

Waltham Abbey Tourist Informa-tion Centre, 4 Highbridge Street, Waltham Abbey EN9 1DG
Tel: (01992) 652295

Follow the A121 north (Signposted 2.2 Miles)
The town of Waltham began as a small Roman settlement on the site of the present-day Market Square. Early Saxon kings maintained a hunting lodge here and a town formed around it with the first church being erected in the 6thC. By the 8thC and during the reign of Cnut, the town had a stone minster church, the main feature of which was a great stone crucifix that had been brought from Somerset where it had been found buried in land owned by Tovi, a trusted servant of the king. This cross became the focus of pilgrims seeking healing and one of those cured of a serious illness, Harold Godwinsson, built a new church, the third on the site. Harold became king of England and the new building was consecrated in 1060, just six years before he was buried in the church following his demise at the Battle of Hastings. The Waltham Abbey Church (Tel: 01992-767897) that exists today was built in the 12thC and was some three times its present length having incorporated an Augustine Abbey built by Henry II in 1177. The remains of this Abbey today can be seen in the Abbey Gardens, adjacent to the Church in the town centre. The main street in the town, Sun Street, is now pedestrianized and contains many buildings from the 16thC onwards. It sits on the Greenwich Meridian (0° Longitude) and this is marked out on the pavement and through the Abbey Gardens. The Market Square boasts many fine and interesting buildings such as the Lych-gate of the 17thC and The Welsh Harp from the 16thC whilst the

Town Hall, which houses the Tourist Information Office, is a fine example of Art Nouveau design.

Within the town centre ...

Epping Forest District Museum

39/41 Sun Street, Waltham Abbey EN9 1EL

Tel: (01992) 716882

Partially housed within a Tudor timber-framed building, the museum has a wide range of exhibits dealing with the history of the area from the Stone Age through to the 20thC. Tudor and Victorian times are well represented with oak panelling dating from the reign of Henry VIII and re-creations of Victorian rooms and shops. There is also an archaeological feature, a Time Zone and temporary exhibitions from time to time as well as a number of hands-on displays. Herb Garden. Café. Shop. Some disabled access.

Lee Valley Regional Park

Lee Valley Park Information Centre, Waltham Abbey EN9 1XQ Tel: (01992) 702200 website: www.leevalleypark.org.uk

Stretching 26 miles along the River Lea from East India Dock Basin in East London to Hertfordshire, Lee Valley Park offers a huge range of facilities including every facet of sport, countryside, leisure and heritage. The Lee Valley is an important area of high biodiversity, sustaining a large range of wildlife including some 200 species of birds embracing internationally important populations of Gadwall and Shoveller ducks. Incorporated within its boundaries, the River Lee Country Park, which has been transformed from old gravel pits into attractive countryside

and lakes, features a number of themed walks; Grasshopper, Water Lily, Waterbirds, Orchid and Dragonfly, each of varying length and duration. Of national importance for overwintering waterbirds, this fine park is an ideal place to unwind, take a leisurely stroll or organize a picnic. Varying disabled access.

JUNCTION 27

THIS JUNCTION IS A MOTORWAY INTERCHANGE WITH THE M11 ONLY AND THERE IS NO ACCESS TO ANY FACILITIES.

Nearest Clockwise A&E Hospital

King George's Hospital

Barley Lane, Goodmayes, Ilford IG3 8YB Tel: (020) 8983 8000

Proceed south along the M11 to Junction 4, follow the A406 south and, at the first exit, turn left along the A12 (Signposted along A12. Distance Approx 9.6 miles)

Nearest Anti-Clockwise A&E Hospital

Barnet Hospital

Wellhouse Lane, Barnet EN5 3DJ Tel: (020) 8216 4000

Proceed west to Junction 24, follow the A111 north, turn left along the A1000 to Barnet, turn right along the A411 and the hospital is signposted along this route. (Distance Approx 17.5 miles)

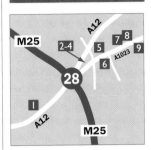

Nearest A&E Hospital

Oldchurch Hospital

Waterloo Road, Romford RM7 0BE Tel: (01708) 746090

Follow the A12 west, continue along the A118 into Romford and it is signposted along the route (Distance Approx 4.9 miles)

FACILITIES

1 Harold Park Service Station (Esso)

Tel: (01708) 342595

0.8 miles west along the A12, on the right (Actual distance 1.6 miles)

LPG. Access, Visa, Delta, Mastercard, Switch, Amex, Overdrive, All Star, Dial Card, BP Supercharge, Esso Cards.

2 South Weald Service Station (Total)

Tel: (01277) 233819

0.1 miles east along the A1023, on the left

Access, Visa, Delta, Mastercard, Switch, Diners Club, Amex, Overdrive, All Star, Dial Card, Total/Fina/Elf Cards.

3 Little Chef

Tel: (01277) 201519
0.1 miles east along the
A1023, on the left
Open; 07.00-22.00hrs daily

4 Burger King

Tel: (01277) 201519
0.1 miles east along the
A1023, on the left
Open; 10.00-22.00hrs daily

5 Holiday Inn, Brentwood

Tel: 0870 400 9012
0.3 miles east along the
A1023, on the left
Traders Bar & Grill Open;
Breakfast; Mon-Fri; 06.30-
10.00hrs, Sat & Sun; 07.00-
10.30hrs, Dinner; 18.00-
22.15hrs daily. Bar meals
available 11.00-23.00hrs daily

6 The Nag's Head

Tel: (01277) 260005
0.4 miles east along the
A1023, on the right
(Six Continents) Open all day.
Meals served; Mon-Fri; 12.00-
22.00hrs, Sat & Sun; 12.00-
21.30hrs

7 The Bull

Tel: (01277) 210445
0.6 miles east along the
A1023, on the left
(Scottish & Newcastle) Open all
day. Meals served; 12.00-
22.00hrs daily

8 The Golden Fleece Harvester

Tel: (01277) 224511
0.7 miles east along the
A1023, on the left
(Six Continents) Open all day.
Meals served; 12.00-21.30hrs
daily

9 Marygreen Manor Hotel & Restaurant

Tel: (01277) 225252
0.8 miles east along the
A1023, on the right
Restaurant Open; Breakfast;
Mon-Fri; 07.00-09.30hrs, Sat &
Sun; 08.00-10.00hrs, Lunch;
Mon-Fri; 12.15-14.15hrs, Sat &
Sun; 12.30-14.15hrs, Dinner;
19.30-21.30hrs only

PLACES OF INTEREST

Weald Country Park

South Weald, Brentwood
CM14 5QS Tel: (01277) 261343
website: www.essexcc.gov.uk/
countryparks

**Follow the A1023 east and
turn left towards South Weald
(1.4 Miles)**

Consisting of nearly 500 acres,
it was established as a
mediaeval deer park over 700
years ago. Today the lakes,
tree-lined avenues and large
parkland trees on view are the
result of extensive landscaping
in the 18thC and the facilities
include a Visitor Centre,
landscapes exhibition and
there are guided tours and
events throughout the year.
Refreshments. Picnic area. Gift
Shop. Disabled access
(Mobility Buggy available if
booked in advance)

Kelvedon Hatch Secret Nuclear Bunker

Kelvedon Hatch, Nr Brentwood
CM14 5TL Tel: (01277) 364883
website: www.japar.demon.co.uk

**Follow the A1023 east into
Brentwood and turn left along
the A128 towards Ongar (6.7
Miles)**

A large three storey ex-
Government regional HQ
nuclear bunker, buried some

100ft underground and
accessed via a 360ft long
entrance tunnel. Built in 1952
it is stocked with over 110 tons
of equipment and was
designed to support 600
personnel but has since
become redundant. Picnic
area. Gift Shop. Café.

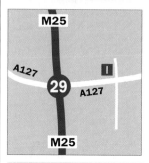

JUNCTION 29

Nearest A&E Hospital

Oldchurch Hospital
Waterloo Road, Romford
RM7 0BE
Tel: (01708) 746090
Follow the A127 west, turn left
along the A118 into Romford
and it is signposted along the
route (Distance Approx 6.1
miles)

FACILITIES

1 The Brick House Hotel

Tel: (01277) 217107
0.8 miles north along the
B186, on the left

JUNCS 30 AND 31 (A282)

THESE TWO JUNCTIONS ARE ADJACENT. ALTHOUGH EACH ONE HAS RESTRICTED ACCESS, THE COMBINATION IS SUCH THAT VEHICLES ARE ABLE TO ENTER AND EXIT IN BOTH DIRECTIONS.

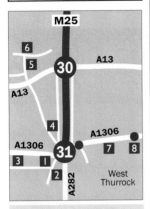

Nearest Clockwise A&E Hospital

Darent Valley Hospital

Darenth Wood Road, Dartford DA2 8DA
Tel: (01322) 428100

Proceed south to Junction 1B (A282) and follow the A296 east (Signposted. Distance approx 6 miles)

Nearest Anti-Clockwise A&E Hospital

Oldchurch Hospital

Waterloo Road, Romford RM7 0BE
Tel: (01708) 746090

Proceed north to Junction 29, follow the A127 west, turn left along the A118 into Romford and it is signposted along the route (Distance Approx 12.2 miles)

FACILITIES

(From Junction 31)

THURROCK (SERVICES) (MOTO)
Tel: (01708) 865487 Fresh

Express 24hr Self Service Restaurant, Little Chef, Burger King, Travelodge & Esso Fuel.

1   Premier Lodge

Tel: 0870 700 1380
Adjacent to roundabout

2   Concord Inn Restaurant & Hotel

Tel: (01708) 866584
0.6 miles south along the A1090, on the left

3   Meads Service Station (Esso)

Tel: (01708) 861707
0.9 miles west along the A1306, on the left

Access, Visa, Delta, Mastercard, Switch, Diners Club, Amex, Overdrive, All Star, Dial Card, Shell Gold, Esso Cards.

4   The Thurrock Hotel

Tel: (01708) 860222
0.2 miles north along the Aveley Road, on the right
Restaurant Open; Breakfast; 07.00-09.00hrs, Lunch; 12.00-14.30hrs, Dinner; 19.00-21.45hrs daily.

5   The Old Ship

Tel: (01708) 865647
1 mile north along the Aveley Road, in Aveley
(Carlsberg Tetley)

6   The Old Clock Hotel

Tel: (01708) 865102
1 mile north along the Aveley Road, in Aveley

7   Lakeside Shopping Centre

Tel: (01708) 869933

0.6 miles east along the A1306, on the right (Access slip road on left)
There are numerous Cafés and Restaurants within the shopping centre.
Open; Mon-Fri; 10.00-22.00hrs, Sat; 09.00-19.30hrs, Sun; 11.00-17.00hrs

8   Safeway Filling Station

Tel: (01375) 480424
1 mile east along the A1306, on the right

LPG. Access, Visa, Delta, Mastercard, Switch, Amex, Electron, Solo, Overdrive, All Star, Dial Card, Safeway Card. Open; Mon-Fri; 06.00-22.30hrs, Sat & Sun; 08.00-20.00hrs. Disabled Toilets and Cash Machines available in adjacent store.

PLACES OF INTEREST

Lakeside Shopping Centre

West Thurrock Way, Grays RM20 2ZP Tel: (01708) 869933 website: www.lakeside-shopping-centre.co.uk

Follow the A1306 east (Signposted 1.5 miles)

With 300 stores and numerous cafés, restaurants and bars in the Shopping Centre and 40 superstores in the adjacent Retail Park, Lakeside is Europe's largest retail destination. Creche. Disabled access. Free wheelchair and pushchair loan.

MOTORWAY ENDS
(Continues via A282 and Dartford Crossing to Junction 2)
(Total Length of Motorway 117 miles)

the **M27**

As a by-pass of Southampton and Portsmouth, this 27.5 miles long motorway forms an important link in the high speed southern coastal route.

Commencing at Junction 1 at **Cadnam**, where it has an end-on connection with the A31 from Bournemouth, between here and Junction 2, the motorway cuts through the northern extremities of the **New Forest**. Created by William the Conqueror as a Royal hunting ground, the New Forest encompasses some 150 square miles. The **River Test** is bridged before the carriageways connect with the M271 at Junction 3.

Between Junctions 3 and 7 the motorway by-passes **Southampton** on the south side. Southampton has been a major seaport since Henry V set sail for Agincourt in 1415 and the Pilgrim Fathers embarked on their voyage to the New World in 1620. During

Sailing, River Hamble

the 20thC the largest Atlantic Passenger liners were deployed from the city's historic docks. The motorway links up with the M3 at Junction 4, passes **Southampton (Eastleigh) Airport**, which opened in 1994, on the north side and then bridges the River Itchen. As the carriageways veer south east, **Hedge End** is passed on the east side and **Bursledon Windmill** is on the south side of Junction 8. Built in 1813/14 it is a fine example of a restored working wind-powered tower mill and is still utilized today to produce stoneground wholemeal flour. The **River Hamble** is bridged just after Junction 8 as the carriageways bear east and **Fareham**, a charming town which was once a prosperous shipbuilding centre, is on the south side of Junction 10.

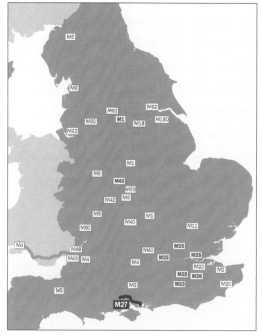

Approaching Junction 11 **Portsmouth Harbour** is in view on the south side. At the east end of the section between Junctions 11 and 12 Portsmouth is visible to the south. Portsmouth is the country's leading naval base which Richard the Lionheart ordered to be built in 1194. It was fortified and enlarged by subsequent monarchs to create a huge naval depot and harbour measuring some 2 miles wide and 4 miles long. **Portsdown Hill** with **Fort Southwick** and the **Admiralty Surface Weapons Establishment** are in view on the

Port Solent, Portsmouth

north side. Portsdown Hill was the site of the first oil drillings in this country under the 1934 Act of Parliament. The motorway ends at Junction 12 in **Cosham** and diverges into the M275 to Portsmouth and the A27 to Chichester.

Location of Places of Interest

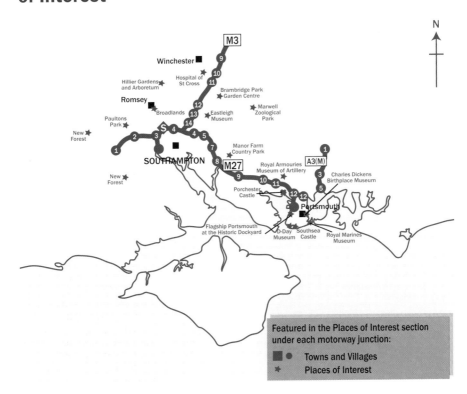

Featured in the Places of Interest section under each motorway junction:

■ ● Towns and Villages

★ Places of Interest

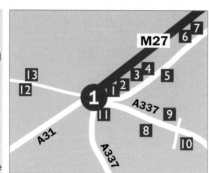

M27 — JUNCTION 1

Nearest A&E Hospital

Southampton General Hospital

Tremona Road, Shirley
SO16 6YD
Tel: (023) 8077 7222

Proceed east to Junction 3, follow the M271 south, continue along the A35 east (Tebourba Way) and it is signposted along the route (Distance Approx 9.8 Miles)

FACILITIES

1 Sir John Barleycorn

Tel: (023) 8081 2236
0.1 miles east along the A337, on the left in Southampton Road.
(Laurel Pub Company) Open all day. Meals served; Mon-Sat; 11.00-23.00hrs, Sun; 12.00-22.30hrs

2 Twin Oaks Guest House

Tel: (023) 8081 2305
0.1 miles east along the A337, on the left in Southampton Road.

3 The White Hart

Tel: (023) 8081 2277
0.3 miles north along the A337, on the left
(Laurel Pub Company) Meals served; Mon-Sat; 12.00-14.00hrs & 17.30-21.30hrs, Sun; 12.00-14.00hrs & 17.30-21.00hrs

4 Green Gables

0.5 miles north along the A337, on the left

5 Courtesy Filling Station (BP)

Tel: (023) 8081 3303
0.5 miles north along the A337, on the right
Access, Visa, Overdrive, All Star, Switch, Dial Card, Mastercard, Amex, Diners Club, Delta, Routex, AA Paytrak, Shell Agency, BP Cards. Open; 06.30-22.00hrs daily

6 Crossway Garage (Murco)

Tel: (023) 8081 2970
0.7 miles north along the A337, on the left
Access, Visa, Mastercard, Switch, Diners Club, Amex, All Star, Delta, Murco Cards. Open; Mon-Sat; 08.00-18.00hrs, Sun; Closed.

7 Le Chanteclerc Restaurant

Tel: (023) 8081 3271
0.7 miles north along the A337, on the left
Restaurant Open; Tues-Fri; 12.00-14.00hrs & 19.00-21.30hrs, Sat; 19.00-21.30hrs. Bistro Open; Mon; 19.00-21.30hrs, Tues-Sat; 12.00-14.00hrs & 19.00-21.30hrs

8 Coach & Horses

Tel: (023) 8081 3120
0.8 miles east along the A336, on the right, in Cadnam (Free House) Open all day. Meals served; 12.00-21.00hrs daily

9 Cadnam Garage (Power)

Tel: (023) 8081 2159
0.9 miles east along the A336, on the left, in Cadnam
Access, Visa, Mastercard, Switch, Electron, Diners Club, Amex, Overdrive, All Star, Dial Card, Delta, AA Paytrak, BP Supercharge. Open; Mon-Fri; 08.00-19.00hrs, Sat; 08.30-18.00hrs

10 The Haywain

Tel: (023) 8081 2243
1 mile east along the A336, on the right, in Cadnam (Brewers Fayre) Open all day. Meals served; Mon-Sat; 11.30-21.00hrs, Sun; 12.00-21.00hrs

11 The Bartley Lodge Country House

Tel: (023) 8081 2248
0.4 miles south along the A337, on the left
(Care Hotels) Restaurant Open; Sun; 12.30-13.45hrs

12 The Green Dragon

Tel: (023) 8081 3359
1 mile west along the B3078, on the left, in Brook
(Laurel Pub Company) Meals Served; Mon-Sat; 12.00-14.00hrs & 18.30-21.00hrs,

Sun; 12.00-14.00hrs & 19.00-21.00hrs

13 The Bell Inn

Tel: (023) 8081 2214

1 mile west along the B3078, on the right, in Brook

(Free House) Open all day. Meals served; Mon-Fri; 12.00-14.30hrs & 18.30-21.30hrs, Sat; 11.00-21.30hrs, Sun; 12.00-21.30hrs.

PLACES OF INTEREST

The New Forest

Follow the B3078 north or A337 south towards Lyndhurst. (The New Forest is on both sides of the motorway)

Neither "new" nor a "forest", but attractively wooded in many places, the term New Forest came into use when William the Conqueror seized the land to create a royal hunting ground. The total area is of 150 miles^2, of which 15,000 acres had been laboriously reclaimed from heathland by Saxon farmers, only to be seized by the new king and planted with thousands of trees.

This domain was protected by Draconian laws including death for killing a deer, the severence of hands for attempting to kill one and the putting out of eyes for disturbing a deer during the mating season. Remaining largely intact and virtually unspoilt since mediaeval times, the forest consists of five specific areas dispersed within its boundaries; Timber Inclosures (established in 1483 to protect woodlands), Ancient & Ornamental Woodlands for deer and grazing animals, Heathland, Pasture Land and Settlements.

The ancient system of protection for the New Forest still exists today (although the original laws have thankfully been abandoned) with Verderers (installed to administer the king's justice but now just required to meet six times a year to supervize the commoning system), Agisters (Five people appointed by the Verderers to deal with the daily management of 5,000 ponies and cattle) and Keepers (Twelve people employed by the Forestry Commission on behalf of the Crown for matters of conservation) effecting the running of the forest whilst the land and animals, including the New Forest Ponies, are owned by some 300 Commoners. This is the largest wild area in lowland Britain, with many excellent walks, and The New Forest Museum & Visitor Centre (Tel: 023-8028 3914) in the small town of Lyndhurst contains a wealth of information and artefacts about the area.

JUNCTION 2

Nearest A&E Hospital
Southampton General Hospital
Tremona Road, Shirley
SO16 6YD
Tel: (023) 8077 7222
Proceed east to Junction 3, follow the M271 south, continue along the A35 east (Tebourba Way) and it is signposted along the route (Distance Approx 6.5 Miles)

FACILITIES

1   The Vine Inn

Tel: (023) 8081 4333

0.7 miles west along the Ower Road, on the right

(Scottish & Newcastle) Open all day. Meals served; Sun-Thurs; 12.00-21.30hrs, Sat & Sun; 12.00-22.00hrs

2   Travelodge

Tel: (023) 8081 4333

0.7 miles west along the Ower Road, on the right

3   The Mortimer Arms Hotel

Tel: (023) 8081 4379

1 mile west along the Ower Road, on the right

(Free House) Open all day. Meals served; 12.00-14.30 hrs & 18.30-21.30hrs daily

4   Star West Wellow (Texaco)

Tel: (023) 8081 7100

0.5 miles north along the A36, on the north side of the roundabout.

Access, Visa, Mastercard, Switch, Electron, Diners Club, Amex, Overdrive, All Star, Dial Card, Delta, AA Paytrak, Securicor Fuelserv, Keyfuels, Texaco Cards.

5   McDonald's

Tel: (023) 8081 4487

0.5 miles north along the A36, on the north side of the roundabout.

Open; 07-00-23.00hrs daily

PLACES OF INTEREST

Paultons Park,

Ower, Hampshire SO51 6AL Tel: (023) 8081 4442

Follow the A36 north (Signposted 1.2 miles)
A family theme park with 140 acres of gardens, animals, birds and wildfowl as well as over 40 attractions and rides. Restaurants. Café. Gift Shop. Disabled access.

JUNCTION 3

THIS JUNCTION IS ALSO PART OF A MOTORWAY INTERCHANGE WITH THE M271

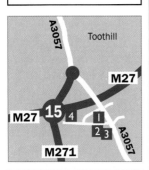

Nearest A&E Hospital
Southampton General Hospital
Tremona Road, Shirley SO16 6YD
Tel: (023) 8077 7222
Follow the M271 south, continue along the A35 east (Tebourba Way) and it is signposted along the route (Distance Approx 4.2 Miles)

FACILITIES

1   Horns Inn

Tel: (023) 8074 2910
0.8 miles south along the A3057, on the right
(Bass) Open all day. Meals served; Mon-Sat; 12.00-14.00hrs & 18.00-21.00hrs, Sun; 12.00-21.00hrs

2   The Balmoral

Tel: (023) 8073 2262
0.8 miles south along the A3057, on the right.
(Beefeater) Open all day. Restaurant Open; Mon-Fri; 12.00-14.30hrs & 17.00-22.00hrs, Sat, Sun & Bank Holiday Mondays; 12.00-22.00hrs. Bar meals served; 12.00-22.00hrs daily

3   Travel Inn

Tel: (023) 8073 2262
0.8 miles south along the A3057, on the right

4   The Four Horseshoes

Tel: (023) 8073 2371
1 mile south along Nursling Street, on the right. (NB. This is adjacent to the motorway junction but is directly inaccessible)
(Wadsworth) Open all day. Meals served; Mon-Sat; 12.00-14.00hrs & 18.00-21.00hrs, Sun; 12.00-14.30hrs.

PLACES OF INTEREST

Southampton

Follow the M271 south (Signposted 4 miles)
For details please see Junction 5 information

Romsey

Tourist Information Office, Romsey Heritage & Visitor Centre, 13 Church St, Romsey SO51 8BT. Tel: (01794) 512200 website; www.exploretestvalley.com

Follow the A3057 north (Signposted 2.7 miles)
Sited on the River Test, the market town of Romsey with mediaeval walkways and streets can trace its history to at least Roman times. Dominating the town with a 70ft high nave stretching for 76ft, the Abbey seen today was built between 1120 and 1230 and is considered to be one of the finest Norman buildings in England. It had been founded by Edward the Elder, son of Alfred the Great in 907AD and refounded in the 960s by King Edgar who established the Benedictine Order. By 1300 it had 100 nuns but following the Black Death only 25 remained when it was dissolved by Henry VIII in 1539.

However, instead of being demolished (a fate suffered by many monastic buildings in this period) the townspeople negotiated a deal with the king and purchased it for £100 in 1544, ensuring that the superb examples of 12thC and 13thC architecture encompassed within the Abbey are still extant today. On the opposite side of Church Court stands King John's House dating back to 1240 and built for a merchant. Despite its name it was never used by King John (whose death preceded it by some 14 years!) but may have occupied the site of a royal hunting lodge and the building today is in use as the Romsey Heritage & Visitor Centre.

Adjacent to the south side of the town ....

Broadlands

Romsey SO51 9ZD
Tel: (01794) 505010

website;
www.hants.gov.uk/leisure/
house/broadlands

Once the property of Romsey Abbey, following the Dissolution it became the home of the St Barbe family for a hundred years before being sold to Henry Temple, 1st Viscount Palmerston. Set in a 400 acre wooded park and on the River Test the mansion was extended and rebuilt in Palladian style in 1770 by Henry Holland whilst the grounds were landscaped by Capability Brown. The important collections of furniture, porcelain and sculpture were acquired by the 2nd Viscount Palmerston before Broadlands was passed on to the Mountbatten family. An exhibition established by the present Lord Romsey traces the lives of Lord & Lady Mountbatten and there is a Tea Room, Gift Shop and Picnic Area.

The Sir Harold Hillier Gardens & Arboretum

Jermyns Lane, Ampfield, Romsey
SO51 0QA
Tel: (01794) 368787
website; www.hillier.hants.gov.uk

Follow the A3057 north (Signposted along the A3090 & A3057. 5 miles)

Established in 1953 this 180 acre garden contains the greatest collection of hardy trees and shrubs in the world and features 11 National Plant Collections, the Ghurka Memorial Garden and the largest Winter Garden in Europe. Tea Room. Disabled access

M27 BETWEEN JUNCS 3 & 4

ROWNHAMS SERVICES (EASTBOUND) (ROADCHEF)
Tel: (023) 8073 4480
Food Fayre Self-Service Restaurant, Wimpy Bar & Esso Fuel

ROWNHAMS SERVICES (WESTBOUND) (ROADCHEF)
Tel: (023) 8073 4480
Food Fayre Self-Service Restaurant, Wimpy Bar, Travel Inn & Esso Fuel

FOOTWAY TUNNEL CONNECTION BETWEEN SITES

M27 JUNCTION 4

THIS JUNCTION IS A MOTORWAY INTERCHANGE ONLY WITH THE M3 AND THERE IS NO ACCESS TO ANY FACILITIES

Nearest Northbound A&E Hospital (Via M3)
Royal Hampshire County Hospital
Romsey Road, Winchester
SO22 5DG
Tel: (01962) 863535
Proceed north to Junction 11 (M3), follow the A3090 north and turn right along the B3040 (Signposted along route. Distance Approx 9.2 Miles)

Nearest Westbound A&E Hospital
Southampton General Hospital
Tremona Road, Shirley

SO16 6YD
Tel: (023) 8077 7222
Proceed west to Junction 3, follow the M271 south, continue along the A35 east (Tebourba Way) and it is signposted along the route (Distance Approx 7.7 Miles)

Nearest Eastbound A&E Hospital
Southampton General Hospital
Tremona Road, Shirley
SO16 6YD
Tel: (023) 8077 7222
Proceed east to Junction 5, follow the A35 south and it is signposted along the route (Distance Approx 4.5 Miles)

M27 JUNCTION 5

Nearest A&E Hospital
Southampton General Hospital
Tremona Road, Shirley
SO16 6YD
Tel: (023) 8077 7222
Follow the A35 south and it is signposted along the route (Distance Approx 3.2 Miles)

FACILITIES

1 McDonald's

Tel: (023) 8058 4733

0.8 miles south along the A35, on the left
Open; 08.00-23.00hrs daily

2 Shell Swaythling

Tel: (023) 8051 6930
0.8 miles south along the A335, on the right
LPG. Access, Visa, Mastercard, Switch, Diners Club, Amex, Overdrive, All Star, Dial Card, Delta, AA Paytrak, UK Fuelcard, Shell Cards.

3 The Concorde Hotel

Tel: (023) 8065 1478
0.4 miles north along Stoneham Lane on the right
The Moudly Fig (Wine Bar); Meals Served; Mon-Fri; 11.00-15.00hrs

4 Stoneham Service Station (Automatic) (Esso)

1 mile north along the A335, on the left
Visa, Switch, Mastercard, Delta, Amex, Diners Club, Shell Gold, All Star, Overdrive, Dial Card, Esso Cards. (NB. 24hr Credit Card operated pumps only)

PLACES OF INTEREST

Southampton

Tourist Information Office, 9 Civic Centre Road, Southampton SO14 7FJ
Tel: (023) 8083 3333 website; www.Southampton.gov.uk

Follow the A335 south (Signposted 3.5 miles)
The city is at least of Saxon origin and although the castle was razed to the ground in 1863, the mediaeval town walls are some of the best preserved in England with over half its length, 13 of the

original 29 towers and three town gates still extant. It had been used as a deep sea harbour since Norman times with Henry V setting sail from here to the Battle of Agincourt in 1415 and developed as a major sea port in the 16thC. Subsequent historical events include the embarkation of the Pilgrim Fathers to the New World in 1620 and the maiden voyage of the RMS Titanic on April 10th, 1912. The city contains many fine museums including the Hall of Aviation (Tel: 023-8063 5830) housing the RJ Mitchell Memorial Museum (designer of the Spitfire Fighter Plane), the Mediaeval Merchants House (Tel: 023-8022 1503) dating back to 1290, the Museum of Archaeology (Tel: 023-8063 5904) and the Southampton Maritime Museum (Tel: 023-8022 3941)

Marwell Zoological Park

Colden Common,
Nr Winchester SO21 1JH

Follow the A335 north (Signposted 6.1 Miles)
For details please see Junction 11 (M3) information

JUNCTION 6

THERE IS NO JUNCTION 6

JUNCTION 7

Nearest A&E Hospital
Southampton General Hospital
Tremona Road, Shirley
SO16 6YD
Tel: (023) 8077 7222
Proceed west to Junction 5,

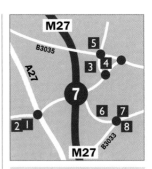

follow the A35 south and it is signposted along the route (Distance Approx 7 Miles)

FACILITIES

1 Eastern Nights Indian Restaurant

Tel: (023) 8047 3269
0.9 miles west along the A334, on the left.
Open; 17.30-23.30hrs daily

2 Star Thornhill (Texaco)

Tel: (023) 8047 0181 or 8046 7940
1 mile west along the A334, on the left.
Access, Visa, Mastercard, Switch, Electron, Diners Club, Amex, Overdrive, All Star, Dial Card, Delta, UK Fuelcard, Texaco Cards. Open; 06.00-22.00hrs daily

3 Sainsbury's Filling Station

Tel: (01489) 790452
0.6 miles north in Hedge End Park, on the left
LPG. Access, Visa, Mastercard, Switch, Amex, Overdrive, All Star, Dial Card, Delta, Sainsbury's Fuel Card. Disabled Toilets available in adjacent store during store opening hours.

4 McDonald's

Tel: (01489) 799080
0.7 miles north in Hedge End Park, on the right
Open; 06.00-0.00hrs daily

5 Burger King

Tel: (01489) 799113
1 mile north in Centre 27 Retail Park, on the left.
Open; 09.00-22.00hrs

6 Twin Oaks Guest House

Tel: (01489) 690054
0.6 miles east along Upper Northam Road, on the left, in Hedge End

7 Purbani Tandoori Restaurant

Tel: (01489) 799382
1 mile east along Upper Northam Road, on the left, in Hedge End
Open; 18.00-0.00hrs daily

8 The Barleycorn

Tel: (01489) 784171
1 mile east along Upper Northam Road, on the right, in Hedge End
(Greene King) Open all day. Meals served; Mon-Sat; 11.30-14.30hrs

PLACES OF INTEREST

Southampton

Follow the A334 west (Signposted 4 miles)
For details please see Junction 5 information

JUNCTION 8

Nearest Eastbound A&E Hospital

Queen Alexandra Hospital
Southwick Hill Road, Cosham, Portsmouth PO6 3LY
Tel: (023) 9228 6000
Proceed east to Junction 12, leave via the westernmost exit (Signposted Cosham A27) and take the second exit at the roundabout along Southampton Road, turn left along the A3, first left along Southwick Hill Road (B2177) and the hospital is on the left. (Distance Approx 12.9 miles)

Nearest Westbound A&E Hospital

Southampton General Hospital
Tremona Road, Shirley SO16 6YD
Tel: (023) 8077 7222
Proceed west to Junction 5, follow the A35 south and it is signposted along the route (Distance Approx 8.6 Miles)

FACILITIES

1 Windhover Manor

Tel: (023) 8040 3500
0.4 miles south along the A27, on the left
(Brewers Fayre) Open all day. Meals served; Mon-Sat; 11.30-22.00hrs, Sun; 12.00-21.30hrs

2 Acacia Lodge Guest House

Tel: (023) 8056 1155
0.6 miles south along the A27, on the right

3 The Crows Nest

Tel: (023) 8040 3129
1 mile south along the A27, on the left
(Merlin Inns) Open all day Mon-Sat. Meals served; Mon-Fri; 12.00-14.00hrs & 18.30-21.00hrs, Sat; 12.00-14.30hrs & 18.30-21.00hrs, Sun; 12.00-14.30hrs.

4 Tesco Filling Station

Tel: (023) 8029 7500
0.5 miles south along the A3025, on the left
Access, Visa, Mastercard, Switch, Electron, Amex, Overdrive, All Star, Dial Card, Delta, Tesco Fuel Card. Toilets and Cash Machines available in the adjacent store (Open 24 hours)

5 BP Safeway Filling Station

Tel: (023) 8040 4420
1 mile north along the A27, on the left
LPG. Access, Visa, Mastercard, Switch, Electron, Diners Club, Amex, Overdrive, All Star, Dial Card, Delta, AA Paytrak, UK Fuelcard, BP Cards. Open 07.30-23.30hrs daily

6 Sunday's Hill Service Station (BP)

Tel: (023) 8040 5958
0.6 miles north along Dodwell Lane, on the left

Access, Visa, Mastercard, Switch, Diners Club, Amex, Overdrive, All Star, Dial Card, Delta, Shell Gold, BP Cards. Open; Mon-Fri; 06.30-22.00hrs, Sat; 07.00-21.00hrs, Sun; 08.00-21.00hrs.

PLACES OF INTEREST

Southampton

Follow the A3024 west (Signposted 5 miles)
For details please see Junction 5 information

Manor Farm Country Park

Pylands Lane, Bursledon
SO31 1BH Tel: (01489) 787055
website; www.eastleigh.gov.uk/tourism/manor.html

Take the north exit off the roundabout and continue along Pylands Lane (Signposted 0.4 miles)
Manor Farm consists of a number of delightful woodland and riverside walks based around a traditional working farm with lots of animals in view. There are numerous craft displays and activities available including boat trips along the River Hamble during the summer. Café. Gift Shop. Disabled access.

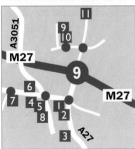

JUNCTION 9

Nearest Eastbound A&E Hospital

Queen Alexandra Hospital
Southwick Hill Road, Cosham, Portsmouth
PO6 3LY
Tel: (023) 9228 6000
Proceed east to Junction 12, leave via the westernmost exit (Signposted Cosham A27) and take the second exit at the roundabout along Southampton Road, turn left along the A3, first left along Southwick Hill Road (B2177) and the hospital is on the left. (Distance Approx 10 miles)

Nearest Westbound A&E Hospital

Southampton General Hospital
Tremona Road, Shirley
SO16 6YD
Tel: (023) 8077 7222
Proceed west to Junction 5, follow the A35 south and it is signposted along the route (Distance Approx 11.5 Miles)

FACILITIES

1   TGI Friday's

Tel: (01489) 577533
0.4 miles south along the A27, on the west side of the roundabout
Open; Mon-Thurs; 07.30-09.00hrs & 12.00-23.00hrs, Fri; 07.30-09.00hrs & 12.00-23.30hrs, Sat; 08.30-10.00hrs & 12.00-23.30hrs, Sun; 08.30-10.00hrs & 12.00-23.00hrs.

2   Travel Inn

Tel: (01489) 579857
0.4 miles south along the A27, on the west side of the roundabout

3   Star Heath (Texaco)

Tel: (01489) 589056
0.9 miles south along the A27, on the right
Access, Visa, Mastercard, Switch, Electron, Solo, Diners Club, Amex, Overdrive, All Star, Dial Card, Delta, AA Paytrak, UK Fuelcard, BP Supercharge, Texaco Cards. Open; 06.00-21.00hrs daily.

4   Kams Palace Restaurant

Tel: (01489) 583328
0.8 miles west along the A27, on the left
Open; 18.00-23.15hrs daily

5   The Talisman

Tel: (01489) 572614
0.8 miles west along the A27, on the left
(Halls & Woodhouse) Open all day. Meals served; 12.00-15.00hrs & 18.00-21.00hrs daily.

6   Xpress Budgens (Q8)

Tel: (01489) 557410
0.8 miles west along the A27, on the right
Access, Visa, Mastercard, Switch, Diners Club, Amex, Overdrive, All Star, Dial Card, Delta, Q8 Cards.

7   Locksheath Service Station (Esso)

Tel: (01489) 581034
1 mile west along the A27, on the left
Access, Visa, Mastercard, Switch, Diners Club, Amex, Overdrive, All Star, Dial Card, Delta, AA Paytrak, Shell Gold, BP Supercharge, Esso Cards.

8   Ambleside Lodge

Tel: (01489) 480974
0.9 miles south along Hunts Pond Road, on the right

9 Parsons Collar

Tel: (01489) 880035

0.5 miles north along Rookery Avenue in Solent Business Park, on the right

(Thwaites) Open all day. Meals served; Mon-Sat; 12.00-14.00hrs & 19.30-21.30hrs, Sun; 12.00-14.00hrs.

10 Solent Hotel

Tel: (01489) 880000

0.5 miles north along Rookery Avenue in Solent Business Park, on the right

Restaurant Open; Mon-Fri; 07.00-09.30hrs, 12.30-14.00hrs & 19.15-22.00hrs, Sat & Sun; 08.00-10.00hrs & 19.15-22.00hrs.

11 Whiteley Shopping Village Outlet

Tel: (01489) 886886

1 mile north along road to Whiteley in Solent Business Park.

There are two coffee shops, Boswell's and Starbuck's, within the Village. Open; Mon-Sat; 10.00-18.00hrs, Sun; 11.00-17.00hrs.

M27
JUNCTION 10

THIS IS A RESTRICTED ACCESS JUNCTION.

- Westbound vehicles can only exit along the northbound carriageway of the A32
- Vehicles can only enter the motorway (eastbound) from the southbound carriageway of the A32

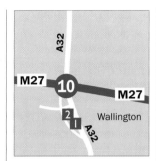

Nearest Eastbound A&E Hospital

Queen Alexandra Hospital

Southwick Hill Road, Cosham, Portsmouth PO6 3LY

Tel: (023) 9228 6000

Proceed east to Junction 12, leave via the westernmost exit (Signposted Cosham A27) and take the second exit at the roundabout along Southampton Road, turn left along the A3, first left along Southwick Hill Road (B2177) and the hospital is on the left. (Distance Approx 7 miles)

Nearest Westbound A&E Hospital

Southampton General Hospital

Tremona Road, Shirley SO16 6YD

Tel: (023) 8077 7222

Proceed west to Junction 5, follow the A35 south and it is signposted along the route (Distance Approx 14.5 Miles)

FACILITIES

1 Yeoman's (Total)

Tel: (01329) 823458

0.6 miles south along the A32, on the right (Involves reversal)

Access, Visa, Mastercard, Switch, Diners Club, Overdrive, All Star, Dial Card, Delta, Total/Fina/Elf Cards. NB. Closed on Christmas Day, Boxing Day, New Year's Eve and New Year's Day.

2 The Turnpike

Tel: (01329) 287300

0.7 miles south along Old Turnpike, on the left. (Involves reversal)

(Laurel Pub Company) Open all day. Meals served; 12.00-15.00hrs & 18.00-21.00hrs daily.

M27
JUNCTION 11

FAREHAM IS WITHIN ONE MILE OF THIS JUNCTION

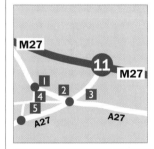

Nearest Eastbound A&E Hospital

Queen Alexandra Hospital

Southwick Hill Road, Cosham, Portsmouth PO6 3LY

Tel: (023) 9228 6000

Proceed east to Junction 12, leave via the westernmost exit (Signposted Cosham A27) and take the second exit at the roundabout along Southampton Road, turn left along the A3, first left along Southwick Hill Road (B2177) and the hospital is on the left. (Distance Approx 5.6 miles)

Nearest Westbound A&E Hospital

Southampton General Hospital

Tremona Road, Shirley
SO16 6YD
Tel: (023) 8077 7222

Proceed west to Junction 5, follow the A35 south and it is signposted along the route (Distance Approx 15.9 Miles)

FACILITIES

1 Sainsbury's Filling Station

Tel: (01329) 827936
1 mile west along Wallington Way (A32), on the right
Access, Visa, Mastercard, Switch, Electron, Solo, Amex, Overdrive, All Star, Dial Card, Delta, Sainsbury's Fuel Card.

2 The Roundabout Hotel

Tel: (01329) 822542
0.7 miles south along the A27, on the north side of the roundabout
Restaurant Open; 12.00-15.00hrs & 18.00-22.00hrs daily

3 The Delme Arms

Tel: (01329) 232638
0.8 miles east along the A27, on the left
(Punch Taverns) Open all day Fri, Sat & Sun. Meals served; Mon; 12.00-14.00hrs, Tues-Sat; 12.00-14.00hrs & 19.00-20.45hrs.

4 The Carrick House Hotel

Tel: (01329) 234678
0.8 miles west along West Street, on the right in Fareham

5 The Red Lion Hotel

Tel: (01329) 822640
0.9 miles west along West Street, on the left in Fareham
(Greene King) Restaurant Open; Mon-Sat; 19.00-22.00hrs, Sun; 12.00-14.00hrs & 19.00-22.00hrs. Bar Meals served; 12.00-14.00hrs daily.

PLACES OF INTEREST

Portchester Castle

Portchester, Hampshire
PO16 9QW
Tel: (023) 9237 8291 website; www.portchester.vir.co.uk

Follow the A27 south, turn left along the A27 into Portchester and turn right along Castle Street. (3.4 Miles)

Standing at the head of Portsmouth Harbour, a fort has occupied this site since c280AD when the Romans enclosed 8 acres to create a base for their ships patrolling the Channel. The original walls were 20ft high and 10ft thick and although much of it was later pillaged to facilitate the construction of buildings by local people it is still the best preserved site of a Roman fort in northern Europe.

The Normans reinforced the castle in 1120 and the Church of St Mary was constructed within the perimeter between 1133 and 1150 as part of a Priory founded by Henry I but was abandoned almost immediately when the Priory moved to Southwick. By the end of the 14thC much of the castle had been converted into a small palace for Richard II and whilst only substantial ruins of this building remain today, the church, restored in the 18thC, is virtually intact. Gift Shop

Royal Armouries Museum of Artillery,

Fort Nelson, Down End Road, Fareham PO17 6AN
Tel: (01329) 233734 website; www.armouries.org.uk/fort/

Take the northbound exit off the roundabout, turn right along Boarhunt Road, right along Swivelton Lane and left along Portsdown Road. (1.5 miles)

Fort Nelson, a huge Victorian military establishment, is claimed to be "Britain's loudest museum" with live firings every day. As well as the Iraqi "Supergun" there are extensive exhibits of artillery, displays of how the soldiers lived and worked around the ramparts and tunnels. Café. Gift Shop. Picnic areas

THIS JUNCTION IS ALSO PART OF A MOTORWAY INTERCHANGE WITH THE M275

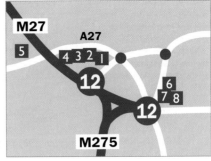

Nearest A&E Hospital

Queen Alexandra Hospital

Southwick Hill Road,
Cosham, Portsmouth
PO6 3LY
Tel: (023) 9228 6000
Leave via the westernmost exit
(Signposted Cosham A27) and
take the second exit at the
roundabout along
Southampton Road, turn left
along the A3, first left along
Southwick Hill Road (B2177)
and the hospital is on the left.
(Distance Approx 1.2 miles)

FACILITIES

(From Western Exit)

1   Portsmouth Marriott

Tel: (023) 9238 3151
**Adjacent to the west side of
the roundabout.**
Mediterrano Restaurant Open;
Mon-Thurs; 06.30-10.30hrs,
12.30-13.30hrs & 18.30-
22.00hrs, Fri; 06.30-10.30hrs,
12.30-13.30hrs & 18.00-
22.00hrs, Sat; 07.00-11.00hrs,
12.30-14.00hrs & 18.00-
22.00hrs, Sun; 07.00-
11.00hrs, 13.00-15.00hrs &
18.30-22.00hrs

2   Banter

Tel: (023) 9232 1122
**0.1 miles west along the A27,
on the left**
(Whitbread) Open all day.
Restaurant Open; Mon-Fri;
12.00-14.00hrs & 17.00-
21.30hrs, Sat; 12.00-22.15,
Sun; 12.00-21.30hrs. Bar
meals served all day.

3   Travel Inn

Tel: (023) 9232 1122
**0.1 miles west along the A27,
on the left**

4   Tesco Filling Station

Tel: (023) 9230 7800
**0.2 miles west along the A27,
on the left in North Harbour
Business Park**
Access, Visa, Mastercard,
Switch, Electron, Amex,
Overdrive, All Star, Dial Card,
Delta, AA Paytrak, Tesco Fuel
Card. Toilets and Cash Machine
available in the adjacent store.

5   Tasman Service
Station (Total)

Tel: (023) 9237 2943
**0.8 miles west along the A27,
on the right**
Access, Visa, Overdrive, All
Star, Switch, Dial Card,
Mastercard, Amex, Diners Club,
Delta, Routex, Total/Fina Card.
Open; Mon-Sat; 07.00-
22.00hrs, Sun; 08.00-
22.00hrs

6   McDonald's

Tel: (023) 9238 6173
**0.9 miles east along the A27,
on the north side of the
roundabout**
Open; 07.00-23.00hrs daily

7   The Portsbridge

Tel: (023) 9237 6653
**1 mile east along Portsmouth
Road, on the right**
(Laurel Pub Company) Open all
day. Meals served; Mon-Sat;
11.00-22.00hrs, Sun; 12.00-
22.00hrs

8   Portsbridge Service
Station (Jet)

Tel: (023) 9221 0120
**1 mile east along Portsmouth
Road, on the right**
Access, Visa, Mastercard,
Switch, Diners Club, Amex,
Overdrive, All Star, Dial Card,
Delta, BP Supercharge, Jet

Cards. Open; Mon-Fri; 06.30-
22.00hrs, Sat; 07.00-22.00hrs,
Sun; 08.00-21.00hrs.

PLACES OF
INTEREST

Portsmouth & Southsea

Tourist Information Office, The
Hard, Portsmouth PO1 3QJ
Tel: (023) 9282 6722 website:
www.portsmouthcc.gov.uk/visitor

Follow the M275 (Signposted
2 Miles)

Portsmouth, of importance
even in the days of Henry I, was
a naval station in the reign of
King John, and was fortified
and enlarged by Edward IV and
subsequent monarchs to
create a huge naval depot.
Although only accessed by a
narrow inlet, the bay opens out
to a harbour measuring some
2 miles wide and 4 miles long
and its major role in shaping
world events is reflected in a
number of museums and sites
around the city. Portsmouth is
also the birthplace of several
renowned figures including the
Victorian engineer Isambard
Kingdom Brunel and the
novelists Charles Dickens,
George Meredith and Sir
Walter Besant. Southsea,
contiguous to Portsmouth on
the south western side of
Portsea Island and the site of a
castle dating back to Henry VIII,
also contains a number of
interesting museums.

Located within
Portsmouth ....

Charles Dickens
Birthplace Museum

393 Old Commercial Road,
Portsmouth PO1 4QL
Tel: (023) 9282 7261 website:
www.portsmouthmuseums.co.uk

John Dickens, a pay clerk in the
Navy Office, moved here with
his wife Elizabeth in 1809 and

this modest house has been restored and furnished to show how it would have looked when the great novelist was born here in 1812. Three rooms, the parlour, dining room and bedroom where Charles was born, are on view and there is a small collection of memorabilia.

Flagship Portsmouth at the Historic Dockyard

Porter's Lodge, 1/7 College Road, HM Naval Base PO1 3LJ
Tel: (023) 9286 1512 website: www.flagship.org.uk

Three of the most important ships in Britain's naval history can be seen here; HMS Victory, possibly the world's most renowned warship and Lord Nelson's flagship; HMS Warrior, commissioned in 1860 as the first steam powered ironclad battleship and the Mary Rose which sank in 1545 with all hands on board and was recovered from the seabed in 1982. The Royal Naval Museum, located in former Georgian storehouses sited opposite to HMS Victory, contains ships models, figureheads, uniforms and the Victory Gallery featuring the famous flagship and Lord Nelson. Gift Shop

Located within Southsea ......

D-Day Museum,

Clarence Esplanade, Southsea
PO5 3NT Tel: (023) 9282 7261
website:
www.portsmouthmuseums.co.uk

Opened in 1984 to commemorate the Allied invasion of Europe in 1943, the centrepiece of the museum is the 272ft long Overlord Embroidery, a 20thC equivalent of the Bayeux Tapestry, commissioned by Lord Dulverton of Batsford and designed by Sandra Lawrence.

There are numerous exhibits including archive films and displays recreating features of the daily life of the civil and military populations of Portsmouth. Café. Gift Shop. Disabled access

Royal Marines Museum

Eastney Esplanade, Southsea
PO4 9PX Tel: (023) 9281 9385
website:
www.royalmarinesmuseum.co.uk

Located in Eastney Barracks, a fine Victorian building on a seven acre seafront site and the former home of the Royal Marines for over 120 years, this award winning museum relates their 330 year history through lifelike recreations, special effects and the latest in audio visual technology and interactives. Tea Rooms. Gift Shop. Some disabled access.

Southsea Castle

Clarence Esplanade, Southsea
PO5 3PA Tel: (023) 9282 7261
website:
www.portsmouthmuseums.co.uk

Built in 1546 by Henry VIII as one of a chain of coastal forts to protect England from French raids, it was enlarged in the early 19thC and was in active service until as recently as 1960.

It is now in use as a museum with displays of the castle's history as well as Portsmouth's role as a harbour and military establishment. Tea Shop. Some limited disabled access.

MOTORWAY ENDS
(Total Length of Motorway 27.5 Miles)

the **M40**

This 87.7 miles long motorway forms a second major route between London, Birmingham and the North West, through the Chilterns, Oxfordshire and Warwickshire. The M40, at first only connected Oxford to London, with the section between Junctions 1 and 7 opening in March 1974, and it was not until January 16th, 1991 that it saw completion through to its link with the M42 at Junction 3A, south east of Birmingham.

Commencing near **Uxbridge** with an end-on connection to the A40 at Junction 1, the motorway heads north west, crossing the M25 at Junction 1A and passing **Gerrards Cross** on the north side before by-passing **Beaconsfield**, a town dating back to medieval times and the home of the famous writer G K Chesterton, to the north between Junctions 2 and 3. Beaconsfield is in the centre of the area known as the "Chiltern Hundreds" which, prior to the Parliamentary reforms was one of the "rotten boroughs". It is still remembered today as MPs who wish to resign their seat in the House of Commons have to follow a Resolution of the House of March 2nd,

Hughenden Manor, Wycombe

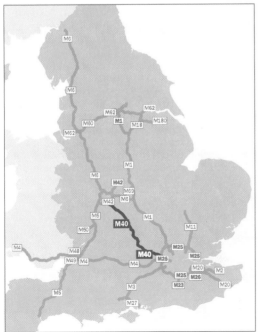

1623, and apply for an office of profit under the Crown which technically disqualifies him from sitting. Since the first instance, when John Pitt resigned on January 17th, 1751, famous incumbents have included John Stonehouse, Roy Jenkins, Brian Walden and Neil Kinnock.

Continuing north westwards, the carriageways skirt around the south side of **High Wycombe**, the largest town in Buckinghamshire and traditionally known for the manufacture of chairs, at Junction 4 where the River Wye and the trackbed of the former Great Western Railway High Wycombe to Bourne End line are bridged. Beyond Junction 4 **Wycombe Air Park**, home of the Booker-Blue Max Collection of historical aircraft including a Sopwith Camel and a Spitfire, is on the south side and approaching Junction 5 **Stokenchurch** is to the north. Between Junctions 5 and 6 the 985ft high **BT Tower**, for which planning permission was granted as long ago as 1956 and now also carries mobile phone signals, is on the north side of the carriageway and the motorway grades steeply through a deep cutting made through the western edge of the **Chiltern Hills**. For those travelling west there is a panoramic view across to the **Cotswold Hills** with the cooling towers of **Didcot Power Station** clearly visible to the south.

Magdelen College, Oxford

The motorway reaches the A40 to Oxford at Junction 8 before turning north and bridging Danes Brook with the town of **Brill** and the 645ft high **Muswell Hill** visible on the east side. Towards the northern end of this section, and to the west, Oxford is just visible on the far side of **Ot Moor** which comprises several square miles of very poorly drained flatland, virtually impossible to farm and a home for a wide variety of wildlife. The historic city of **Oxford** dates back to Saxon times, having been captured from the Danish invaders in 912. The Normans built a castle here in 1067 and the University dates from 1229. The ex-London & North Western Railway Oxford to Bicester line is bridged as the motorway approaches Junction 9. Continuing north to Junction 10, **Bicester**, a market town established in Saxon times, is passed on the eastern side and an imposing **water tower** can be seen adjacent to the west side of the motorway. This tower was originally built in 1909 to supply water to the Bicester area but was never utilized as a supply was found nearer to the town. It was later used to supply water to Bucknell under a private scheme but has since been abandoned. Between Junctions 10 and 11, the carriageways run alongside of, and cross from time to time, the former Great Western Railway line between Birmingham and Paddington, the River Cherwell and the **Oxford Canal**. The southern section of this canal, from Banbury to Oxford, was opened in 1790. At the north end of this section, **Banbury** is passed on the west side. The original cross at Banbury, immortalized in the children's nursery rhyme, was destroyed by the Puritans in the 17thC but later replaced with a more ornate structure.

Continuing north westwards from Junction 11, the carriageways cross the **Oxford Canal** once more. This section of the canal, from Coventry to Banbury was originally opened in 1778 and followed a very circuitous route to avoid extensive earthworks. This was rectified by the Oxford Canal Company in 1830 who rebuilt the waterway and reduced the overall distance by 14 miles. Approaching Junction 12, **Burton Dassett** on Church Hill and the 14thC beacon in **Burton Hills Country Park** are visible on the east side and in the

Warwick Castle

section between Junctions 12 and 13 **Chesterton Windmill**, a cylindrical building constructed in stone and surmounted on arches, can be seen on top of Windmill Hill on the east side. The windmill was commissioned and built by the Peyto family in 1632 and is currently owned by the Warwickshire County Council. It is the only one of its design in the world and is opened just once a year to visitors.

As the carriageways continue north westwards between Junctions 13 and 15, the historic towns of

Warwick and Royal Leamington Spa are passed on the east side and the River Avon is bridged. **Warwick** dates back to mediaeval times with its impressive castle and spectacular Lord Leycester's Hospital being prominent historic structures. **Leamington Spa** was popularised during the 17th and 18th centuries for its spa waters and contains many fine Regency buildings. Approaching Junction 16 the ex-Great Western Railway Birmingham to Paddington line runs alongside the carriageways on the east side and the Stratford Upon Avon Canal is bridged whilst **Bushwood Grange** is visible on the west side. The southern section of the **Stratford upon Avon Canal** between Kingswood and the River Avon opened in 1816 and was abandoned by the 1940s. It has since been restored and now forms part of the popular "Avon Ring" circuit of waterways. The motorway continues north westwards and, just before it ends and merges with the M42, an **obelisk** is visible on the north side of the carriageway. The reason for its construction is not known but it was built in 1749 and is one of six such structures erected by Thomas Carver.

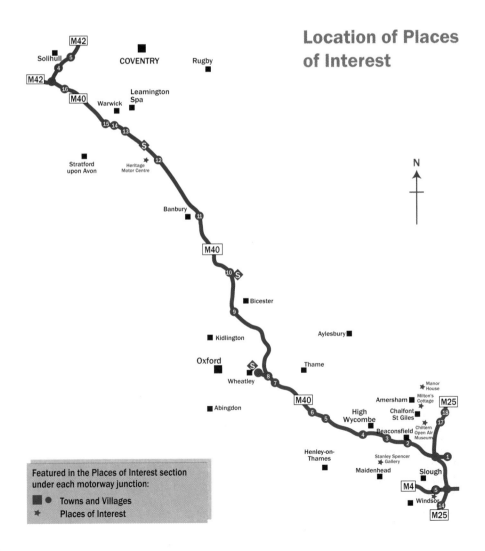

Location of Places of Interest

Featured in the Places of Interest section under each motorway junction:

■ ● Towns and Villages
✴ Places of Interest

JUNCTION 1A

THIS JUNCTION IS A MOTORWAY INTERCHANGE WITH THE M25 ONLY AND THERE IS NO ACCESS TO ANY FACILITIES

JUNCTION 2

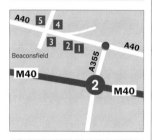

Nearest Northbound A&E Hospital

Wycombe General Hospital

Queen Alexandra Road, High Wycombe HP11 2TT
Tel: (01494) 526161
Proceed to Junction 4 and take the A404 north towards High Wycombe. Turn first left at the bottom of the hill and the Hospital is on the left. (Distance Approx 7.8 miles)

Nearest Southbound A&E Hospital

Wexham Park Hospital

Wexham Road, Slough
SL2 4HL Tel: (01753) 633000
Take the A355 south towards Slough and turn left at the first roundabout (at Farnham Royal) along the B412. Turn right at the end of this road and left to Stoke Green. Turn left at the roundabout along Wexham Street and the hospital is on the right. (Distance Approx 6.5 miles)

FACILITIES

1   Loch Fine Fishery Restaurant

Tel: (01494) 679960
0.9 miles north along the A40, in Beaconsfield, on the left.
Open; 10.00-22.00hrs daily

2   The Old White Swan

Tel: (01494) 673800
0.9 miles north along the A40, in Beaconsfield, on the left (Laurel Pub Company) Open all day. Meals served; Mon-Fri; 12.00-14.30hrs & 18.00-20.45hrs, Sat; 12.00-14.30hrs, Sun; 12.00-15.00hrs

3   The Royal Saracens Head

Tel: (01494) 674119
1 mile north along the A40, in Beaconsfield, on the left (Whitbread) Open all day. Meals served; Sun-Thurs; 12.00-22.00hrs, Fri & Sat; 12.00-22.30hrs.

4   White Hart Hotel

Tel: (01494) 671211
1 mile north along the A40, in Beaconsfield, on the right (Six Continents) Open all day. Restaurant Open; 12.00-22.00hrs daily.

5   The George Hotel

Tel: (01494) 673086
1 mile north along the A40, in Beaconsfield, on the right.
Wine Bar; Meals served; 10.00-16.00hrs daily.

JUNCTION 3

THIS IS A RESTRICTED ACCESS JUNCTION
- Vehicles can only exit from the northbound lanes
- Vehicles can only enter along the southbound lanes

Nearest Northbound A&E Hospital

Wycombe General Hospital

Queen Alexandra Road, High Wycombe HP11 2TT
Tel: (01494) 526161
Proceed to Junction 4 and take the A404 north towards High Wycombe. Turn first left at the bottom of the hill and the Hospital is on the left. (Distance Approx 4.6 miles)

Nearest Southbound A&E Hospital

Wexham Park Hospital

Wexham Road, Slough
SL2 4HL Tel: (01753) 633000
Proceed to Junction 2, take the A355 south towards Slough and turn left at the first roundabout (at Farnham Royal) along the B412. Turn right at the end of this road and left to Stoke Green. Turn left at the roundabout along Wexham Street and the hospital is on the right. (Distance Approx 8.7 miles)

FACILITIES

1   Browns Skoda Centre (Shell)

Tel: (01494) 678881
0.5 miles east along the A40, on the right.
Access, Visa, Delta, Mastercard, Switch, Diners Club, Amex, Overdrive, All Star, Dial Card, Shell Cards. Open; Mon-Fri; 07.00-22.00hrs, Sat & Sun; 07.00-21.00hrs.

2   The Rose & Crown

Tel: (01628) 520681
1 mile south along the A4034, in Wooburn Green, on the left.
(Punch Taverns) Open all day. Meals served; 12.00-18.30hrs daily

3   The Happy Union

Tel: (01628) 520972
0.6 miles along Loudwater Road, on the left.
(Laurel Pub Company) Open all day on Sat & Sun. Meals served; Mon-Sat; 12.00-14.00hrs, Sun; 12.00-15.00hrs

4   The Paper Mill

Tel: (01494) 537080
0.1 miles west along the A40, on the right.
(Brewers Fayre) Open all day. Meals served; 11.30-22.00hrs daily.

5   Travel Inn

Tel: (01494) 537080
0.1 miles west along the A40, on the right.

6   Shell Loudwater

Tel: (01494) 894710

1 mile west along the A40, on the left.
Access, Visa, Delta, Mastercard, Switch, Diners Club, Amex, Overdrive, All Star, Dial Card, BP Supercharge, BP Agency, Shell Cards. Open; 06.00-23.00hrs daily

7   King George V

Tel: (01494) 520928
1 mile west along the A40, on the left.
(Courage) Open all day. Meals served; 12.00-14.30hrs daily

JUNCTION 4

Nearest A&E Hospital

Wycombe General Hospital
Queen Alexandra Road, High Wycombe HP11 2TT
Tel: (01494) 526161
Take the A404 north exit towards High Wycombe. Turn first left at the bottom of the hill and the Hospital is on the left. (Distance Approx 1.1 miles)

FACILITIES

1   The Blacksmiths Arms

Tel: (01494) 525323
0.2 miles south along the Marlow Bottom Road, on the right.

(Beefeater) Open all day. Bar Meals served 12.00-21.00hrs daily, Restaurant Open; Mon-Fri; 12.00-14.30hrs & 17.00-22.30hrs, Sat; 12.00-23.00hrs, Sun; 12.00-22.30hrs.

2   Holiday Inn, High Wycombe

Tel: 0870 400 9042
0.1 miles north along the A4010, on the left.
The Junction Restaurant; Breakfast; Mon-Fri; 06.30-10.00hrs, Sat & Sun; 07.30-11.00hrs, Lunch; Sun-Fri; 12.30-14.30hrs, Dinner; Mon-Sat; 18.30-22.30hrs, Sun; 19.00-22.00hrs. Bar Meals available 24hrs.

3   Frankie & Benny's

Tel: (01494) 511958
0.2 miles north along the A4010, in Crest Road, on the left.
Open; 12.00-23.00hrs daily

4   TGI Fridays

Tel: (01494) 450067
0.2 miles north along the A4010, in Crest Road, on the left.
Open; Mon-Sat; 12.00-23.30hrs, Sun; 12.00-22.30hrs.

5   Asda Filling Station

Tel: (01494) 441611
0.2 miles north along the A4010, in Crest Road, on the left.
Access, Visa, Delta, Mastercard, Switch, Diners Club, Amex, Electron, Solo, Overdrive, All Star, Dial Card, Asda Business Card. Open: Mon-Fri; 06.00-23.00hrs, Sat; 06.30-22.00hrs, Sun; 08.00-18.00hrs. Disabled Toilets and Cash Machines available in adjacent store during opening hours.

6 Elaichai Tandoori Restaurant

Tel: (01494) 510710
0.7 miles north along the
A4010, on the right.
Open; 12.00-14.00hrs &
18.00-23.30hrs daily

7 Turnpike Petrol Station (Esso)

Tel: (01494) 523471
0.7 miles north along the
A4010, on the left.
Access, Visa, Delta,
Mastercard, Switch, Diners
Club, Amex, Electron, Solo,
Overdrive, All Star, Dial Card,
BP Supercharge, Shell Gold,
Esso Cards. Open; 07.00-
23.00hrs daily.

8 The Turnpike

Tel: (01494) 529419
0.8 miles north along the
A4010, on the right.
(Hungry Horse) Open all day.
Meals served; Mon-Sat; 12.00-
22.00hrs, Sun; 12.00-21.00hrs.

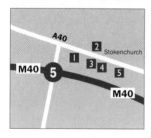

Nearest Northbound A&E Hospital

John Radcliffe Hospital
Headley Way, Headington,
Oxford OX3 9DU
Tel: (01865) 741166

Proceed to Junction 8 and take
the A40 west to Oxford. At the
first roundabout take the
second exit towards Oxford and
turn right at the second set of
traffic lights into Headley Way.
The hospital entrance is on the
right. (Distance Approx 16.4
miles)

Nearest Southbound A&E Hospital

Wycombe General Hospital
Queen Alexandra Road, High
Wycombe HP11 2TT
Tel: (01494) 526161
Proceed to Junction 4 and take
the A404 north towards High
Wycombe. Turn first left at the
bottom of the hill and the
Hospital is on the left.
(Distance Approx 8.7 miles)

FACILITIES

1 TCS Stokenchurch (Total)

Tel: (01494) 480950
0.4 miles east along the A40,
in Stokenchurch, on the right.
Access, Visa, Overdrive, All
Star, Switch, Dial Card,
Mastercard, Amex, Diners Club,
Delta, Total/Fina/Elf Cards.
Open; Mon-Sat; 06.00-
22.00hrs, Sun; 07.00-22.00hrs

2 The Kings Arms Hotel

Tel: (01494) 609090
0.5 miles east along the A40,
in Stokenchurch, on the left.
(Dhillon Hotels/Best Western)
The Black Olive Restaurant
Open; Breakfast; Mon-Fri;
07.00-09.00hrs, Sat & Sun;
08.00-10.00hrs, Meals then
served 11.00-22.00hrs daily.

3 Ye Fleur de Lis

Tel: (01494) 482269
0.5 miles east along the A40,

in Stokenchurch, on the right.
(Laurel Pub Company) Open all
day Fri, Sat & Sun. Meals
served; Mon-Thurs; 12.00-
15.00hrs & 17.30-21.00hrs, Fri
& Sat; 12.00-15.00hrs &
18.00-21.00hrs, Sun; 12.00-
19.00hrs.

4 The Four Horse Shoes

Tel: (01494) 482265
0.5 miles east along the A40,
in Stokenchurch, on the right.
(Pubmaster) Open all day.
Meals served; 09.30-22.00hrs
daily

5 Mowchak Bar & Indian Restaurant

Tel: (01494) 485005
0.9 miles east along the A40,
in Stokenchurch, on the right.
Open; 12.00-14.00hrs & 17.30-
23.30hrs daily

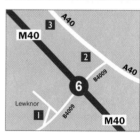

Nearest Northbound A&E Hospital

John Radcliffe Hospital
Headley Way, Headington,
Oxford OX3 9DU
Tel: (01865) 741166
Proceed to Junction 8 and take
the A40 west to Oxford. At the
first roundabout take the
second exit towards Oxford and
turn right at the second set of
traffic lights into Headley Way.

The hospital entrance is on the right. (Distance Approx 13.9 miles)

Nearest Southbound A&E Hospital

Wycombe General Hospital

Queen Alexandra Road, High Wycombe HP11 2TT
Tel: (01494) 526161
Proceed to Junction 4 and take the A404 north towards High Wycombe. Turn first left at the bottom of the hill and the Hospital is on the left.
(Distance Approx 11.2 miles)

FACILITIES

1   Ye Olde Leathern Bottel

Tel: (01844) 351482
0.6 miles west, in Lewknor, along the High Street.
(Brakspears Henley Brewery) Meals served: Sun-Thurs; 12.00-14.00hrs & 19.00-21.30hrs, Fri & Sat; 12.00-14.00hrs & 18.00-22.00hrs.

2   The Lambert Arms

Tel: (01844) 351496
0.4 miles north along the A40, on the left.
(Laurel Pub Company) Open all day. Meals served; Mon-Sat; 12.00-14.00hrs & 19.00-21.00hrs, Sun; 12.00-14.00hrs

3   Peel Guest House

Tel: (01844) 351310
1 mile north along the A40, on the left.

JUNCTION 7

THIS IS A RESTRICTED ACCESS JUNCTION
- Vehicles can only exit from the northbound lanes
- Vehicles can only enter along the southbound lanes

Nearest Northbound A&E Hospital

John Radcliffe Hospital

Headley Way, Headington, Oxford OX3 9DU
Tel: (01865) 741166
Proceed to Junction 8 and take the A40 west to Oxford. At the first roundabout take the second exit towards Oxford and turn right at the second set of traffic lights into Headley Way. The hospital entrance is on the right. (Distance Approx 8.2 miles)

Nearest Southbound A&E Hospital

Wycombe General Hospital

Queen Alexandra Road, High Wycombe HP11 2TT
Tel: (01494) 526161
Proceed to Junction 4 and take the A404 north towards High Wycombe. Turn first left at the bottom of the hill and the Hospital is on the left.
(Distance Approx 16.9 miles)

FACILITIES

1   The Three Pigeons Inn

Tel: (01844) 279247
0.1 miles north along the A40, in Milton Common, on the right.
(Tetley Carlsberg) Meals served; Mon-Thurs; 18.00-21.00hrs, Fri-Sun; 12.00-15.00hrs & 18.00-21.30hrs

2   The Oxford Belfry

Tel: (01844) 279381
0.2 miles north along the A40, in Milton Common, on the right.
The Terrace Restaurant Open; Breakfast; Mon-Fri; 07.00-09.30hrs, Sat & Sun; 08.00-10.00hrs, Lunch; Sun-Fri; 12.30-14.00hrs, Dinner; Sun-Fri; 19.00-21.30hrs, Sat; 19.00-22.00hrs

3   Lantern Service Station

Tel: (01844) 279336
0.5 miles north along the A40, on the right.
Diesel Fuel Only. Access, Visa, Amex, Keyfuels Open; Mon-Sat; 09.00-18.00hrs.

JUNCS 8 & 8A

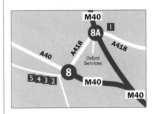

Nearest A&E Hospital

John Radcliffe Hospital

Headley Way, Headington,
Oxford OX3 9DU
Tel: (01865) 741166

Proceed along the A40 west to
Oxford and at the first
roundabout take the second
exit towards Oxford. Turn right
at the second set of traffic
lights into Headley Way and the
hospital entrance is on the
right. (Distance Approx 6.7
miles)

FACILITIES

> OXFORD SERVICES
> (WELCOME BREAK)
> Tel: (01865) 877000
> Red Hen, Food Connection, KFC,
> Burger King, Days Inn & BP Fuel.

1 Waterstock Golf Club

Tel: (01844) 338093
0.1 miles east along the
A418, on the left.
Restaurant Open (Summer);
08.00-20.00hrs daily. (Winter);
08.00-17.00hrs daily

2 The Wheatley Harvester

Tel: (01865) 875270
0.8 miles west along London
Road, in Wheatley, on the
left.
(Six Continents) Open all day.
Meals served; 12.00-22.00hrs
daily

3 Travelodge Oxford East

Tel: (01865) 875705
0.8 miles west along London
Road, in Wheatley, on the left

4 Asda Filling Station

Tel: (01865) 873888
0.8 miles west along London
Road, in Wheatley, on the
left.
Access, Visa, Delta,
Mastercard, Switch, Diners
Club, Amex, Overdrive, All Star,
Dial Card, Asda Business Card.
Disabled Toilets and Cash
Machines available in adjacent
store. Open; Mon-Sat; 07.00-
22.00hrs, Sun; 09.00-
16.00hrs.

5 The Plough

Tel: (01865) 872949
1 mile west along London
Road, in Wheatley, on the
left.
(Morrell's) Open all day Mon-
Sat. Meals served; Mon-Sat;
11.00-21.00hrs, Sun; 12.00-
15.00hrs

PLACES OF INTEREST

Oxford

Oxford Tourist Information Office,
The Old School, Gloucester Green,
Oxford OX1 2DA
Tel: (01865) 726871
website: www.visitoxford.org

**Follow the A40 west
(Signposted 7.4 Miles)**
Of Saxon origin, it was
captured from the Danish
invaders in 912 by Edward the
Elder and his son, Athelstan
established a mint in the town
in 924. The city was taken by
William the Conqueror in 1067
and he established a castle,
the remains of which adjoin
the County Hall.

Many historical events took
place here; Maud surrendered to
Stephen in 1142, in 1258 the

"Mad Parliament" under Henry III
passed the "Provisions of Oxford"
and Ridley, Latimer and Cranmer
were martyred within a few years
of the founding of the see in
1542. The city and colleges
abound with many of the finest
period buildings in the country,
dating from the 13thC through
the subsequent centuries and
embracing some of the best
examples of the classical styles of
architecture.

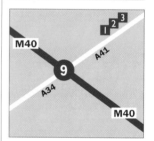

Nearest Northbound A&E Hospital

Horton General Hospital

Oxford Road (A4260),
Banbury OX16 9AL
Tel: (01295) 275500

Proceed to Junction 11 and
take the A422 west towards
Banbury and turn left at the
second roundabout. Follow this
route and turn left at the end
along the A4260. The hospital
is on the left along this road.
(Distance Approx 18 miles)

Nearest Southbound A&E Hospital

John Radcliffe Hospital

Headley Way, Headington,
Oxford OX3 9DU
Tel: (01865) 741166
Take the A34 south west
towards Oxford and turn left

along the A44. At the first roundabout turn left along the A40 and then follow the slip road to the B4150. Turn right at the first roundabout along the B4495 and the hospital is along this road. (Distance Approx 10.3 miles)

FACILITIES

THERE ARE NO FACILITIES WITHIN ONE MILE OF THIS JUNCTION

1 Bicester Services (Esso)

 WC 24HOUR

Tel: (01869) 324451
2.5 miles north along the A41, on the left.
Keyfuels, Access, Visa, Delta, Mastercard, Switch, Diners Club, Amex, Overdrive, All Star, Dial Card, BP Supercharge, Shell Gold, Esso Cards.

2 Little Chef

Tel: (01869) 248176
2.5 miles north along the A41, on the left.
Open; 07.00-22.00hrs daily.

3 Burger King

Tel: (01869) 248176
2.5 miles north along the A41, on the left.
Open; 10.00-22.00hrs daily.

PLACES OF INTEREST

Oxford

Follow the A34 west
(Signposted 10.5 Miles)
For details please see Junction 8 information.

JUNCTION 10

Nearest Northbound A&E Hospital

Horton General Hospital
Oxford Road (A4260), Banbury OX16 9AL Tel: (01295) 275500
Proceed to Junction 11 and take the A422 west towards Banbury and turn left at the second roundabout. Follow this route and turn left at the end along the A4260. The hospital is on the left along this road. (Distance Approx 12.4 miles)

Nearest Southbound A&E Hospital

John Radcliffe Hospital
Headley Way, Headington, Oxford OX3 9DU
Tel: (01865) 741166
Proceed to Junction 9, take the A34 south west towards Oxford and turn left along the A44. At the first roundabout turn left along the A40 and then follow the slip road to the B4150. Turn right at the first roundabout along the B4495 and the hospital is along this road. (Distance Approx 15.9 miles)

FACILITIES

CHERWELL VALLEY SERVICES (MOTO)
Tel: (01869) 346060

Fresh Express, Burger King, Little Chef, Travelodge & Esso Fuel

1 Fox & Hounds

Tel: (01869) 346883
0.3 miles south along the B430, in Ardley, on the left.
(Avesbury) Meals served; Mon-Sat; 12.00-14.30hrs & 18.00-21.30hrs, Sun; 12.00-14.30hrs

2 The Old Post Office B&B

Tel: (01869) 345958
0.5 miles south along Church Road, in Ardley, on the left.

3 Baynards Green Service Station (Esso)

WC 24HOUR

Tel: (01869) 345312
0.6 miles north along the A43, on the right.
Access, Visa, Delta, Mastercard, Switch, Diners Club, Amex, Electron, Solo, Overdrive, All Star, Dial Card, UK Fuelcard, Shell Gold, BP Supercharge, Esso Cards.

JUNCTION 11

Nearest A&E Hospital

Horton General Hospital
Oxford Road (A4260), Banbury OX16 9AL
Tel: (01295) 275500

Take the A422 west towards Banbury and turn left at the second roundabout. Follow this route and turn left at the end along the A4260. The hospital is on the left along this road. (Distance Approx 2.2 miles)

FACILITIES

1   Tesco Filling Station

Tel: (01295) 457400
1 mile west along the A422, in Banbury Cross Retail Park, on the right.
Visa, Delta, Mastercard, Switch, Amex, Electron, Overdrive, All Star, Dial Card, Tesco Fuel Card. Disabled Toilets and Cash Machine available in adjacent store

2   Burger King

Tel: (01295) 275744
1 mile west along the A422, in Banbury Cross Retail Park, on the right.
Open; Mon-Fri; 09.00-22.00hrs, Sat; 09.00-21.00hrs, Sun; 10.00-21.00hrs.

3   Ermont Way Service Station (Esso)

Tel: (01295) 279989
0.4 miles south along Ermont Way, in Banbury, on the left.
Access, Visa, Delta, Mastercard, Switch, Diners Club, Amex, Overdrive, All Star, Dial Card, Shell Gold, BP Supercharge, Esso Cards.

4   The Pepper Pot

Tel: (01295) 261790
0.7 miles along Middleton Road, on the right.
(Banks's) Open all day. Meals served; Mon-Sat; 12.00-

14.00hrs & 18.00-20.30hrs, Sun; 12.00-14.00hrs.

5   Blacklock Arms

Tel: (01295) 263079
0.8 miles along Middleton Road, on the right.
(Voyager) Open all day Fri, Sat & Sun. Meals served; Mon-Sat; 12.00-14.00hrs & 18.00-21.30hrs, Sun; 12.00-20.30hrs.

PLACES OF INTEREST

Banbury

Banbury Tourist Information Centre, 8 Horsefair, Banbury OX16 0AA Tel: (01295) 259855 website www.cherwell-dc.gov.uk

Follow the A422 west. (Signposted 1.8 Miles)
Banbury dates from Saxon times and it was during the Mediaeval period that the town expanded. A castle was erected in Banbury in 1125 and this was twice beseiged, latterly during the Civil War, culminating in its near total demolition. There are several old buildings surviving in the town including Ye Olde Reindere Inn from the 16thC and No.16 Market Place, a timber framed structure dating from the late 15thC.

Within the town there was a strong connection with the Puritan movement and the original legendary cross of nursery rhyme fame was destroyed by them in the 17thC. A Victorian Gothic replacement, in the style of an Eleanor Cross, was installed to commemorate the wedding of Queen Victoria's eldest daughter to the Crown Prince of Prussia.

JUNCTION 12

Nearest Northbound A&E Hospital

Warwick Hospital
Lakin Road, Warwick
CV34 5BW
Tel: (01926) 495321
Proceed to Junction 13, take the A452 and then the A425 north into Warwick. Follow the A429 towards Coventry and bear left immediately after the railway bridge. The hospital is on the left side of this road. (Distance Approx 9.2 miles)

Nearest Southbound A&E Hospital

Horton General Hospital
Oxford Road (A4260), Banbury OX16 9AL
Tel: (01295) 275500
Proceed to Junction 11 and take the A422 west towards Banbury and turn left at the second roundabout. Follow this route and turn left at the end along the A4260. The hospital is on the left along this road. (Distance Approx 12.8 miles)

FACILITIES

1   Gaydon Service Station (Esso)

Tel: (01926) 642278
0.7 miles south along the

B4100, on the left.
Access, Visa, Delta, Mastercard, Switch, Diners Club, Amex, Overdrive, All Star, Dial Card, Shell Gold, BP Supercharge, Esso Cards. Open; 06.00-23.00hrs daily.

2   Gaydon Inn

Tel: (01926) 640388
0.7 miles south along the B4100, on the right.
(Punch Taverns) Meals served; Mon-Sat; 12.00-14.30hrs & 18.00-21.00hrs, Sun; 12.00-15.00hrs

3   Malt Shovel

Tel: (01926) 641221
0.8 miles west, in Gaydon Village.
Open all day Fri-Sun. Meals served; 12.00-14.00hrs & 18.30-21.00hrs daily.

PLACES OF INTEREST

The Heritage Motor Centre

Banbury Road, Gaydon CV35 0BJ

Tel: (01926) 641188. website: www.heritage.org.uk

Signposted from the junction. (3.4 Miles)
This fascinating centre holds the largest exhibition of historic British cars and tells the story of the British motor industry from 1896 to the present day. Over 200 vehicles, embracing the world-famous makes of Austin, Morris, Rover, Wolseley, Riley, Standard, Triumph, MG and Austin-Healey, are on display and the 65 acre site also features a 4x4 off-road demonstration circuit. Gift Shop. Restaurant. Disabled access.

M40 BETWEEN JUNCS 12 & 13

WARWICK SERVICES (NORTHBOUND) (WELCOME BREAK)
Tel: (01926) 651681
The Granary Restaurant, Burger King, Red Hen Restaurant, Days Inn & BP Fuel

WARWICK SERVICES (SOUTHBOUND) (WELCOME BREAK)
Tel: (01926) 651681
The Granary Restaurant, Burger King, Red Hen Restaurant, KFC, La Brioche Doree, Welcome Lodge & BP Fuel

M40 JUNCTION 13

THIS IS A RESTRICTED ACCESS JUNCTION
- Vehicles can only exit from the northbound lanes
- Vehicles can only enter along the southbound lanes

Nearest Northbound A&E Hospital

Warwick Hospital
Lakin Road, Warwick CV34 5BW
Tel: (01926) 495321
Take the A452 and then the A425 north into Warwick. Follow the A429 towards Coventry and bear left immediately after the railway bridge. The hospital is on the left side of this road. (Distance Approx 3.8 miles)

Nearest Southbound A&E Hospital

Horton General Hospital
Oxford Road (A4260), Banbury OX16 9AL
Tel: (01295) 275500

Either;

Proceed to Junction 11 and take the A422 west towards Banbury and turn left at the second roundabout. Follow this route and turn left at the end along the A4260. The hospital is on the left along this road. (Distance Approx 18.2 miles)

Or;

Proceed to Junction 12, return to Junction 13 and follow the above Directions (Distance Approx 14.6 miles)

FACILITIES

THERE ARE NO FACILITIES WITHIN ONE MILE OF THIS JUNCTION

PLACES OF INTEREST

Warwick

Warwick Tourist Information Centre, The Court House, Jury Street, Warwick CV34 4EW
Tel: (01926) 492212 website: www.warwick-uk.co.uk

Follow the A452 north (Signposted 3.2 Miles)
Standing by the River Avon, the mediaeval castle (Tel: 01926-495521) is one of the most splendid and well preserved fortresses in England. Established in Norman times, it was largely destroyed during the Barons' revolt in 1264 and most of the present structure dates from the 14thC. Although the centre of the town was

rebuilt after a fire in 1694 some of the mediaeval structures including Lord Leycester's Hospital (Tel: 01926-491422), a beautiful collection of 15thC half timbered buildings enclosing a galleried courtyard, still remain amongst the elegant Queen Anne edificies.

JUNCTION 14

THIS IS A RESTRICTED ACCESS JUNCTION

- Vehicles can only exit from the southbound lanes
- Vehicles can only enter along the northbound lane

Nearest Northbound A&E Hospital

Warwick Hospital
Lakin Road, Warwick
CV34 5BW
Tel: (01926) 495321
Proceed to Junction 15 and take the A429 north to Warwick. Follow this route through the town centre and bear left immediately after the railway bridge. The hospital is on the left of this road.
(Distance Approx 3.8 miles)

Nearest Southbound A&E Hospital

Warwick Hospital
Lakin Road, Warwick
CV34 5BW
Tel: (01926) 495321
Take the A452 and then the A425 north into Warwick. Follow the A429 towards Coventry and bear left immediately after the railway bridge. The hospital is on the left side of this road. (Distance Approx 3.9 miles)

FACILITIES

THERE ARE NO FACILITIES WITHIN ONE MILE OF THIS JUNCTION

PLACES OF INTEREST

Warwick

Follow the A452 south (Signposted 3.2 Miles)
For details please see Junction 13 information

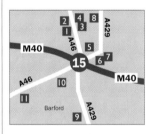

JUNCTION 15

Nearest A&E Hospital

Warwick Hospital
Lakin Road, Warwick
CV34 5BW
Tel: (01926) 495321
Take the A429 north to Warwick follow this route through the town centre and bear left immediately after the railway bridge. The hospital is on the left of this road.
(Distance Approx 2.6 miles)

FACILITIES

1   Little Chef

Tel: (01926) 491764

1 mile north along the A46, on the left.
Open; 07.00-22.00hrs daily.

2   BP Express Shopping, Warwick North

Tel: (01926) 496862
1 mile north along the A46, on the left.
Access, Visa, Delta, Mastercard, Switch, Diners Club, Amex, Overdrive, All Star, Dial Card, Shell Agency, BP Cards. Open; 06.00-22.00hrs daily.

3   Little Chef

Tel: (01926) 491560
1 mile north along the A46, on the right.
Open; 07.00-22.00hrs daily.

4   BP Express Shopping, Warwick South

Tel: (01926) 499932
1 mile north along the A46, on the right.
Access, Visa, Delta, Mastercard, Switch, Diners Club, Amex, Overdrive, All Star, Dial Card, Shell Agency, BP Cards. Open; 06.00-22.00hrs daily.

5   Hilton Warwick

Tel: (01926) 499555
0.1 miles north along the A429, on the left.
The Britisserie Restaurant Open; Breakfast; Mon-Fri; 07.00-09.30hrs, Sat & Sun; 07.30-10.00hrs, Lunch; Sun-Fri; 12.30-14.00hrs, Dinner; 18.30-22.00hrs daily.

6   Express by Holiday Inn, Warwick

Tel: (01926) 483000
0.1 miles north along the A429, on the right.

7 Porridge Pot

Tel: (01926) 401697

0.1 miles north along the A429, on the right.

(Tom Cobleighs) Open all day. Meals served; Mon-Sat; 12.00-22.00hrs, Sun; 12.00-21.30hrs.

8 Stratford Road Filling Station (Jet)

Tel: (01926) 491228

1 mile north along the A429, on the left.

LPG. Access, Visa, Overdrive, All Star, Switch, Dial Card, Mastercard, Amex, Diners Club, Delta, BP Supercharge, Jet Cards. Open; Mon-Fri; 07.00-22.00hrs, Sat; 07.00-21.00hrs, Sun; 08.00-21.00hrs.

9 The Joseph Arch

Tel: (01926) 624365

1 mile south along the A429, in Barford, on the right.

(Punch Taverns) Open all day on Fri-Sun. Meals served; Mon-Sat; 12.00-14.00hrs & 19.00-21.00hrs, Sun; 12.00-15.00hrs

10 The Old Rectory B&B

Tel: (01926) 624562

0.2 miles south along the A46, on the left.

11 Hillcrest Guest House

Tel: (01926) 624386

1 mile south along the A46, on the left

PLACES OF INTEREST

Warwick

Follow the A429 (Signposted 2.2 Miles)

For details please see Junction 13 information

Stratford upon Avon

Stratford upon Avon Tourist Information Centre, Bridgefoot, Stratford upon Avon CV37 6GW Tel: (01789) 293127 website: www.shakespeare-country.co.uk

Follow the A46 south (Signposted 6.2 Miles)

On the banks of the River Avon, Stratford has many interesting features as well as being the home town of William Shakespeare. A market town dating back to at least 1196 when it was granted its charter by King John, the focal point of interest is his birthplace, a small timber framed house in Henley Street, (Tel: 01789-204016) but there are also a considerable number of buildings of the Tudor and Jacobean periods. The Shakespeare Memorial Theatre is the second on the site, the first was built in 1879 and destroyed by a fire in 1926. The current building opened on April 23rd, 1932 but is now the subject of a heated debate as to whether it should be demolished and replaced (Tel: 01789-403403).

M40
JUNCTION 16

THIS IS A RESTRICTED ACCESS JUNCTION

- Vehicles can only exit from the southbound lanes
- Vehicles can only enter along the northbound lanes

Nearest Southbound A&E Hospital

Warwick Hospital

Lakin Road, Warwick CV34 5BW

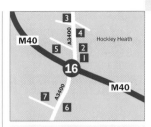

Tel: (01926) 495321

Proceed to Junction 15 and take the A429 north to Warwick. Follow this route through the town centre and bear left immediately after the railway bridge. The hospital is on the left of this road. (Distance Approx 11.4 miles)

Nearest Northbound A&E Hospital

Solihull Hospital

Lode Lane, Solihull B91 2JL Tel: (0121) 424 4226

Proceed north to Junction 5 on the M42 and take the A41 north towards Birmingham. After about 1.5 miles turn left along Lode Lane (B425) and the hospital is on the left. (Distance Approx 8.5 miles)

FACILITIES

1 Old Royal Oak

Tel: (01564) 785252

0.4 miles north along the A3400, on the right.

(Greene King) Open all day. Meals served; 12.00-21.00hrs daily

2 Rose Cottage B&B

Tel: (01564) 782936

0.5 miles north along the A3400, on the right

3 Wharf Tavern

Tel: (01564) 782075

1 mile north along the A3400,

in Hockley Heath, on the left.
(Scottish & Newcastle) Open all
day. Lunch, Mon-Sat; 12.00-
14.00hrs & 18.30-21.00hrs,
Sun; 12.00-20.00hrs.

**4   Hockley Heath Service
Station (Shell)**

Tel: (01564) 782244
1 mile north along the A3400,
in Hockley Heath, on the
right.
Access, Visa, Delta,
Mastercard, Switch, Diners
Club, Amex, Overdrive, All Star,
Dial Card, UK Fuelcard, BP
Supercharge, Shell Cards.
Open; Mon-Sat; 07.00-
23.00hrs, Sun; 08.00-
23.00hrs.

**5   Nuthurst Grange Hotel
& Restaurant**

Tel: (01564) 783972
0.6 miles north along
Nuthurst Grange Lane, on the
left.
Restaurant Open; Breakfast;
Mon-Fri; 07.00-09.30hrs, Sat &
Sun; 07.30-10.00hrs, Lunch;
Sun-Fri; 12.00-14.00hrs,
Dinner; 19.00-21.30hrs daily.

6   Village Garden B&B

Tel: (01564) 783553
1 mile south along the
A3400, on the left

7   Ye Olde Pounde Café

Tel: (01564) 782970
1 mile south along the
A3400, on the right.
Open; Mon-Fri; 08.00-
15.00hrs, Sat & Sun; Closed.

**MOTORWAY MERGES WITH
THE M42**
(Total length opf moteorway 87.7
miles)

the M42

Although only a short motorway of under 40 miles in length, it provides a direct north east-south west connection from the M1 to the M5, links up with the M40 and avoids the need for traffic to go around the north side of Birmingham.

Commencing at its junction with the M5 at Junction 4A at **Lickey End** the motorway heads due east, and passes **Bromsgrove**, a town well-known for the manufacture of nails and the birthplace of the famous poet AE Houseman, on the south side of Junction 1. Continuing east, the 950ft high **Lickey Hills** are on the north side of the motorway, and the Birmingham to Bristol line, which opened in 1840, is bridged. The motorway crosses the line only about 0.8 miles north of the summit of the 2 miles long **Lickey Incline**, which at 1 in 37 is the steepest main line gradient in Britain. The Worcester & Birmingham Canal, completed in 1815, is bridged and **Alvechurch** is on the south side just before Junction 2. The small village of Alvechurch earned national recognition when its football team reached the semi-finals of the FA Amateur Cup in 1966 and later took part in the longest ever FA cup tie, a 4th Qualifying Round fixture against Oxford City in 1971 which took 11 hours (six matches) before they finally won 1-0.

Between Junctions 2 and 3 the **Lickey Hills** can be seen on the north side with part of the **MG Rover Longbridge Plant** visible to the right. The buildings that can be seen include the Central Assembly Building (CAB) on top of the hill and the extraction chimneys of the Cofton Hackett and East Works factories at a lower level. The CAB is built on the site of the flying ground from which aircraft built at the factory during World War II took off. At its connection with the M40 at Junction 3A, the motorway turns north and bridges the **Stratford Canal**. The northern section of this canal, which links the Worcester & Birmingham and Grand Union Canals, opened in 1802. Never officially closed it became difficult to navigate by the 1940s and was restored to operational standard in the early 1950s by the Inland Waterways Association. Just before Junction 4, a **bow string style road bridge** carrying the exit roads from Blythe Valley Business Park spans the carriageways. The 490 tons of steelwork had been transported from the Bolton Works of Watson Steel Ltd and assembled, along with the concrete works and pedestrian parapets, on the east side of the

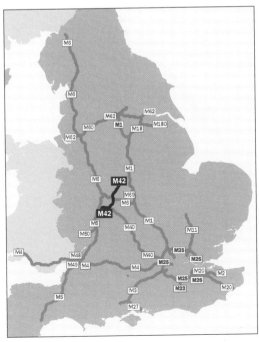

motorway. On the night of November 21st/22nd 1999, the M42 was closed between Junctions 3A and 4 and the bridge, with a combined weight of 1380 tons, was slid across the carriageways utilizing a self-propelled tractor unit with 120 individually computer controlled wheels at the front end and a purpose built slide track at the rear. The overall length of the single span bridge is 214ft which allows for widened slip roads and will also accommodate any possible (and inevitable!) widening of the M42.

The motorway continues northwards past **Solihull**, home of the world famous Land Rover and the Renewal Christian Centre, on the west side and just after Junction 5 crosses the **Grand Union Canal**. This section of the Grand Union Canal, the Warwick & Birmingham, opened in 1800. Between Junctions 5 and 7A, low flying aircraft frequently cross the motorway as they land and take off at **Birmingham International Airport** on the west side of the carriageway and just before Junctions 7A and 8 where it connects with the M6, the suspended roof supports of the **NEC Arena** can be seen on the same side. The NEC, National Exhibition Centre, was opened in February 1976 and is the seventh largest exhibition site in Europe with a total covered floor area of 227,245 square yards.

Immediately north of the M6, the eastern suburbs of **Birmingham** can be seen to the west and the small town of **Coleshill**, which dates back to 799AD, is on the east. At Junction 9 the Birmingham to Derby line is bridged with the site of the former Hams Hall Power Station, now being utilized as an industrial park and Channel Tunnel Rail Freight Depot, on the east side. Also at this junction construction work is under way to provide a connection with the **M6 Toll** (formerly known as the Birmingham Northern Relief Road), Britain's first toll motorway. Continuing northwards towards Junction 10 the Birmingham & Fazeley Canal and the Heart of England Way run adjacent to the west side of the motorway and **Kingsbury Water Park**, partially hidden by a small wood, is on the east side. Beyond Junction 10 on the west side is **Tamworth** which dates back to Saxon days and was once the site of Offa, King of Mercia's Palace and where the remains of the Norman castle are still visible. The motorway ends at Junction 11 where it has an end-on connection with the A42 to the M1 north and Nottingham.

Location of Places of Interest

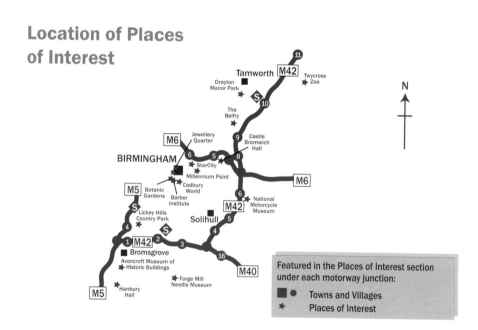

Featured in the Places of Interest section under each motorway junction:

■ ●   Towns and Villages

★   Places of Interest

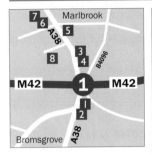

JUNCTION 1

Marlbrook

M42   **1**   M42

Bromsgrove

THIS IS A RESTRICTED ACCESS JUNCTION

- There is no exit for eastbound vehicles.
- There is no access for westbound vehicles

Nearest North & Eastbound A&E Hospital

Selly Oak Hospital

Raddlebarn Road, Selly Oak, Birmingham B29 6JD
Tel: (0121) 627 1627
Take the A38 north to Birmingham and into Selly Oak. The hospital is signposted within the city. (Distance Approx 9.6 miles)

Nearest Southbound A&E Hospital

Worcester Royal Hospital

Charles Hastings Way, Worcester WR5 1DD
Tel: (01905) 763333
Proceed to Junction 6 (M5), take the westbound exit along the A4440 and the route is signposted A&E Hospital. (Distance Approx 14.5 miles)

Nearest Minor Injury Unit

The Princess of Wales Community Hospital

Stourbridge Road, Bromsgrove B61 0BB
Tel: (01527) 488000

Follow the A38 into Bromsgrove. Signposted within the town. Opening Hours; 09.00-17.00, Monday to Friday. (Distance Approx 1 mile)

FACILITIES

1   Bromsgrove Harvester

Tel: (01527) 872063
On the south side of the Roundabout.
(Six Continents) Open all day. Meals served; Sun-Thurs; 12.00-21.00hrs, Fri & Sat; 12.00-22.00hrs

2   Forest Service Station (Esso)

Tel: (01527) 570142
0.1 miles south along the A38, on the left.
Access, Visa, Delta, Mastercard, Switch, Diners Club, Overdrive, All Star, Dial Card, Shell Gold, Esso Cards.

3   Marlgrove Super Stop (Total)

Tel: (01527) 579854
0.3 miles north along the A38, on the right.
LPG. Access, Visa, Delta, Mastercard, Switch, Diners Club, Amex, Overdrive, All Star, Dial Card, Total/Fina/Elf Cards.

4   Marlgrove Club, Motel & Café

Tel: (01527) 872889
0.3 miles north along the A38, on the right.
Café Open: Mon-Fri; 07.00-14.00hrs, Sat; 08.00-14.00hrs, Sun; 08.00-12.00hrs

---

5   Toby Carvery, Marlbrook

Tel: (01527) 878060
0.6 miles north along the A38, on the right.
(Toby Carvery) Open all day. Bar meals served; Mon-Sat; 11.00-23.00hrs. Carvery Open; Mon-Fri; 12.00-14.00hrs & 17.00-22.00hrs, Sat & Sun; 12.00-22.00hrs.

6   Marlbrook Service Station (Total)

Tel: (01527) 570178
0.7 miles north along the A38, on the left.
Access, Visa, Mastercard, Switch, Diners Club, Amex, Overdrive, All Star, Dial Card, Delta, AA Paytrak, BP Supercharge, Total/Fina/Elf Cards. Open; Mon-Fri; 07.00-22.00hrs, Sat; 08.00-22.00hrs, Sun; 08.00-13.00hrs.

7   Hilton Bromsgrove

Tel: (0121) 447 7888
0.8 miles north along the A38, on the left.
The Britisserie Restaurant Open; Mon-Fri; 07.00-10.00hrs, 12.00-14.00hrs, 19.00-21.30hrs, Sat; 07.00-10.00hrs, 19.00-21.30hrs, Sun; 07.30-10.00hrs, 12.00-14.00hrs, 19.00-21.30hrs.

8   The Royal Oak

Tel: (01527) 870141
0.7 miles along Barley Mow Lane, on the left.
(Free House) Open all day. Meals served; Mon-Sat, 12.00-14.00hrs & 18.00-21.00hrs, Sun; 12.00-20.15hrs.

PLACES OF INTEREST

Avoncroft Museum of Historic Buildings

Stoke Heath, Worcestershire

Follow the A38 south. (Signposted 3.4 miles)
For details please see Junction 5 (M5) information

Hopwood

Hopwood Park Services

M42 **2** M42

Nearest North & Eastbound A&E Hospital

Selly Oak Hospital

Raddlebarn Road, Selly Oak, Birmingham B29 6JD
Tel: (0121) 627 1627
Take the A441 north towards Birmingham. In Cotteridge bear left along the Ring Road (A4040) to Selly Oak and after about 1.5 miles turn right into Raddlebarn Road. The hospital is on the left. (Distance Approx 5.9 miles)

Nearest South & Westbound A&E Hospital

Worcester Royal Hospital

Charles Hastings Way, Worcester WR5 1DD
Tel: (01905) 763333
Proceed to Junction 6 (M5) and take the westbound exit along the A4440 and the route is signposted A&E Hospital. (Distance Approx 18.9 miles)

Nearest Minor Injury Unit

The Princess of Wales Community Hospital

Stourbridge Road, Bromsgrove B61 0BB
Tel: (01527) 488000
Proceed west to Junction 1 and follow the A38 into Bromsgrove. Signposted within the town. Opening Hours; 09.00-17.00hrs, Monday to Friday. (Distance Approx 5.2 miles)

FACILITIES

HOPWOOD PARK SERVICES (WELCOME BREAK)

Tel: (0121) 447 4000
La Brioche Doree French Café, Granary Restaurant, Burger King, Red Hen Restaurant and BP Fuel.

1   Petrol Express (Esso)

Tel: (0121) 445 6173
0.8 miles north along the A441, on the right.
Access, Visa, Delta, Mastercard, Switch, Diners Club, Amex, Overdrive, All Star, Dial Card, Shell Agency, Esso Cards. Open; Mon-Fri; 06.00-22.00hrs, Sat & Sun; 07.00-22.00hrs

2   Hopwood House

Tel: (0121) 445 1716
0.8 miles north along the A441, on the left.
(Banks's) Open all day. Meals served; Sun-Thurs; 12.00-21.00hrs, Fri & Sat; 12.00-22.00hrs

3   Westmead Hotel & Restaurant

Tel: (0121) 445 1202
1 mile north along the A441, on the right.

Blakes Restaurant; Open; Breakfast; Mon-Sat; 07.00-09.30hrs, Sun; 08.00-10.30hrs, Lunch; Mon-Fri; 12.00-14.00hrs, Dinner; Mon-Sat; 19.00-21.45hrs. Carvery Bar; Open; Sun; 12.00-16.00hrs.

PLACES OF INTEREST

Birmingham

Follow the A441 north (Signposted 10 Miles)
For details please see Junction 1 (M5) information.

Cadbury World

Bournville, Birmingham B30 2LD

Follow the A441 north (Brown & White tourist boards along the route) (6 Miles).
For details please see Junction 4 (M5) information.

Brindley Place & Broad Street, Birmingham

Follow the A441 north into the city centre. The route is signposted "National Indoor Arena & Convention Centre" (10 Miles)
For details see Junction 1 (M5) information.

Forge Mill Needle Museum

Needle Mill Lane, Riverside, Redditch B98 8HY

Tel: (01527) 62509 website: www.redditchbc.gov.uk

Follow the A441 south to Redditch (3.5 Miles)
Redditch has established a reputation for manufacturing high quality springs and needles and at Forge Mill the history of the latter is described. The displays include water powered machinery and textiles. Picnic Area. Museum Shop. Café. Disabled access.

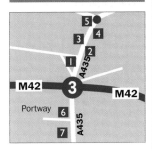

JUNCTION 3

Nearest Northbound A&E Hospital

Solihull Hospital

Lode Lane, Solihull B91 2JL
Tel: (0121) 424 4226

Proceed to Junction 5 and take the A41 north towards Birmingham. After about 1.5 miles turn left along Lode Lane (B425) and the hospital is on the left. (Distance Approx 9.6 miles)

Nearest Southbound A&E Hospital

Selly Oak Hospital

Raddlebarn Road, Selly Oak, Birmingham B29 6JD
Tel: (0121) 627 1627

Proceed to Junction 2 and take the A441 north towards Birmingham. In Cotteridge bear left along the Ring Road (A4040) to Selly Oak and after about 1.5 miles turn right into Raddlebarn Road. The hospital is on the left. (Distance Approx 8.7 miles)

Nearest Minor Injury Unit

The Princess of Wales Community Hospital

Stourbridge Road, Bromsgrove B61 0BB
Tel: (01527) 488000

Proceed to Junction 1 and follow the A38 into Bromsgrove. Signposted within the town. Opening Hours; 09.00-17.00, Monday to Friday. (Distance Approx 8 miles)

FACILITIES

1 TCS Weatheroak Service Station (Total)

Tel: (01564) 824685
0.2 miles north along the A435, on the left.
Access, Visa, Delta, Mastercard, Switch, Diners Club, Amex, Electron, Solo, Overdrive, All Star, Dial Card, Total/Fina/Elf Cards. Open; Mon-Sat; 06.00-22.00hrs, Sun; 07.00-22.00hrs

2 The Horse & Jockey

Tel: (01564) 822308
0.4 miles north along the A435, on the right.
(The Spirit Group) Open all day. Meals served; Mon-Sat; 11.00-22.00hrs, Sun; 12.00-21.30hrs.

3 Inkford Hotel

Tel: (01564) 824330
0.9 miles north along the A435, on the left.

4 Star Market Wythall (Texaco)

Tel: (01564) 825110
0.9 miles north along the A435, on the right.
Access, Visa, Delta, Mastercard, Switch, Diners Club, Amex, Electron, Solo, Overdrive, All Star, Dial Card, UK Fuelcard, Keyfuels, Texaco Cards.

5 Becketts Farm Restaurant

Tel: (01564) 823402

1 mile north along the A435, on the left.
Open; Mon-Thurs; 08.00-17.30hrs, Fri & Sat; 08.00-17.30hrs & 18.00-22.00hrs (Carvery), Sun; 08.00-17.00hrs.

6 The Rose & Crown

Tel: (01564) 822166
0.2 miles south along the A435, on the right.
(Scottish & Newcastle) Open all day. Meals served; Mon-Fri; 12.00-14.30hrs & 18.00-21.30hrs, Sat & Sun 12.00-21.30hrs.

7 Portway House Restaurant (Italian)

Tel: (01564) 824794
0.3 miles south along the A435, on the right.
Open; Lunch; Tues-Fri & Sun; 12.00-14.30hrs, Evening Meals; Tues-Sat; 18.30-22.30hrs

JUNCTION 3A

THIS JUNCTION IS A MOTORWAY INTERCHANGE WITH THE M40 ONLY AND THERE IS NO ACCESS TO ANY FACILITIES

JUNCTION 4

Nearest Northbound A&E Hospital

Solihull Hospital

Lode Lane, Solihull B91 2JL
Tel: (0121) 424 4226

Proceed to Junction 5 and take the A41 north towards Birmingham. After about 1.5 miles turn left along Lode Lane (B425) and the hospital is on the left. (Distance Approx 4 miles)

Nearest Southbound A&E Hospital

Selly Oak Hospital

Raddlebarn Road, Selly Oak, Birmingham B29 6JD
Tel: (0121) 627 1627

Proceed to Junction 2 and take the A441 north towards Birmingham. In Cotteridge bear left along the Ring Road (A4040) to Selly Oak and after about 1.5 miles turn right into Raddlebarn Road. The hospital is on the left. (Distance Approx 14.3 miles)

Nearest Minor Injury Unit

The Princess of Wales Community Hospital

Stourbridge Road, Bromsgrove B61 0BB
Tel: (01527) 488000

Proceed to Junction 1 and follow the A38 into Bromsgrove. Signposted within the town. Opening Hours; 09.00-17.00hrs, Monday to Friday. (Distance Approx 13.6 miles)

FACILITIES

1 Tesco Filling Station

Tel: (0121) 253 7500
0.2 miles north along the A34, on the right.
Access, Visa, Delta, Mastercard, Switch, Amex, Electron, Overdrive, All Star, Dial Card, Tesco Fuelcard. Disabled Toilets and Cash Machines available in adjacent store during store opening hours.

2 McDonald's

Tel: (0121) 733 6327
0.3 miles north along the A34, on the right.
Open; 07.00-23.00hrs daily.

3 The Plough Inn

Tel: (0121) 744 2942
0.6 miles north along the A34, on the left.
(Beefeater) Open all day. Restaurant Open; Mon-Fri; 07.00-09.00hrs, 12.00-14.30hrs & 17.30-22.00hrs, Sat; 08.00-10.00hrs & 12.00-22.00hrs. Sun; 08.00-10.00hrs & 12.00-21.00hrs. Bar Meals served; 12.00-21.00hrs daily.

4 Travel Inn

Tel: (0121) 744 2942
0.6 miles north along the A34, on the left

5 Chez Julien Français

Tel: (0121) 744 7232
0.8 miles north along the A34, on the left.
Open; Mon-Fri; 12.00-14.00hrs & 19.00-22.30hrs, Sat; 19.00-22.30hrs.

6 Jefferson's

Tel: (0121) 733 1666
0.8 miles north along the A34, on the left.
Open all day. Meals served; Mon-Sat; 12.00-23.00hrs, Sun; 12.00-22.30hrs.

7 Da Corrado (Italian)

Tel: (0121) 744 1977
1 mile north along the A34, on the right.
Open; Mon-Sat; 12.00-14.00hrs & 19.00-23.00hrs.

8 The Regency Hotel

Tel: (0121) 745 6119
1 mile north along the A34, on the right.
Copperfields Brasserie Open; Breakfast; 07.00-09.30hrs daily, Lunch; Mon-Fri; 12.00-14.00hrs, Dinner; 19.00-21.30hrs daily

9 Boxtrees Farm B&B and Coffee Shop

Tel: (01564) 782039
0.9 miles south along the A3400, on the left.
Coffee Shop Open; Wed-Mon; 10.00-17.00hrs. (NB. Hot meals served; 12.00-14.30hrs)

10 Boxtrees Filling Station (Total)

Tel: (01564) 782139
1 mile south along the A3400, on the left.
Access, Visa, Delta, Mastercard, Switch, Diners Club, Amex, Electron, Solo, Overdrive, All Star, Dial Card, Total/Fina/Elf Cards. Open: Mon-Fri; 06.00-22.00hrs, Sat & Sun; 07.00-22.00hrs

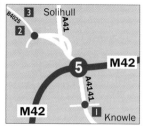

Nearest A&E Hospital

Solihull Hospital

Lode Lane, Solihull B91 2JL
Tel: (0121) 424 4226
Take the A41 north towards
Birmingham. After about 1.5
miles turn left along Lode Lane
(B425) and the hospital is on
the left. (Signposted. Distance
Approx 2 miles)

FACILITIES

THERE ARE NO FACILITIES
WITHIN ONE MILE OF THIS
JUNCTION

1   Wilson Arms

Tel: (01564) 772559
1.3 miles south along the
A4141, in Knowle on the left.
(Toby Carvery) Open all
day. Carvery Open; Mon-
Sat; 12.00-14.00hrs &
17.00-22.00hrs, Sun;
12.00-22.00hrs. Bar
Meals served; 12.00-
22.00hrs daily.

2   Brueton Park Filling Station (BP)

Tel: (0121) 704 0878
1.4 miles north along the
B4025, on the left, in Solihull.
Access, Visa, Delta,
Mastercard, Switch, Diners
Club, Amex, Overdrive, All Star,
Dial Card, BP Cards. Open;
06.00-22.00hrs daily.

3   Bar Co

Tel: (0121) 704 1567
1.5 miles north along the
B4025, on the right, in
Solihull.
(Unique Pub Co) Open all day.
Meals served; Mon-Sat; 11.00-
15.00hrs

PLACES OF INTEREST

Birmingham

Follow the A41 north
(Signposted 9.4 Miles)
For details please see Junction
1 (M5) information.

Brindley Place & Broad Street, Birmingham

Follow the A41 north into the
city centre and the route is
signposted "National Indoor
Arena & Convention Centre"
(10 Miles)
For details please see Junction
1 (M5) information.

Nearest A&E Hospital

Heartlands Hospital

Bordesley Green East,
Birmingham B9 5SS
Tel: (0121) 424 3263
Take the A45 towards
Birmingham and after about 4
miles turn right at Yardley along
the A4040 (Ring Road). Follow
this route for about 1 mile and
turn left along Bordesley Green
East (B4126). The hospital is
on the left. (Distance Approx
6.9 miles)

FACILITIES

1   Arden Hotel & Restaurant

Tel: (01675) 443221
0.5 miles west along the A45,
on the right.
Restaurant Open: Lunch; Sun-
Fri; 12.00-14.30hrs, Dinner;
Sun-Thurs; 18.30-22.00hrs, Fri
& Sat; 18.30-23.00hrs.

2   Bickenhill Service Station (Esso)

Tel: (01675) 443485
0.6 miles west along the A45,
on the right.
Access, Visa, Delta,
Mastercard, Switch, Diners
Club, Amex, Overdrive, All Star,
Dial Card, Shell Gold, BP
Supercharge, Esso Cards.
(NB Closes temporarily
between 22.35 &
23.00hrs to effect shift
changeover)

3   The Clock

Tel: (0121) 782 3434
0.9 miles west along the
A45, on the left.
(Punch Taverns) Open all day.
Meals served; Mon-Thurs;
12.00-21.00hrs, Fri & Sat;
12.00-22.00hrs, Sun; 12.00-
20.30hrs.

4   Anne's Pantry Petrol Station (Total)

Tel: (0121) 782 4498
1 mile west along the A45, on
the left.
Access, Visa, Delta,
Mastercard, Switch, Diners
Club, Amex, Electron, Solo,
Overdrive, All Star, Dial Card,
Total/Fina/Elf Cards. Open:
06.00-21.00hrs daily.

5 Toby Carvery, Stonebridge

Tel: (01675) 442326

0.9 miles east along the A45, on the left.

(Toby Carvery) Open all day. Carvery Restaurant Open; Mon-Thurs; 12.00-14.00hrs & 17.00-22.00hrs, Fri; 12.00-14.00hrs & 17.00-22.30hrs, Sat; 12.00-22.30hrs, Sun; 12.00-22.00hrs. Bar Meals served; Mon-Sat; 11.00-22.00hrs.

6 Hilton Metropole Hotel

Tel: (0121) 780 4242

0.6 miles, within the NEC site. Boulevard Restaurant Open; Breakfast; 07.00-10.30hrs daily, Lunch; Sun-Fri; 12.30-15.00hrs, Dinner; 18.00-22.30hrs daily.

PLACES OF INTEREST

National Motorcycle Museum

Coventry Road, Bickenhill, Solihull B92 0EJ

The entrance is adjacent to the roundabout.
For details please see Junction 4 (M6) information.

JUNCTION 7

THIS JUNCTION IS A MOTORWAY INTERCHANGE WITH THE M6 ONLY AND THERE IS NO ACCESS TO ANY FACILITIES

JUNCTION 8

THIS JUNCTION IS A MOTORWAY INTERCHANGE WITH THE M6 ONLY AND THERE IS NO ACCESS TO ANY FACILITIES

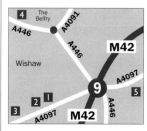

JUNCTION 9

Nearest A&E Hospital

Good Hope Hospital

Rectory Road, Sutton Coldfield B75 7RR.
Tel: (0121) 378 2211
Take the A449 towards Lichfield and after about 2.6 miles turn left along Holly Lane. Turn first right into Lindrige Road and third left into Rectory Road. The hospital is on the right after 1 mile. (Distance Approx 4.9 miles)

FACILITIES

1 The White Horse

Tel: (01675) 470227

0.6 miles south along the A4097, on the right.

(Six Continents) Open all day. Meals served; Mon-Sat; 12.00-22.00hrs, Sun; 12.00-21.00hrs

2 The Old School House Hotel

Tel: (01675) 470177

0.8 miles south along the A4097, on the right.

3 The Kingsley

Tel: (01675) 470808

1 mile south along the A4097, on the right.

(Beefeater) Open all day. Meals served; Mon-Fri; 12.00-14.30hrs & 17.00-22.00hrs, Sat; 12.00-22.30hrs, Sun; 12.00-21.0hrs

4 The Belfry Hotel

Tel: (01675) 470301

1 mile north along the A446, on the right.

(De Vere Hotels) There are five restaurants within the hotel (The Atrium, French, Riley's, Café Bar & Belle Aire Bistro) and food is served between 07.00 & 22.00hrs daily.

5 Water Park Lodge

Tel: (01675) 470533

0.3 miles east along the A4097, on the right.

PLACES OF INTEREST

Drayton Manor Park

Tamworth, Staffordshire B78 3TW

Tel: (01827) 287979 website: www.draytonmanor.co.uk

Follow the A446 north and continue along the A4091 (Signposted 4.9 Miles)

Based around the former home of Sir Robert Peel, Drayton Manor Family Theme Park is the UK's biggest family run Theme Park. The 250 acre site also includes a Zoo, excellent conference and function facilities and over one hundred rides and attractions including Shockwave - the UK's only stand-up Coaster and Stormforce 10, a £4 million wet knuckle ride. Maelstrom, The Jubilee Circus (daily except Mondays) and Fifth Element. Park are three new attractions for 2002. Gift Shops. Cafés. Disabled access.

The Belfry

Wishaw, North Warwickshire B76 9PR

Tel: (01675) 470301 website; www.devereonline.co.uk

Follow the A446 north (Signposted 1 Mile)

Set in 500 acres of North Warwickshire countryside, the world-famous Belfry is a must for golf enthusiasts with its three championship golf courses. Casual visitors are welcome to view the scene of some of the most renowned encounters in the Ryder Cup and browse through the largest on-course Golf, Leisure and Lifestyle Shop in Europe. The complex, the venue for the Ryder Cup in 2002, also includes a 324 bedroom 4-star hotel, 5 restaurants, 8 bars, a night club and a floodlit driving range.

JUNCTION 10

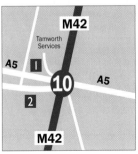

Nearest Northbound A&E Hospital

George Eliot Hospital

College Street, Nuneaton CV10 7DJ
Tel: (024) 7635 1351

Take the A5 east towards Hinckley and at Atherstone bear left along the B4111 to Nuneaton town centre. Follow the A444 south towards Coventry and turn right into College Street. The hospital is on the left. (Distance Approx 11.6 miles)

Nearest Southbound A&E Hospital

Good Hope Hospital

Rectory Road, Sutton Coldfield B75 7RR
Tel: (0121) 378 2211

Proceed to Junction 9, take the A449 towards Lichfield and after about 2.6 miles turn left along Holly Lane. Turn first right into Lindrige Road and third left into Rectory Road. The hospital is on the right after 1 mile. (Distance Approx 10.8 miles)

FACILITIES

TAMWORTH SERVICES (MOTO)

Tel: (01827) 260120
Fresh Express Restaurant, Harry Ramsden's, Burger King, Little Chef, Travelodge and Esso Fuel.

1 Kinsall Green Garage (Murco)

 WC

Tel: (01827) 283838
0.1 miles north along the A5, on the right.
Access, Visa, Delta, Mastercard, Switch, Electron, Solo, Murco Cards. Open; Mon-Sat; 08.00-18.00 hours.

2 Centurion Park

Tel: (01827) 260587
0.3 miles north along the B5404, on the left.
(Brewers Fayre) Open all day. Meals served all day Mon-Sat 11.30-22.00hrs, Sun; 12.00-22.00hrs.

PLACES OF INTEREST

Drayton Manor Park

Tamworth, Staffordshire B78 3TW

Follow the A5 west (Signposted 3.3 Miles)

For details please see Junction 9 information

Tamworth

Tourist Information Office 29 Market Street, Tamworth B79 7LR Tel: (01827) 709581 website: www.tamworth.gov.uk

Follow the A5 west (3.4 Miles)

In the second half of the 8thC Offa, King of Mercia, built a great palace in Tamworth and fortified it by encircling the palace and town with a ditch, of which traces remain as Offa's Dyke and King's Ditch. The town was destroyed twice by the Danes and later invaded by the Scandinavians, with evidence of this occupation being revealed in some of the street names such as Gunlake. Tamworth Castle, sited on an eminence beside the River Anker and close to its junction with the River Thame, was first constructed by Ethelfreda, King Alfred's daughter, in the 10thC. The Normans built a motte and bailey castle in sandstone in the 1180's and the building, set in delightful Pleasure Grounds is open to public view (Tel: 01827-709626). The vast Parish Church was founded in

963, rebuilt by the Normans and rebuilt again after the Great Fire of Tamworth in 1345 and has a fine 15thC tower with a remarkable double staircase. The town has some fine 18thC buildings and, in front of the Town Hall of 1701, there is a bronze statue of Sir Robert Peel, Tamworth's most famous son.

JUNCTION 11

Nearest Northbound A&E Hospital

Queen's Hospital

Belverdere Road, Burton upon Trent DE13 0RB
Tel: (01283) 566333
Take the A444 into Burton and at Stapenhill proceed over St.Peters Bridge and continue to the 2nd roundabout and the hospital is signposted Burton A&E from this point. (Distance Approx 11.5 miles)

Nearest Southbound A&E Hospital

George Eliot Hospital

College Street, Nuneaton CV10 7DJ
Tel: (024) 7635 1351
Take the A444 south into Nuneaton town centre and continue south towards Coventry. Turn right into College Street and the hospital is on the left. (Distance Approx 14.3 miles)

FACILITIES

1   The Four Counties

Tel: (01827) 830243
1 mile south along the B5493, in No Man's Heath, on the left.
(Free House) Lunch; Mon-Sat; 12.00-14.00hrs, Sun; 12.00-14.30hrs, Evening Meals; Mon-Sat; 19.00-22.30hrs, Sun; 19.00-22.00hrs.

2   Four Counties Garage (Murco)

Tel: (01827) 830883
1 mile south along the B5493, in No Man's Heath, on the left.
Access, Visa, Delta, Mastercard, Switch, Amex, Electron, Solo, Overdrive, All Star, Dial Card, Open; Mon-Sat; 08.00-17.30hrs,

3   The Crown Inn

Tel: (01530) 271478
1 mile east, in Appleby Magna, in Church Street.
(Banks's) Open all day. Bar meals served; Mon-Sat; 12.00-21.00hrs.

4   The Black Horse

Tel: (01530) 270588
1 mile east, in Appleby Magna, in Top Street
(Banks's) Open all day Sun. Meals served; Mon-Tues & Thurs-Sat; 18.00-21.00hrs

5   McDonald's

Tel: (01530) 273197
0.1 miles south along the A444, on the right
Open; Sun-Thurs; 06.00-23.00hrs ["Drive Thru" open

until 23.30hrs], Fri & Sat; 06.00-23.30hrs ["Drive Thru" open until 0.00hrs].

6   Appleby Magna Service Area (Total)

Tel: (01530) 273303
0.1 miles south along the A444, on the right.
LPG. Access, Visa, Delta, Mastercard, Switch, Diners Club, Amex, Electron, Solo, Overdrive, All Star, Dial Card, Total/Fina/Elf Cards.

7   Appleby Inn Hotel

Tel: (01530) 270463
0.7 miles south along the A4444, on the left.
(Free House) Breakfast Served; 07.00-09.00hrs daily. Restaurant Open; 19.00-22.00hrs daily, Bar Meals served; 12.00-22.00 daily.

PLACES OF INTEREST

Twycross Zoo

Burton Road, Twycross, Nr Atherstone, Warwickshire CV9 3PX Tel: (01827) 880250 website: www.twycrosszoo.com

Follow the A444 south and turn left along the B4116 (4.1 Miles)
Over 1,000 animals, including many endangered species, are on view at this centre for conservation and education. Other attractions include a pets corner, children's adventure playground and picnic areas. Gift Shop. Café. Licensed Bar.

MOTORWAY ENDS
(Total length of motorway 39.0 miles)

the **M50**

Also known as the Ross Spur, the 21 miles long M50 opened in November 1960 to form part of the dual carriageway route between South Wales, the Midlands and the North. Commencing at its connection to the M5 at Junction 8 at **Strensham** the motorway heads south west to link up with the A40 at Junction 4.

Primarily a rural route, the only significant items of note are **the bridge** over the River Severn at Queenhill between Junctions 1 and 2 and the fine view across the **River Wye**, a mecca for

Ross on Wye

Location of Places of Interest

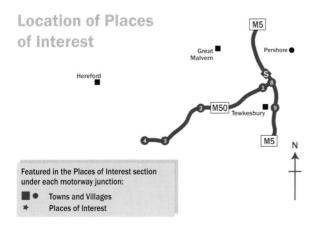

Featured in the Places of Interest section under each motorway junction:

■ ●   Towns and Villages

✱   Places of Interest

anglers and a Site of Special Scientific Interest, to Ross at the south end of the motorway just before Junction 4. **Ross on Wye** is a lovely old market town which is full of interesting buildings including the 15thC St Mary's Church and the 17thC Market House.

Travellers should note that there are no fuel facilities available off the motorway between Strensham on the M5 and Ross on Wye.

M50 JUNCTION 1

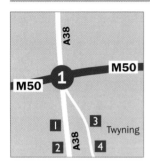

Nearest Northbound A&E Hospital
Worcester Royal Hospital
Charles Hastings Way, Worcester WR5 1DD
Tel: (01905) 763333
Proceed north to Junction 7 on the M5 and take the A44 exit west. The route is signposted A&E Hospital. (Distance Approx 13.7 miles)

Nearest Southbound A&E Hospital
Cheltenham General Hospital
Sandford Road, Cheltenham GL53 7AN
Tel: (01242) 222222
Proceed to Junction 10 on the M5 and follow the A4019 into Cheltenham. The hospital is signposted from within the town. (Distance Approx 14.6 miles)

Nearest Minor Injury Unit
Tewkesbury Hospital
Barton Road, Tewkesbury GL20 5QN
Tel: (01684) 293303.
Follow A38 south into Tewkesbury. Signposted from within the town. Open 24 hours. (Distance Approx 3.3 miles)

Nearest Westbound A&E Hospital
Hereford General Hospital
Nelson Street, Hereford HR1 2PA
Tel: (01432) 355444
Proceed to Junction 2, take the A417 and then the A438 to Hereford. The hospital is signposted within the city. (Distance Approx 27.9 miles)

Nearest Westbound Minor Injury Unit
Ross Community Hospital
Walton Street, Ross on Wye HR9 5AD
Tel: (01989) 562100
Proceed to Junction 4 and take the A449 to Ross. Continue along Broad Street, cross Market Square and go along Walford Street. Turn second left into Walton Street and the hospital is along this road. Open 24 Hours. (Distance Approx 21.5 miles)

FACILITIES

1 Hilton Puckrup Hall Hotel & Golf Club

Tel: (01684) 296200
0.4 miles south along the A38, on the right.
Balharries Restaurant; Open; Breakfast; Mon-Fri; 07.00-10.00hrs, Sat & Sun; 07.30-10.00hrs, Lunch; Mon-Fri; 12.00-14.00hrs, Sun; 12.30-14.00hrs, Dinner; Mon-Sat; 19.00-22.00hrs, Sun; 19.00-21.30hrs.

2 The Crown at Shuthonger

Tel: (01684) 293714
1 mile south along the A38, in Shuthonger, on the right.
(Free House) Evening Meals served daily.

3 The Village Inn

Tel: (01684) 293500
0.8 miles south on Twyning Green, in Twyning, on the left.
(Pubmaster) Meals served; Wed-Sun; 12.00-14.00hrs & 19.00-21.00hrs. (Daily between May and September)

4 The Fleet Inn
Tel: (01684) 274310
1 mile south along Fleet Lane, in Twyning, on the left.
(Whitbread) Open all day. Lunch; 12.00-14.30hrs daily, Evening meals; Sun-Thurs; 18.00-21.00hrs, Fri & Sat; 18.00-21.30hrs. Baguettes and Chips served between 12.00-21.00hrs daily.

M50 JUNCTION 2

> **THERE ARE NO FACILITIES WITHIN ONE MILE OF THIS JUNCTION**

Nearest Eastbound A&E Hospital
Worcester Royal Hospital
Charles Hastings Way, Worcester WR5 1DD
Tel: (01905) 763333
Proceed north to Junction 7 on the M5 and take the A44 exit west. The route is signposted A&E Hospital. (Distance Approx 23 miles)

Nearest Eastbound Minor Injury Unit
Tewkesbury Hospital
Barton Road, Tewkesbury GL20 5QN
Tel: (01684) 293303
Proceed north to Junction 1 and follow the A38 south into Tewkesbury. Signposted from within the town. Open 24

hours. (Distance Approx 12.6 miles)

Nearest Westbound A&E Hospital

Hereford General Hospital

Nelson Street, Hereford
HR1 2PA
Tel: (01432) 355444
Take the A417 and then the A438 to Hereford. The hospital is signposted within the city. (Distance Approx 18.7 miles)

Nearest Westbound Minor Injury Unit

Ross Community Hospital

Walton Street, Ross on Wye
HR9 5AD
Tel: (01989) 562100
Proceed to Junction 4 and take the A449 to Ross. Continue along Broad Street, cross Market Square and go along Walford Street. Turn second left into Walton Street and the hospital is along this road. Open 24 Hours. (Distance Approx 12.2 miles)

Nearest Eastbound A&E Hospital

Gloucestershire Royal Hospital

Great Western Road, Gloucester GL1 3PQ
Tel: (01452) 528555
Take the B4215 south into Gloucester. The hospital is signposted within the town. (Distance Approx 13.5 miles)

Nearest Eastbound Minor Injury Unit

Tewkesbury Hospital

Barton Road, Tewkesbury
GL20 5QN
Tel: (01684) 293303.
Proceed north to Junction 1 and follow the A38 south into Tewkesbury. Signposted from within the town. Open 24 hours. (Distance Approx 19.5 miles)

Nearest Westbound A&E Hospital

Hereford General Hospital

Nelson Street, Hereford
HR1 2PA
Tel: (01432) 355444
Take the B4224 north to Hereford and the hospital is signposted within the city. (Distance Approx 14.4 miles)

Nearest Westbound Minor Injury Unit

Ross Community Hospital

Walton Street, Ross on Wye
HR9 5AD
Tel: (01989) 562100
Proceed to Junction 4 and take the A449 to Ross. Continue along Broad Street, cross Market Square and go along Walford Street. Turn second left into Walton Street and the hospital is along this road. Open 24 Hours. (Distance Approx 5.3 miles)

FACILITIES

1   The Roadmaker Inn

Tel: (01989) 720352
0.4 miles south along the B4221, on the right.
(Free House) Meals served; Tues-Fri; 18.00-21.30hrs, Sat; 12.00-14.00hrs & 18.00-21.30hrs, Sun; 12.00-14.00hrs

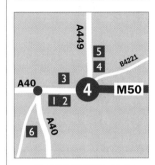

Nearest A&E Hospital

Hereford General Hospital

Nelson Street, Hereford
HR1 2PA
Tel: (01432) 355444
Take the A49 north to Hereford and the hospital is signposted within the city. (Distance Approx 16.3 miles)

Nearest Minor Injury Unit

Ross Community Hospital

Walton Street, Ross on Wye
HR9 5AD
Tel: (01989) 562100
Take the A449 to Ross, continue along Broad Street, cross Market Square and go along Walford Street. Turn second left into Walton Street and the hospital is along this road. Open 24 Hours. (Distance Approx 1.6 miles)

FACILITIES

1   The Granary Restaurant

Tel: (01989) 565301
0.4 miles south along the A449, on the left.
Open; 07.00-22.00hrs daily.

2   BP Ross Spur South

Tel: (01989) 565027
**0.4 miles south along the
A449, on the left.**
Access, Visa, Delta,
Mastercard, Switch, Diners
Club, Amex, Electron, Solo,
Overdrive, All Star, Dial Card.
Routex, Shell Gold, Shell
Agency, BP Cards.

3 BP Ross Spur North

Tel: (01989) 565028
**0.4 miles south along the
A449, on the right.**
Access, Visa, Delta,
Mastercard, Switch, Diners
Club, Amex, Electron, Solo,
Overdrive, All Star, Dial Card.
Routex, Shell Gold, Shell
Agency, BP Cards.

4 The Travellers Rest

Tel: (01989) 563861
**Adjacent to the roundabout,
on the north side.**
(Beefeater) Open all day. Meals
served; Mon-Thurs; 07.00-
09.00hrs & 12.00-22.30hrs,
Fri; 07.00-09.00hrs & 12.00-
23.00hrs, Sat; 08.00-10.00hrs
& 12.00-23.00hrs, Sun; 08.00-
10.00hrs & 12.00-22.30hrs.

5 Travel Inn

Tel: (01989) 563861
**Adjacent to the roundabout,
on the north side**

6 Broadlands B&B

Tel: (01989) 563663
**1 mile south along the
B4234, on the left, in Ross on
Wye.**

the M62

Fully opened in January 1976, this 106 miles long motorway forms the strategic east-west link across northern England, connecting the ports of Liverpool, on the west coast and Kingston upon Hull on the east with Manchester, Huddersfield, Bradford and Leeds.

The motorway commences at Junction 4 on the eastern outskirts of Liverpool where it connects with the A5080 and A5058. As originally designed it was planned to start the M62 in Liverpool at an inner ring motorway but as this was dropped, the section of M62 to join it was also dispensed with in 1976 leaving the motorway to end here. Continuing east the carriageways link up with the M57 at Junction 6 and east of Junction 7, the glass making town of **St Helens** is in view on the north side. Along this stretch the cooling towers of **Fiddlers Ferry Power Station** are on the horizon to the south and just to the west of Burtonwood Services the motorway crosses over the site of **RAF Burtonwood Airfield**. This airfield was utilized by the USAF during World War II and closed as an operational facility on April 3rd, 1959. In 1967 the US Army took it over as the Burtonwood Army Depot before it was finally dispensed with and converted to commercial use in 1992.

Warrington is passed on the south side before the motorway crosses the M6 at Junction 10. Warrington, an important industrial centre since Georgian and Victorian times, was established as a crossing point over the River Mersey with a bridge being constructed here in the 13thC. In 1745 it was deliberately sabotaged to hinder the march south of the Young Pretender. As the motorway continues east towards Manchester it crosses the south edge of **Chat Moss**. This is a huge boggy area which was a major engineering problem for George Stephenson as he constructed the Liverpool & Manchester Railway in the 1820s, and he was forced to use many tons of ballast to infill and create a solid base upon which to lay the rails. Just before it reaches Junction 12, the motorway is bridged by the **ex-Liverpool & Manchester Railway** main line. This was opened on September 15th, 1830 by the Duke of Wellington and was the first full-scale

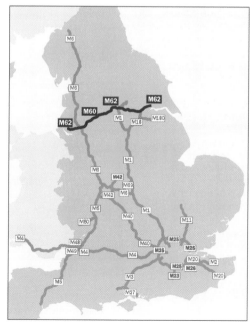

inter city railway, exclusively powered by locomotives and providing a strictly timetabled service for both passengers and freight, the prototype on which all subsequent railways throughout the world were modelled.

At Junction 12 the motorway forms an end-on connection with the M602 into Manchester and turns north as it joins the M60. The M60 north from this junction to Junction 18 was originally part of the M62 but has been re-classified as the M60 (Manchester Outer Ring Road). The north end of Junction 14 has been renumbered as Junction 15 and Junction 15 as Junction 16. The Bridgewater Canal is bridged at Junction 12 and the motorway connects with the M61 at Junctions 14, 15 and 16 and turns east whilst, just after Junction 16, the Manchester to Bolton railway line, Fletcher's Canal and the River Sankey are all bridged with Kearsley and Bolton in view to the north and Clifton Green to the south. **Bolton** was first settled during the Bronze Age but it was the wealth and prosperity generated by spinning high quality yarn which led to its growth in the 19thC and which endowed the town with many fine Victorian buildings. The motorway links up with the M66 at Junction 18 and continues eastwards, reverting to its M62 classification as the M60 turns south. At the west end of the section between here and Junction 19, Bury, with the 1,350ft high **Holcombe Moor** beyond, can be viewed to the north. **Bury**, a typical mill town and the birthplace of Sir Robert Peel, dates from the Bronze Age and a castle was constructed here under the stewardship of the Pilkington family. Bury Castle was demolished following the Battle of Bosworth in 1485 and the Pilkingtons, centuries later, established the world famous glass company at St Helens. Just east of Junction 19, **Heywood** is on the north side the 1,375ft high **Knowl Moor** is in view with the town of **Ramsbottom** visible beyond whilst at Junction 20 the town of **Rochdale**, the birthplace of the Co-operative Movement, is passed on the north side as a connection is made with the A627(M) to Oldham.

Beyond Junction 21, **Clegg Moor** is on the north side and the 1,330ft high **Bleakedgate Moor** is to the south, whilst approaching Junction 22 a footbridge carries the **Pennine Way** high over the carriageways. The Pennine Way is a 256 miles long footpath linking Edale in Derbyshire and Kirk Yetholm in Scotland. It was the brainchild of Tom Stephenson, a journalist and rambler, and after years of campaigning, lobbying and fighting the inertia of bureaucracy, it was officially opened at a ceremony near Malham in North Yorkshire in April 1965. The M62, the highest motorway in Britain, attains a height of 1,221ft at Junction 22 some 188ft higher than Shap Summit on the M6. As it continues east the motorway skirts past **Booth Valley Reservoir** in the valley below before it splits and **Stott Hall Farm** can be seen between the carriageways, the only instance of a dwelling occupying the central reservation of a motorway.

Shibden Hall, Halifax

Approaching Junction 23, **Scammonden Water** is adjacent to the carriageways on the south side. This reservoir was built jointly by the Huddersfield Borough Council and the

Ministry of Transport in 1970 using the motorway, on a 7,000ft long, 220ft high embankment, 129ft wide at the top and 1,100ft wide at the base, as the dam. Between Junctions 24 and 25 a panoramic view across to **Elland**, **Halifax**, boasting some fine examples of municipal architecture, and the **South Pennines** can be seen from the north side and the River Calder, the Calder & Hebble Navigation and the ex-Lancashire & Yorkshire Railway Mirfield to Halifax line are all bridged by a viaduct. Turning north, the motorway links up with the M606 at Junction 26 and, as the carriageways bear east, **Bradford**, famous for the National Museum of Photography, Film and Television, is in view on the north side between Junctions 26 and 27, where it connects with the M621. Continuing east the motorway passes **Leeds**, a former industrial city which has been transformed into a thriving commercial and cultural centre, to the north before crossing the M1 at Junction 29.

The Aire & Calder Navigation is bridged between Junctions 30 and 31. The Aire & Calder Navigation was constructed in the 1790s to connect the West Riding of Yorkshire to the River Ouse at Goole. It was modernized in the 1970s and is now capable of handling 700 tons vessels. Also on this section the town of **Wakefield**, one of the oldest towns in Yorkshire, is in view to the south. Between Junctions 31 and 32 **Pontefract Racecourse** is on the south side of the carriageways. Pontefract Racecourse is sited within Pontefract Park, a Norman hunting estate which stretched from the northern reaches of the castle to Featherstone in the west and Glasshoughton to the north. Horse races had taken place here as long ago as 1738 before the first formal track was laid out in 1790. This was a complete circuit but it was adjusted when the arrival of the Pontefract to Methley line in 1849 sliced off the north east corner of the park. The track saw additional modifications in 1971 when the M62 was built across the

Arnley Mills, Leeds

north end of the park and the current 2 miles 121yds 1 ft long circuit, which was completed in 1983, is the longest continuous Flat Racing circuit in Britain.

Between Junctions 32 and 33 **Castleford** is on the north side and **Pontefract** is on the south side. Pontefract, originally known as Pomfret and renowned for its "cakes", is on an eminence near to the junctions of the Rivers Aire and Calder. Pomfret Castle, of which little remains, was constructed in 1069 to protect the crossing of the Aire. Approaching Junction 33, **Ferrybridge Power Station** is in view to the north and the Mexborough to Knottingley railway line is bridged. The landscape is now in complete contrast to the rocky Pennines over which the motorway has traversed and beyond Junction 34, the cooling towers of **Thorpe Marsh Power Station**, to the south, and **Drax Power Station**, to the north are visible in the distance before the carriageways cross over the East Coast Main Line between London (Kings Cross) and Edinburgh. The motorway links up with the M18 at Junction 36 beyond which the River Ouse is bridged by a 1,320 ft long viaduct with views across to **Selby**, famous for its Abbey which has 12[th]C origins, to the north and **Goole**, Britain's most inland port, to the south. Just past Junction 37, the town of **Howden** and its 130ft high Minster can be seen on the north side and the motorway terminates at Junction 38 with an end-on connection with the A63 to Kingston upon Hull.

Location of Places of Interest

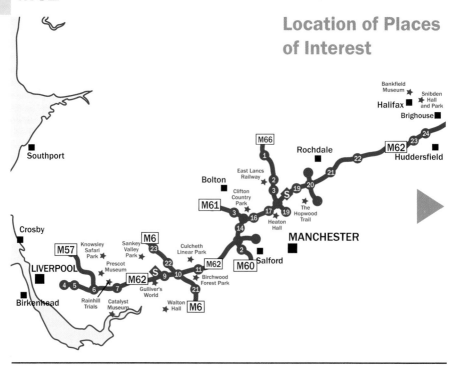

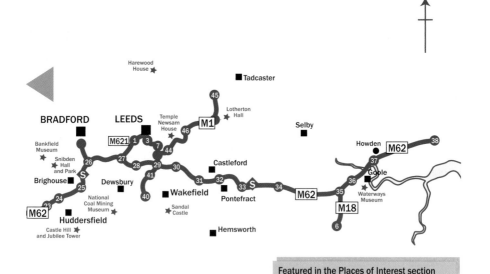

Featured in the Places of Interest section under each motorway junction:

■ ● Towns and Villages
★ Places of Interest

JUNCTION 4

Nearest A&E Hospital
The Royal Liverpool University Hospital
Prescot Street, Liverpool
L7 8XP
Tel: (0151) 706 2000
Follow the A5080 west into Liverpool (Signposted in city. Distance Approx 2.8 miles)

JUNCTION 5

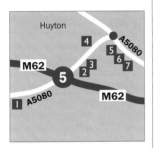

Nearest Eastbound A&E Hospital
Whiston Hospital
Prescot, Merseyside L35 5DL
Tel: (0151) 426 1600
Proceed to Junction 6 and take the exit north to Prescot. (Signposted within town. Distance Approx 4.4 miles)

Nearest Westbound A&E Hospital
The Royal Liverpool University Hospital
Prescot Street, Liverpool
L7 8XP
Tel: (0151) 706 2000
Proceed to Junction 4 and follow the A5080 west into Liverpool (Signposted in city. Distance Approx 4.1 miles)

FACILITIES

1   Turnpike Tavern

Tel: (0151) 738 2921
1 mile west along the A5080, on the left.
(Six Continents) Open all day. Meals served; Mon-Thurs; 12.00-14.30hrs & 17.00-19.00hrs, Fri; 12.00-19.00hrs, Sat; 12.00-18.30hrs, Sun; 12.00-16.30hrs

2   Derby Lodge

Tel: (0151) 480 4440
0.3 miles east along the A5080 on the right.
(Scottish & Newcastle) Open all day. Meals served; Mon-Fri; 07.00-09.30hrs & 12.00-22.00hrs, Sat & Sun; 07.00-10.00hrs & 12.00-22.00hrs.

3   Premier Lodge
Tel: (0151) 480 4440
0.3 miles east along the A5080 on the right

4   The Stanley Arms
Tel: (0151) 480 1651
0.6 miles east along the A5080 on the left.
(Six Continents) Open all day. Meals served; Mon-Fri; 12.00-14.00hrs & 17.00-20.00hrs, Sat & Sun; 12.00-20.00hrs

5   The Crofters

Tel: (0151) 482 4951
0.8 miles east along the A5080 on the right.
(Six Continents) Meals served; 12.00-15.00hrs daily

6   Repsol Service Station

Tel: (0151) 489 6246
0.8 miles east along the A5080 on the right.
Access, Visa, Overdrive, All Star, Switch, Dial Card, Mastercard, Amex, Diners Club, Delta, BP Supercharge, Repsol Card. Open; 07.00-23.00hrs

7   Save Petrol Station
Tel: (0151) 481 0188
0.9 miles east along the A5080 on the right.
Access, Visa, Overdrive, All Star, Switch, Dial Card, Mastercard, Amex, Diners Club, Delta, Save Card. Open; 06.00-23.00hrs

JUNCTION 6

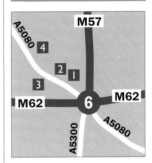

Nearest A&E Hospital
Whiston Hospital
Prescot, Merseyside L35 5DL
Tel: (0151) 426 1600
Take the M57 exit north to Prescot and follow the A57 east. (Signposted within town. Distance Approx 1.8 miles)

FACILITIES

1   Travel Inn

Tel: (0151) 480 9614
0.2 miles west along the
A5080, on the right

2   Chapel Brook

Tel: (0151) 480 9614
0.2 miles west along the
A5080, on the right.
(Whitbread) Open all day.
Meals served; Mon-Sat; 11.30-
22.00hrs, Sun; 12.00-
22.00hrs

3   Woodlands Service Station (Esso)

Tel: (0151) 480 6284
0.3 miles west along the
A5080, on the left.
Access, Visa, Mastercard,
Switch, Diners Club, Amex,
Overdrive, All Star, Dial Card,
BP Supercharge, Shell Gold,
Esso Cards

4   Hare & Hounds

Tel: (0151) 489 3046
0.5 miles west along the
A5080, on the right.
(Scottish & Newcastle) Open all
day. Meals served; Mon-Sat;
12.00-21.00hrs, Sun; 12.00-
20.00hrs

PLACES OF INTEREST

Knowsley Safari Park

Prescot, Merseyside L34 4AN
Tel: (0151) 430 9009
website; www.knowsley.com

**Follow the M57 north and
take the A58 east at Junction
2. (Signposted from junction
3.7 Miles)**

A huge variety of animals are in
view along the 5-mile long
safari drive. Other attractions
include a miniature railway,
Lake farm, Seal & Parrot
Shows, Reptile house,

amusement park and picnic
areas. Gift Shop. Restaurant.
Disabled access.

The Prescot Museum

34 Church Street, Prescot,
Merseyside L34 3LA
Tel: (0151) 430 7787
website: www.knowsley.gov.uk/
leisure/museum

**Follow the M57 north and
take the A57 east at Junction
2. (2.6 Miles)**

By 1800 Prescot had become
the principal UK manufacturing
base for the production of
watch movements, watch and
clock components and
horological and precision tools,
but by the end of the century
the mass production of
watches in the USA and the
improvements made to the
Swiss cottage industry of watch
manufacture all but wiped it
out. Not just a museum for the
study of Prescot's local history,
it is also a centre of national
importance for the study,
interpretation and display of
the watchmaking craft for
which the area was once
famous. The exhibits include a
reconstruction of a
watchmakers workshop and
watchmaking factory. Gift
Shop. Limited disabled access.

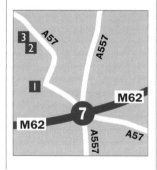

Nearest Eastbound A&E Hospital

Warrington Hospital

Lovely Lane, Warrington
WA5 1QG
Tel: (01925) 635911

Proceed to Junction 9 and
follow the A49 south, at the
roundabout junction of the
A49, A570 and the A50 turn
right along the A570 and
proceed through the town
centre towards Prescot. At the
junction with the B5210, the
first major roundabout, turn
right into Lovely Lane and the
hospital is on the right.
(Distance Approx 8.9 miles)

Nearest Westbound A&E Hospital

Whiston Hospital

Prescot, Merseyside L35 5DL
Tel: (0151) 426 1600

Follow the A57 north to
Prescot. (Signposted within
town. Distance Approx 3.1
miles)

FACILITIES

1   Stoops Filling Station (Shell)

Tel: (0151) 426 4199
0.2 miles north along the
A57, on the left.
Access, Visa, Delta,
Mastercard, Switch, Diners
Club, Amex, Overdrive, All Star,
Dial Card, BP Supercharge,
Shell Cards, Smartcard.

2   The Ship

Tel: (0151) 426 4165
0.4 miles north along the
A57, on the left.
(Henry's Table) Open all day.
Meals served; 12.00-22.00hrs
daily

3   Premier Lodge

Tel: (0151) 426 4165
0.4 miles north along the A57, on the left

PLACES OF INTEREST

The Rainhill Trials Exhibition

The Library, View Road, Rainhill L35 0LE Tel: (0151) 426 4269 website: www.angelfire.com/pq/rainhill/

Follow the A57 north into Rainhill and View Road is on the left. (1.2 Miles)

In 1829 the directors of the Liverpool & Manchester Railway held a competition at Rainhill to decide whether their railway would be powered by the preferred method of stationary steam winding engines and cables or by a steam locomotive capable of hauling a load 3 times its own weight for a total distance of 70 miles at 10 mph. Up to this point steam locomotives had been crude and unreliable but Stephenson's "Rocket" proved to be more than adequate for the task and, once and for all, eliminated all doubts that they could provide the motive power on railways. The Rainhill Trials Exhibition, located in a railway carriage adjacent to the library, contains many fascinating artefacts associated with this epoch making event that shaped transport across the world for the next 100 years.

JUNCTION 8

THERE IS NO JUNCTION 8

BETWEEN JUNCS 7 & 9

BURTONWOOD (EASTBOUND) (WELCOME BREAK)
Tel: (01925) 651656 Red Hen Restaurant & Shell Fuel

BURTONWOOD (WESTBOUND) (WELCOME BREAK)
Tel: (01925) 651656 Granary Restaurant, Welcome Lodge & Shell Fuel

FOOTWAY TUNNEL CONNECTION BETWEEN SITES.

JUNCTION 9

Nearest A&E Hospital
Warrington Hospital
Lovely Lane, Warrington WA5 1QG
Tel: (01925) 635911
Follow the A49 south and at the roundabout junction of the A49, A570 and the A50 turn right along the A570 and proceed through the town centre towards Prescot. At the junction with the B5210, the first major roundabout, turn right into Lovely Lane and the hospital is on the right. (Distance Approx 2.6 miles)

FACILITIES

1 Winwick Quay

Tel: (01925) 414417
0.1 miles south along the A49, on the right.
(Brewer's Fayre) Open all day. Meals served; Mon-Fri; 07.00-09.00hrs & 11.00-22.00hrs, Sat; 08.00-10.00hrs & 11.00-22.00hrs, Sun; 08.00-10.00hrs & 12.00-22.00hrs.

2 Travel Inn

Tel: (01925) 414417:
0.1 miles south along the A49, on the right

3 Winwick Filling Station (Texaco)

Tel: (01925) 638240
0.2 miles south along the A49, on the left.
Access, Visa, Mastercard, Switch, Amex, Electron, Solo, Overdrive, All Star, Dial Card, Fast Fuel, Texaco Cards.

4 KFC
Tel: (01925) 419786
0.9 miles south along the A49, on the right in Alban Retail Park.
Open; 11.00-23.00hrs daily

5 Pizza Hut
Tel: (01925) 574220
0.9 miles south along the A49, on the right in Alban Retail Park.
Open; 12.00-23.00hrs daily

6 BP Longford

Tel: (01925) 633983
1 mile south along the A49, on the right.
Access, Visa, Delta, Mastercard, Switch, Diners

Club, Amex, Overdrive, All Star, Dial Card, BP Cards.

7 Burger King

Tel: (01925) 573387
0.1 miles north along the A49, on the left.
Open; 08.00-21.00hrs daily.
(Drive-Thru open until 22.00hrs daily)

8 Premier Lodge

Tel: (01925) 631416
0.6 miles north along the A573, on the right

9 The Swan

Tel: (01925) 631416
0.6 miles north along the A573, on the right.
(Scottish & Newcastle) Open all day. Meals served; 12.00-22.00hrs daily

PLACES OF INTEREST

Gullivers World

Warrington, Cheshire WA5 5YZ

(Signposted from Junction 2.9 Miles)
For details please see Junction 22 (M6) information.

Sankey Valley Park

Bewsey Old Hall, Bewsey Farm Close, Old Hall, Warrington WA5 5PB Tel: (01925) 571836 website: www.warrington.gov.uk

Follow the A49 south and turn right along the A574 (Signposted Bewsey 2.7 Miles)
Centred around Sankey Canal, opened in 1757 and claimed to be the country's first true canal, Sankey Valley Park is part of the Mersey Forest. Within the park, which also contains Bewsey Old Hall, the family seat of the Botelers, Lords of Warrington, mosaics

of woodlands, grasslands, and ponds allow a variety of wildlife, insects and flowers to flourish. There are excellent walks, including the Sankey Canal Trail, and a childrens play area. Disabled access.

THIS JUNCTION IS A MOTORWAY INTERCHANGE ONLY WITH THE M6 AND THERE IS NO ACCESS TO ANY FACILITIES

Nearest Westbound A&E Hospital
Warrington Hospital
Lovely Lane, Warrington WA5 1QG
Tel: (01925) 635911
Proceed to Junction 9 and follow the A49 south, at the roundabout junction of the A49, A570 and the A50 turn right along the A570 and proceed through the town centre towards Prescot. At the junction with the B5210, the first major roundabout, turn right into Lovely Lane and the hospital is on the right.
(Distance Approx 4.3 miles)

Nearest Eastbound A&E Hospital
Hope Hospital
Stott Lane, Salford M6 8HB
Tel: (0161) 789 7373
Proceed to Junction 12 and follow the M602 east (Signposted within city. Distance Approx 11.1 miles)

THERE ARE NO FACILITIES WITHIN ONE MILE OF THIS JUNCTION

Nearest Westbound A&E Hospital
Warrington Hospital
Lovely Lane, Warrington WA5 1QG
Tel: (01925) 635911
Proceed to Junction 9 and follow the A49 south, at the roundabout junction of the A49, A570 and the A50 turn right along the A570 and proceed through the town centre towards Prescot. At the junction with the B5210, the first major roundabout, turn right into Lovely Lane and the hospital is on the right.
(Distance Approx 6.8 miles)

Nearest Eastbound A&E Hospital
Hope Hospital
Stott Lane, Salford M6 8HB
Tel: (0161) 789 7373
Proceed to Junction 12 and follow the M602 east (Signposted within city. Distance 9.2 miles)

PLACES OF INTEREST

Culcheth Linear Park

Wigshaw Lane, Culcheth, Warrington WA3 4AB
Tel: (01925) 765064. website: www.warrington.gov.uk

Follow the A574 south and then right towards Culcheth. (4 Miles)
Following part of the trackbed of the former Cheshire Lines Committee railway line between Wigan and Glazebrook, the Culcheth Linear Park offers a delightful and pleasant walk. Picnic Areas. Disabled access.

Birchwood Forest Park & Risley Moss

Ordnance Avenue, Birchwood,

Warrington WA3 6QX Birchwood Forest Park Tel: (01925) 824239,

Risley Moss Tel: (01925) 824339
website: www.warrington.gov.uk

Follow the A574 south. Turn left at the first roundabout along Moss Gate. (1 Mile)
Birchwood Forest Park is the name given to all the green areas throughout Birchwood. The town is made up of three villages; Gorse Covert, Oakwood and Locking Stumps and these and the surrounding countryside are linked by a comprehensive network of footpaths creating a 550 acre parkland. There are many pleasant walks which include beautiful parkland, secluded ponds, mosses and birch woodland, providing ideal habitats for wildlife. Playgrounds. Visitor Centre. Disabled access.

JUNCTION 12

THIS JUNCTION IS A MOTORWAY INTERCHANGE WITH THE M63 AND M602 ONLY AND THERE IS NO ACCESS TO ANY FACILITIES

Nearest A&E Hospital
Hope Hospital
Stott Lane, Salford M6 8HB
Tel: (0161) 789 7373
Follow the M602 east
(Signposted within city.
Distance 2.5 miles)

M62 BETWEEN JUNCS 13 & 18

BETWEEN JUNCTIONS 13 AND 18 THE M62 MOTORWAY HAS BEEN RECLASSIFIED AS THE M60

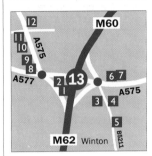

JUNCTION 13

Nearest A&E Hospital
Hope Hospital
Stott Lane, Salford M6 8HB
Tel: (0161) 789 7373
Proceed to Junction 12 and follow the M602 east (Signposted within city. Distance 3.5 miles)

FACILITIES

1   The John Gilbert
Tel: (0161) 703 7733
Adjacent to south side of west roundabout.
(Hardys & Hansons) Open all day. Meals served; 12.00-21.00hrs daily (NB. Carvery also available on Sun; 12.00-19.00hrs)

2   Novotel Manchester West Hotel
Tel: (0161) 799 3535
Adjacent to south side of west roundabout.
The Garden Brasserie; Open; 06.00-0.00hrs daily

3   The Bridgewater Hotel
Tel: (0161) 794 0589
0.3 miles south along the B5211, on the right.

(Scottish & Newcastle) Open all day. Meals served; Mon-Sat; 11.00-21.30hrs, Sun; 12.00-21.30hrs

4   The Barton Arms
Tel: (0161) 727 9318
0.5 miles south along the B5211, on the left.
(Six Continents) Open all day. Meals served; 12.00-20.00hrs daily.

5   Alder Service Station (Texaco)
Tel: (0161) 789 4665
0.8 miles south along the B5211, on the left.
Access, Visa, Delta, Mastercard, Switch, Diners Club, Amex, Electron, Solo, Overdrive, All Star, Dial Card, Texaco Cards. Open; 07.00-22.00hrs daily

6   Tung Fong Chinese Restaurant
Tel: (0161) 794 5331
0.2 miles east along the A572, on the left.
Open; Mon-Thurs; 17.30-23.15hrs, Fri & Sat; 17.30-23.45hrs, Sun; 17.30-22.45hrs

7   Café Bar Rioja Tapas Bar
Tel: (0161) 793 6003
0.2 miles east along the A572, on the left.
Open; Tues-Fri; 12.00-15.00hrs & 17.30-23.00hrs, Sat & Sun; 17.30-23.00hrs

8   Worsley Old Hall
Tel: (0161) 799 2960
0.3 miles north along the A575, on the left.
(Brewers Fayre) Open all day. Meals served; Mon-Sat; 11.30-22.00hrs, Sun; 12.00-22.00hrs

9 Marriott Worsley Park Hotel & Country Club

Tel: (0161) 975 2000
0.3 miles north along the A575, on the left.
Brindley's Restaurant; Breakfast; Mon-Thurs; 06.30-10.30hrs, Fri-Sun; 07.00-11.00hrs, Lunch; Mon-Fri; 12.00-14.00hrs, Sun; 13.00-14.30hrs, Dinner; 19.00-22.00hrs daily

10 The Cock

Tel: (0161) 790 2381
0.8 miles north along the A575, on the left.
(Henry's Table) Open all day. Meals served; 12.00-22.00hrs daily

11 Worsley Service Station (Esso)

Tel: (0161) 702 0370
0.9 miles north along the A575, on the left.
Access, Visa, Delta, Mastercard, Switch, Diners Club, Amex, Overdrive, All Star, Dial Card, Shell Gold, Esso Cards

12 The Willows

Tel: (0161) 790 4951
1 mile north along the A575, on the right

JUNCTION 14

THIS IS A RESTRICTED ACCESS JUNCTION AND INTERCHANGE WITH THE M61
- Vehicles can only exit from the southbound lanes and travel west along the A580
- Vehicles can only enter the motorway along the northbound lanes from the A580 east carriageway

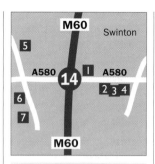

Nearest A&E Hospital

Hope Hospital
Stott Lane, Salford M6 8HB
Tel: (0161) 789 7373
Proceed to Junction 12 and follow the M602 east (Signposted within city. Distance 4.5 miles)

FACILITIES

1 XS Superbowl

Tel: (0161) 794 3374
0.2 miles east along the A580, on the left.
Within the building: Wimpy Restaurant; Open 10.00-0.00hrs daily & Bridgewater Bar; Open during licensing hours.

2 Deansbrook Service Station (Total)

Tel: (0161) 727 7072
0.9 miles east along the A580, on the right.
Access, Visa, Delta, Mastercard, Switch, Diners Club, Amex, Overdrive, All Star, Dial Card, BP Supercharge, Total/Fina/Elf Card.

3 The New Ellesmere

Tel: (0161) 728 2791
1 mile east along the A580, on the right.
(Scottish & Newcastle) Open all day. Meals served; 07.30-09.30 & 12.00-21.30hrs daily

4 Premier Lodge

Tel: (0161) 728 2791
1 mile east along the A580, on the right.

5 The Willows

Tel: (0161) 790 4951
1 mile north along the A575, on the right

6 Worsley Service Station (Esso)

Tel: (0161) 702 0370
0.9 miles south along the A575, on the right.
Access, Visa, Delta, Mastercard, Switch, Diners Club, Amex, Overdrive, All Star, Dial Card, Shell Gold, Esso Cards

7 The Cock

Tel: (0161) 790 2381
1 mile south along the A575, on the right.
(Henry's Table) Open all day. Meals served; 12.00-22.00hrs daily

JUNCTION 15

THIS JUNCTION IS A MOTORWAY INTERCHANGE ONLY WITH THE M61 AND THERE IS NO ACCESS TO ANY FACILITIES

M60
JUNCTION 16

THIS IS A RESTRICTED ACCESS JUNCTION
- Vehicles can only exit from the southbound lanes.
- Vehicles can only enter the motorway along the northbound lanes.

Nearest Westbound A&E Hospital

Hope Hospital

Stott Lane, Salford M6 8HB
Tel: (0161) 789 7373
Proceed to Junction 12 and follow the M602 east (Signposted within city. Distance 6.3 miles)

Nearest Eastbound A&E Hospital

North Manchester General Hospital

Delauneys Road, Crumpsall, Manchester M8 5RB
Tel: (0161) 795 4567
Proceed to Junction 17, follow the A56 south and turn left along the A576 and right along the A6010 (Signposted along this route. Distance Approx 7.5 miles)

FACILITIES

1   The Robin Hood

Tel: (0161) 794 2906
Adjacent to south side of motorway junction.
(Spirit Retail) Open all day. Meals served; Mon-Sat; 11.00-21.30hrs, Sun; 12.00-21.30hrs.

2   Golden Lion

Tel: (0161) 794 3016
0.1 miles south along the A666, on the right.
(Brewers Fayre) Open all day. Meals served; Mon-Sat; 11.30-22.00hrs, Sun; 12.00-22.00hrs

3   Oddfellows Arms

Tel: (0161) 794 5691
0.4 miles south along the A666, on the right.
(Unique Pub Company) Open all day Sat & Sun. Meals served; Mon-Fri 12.00-14.00hrs. (NB Accommodation is Bed & Evening Meal)

4   Pendle Hill Service Station (Esso)

Tel: (0161) 281 7989
0.7 miles south along the A666, on the left.
Access, Visa, Delta, Mastercard, Switch, Diners Club, Amex, Electron, Solo, Overdrive, All Star, Dial Card, Shell Gold, Esso Cards

5   Dilash Balti House

Tel: (0161) 728 5333
0.8 miles south along the A666, on the left.
Open; Sun-Thurs; 17.00-0.00hrs, Fri/Sat & Sat/Sun; 17.00-01.00hrs

6   McDonald's

Tel: (0161) 794 7415
1 mile south along the A666, on the left.
Open; 07.30-23.00hrs daily

7   Clifton Park Hotel

Tel: (0161) 794 3761
0.4 miles north along the A666, on the right.
Restaurant Open; Mon-Sat; 12.00-14.00hrs & 17.30-20.30hrs, Sun; 12.00-17.00hrs

8   Save Service Station

Tel: (0161) 794 4063
0.8 miles north along the A666, on the left.
Access, Visa, Overdrive, All Star, Switch, Dial Card, Mastercard, Delta, Save Card. Open: 07.00-23.00hrs daily.

9   Unity Brook

Tel: (01204) 797831
1 mile north along the A666, on the left.
(Six Continents) Open all day. Meals served; Mon-Sat; 12.00-19.45hrs, Sun; 12.00-18.45hrs

PLACES OF INTEREST

Clifton Country Park

Clifton House Road, Swinton M27 6NG
Tel: (0161) 793 4219
website: www.salford.org.uk
Follow the A666 north (0.7 Miles)

Set within 80 acres of countryside, this beautiful park features a wide variety of different wildlife habitats; woodland, open grassland, wetland areas, a pond and a lake. Gift Shop.

JUNCTION 17

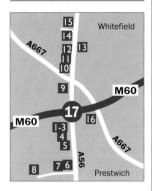

Nearest A&E Hospital

North Manchester General Hospital

Delauneys Road, Crumpsall, Manchester M8 5RB
Tel: (0161) 795 4567
Follow the A56 south and turn left along the A576 and right along the A6010 (Signposted along this route. Distance Approx 5.3 miles)

FACILITIES

1   Paddock Filling Station (BP)

Tel: (0161) 772 9969
0.1 miles south along the A56, on the right.
Access, Visa, Delta, Mastercard, Switch, Diners Club, Amex, Overdrive, All Star, Dial Card, Shell Agency, BP Cards.

2   Travel Inn

Tel: (0161) 798 0827
0.1 miles south along the A56, on the right

3   TGI Fridays

Tel: (0161) 798 7125
0.1 miles south along the A56, on the right.
Open; Mon-Fri; 11.00-23.00hrs, Sat; 11.30-23.30hrs, Sun; 11.30-22.00hrs

4   Tesco Filling Station

Tel: (0161) 910 9400
0.2 miles south along the A56, on the right.
Access, Visa, Delta, Mastercard, Amex, Solo, Overdrive, All Star, Dial Card, Tesco Fuelcard. Disabled Toilets and Cash machines available in adjacent store (Open 24 hours)

5   Grapes of Prestwich

Tel: (0161) 773 2570
0.4 miles south along the A56, on the right.
(Inn Partnership) Open all day. Meals served; 12.00-14.30hrs daily

6   Royal Bengal Tandoori Restaurant

Tel: (0161) 773 6311
0.7 miles south along the A56, on the right.
Open; 18.00-01.00hrs daily

7   The Cottage Café

Tel: (0161) 773 6022
0.7 miles south along the A56, on the right, in Church Lane.
Open; Mon-Fri; 08.00-14.00hrs, Sat; 09.00-12.00hrs

8   The Church

Tel: (0161) 798 6727
0.7 miles south along the

A56, on the right in Church Lane.
(John Smith's) Open all day. Meals served; Mon & Tues; 12.00-14.30hrs, Wed-Fri; 12.00-14.30hrs & 17.00-22.00hrs, Sat & Sun; 12.00-16.00hrs & 17.00-22.00hrs

9   McDonald's

Tel: (0161) 767 9731
0.3 miles north along the A56, on the left.
Open; Mon-Wed; 08.000-2.00hrs [Drive-Thru until 23.00hrs], Thurs-Sun; 08.00-22.00hrs [Drive-Thru until 0.00hrs]

10 Khan Saab

Tel: (0161) 766 2148
0.4 miles north along the A56, on the left.
Open; Sun-Thurs; 18.00-23.30hrs, Fri & Sat; 18.00-0.00hrs

11 The Mogul Restaurant

Tel: (0161) 796 0403
0.5 miles north along the A56, on the left.
Open; Sun-Fri; 18.00-23.30hrs, Sat; 18.00-0.00hrs

12 The Masons

Tel: (0161) 766 2713
0.7 miles north along the A56, on the left.
(Whitbread) Open all day. Meals served; 12.00-15.30hrs daily

13 Roma Coffee Lounge & Restaurant

Tel: (0161) 766 2941
0.8 miles north along the A56, on the right.
Open; Mon-Fri; 09.15-18.45hrs, Sat; 09.00-16.50hrs

14 Bulls Head

Tel: (0161) 766 5968
0.9 miles north along the A56, on the left.
(Laurel Pub Company) Open all day Sat & Sun. Meals served; Mon-Fri; 11.30-14.00hrs

15 Total Whitefield

Tel: (0161) 796 3932
1 mile north along the A56, on the left.
Access, Visa, Delta, Mastercard, Switch, Diners Club, Amex, Electron, Solo, Overdrive, All Star, Dial Card, BP Supercharge, Total/Fina/Elf Cards. Open; 06.00-23.00hrs daily

16 Kirkhams Service Station (Esso)

Tel: (0161) 773 2486
0.7 miles east along the A667, on the right.
Access, Visa, Delta, Mastercard, Switch, Diners Club, Amex, Overdrive, All Star, Dial Card, Shell Gold, Esso Cards

PLACES OF INTEREST

Heaton Hall

Heaton Park, Prestwich, Manchester M25 5SW
Tel: (0161) 773 1231

Follow the A56 south and turn left along Scholes Lane (A6044) (Signposted 2 miles)
Built by James Wyatt in 1722 and set in a large parkland, it was a former residence of the Earls of Wilton. The Hall contains one of the few remaining Etruscan rooms, with painted walls and ceiling by Biagio Rebecca. Other contents include an organ built by Samuel Green in 1790, 17thC Dutch paintings, furniture and paintings of the 18thC and the Assheton Bennett Collection of English silver. Café. Disabled access.

East Lancs Railway

Bolton Street Station, Bury BL9 0EY Tel: (0161) 764 7790 website; www.east-lancs-rly.co.uk

Follow the A56 north to Bury (4.1 miles)
An 8 miles long steam railway linking Bury and Rawtenstall via the pretty Irwell Valley. Opens at weekends and Bank Holidays. Café. Gift Shop. Disabled access.

M62 JUNCTION 18

THIS JUNCTION IS A MOTORWAY INTERCHANGE ONLY WITH THE M66 NORTH AND M60 SOUTH, AND THERE IS NO ACCESS TO ANY FACILITIES

Nearest A&E Hospital
North Manchester General Hospital
Delauneys Road, Crumpsall, Manchester M8 5RB
Tel: (0161) 795 4567
Follow the M60 south to Junction 19, take the A576 exit west and turn left along Blackley New Road (Signposted along this route. Distance Approx 4.1 miles)

M62 BETWEEN JUNCS 18 & 19

BIRCH SERVICES (WESTBOUND) (MOTO)
Tel: (0161) 643 0911 Upper Crust Restaurant, Burger King, Little Chef, Travelodge & Esso Fuel

BIRCH SERVICES (EASTBOUND) (MOTO)
Tel: (0161) 643 0911 Fresh Express Self Service Restaurant, Burger King, Travelodge & Esso Fuel

FOOTBRIDGE CONNECTION BETWEEN SITES

M62 JUNCTION 19

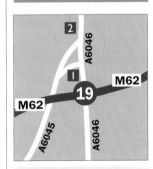

Nearest Westbound A&E Hospital
Royal Oldham Hospital
Rochdale Road, Oldham OL1 2JH
Tel: (0161) 624 0420
Proceed to Junction 20, follow the A627 (M) south and turn left along the A6048. (Distance Approx 5.8 Miles)

Nearest Eastbound A&E Hospital
North Manchester General Hospital

Delauneys Road, Crumpsall, Manchester M8 5RB
Tel: (0161) 795 4567

Proceed to Junction 18, follow the M60 south to Junction 19, take the A576 exit west and turn left along Blackley New Road (Signposted along this route. Distance Approx 6.9 miles)

FACILITIES

1   Hopwood Service Station (Texaco)

Tel: (01706) 692100

0.4 miles north along the A6046, on the left.

Access, Visa, Delta, Mastercard, Switch, Diners Club, Amex, Electron, Solo, Overdrive, All Star, Dial Card, Fast Fuel, Texaco Cards.

2   Starkey Arms

Tel: (01706) 622301

0.9 miles north along the A6046, on the left.

(Joseph Holt) Open all day. Meals served 12.00-14.30hrs daily

PLACES OF INTEREST

The Hopwood Trail

Rochdale Road, Middleton M24 2GL Tel: (01706) 356592 website: www.rochdale.gov.uk

Follow the A6046 south into Middleton and turn left along the A664 (2.5 Miles)

Following a circular route of nearly 2 miles through the former Hopwood Estate, the trail consists of 12 easily identified points and passes through oak and birch woodlands, ancient clay pits and coal mining areas.

M62
JUNCTION 20

THIS JUNCTION IS A MOTORWAY INTERCHANGE ONLY WITH THE A627 (M) AND THERE IS NO ACCESS TO ANY FACILITIES

Nearest A&E Hospital
Royal Oldham Hospital
Rochdale Road, Oldham OL1 2JH
Tel: (0161) 624 0420

Follow the A627 (M) south and turn left along the A6048. (Distance Approx 3.6 Miles)

PLACES OF INTEREST

Rochdale

Rochdale Tourist Information Cente, The Clock Tower, Rochdale OL16 1AB Tel: (01706) 356592 website: www.rochdale.gov.uk

Follow the A627 (M) north (Signposted 2.4 Miles)

Lying in a shallow valley formed by the little River Roch, the town is surrounded to the north and east by the Pennines and, with its origins in mediaeval times, it expanded with the booming cotton industry. Rochdale was the birthplace of the Co-operative Movement and the first Co-op shop, opened on December 21st, 1844 and sited in Toad Lane, still exists as the Rochdale Pioneers Museum (
Tel: 01706-524920). The town has some famous sons and daughters and these include John Bright, the renowned 19thC political thinker and Gracie Fields, the celebrated singer.

M62
JUNCTION 21

Nearest A&E Hospital
Rochdale Infirmary
Whitehall Street, Rochdale OL12 0NB
Tel: (01706) 377777

Follow the A640 north and turn right along the A671. (Signposted within town. Distance Approx 3.3 Miles)

FACILITIES

1   The Ladybarn

Tel: (01706) 355402

0.3 miles north along the A640, on the left, in Harbour Lane.

(Hungry Horse) Open all day. Meals served 12.00-21.30hrs daily

2   Tim Bobbin

Tel: (01706) 658992

0.6 miles east along the B6225, on the left, in Milnrow.

(Unique Pub Co) Open all day. Meals served Mon-Sat; 12.00-19.00hrs, Sun; 12.00-15.00hrs

3   Milnrow Balti Restaurant

Tel: (01706) 353651

0.7 miles east, on the right in Milnrow.

Open; Mon-Sat; 17.00-0.00hrs, Sun; 15.00-23.00hrs

4 BP Milnrow

Tel: (01706) 641132

1 mile east, on the right in Milnrow.

Access, Visa, Delta, Mastercard, Switch, Diners Club, Amex, Overdrive, All Star, BP Cards

5 The John Milne

Tel: (01706) 299999

0.4 miles south along the (B6225), on the left in Milnrow.

(Brewers Fayre) Open all day. Meals served; Mon-Fri; 07.00-09.00hrs & 11.30-22.00hrs, Sat; 08.00-10.00hrs & 11.30-22.00hrs, Sun; 08.00-10.00hrs & 12.00-22.00hrs.

6 Travel Inn

Tel: (01706) 299999

0.4 miles south along the (B6225), on the left in Milnrow

7 Waggon & Horses

Tel: (01706) 844248

0.5 miles south along the A640, on the left

(JW Lees) Open all day Fri-Sun.

PLACES OF INTEREST

Rochdale

Follow the A640 north (Signposted 3.1 Miles)

For details please see Junction 20 information

M62 JUNCTION 22

THERE ARE NO FACILITIES WITHIN ONE MILE OF THIS JUNCTION

Nearest Westbound A&E Hospital

Rochdale Infirmary

Whitehall Street, Rochdale OL12 0NB

Tel: (01706) 377777

Proceed to Junction 21, follow the A640 north and turn right along the A671. (Signposted within town. Distance Approx 7.8 Miles)

Nearest Eastbound A&E Hospital

Huddersfield Royal Infirmary

Acre Street, Lindley, Huddersfield HD3 3EA

Tel: (01484) 342000

Proceed to Junction 23 and follow the A640 east (Signposted. Distance Approx 9 miles)

M62 JUNCTION 23

THIS IS A RESTRICTED ACCESS JUNCTION

- Vehicles can only exit from the eastbound lanes.
- Vehicles can only enter the motorway along the westbound lanes.

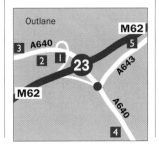

Nearest Westbound A&E Hospital

Rochdale Infirmary

Whitehall Street, Rochdale OL12 0NB

Tel: (01706) 377777

Proceed to Junction 21, follow the A640 north and turn right along the A671.(Signposted within town. Distance Approx 14.9 Miles)

Nearest Eastbound A&E Hospital

Huddersfield Royal Infirmary

Acre Street, Lindley, Huddersfield HD3 3EA

Tel: (01484) 342000

Follow the A640 east (Signposted. Distance Approx 1.9 miles)

FACILITIES

1 The Swan Inn

Tel: (01422) 379007

0.3 miles west along the A640, on the left, in Outlane

(Enterprise Inns) Open all day. Meals served; Tues-Sat; 12.00-15.00hrs & 17.00-21.00hrs, Sun; 12.00-18.00hrs

2 The Old Golf House Hotel

Tel: (01422) 379311

0.5 miles west along the A640, on the left, in Outlane.

The Grangemoor Restaurant; Open; 12.00-14.00hrs & 19.00-21.30hrs daily

3 The Highlander

Tel: (01422) 370711

1 mile west along the A640, on the right, in Outlane.

(Free House) Meals served; Tues-Fri; 18.00-21.00hrs, Sat & Sun; 12.00-14.00hrs & 18.00-21.00hrs

4 Salendine Service Station (Total)

Tel: (01484) 460267
0.9 miles south along the A640, on the right.
Access, Visa, Delta, Mastercard, Switch, Diners Club, Amex, Electron, Solo, Overdrive, All Star, Dial Card. Total/Fina/Elf Cards. Open; 06.00-23.00hrs daily

5 The Wappy Spring Inn

Tel: (01422) 372324
0.8 miles east along the A643, on the left.
(Pubmaster) Meals served; Tues-Fri; 17.30-21.00hrs, Sat; 18.30-21.30hrs, Sun; 16.30-20.00hrs

PLACES OF INTEREST

Castle Hill & Jubilee Tower

Off Lumb Lane, Almondbury, Huddersfield HD4 6SZ
Tel: (01484) 223830

Follow the A640 east, turn right along the A62 and right along the A616 (6 Miles)
Considered to be one of the most important archaeological sites in Yorkshire, the hill, a high moorland ridge overlooking the Colne and Holme Valleys, has been occupied as a place of defence since c20,000BC, by what are believed to be Neolithic herdsmen from mainland Europe, and the magnificent ramparts of an Iron Age Fort, built in 600BC and later destroyed by fire, can still be seen here. In 1147 the Normans restored the earthworks, building a motte and bailey castle and the hill was used as a beacon during

the times of the Armada and the Napoleonic Wars. In 1897 the Jubilee Tower was built to commemorate the 60th anniversary of Queen Victoria's reign and, at a height of 1,000ft above sea level, the top of the tower affords splendid panoramic views. An exhibition tracing the hill's history is contained within the tower.

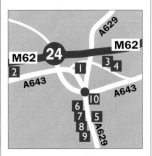

Nearest A&E Hospital
Huddersfield Royal Infirmary
Acre Street, Lindley, Huddersfield HD3 3EA
Tel: (01484) 342000
Follow the A629 south (Signposted within town. Distance Approx 1.7 miles)

FACILITIES

1 Cedar Court Hotel

Tel: (01422) 375431
0.1 miles west along the A643, on the right.
Restaurant Open; Breakfast; Mon-Fri; 07.00-10.00hrs, Sat & Sun; 07.30-10.0hrs, Lunch; Sun-Fri; 12.30-14.00hrs, Dinner; 19.00-22.00hrs daily.

2 The Wappy Spring Inn

Tel: (01422) 372324
1 mile west along the A643, on the right.
(Pubmaster) Meals served; Tues-Fri; 17.30-21.00hrs, Sat; 18.30-21.30hrs, Sun; 16.30-20.00hrs

3 Nags Head Country Carvery

Tel: (01422) 373758
1 mile east along the A643, in New Hay Road, Ainley Top.
(Scottish & Newcastle) Restaurant Open; Mon-Fri; 07.00-09.30hrs, 12.00-14.00hrs & 18.00-21.30hrs, Sat; 08.00-10.00hrs, 12.00-14.00hrs & 18.00-21.30hrs, Sun; 08.00-10.00hrs & 12.00-21.00hrs. Bar meals available, Mon-Sat; 12.00-21.00hrs, Sun; 12.00-19.300hrs.

4 Premier Lodge

Tel: (01422) 373758
1 mile east along the A643, in New Hay Road, Ainley Top.

5 Birchencliffe BP Petrol Station

Tel: (01484) 451362
0.3 miles south along the A629, on the left.
Access, Visa, Delta, Mastercard, Switch, Diners Club, Amex, Overdrive, All Star, Dial Card, Shell Gold, BP Cards.

6 Briar Court Hotel

Tel: (01484) 519902
0.3 miles south along the A629, on the right

7 Da Sandro Pizzeria Restaurant

Tel: (01484) 519902
0.3 miles south along the

A629, on the right.
Open; Mon; 12.00-14.00hrs &
18.00-22.30hrs, Tues-Fri;
12.00-14.00hrs & 18.00-
23.00hrs, Sat; 12.00-14.00hrs
& 18.00-23.30hrs, Sun; 12.30-
21.45hrs.

8   Monza BP Petrol Station

Tel: (01484) 435152
0.6 miles south along the
A629, on the right.
Access, Visa, Delta,
Mastercard, Switch, Diners
Club, Amex, Overdrive, All Star,
Dial Card, Shell Agency, BP
Cards.

9   The Cavalry Arms

Tel: (01484) 530812
0.7 miles south along the
A629, on the right.
(Pubmaster) Meals served;
Mon-Sat; 12.00-14.00hrs &
17.00-20.00hrs, Sun; 12.00-
20.00hrs.

10 The Ainley Top

Tel: (01422) 374360
Adjacent to east side of
roundabout
(Brewster's) Open all day.
Meals served; Mon-Sat; 11.30-
22.00hrs, Sun; 12.00-
22.00hrs

PLACES OF INTEREST

Halifax

Halifax Tourist Information Centre,
Piece Hall, Halifax HX1 1RE
Tel: (01422) 368725
website: www.calderdale.gov.uk

**Follow the A629 north
(Signposted 5.6 Miles)**
In the valley of the River
Hebble and built upon a rise
that ascends sharply towards a

range of hills, Halifax has one
of Yorkshire's most impressive
pieces of municipal
architecture, the large and
beautiful Piece Hall. Built in
1779 the classically styled
edifice consists of colonnades
and balconies surrounding a
large quadrangle and originally
housed 315 merchant's rooms
for the selling of cloth or
pieces. A replica of a guillotine
can be found in Gibbet Street,
an old thoroughfare where
executions took place, and the
Church of St John the Baptist
which dates from the 12th and
13thC's with most of the
present building of 15thC
origin, is the largest Parish
Church in England.

Also in the town centre ...

Eureka!

Discovery Road, Halifax HX1 2NE
Tel: (01422) 330069
website: www.eureka.org.uk

Britain's first interactive
museum designed especially
for children aged between 3
and 12 years. Over 400
exhibits of hands-on displays
that allow visitors to touch,
listen and smell as well as look
are available. Gift Shop. Café.
Disabled access.

Bankfield Museum

Akroyd Park, Boothtown Road,
Halifax HX3 6HG
Tel: (01422) 354823
website: www.calderdale.gov.uk

**Follow the A629 north into
Halifax and take the A647
north (5.9 Miles)**
Set in a Victorian millowner's
house, Bankfield is a centre for
textiles and contemporary
craft. The collection includes
textiles and weird and
wonderful objects and displays
include the Toy Gallery and the
Duke of Wellington's
Regimental Museum. Disabled
access

Shibden Hall & Park

Listers Road, Halifax HX3 6AG
Tel: (01422) 352246 website:
www.calderdale.gov.uk

**Follow the A629 north into
Halifax and take the A58 east
(Signposted along A58, 6.2
Miles)**
The Old Hall lies in a valley on
the outskirts of Halifax and is
situated in 90 acres of
parkland. The distinctive
timber framed house dates
from 1420 and is furnished to
reflect the various periods of
its history. The 17thC barn,
behind the hall, houses a fine
collection of horse drawn
vehicles and the original
buildings have been
transformed into a 19thC
village centre with a pub,
estate worker's cottage and
saddler's, blacksmith's,
wheelwright's and potter's
workshops. Other attractions
include children's rides, a
miniature railway, pitch and
putt and a boating lake. Gift
Shop. Café.

Castle Hill & Jubilee Tower

Off Lumb Lane, Almondbury
Huddersfield HD4 6SZ

**Follow the A640 east, turn
right along the A62 and right
along the A616 (6 Miles)**
For details please see Junction
23 information.

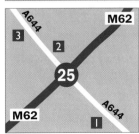

Nearest Westbound A&E Hospital
Huddersfield Royal Infirmary
Acre Street, Lindley,
Huddersfield HD3 3EA
Tel: (01484) 342000
Proceed to Junction 24 and
follow the A629 south
(Signposted within town.
Distance Approx 5.5 miles)

Nearest Eastbound A&E Hospital
Bradford Royal Infirmary
Duckworth Lane, Bradford
BD9 6RJ
Tel: (01274) 542200
Proceed to Junction 26, follow
the M606 north, continue
along the A6177 and turn right
along the A641 (Signposted
along route. Distance Approx
10 Miles)

FACILITIES

1   The Old Corn Mill

Tel: (01484) 400069
0.5 miles east along the
A644, on the right.
(Independent) Open all day.
Meals served; 12.00-18.00hrs
daily

2   Holiday Inn Leeds/ Brighouse

Tel: 0870 400 9013
0.2 miles west along the
A644, on the right.
The Junction Restaurant Open;
Mon-Fri; 06.30-09.30hrs,
12.00-14.30hrs & 18.30-
22.30hrs Sat; 07.00-11.00hrs
& 18.30-22.30hrs, Sun; 07.00-
11.00hrs, 12.00-15.30hrs &
18.30-22.30hrs.

3   Crown Service Station (Shell)

Tel: (01484) 720371
0.8 miles west along the

A644, on the left.
Access, Visa, Delta,
Mastercard, Switch, Diners
Club, Amex, Overdrive, All Star,
Dial Card, Keyfuels, Diesel
Direct, Shell Cards. Open; Mon-
Fri; 06.30-21.30hrs, Sat & Sun;
07.00-21.00hrs.

M62
BETWEEN JUNCS 25 & 26

**HARTSHEAD MOOR
SERVICES (EASTBOUND)
(WELCOME BREAK)**
Tel: (01274) 876584 Days Inn,
Burger King, The Granary
Restaurant & Shell Fuel

**HARTSHEAD MOOR
SERVICES (WESTBOUND)
(WELCOME BREAK)**
Tel: (01274) 876584 KFC, The
Granary Restaurant & Shell Fuel

**FOOTBRIDGE CONNECTION
BETWEEN SITES**

M62
JUNCTION 26

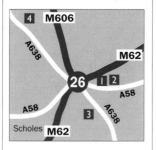

Nearest A&E Hospital
Bradford Royal Infirmary
Duckworth Lane, Bradford
BD9 6RJ
Tel: (01274) 542200

Follow the M606 north,
continue along the A6177 and
turn right along the A641.
(Signposted along route.
Distance Approx 6.9 Miles)

FACILITIES

1   The Hunsworth

Tel: (01274) 862828
0.2 miles east along the A58,
on the left.
(Brewers Fayre) Open all day.
Meals served; Mon-Sat; 11.00-
23.00hrs, Sun; 12.00-
22.30hrs.

2   Travel Inn

Tel: (01274) 862828
0.2 miles east along the A58,
on the left

3   The Horncastle

Tel: (01274) 875444
0.5 miles south along the
A638, on the right.
(Free House) Open all day.
Meals served; Mon-Fri; 07.30-
19.00hrs, Sat & Sun; 07.30-
16.00hrs.

4   Richardsons Arms

Tel: (01274) 675722
0.7 miles north along
Oakenshaw Road, in
Oakenshaw, on the right.
(Laurel Pub Company) Open all
day. Meals served; Tues-Sun;
12.00-15.00hrs & 17.00-
20.00hrs

PLACES OF INTEREST

Bradford

Bradford Tourist Information
Centre, Central Library, Princes
Way, Bradford BD1 1NN

Tel: (01274) 753678 website: www.visitbradford.com

Follow the M606 north (Signposted 4.6 Miles)

On a tributary of the River Aire, Bradford was established prior to 1066 but it was during the 18thC that it developed into a major centre of trade in worsted and wool, with the first mill being erected in 1798. It reached its pinnacle of wealth in the mid-19thC and many fine buildings constructed during this period can be seen, especially in Little Germany. Of particular note is the Town Hall of 1873, with an exterior ornamented with statues of English monarchs.

Also in the city centre …

The National Museum of Photography, Film & Television

Pictureville, Bradford BD1 1NQ
Tel: (01274) 202030
website: www.nmpft.org.uk

Recently extended, the six floors include the Kodak and TV Heaven galleries, displays on animation and film-making, advertising and, in the Magic Factory, a hands-on exhibition. There is also an IMAX cinema, shop and full catering facilities.

Bradford Industrial & Horses at Work Museum

Moorside Mills, Moorside Road, Eccleshill, Bradford BD2 3HP
Tel: (01274) 435900
website: www.visitbradford.com

Follow the M606 north and turn right along the A6177 (Signposted along A6177, 6.3 Miles)

An original worsted spinning mill complex built in 1875 and now in use as a working museum recreating life in Bradford at the turn of the 19thC. The displays include live steam workings every Wednesday, the mill stables, complete with Shire horses, mill owner's house, transport gallery and back to back cottages with working demonstrations of horse drawn buses and trams. Café. Shop. Disabled access.

Nearest Westbound A&E Hospital

Bradford Royal Infirmary
Duckworth Lane, Bradford
BD9 6RJ
Tel: (01274) 542200
Proceed to Junction 26, follow the M606 north, continue along the A6177 and turn right along the A641 (Signposted along route. Distance Approx 11.2 Miles)

Nearest Eastbound A&E Hospital

Leeds General Infirmary
Great George Street, Leeds
LS1 3EX
Tel: (0113) 243 2799
Follow the M621 north, leave at Junction 2, take the A643 north and continue along the A58. (Signposted. Distance Approx 5.7 Miles)

FACILITIES

1   Bella Pasta

Tel: (01924) 422374
0.3 miles east along the A62, in Centre 27, on the left.
Open; Sun-Thurs; 12.00-23.00hrs, Fri & Sat; 12.00-23.30hrs

2   Frankie & Benny's

Tel: (01924) 423747
0.3 miles east along the A62, in Centre 27, on the left.
Open; Mon-Sat; 12.00-23.00hrs, Sun; 12.00-22.30hrs.

3   Chiquito's

Tel: (01924) 359292
0.3 miles east along the A62, in Centre 27, on the left.
Buffet Meals served; 12.00-18.00hrs daily, A la carte Menu available; 12.00-23.00hrs daily.

4   KFC

Tel: (01924) 422634
0.3 miles east along the A62, in Centre 27, on the left.
Open; 11.00-0.00hrs daily.

5   Pizza Hut

Tel: (01924) 420460
0.3 miles east along the A62, in Centre 27, on the left.
Open; Sun-Fri; 11.30-23.00hrs, Sat; 11.30-0.00hrs.

6   McDonald's

Tel: (01924) 456833
0.3 miles east along the A62, in Centre 27, on the left.
Open; Sun-Thurs; 07.30-23.00hrs, Fri & Sat; 07.30-0.00hrs

7   Exchange Bar

Tel: (01924) 422120
0.3 miles east along the A62, in Centre 27, on the left.
Meals served; Mon-Sat; 12.00-23.00hrs, Sun; 12.00-22.30hrs

8 TGI Friday's

Tel: (01924) 475000

0.3 miles east along the A62, in The West Yorkshire Retail Park, on the right.
Open; Mon-Sat; 12.00-22.30hrs, Sun; 12.00-22.00hrs

9 Murco Service Station

Tel: (01924) 422077

0.3 miles east along the A62, in The West Yorkshire Retail Park, on the right.
Access, Visa, Overdrive, All Star, Switch, Dial Card, Mastercard, Amex, AA Paytrak, Diners Club, Delta, Murco Cards. Open; Mon-Fri; 06.00-23.00hrs, Sat; 07.00-23.00hrs, Sun; 08.00-22.00hrs.

10 Harry Ramsden's

Tel: (01924) 440621

0.6 miles east along the A62, on the right.
Open; 07.00-22.00hrs daily

11 The Pheasant

Tel: (01924) 473022

0.8 miles east along the A62, on the right.
(Laurel Pub Company) Open all day. Meals served; 12.00-21.00hrs daily

12 The Old Brickworks

Tel: (0113) 287 9132

0.6 miles west along the Wakefield Road, in Drighlington, on the left.
(Whitbread) Meals served; 12.00-22.00hrs daily.

13 Travel Inn

Tel: (0113) 287 9132

0.6 miles west along the Wakefield Road, in Drighlington, on the left.

14 The New Inn

Tel: (0113) 285 2447

1 mile west along the Wakefield Road, in Drighlington, on the left.
(Enterprise Inns) Meals served; Mon-Sat; 12.00-14.00hrs & 18.00-21.00hrs, Sun Carvery; 12.00-16.00hrs

15 Hadleys Hotel & Bistro

Tel: (0113) 252 1828

0.6 miles north along the A62, in Gildersome, on the left.
Meals served in Bistro; Thurs; 18.00-21.30hrs, Fri & Sat; 19.00-21.30hrs, Sun; 12.30-15.00hrs. (Bar Meals served; Mon-Wed; 18.00-20.00hrs)

16 Gildersome Service Station (Total)

Tel: (0113) 238 3343

0.6 miles north along the A62, in Gildersome, on the left.
Access, Visa, Delta, Mastercard, Switch, Diners Club, Amex, Electron, Solo, Overdrive, All Star, Dial Card, Total/Fina/Elf Cards.

17 The Mill House Bar & Family Restaurant

Tel: (0113) 238 3810

0.7 miles north along the A62, in Gildersome, on the right.
(Mill House Inns) Meals served; Mon-Sat; 12.00-21.00hrs, Sun; 12.00-20.00hrs

18 Toby Carvery

Tel: (0113) 253 3115

0.7 miles east along the A650, on the left.
(Six Continents) Open all day Meals served; Mon-Fri; 07.00-09.30hrs & 12.00-22.00hrs, Sat & Sun; 08.00-10.00hrs & 12.00-22.00hrs

19 Innkeeper's Lodge

Tel: (0113) 253 3115

0.7 miles east along the A650, on the left.

20 Victoria Filling Station (Shell)

Tel: (0113) 252 7538

0.9 miles east along the A650, on the left.
LPG. Access, Visa, Delta, Mastercard, Switch, Diners Club, Amex, Overdrive, All Star, Dial Card Routex, Keyfuels, Securicor Fuelserv, BP Agency, Shell Cards.

PLACES OF INTEREST

Leeds

Leeds Tourist Information Centre, The Arcade, Leeds City Station, Leeds LS1 1PL
Tel: (0113) 242 5242
website: www.leeds.gov.uk

Follow the M621 north (Signposted 5 Miles)

On the River Aire, there were primitive lake dwellings here and the site was in use by Norman times. In the reign of Edward III Flemish emigrants arrived here and brought with them their trade of cloth making, establishing it as a major industry within the area. The city developed rapidly in the early 19thC as the inland port on the Leeds to Liverpool and Aire & Calder Navigation canals, forming a central link between Liverpool and Hull, from where goods were exported world wide. The Canal Basin, an integral part of this system which provided extensive wharves, warehouses, boat building yards and wet and dry docks, fell into disuse as other modes of transport took over but it has, recently, been sympathetically restored and designated as a Conservation Area. The city centre contains a number of buildings from varying periods throughout its history but most of the outstanding edifices are of the classical baroque style favoured in the Victorian era.

Within the city centre ...

Royal Armouries

Armouries Drive, Leeds LS10 1LT
Tel: (0113) 220 1999
website; www.armouries.org.uk

3,000 years of history is displayed within five galleries themed on War, Tournament, The Orient, Self-Defence and Hunting. Over 8,000 exhibits are on display including Henry VIII's tournament armour and 16thC Indian elephant armour. There are displays, dramatic interpretations, live action events, interactive technology and a continuous daily showing of 42 specially commissioned films. Shops. Restaurants. Bars. Disabled access.

Thackray's Medical Museum

Beckett Street, Leeds LS9 7LN
24hr Information Line
Tel: (0113) 245 7084
Tel: (0113) 244 4343 website: www.thackraymuseum.org

Follow the M621 and A653 into Leeds and take the A58 east (Signposted along A58, 6.7 Miles)

Housed in the old Leeds Union Workhouse and utilizing state of the art interactive exhibits, the museum traces the history of medicine and its impact on every day life. Displays include Victorian slum life, surgical operations and a fascinating collection of objects and gadgets. Gift Shop. Café. Disabled access.

M62
JUNCTION 28

Nearest A&E Hospital
Leeds General Infirmary

Great George Street, Leeds LS1 3EX Tel: (0113) 243 2799
Follow the A653 north, bear left along the A6110, continue along the A643 north and the A58. (Signposted. Distance Approx 5.5 Miles)

FACILITIES

1 The White Bear

Tel: (0113) 253 2768
Adjacent to south side of the roundabout.
(Beefeater) Open all day. Meals served; Mon-Fri; 12.00-14.00hrs & 17.00-22.00hrs, Sat: 12.00-22.00hrs, Sun; 12.00-21.00hrs.

2 Tingley Bar Fish Restaurant

Tel: (0113) 253 3774
0.8 miles west along the A650, on the right.
Open; 11.30-20.30hrs daily. (NB Takeaway open until 22.00hrs daily)

3 White Rose

Tel: (0113) 252 3720
1 mile north along the A653, on the left.

(Brewsters) Open all day. Meals served; Mon-Sat; 11.30-22.00hrs, Sun; 12.00-22.00hrs.

PLACES OF INTEREST

Leeds

Follow the A653 and M621 north (Signposted 4.8 Miles)
For details please see Junction 27 information

Within the city centre ...

Royal Armouries

Armouries Drive, Leeds LS10 1LT
For details please see Junction 27 information

Thackray's Medical Museum

Beckett Street, Leeds LS9 7LN

Follow the A653, M621 and A653 into Leeds and take the A58 east (Signposted along A58, 6.5 Miles)
For details please see Junction 27 information

M62
JUNCTION 29

THIS IS A MOTORWAY INTERCHANGE ONLY WITH THE M621 AND THERE IS NO ACCESS TO ANY FACILITIES

Nearest Westbound A&E Hospital
Leeds General Infirmary

Great George Street, Leeds LS1 3EX
Tel: (0113) 243 2799
Proceed north to Junction 7 (M621) and take the A61 north into Leeds city centre. The hospital is signposted in the city. (Distance Approx 6.8 miles)

Nearest Eastbound A&E Hospital

Pinderfield Hospital

Aberford Road, Wakefield
WF1 4DG
Tel: (01924) 201688
Proceed south to Junction 41 (M1), take the A650 exit east and continue along the A61. At the junction of the A642 and A61 turn left along the A642 and the hospital is along this road. (Distance Approx 4.6 miles)

PLACES OF INTEREST

Leeds

Follow the M1 and M621 north (Signposted 6 Miles)
For details please see Junction 27 information

Within the city centre ...

Royal Armouries

Armouries Drive, Leeds LS10 1LT
For details please see Junction 27 information

Thackray's Medical Museum

Beckett Street, Leeds LS9 7LN

Follow the M1 north, take the A61 north exit at Junction 7 (M621) and continue along the A58 (5.7 Miles)
For details please see Junction 27 information

JUNCTION 30

THERE ARE NO FACILITIES WITHIN ONE MILE OF THIS JUNCTION

Nearest A&E Hospital
Pinderfield Hospital
Aberford Road, Wakefield

WF1 4DG
Tel: (01924) 201688
Follow the A642 south.
(Distance Approx 2.8 miles)

PLACES OF INTEREST

Wakefield

Follow the A 642 south (Signposted 3.7 Miles)
For details please see Junction 40 (M1) information

Within the city centre ...

The Cathedral Church of All Saints

Northgate, Wakefield WF1 1HG
For details please see Junction 40 (M1) information

The Chantry Chapel of St Mary

On Wakefield Bridge
For details please see Junction 40 (M1) information

JUNCTION 31

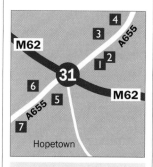

Hopetown

Nearest Westbound A&E Hospital

Pinderfield Hospital
Aberford Road, Wakefield
WF1 4DG
Tel: (01924) 201688
Proceed to Junction 30 and follow the A642 south.
(Distance Approx 5.9 miles)

Nearest Eastbound A&E Hospital

Pontefract General Infirmary

Friarwood Lane, Pontefract
WF8 1PL
Tel: (01977) 600600
Proceed to Junction 32 and follow the A639 south (Signposted in town. Distance Approx 4.1 miles)

FACILITIES

1   Premier Lodge Castleford

Tel: (01977) 665400
0.5 miles north along the A655, on the right.
Little Red Lion Restaurant Open; 07.00-10.00hrs & 18.00-22.00hrs daily.

2   Trading Post, Castleford

Tel: (01977) 519587
0.5 miles north along the A655, on the right.
(Mill House Inns) Open all day. Meals served; Mon-Sat; 11.00-21.30hrs, Sun; 12.00-21.00hrs

3   Rising Sun

Tel: (01977) 554766
0.6 miles north along the A655, on the left.
(Free House) Open all day. Meals served; Mon-Sat; 12.00-22.00hrs, Sun; 12.00-21.00hrs

4   Q8 Garage, Castleford

Tel: (01977) 512078
0.9 miles north along the A655, on the left.
Access, Visa, Delta, Mastercard, Switch, Diners Club, Amex, Overdrive, All Star, Dial Card, Q8 Cards.

5   The Village Motel

Tel: (01924) 897171
0.2 miles along the
Normanton Road, on the left.
(Mill House Inns) Open all day.
Meals served; 12.00-21.00hrs
daily

6   Prospect Garage (Texaco)

Tel: (01924) 895840
0.5 miles along the
Normanton Road, on the
right.
Access, Visa, Delta,
Mastercard, Switch, Diners
Club, Amex, Electron, Solo,
Overdrive, All Star, Dial Card,
Texaco Cards. Open; Mon-Fri;
06.30-22.00hrs, Sat; 07.00-
22.00hrs, Sun; 09.00-
22.00hrs.

7   Q8 Garage, Normanton

Tel: (01924) 893579
1 mile along the Normanton
Road, on the left.
Access, Visa, Delta,
Mastercard, Switch, Diners
Club, Amex, Overdrive, All Star,
Dial Card, Q8 Cards. Open:
Mon-Sat; 06.00-23.00hrs, Sun;
07.00-23.00hrs.

PLACES OF INTEREST

Castleford

**Follow the A655 east
(Signposted 2.3 Miles)**
Sited on the River Aire the
Romans established a crossing
here and built a notable fort
and settlement known as
Lagentium or Legioleum.
Archaeological finds from this
period can be seen at the
Library Museum. Known as the
birthplace of the famous

sculptor Henry Moore, the town
is renowned for its excellent
18thC pottery and glassware.

**Nearest A&E Hospital
Pontefract General
Infirmary**
Friarwood Lane, Pontefract
WF8 1PL
Tel: (01977) 600600
Follow the A639 south
(Signposted in town. Distance
Approx 1.6 miles)

FACILITIES

1   Parkside International

Tel: (01977) 709911
0.2 miles south along the
A639, on the left.
(Independent) Carvery Open;
Mon-Fri; 12.00-14.00hrs &
19.00-21.30hrs, Sat; 12.00-
14.00hrs & 19.00-21.30hrs,
Sun; 12.00-17.00hrs.
Restaurant Open; Mon-Sat;
19.00-21.30hrs, Sun; 12.00-
14.30hrs & 19.00-21.30hrs.
Bar Meals served; Mon-Sat;
19.00-21.30hrs, Sun; 19.00-
21.00hrs.

2   McDonald's

Tel: (01977) 602919

0.9 miles south along the
A639, in the Racecourse
Retail Park, on the left.
Open; Sun-Thurs; 07.30-
23.00hrs, Sat & Sun; 07.30-
0.00hrs

3   Save Glasshoughton Filling Station

Tel: (01977) 553489
0.2 miles north along the
A639, on the left.
Access, Visa, Delta,
Mastercard, Switch, Amex,
Electron, Solo, Overdrive, All
Star, Dial Card, Save Card.
Open; 06.00-23.00hrs daily.

4   Singing Choker

Tel: (01977) 668383
0.3 miles north along the
A639, on the left.
(Tom Cobleigh's) Open all day.
Meals Served; Mon-Sat; 12.00-
22.00 hrs, Sun; 12.00-
21.30hrs.

5   Petrol Express Castleford (Texaco)

Tel: (01977) 552718
0.4 miles north along the
A639, on the left.
Access, Visa, Delta,
Mastercard, Switch, Diners
Club, Amex, Electron, Solo,
Overdrive, All Star, Dial Card,
Fast Fuel, Texaco Cards.

6   The Royal Oak

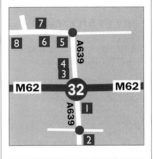

Tel: (01977) 553610
0.7 miles north along the
A639, on the left.
(Punch Taverns) Open all day.
Meals served; Mon-Sat; 12.00-
20.00hrs, Sun; 12.00-16.00hrs

7   TCS Glasshoughton (Total)

Tel: (01977) 516578
0.7 miles north along the

A639, on the right.
Access, Visa, Delta, Mastercard, Switch, Diners Club, Amex, Electron, Solo, Overdrive, All Star, Dial Card, Total/Fina/Elf Cards. Open; 06.00-23.00hrs daily

8   Mirage Hotel

Tel: (01977) 553428
1 mile north along the A639, on the left

PLACES OF INTEREST

Castleford

Follow the A639 north (Signposted 1.7 Miles)
For details please see Junction 31 information.

Pontefract

Follow the A639 south (Signposted 1.6 Miles)
The town of Pontefract, or "Pomfret" as it was known and so called in Shakespeare, was an important crossing point over the River Aire. Pomfret Castle, constructed by the Normans just after 1069, was a Royal stronghold and used to imprison Richard II who died here. In 1649, during the Civil War, the castle was finally taken by the Parliamentary forces and they subsequently demolished it just leaving some underground passages, dungeons and a keep which is now utilized as a museum (Tel: 01977-723440). The mixture of spacious precincts and narrow streets reflects its history with the Town Hall of 1785, the Buttercross and timber framed building providing an attractive setting in the town centre. The town is renowned for a variety of sweets known as Pontefract Cakes, made from locally grown liquorice.

M62
JUNCTION 33

FACILITIES

FERRYBRIDGE SERVICES (MOTO)
Tel: (01977) 672767 Fresh Express Self Service Restaurant, Harry Ramsden's, Burger King, Little Chef, Travelodge, Esso Fuel.

Nearest A&E Hospital
Pontefract General Infirmary
Friarwood Lane, Pontefract WF8 1PL.
Tel: (01977) 600600
Follow the A1 north and turn left along the A628. (Signposted in town. Distance Approx 2.5 miles)

PLACES OF INTEREST

Pontefract

Follow the A1 north and turn left along the A628. (Signposted 2.5 Miles)
For details please see Junction 32 information.

M62
JUNCTION 34

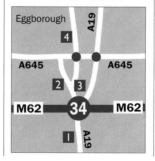

Nearest Westbound A&E Hospital
Pontefract General Infirmary
Friarwood Lane, Pontefract WF8 1PL
Tel: (01977) 600600
Proceed to Junction 33, follow the A1 north and turn left along the A628. (Signposted in town. Distance Approx 7 miles)

Nearest Eastbound A&E Hospital
Goole & District Hospital
Woodland Avenue, Goole DN14 6RX
Tel: (01724) 282282
Proceed to Junction 36 and follow the A614 east (Signposted. Distance Approx 12.6 miles)

FACILITIES

1   George & Dragon

Tel: (01977) 661319
0.6 miles south along the A19, on the right.
(Independent) Open all day Fri-Sun. Meals served; Sun-Fri; 12.00-14.00hrs & 19.00-21.00hrs, Sat; 12.00-14.00hrs & 19.00-21.30hrs.

2   The Jolly Miller

Tel: (01977) 661348
0.4 miles north along the Selby Road, in Eggborough, on the left.
(Pubmaster) Open all day. Meals served; 12.00-21.00hrs daily

3   Station Garage

Tel: (01977) 661256
0.4 miles north along the Selby Road, in Eggborough, on the right.
Access, Visa, Delta,

Mastercard, Switch, Diners Club, Amex, Electron, Solo, Overdrive, All Star, Dial Card. Open; Mon-Fri; 07.30-18.30hrs, Sat; 07.30-15.00hrs, Sun; 09.00-12.30hrs.

4   Selby Road Filling Station

 WC

Tel: (01977) 661651
1 mile north along the Selby Road, in Eggborough, on the left.
Access, Visa, Delta, Mastercard, Switch, Solo, Overdrive, All Star, Dial Card. Open; Mon-Fri; 08.00-18.00hrs, Sat; 08.00-15.00hrs.

M62
JUNCTION 35

THIS JUNCTION IS A MOTORWAY INTERCHANGE WITH M18 ONLY AND THERE IS NO ACCESS TO ANY FACILITIES

Nearest Westbound A&E Hospital
Pontefract General Infirmary
Friarwood Lane, Pontefract WF8 1PL
Tel: (01977) 600600
Proceed to Junction 33, follow the A1 north and turn left along the A628. (Signposted in town. Distance Approx 15 miles)

Nearest Eastbound A&E Hospital
Goole & District Hospital
Woodland Avenue, Goole DN14 6RX
Tel: (01724) 282282
Proceed to Junction 36 and follow the A614 east (Signposted. Distance Approx 4.6 miles)

M62
JUNCTION 36

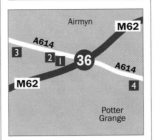

Nearest A&E Hospital
Goole & District Hospital
Woodland Avenue, Goole DN14 6RX
Tel: (01724) 282282
Follow the A614 east (Signposted. Distance Approx 1.9 miles)

FACILITIES

1   Glews Garage (Shell)

Tel: (01405) 764525
0.2 miles west along the A614, on the left.
Access, Visa, Delta, Mastercard, Switch, Diners Club, Amex, Overdrive, All Star, Dial Card, Shell Cards. Food available Mon-Sat; 08.00-17.00hrs.

2   McDonald's

Tel: (01405) 766747
0.2 miles west along the A614, on the left.
Open; Sun-Thurs; 07.30-23.00hrs, Fri & Sat; 07.30-0.00hrs

3   Woodside Café (Transport)

Tel: (01405) 839321
0.9 miles west along the A614, on the right.
Open; Mon-Fri; 06.00-17.00hrs

4   TCS Rawcliffe Road (Total)

Tel: (01405) 763445
1 mile east along the A614, in Goole, on the right.
Access, Visa, Delta, Mastercard, Switch, Diners Club, Amex, Electron, Solo, Overdrive, All Star, Dial Card, Total/Fina/Elf Cards. Open; 06.00-22.00hrs daily

PLACES OF INTEREST

The Waterways Museum & Adventure Centre

Dutch River Side, Goole DN14 5TB Tel: (01405) 768730
website: www.waterwaysmuseum andadventurecentre.co.uk

Follow the A614 east and turn right along the A161. (Signposted 2.4 Miles)
The collection tells the story of Goole's development as a canal terminus to the Aire & Calder Navigation and as a port connecting to the North Sea. The displays include contemporary social history and interactive exhibitions. There is a nature trail and boat trips are available on summer Sundays (Also at other times if pre-booked). Café. Gift Shop. Disabled access.

M62
JUNCTION 37

Nearest Westbound A&E Hospital

Goole & District Hospital

Woodland Avenue, Goole
DN14 6RX
Tel: (01724) 282282
Proceed to Junction 36 and
follow the A614 east
(Signposted. Distance Approx
4.7 miles)

Nearest Eastbound A&E Hospital

The Hull Royal Infirmary

Anlaby Road, Kingston upon
Hull HU3 2JZ
Tel: (01482) 328541
Proceed to Junction 38, follow
the A63 east and continue
along the A164 and A1105.
(Distance Approx 23.1 miles)

FACILITIES

1   Junction 37 Service Station (Rix)

Tel: (01430) 430388
**0.6 miles west along the
A614, on the right.**
Access, Visa, Delta,
Mastercard, Switch, Overdrive,
All Star, Dial Card, Securicor
Fuelserv, UK Fuelcard,
Keyfuels. Open; Mon-Fri; 07.00-
22.00hrs, Sat; 07.30-20.30hrs,
Sun; 08.30-20.30hrs.

2   The Ferryboat Inn

Tel: (01430) 430300
**1 mile west along the A614,
on the left.**
(Free House) Open all day.
Meals served; Mon-Fri; 12.00-
14.00hrs & 18.00-22.00hrs,
Sat; 12.00-22.00hrs, Sun;
12.00-21.00hrs

3   Brian Leighton Garages (BP)

Tel: (01430) 430717
**1 mile north along the A614,
on the right.**

Access, Visa, Delta,
Mastercard, Switch, Diners
Club, Amex, Overdrive, All Star,
Dial Card, Shell Agency, BP
Cards

4   The Wellington Hotel

Tel: (01430) 430258
**1 mile north along the A614,
in Howden, on the right.**
(Independent) Open all day.
Meals served; 12.00-14.00hrs
& 18.30-21.30hrs daily

5   Bowmans Hotel

Tel: (01430) 430805
**1 mile north along the A614,
in Howden, on the right.**
(Independent) Open all day.
Meals served; Mon-Fri; 12.00-
14.30hrs & 17.00-21.30hrs,
Sat; 12.00-22.00hrs, Sun;
12.00-21.30hrs.

6   The Wheatsheaf

Tel: (01430) 432334
**1 mile north along the A614,
in Howden, on the right.**
(Unique Pub Co) Meals served;
Wed-Sun; 12.00-18.30hrs

7   The White Horse Inn

Tel: (01430) 430326
**1 mile north along the A614,
in Howden, on the right.**
(Laurel Pub Company) Meals
served; Mon-Thurs; 12.00-
14.30hrs & 17.30-19.30hrs,
Fri-Sun; 12.00-14.30hrs

8   The Station

Tel: (01430) 431301
**1 mile north along the A614,
in Howden, on the right**
(Free House)

Nearest A&E Hospital

The Hull Royal Infirmary

Anlaby Road, Kingston upon
Hull HU3 2JZ
Tel: (01482) 328541
Follow the A63 east and
continue along the A164 and
A1105. (Distance Approx 14.7
miles)

FACILITIES

1   Triangle Motors (BP)

Tel: (01430) 424119
**0.1 miles west along the
B1230, on the left.**
Access, Visa, Delta,
Mastercard, Switch, Diners
Club, Amex, Overdrive, All Star,
Dial Card, BP Cards. Open;
Mon-Sat; 07.00-22.00hrs, Sun;
08.00-22.00hrs.

2   Crown & Anchor

Tel: (01430) 449757
**1 mile west along the B1230,
in Newport, on the right.**
(Free House) Open all day Fri-
Sun. Meals served; Mon-Thurs;
17.00-20.00hrs, Fri-Sun;
12.00-14.00hrs & 17.00-
20.00hrs

3   Kings Arms

Tel: (01430) 440289
**1 mile west along the B1230,
in Newport, on the right.**
(Pubmaster) Meals served;
12.00-14.00hrs daily

MOTORWAY ENDS
(Total length of motorway 106.0
miles)

the M69

A 15.7 miles long motorway which opened in July 1977 to link Coventry and Leicester and provide a useful connection between the M1 and M6.

Commencing at Junction 2 of the M6, north west of Coventry, where it also has an end-on connection with the A46, it heads north east to join up with the M1 at Junction 21 and link up with the A5460 into Leicester. Although there is nothing of great significance to note along the route, the junction with the M1 at the north end still remains as a monument to world events that shaped strategic planning decisions in the 1970s. The earthworks were constructed in 1976 to lead to a flyover and clover leaf junction on the east side of the M1 (the site now partially occupied by Fosse Park) but, with a fuel crisis escalating daily, they were abandoned in the same year as it was felt that traffic levels would never warrant the investment!

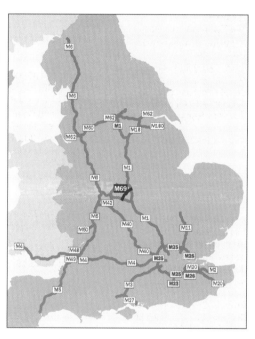

Location of Places of Interest

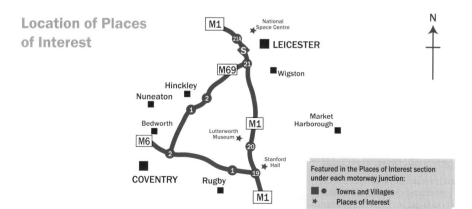

M69

JUNCTION 1

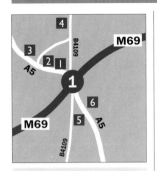

Nearest Northbound A&E Hospital

Leicester Royal Infirmary

Infirmary Square, Leicester
LE1 5WW
Tel: (0116) 254 1414

Proceed to Junction 21 (M1) and take the exit to Leicester. Follow the A5460 into the city and turn right along Upperton Road. Turn left at the end and the hospital is on the left. (Distance Approx 13.5 miles)

Nearest Southbound A&E Hospital

George Eliot Hospital

College Street, Nuneaton
CV10 7DJ
Tel: (024) 7635 1351

Take the A5 west towards Atherstone and after about 2.9 miles turn left along the A47 to Nuneaton town centre. Follow the A444 south towards Coventry and turn right into College Street. The hospital is on the left. (Distance Approx 6.1 miles)

FACILITIES

1　Star Three Pots Service Station (Texaco)

Tel: (01455) 620940
0.2 miles north along the A5, on the right.

Access, Visa, Delta, Mastercard, Switch, Diners Club, Amex, Electron, Solo, Overdrive, All Star, Dial Card, UK Fuelcard, Keyfuels, Texaco Cards.

2　The Three Pots Harvester

Tel: (01455) 615408
0.3 miles north along the A5, on the right.

(Six Continents) Open all day. Restaurant Open; Sun-Fri 12.00-21.00hrs, Sat; 12.00-22.00hrs. Bar Meals served; 12.00-21.00hrs daily.

3　The Hinckley Knight

Tel: (01455) 610773
0.4 miles north along the A5, on the right.

(Noble House Company) Open all day Thurs-Sun. Meals served; Mon-Wed; 12.00-14.00hrs & 17.00-21.00hrs, Thurs-Sat; 12.00-14.30hrs & 17.00-21.00hrs, Sun; 12.00-20.30hrs.

4　Sketchley Grange Hotel

Tel: (01455) 251133
0.9 miles north along the B4109, on the left.

(Best Western) The Terrace Bistro; Open; Mon-Sat; 12.00-23.00hrs, Sun; 12.00-22.30hrs. The Willow Restaurant; Open; Mon-Fri; 12.00-14.00hrs & 19.00-21.30hrs

5　Barnacles Restaurant

Tel: (01455) 633220
0.1 miles south along the A5, on the right.

Open; Mon- Fri; 12.00-

14.00hrs & 18.30-21.30hrs, Sat; 18.30-21.30hrs, Sun; 12.00-14.00hrs

6　Hanover International Hotel & Club

Tel: (01455) 631122
0.2 miles south along the A5, on the left.

The Brasserie Open; Mon-Sat; 07.00-10.00hrs, 12.00-14.00hrs & 19.00-22.00hrs, Sun; 07.00-10.00hrs, 12.30-15.00hrs & 19.00-22.00hrs. The Conservatory Restaurant Open; 19.00-22.00hrs daily. (NB. There is also an all day menu from 12.00-19.00hrs daily).

JUNCTION 3

> **THIS IS A RESTRICTED ACCESS JUNCTION**
> - There is no exit for northbound vehicles
> - There is no access for southbound vehicles

Nearest Northbound A&E Hospital

Leicester Royal Infirmary

Infirmary Square, Leicester
LE1 5WW
Tel: (0116) 254 1414

Proceed to Junction 21 (M1) and take the exit to Leicester.

Follow the A5460 into the city and turn right along Upperton Road. Turn left at the end and the hospital is on the left. (Distance Approx 10.6 miles)

Nearest Southbound A&E Hospital

George Eliot Hospital

College Street, Nuneaton CV10 7DJ

Tel: (024) 7635 1351

Proceed to Junction 1, take the A5 west towards Atherstone and after about 2.9 miles turn left along the A47 to Nuneaton town centre. Follow the A444 south towards Coventry and turn right into College Street. The hospital is on the left. (Distance Approx 8.7 miles)

FACILITIES

1 Woodside Garage (Independent)

Tel: (01455) 632253

0.6 miles west along the A5070, on the left.

Access, Visa, Delta, Mastercard, Switch, Diners Club, Amex, Overdrive, All Star, Dial Card. Open; Mon-Fri; 06.00-18.00hrs, Sat; 07.00-18.00hrs, Sun; 08.00-17.30hrs. Attended Service available.

2 Wynnes Motor Services (Jet)

Tel: (01455) 610213

1 mile west along the A5070, on the right.

Access, Visa, Delta, Mastercard, Switch, Diners Club, Amex, Overdrive, All Star, Dial Card, Jet Cards. Open; Mon-Sat; 07.00-20.00hrs, Sun; 08.30-16.30hrs. Attended Service.

the **M180**

This 25.5 miles long motorway was fully opened during July 1979 and connects Scunthorpe and, via the A180, Grimsby, Immingham and Cleethorpes to the motorway network through the M18.

Commencing with its connection with Junction 5 of the M18 at **Hatfield**, the motorway heads east across the Low Levels of the Hatfield Chase to the **Isle of Axholme** at Junction 2. Much of this area was under water and Axholme was literally an island before the Dutch draining schemes in the 17thC. Continuing east, the motorway bridges the River Trent before linking up with the M181 at Junction 3.

Between here and Junction 4 it by-passes the steel making town of **Scunthorpe** on the north side. Scunthorpe changed from a rural farming community to a centre of the steel industry after 1860, when large deposits of ironstone were found beneath the five villages that made up the parish: Appleby, Ashby, Brumby, Crosby and Frodingham. The motorway then passes through **Manby Wood**, to the north and **High Wood**, to the south, as it reaches Junction 4.

Beyond Junction 4 the carriageways cross the New and Old River Ancholmes before passing **Brigg** on the south side. Brigg is famous for its fair which was established by a Royal Charter from King John and celebrated in word and song by Delius and Percy Grainger. The Scunthorpe to Grimsby line crosses the motorway just before it continues past the grounds of **Elsham Hall**, containing a Country and Wildlife Park, on the north side and ends as it connects with the A15 to Kingston upon Hull and the A180 to Grimsby at Junction 5.

Location of Places of Interest

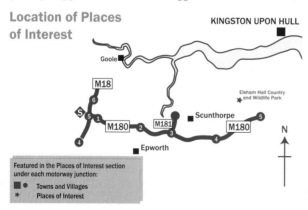

Featured in the Places of Interest section under each motorway junction:

■ ● Towns and Villages
✷ Places of Interest

M180

THIS IS A RESTRICTED ACCESS JUNCTION.

■ Vehicles can only exit from the eastbound lanes.

■ Vehicles can only enter the motorway along the westbound lanes

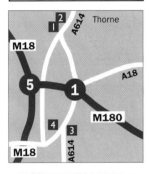

Nearest Eastbound A&E Hospital

Scunthorpe General Hospital

Cliff Gardens, Scunthorpe
DN15 7BH
Tel: (01724) 282282

Proceed east to Junction 3, follow the M181 north and turn right along the A18 (Signposted. Distance Approx 15 miles)

Nearest Westbound A&E Hospital (Via M18)

Doncaster Royal Infirmary

Armthorpe Road, Doncaster
DN2 5LT
Tel: (01302) 366666

Proceed south to Junction 4 (M18), follow the A630 west, continue along the A18, turn right at the second roundabout along Armthorpe Road and the hospital is signposted. (Distance Approx 10.5 miles)

FACILITIES

1   The Rising Sun

Tel: (01405) 812688

0.9 miles north along the A614, on the left in Thorne

(Pubmaster) Open all day Thurs-Sun. Meals served; Tues-Sat; 12.00-14.00hrs & 18.00-20.00hrs, Sun; 12.00-15.00hrs

2   Canal Tavern

Tel: (01405) 813688

1 mile north along the A614, on the left in Thorne

(Enterprise Inns) Open all day Fri-Sun; Meals served; Mon-Sat; 12.00-14.30hrs & 17.30-22.00hrs, Sun; 12.00-14.30hrs & 19.00-21.00hrs

3   Green Tree Garage (Independent)

 |WC|

Tel: (01302) 840488

0.8 miles south along the A18, on the left

Access, Visa, Overdrive, All Star, Switch, Dial Card, Mastercard, Diners Club, Delta. Open; Mon-Fri; 07.00-21.00hrs, Sat; 08.00-21.00hrs, Sun; 09.00-20.00hrs

4   Green Tree

Tel: (01302) 840305

0.8 miles south along the A18, on the right

(Whitbread) Open all day. Meals served; 12.00-22.00hrs daily

M180

Nearest Eastbound A&E Hospital

Scunthorpe General Hospital

Cliff Gardens, Scunthorpe
DN15 7BH
Tel: (01724) 282282

Proceed east to Junction 3, follow the M181 north and turn right along the A18 (Signposted. Distance Approx 8.3 miles)

Nearest Westbound A&E Hospital (Via M18)

Doncaster Royal Infirmary

Armthorpe Road, Doncaster
DN2 5LT
Tel: (01302) 366666

Proceed south to Junction 4 (M18), follow the A630 west, continue along the A18, turn right at the second roundabout along Armthorpe Road and the hospital is signposted. (Distance Approx 17.2 miles)

FACILITIES

1   Sir Solomon

Tel: (01427) 873522

0.9 miles south along the A161 on the left in King Edward Street, Belton

(Pubmaster) Open all day Fri-Mon. Meals served; Tues-

Thurs; 17.30-20.30hrs, Fri-Mon; 12.00-14.00hrs & 17.30-20.30hrs

2 Leyland Central Filling Station (Jet)

 WC

Tel: (01427) 874449
1 miles south along the A161 on the right in Belton
Access, Visa, Overdrive, All Star, Switch, Dial Card, Mastercard, Amex, Diners Club, Delta, Solo, BP Supercharge, Jet Cards. Open; 06.00-22.00hrs daily

PLACES OF INTEREST

Epworth

Epworth Local Link, Chapel Street, Epworth DN9 1HQ
Tel: (01724) 296870

Follow the A161 south (Signposted 3.4 miles)
This small town could be found on an island until the 17thC when the surrounding area was drained by Vermuyden, a Dutch engineer specializing in land reclamation, and opened up for agricultural use. This district is still known as the Isle of Axholme and is traditionally shrouded in mystery and strange local customs. Epworth holds a special place in the history of Christianity in England as the birthplace of John and Charles Wesley, founders of Methodism, and buildings that reflect this period include The Old Rectory where they were brought up (now a museum, Tel: 01427-872268) and St Andrew's Church (Tel: 01427-872080) where their father, Samuel, was Rector and his sons were baptized, whilst a later monument to their achievements, the Wesley

Memorial Church, was constructed in 1889.

JUNCTION 3

THIS JUNCTION IS A MOTORWAY INTERCHANGE WITH THE M181 ONLY AND THERE IS NO ACCESS TO ANY FACILITIES

Nearest A&E Hospital
Scunthorpe General Hospital
Cliff Gardens, Scunthorpe DN15 7BH
Tel: (01724) 282282
Follow the M181 north and turn right along the A18 (Signposted. Distance Approx 3.5 miles)

JUNCTION 4

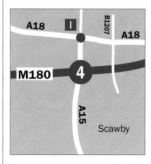

Nearest A&E Hospital
Scunthorpe General Hospital
Cliff Gardens, Scunthorpe DN15 7BH
Tel: (01724) 282282
Follow the A18 west (Signposted along route. Distance Approx 5.9 miles)

1 Forest Pines Hotel & Restaurant

Tel: (01652) 650770
0.3 miles north along the A15, on the north side of the roundabout
(Best Western) Mulligan's Restaurant Open; 07.30-19.30hrs daily, Beech Tree Restaurant Open; Breakfast; 07.00-09.30hrs daily, Lunch; 12.00-14.00hrs daily, Dinner; 19.00-22.00hrs daily. The Garden Room Open; 11.00-23.00hrs daily

JUNCTION 5

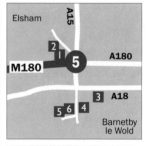

Nearest A&E Hospital
Scunthorpe General Hospital
Cliff Gardens, Scunthorpe DN15 7BH
Tel: (01724) 282282
Proceed west to Junction 4 and follow the A18 west (Signposted along route. Distance Approx 12.7 miles)

1 Little Chef

Tel: (01652) 680798

Adjacent to the north side of the roundabout
Open; 07.00-23.00hrs daily

2 Barnetby Jet Service Station

Tel: (01652) 688409
Adjacent to the north side of the roundabout
Access, Visa, Overdrive, All Star, Switch, Dial Card, Mastercard, Amex, AA Paytrak, Diners Club, Delta, Keyfuels, Securicor Fuelserv, UK Fuelcard, Jet Cards

3 Barny's Café

Tel: (01652) 680966
0.3 miles east along the A18, on the right
Open; Mon-Fri; 06.00-21.00hrs, Sat; 06.00-14.00hrs

4 Railway Inn

Tel: (01652) 688284
0.6 miles south along Barnetby Road, on the left
(Enterprise Inns) Meals served; Mon-Fri; 14.00-21.00hrs, Sat & Sun; 12.00-14.00hrs & 19.00-21.00hrs

5 Whistle & Flute Hotel

Tel: (01652) 688238
0.7 miles south along Barnetby Road, on the right
Bar open all day. Restaurant Open; 12.00-14.00hrs & 18.00-21.30hrs daily

6 Public Toilets

0.7 miles south along Barnetby Road, on the right

PLACES OF INTEREST

Elsham Hall Country & Wildlife Park

Nr Brigg, North Lincolnshire
DN20 0QZ
Tel: (01652) 688698 website;
www.brigg.com/elsham.htm

Follow the signposts to Elsham (1.9 miles)
A huge variety of attractions can be found within the Park, including a Children's Animal Farm, Miniature Walled Garden Zoo, Wild Butterfly Garden, Arboretum & Woodland Bulb Garden, Garden Centre, Lakeside Gardens, Adventure Playground, Falconry & Conservation Centre and a Working Craft Centre. Granary Tea Rooms, Restaurant, Disabled Access.

MOTORWAY ENDS
(Total Length of Motorway 25.5 Miles)